INTERNATIONAL MIGRATION LAW: DEVELOPING PARADIGMS AND KEY CHALLENGES

INTERNATIONAL MIGRATION LAW: DEVELOPING PARADIGMS AND KEY CHALLENGES

edited by

Ryszard Cholewinski
Richard Perruchoud
Euan MacDonald

T·M·C·ASSER PRESS
The Hague

Published by T.M.C. ASSER PRESS
P.O. Box 16163, 2500 BD The Hague, The Netherlands
<www.asserpress.nl>

T.M.C. ASSER PRESS' English language books are distributed exclusively by

Cambridge University Press, The Edinburgh Building, Shaftesbury Road,
Cambridge CB2 2RU, UK,
or,
for customers in the USA, Canada and Mexico:
Cambridge University Press, 100 Brook Hill Drive, West Nyack, NY 10994-2133, USA
<www.cambridge.org>

ISBN 10: 90-6704-232-3
ISBN 13: 978-90-6704-232-1

SUMMARY OF CONTENTS

Forced Migration

Human Rights of Specific Migrant Groups

Free Movement Regimes and Other Regional Developments

FOREWORD

The International Organization for Migration (IOM) is dedicated to promoting humane and orderly migration worldwide by serving the policy and programme needs of governments and migrants. The challenges of migration management reflect the contemporary challenges posed by migration itself, many of which can be turned into opportunities that can benefit countries of origin, countries of destination and migrants themselves. To be effectively managed, migration has to be looked at comprehensively, taking into account its economic, social, humanitarian, demographic, development, security and normative aspects.

The normative approach to migration can be viewed mainly from two different, but complementary angles. Firstly, there are the principles and standards deriving from State sovereignty, among which are the right to protect borders, to confer nationality, to admit and expel foreigners, to combat trafficking and smuggling and to safeguard national security. Secondly, there are the human rights of the persons involved in migration. These two elements constitute the main pillars of what is generally known and accepted today as 'international migration law'.

International migration law instruments are spread across various branches of international law, such as human rights law, humanitarian law, refugee law, criminal law and labour law; the relevant norms are therefore dispersed throughout a wide range of texts. This disparity or dispersion of norms contributes to the belief that there are gaps in the set of norms protecting migrants and/or regulating migration. Occasionally, it is argued that the major gap in the current international structure is the absence of a multilateral framework for governing the movement of people.

The IOM plays an increasing role in promoting understanding and effective practices in migration management, including in the promotion of international migration law. To streamline and strengthen its growing involvement in this field, the IOM established in 2005 the International Migration Law and Legal Affairs Department. Its objective is to increase awareness and knowledge on international migration law and contribute to a better understanding of the legal instruments that govern migration at the national, regional and international level. It has, for example, created an online database on migration law; it organizes training and capacity building activities for government officials and other stakeholders in migration in all regions of the world, and it conducts research on selected migration law topics and general issues concerning international migration law.

This publication is an outcome of the Department's involvement in research activities. *International Migration Law: Developing Paradigms and Key Challenges* encapsulates the current state of international migration law by re-visiting key topics first addressed in a companion volume, *Migration and International Legal Norms*, published by T.M.C. Asser Press in 2003, and by addressing the substantial developments that have since taken place and investigating new issues.

This book analyzes the legal framework related to matters such as trafficking, multiple nationality, consular protection, biometrics, remittances, trade, terrorism, and detention. It also maps out recent developments as well as current and future challenges. In our globalized world, in which international movements of people are growing and diversifying and thus moving up the policy agendas of governments, international organizations, the private sector and civil society, my hope is that this body of work will contribute to a better understanding of international migration law, particularly among stakeholders such as policy makers, academics, civil society representatives and students of the subject. It will also no doubt stimulate further thinking and work in this important field and help to promote international migration law as an essential component of comprehensive migration management frameworks.

Geneva, January 2007

Brunson McKinley
Director General
International Organization for Migration

ACKNOWLEDGEMENTS

The decision to write this book under the auspices of the IOM's newly created International Migration Law and Legal Affairs Department came about as a result of discussions held with the Migration Policy, Research and Communications Department of the IOM and a number of external interlocutors. The discussions crystallized in the need to prepare a new text with a view to analysing and taking account of significant developments and emerging issues in international migration law since the publication in 2003 by T.M.C. Asser Press of *Migration and International Legal Norms*, in which the IOM was also involved in collaboration with the Migration Policy Institute in Washington, DC and the Graduate Institute of International Studies in Geneva, with the support of the Swiss Federal Office for Refugees (since renamed the Federal Office for Migration). An important external interlocutor in these discussions was Alexander Aleinikoff, one of the editors of *Migration and International Legal Norms*, and the author of the concluding chapter to the present volume.

The publication of this book would not have been possible without the contribution of a broad range of persons in addition to the authors of the chapters in this volume. First of all, generous financial assistance provided by the Swiss Federal Office for Migration, through the conduit of the head of International Affairs of the Office, Anne-Grethe Nielsen, who also authored a chapter in the book, was indispensable for getting this project off the ground and for ensuring that most of the authors were able to participate in a November 2005 workshop, held in Geneva, at which the themes of the volume were discussed. These discussions were greatly facilitated by the following persons from the IOM, other international organizations, academia and civil society, who participated in this workshop, either as Chairs or Discussants: Nilim Baruah (Head of the Labour Migration Service Area, Migration Management Services, IOM), Vincent Chetail (Graduate Institute of International Studies), Carla Edelenbos (Secretary, Committee of Migrant Workers, Office of the UN High Commissioner for Human Rights), Bill Frelick (Human Rights Watch), Philippe Leclerc (Head of the Statelessness Unit, Department of International Protection, UNHCR), Grainne O'Hara (Legal Officer, Protection Policy and Legal Advice Section, Department of International Protection, UNHCR), José-Angel Oropeza (Senior Regional Adviser for the Americas, IOM), John Packer (Former Senior Advisor to the OSCE High Commissioner on National Minorities), and Linda Taylor (Chief of the Legal Services Branch, UN Compensation Commission).

In addition to the eight members of IOM staff who contributed a chapter to this volume, its publication was strongly supported by IOM's Director General, Brunson McKinley, who provided helpful advice at the outset on the topics and structure for the book. In the IOM's International Migration Law and Legal Affairs Department, Kerstin Bartsch provided invaluable assistance at various stages of the project, particularly in the organization of the November 2005 workshop, while Hasmig Schaeffer afforded essential administrative support throughout the course of the project.

Last but not least, the patience and support of the publisher, T.M.C. Asser Press, were key to bringing this project to fruition in the present volume.

Geneva
February 2007

Ryszard Cholewinski
Richard Perruchoud
Euan MacDonald

TABLE OF CONTENTS

LIST OF CONTRIBUTORS

T. Alexander Aleinikoff is Dean and Executive Vice President for Law Center Affairs at Georgetown University in Washington DC. He teaches and writes in the fields of immigration, refugee, and citizenship law and policy. Dean Aleinikoff has served in senior level positions at the US Immigration and Naturalization Service (1994-97) and as a consultant to UNHCR and IOM in Geneva. He is the co-editor of *Migration and International Legal Norms* (2003, with V. Chetail).

Simon Bagshaw is a Protection Officer in the Inter-Agency Internal Displacement Division of the UN Office for the Coordination of Humanitarian Affairs in Geneva. Prior to this, he worked for three years as a Senior Research Associate in the Office of the Representative of the Secretary-General on Internally Displaced Persons in the UN Office of the High Commissioner for Human Rights. He has a Ph.D. in Law from the European University Institute in Florence. His thesis was published in 2005 as *Developing a Normative Framework for the Protection of Internally Displaced Persons*. He has written extensively on internal displacement including co-authoring, with Diane Paul, *Protect or Neglect – Toward a More Effective United Nations Approach to the Protection of Internally Displaced Persons* (2004).

Rosemary Byrne teaches international and human rights law at Trinity College Dublin, where she is also a Research Fellow at the Institute of International Integration Studies. She has worked extensively with non-governmental organizations, is the director of the International Process and Justice Project, and is a founding member of the Refugee Policy Protection Group. She has been a Government of Ireland Research Fellow and a Visiting Fellow at the Harvard Law School Human Rights Programme. She earned her BA from Barnard College, Columbia University and her JD from Harvard Law School.

Ryszard Cholewinski works for the Migration Policy, Research and Communications Department in the IOM, Geneva. He has published widely on international and European migration law, including *Migrant Workers in International Human Rights Law: Their Protection in Countries of Employment* (1997); *Borders and Discrimination in the European Union* (2002); *The Legal Status of Migrants Admitted for Employment: A Comparative Study of Law and Practice in Selected European States* (2004); and *Study on Obstacles to Effective Access of Irregular Migrants to Minimum Social Rights* (2005). Prior to joining IOM, Ryszard was Reader in Law at the University of Leicester in the United Kingdom. He holds degrees from the Universities of Ottawa (LL.D.), Saskatchewan (LL.M.) and Leicester (LL.B.).

Philippe De Bruycker is Professor and Researcher at the Institute for European Studies and the Law Faculty of the Université Libre de Bruxelles in Belgium. In 1999, he founded, with the financial support of the European Commission, the 'Odysseus' Academic Network for Legal Studies on Immigration and Asylum in Europe, which has organized a summer school on 'European Union Law and Policy on Immigration and Asylum' every year since 2001. From 2001 until 2003 he was principal administrator in the General Directorate Justice and Home Affairs of the European Commission, where he was in charge of drafting proposals for directives on immigration.

Betty de Hart is Senior Researcher at the Centre for Migration Law of the Radboud University Nijmegen. Her Ph.D. (2003) was on mixed nationals in nationality and immigration law. Her publications include 'The Morality of Maria Toet: Gender, Citizenship and the Construction of the Nation-State', 32 *Journal of Ethnic and Migration Studies* (2006); *Migration and the Regulation of Social Integration* (2004, co-edited with A. Böcker and I. Michalowski); 'Political Debates on Dual Nationality in the Netherlands (1990-2003)', in A. Böcker, B. De Hart and I. Michalowski (eds.), *Migration and the Regulation of Social Integration* (2004); and 'Not Without My Daughter: On Parental Abduction, Orientalism and Maternal Melodrama', 8 *European Journal of Women's Studies* (2001).

Gustavo A. Flores-Macías is a doctoral fellow in Government and Instructor of Globalization at Georgetown University. Previously, he received a Masters Degree in Public Policy from Duke University, where he was a Fulbright scholar. Before coming to Washington, DC, he worked in Geneva, Switzerland as a trade consultant and in Mexico City, Mexico, where he worked for the Federal Government.

Nida Gelazis is Program Associate and Editor of the East European Studies Program at the Woodrow Wilson International Center for Scholars in Washington, DC. Previously, she was managing editor of the *East European Constitutional Review,* initially at the University of Chicago Law School and then transferred to the Open Society Institute's Constitutional and Legislative Policy Institute in Budapest, Hungary. She also served as Research Associate for the East European Programme at the Robert Schuman Centre for Advanced Studies in Florence.

Stefanie Grant is a lawyer specializing in human rights, migration, nationality and refugees. She has directed the Research and Right to Development branch of the UNHCR in Geneva, was Director of Research at Amnesty International's International Secretariat, and practised law as a partner with Bindman & Partners in London.

Kees Groenendijk is Professor of Sociology of Law at the Radboud University Nijmegen, Chairman of its Centre for Migration Law, Chairman of the Standing Committee of Experts on international immigration, refugee and criminal law, and Co-Director of the European Commission's Network on the Free Movement of Workers within the European Union. His publications include *Temporary Employment of Migrants in Europe* (1995); *Regulating Ethnic Migration: the Aussiedler* (1997); *Security of Residence of Long-Term Migrants: Law and Practice in European Countries* (1998, with E. Guild and H. Dogan); *Immigration, Migrants and Naturalization in the Netherlands 1945-1998* (1999, with E. Heijs); *Western Europe and its Islam* (2001, with others); *The Legal Position of Third Country Nationals in the Member States of the European Union* (2001); *In Search of Europe's Borders* (2003, with E. Guild and P. Minderhoud); and *Legal Concepts of Integration in EU Migration Law* (2004).

Kay Hailbronner has been Professor of Public, International and European law at the University of Konstanz since 1979. He is Director of the Centre for International and European Law on Immigration and Asylum at the University of Konstanz. Since 1990, he has acted as Legal Counsel for the Federal Government in asylum and immigration law and European law. Moreover, he was Chairman of the International Law Association Committee on Refugee Procedures from 1998 until 2002, was a member of the Governmental Commission on Immigration Issues from 2000 until 2001, and since 2000 has been a member of the Advisory Board of the German Federal Office for Migration and Refugees. His major English-language publication is *Immigration and Asylum Law and Policy of the European Union* (2000). Other principal publications include his Commentary on Aliens Law (*Kommentar Ausländerrecht*) and the Commentary on Citizenship (*Kommentar zum Staatsangehörigkeitsrecht*, together with G. Renner).

Michele Klein Solomon is Director of the Migration Policy, Research and Communications Department at the IOM, where she has been instrumental in building the Organization's migration policy expertise and profile, including by creating and leading the International Dialogue on Migration, and serving as a key member of the secretariat to and producing the Berne Initiative's International Agenda on Migration Management. Prior to joining IOM, she served as an Attorney Adviser with the US Department of State from 1989-2000, and served as the Department's principal refugee and migration lawyer from 1991-1996. She received her JD and Masters degrees from the Georgetown University Law Center and Georgetown University School of Foreign Service respectively. She has published on a range of migration-related subjects.

Stephen H. Legomsky is the Charles Nagel Professor of International Law at Washington University, in St. Louis, and the founding Director of the Harris Institute for Global Legal Studies. He is the author of *Immigration and Refugee Law and Policy* (4th edn. 2005) a leading law school textbook on US immigration and refugee law; *Specialised Justice: Courts, Administrative Tribunals, and a Cross-National Theory of Specialization* (1990); and *Immigration and the Judiciary: Law and Politics in Britain and America* (1987). Moreover, he has acted as consultant or advisor to President Clinton's transition team, President George

H.W. Bush's Commissioner of Immigration, the UNHCR, the IOM, and several foreign governments.

Euan MacDonald graduated in Law from the University of Edinburgh in 1999, and also gained a Masters degree from the same institution in 2000, focusing on public international law and legal theory. He went on to obtain a PhD in law from the European University Institute in Florence, Italy, in October 2006, with a thesis on critical approaches to international legal theory, which is scheduled for publication in 2007. He has also been a Visiting Fellow on the Programme for the Study of International Organizations at the Graduate Institute for International Studies in Geneva.

Jonathan Martens graduated from the University of Winnipeg (1996) and the Faculty of Law at McGill University in Montreal (2000) before joining the IOM in Bosnia as Legal Programme Development Officer, where he was part of an inter-agency working group drafting by-laws to the country's new Law on Immigration and Asylum, and co-authored a chapter entitled 'Irregular Migration Through Bosnia and Herzegovina' in *New Challenges for Migration Policy in Central and Eastern Europe* (2002). In 2001, he took up a position with the IOM's regional office for Southern Africa, and has since co-authored *Seduction, Sale and Slavery: Trafficking in Women and Children for Sexual Exploitation in Southern Africa* and developed several project initiatives to address the challenges of irregular migration, including the IOM's Southern African Counter-Trafficking Assistance Programme, which he currently manages.

Anne-Grethe Nielsen, LL.M., served for several years as a lawyer for the UNHCR, and is at present Director of International Affairs at the Swiss Federal Office for Migration (previously the Federal Office for Refugees). As such she was in charge of the development of the Berne Initiative, among other projects. She is also Chairperson of the Refugee Law Commission of the International Institute of Humanitarian Law, and has authored various policy papers for the Swiss Minister for Justice and Police.

Sophie Nonnenmacher is a Migration Policy Specialist in the Migration Policy Research and Communications Department, IOM Geneva. She specializes in all aspects of international labour migration, and has developed expertise on workers' mobility as dealt with in GATS Mode 4 and other regional free trade arrangements. She has also played a central role in the development of the IOM's International Migration and Development Initiative. She has Masters degrees in International Cooperation and Development from the Department of Political Science, University of Paris 1 (Sorbonne) and in Social Anthropology from the *École des Hautes Études en Sciences Sociales*, Paris.

Manuel Orozco is Director of Remittances and Development at the Inter-American Dialogue, where he also heads the Central America program. He was previously chair of Central America and the Caribbean at the United States Foreign Service Institute, and is currently a senior researcher at the Institute for the Study of International Migration at Georgetown University. His most recent publications include *Remittances: Global Opportunities for International Person-to-person Money Transfers* (2005); 'Markets and Financial Democracy: The Case for Remittance Transfers', 1 *Journal of Payment Systems Law* (2005); *International Norms and Mobilization for Democracy* (2002); and *The Remittance Marketplace: Prices, Policy and Financial Institutions* (2004).

Steve Peers is a Professor of Law at the Human Rights Centre at the University of Essex. He has written extensively on EU immigration and asylum law and other EU law issues. In particular, he is the author of *EU Justice and Home Affairs Law* (2nd edn. 2006), and the co-editor (with A. Ward) of *The EU Charter of Rights* (2004) and (with N. Rogers) of *EU Immigration and Asylum Law: Text and Commentary* (2006).

Richard Perruchoud is Director of the International Migration Law and Legal Affairs Department at the IOM, in Geneva. Before joining the IOM in 1982, he was Adjunct Professor of International Law at the Graduate Institute of International Studies in Geneva and visiting scholar at the Harvard Law School. He has published widely on international humanitarian law, human rights and migration law. He holds degrees from the University of Geneva (LL.D., LL.M., and LL.B.).

Ryszard Piotrowicz has been Professor of Law at the University of Wales, Aberystwyth since 1999. He was previously Professor and Dean of Law at the University of Tasmania. He has also taught at the Universities of Durham and Glasgow. He is an Alexander-von-Humboldt Research Fellow. He has published extensively on refugee and trafficking issues and worked as a consultant to various international organisations and other bodies. He is also Book Reviews Editor for the *International Journal of Refugee Law*.

Nicola Piper is Senior Research Fellow at the Asia Research Institute, National University of Singapore. She holds a Ph.D. in Sociology from the University of Sheffield in the United Kingdom and had previous appointments with the Nordic Institute of Asian Studies in Copenhagen and the Australian National University in Canberra. She is the author of the book *Racism, Nationalism and Citizenship* (1998), the co-editor of the volumes *Women and Work in Globalising Asia* (2002), *Wife or Worker? Asian Women and Migration* (2003), *Transnational Activism in Asia – Problems of power and democracy* (2004), as well as various journal articles. Her current projects are on the rights of migrants and the political organizing of migrant labour from a transnational as well as gender perspective.

Jillyanne Redpath is a Senior Legal Officer in the Department of International Migration Law and Legal Affairs, IOM Geneva. During her time at the IOM she has worked on issues such as migrants' rights, comparative immigration law and policies, migration and security and trafficking in human beings. Prior to joining the IOM, Jillyanne worked in Australia as a university lecturer and as an attorney. She has completed an LL.M. at the University of Cambridge, United Kingdom, and a BA/LL.B. at Monash University, Australia.

Ana María Santestevan is a lawyer with a Diploma in Diplomacy. She is currently Professor of Labour and Social Security Law at the Law School of the Republic of Uruguay, and Legal Consultant at the Office of Planning and Budget of the Presidency of the Republic of Uruguay. She also acts as a Government delegate to various MERCOSUR bodies, such as Working Sub-Group No. 10, the Social-Labour Commission, and the High Level Employment Group. Moreover, she has worked as a consultant for both the ILO and the IOM, and is the author of various articles, including (with H. Barretto) 'Los problemas laborales y de seguridad social que se plantean respecto de la migración de trabajadores fronterizos' [Labour and Social Security Problems regarding the Migration of Border Workers] *XI Jornadas rioplatenses de Derecho del Trabajo y de la Seguridad Social* (2000). She also co-authored *Migraciones laborales en Sudamérica: el Mercosur ampliado* [Labour Migration in South America: The Expanded Mercosur] (2003).

Margaret Satterthwaite is an Assistant Professor of Clinical Law at New York University School of Law, where she teaches international human rights and is Faculty Director of the Center for Human Rights and Global Justice. Her scholarship focuses on using feminist methodologies in international human rights law, the rights of migrants, and human rights in the 'war on terror'. Recent articles include 'Extraordinary Renditions: Testing the Limits of Human Rights Law' (in progress); 'Crossing Borders, Claiming Rights: Using Human Rights Law to Empower Women Migrant Workers', 8 *Yale Human Rights and Development Law Journal* (2005), and 'Women Migrants' Rights Under International Human Rights Law', 77 *Feminist Review* (2004).

Andrew I. Schoenholtz is the Deputy Director of Georgetown University's Institute for the Study of International Migration, Visiting Professor at the Georgetown University Law Center and School of Foreign Service, and Co-Director of the Graduate Certificate in Refugees and Humanitarian Emergencies. His publications include numerous articles and chapters on asylum and refugee protection, international migration and security, and the integration of immigrants. He holds a JD from Harvard Law School and a Ph.D. from Brown University and teaches courses on refugee and immigration law and policy.

Shyla Vohra obtained a Master of Laws *Cum Laude* from Leiden University in the Netherlands, focusing on the law of international institutions, following completion of a Bachelor of Arts and a Bachelor of Laws degree from Monash University in Australia. From 1995, she has worked with the IOM in Geneva and is currently Senior Legal Officer of the International Migration Law and Legal Affairs Department. She has also obtained a qualification to practice law as a barrister and solicitor in Australia, and has worked there as an immigration lawyer, representing both applicants and the Government, in refugee and migration cases in the Federal Court of Australia.

David Weissbrodt is the Regents Professor of Law and the Fredrikson & Byron Professor of Law at the University of Minnesota Law School. He has also been a Visiting Professor/Fellow at the Graduate Institute of International Studies in Geneva; Keio University and the UN University in Tokyo; Monash University in Melbourne; and Kellogg College, Oxford University. In 1996 he was elected and in 2000 he was re-elected by the UN Commission on Human Rights to serve as a member of the Sub-Commission on the Promotion and Protection of Human Rights. In 2001-02, he became the first US citizen since Eleanor Roosevelt to head a UN human rights body when he served as chairperson for the UN Sub-Commission on the Promotion and Protection of Human Rights. During the period 2000-03 he also served as the UN Special Rapporteur on the Rights of Non-Citizens.

Norbert Wühler is currently Director of Claims and Compensation Programmes at the IOM in Geneva. Previously, he was Chief of the Legal Services Branch of the UN Compensation Commission in Geneva, Legal Advisor to the President and Deputy Secretary-General of the Iran-United States Claims Tribunal in The Hague, and research fellow at the Max Planck Institute for Comparative Public Law and International Law in Heidelberg. Moreover, he has been an adviser to several international claims commissions and both member and chairman of a number of international arbitral tribunals. He graduated and received his doctorate in law from Heidelberg University in Germany.

LIST OF ABBREVIATIONS

ACHR	American Convention on Human Rights
ACHRPR	African Charter on Human Rights and People's Rights
ADB	Asian Development Bank
AEC	African Economic Community
AI	Amnesty International
ALO	Airline Liaison Officer
APC	The Asia-Pacific Consultations on Refugees, Displaced Persons and Migrants
APEC	Asia-Pacific Economic Cooperation
APIS	Advance Passenger Information System
APMRN	Asia Pacific Migration Research Network
ASEAN	Association of Southeast Asian Nations
C97	ILO Convention No. 97 (1949)
C143	ILO Convention No. 143 (1975)
CAFTA	Central American Free Trade Agreement
CAFTA-DR	Central American Free Trade Agreement since the accession of the Dominican Republic
CAN	Andean Community of Nations
CARAM	Coordination of Action Research on AIDS and Mobility
CARICOM	Caribbean Community and Common Market
CARIFTA	Caribbean Free Trade Association
CAT	Convention against Torture and Other Cruel, Inhuman or Degrading Treatment or Punishment
CEDAW	Convention on the Elimination of All Forms of Discrimination Against Women
CEDEAO	*Communauté économique de l'Afrique de l'Ouest*
CERD	Committee on the Elimination of Racial Discrimination
CFA F	*Franc de la Communauté Financière d'Afrique*
CINTERFOR	Inter-American Research and Documentation Centre on Vocational Training
CIREFCA	International Conference on Central American Refugees
CIS	Commonwealth of Independent States
CMC	*Consejo del Mercado Común* [MERCOSUR Council of the Common Market]
COMESA	Common Market for East and Southern Africa
CPA	Comprehensive Plan of Action for Indo-Chinese Refugees
CPC	*Comisión Parlamentaria Conjunta* [MERCOSUR Joint Parliamentary Commission]
CPT	European Committee for the Prevention of Torture and Inhuman or Degrading Treatment or Punishment
CRC	Convention on the Rights of the Child
CROSQ	CARICOM Regional Organization for Standards and Quality
CRPC	Commission for Real Property Claims of Displaced Persons and Refugees in Bosnia
CRRPD	Commission for the Resolution of Real Property Disputes (Iraq)
CRS	Convention on the Reduction of Statelessness
CRSSP	Convention Relating to the Status of Stateless Persons

CSL	*Comisión Sociolaboral* [MERCOSUR Social-Labour Commission]
CSME	Carribean Single Market and Economy
EAC	East African Community
ECCAS	Economic Community of Central African States
ECLAC	United Nations Economic Commission for Latin America and the Caribbean
EC	European Community
ECHR	European Convention for the Protection of Human Rights and Fundamental Freedoms (The European Convention on Human Rights)
ECOSOC	Economic and Social Council (UN)
ECOWAS	Economic Community of West African States
ECRE	European Council on Refugees and Exiles
ECRI	European Commission against Racism and Intolerance
ECtHR	European Court of Human Rights
EEC	European Economic Community
EECC	Eritrea Ethiopia Claims Commission
EP	European Parliament
EPFSF	European Parliamentary Financial Services Forum
ETS	European Treaty Series
EU	European Union
EUROPOL	European Police Office
EXCOM	Executive Committee of the United Nations High Commissioner for Refugees
FATF	Financial Action Task Force
FCNM	Framework Convention for the Protection of National Minorities
FDI	Foreign Direct Investment
FTA	Free Trade Agreement
GATS	General Agreement on Trade in Services
GCC	Gulf Cooperation Council
GCIM	Global Commission on International Migration
GENPROM	ILO Gender Promotion Programme
GFLCP	German Forced Labour Compensation Programme
GMC	*Grupo Mercado Común* [MERCOSUR Common Market Group]
GMG	Global Migration Group
GISTI	*Groupe d'information et de soutien des immigrés*
HLD	High Level Dialogue (on International Migration and Development) (UNGA)
HPCC	Housing and Property Claims Commission (Kosovo)
HPD	Housing and Property Directorate (Kosovo)
HRW	Human Rights Watch
HVAP	Holocaust Victim Assets Programme
IACtHR	Inter-American Court of Human Rights
IAML	*Instrumento Andino de Migración Laboral* [Andean Labour Migration Instrument]
IAMM	International Agenda for Migration Management
IASC	Inter-Agency Standing Committee (UN)
ICAO	International Civil Aviation Organization
ICC	International Criminal Court
ICCPR	International Covenant on Civil and Political Rights
ICERD	International Convention on the Elimination of All Forms of Racial Discrimination

ICESCR	International Covenant on Economic, Social and Cultural Rights
ICMC	International Catholic Migration Commission
ICMPD	International Centre for Migration Policy Development
ICRC	International Committee of the Red Cross
ICRMW	International Convention on the Protection of the Rights of All Migrant Workers and Members of Their Families
ICT	Intra-Corporate Transferee
IDM	International Organization for Migration's International Dialogue on Migration
IDPs	Internally Displaced Persons
IGAD	Inter-Governmental Authority on Development
IGC	Inter-Governmental Consultations on Asylum, Refugee and Migration Policies in Europe, North America and Australia
ILC	International Labour Conference
ILO	International Labour Organization
ILPA	Immigration Law Practitioners' Association
IMP	International Migration Policy Programme
INEGI	*Instituto Nacional de Estadística, Geografía e Informática* [National Institute of Statistics, Geography and Informatics] (Mexico)
IOM	International Organization for Migration
IPCC	Iraq Property Claims Commission
ISS	Institute for Security Studies
LDCs	Least Developed Countries
	Less Developed Countries
LNTS	League of Nations Treaty Series
MERCOSUR	Common Market of the South
MIDWA	Migration Dialogue for West Africa
MIDSA	Migration Dialogue for Southern Africa
MPG	Migration Policy Group
MRI	Migrants Rights International
NAALC	North American Agreement for Labor Cooperation
NAFTA	North American Free Trade Agreement
NGO	Non-Governmental Organization
NHLA	National Hispanic Leadership Agenda
OAS	Organization of American States
OAU	Organization for African Unity
OCHA	United Nations Office for the Coordination of Humanitarian Affairs
OECD	Organization for Economic Cooperation and Development
OECS	Organization of Eastern Caribbean States
OHCHR	Office of the United Nations High Commissioner for Human Rights
OSCE	Organization for Security and Cooperation in Europe
RCP	Regional Consultative Process
RFID	Radio Frequency Identification
RNCOM	Regional Network of Civil Organizations for Migration
SAARC	South Asian Association for Regional Cooperation
SADC	Southern African Development Community
SADCC	Southern African Development Coordination Conference
SAFTI	Secure and Facilitated International Travel Initiative (G8)
SIS	Schengen Information System
SIS II	Schengen Information System II

SGT10	MERCOSUR, *Subgrupo de Trabajo No. 10 sobre Relaciones Laborales, Empleo y Seguridad Social* [Working Subgroup No. 10 on Labour Relations, Employment and Social Security]
SPP	Security and Prosperity Partnership (US-Canada-Mexico)
UAMT	Union African Money Transfers
UDHR	Universal Declaration of Human Rights
UEMOA	*Union Economique et Monétaire Ouest Africaine*
UN	United Nations
UNCC	United Nations Compensation Commission
UNCHR	United Nations Commission on Human Rights
UNCTAD	United Nations Conference on Trade and Development
UNCTOC	United Nations Convention against Transnational Organized Crime
UNDAW	United Nations Division for the Advancement of Women
UNDESA	United Nations Department of Economic and Social Affairs
UNDP	United Nations Development Programme
UNECA	United Nations Economic Commission for Africa
UNESCO	United Nations Educational, Scientific and Cultural Organization
UNFPA	United Nations Population Fund
UNGA	United Nations General Assembly
UNGAOR	United Nations General Assembly Official Records
UNHCHR	United Nations High Commissioner for Human Rights
UNHCR	United Nations High Commissioner for Refugees
UNIFEM	United Nations Development Fund for Women
UNODC	United Nations Office on Drugs and Crime
UNRISD	United Nations Research Institute for Social Development
UNSC	United Nations Security Council
UNTS	United Nations Treaty Series
VCCR	Vienna Convention on Consular Relations
VIS	(European) Visa Information System
WAEMU	West African Economic and Monetary Union
WTO	World Trade Organization

PREFACE

The purpose of this book is to encapsulate the current state of international migration law by addressing the substantial developments that have taken place since the publication of *Migration and International Legal Norms* by T.M.C. Asser Press in 2003.[1] This was the first recent volume that purported to examine the international legal norms relating to migration in a comprehensive fashion,[2] with the assistance of renowned experts working in the diverse fields covered by the topic. While there are also now a number of authoritative texts which address specific groups of migrants encompassed by international migration law, such as non-citizens generally,[3] refugees,[4] migrant workers,[5] irregular migrants,[6] and internally displaced persons,[7] as well as pertinent themes, such as the human rights of migrants,[8] there remains a need to consider all these groups and themes from a

[1] T.A. Aleinikoff and V. Chetail (eds.), *Migration and International Legal Norms* (The Hague, T.M.C. Asser Press 2003). This volume was published with the support of the International Organization for Migration (IOM), the Graduate Institute of International Studies in Geneva and the Migration Policy Institute in Washington, under the sponsorship of the Swiss Government's Berne Initiative.

[2] However, international migration law is not a new term and, to the best of our knowledge, was first used in the academic literature by Richard Plender in his seminal work on the issue in the 1970s (a second edition was produced in the 1980s) as well as in the text of basic documents that accompanied it. See R. Plender on *International Migration Law*, 2nd rev. edn. (Dordrecht, Martinus Nijhoff 1988) and R. Plender, *Basic Documents on International Migration Law* (Dordrecht, Martinus Nijhoff 1988), with revised editions published in 1997 and 2006. For other broad legal perspectives on the movement of persons across international borders, see L. Sohn and T. Buergenthal, *The Movement of Persons Across Borders* (Washington DC, American Society of International Law 1992) and G. Goodwin-Gill, *International Law and the Movement of Persons Between States* (Oxford, Clarendon Press 1978).

[3] R. Lillich, *The Human Rights of Aliens in Contemporary International Law* (Manchester, Manchester University Press 1984); C. Tiburcio, *The Human Rights of Aliens under International and Comparative Law* (The Hague, Martinus Nijhoff 2001).

[4] G. Goodwin-Gill, *The Refugee in International Law*, 2nd edn. (Oxford, Clarendon Press 1996); J. Hathaway, *The Law of Refugee Status* (Toronto, Butterworths 1991); J. Hathaway, *The Rights of Refugees under International Law* (Cambridge, Cambridge University Press 2005).

[5] R. Cholewinski, *Migrant Workers in International Human Rights Law: Their Protection in Countries of Employment* (Oxford, Clarendon Press 1997).

[6] B. Bogusz, R. Cholewinski, A. Cygan and E. Szyszczak (eds.), *Irregular Migration and Human Rights: Theoretical, European and International Perspectives* (Leiden, Martinus Nijhoff 2004).

[7] S. Bagshaw, *Developing a Normative Framework for the Protection of Internally Displaced Persons* (New York, Transnational Publishers 2005); C. Phoung, *International Protection of Internally Displaced Persons* (Cambridge, Cambridge University Press 2005).

[8] B. Ghosh, *Elusive Protection, Uncertain Lands: Migrants' Access to Human Rights* (IOM, Geneva 2003). The human rights of victims of trafficking and human smuggling are also covered in recent scholarly literature. See, e.g., R. Piotrowicz, 'Irregular Migration Networks: The Challenge Posed by People Traffickers to States and Human Rights', in B. Bogusz, et al., op. cit. n. 6, p. 137; T. Obokata, 'Smuggling of Human Beings from a Human Rights Perspective: Obligations of Non-State and State Actors under International Human Rights Law', 17 *International Journal of Refugee Law* (2005) p. 394.

broader international legal perspective with a view to providing a more comprehensive, coherent and contextual analysis of the impact of international migration law at the global, regional, sub-regional, and national level.

The contributors to this volume comprise scholars and practitioners researching and working in the field of international migration law, including promising younger researchers who have already made original contributions to specific aspects of this field, and a number of policy makers and researchers working for international organizations with international migration law as part of their mandate. The contributors were requested to draft short chapters summarizing the core of international migration law existing in their field of expertise, including analyses of the principal developments and anticipated future trends. With the generous financial support of the Swiss Federal Office for Migration, most of the contributors were then able to participate in a workshop in Geneva at the beginning of November 2005 to discuss their chapters with a view to improving their content and structure. Other experts in international migration law, officials working on migration from international organizations, government policy makers, and prominent representatives from civil society organizations also took part in the workshop to ensure that the input into the discussions was as pertinent and wide-ranging as possible. The workshop also provided the authors with a good opportunity to see how their work complemented the overall structure of the book, and the editors of the volume with the chance to discuss the overarching themes and to try to ensure that the text would take on a coherent shape. We hope that these objectives have been achieved in the final product and that the text will appeal to a diverse group of readers: i.e., academics and advanced students; government policy makers and officials working for international and regional organizations; migration practitioners; and representatives of civil society.[9]

This edited collection of articles attempts to build upon and deepen consideration of a number of the legal issues addressed in the 2003 volume, and also deals with subject areas not addressed in the earlier text, thereby seeking to further the project of defining and improving the understanding of the principal international legal norms relating to migration. The book contains chapters grouped under similar topics, such as state sovereignty, forced migration, human rights of migrants and migration and trade, but often from rather different and broader perspectives, and considers new emerging issues. It also devotes, for example, a whole part to the development in a number of world regions of free movement regimes, which are having an increasing impact on the nature of migratory movements in those regions, and on the perception of migrants and their treatment in countries of destination.

The first part of the book, concerned with state sovereignty and responsibility, contains an in-depth analysis of the challenges posed by migration to state sovereignty, such as the increasing tensions between the content of security or anti-

[9] To accompany this book, IOM's International Migration Law and Legal Affairs Department is also preparing a compendium of instruments on international migration law.

terrorism legislation and the legal framework for international migration (Schoenholtz); the legal protection of stranded migrants (Grant), who are often caught in a legal void when transiting countries or when conditions in the countries in which they are residing deteriorate; the difficult legal questions arising from the detention of migrants and asylum seekers (Vohra); recent advances in consular protection and assistance to migrants (Perruchoud); and the vexed issue of multiple nationality (de Hart and Groenendijk), which, despite the existence of nascent norms at the regional level among a number of Council of Europe Member States, is still largely regulated at the national level, with diverging results for the migrants concerned as demonstrated by the practices in Germany and the Netherlands.

The second part of the book examines the interrelationship between trade and labour migration. It looks at developments in World Trade Organization (WTO) negotiations on the movement of service providers under Mode 4 of the General Agreement on Trade in Services (Klein Solomon), focusing also on what has occurred in this area outside of these negotiations. The international regulatory framework governing the transfer of remittances, which constitute such a significant source of revenue for many countries of origin whose nationals work abroad, is analysed from the perspective of different regional approaches (Orozco). The North American Free Trade Agreement (NAFTA) and the recently adopted Central America-Dominican Republic-United States Free Trade Agreement (CAFTA-DR) (Flores-Macías) offer an important regional perspective on the migration-trade nexus.

The issue of forced migration comprises the third part of the book. In addition to a critical overview of changing paradigms in refugee law (Byrne), this section addresses specific developments, such as actions undertaken to address secondary movements of refugees and asylum seekers (Legomsky), which are increasingly occupying the minds of policy makers working in this field. It also discusses one particular group of forced migrants not covered in the 2003 volume, namely internally displaced persons (Bagshaw), with a focus on the activities undertaken at the level of the international community and in individual states to implement the landmark Guiding Principles on Internal Displacement.[10] While forced migration has a number of repercussions in international law, including human rights violations, one often neglected consequence concerns claims for restitution and compensation by those migrants required to leave their properties behind, and the international regime relating to such claims is considered in a separate chapter (Wühler).

The fourth part of the book undertakes an in-depth examination of the human rights of migrants with a focus on specific migrant groups. The starting-point is the application of international human rights norms to non-citizens generally

[10] *Report of the Representative of the Secretary-General, Mr. Francis M. Deng, submitted pursuant to Commission on Human Rights resolution 1997/39. Addendum. Guiding Principles on Internal Displacement.* UN Doc. E/CN.4/1998/53/Add.2 (11 Feb. 1998).

(Weissbrodt). The increasing feminization of migration and the fact that about half of today's economic migrants are women warrants a separate chapter on migrant women (Piper and Satterthwaite) and the specific challenges of their protection. Further contributions in this section include an overview of the rights of migrant workers under international human rights and labour law (Cholewinski), but also with a focus on supplementary means of protection currently being developed under non-binding mechanisms, and the human rights of victims of trafficking in the migration context (Piotrowicz). The final chapter in this section examines the treatment of stateless persons under pertinent international legal instruments with specific reference to the situation in Estonia and Latvia (Gelazis).

The expansion of regional legal frameworks concerned with migration, particularly in the European Union (EU) but also other regions of the globe, has been incorporated into the analysis of the growing body of international migration law as the fifth part to this volume. The EU is the most developed system, and two chapters are devoted to developments there: the first on the evolving concept of European Citizenship in the context of the free movement of EU nationals (Hailbronner), with a focus on the recent judicial pronouncements on the content of Union Citizenship by the European Court of Justice; and the second examining the rapid pace of change in the design of the European immigration policy in respect of non-EU or third-country nationals (De Bruycker). While free movement regimes elsewhere have not evolved as quickly or had the same profound impact as that of the EU, there has been progress nonetheless, and these developments are discussed with regard to three regions, Africa (Martens), with particular reference to West and Southern Africa, South America (Santestevan), and the Caribbean (Nonnenmacher).

Since the publication of *Migration and International Legal Norms* in 2003, a number of significant issues continue to develop and new complex legal areas, which will have an important impact on the international movement of persons, have evolved, and these are analysed in the sixth part of the book, 'Continuing and Emerging Issues of Significance'. In the absence of a universal legal framework regulating international migration, inter-state cooperation mechanisms at the global, regional and bilateral level (Nielsen) will continue to be important for the better understanding of the diverse components of international migration law and its improved implementation in practice. The second chapter in this section examines the development and application of biometrics technology to the transnational movement of persons (Redpath), and the human rights and data protection implications of this technology. Finally, in the EU, enhanced cooperation on border controls (Peers) is moving apace resulting in new legal instruments and mechanisms, particularly the adoption of the EU Borders Code and the establishment of the European Border Agency.

The concluding chapter in this book, written by one of the editors of *Migration and International Legal Norms* (Aleinikoff), takes stock of the principal trends and themes identified. It contends that a global normative regime regulating international migration is probably a rather unrealistic goal given that states jealously guard their sovereignty in this area, but also asks whether it might be possible to move towards consensus on a non-binding bill of rights for migrants, outlining the basic rights to which they are entitled in a clear and concise manner.

We hope this book succeeds in its objectives of encapsulating the current state of international migration law and assisting readers, both experts and non-experts alike, in developing a more in-depth understanding of this important field, which continues to move up the policy agendas of governments, the private sector and civil society. The emerging global labour market, increased opportunities for faster and cheaper travel, and better communications and technological advances mean that international movements of persons are likely to grow and diversify. Consequently, it is not surprising that the legal norms relating to these movements, whether comprising 'hard' or 'soft' law, are also becoming more complex. In due course, there may well be a need for the preparation of another study on this subject to take account of developments and to discuss new issues but, in the meantime, we trust that this book will make a worthy and authoritative contribution to this increasingly important field of international law.

Ryszard Cholewinski, Richard Perruchoud and Euan MacDonald

State Sovereignty and Responsibility

Chapter 1
ANTI-TERRORISM LAWS AND THE LEGAL FRAMEWORK FOR INTERNATIONAL MIGRATION

Andrew I. Schoenholtz*

1. Introduction

The development of explicit anti-terrorism laws that enable states to attempt to control the international movement of suspected terrorists is a relatively recent phenomenon. In 1990, for example, the US Congress for the first time enacted a law providing for the exclusion and deportation of a non-citizen who has 'engaged in terrorist activity'. The 21st century has witnessed major anti-terrorist developments in a variety of national migration laws, policies and practices, as states throughout the world have responded to an increase in the level of terrorist acts. The analysis that follows will focus particularly on these national developments, with due attention where appropriate to the more limited regional and global legal changes that have occurred in this area.[1]

This chapter examines the four major ways in which states employ migration laws to control the international movement of suspected terrorists. First, they enact laws to exclude terrorists from entering their territories and remove those who have successfully entered. These statutes define who is a terrorist and substantively authorize the state to prevent their entry and prosecute them for violating migration laws after entry. Second, states impose many controls to prevent the actual entry of terrorists. Third, states detain and remove suspected terrorists found within their territories. Finally, states employ practices, such as profiling, that adversely affect targeted communities.

What follows raises issues regarding the impact of anti-terrorist laws and policies on the international movement of people. The focus remains on the legal and

* Deputy Director of Georgetown University's Institute for the Study of International Migration, Visiting Professor at the Georgetown University Law Center and School of Foreign Service, and Co-Director of the Graduate Certificate in Refugees and Humanitarian Emergencies. The author wishes to thank his very able research assistant, Daniel McLaughlin, for his outstanding help in researching the developments discussed in this chapter.

[1] For an analysis of how international law addresses the full range of security matters, see D. Fisher, S. Martin, and A. Schoenholtz, 'Migration and Security in International Law', in T.A. Aleinikoff, et al. (eds.), Migration and International Legal Norms (The Hague, T.M.C. Asser Press 2003) p. 87.

R. Cholewinski, R. Perruchoud and E. MacDonald, eds., International Migration Law

policy level, as an empirical study of such issues – which would be quite useful – is beyond the scope of this chapter. While this study attempts to cover developments throughout the world, the research has predictably uncovered considerably more information regarding some states than others. Still, recognizing such limitations, the analysis identifies trends and questions certain ways in which states have tried to accomplish the major goals of international migration: facilitating the entry of non-citizens whose presence is desired, while identifying and deterring the entry of unwanted foreigners – in this case, terrorists.

2. Terrorism and Laws of Admission and Exclusion

Since the end of the Cold War, states have enacted international migration laws that explicitly provide for the exclusion and deportation of terrorists. As international terrorist activity has expanded, so have state attempts to exclude and remove such foreigners. The lack of an internationally agreed upon definition of terrorism has not hindered this trend.

The development of terrorist exclusion laws in the United States provides a good example of this phenomenon. While the exclusion of subversives from the United States dates back over a century, it was not until 1990 that its immigration laws provided for the exclusion and deportation of those 'engaged in terrorist activity'.[2] Generally, any such non-citizen, regardless of political motive, is permanently excluded from the United States. In limited circumstances, certain forms of relief from deportation were available under the 1990 law.

Following the first World Trade Center terrorist attack in 1993, Congress expanded the grounds for exclusion of non-citizens twice in 1996. Under the Anti-terrorism and Effective Death Penalty Act (AEDPA), Congress defined the phrase 'engaged in terrorist activity' to include representatives and members of organizations designated as 'terrorist organizations' by the US Department of State. The AEDPA also barred aliens who can be deported for having 'engaged in terrorist activity' from most forms of relief.[3] Later in 1996, the Illegal Immigration Reform and Immigrant Responsibility Act (IIRIRA) amended the definition of 'engaging in terrorist activity' in two respects: (1) by adding a new provision to include an alien who, 'under circumstances indicating an intention to cause death or serious bodily harm, incited terrorist activity'; and (2) by providing that a representative of a foreign terrorist organization as designated by the Secretary of State is removable only if the alien 'knows or should have known' that the organization is a terrorist organization. In addition, the IIRIRA repealed the AEDPA provision that had allowed, in highly limited circumstances, withholding of deportation (now withholding of removal) in cases where there is a probability

[2] The Immigration Act of 1990, Pub. L. No. 101-649, 104 Stat. 4978, Section 601.

[3] The Anti-terrorism and Effective Death Penalty Act of 1996, Pub. L. No. 104-132, 110 Sta. 1214, Title IV.

that the individual to be removed would be persecuted should it be carried out.[4]

The net result, according to David Martin, was a highly stringent statutory scheme applicable to persons who meet the broad definition of having 'engaged in a terrorist activity', with virtually no possibility for asylum or other relief from removal. These grounds for removal of terrorists apply broadly and leave little room for case-by-case treatment of claims for relief from removal, which were previously judged based on individual factors.[5]

Nonetheless, the Uniting and Strengthening America By Providing Appropriate Tools Required to Intercept and Obstruct Terrorism Act (USA Patriot Act) expanded the security-related grounds for denial of entry, removal, and mandatory detention shortly after the attacks of 11 September 2001.[6] The Act broadened the scope of what is defined as terrorism-related activity, and included providing material support for humanitarian projects of groups that are named on the Secretary of State's list of designated terrorist organizations. The Act also allowed for the detention and deportation of non-citizens who provide lawful assistance to groups that are not officially designated as terrorist organizations. The burden is on the non-citizen to prove that he did not know and should not have known that his assistance would further terrorist activity. Persons certified by the Attorney General as suspected terrorists or terrorist supporters face mandatory detention.[7]

While the trend has been heavily towards state expansion of anti-terrorism laws in the migration context,[8] at least one major international migration state,

[4] The Illegal Immigration Reform and Immigrant Responsibility Act of 1996, Pub. L. No. 104-208, 110 Stat. 3009, Sections 304, 342 and 355.

[5] D. Martin, 'Testimony Before the Ad Hoc Committee on Irish Affairs Concerning the Deportation and Exclusion of Persons Who May Have Committed Criminal or Terrorist Acts', US Department of Justice, Immigration and Naturalization Service (INS) (6 Feb. 1997) <http://www.uscis.gov/graphics/aboutus/congress/testimonies/1997/970206.pdf> pp. 5, 7 ('The definition of "engaging in terrorist activity" is also very broad. This term "means to commit, in an individual capacity or as a member of an organization, an act of terrorist activity or an act which the actor knows, or reasonably should know, affords material support to any individual, organization, or government in conducting a terrorist activity at any time..."').

[6] Uniting and Strengthening America By Providing Appropriate Tools Required to Intercept and Obstruct Terrorism Act of 2001, Pub. L. No. 107-56, 115 Stat. 272.

[7] Immigration and Nationality Act, 8 USC 236A, Section 236A.

[8] In the period after 9/11, European states also broadened their terrorist laws affecting the rights of admission of third country nationals. For example, the German Prevention of Terrorism Act 2002 [*Gesetz zur Bekämpfung des internationalen Terrorismus (Terrorismusbekämpfungsgesetz)*], BGBl I, v. 11, p. 361 (2002) amended the Aliens Act [*Gesetz über die Einreise und den Aufenthalt von Ausländern im Bundesgebiet (Ausländergesetz)*], BGBl I, v. 9, p. 1354 (1990) by providing for new mandatory refusal grounds for a residence permit or visa and mandatory expulsion grounds if the third country national is a threat to the free democracy or security of Germany, is a member of an association which supports international terrorism, or supports such an association. The UK's Anti-Terrorism, Crime and Security Act (ATCSA) 2001 (c. 24) provides that a person certified by the Home Secretary as an international terrorist can be refused entry or leave to remain or given an order of deportation. The definition of 'suspected international terrorist' widened the definition of the Terrorism Act 2000 (c. 11) to include people who the Secretary reasonably believes to be national security risks and reasonably suspects to

India, has taken steps at different times to repeal such laws. The Terrorist and Disruptive Activities (Prevention) Act (TADA) lapsed in 1995 after widespread abuse. India's Union Cabinet issued the temporary Prevention of Terrorism Ordinance (POTO) in October 2001, and, following the attack on the Indian Parliament in December of that year, the Cabinet passed the Prevention of Terrorism Act (POTA) in a rare joint session convened at the Prime Minister's request. While these measures particularly addressed insurgent groups, they also purported to respond to an 'intensification of cross border terrorism'.[9] Like the USA Patriot Act, POTA defines terrorism broadly, but with even less precision, referring only to any violence committed 'with intent to threaten the unity, integrity, security or sovereignty of India or to strike terror in the people or any section of the people'. Though POTA provided some safeguards to address the widespread abuse of TADA, the later law also suffered from similar problems. Following significant political misuses of the detention powers under POTA, a new central Government repealed the law in 2004.[10]

The only significant international law regarding the exclusion of terrorists is found in the 1951 Refugee Convention and the 1967 Refugee Protocol. Terrorism is not explicitly mentioned, but Article 1F formally excludes from international protection any person 'with respect to whom there are serious reasons for considering' that he has committed a crime against peace, a war crime, or a crime against humanity; acts contrary to the purposes and principles of the United Nations; or a serious non-political crime outside the country of refuge.[11] Recent UNHCR Guidelines state that 'acts commonly considered to be terrorist in nature are likely to fall within the exclusion clauses', noting that

> '[c]onsideration of the exclusion clauses is, however, often unnecessary as terrorists may not be eligible for refugee status in the first place, their fear being of legitimate prosecution as opposed to persecution for Convention reasons'.[12]

Two other provisions of this Convention very generally address terrorists. Article 32(1) prohibits the expulsion of refugees lawfully present, but provides for a se-

---

be terrorists. The word 'terrorist' is defined as a person who is involved in acts of international terrorism or supports or assists or is a member of 'an international terrorist group'. E. Brouwer, 'Immigration, Asylum and Terrorism: A Changing Dynamic – Legal and Practical Developments in the EU in Response to the Terrorist Attacks of 11.09', 4 *European Journal of Migration and Law* (2002) p. 399 at pp. 404, 409-410.

[9] C. Gagne, 'Immigration Law and Human Rights: Legal Line Drawing Post-September 11: Note: POTA: Lessons Learned From India's Anti-Terror Act', 25 *Boston College Third World Law Journal* (2005) p. 261 at p. 263.

[10] Ibid., at p. 265.

[11] Convention Relating to the Status of Refugees, 28 July 1951, 189 *UNTS* 150 (hereafter 'Refugee Convention'), Art. 1F, and Protocol Relating to the Status of Refugees, 31 Jan. 1967, 606 *UNTS* 267.

[12] UNHCR, *Guidelines on International Protection No. 5: Application of the Exclusion Clauses: Article 1F of the 1951 Convention relating to the Status of Refugees*, Doc. HCR/GIP/03/05 (4 Sept. 2003) <http://www.unhcr.ch/cgi-bin/texis/vtx/publ/opendoc.pdf?tbl=PUBL&id=3f7d48514>.

curity exception; and Article 33(1) requires states to respect the most fundamental commitment in international refugee law, *non-refoulement*. But Article 33(2) provides for an exception to this obligation where there are 'reasonable grounds' for regarding a refugee 'as a danger to the security of the country in which he is'.

Experts have expressed serious concern that states will expand the use of the exclusion clause (Article 1F) and the security exception (Article 33(2)) of the Refugee Convention in an overbroad manner. One commentator has argued that the adoption of Security Council Resolution 1377 in 2001, which notes that acts of international terrorism are contrary to the purpose and principles of the UN Charter,[13] is 'likely to lead to a significant expansion in the use of this clause to exclude refugees accused of terrorism'.[14]

The significant expansions in the definition of 'terrorist activity' in national laws discussed above provide states with an exceptional degree of authority to make such determinations. Moreover, even though Articles 1(F) and 33(2) of the Refugee Convention provide states with the means of excluding terrorists, certain states have also made changes to domestic asylum law, citing terrorist control as justification. UK law provides, in Section 33 of the Anti-Terrorism, Crime and Security Act 2001, for significant deference to an executive certification that an asylum claimant is not entitled to protection from *refoulement* under Article 33(1) of the Refugee Convention because of the exceptions contained in Article 1F or Article 33(2).[15] In May 2005, the United States revised its asylum laws through the Real ID Act, purportedly to 'prevent terrorists from obtaining relief from removal'.[16] While many observers contend that these changes have no serious connection to security issues, the thrust of the legislation provides Immigration Judges with greater authority to make credibility determinations and to require corroboration of an asylum claim, and broadens bars to asylum for those who in some way support terrorist activities. The new law expands the definition of terrorism, and what constitutes 'supporting' terrorism, to the extent that human rights organizations are very concerned that 'people who bear no personal responsibility for terrorist acts – even the wives and children of victims of extortion by militant groups' are being barred from protection and subject to removal.[17]

---

[13] UNSC Res. 1377 on threats to international peace and security caused by terrorist acts, UNSC, 56th Sess., 4413th Mtg at 1, UN Doc. S/RES/1377 (12 Nov. 2001).

[14] M. Zard, 'Exclusion, Terrorism and the Refugee Convention', 13 *Forced Migration Review* (2002) p. 32 at pp. 33-34.

[15] D. Bonner and R. Cholewinski, 'Immigration and Asylum Law: The Impact of Terrorism – The United Kingdom', in A. Baldaccini and E. Guild (eds.), *Terrorism and the Foreigner: A Decade of Tension around the Rule of Law in Europe* (Leiden, Brill forthcoming 2006) p. 48; M. Zard, loc. cit. n. 14, at p. 34.

[16] The Real ID Act of 2005, Division B of An Act making Emergency Supplemental Appropriations for Defense, the Global War on Terror, and Tsunami Relief, for the fiscal year ending September 30, 2005, and for other purposes, Pub. L. No. 109-13.

[17] Human Rights First, 'Real ID Endangers People Fleeing Persecution', (2005) <http://www.humanrightsfirst.org/asylum/asylum_10_sensenbr.asp>.

As David Bonner and Ryszard Cholewinski observe, however, international human rights law has curtailed the operation of Article 33(2) of the Refugee Convention considerably, in connection with the prohibitions on torture and inhuman and degrading treatment and punishment found in the UN Convention against Torture (CAT),[18] which has no security exception to *non-refoulement*, and the International Covenant on Civil and Political Rights (ICCPR).[19] They also point out that the European Court of Human Rights (ECtHR) has established an absolute prohibition on the return of persons to countries where they face a real risk of torture or degrading treatment at the hands of governmental authorities or non-state actors in contravention of the European Convention on Human Rights (ECHR),[20] Article 3.[21] This prohibition also extends to those considered to constitute a risk to the national security of the state of asylum.[22]

In developing laws aimed at the exclusion and removal of those involved in terrorist activities, therefore, states have generally created broad definitions that provide them with considerable discretion. As international terrorists strike with greater effect, many states have expanded their legal abilities to exclude and deport. While this power enables them to protect citizens and residents from security threats with greater ease, such authority is open to serious misuse. On occasion, states have reacted to such abuse by scaling back the powers they grant. International human rights law may, to some degree in certain states, keep such powers somewhat in check. As of now, however, most states that have developed anti-terrorism laws possess exceptional authority to exclude and remove those believed to be involved in international terrorist activities. Furthermore, as the discussion in Section 4 below on interior control and prosecution demonstrates, states have used these powers aggressively.

[18] Convention Against Torture and Other Cruel, Inhuman or Degrading Treatment or Punishment, 10 Dec. 1984, 1465 *UNTS* 85.

[19] International Covenant on Civil and Political Rights, UNGA Res. 2200A (XXI) of 16 Dec. 1966, 21 UN GAOR Supp. (No. 16) p. 52, UN Doc. A/6316 (1966), 999 *UNTS* 171.

[20] Convention for the Protection of Human Rights and Fundamental Freedoms, 4 Nov. 1950, 213 *UNTS* 222, *ETS* No. 5; entered into force 3 Sept. 1953.

[21] D. Bonner and R. Cholewinski, loc. cit. n. 15, at p. 16.

[22] *Chahal* v. *The United Kingdom* (1997) 23 *EHRR* 413, paras. 79 and 80. The ECtHR has said that 'Article 3 enshrines one of the most fundamental values of democratic society … The Court is well aware of the immense difficulties faced by States in modern times in protecting their communities from terrorist violence. However, even in these circumstances, the Convention prohibits in absolute terms torture or inhuman or degrading treatment or punishment, irrespective of the victim's conduct … The prohibition provided by Article 3 against ill-treatment is equally absolute in expulsion cases. Thus, whenever substantial grounds have been shown for believing that an individual would face a real risk of being subjected to treatment contrary to Article 3 if removed to another State, the responsibility of the Contracting State to safeguard him or her against such treatment is engaged in the event of expulsion … In these circumstances, the activities of the individual in question, however undesirable or dangerous, cannot be a material consideration. The protection afforded by Article 3 is thus wider than that provided by Articles 32 and 33 of the United Nations 1951 Convention on the Status of Refugees …'

3. Prevention: Controlling the Entry of Terrorists

Many of the developments in migration law and policy regarding terrorists have focused on controlling entry.[23] The impetus for this clearly derived from the way in which the September 11 terrorists traveled internationally, entering on tourist and student visas under false pretenses or with fraudulently altered passports.[24]

The UN has emphasized the responsibility of states to control the international movement of terrorists. Passed in response to the 9/11 attacks, UN Security Council Resolution 1373 requires states to

> '[p]revent the movement of terrorists or terrorist groups by effective border controls and controls on issuance of identity papers and travel documents, and through measures for preventing counterfeiting, forgery or fraudulent use of identity papers and travel documents'.[25]

3.1 Visa procedures and policies

Visa procedures and policies have been heavily affected by the security concerns generated by the 21st century terrorist attacks in various states. According to one US State Department official, the goal is 'to "push out" our border security beyond the United States to the maximum extent possible, while at the same time facilitating legitimate travel'.[26] The additional security checks in the US visa process put into place in the aftermath of September 11 have caused significant delays.[27] Personal interviews

---

[23] No international or regional human rights instrument expressly provides for the right of non-citizens to enter a foreign state. For a full discussion of security issues regarding the control of entry under international law, see D. Fisher, loc. cit. n. 1, at pp. 99-111.

[24] 'The 19 hijackers who attacked the World Trade Center and the Pentagon entered the US on tourist and student visas under false pretenses and used the same modalities of travel document fraud and visa abuse characteristic of illegal migration to the US. Al-Qaeda operated a "passport office" at the Kandahar airport to alter travel documents… and at least two, and perhaps as many as eleven, of the September 11th hijackers used fraudulently altered passports'. R. Koslowski, 'Possible Steps towards an International Regime for Mobility and Security', *Global Migration Perspectives No. 8* (2004) <http://www.gcim.org/en/ir_gmp.html> p. 3.

[25] UNSC Res. 1373, UNSC, 56th Sess., 4385th Mtg at 2, UN Doc. S/RES/1373 (28 Sept. 2001).

[26] Testimony of T. Edson, Deputy Assistant Secretary for Visa Services, US State Department, Before the US House Subcommittee on National Security, Emerging Threats, and International Relations of the Committee on Government Reform, 13 Sept. 2005, p. 1.

[27] See US General Accounting Office, *Border Security: Strengthened Visa Process Would Benefit From Improvements in Staffing and Information Sharing* GAO-05-859, 13 Sept. 2005 <http://www.gao.gov/new.items/d05859.pdf> pp. 1, 16-17, 23-26. A high ranking State Department official has observed that '[t]he implementation of the numerous post 9/11 changes to the visa process has resulted in significantly increasing the complexity of the visa adjudication process and therefore also increasing the average time necessary to adjudicate a visa'. Testimony of T. Edson, loc. cit. n. 26, at p. 4. Post-9/11 US visa procedures also changed the handling of cases requiring Security Advisory Opinions (SAOs). According to the Consul General at the US Embassy in Beijing during this period, SAOs are broad categories of cases involving potential 'security-related' matters regarding which Consular Officers

and background checks in particular have considerably lengthened the process.[28]

European visa procedures are also changing in the new security environment. The EU is creating a European Visa Information System (VIS) that will contain data from every visa application for a short visit of up to 3 months made to an EU Member State, whether successful or not. All visa applicants will have to provide two forms of biometric data – digital photos and fingerprints – which will also be stored in the VIS.[29] Analysts observe that the VIS has not been seriously assessed to determine whether the goal of reducing the risk of terrorists entering the EU on a visa, and the other goals of the system, could be accomplished by less expensive and less 'far-reaching means than by establishing such an intrusive system'.[30]

With regard to visa eligibility, states have also at times responded to terrorist threats by clamping down on specific groups. For example, UK Immigration Rules were amended in 1990 during the First Gulf War to prevent the admission of new Iraqi students.[31] After 9/11, the exponential growth of on- and offshore US visa screening mechanisms, some of which directly targeted Arab and Muslim nationals, created massive delays and considerable frustration for Arab and Muslim students seeking an American education.[32]

3.2 Airline Liaison Officers

In the 1990's, several European, North American and South Pacific states deployed Airline Liaison Officers (ALOs) abroad to intercept travellers without valid documents. This was another means of pushing the border back to where

cannot issue visas without clearance from Washington. There are several thousand SAO cases each year in China, mostly involving potential illicit technology transfer matters, not terrorism. Significant delays started to adversely affect many legitimate scientific and academic exchanges, but, in time, significant improvements occurred for most cases. See the Testimony of J.D. Morris, Consul General, US Embassy Beijing, Before the US House Subcommittee on National Security, Emerging Threats, and International Relations of the Committee on Government Reform, 13 Sept. 2005, pp. 2-3.

28 For example, once there is a 'hit' between the visa applicant's information and the FBI criminal records information system, the data needed to make visa determinations is not electronically available to the Consular Officer. Experts have recommended that the law be changed to enable these visa officials to access such information and thus eliminate major delays in the visa determination process. See the Testimony of S. Ginsburg Before the U.S. House Subcommittee on National Security, Emerging Threats, and International Relations of the Committee on Government Reform, 13 Sept. 2005, p. 6.

29 B. Hayes, 'SIS II: *fait accompli?* Construction of EU's Big Brother database underway', *Statewatch Analysis* (May 2005) <http://www.statewatch.org/news/2005/may/sisII-analysis-may05.pdf> p. 6.

30 S. Peers, 'Key Legislative Developments on Migration in the European Union', 6 *European Journal of Migration and Law* (2004) p. 243 at p. 256.

31 D. Bonner and R. Cholewinski, loc. cit. n. 15, at p. 5.

32 R. Sedgwick. 'Middle Eastern Students Find Options at Home and Elsewhere', *World Education News and Review* (Nov. 2004) <http://www.wes.org/ewenr/04Nov/feature.htm>; S. Yale-Loehr, et al., *Secure Borders, Open Doors: Visa Procedures in the Post-September 11 Era* (Washington DC, Migration Policy Institute 2005).

it is easier to control the travel of individuals whom the state does not want to admit. In the aftermath of 9/11, states have developed this means of control more seriously.[33]

The main role of ALOs is to assist airline and airport staff in document examination, to check passengers' documents for irregularities, and to provide training to host nation immigration authorities as well as airline and airport security staff on entry requirements. Although airlines decide whether to allow passengers to board their intended flight, these decisions are often made following ALO advice regarding the authenticity of the passengers' travel documents.[34]

By maintaining a visible presence at international airports, ALOs may also act as a deterrent to people smugglers and inadequately documented passengers. As part of the international cooperative efforts to combat people smuggling and illegal migration, ALOs participate in short-duration multi-national exercises held at select airports overseas and aimed at stopping irregular travellers.[35]

The UK's 27 ALOs, based in 25 posts across Europe, Asia and Africa, were expanded to 42 in 2004; this is because their advice led airlines to prevent over 30,000 passengers from embarking on flights at ALO locations, including over 800 improperly documented children.[36] Other states increasingly employing ALOs include Canada, Australia, and the US.[37]

3.3 Pre-departure travel information and documents

In their efforts to prevent the entry of terrorists, states have focused particularly on pre-departure traveller information and biometrics.[38] Pursuant to the

---

[33] UK Home Office, 'UK Borders further strengthened with Expansion of Airline Liaison Officer Network' (21 Feb. 2005) <http://www.ind.homeoffice.gov.uk/ind/en/home/news/press_releases/uk_borders_further.html>.

[34] Overseas immigration officers operate under the guidelines for airline liaison officers developed by the International Air Transport Association/Control Authorities Working Group available at <http://www.iata.org/WHIP/_Files/WgId_0014/ALOconductOct02.pdf>.

[35] Australian Department of Immigration and Multicultural and Indigenous Affairs, 'Border Control' (2005) <http://www.immi.gov.au/illegals/border.htm>.

[36] UK Home Office, loc. cit. n. 33.

[37] Canada has deployed 45 immigration officers, called Migration Integrity Officers, to 39 key locations overseas. Australia's 17 ALOs work at 12 strategically placed international airports with direct flights to Australia. The United States has developed a pre-9/11 ALO programme into the Immigration Security Initiative (ISI). Modelled on programmes in Australia, Canada, the United Kingdom and the Netherlands, this initiative will station teams of Customs and Border Protection officers in the key airports from which the majority of US-bound passengers depart. These officers will use advanced passenger manifest data to identify high-risk travellers before they board planes. See R. Koslowski, loc. cit. n. 24, at p. 7. According to the US Customs and Border Protection, '[t]he program would thus provide a middle layer of defense between the American consular office abroad, which issues visas, and the US port of arrival'; L. Woolf, US Department of Homeland Security, 'Immigration Security Initiative: New layer in homeland security defense', *Customs and Border Protection Today* (May 2004) <http://www.customs.gov/xp/CustomsToday/2004/May/isi.xml>.

[38] While most of this activity has occurred in response to the September 11 attacks, Australia had developed before this date, for general immigration control purposes, an electronic visa (the Electronic

Enhanced Border Security and Visa Entry Reform Act of 2002, US authorities require passenger manifests and passenger name records of all US-bound travellers.[39] All non-immigrant (temporary) visa applicants must now be interviewed at US consulates, and submit a biometric identifier at that time and then again upon entering. Other nations are adopting similar visa and border control policies.[40]

While these developments occurred quickly, some European states whose airlines were required to provide passenger name record (PNR) information raised major privacy concerns, contending that such sharing of information would violate EU data protection rules. Partly motivated by the fact that Canada and Australia also passed legislation requiring advanced submission of PNR data, however, the European Commission opted 'to take a global approach to the issue'.[41] Negotiations resulted in an agreement between the European Commission and US Customs and Border Protection (CBP) in the form of a Commission 'adequacy decision' that data were adequately protected, and corresponding undertakings issued by CBP, which promised that data would be treated in a manner agreed upon by the parties.[42] In October 2005, CBP added a new rule requiring carriers to include addresses of where visitors will be staying while in the US along with other passenger manifest data through the Advance Passenger Information System (APIS).[43]

Travel Authority, or ETA) as well as the Advance Passenger Processing system, which allows Australian officials to pre-process travellers before their flight reaches Australia. In advance of travel, an ETA is issued after checking the traveller's information through security systems. Then, when the traveller arrives at check-in, the airline can check electronically with the ETA system and will receive a message back saying that the individual is clear to board. The check-in data is then delivered to the destination country, and Australian inspectors have that information when the passenger arrives. See A. Schoenholtz, 'Transatlantic Dialogue on Terrorism and International Migration', 41(4) *International Migration* (2003) p. 173 at pp. 176-177.

[39] The Enhanced Border Security and Visa Entry Reform Act of 2002, Public Law 107-173, May 14, 2002, 116 Stat. 543, Section 402.

[40] For example, Canada implemented a Passenger Information System at Canadian airports in October 2002 to collect advanced passenger information. Canada and the United States agreed to share advanced passenger information and passenger name records on high-risk travellers and implemented an automated data-sharing program in 2003. See IOM, *International Terrorism and Migration*, (Geneva, IOM 2003) pp. 1, 8 <http://www.iom.int/en/PDF_Files/tcm/Int_terrorism_migration.pdf>. Koslowski reports that Member States of the International Civil Aviation Organization (ICAO) have agreed to issue machine-readable travel documents with biometric details stored on Radio Frequency Identification chips. ICAO Members are also considering proposals for international cooperation on electronic submission of advanced passenger information and the sharing of passenger name record data. See R. Koslowski, loc. cit. n. 24, at p. 4.

[41] R. Koslowski, loc. cit. n. 24, at p. 16.

[42] The EU Parliament has objected to this agreement. While it has no authority to stop its implementation, persistent attention to this matter may undermine support in some EU states. The Parliament has also referred the agreement to the European Court of Justice. See R. Koslowski, loc. cit. n. 24, at pp. 13-14.

[43] US Department of Homeland Security, 'US-VISIT UPDATE', 29 Sept. 2005. Under the US-

Separate from the EU-US agreement on the transfer of passenger data to the latter, the EU Council adopted a Directive on passenger data transmission in April 2004,[44] which Member States will have to implement by 5 September 2006. The core obligation is for carriers to transmit information at the request of external border control authorities before the end of passenger check-in at the latest. The requirement applies to all passengers, not just non-EU nationals. Analysts have questioned whether it is necessary or proportionate to require transmission of data on EU citizens and to permit continued storage of this information for law enforcement purposes.[45]

3.4 Biometric controls at entry and exit

Countries in different parts of the world have started to put in place computer systems that use biometric information at ports of entry to identify security threats.[46] The Philippine Bureau of Immigration, for example, is using facial recognition at Mactan-Cebu International Airport.[47] East African nations have begun to implement the US-funded Terrorist Interdiction Program to collect and analyze passport data. Kenya, Tanzania and Uganda are participating in this system to monitor cross-border movements at land and air ports of entry.[48]

The United Arab Emirates, which depends heavily on migrant labour (only 20 per cent of its workforce are UAE citizens), is one of the first countries to use an iris scan at most points of entry. Dubai airport is one of the busiest in the world, and all arriving passengers have their eyes scanned.[49] Canada and the Netherlands also use iris scanning as a border control method.[50]

VISIT Program, information collected on individuals 'consists of complete name, date of birth, gender, country of citizenship/nationality, passport number and country of issuance, country of residence, travel document type (e.g., visa), number, date and country of issuance, complete US destination address, arrival and departure information, a digital photograph, digital fingerscans, and for travelers using land POEs [ports of entry] after implementation of RFID [radio frequency identification], a unique and individually assigned RFID tag number for each traveler'. *Privacy Impact Assessment for the United States Visitor and Immigrant Status Indicator Technology (US-VISIT) Program* (22 Dec. 2005) p. 5.

[44] Council Directive 2004/82/EC of 29 April 2004 on the obligation of carriers to communicate passenger data, OJ 2004 L 261/24.

[45] S. Peers, loc. cit. n. 30, at p. 256.

[46] For a full discussion of biometrics and international migration, see the contribution to this volume by Jillyanne Redpath.

[47] 'Philippines Upgrades Airport Computers in Anti-terrorism Drive', *Asia Pulse*, 25 April 2005.

[48] 'Uganda Starts Using Hi-tech Immigration System to Counter Terrorism', *Agence France Presse*, 17 June 2005.

[49] The UAE also has installed an 'e-gate' at Dubai airport, which speeds up entry and exit procedures. Passengers use a card that stores their fingerprints, photo, and scanned passport for about $40 to enter via the 'e-gate'. See R. Tiron, 'Biometrics Systems Help Strengthen Border Security in Persian Gulf Nation', 89 *National Defense* (2005) p. 54.

[50] Ibid.

In the United States, the Enhanced Border Security Act mandates an automated entry-exit tracking system.[51] While Congress had required such a system in 1996, major concerns regarding long delays in Canadian-US crossings connected to trade held up its development. The Act requires the use of biometrics to verify the identity of non-citizens. Pursuant to that legislation, the United States Visitor and Immigrant Status Indicator Technology (US-VISIT) Program collects digital photographs and fingerprint scans from those individuals arriving on a non-immigrant visa to the United States, in order to prevent the use of fraudulent identities and travel documents, including visas. The purpose of the biometric identifier is to verify a person's identity, run criminal background checks, and ensure that an individual cannot apply or be granted welfare benefits, a visa, or admission to the United States under different names. The biometric information is checked against multiple databases, which contain visa issuance information, terrorist and criminal watchlists, and immigration status information. Those entering on the Visa Waiver programme are also subject to the entry-exit tracking system.[52]

Two regional developments are noteworthy here. The EU has also focused on using information technology to strengthen border controls. The European Commission proposed the expansion of the Schengen Information System (SIS), designed to enforce the common external border, to handle the increased data processing demands of EU enlargement. SIS II, scheduled to be operational in 2007, will also store digital images and biometric data, and will answer requests within five seconds.[53] While access to SIS under the Schengen Convention was restricted to immigration and customs enforcement officials (police, border guards, and immigration and customs officers), security and intelligence services will have access to SIS II pursuant to a reinterpretation of the Convention.[54]

Within months of the 9/11 attacks, Canada and the United States signed the Smart Border Declaration, which resulted in a Smart Border Action Plan.

---

[51] The Enhanced Border Security Act, loc. cit. n. 39, Section 302.

[52] As of December 2005, US-VISIT entry procedures are in place at 115 airports, 15 seaports, and in the secondary inspection areas of the 50 busiest land ports of entry. US-VISIT exit procedures are operating at 12 airports and two seaports. Entry procedures were expected to be in place at the remaining land ports of entry by 31 December 2005. See the website of the Department of Homeland Security, <http://www.dhs.gov/dhspublic/interapp/editorial/editorial_0685.xml>. As of August 2005, over 36 million foreign visitors have been processed under these entry procedures 'without adversely impacting wait times. In addition, the DHS (Department of Homeland Security) has taken adverse action against more than 800 criminals and immigration violators'. See the Testimony of E. Dezenski, Acting Assistant Secretary for Border and Transportation Security, Policy and Planning, Department of Homeland Security, Before the US House Subcommittee on National Security, Emerging Threats, and International Relations of the Committee on Government Reform, 13 Sept. 2005, pp. 8-9. Although Congress did not require US citizens to enroll in the program, the 9/11 Commission has recommended that all US, Canadian and Mexican nationals be required to participate. These nationals make up the vast majority of the 500,000 million crossings into the US every year.

[53] R. Koslowski, loc. cit. n. 24, at p. 9.

[54] B. Hayes, loc. cit. n. 29, at p. 6.

US$1.4 billion in trade crosses this border on a daily basis, so a great deal is at stake economically in ensuring that the border remains open to the desirable movement of goods and people and closed to the movement of security threats. Pre-screening goods, cargo, and people that cross the border is part of a risk management strategy that enables authorities to focus their efforts on movements of goods and people that represent the highest risk.[55] In short, the 'smarter' approach reflects an increased reliance on intelligence and information-sharing; common visa policies; shared lookout lists; pre-clearance of low-risk border crossers and dedicated travel lanes to facilitate their reasonably fast entry; advance sharing of airline passenger manifests prior to landing; common biometric identifiers; and joint operations/integrated enforcement teams.[56] While this approach has promise both in terms of facilitating desirable movements and preventing undesirable ones, the governments in this region face a difficult challenge in keeping up with the high and growing levels of land border crossings, which number more than 500 million across the US border annually.[57]

Prior to 9/11, states had developed a variety of entry control laws and mechanisms in response to irregular movements, smuggling and trafficking of persons across borders. As discussed above, 21st century terrorist attacks stimulated states to develop the next generation of controls. Despite fears of substantial adverse impact on desired international migration as well as serious concerns about privacy, states have begun to establish extensive entry control systems, on their own and in cooperation with others, that aim to prevent the international movement of those engaged in terrorism. Coupled with good intelligence, such systems could help states prevent potential terrorists from crossing international borders. Particularly where states understand the potentially significant economic impact of entry controls, some attempts are being made to focus not only on the restriction of unwanted movement but also on the facilitation of desired international migration. The risk management approach of facilitating the legal movement of

[55] A. Belelieu, 'Canada Alert: The Recent Evolution in Canadian Security Policy', XII *CSIS Hemisphere Focus* No. 12 (2 Sept. 2004) p. 1 at p. 2.

[56] D. Meyers, 'Security at US Borders: A Move Away from Unilateralism?', *Migration Information Source* (1 Aug. 2003) p. 2; A. Belelieu, loc. cit. n. 55, at p. 3; see also 'Smart Border Action Plan: Status Report', *Migration News*, 17 Dec. 2004 <http://migration.ucdavis.edu/rs/more.php?id=170_0_2_0>.

[57] At the insistence of Canada, both countries also agreed to implement controversial 'safe third country' policies. In 2005, Canada, Mexico and the United States agreed to strengthen information sharing on terrorists as part of the Security and Prosperity Partnership (SPP). According to the Acting Assistant Secretary for Border and Transportation Security, '[t]he SPP will enable all three countries to address and resolve gaps in cross-border information sharing. Ultimately, our goal is to ensure that all travellers arriving in North America will experience a comparable level of screening'. See the Testimony of E. Dezenski, loc. cit. n. 52, at p. 10. The United States is also working with other international partners, such as the G-8 Secure and Facilitated International Travel Initiative (SAFTI) (White House Press Release, <http://www.whitehouse.gov/news/releases/2004/06/20040609-51.html> (9 June 2004)), to improve information sharing.

low-risk migrants and focusing limited resources on high-risk threats may strike a reasonable balance in terms of state interests in this regard.

One group, however, that has already been adversely impacted by these changes are those fleeing persecution, civil conflict and other serious harms.[58] Since 9/11, the number of asylum seekers who manage to cross developed state borders and apply for protection has been halved.[59] Given that the entry control changes described above are here to stay, and are likely to make it more and more difficult for those in need of protection to find it in the developed world, states need also to develop mechanisms to identify and protect such individuals and not simply prevent their entry. Both states and the UNHCR will need to be thoughtful and creative in developing mechanisms for protection of the vulnerable in an age of terrorism.

4. Interior Controls and the Prosecution of Terrorists

Perhaps the most controversial state actions in response to terrorist acts or threats have been the aggressive use of extraordinary interior controls. States have relied particularly on detention, special courts to hear secret evidence, deportation, and registration. As the most important legal developments to date concern detention powers, this section will focus especially on the use of detention and some limits imposed thereon by human rights law.

In contrast with its use in the United Kingdom during the first Gulf War,[60] detention powers have been used sparingly since 9/11 by the Home Office – at least until the July 2005 terrorist attacks in London. According to Bonner and Cholewinski, the adoption of the Human Rights Act in 1998 and the articulation of the ECHR standards in immigration and asylum law by the European Court of Human Rights contributed to a shift in the use of detention powers between the Gulf War and 9/11. The Court's *Chahal* decision, in particular, set substantive and procedural limits on the power to detain and deport.[61]

---

[58] A. Schoenholtz, 'Refugee Protection in the United States Post-September 11', 36 *Columbia Human Rights Law Review* (2005) p. 323.

[59] See UNHCR, *Asylum Levels and Trends in Industrialized Countries, 2005* <http://www.unhcr.org/cgi-bin/texis/vtx/statistics/opendoc.pdf?tbl=STATISTICS&id=44153f592> p. 3.

[60] Prior to and during the First Gulf War, UK immigration rules required Iraqi nationals to register with the police or face criminal sanctions. While this appears to have encouraged public hostility towards these non-citizens, deportation of those thought to be a security risk was the most controversial power. Under the Immigration Act 1971, a non-citizen and his family members may be subject to deportation if the Home Secretary deems the principal's deportation to be conducive to the public good. As deportation to Iraq was generally not feasible, such determinations resulted in detention without trial. Non-judicial review of these determinations and detentions resulted in some releases largely due to the weakness of the intelligence against the individuals. See D. Bonner and R. Cholewinski, loc. cit. n. 15, at pp. 6, 9.

[61] D. Bonner and R. Cholewinski, loc. cit. n. 15, at pp. 3-4.

With regard to the requirement of the ECHR's Article 5(4) that everyone is entitled to challenge the lawfulness of his detention in court, the ECtHR ruled that courts must be able to review the evidence related to the supposed national security threat posed by the detainee.[62] The Court also found that the UK Advisory Panel, a body of three advisors appointed by the Home Secretary to review deportation (and detention) and to advise him or her accordingly, had serious shortcomings: the non-citizen was not entitled to legal representation before the panel; he/she was only given an outline of the grounds for deportation; the panel had no power of decision; and its advice to the Home Secretary was not disclosed. In contrast with the UK procedures, the Court looked favourably to the Canadian model of holding *in camera* hearings of such evidence, whereby the confidentiality of the information is maintained by appointing security-cleared counsel who cross-examine the witnesses and generally assist the court to test the strength of the Government's case.[63]

The Court also ruled that Article 13's guarantee of the right to an effective remedy of a Convention violation requires

> 'independent scrutiny of the claim that there exist substantial grounds for fearing a real risk of treatment contrary to Article 3. This scrutiny must be carried out without regard to what the person may have done to warrant expulsion or to any perceived threat to the national security of the expelling State'.[64]

The ECtHR found the British courts' approach wanting in this regard, because of an attempt to balance the risk to the detainee/deportee against the danger to national security. The ECtHR also found that the UK Advisory Panel did not provide sufficient procedural safeguards to comply with Article 13, due to the shortcomings discussed above with regard to Article 5(4).[65] On the other hand, the ECtHR did not find an Article 5(1) violation in the length of the detention (six years), which suggests that the international standards regarding arbitrary detention in terrorist cases may be rather low.[66]

Following the September 11 attacks, the United Kingdom passed the Anti-Terrorism, Crime and Security Act (ATCSA), which provided for the indefinite detention of non-citizen terrorists.[67] The UK Home Secretary certified a small

---

[62] *Chahal*, loc. cit. n. 22, para. 130.

[63] Ibid., at paras. 131, 144.

[64] Ibid., at para. 151.

[65] For a discussion of the procedural shortcomings of the UK advisory panel and the Canadian model, see I. Cameron, *National Security and the European Convention on Human Rights* (The Hague, Kluwer Law International 2000) pp. 271-274.

[66] Article 5(1) of the Convention enshrines the basic right to liberty, and freedom from arbitrary deprivation thereof. For a fuller discussion of the prohibition against arbitrary detention in the migration context, see Fisher, loc. cit. n. 1, at pp. 113-115.

[67] UK Anti-Terrorism, Crime and Security Act 2001, loc. cit. n. 8. To detain after 9/11 those non-

number of suspected international terrorists as threats to national security, and used the detention powers under ATCSA to hold those individuals who could not be deported for legal or practical reasons in indefinite detention without trial. The Home Secretary can certify a person as such based on secret evidence, where he suspects that the person is a terrorist and reasonably believes that the individual's presence in the United Kingdom is a risk to national security.[68]

In response to the *Chahal* ruling regarding legal shortcomings of the UK procedure used during the Gulf War, the United Kingdom established the Special Immigration Appeals Commission (SIAC). The SIAC can see all the material on which the Home Secretary's decision is based. The individual can be represented and present in open sessions. A security-cleared special advocate and immigration law expert, appointed by the Attorney General, acts as counsel to the Commission to probe the weaknesses of the security-related evidence. The special advocate is not instructed by the individual or his lawyer and cannot communicate with them without the Commission's approval after seeing the security evidence. The ATCSA made the SIAC a superior court of record and the sole means of appealing against and reviewing these detention decisions. Appeal from SIAC to the Court of Appeal and then the House of Lords is limited to points of law.[69] While an improvement on the previous review arrangement, according to Human Rights Watch (HRW), SIAC is a tribunal with limited procedural guarantees and a low standard of proof.[70]

Parliamentary scrutiny of these emergency detention powers pushed the Home Office to use them in a more limited way and subject them to a sunset clause.[71] Human rights organizations and the Islamic Human Rights Commission criticized the Home Office use of the detention powers and called for their repeal. They also expressed serious concern about 'their discriminatory use and the damaging focus on the Islamic community as contributing to a climate of Islamaphobia'.[72]

While the Home Office perceived ATCSA detention as essential, in December 2004 the UK House of Lords ruled that indefinite detention without trial of non-citizen terrorist suspects was contrary to the ECHR because it discriminated on

---

citizens who could not be deported, the United Kingdom had to suspend, or derogate from, certain of its obligations under the ECHR (loc. cit. n. 20) and the ICCPR (loc. cit. n. 19) by formally declaring 'a public emergency threatening the life of the nation'. The United Kingdom is the only Council of Europe and UN Member State to declare such an emergency. Human Rights Watch, 'European Union', *World Report* (2005) <http://www.reliefweb.int/library/documents/2005/hrw-gen-14jan.pdf> p. 369 at p. 375.

[68] D. Bonner and R. Cholewinski, loc. cit. n. 15, at p. 26.

[69] Ibid., at p. 25.

[70] Human Rights Watch, 'European Union', loc. cit. n. 67, at p. 375.

[71] A sunset clause, or sunset provision, is a clause of statute that provides for the repeal of all or sections of that statute at a later set date unless those sections are re-authorized by further legislative action.

[72] D. Bonner and R. Cholewinski, loc. cit. n. 15, at pp. 38-39.

the basis of nationality, and that the Government's derogation under Article 15 of the ECHR from the right to liberty constituted a disproportionate response to the emergency situation.[73] In reaction to this judgment, the Home Secretary looked for ways to reduce reliance on detention by utilizing criminal and deportation laws. Legislation in March 2005 repealed the detention without trial powers. Detainees were released, subject to varying degrees of restriction on free movement, assembly, expression and association, under the 'non-derogating' and 'derogating' control order regime instituted by the new legislation: the Prevention of Terrorism Act 2005.[74] The new regime requires the Home Secretary to seek approval from the High Court for making a non-derogating control order, whereas he must apply to the Court for the issue of an order which involves derogating from the ECHR.

Under this new regime, the Home Office has focused on prosecution on criminal grounds, as well as obtaining diplomatic assurances in writing from destination states in North Africa and the Middle East that the deportee will not, if returned, be subject to mistreatment contrary to Article 3 of the ECHR or to the death penalty. There is serious concern that such assurances will not be meaningful.[75] A Human Rights Watch report in 2004 revealed that such assurances provide no guarantee against torture, documenting cases where persons returned based on such assurances were tortured or mistreated. The report also pointed to cases in several European countries where courts intervened and ruled that the assurances from governments in states where torture is a serious problem were not reliable.[76] Indeed, the ECtHR made its own assessment of the assurances provided by the Indian Government in the *Chahal* case, and determined that

> 'despite the efforts of that Government, the NHRC [National Human Rights Commission] and the Indian courts to bring about reform, the violation of human rights by certain members of the security forces in Punjab and elsewhere in India is a recalcitrant and enduring problem'.[77]

Human Rights Watch reports a growing reliance on diplomatic assurances in Germany and the Netherlands, in addition to the United Kingdom.[78]

In response to the July attacks in London that killed 52 subway and bus passengers, Prime Minister Tony Blair announced plans for harsh new anti-terror laws, including deportation powers that may contravene the ECHR. Since the

[73] *A and Others* v. *Secretary of State for the Home Department* (2004) UKHL 56 (judgment of 16 Dec. 2004).

[74] Prevention of Terrorism Act 2005 (c. 2); for a detailed discussion of this regime, see D. Bonner and R. Cholewinski, loc. cit. n. 15, at pp. 41-47.

[75] Ibid., at pp. 40-41.

[76] Human Rights Watch, *'Empty Promises': Diplomatic Assurances No Safeguard against Torture* (April 2004) <http://hrw.org/reports/2004/un0404/> p. 6.

[77] *Chahal*, loc. cit. n. 22, at para. 105.

[78] Human Rights Watch, *'Empty Promises'*, loc. cit. n. 76, at p. 7.

attacks, the United Kingdom has stepped up its use of deportation and detention powers, and its attempts to obtain diplomatic assurance agreements from Middle Eastern and North African states.[79] In proposed legislation, the UK Government originally backed a police proposal to hold terrorism suspects for as long as three months without charge, a proposal criticized by civil rights groups.[80]

Incommunicado detention of suspected terrorists in Spain has led human rights organizations to raise significant due process concerns. Now deployed against non-citizens, Spain's anti-terrorism measures have been shaped by years of addressing Basque separatist violence. Soon after the World Trade Center and Pentagon attacks, Spanish police launched efforts to dismantle an alleged al-Qaeda cell located in their country. The Code of Criminal Procedure enables Spanish authorities to hold those suspected of membership in an armed group in incommunicado detention for up to thirteen days and in pre-trial detention for up to four years.[81] Other states also allow for the use of incommunicado detention for varying periods pursuant to their anti-terrorism laws.[82]

Spanish authorities applied the same detention powers to those who allegedly participated in the '11-M' acts of terror: the ten explosions on four different commuter trains in Madrid on 11 March 2004, which resulted in the death of 191 people and the injury of over 1,400 individuals – the worst terrorist attack in modern European history. According to Human Rights Watch, the law and practice of incommunicado detention in Spain renders the right of detainees to file a writ of *habeas corpus* challenging the lawfulness of their detention essentially meaningless. A second major procedure in the Spanish system of concern to Human Rights Watch is the use of secret legal proceedings. Judges may and often do impose secrecy on the investigation and judicial proceedings in whole or in part, impairing the right to a fair trial.[83]

The United States has used several other immigration-related enforcement initiatives as part of a sweeping anti-terrorist investigation: voluntary interviews,[84]

---

[79] R. Barr, 'Seven Men Detained in Britain As Threats', *Associated Press*, 15 Sept. 2005 <http://abcnews.go.com/International/wireStory?id=1128238&CMP=OTC-RSSFeeds0312>.

[80] E. Johnson, '7 Detained in Britain as Security Threats', *Washington Post*, 16 Sept. 2005, p. A25. This proposed length of detention without charge for persons suspected of terrorism was reduced to a maximum of 28 days in new anti-terrorism legislation passed at the end of March 2006. See Terrorism Act 2006 (c. 11), s. 23.

[81] Human Rights Watch, *Setting an Example? Counter-Terrorism Measures in Spain* (2005) <http://hrw.org/reports/2005/spain0105/> p. 1.

[82] For example, incommunicado detention is limited to two days under the UK Terrorism Act 2000, and seven days with extensions under Australia's Terrorism Act. See the section on 'The Use of Incommunicado Detention', in Human Rights Watch, *Setting an Example?*, loc. cit. n. 81, at p. 23.

[83] Human Rights Watch, *Setting an Example?*, loc. cit. n. 81, at pp. 1-3.

[84] The first initiative in 2001 involved conducting voluntary interviews of up to 5,000 young men (aged 18 to 33) from countries suspected of harbouring terrorists who had entered the United States as temporary visitors since 1 January 2000. Of the first group of 2,261 men interviewed, twenty were arrested, most for alleged immigration violations and none on charges related to terrorism. See D. Kerwin, 'Migrants, Borders, and National Security: US Immigration Policy Since September 11, 2001', *CMS Occasional Paper Series No. 12* (2002) p. 26.

registration,[85] detention, closed hearings,[86] and deportation.[87] The investigation into the 9/11 attacks ushered in a new form of detention, not primarily to ensure the removal of immigration law violators, nor to protect the public from dangerous individuals, but to secure information about terrorists in the United States. During this investigation, the United States detained some 1,200 Middle Eastern and South Asian immigrants and held them for long periods without a showing of probable cause or a charge.[88] A Justice Department rule, issued shortly after the September 11 attacks, increased the permissible period of pre-charge detention for certain non-citizens from 24 to 48 hours, or for an undefined 'reasonable period of time' in 'an emergency or other extraordinary circumstances'.[89] The overwhelming majority were ultimately charged with breaches of immigration laws as opposed to security violations. Even where a non-citizen is suspected of engaging in or supporting terrorist activity, it is considerably easier for prosecutors to detain that individual on an immigration law violation, which in the United States is a civil, not a criminal, law matter.[90] A much smaller number of non-citizens were

[85] Starting in September 2002, another initiative required special registration of male visitors from specified countries, beginning with Iraq, Iran, Libya, Sudan and Syria. Another 20 countries were later added to this list. The National Security Entry-Exit Registration System (NSEERS) required non-immigrant aliens to report to the immigration authorities upon arrival, thirty days after arrival, and every twelve months thereafter. The Government dropped the registration programme a little over a year later, perhaps recognizing that it had resulted in an 'alienated Arab and Muslim community that mistrusted government authorities, and especially the INS [Immigration and Naturalization Service], and had lost any incentive to cooperate'. N. Demleitner, 'Misguided Prevention: The War on Terrorism as a War on Immigrant Offenders and Immigration Violators', 40 *Criminal Law Bulletin* (2004) p. 550 at p. 555.

[86] 'Special interest' non-citizens in administrative removal proceedings were subject to closed immigration hearings in the United States. The Attorney General asserted the need to withhold valuable intelligence from the enemy (i.e., which of their agents may have been detained and which remained free) and a respect for the privacy of those detained. Federal Circuit Courts of Appeals issued conflicting decisions in media challenges to these closed hearings. See the Statement of Jan Ting to the National Commission on Terrorist Attacks Upon The United States (2003) <http://www.fpri.org/transcripts/testimony.20031208.ting.911commission.html> pp. 6-8.

[87] Another controversial initiative prioritized the arrest and removal of four to six thousand men from particular countries of origin, out of hundreds of thousands of 'absconders' whose deportability had been finalized and who had exhausted their administrative and judicial appeal rights. Less than 600 had been arrested by May 2002, and none of them were terrorists or their associates. See D. Kerwin, loc. cit. n. 84, at p. 27. In response to terrorist abuse of the student visa system, the United States also established the Student and Exchange Visitor Information System to track the whereabouts and ensure the *bona fides* of foreign students. The Internet-based system stores data from colleges and universities about the current enrollment status, area of study, and nationality of the student. Educational institutions are required by federal law to provide the US Government with this information within 30 days of the student's arrival and then generally every semester thereafter. See generally <http://www.ice.gov/graphics/sevis/index.htm>.

[88] Kerwin, loc. cit. n. 84, at p. 23.

[89] 66 Fed. Reg. 48334 (20 Sept. 2001).

[90] Federal criminal prosecutions for immigration violations more than doubled in the four years after the 9/11 attack, though a significant portion of this increase came from prosecutors in South Texas. While most of these prosecutions targeted illegal migration, the number of cases brought by the Justice

charged with criminal law violations, or held as material witnesses as authorized by a federal court.[91] Reportedly, none were charged with terrorist activities. The Justice Department claimed that a substantial number of the individuals deported could have been held accountable in anti-terrorism prosecutions.[92]

The Inspector General of the US Department of Justice issued a 'Report on the September 11 Detainees', which identified numerous problems in the way in which detainees were subjected to long periods of detention because of delays in FBI clearances of suspected individuals, the unavailability of bond determinations (a type of bail hearing commonly available in regular immigration proceedings), and the conditions of confinement. The Inspector General found that arrests were 'indiscriminate' and 'haphazard', and that the immigration authorities routinely arrested people who had no connection to criminal activity, let alone terrorism.[93] According to the report, immigrants were refused release on bond, denied access to counsel and to consular officials, interrogated about their religious and political views, and held in degrading conditions. Some prison staff verbally and physically abused the detainees.[94]

The interior control and prosecution devices that states have used since 9/11 are extraordinary. How effectively have these enforcement tools protected the security of these states? Could more targeted and less draconian powers have accomplished at least the same degree of effectiveness? Better intelligence surely would enable states to use more precise and measured enforcement measures. Many experts in the security and international migration fields observe that states are alienating the very populations whose loyalty and cooperation they desire by using exceptional enforcement measures in such a broad manner that many who are wholly unconnected to any terrorist activities are seriously harmed. As discussed more fully below, states must find better ways to balance their responsibility to control and prosecute international terrorists with their obligation and need to respect the rights and dignity of non-citizens.

5. Protecting Non-citizens

When states use extraordinary measures focused on broad groups of non-citizens in order to 'ferret out' the small number of security threats, such enforcement actions end up harming both individuals and whole communities. Profiling has been at the centre of these enforcement actions. As Stephen Legomsky explains, profiling means

---

Department related to terrorism rose to nearly 800 in 2004 from 115 in 2001. See E. Lichtblau, 'Prosecutions in Immigration Doubled in Last Four Years', *New York Times*, 29 Sept. 2005, p. A16.

[91] See Statement of J. Ting, loc. cit. n. 86, at p. 4.

[92] N. Demleitner, loc. cit. n. 85, at p. 5.

[93] Office of the Inspector General/ Department of Justice (OIG/DOJ), *The September 11 Detainees: A Review of the Treatment of Aliens Held on Immigration Charges in Connection with the Investigation of the September 11 Attacks*, (April 2003) <http://www.usdoj.gov/oig/special/0306/full.pdf> p. 70.

[94] Ibid., at p. 162.

> 'specially targeting individuals who possess identifiable attributes that are believed to bear positive statistical correlations to particular kinds of misconduct – in this case, involvement in terrorism'.[95]

While governments assert that this profiling is driven by nationality, age and gender reflected in the characteristics of the terrorists, the practical impact of these initiatives falls on particular ethnic and religious groups. Due to this disproportionate impact, many members of the affected communities and other concerned citizens perceive, rightly or wrongly, that the country-of-nationality distinction is just a façade for anti-Arab and anti-Muslim sentiments.[96] While the profiling may be rationally based on the characteristics of the attackers, 'many of the specific profiling programs carry social costs ... excessive in relation to any law enforcement gains they might be thought to yield'.[97]

The prosecution measures described in the previous section came with significant social costs. In New York, for example, federal agents began 'pounding on doors in the middle of the night and detained hundreds of Pakistanis in the Little Pakistan area' in the tense weeks after 9/11. 'Thousands of people, gripped with fear, soon bolted. Many of them went to other states, back to their homeland, to Canada or even Western Europe. Few have returned, by all accounts'.[98] Again, in the late Fall of 2002, when the US Government required special registration of certain groups of non-citizens,[99] an even larger exodus reportedly occurred. Over the next year, some 13,000 Muslims were placed in deportation proceedings when they registered. The largest single nationality affected was Pakistani. Authorities said that they were looking, in part, for any ties between Islamic terrorists in Pakistan and the estimated 500,000 Pakistani immigrants in the United States. About 120,000 lived in New York City. In the summer of 2003, a survey by a local resettlement group estimated that 18,000 Pakistanis had left Little Pakistan and the vicinity.[100]

The London attacks have refuelled worries that South Asians and Arabs across New York and the United States will incur new suspicion and backlash. 'Everyone's scared', reported one local leader.

> 'Women and girls in particular, given their mode of dress – their head scarves, for example – tell me that they feel they would be the first to be singled out for a hate crime or a deportation-type arrest. Some are actually afraid to go outside right now'.

The FBI in New York reports periodic meetings with Little Pakistan community leaders and neighborhood forums to give people an opportunity to air grievances

---

95 S. Legomsky, 'The Ethnic and Religious Profiling of Non-citizens: National Security and International Human Rights', 25 *Boston College Third World Law Journal* (2005) p. 161.

96 Ibid., at p. 185.

97 Ibid., at p. 196.

98 R. Polner, 'A Neighborhood in a Fishbowl; Little Pakistan has lost Plenty of Residents since 9/11, and Many who Stayed Behind are Struggling to Adapt', *Newsday*, 2 Aug. 2005, p. A34.

99 See *supra* n. 85, on NSEERS.

100 R. Polner, loc. cit. n. 98, at p. A34.

and hear about the agency's counterterrorism strategies. 'We don't want to be seen as the enemy', said an FBI spokesman.[101] It is extremely difficult, however, for government authorities to redress excessive measures after the fact.

Canada did not employ as harsh a set of measures as some other states, but did use profiling in its post-9/11 security investigations. In connection with such enforcement activities, the Canadian Government has tried to find a way to work with Muslim communities. Mandated as part of its national security strategy in 2004, the Government has established a cross-cultural roundtable on security. The goal is to ensure that the views of Canada's ethnocultural and religious communities on managing security interests in a diverse society are heard by the Government.[102] Belelieu asserts that, should this outreach and inclusion approach be successful in getting ethnic and cultural communities to 'buy into' security policies, Canadian efforts could serve as a model for future US homeland security initiatives, particularly in light of the alienation of Arab-Americans incurred by the existing policies.[103] 'Buying in' only works, however, when the concerns of the alienated community are addressed in a reasonable fashion.

Keeble asserts that the difference in the Canadian and American approaches derives from US Government immigration policies that have undermined the sense of belonging of many ethnic communities, particularly since 1996.[104] In broad terms, according to Keeble, Canada views immigrants as citizens-in-waiting, with the Government actively promoting integration, whereas the United States sees immigrants as non-citizens, restricting their legal and socio-economic rights even before the events of 11 September 2001. She suggests that, from a security perspective, the exclusionary, hands-off nature of American immigration policy may in the end detract from the US Government's efforts to map out communities and identify terrorists in its midst.[105]

In the US context, it is important to note that the impact of the enforcement measures implemented following 9/11 was not limited to Arab or Muslim communities. A major Hispanic leadership organization reported, in June 2004, that:

> '[t]he federal government has taken actions in the name of protecting national security, which have had harmful effects on undocumented immigrants, legal permanent residents, and even US citizens. In order to fight terrorism, the US government has adopted measures that are carried out by casting a wide net to catch immigrants – hoping that, among the many immigrants, there will be terrorists or persons with links to terrorists.'[106]

---

[101] Ibid., at p. A34.

[102] E. Keeble, 'Immigration, Civil Liberties, and National/Homeland Security', 60 *Canadian Business and Current Affairs* (1 April 2005) p. 359 at p. 363.

[103] A. Belelieu, loc. cit. n. 55, at p. 7.

[104] E. Keeble, loc. cit. n. 102, at pp. 360, 364.

[105] Ibid., at p. 360.

[106] National Hispanic Leadership Agenda (NHLA), *How the Latino Community's Agenda on Im-*

The report argues that these measures are both ineffective in preventing terrorist acts and harmful to American communities.[107]

In addition to affecting communities, prosecutions have also harmed innocent individuals in the United States. In May 2005, for example, a Lebanese-born US citizen was arrested during a night time helicopter raid by gun-toting agents who smashed down the door to his home. The 37-year-old was charged with immigration fraud. A spokesman for the US attorney's office said that after an investigation, authorities discovered that the charge was a mistake in the individual's immigration records. The raid left a family traumatized; the 7-year-old daughter of this citizen was so frightened that she refused to sleep alone. US authorities provided no explanation to this individual as to why this happened. According to the American-Arab Anti-Discrimination Committee, this case appeared to be part of a pattern of dramatic anti-terrorism arrests that resulted in immigration allegations or other charges that were later dropped.[108]

With regard to a different enforcement initiative, Human Rights Watch has accused the US Government of serious misuse of the federal material witness law[109] since 11 September 2001. Over ninety men living in the United States, all Muslim but one, 'have been thrust into a Kafkaesque world of indefinite detention without charges, secret evidence, and baseless accusations of terrorist links'.[110] Human Rights Watch contends that the material witness law has been used to detain indefinitely those the Justice Department wants to investigate as possible terrorist suspects. No showing of probable cause that they had committed crimes is required. The Justice Department has reportedly refused to respect fundamental constitutional and human rights of detainees, such as the right to be notified of charges, to have prompt access to counsel, to view exculpatory evidence, and to know and be able to challenge the basis for arrest and detention.[111]

This Justice Department initiative resulted in a small number of terrorist-related convictions. Seven detainees were charged with providing material support to terrorist organizations, four of whom had been convicted as of June 2005. Two

---

migration Enforcement and Reform Has Suffered Since 9/11 (June 2004) <www.nclr.org/files/26073_file_NHLA_report.pdf> p. 7.

[107] While recognizing that the most visible impact of post-9/11 strategies has been on the Arab, Muslim and Sikh communities in the United States, the report cites a number of ways in which the security focus of immigration enforcement has harmed Latino communities. For example, Federal Government efforts to enlist state and local law enforcement officers unfamiliar with immigration law in a variety of immigration enforcement activities has created fear and distrust of the police in the Latino community. See the NHLA report, op. cit. n. 106, at p. 8. The report documents profiling of Latinos, both citizens and non-citizens, by local police in different parts of the country. Ibid., at pp. 11-13.

[108] M.B. Sheridan, 'Immigration Charge Dropped in Va. Terror Case', *Washington Post*, 5 Sept. 2005, p. A4.

[109] 18 USC § 3144.

[110] Human Rights Watch and the American Civil Liberties Union, *Human Rights Abuses under the Material Witness Law since September 11*, 17 *Witness to Abuse* (June 2005) <http://hrw.org/reports/2005/us0605/> p. 1.

[111] Ibid., at pp. 1-2.

more were designated as 'enemy combatants' and removed from the criminal justice system, turned over to the Department of Defense, and held without charge in solitary confinement in military brigs. Another twenty were charged with non-terrorist-related crimes, such as bank or credit card fraud or making false statements to the FBI. Twenty-four were deported. Forty-two were ultimately released without any charges. The US Government has apologized to at least thirteen material witnesses for wrongfully detaining them.[112]

The adverse impact of the wrongful arrests and detentions begins with the individual's loss of liberty, and includes abuse by guards and traumatization by being held in solitary confinement with no understanding of why they are there. The families of the wrongfully detained are traumatized as well, and the highly public arrests and Government suggestions of links to terrorism damages businesses and community reputations. Finally, their incarceration has aggravated distrust towards the Government in Muslim communities in the United States.[113]

States, then, have faced challenging balancing acts in their efforts to prevent terrorist attacks and protect innocent non-citizen populations. Unfortunately, many states have prioritized security concerns to such an extent that they have become counterproductive. Some, however, have demonstrated that a better balance between prosecuting suspected terrorists and protecting targeted communities is possible and warranted.

6. Conclusion

Laws, policies and practices established by states in response to international terrorist attacks have changed the legal framework of migration in serious ways. This is an age of terrorism, and states have adopted and employed extraordinary powers to exclude, detain and remove non-citizens, many of whom are wholly unconnected to any terrorist activity. To prevent the entry and stay of terrorists, tracking the legal international movement of people has become the order of the day.

In using certain of these authorities in an overbroad fashion and wrongfully detaining non-citizens, states have acted in ways that run counter to two important interests. First, by alienating the very communities in which the small number of terrorists reside, states have lost the potentially valuable cooperation of their citizen and non-citizen members in efforts to prevent further terrorist attacks. Second, excessive efforts to control international migration come with costs to the lawful and desirable movements of people across borders. Today, more and more states look at international migration first and foremost as a matter of security. These governments may recognize that facilitation of cross-border movement is a value, but anti-terrorism measures are the higher priority by far.

112 Ibid., at p. 5.

113 Ibid., at pp. 5-6.

This chapter has questioned the efficacy of certain anti-terrorist measures. States can better achieve their security and international migration goals, but only if they develop considerably more measured and accurate ways to control and prosecute non-citizens engaged in terrorist activities. By using more precise, targeted enforcement measures, states can fulfill their responsibilities to protect their residents from terrorist attacks while facilitating desirable international migration and respecting the rights of non-citizens.

Selected Bibliography

Belelieu, A., 'Canada Alert: The Recent Evolution in Canadian Security Policy', XII *CSIS Hemisphere Focus* No. 12 (2 Sept. 2004) p. 1.

Bonner, D., and R. Cholewinski, 'Immigration and Asylum Law: The Impact of Terrorism – The United Kingdom', in A. Baldaccini and E. Guild (eds.), *Terrorism and the Foreigner: A Decade of Tension around the Rule of Law in Europe* (Leiden, Brill forthcoming 2006).

Brouwer, E., 'Immigration, Asylum and Terrorism: A Changing Dynamic – Legal and Practical Developments in the EU in Response to the Terrorist Attacks of 11.09', 4 *European Journal of Migration and Law* (2002) p. 399.

Keeble, E., 'Immigration, Civil Liberties, and National/Homeland Security', 60 *Canadian Business and Current Affairs* (1 April 2005) p. 359.

Kerwin, D., 'Migrants, Borders, and National Security: US Immigration Policy Since September 11, 2001', 12 *CMS Occasional Paper Series* (2002).

Koslowski, R., 'Possible Steps towards an International Regime for Mobility and Security', *Global Migration Perspectives No. 8* (2004) <http://www.gcim.org/en/ir_gmp.html>.

Legomsky, S., 'The Ethnic and Religious Profiling of Non-citizens: National Security and International Human Rights', 25 *Boston College Third World Law Journal* (2005) p. 161.

Martin, S., and P. Martin, 'International Migration and Terrorism: Prevention, Prosecution and Protection', 18 *Georgetown Immigration Law Journal* (2004) p. 329.

Office of the Inspector General/ Department of Justice (OIG/DOJ), *The September 11 Detainees: A Review of the Treatment of Aliens Held on Immigration Charges in Connection with the Investigation of the September 11 Attacks* (April 2003) <http://www.usdoj.gov/oig/special/0306/full.pdf>.

Schoenholtz, A., 'Transatlantic Dialogue on Terrorism and International Migration', 41(4) *International Migration* (2003) p. 173.

Zard, M., 'Exclusion, Terrorism and the Refugee Convention', 13 *Forced Migration Review* (2002) p. 32.

Chapter 2
THE LEGAL PROTECTION OF STRANDED MIGRANTS

Stefanie Grant[*]

1. Introduction

At its first session, in 1947, the UN Human Rights Commission identified statelessness as a first priority.[1] The problem then affected millions in Europe, displaced by new frontiers and political divisions in the aftermath of war. The Commission's work led to an international refugee protection regime for refugees who were *de facto* stateless and to international rules on legal – *de jure* – statelessness.

This paper examines a different, but related, phenomenon in which migrants find themselves legally 'stranded', because they are unable to remain lawfully in the country in which they are physically present, or move to another country, or return to their home country. Some are legally stateless, but for others the problem is that their nationality is not effective in enabling them to return home, or in giving them diplomatic protection and assistance while they are abroad. At its most acute, migrants who are stranded find themselves without protection in the country in which they are physically present, without protection from their country of nationality, and without international protection. For many of those who are not legally stateless, this situation can amount to *de facto* statelessness.[2]

While the fact of migrants being 'stranded' is not new, it seems that the scale and complexity of the phenomenon have grown. Both present new challenges to governments in terms of human rights protection. This is one outcome of the often acute discordance between, on the one hand, international migration driven by poverty, human insecurity, and the economics of globalization, and, on the other, national laws which restrict the movement of people across borders. The

[*] Lawyer specializing in human rights, migration, nationality and refugees.

[1] In a report to the Commission, the UN Secretary-General described the situation of a stateless person faced with expulsion, who 'is unable to enter another country legally, [and] is obliged either to remain in hiding, disobeying the order, or to enter the territory of a neighboring country by fraudulent means'. The report commented that '[t]he desire to guarantee order and security' led to 'outlaws'. UN, *A Study of Statelessness*, UN Docs. E/1112; E/1112/Add.1 (Aug. 1949).

[2] The UN Study, loc. cit. n. 1, identified two forms of statelessness: *de jure* and *de facto*. Stateless persons *de jure* were those who are not nationals of any state. Stateless persons *de facto* were those who, 'having left the country of which they were nationals, no longer enjoy the protection and assistance of their national authorities …'. See also the discussion of 'effective nationality' in R. Piotrowicz, 'Victims of Trafficking and de Facto Statelessness', 21 *Refugee Survey Quarterly* (2002) p. 50.

R. Cholewinski, R. Perruchoud and E. MacDonald, eds., International Migration Law

Global Commission on International Migration has described irregular migration as 'inextricably linked' to human security, noting that many who migrate in an irregular manner do so because their own countries are affected by armed conflict, political instability and economic decline. While in transit, they often become stranded while en route to their final destination.[3]

Situations where migrants are stranded because of a lost passport or lack of funds, and where the problem can be solved with assistance from their national consulates, are outside the scope of this paper.[4] The focus is rather on individuals who are not refugees but who are unable to return to a country of nationality or former residence for legal, or intractable humanitarian or logistical, reasons.[5]

2. The Problem of Data

By its nature, the population of stranded migrants is a hidden one, and there is little – if any – reliable statistical data. Available information tends to focus on rejected asylum seekers, both because their identity is known to the state authorities through their asylum applications, and because the UNHCR and NGOs monitor refugee protection issues with a diligence which is generally lacking for migrants, and even for stateless persons.[6] Information on migrants who initially moved in search of employment, or to escape poverty, conflict and insecurity, is thus harder to find, although there is growing attention to migrant women, including domestic workers and victims of trafficking.

3. Who are Stranded Migrants?

The term 'stranded migrant' has no generally accepted definition.[7] In practice, migrants become legally stranded where they are caught between removal from the state in which they are physically present, inability to return to their state

[3] Global Commission on International Migration (GCIM), *Migration in an Interconnected World: New directions for action* (GCIM, Geneva 2005) (hereafter, GCIM Report) p. 33.

[4] Nor does the paper focus on recent cases involving national security, except where these have relevance for broader migration issues.

[5] While many of those who are stranded may have sought refugee status, rejection of their applications through a fair determination process means they are not entitled to international protection as refugees. In addition, although rarely, refugees may be excluded from protection; see generally *International Journal of Refugee Law*, Vol. 12, Special Supplementary Issue 2000, *Exclusion from Protection.*

[6] But even in this area official data is often weak, including data for states with tight immigration controls. 'The actual number of failed asylum seekers still in the UK is not known and therefore the number of people due for removal is not known'. *Returning Failed Asylum Applicants*, Report by the Comptroller and Auditor General, House of Commons, HC 76, Session 2005-2006, London, 14 July 2005, para. 8.

[7] It does not appear, for example, in the International Migration Law *Glossary on Migration* (IOM, Geneva 2004).

of nationality or former residence, and refusal by any other state to grant entry. They may also be stranded where there are practical or humanitarian reasons which prevent them from returning home. Many of those who become stranded – including rejected asylum seekers, migrant workers or other economic migrants – entered a country illegally, assisted by smugglers or transported at the hands of traffickers. Some are legally stateless. Because little attention has been paid to this group, its numbers and condition are not well documented or understood in any region, and this is particularly so in Africa,[8] Asia and the Middle East.

An early use of the term 'stranded' in this context was to characterize a migrant who had left the United States after a period of legal residence, and on return was excluded from entering, and held in detention – in the Supreme Court's words 'stranded' – on Ellis Island. He had been 'shipped and reshipped to France', which twice refused him entry, as did several European and twelve Latin American countries. No country could be found to accept him and he remained in indefinite detention.[9] Similar facts can be found in contemporary cases. The term 'stranded' is clearly applicable to, for example, the case of a Palestinian who arrived in Australia without a visa, was detained, and, upon the refusal of his visa application, asked to be removed. Without any country of nationality, removal could not take place, and nor was it likely in the foreseeable future, because he was stateless. He therefore remained in detention, under national legislation requiring that an 'unlawful non citizen' be held until either removal (which was impossible) or the grant of a visa (which had been refused).[10] The term has also been used to refer to more than 240,000 stateless Biharis, who remained in West Bengal when Bangladesh seceded from Pakistan in 1971; most of these so-called 'stranded Pakistanis' continue to live in camps, without effective nationality.[11]

3.1 Legally stranded migrants

Legally stranded migrants are typically irregular migrants, without a lawful immigration status. Available data suggests that many are held in detention, often for long periods: over the last decade, some states have resorted to action which can constitute arbitrary detention under international human rights law. Where they are not held in custody, they are likely to have at best a temporary immigra-

[8] One example of the complex legal and political factors underlying situations where non citizens are stranded is the case of some 50,000 Mauritanians, who were declared stateless in 1989 and expelled, many to Senegal. They have since remained there, initially as refugees, and later with an indeterminate status while they await active steps by the Mauritanian authorities to restore their citizenship and ensure their safe return. See *Report of a Mission to Senegal held on August – September 2005* (New York, Open Society Justice Initiative 2005).

[9] *Shaughnessy* v. *US ex rel. Mezei*, 345 US 206 (1953).

[10] *Al-Kateb* v. *Godwin* [2004] HCA 37.

[11] The term is controversial in that it implies that they remain Pakistani citizens. See, e.g., the Refugees International Report by M. Lynch and T. Cook, *Citizens of Nowhere: The Stateless Biharis of Bangladesh,* (Washington DC, Refugees International 2006).

tion status which may restrict movement, employment, and access to social and economic benefits.

States' practice of detaining migrants who cannot be removed is not new, but appears to be on the increase.[12] The IOM points to situations where migrants who are stranded become 'locked in a cycle of detention': detained for entering the country illegally, they have no means of leaving it upon being released, and are therefore returned to detention.[13] The UNHCR reports that it is regularly confronted with cases of individuals 'languishing in indefinite detention for years, turning often to decades', because they have no recognized legal status in any country.[14] The UNHCR also reports that trafficked women without documents are detained in the country to which they have been transported, and

> 'remain there for years because of the refusal by their country of citizenship to readmit in the absence of evidence of their nationality, and because of the refusal by the detaining country to release without proper documentation'.[15]

Mexican law, to take one example, allows prolonged detention, *inter alia*, where the individual's country has no consulate, or where he is entitled to international protection, or where false information about identity has been provided.[16]

The detention of migrants who cannot be removed has been reviewed over the last decade by national courts in a number of countries.[17] In the United States, those non-citizen detainees are sometimes referred to as 'lifers' or 'unremovables'; some have criminal records, others lack immigration status and the ability to return to their country of origin.[18] An appeal by the United States to China to

[12] For a detailed examination of the detention of irregular migrants, see the chapter by Shyla Vohra in this volume. See also A. de Zayas, 'Human Rights and Indefinite Detention', 87 *International Review of the Red Cross* (2005) p. 15.

[13] IOM, *Stranded Migrants Facility: Briefing Note*, Doc. IC/2005/11 (14 Oct. 2005).

[14] UNCHR, *Progress Report on UNHCR Activities in the Field of Statelessness*, Doc. EC/49/SC/CRP.15 (4 June 1999), para. 15.

[15] UNHCR, *UNHCR's Activities in the Field of Statelessness: Progress Report*, Doc. EC/55/SC/CRP.13/Rev.1 (20 June 2005).

[16] 'The detention of a person cannot exceed 90 days, except in the following situations: (1) there is no diplomatic representation of the state of which the person is a national; (2) the person does not have identification papers or travel documents; … (12) the person detained provides false information about his or her identity, nationality, etc.; (13) a request for protection from national or international agencies; (14) the person does not have identification papers or travel documents due to the responsibility of his or her diplomatic or consular representation …'. Inter-American Commission on Human Rights Special Rapporteur on Migrant Workers and Their Families, *Report on Mexico*, Pt V, 2003.

[17] See, e.g., the review of UK law in *A(FC) and others (FC) (Appellants)* v. *Secretary of State for the Home Department (Respondents)* [2004] UKHL 56, paras. 8-15.

[18] 'Most indefinite detainees are from countries that lack normal diplomatic relations with the US (e.g., Cuba, Iran or North Korea) … The majority of 'lifers' are Cubans who came during the Mariel boatlift … in 1980, when approximately 125,000 Cubans … arrived by boat in Florida … Other indefinite detainees are stateless persons (e.g., Palestinians and persons from the former Soviet Union who do not meet the citizenship requirements of any of the newly independent states) or persons whose nationality cannot be determined. Other indefinite detainees are from countries that refuse to accept

'take back' some 40,000 Chinese immigrants, who had been denied permission to stay in the United States, indicates the potential scale of these situations.[19]

The Supreme Court has considered a number of cases where aliens were held in indefinite administrative detention, having been issued with removal orders to leave the United States, but with no possibility of being sent to another country.[20] In *Zadvydas*, the Court held that persons could only be detained, after being issued with a removal order, for a period that was reasonably necessary to effect the removal. It held that 6 months was a presumptively reasonable period. The case concerned a migrant who had been legally admitted to the United States as a child, then acquired a serious criminal record as an adult; he was ordered removed from the United States and held in detention, but without any foreseeable prospect of removal because he was stateless. The US Department of Justice interpreted the Court's decision as applying only to those who had entered the United States legally, but in a subsequent decision – *Benitez* – the Supreme Court held that the same (*Zadvydas*) rules applied to Cuban Mariels and other arriving aliens who had not been admitted to the United States and who could not be returned.[21]

By contrast, Australian courts upheld the indefinite detention of a Palestinian who could not be removed, again because he was stateless. Describing his situation as 'tragic', the High Court nonetheless held it could not challenge national legislation which made detention mandatory. It characterized detention as 'non punitive', as long as its purpose was 'to make the alien available for deportation or to prevent [him] from entering … the Australian community'.[22] The Human Rights Committee has questioned the Australian legislation's compliance with international human rights law (see below).

Even where states do not resort to detention of 'unremovable' stranded migrants, there is often a clear reluctance to regularize their status. Dismissing the claim of an Iraqi Kurd to be granted a legal immigration status, despite the impossibility of safe removal to northern Iraq, the UK House of Lords commented that

> '[t]here may come a time when the prospects of a person ever being able safely to return, whether voluntarily or compulsorily, are so remote that it would be irrational

---

the return of their nationals (e.g., Vietnam, Laos, Cambodia and the Peoples' Republic of China) or from countries experiencing immense upheaval. Others may be indefinitely detained because the alien has strong ties to the US, and only attenuated connections to their country of origin. For example, an alien may be brought by his parents to the US as a two-year old, and live in the US for 40 years without naturalizing. If the person commits a crime and is removable, his birth country may refuse to take him'. *Immigration Related Detention: current legislative issues*, US Congressional Research Service Report, Washington DC, 28 April 2004, n. 38. See S. Legomsky, *Immigration and Refugee Law and Policy* (New York, Foundation Press 2005) pp. 144-158, 191-207.

[19] Homeland Security Secretary Michael Chertoff said illegal immigrants were 'clogging' detention centres, and the American Government had spent an estimated $667m in detention costs. 'US says China refuses deportees', BBC News report, 16 March 2006.

[20] E.g., *Shaughnessy* v. *US ex rel. Mezei*, loc. cit. n. 9.

[21] *Zadvydas* v. *Davis*, 533 US 678 (2001); *US* v. *Benitez*, 542 US 74 (2004).

[22] *Al-Kateb* v. *Godwin* [2004] HCA 37 (6 Aug. 2004), decided by a majority (5:4) in the High Court of Australia.

to deny him the status which would enable him to make a proper contribution to the community here, but that is another question. It certainly did not arise on the facts of this case.'[23]

Migrants may also become stranded 'in orbit' in ways which are similar to the situation of a refugee in orbit. One Indian national, who left India with the assistance of a recruitment agent, travelled to Turkey, where he was refused entry and sent to Iran, where he was again refused entry and sent on to Pakistan, where he was detained in Queta Jail and sentenced to imprisonment on charges of violating immigration laws.[24]

3.2 Migrants stranded for humanitarian reasons

Migrants may become stranded for a range of humanitarian as well as legal reasons: for example, where they are abandoned by traffickers or smugglers without travel documents or the means of paying for return travel; or become stranded in conflict or disputed areas; or are unaccompanied minors smuggled abroad and abandoned with no protection or means of earning a living.[25] This also occurs where migrants enter transit countries but cannot proceed with their journeys, and find themselves stranded for long periods of time while en route to their final destination.

Morocco is a country of transit for migration flows originating in sub-Saharan Africa. For example, nationals of Côte d'Ivoire, Congo, Sudan, Liberia, or the Democratic Republic of Congo pass through the Maghreb on their way to Spain and the southernmost frontiers of the EU. Their journeys may take several years, and involve difficult and dangerous travel through a number of countries. Some migrants are fleeing persecution and conflict. Others are escaping poverty, and hope to enter Spain, get work, and support their families through the remittances they send home. Noting the 'poverty gap' between Morocco and Spain, the Spanish Prime Minister has described the root of the problem as drought and famine in sub-Saharan Africa.[26]

In September 2005, migrants from a number of sub-Saharan African countries scaled the border fence between Morocco and Spain at Ceuta, a Spanish enclave on the Mediterranean coast of Morocco. They were expelled back to Morocco by the Spanish authorities under a readmission agreement. Some hundreds were then moved to an isolated part of southeast Morocco, in the Sahara Desert, where the

---

[23] The applicant in this case was from the Kurdish Autonomous Area of northern Iraq, and unable to return because there was no safe means to do so. *R* v. *Secretary of State for the Home Department ex parte Khadir* [2005] UKHL 39.

[24] UN, ECOSOC, Commission on Human Rights, *Report of the Special Rapporteur on the Human Rights of Migrants*, UN Doc. E/CN.4/2004/85/Add.1 (4 Feb. 2005), paras. 108-109.

[25] IOM, loc. cit. n. 13.

[26] BBC News, 6 Oct. 2005.

aid agency Médecins sans Frontières reported they had been 'abandoned' without adequate food, water or medical support.[27] One migrant had earlier described how he stayed in a pine forest as he waited to cross the frontier, hiding from police during the day, and 'sneaking out at night to eat from trash cans and dodging bandits'.[28] A UN expert characterized the conditions of such groups, living 'in the shadows, isolated and abandoned', as 'appalling'.[29]

Some of these sub-Saharan nationals were then flown to Senegal, under a re-admission agreement. Others were assisted by IOM to return to Mali. Since none had travel documents, a collective *laissez passer* was signed, after a Malian consul had met with migrants to assess if they were in fact Malian nationals, and after each had signed a declaration of voluntary return.[30]

4. The State's Duty to Protect the Human Rights of Stranded Migrants

In their dealings with migrants who they have determined may not legally remain, states have a double responsibility – and challenge: to respect and protect the migrants' rights while they remain within the national territory, and to facilitate their safe return to a home country or country of former residence in safety and dignity.

This duty of protection can be clearly understood in relation to the prohibition of torture, where it is rooted both in customary international law which binds all states, and in international treaties which are binding on their States Parties. The prohibition of torture is at the same time a peremptory norm of customary international law and an obligation under all international human rights treaties. The International Criminal Tribunal for the Former Yugoslavia has characterized this prohibition as

> '… particularly stringent and sweeping. States are obliged not only to prohibit and punish torture, but also to forestall its occurrence: it is insufficient merely to intervene after the infliction of torture, when the physical or moral integrity of human beings has already been irreparably harmed. Consequently, States are bound to put in place all those measures that may pre-empt the perpetration of torture.'[31]

---

[27] The Moroccan Human Rights Association told Reuters that '[t]he authorities then cut electricity in the nearest towns like Bouarfa. It was a deliberate move so the migrants would not be able to see town lights and would have no direction to follow so they would get lost in the desert'. Despite this, many found their way to Bouafara, to 'makeshift camps'. *Reuters report*, 10 Oct. 2005.

[28] See Commission on Human Rights, op. cit. n. 24.

[29] In the forest of Gourougou women gave birth in 'unacceptable conditions of hygiene and without any medical attention', UN, ECOSOC, Commission on Human Rights, *Report on Visit to Morocco of the Special Rapporteur on the Human Rights of Migrants*, UN Doc. E/CN.4/2004/76/Add.3 (15 Jan. 2004), para. 55.

[30] Reported in *Migration* (Geneva, IOM, Dec. 2005).

[31] *Prosecutor v Furundzija* (1998) ICTY 3, 10 Dec. 1998.

Over the last three decades, the protection of rights under the international human rights treaty system has strengthened. As more states have become bound by these treaties, a major change has taken place, 'the significance of which cannot be overstated',[32] in the way in which the rights of aliens are protected. This has involved a shift 'from the classic system of diplomatic protection by the alien's state of nationality, to the direct protection of the individual alien's rights through … a set of reformulated international norms'.[33] The result is an international legal regime which goes some way towards 'decoupling' the right to have rights from an individual's nationality status.[34] It is now the case that while states may expel or remove migrants who are illegally present on their territory, international law requires generally that the state should protect their rights without discrimination for as long as they remain. The Human Rights Committee has underscored that the enjoyment of ICCPR[35] rights

> 'is not limited to citizens of State parties but must also be available to all individuals, regardless of nationality or statelessness, such as asylum-seekers, refugees, migrant workers and other persons, who may find themselves in the territory or subject to the jurisdiction of the State party.'[36]

The basic principle underlying the international human rights protection of migrants is that entering a country in violation of national immigration law does not deprive an irregular migrant of his or her most fundamental human rights, nor does it nullify the duty of the host state to protect the rights of these individuals.[37] An analogy may be made with the treatment of individuals within a national criminal justice system: they may be prosecuted for criminal offences, but they are nonetheless entitled to rights protection – including to due process and humane treatment – throughout the legal process, and after conviction. Recent international criminal law is explicit in its recognition that the human rights of those who are smuggled or trafficked should be protected.[38]

---

[32] R. Lillich, *The Human Rights of Aliens* (Manchester, Manchester University Press 1984) p. 3. The older international law institution of consular protection and assistance is examined in the chapter by Richard Perruchoud in this volume.

[33] Lillich, ibid.

[34] 'The right to have rights today means the recognition of the universal status of personhood of each and every human being independently of their national citizenship. Whereas for [Hannah] Arendt, ultimately citizenship was the prime guarantor for the protection of one's human rights, the challenge ahead is to develop an international regime which decouples the right to have rights from one's nationality status'. S. Benhabib, *The Rights of Others: Aliens, Residents and Citizens* (Cambridge, Cambridge University Press 2004) p. 68.

[35] International Covenant on Civil and Political Rights, 16 Dec. 1966, 999 *UNTS* 171.

[36] UN, Human Rights Committee, General Comment 31 on The Nature of the General Legal Obligation Imposed on States Parties to the Covenant, UN Doc. CCPR/C/21/Rev.1/Add.13 (26 May 2004), para. 10.

[37] See e.g., GCIM Report, loc. cit. n. 3, at p. 55.

[38] Protocol against the Smuggling of Migrants by Land, Sea and Air to the UN Convention against Transnational Organized Crime, UNGA Res. 55/25 of 15 Nov. 2000. The Protocol makes specific

It follows that stranded migrants are entitled to human rights protection regardless of their immigration status, or of whether they have been legally admitted to a country.[39] Their basic rights are defined in six 'core' human rights treaties, which are legally binding on most states. A seventh, the Convention on the Rights of Migrant Workers (ICRMW),[40] is less widely ratified, but most states are nonetheless bound – regardless of accession – by the majority of its provisions, insofar as these mirror rights protected under the other 'core' treaties to which they are already parties. Thus, the ICRMW's prohibition of torture or cruel, inhuman or degrading treatment or punishment[41] reflects the universal prohibition in the ICCPR,[42] and the prohibition in relation to children in the Convention on the Rights of the Child (CRC).[43] States Parties to the ICCPR and to the CRC[44] are thus bound by this prohibition in relation to migrants, regardless of whether they have ratified the ICRMW, and in addition to their obligations under customary international law.

The ICCPR gives 'everyone' protection from abuses such as arbitrary killing, torture and inhuman treatment, slavery, forced labour, child labour, arbitrary arrest, unfair trial, and invasions of privacy. Moreover, all persons have the right to marry; to be protected as minors; to enjoy peaceful association and assembly; to equality; and to freedom of religion and belief. Except in a narrowly defined area of immigration control, these rights apply to 'everyone ... irrespective or his or her nationality ... [and] must be guaranteed without discrimination between citizens and aliens'.[45]

Applying the ICCPR, the Human Rights Committee found the detention of a woman and her children, rejected asylum seekers, for more than two years in Australia to be arbitrary and in breach of Article 9 which protects the right to liberty and security of person. It has questioned the compatibility of Australian detention legislation with the Covenant.[46]

---

reference to the right to life, to the right not to be subjected to torture, or other cruel, inhuman or degrading treatment or punishment, and to non-discrimination; it also makes general reference to the obligations of states under international human rights law (Art. 19). There is a similar provision in the Protocol to the same Convention to Prevent, Suppress and Punish Trafficking in Persons, Especially Women and Children, Art. 14.

[39] ICCPR, loc. cit. n. 35, Art. 2(1).

[40] International Convention on the Protection of the Rights of All Migrant Workers and Members of Their Families, UNGA Res. 45/158 of 18 Dec. 1990.

[41] Ibid., Art. 10.

[42] ICCPR, loc. cit. n. 35, Art. 7.

[43] Convention on the Rights of the Child, 20 Nov. 1989, 1577 *UNTS* 3, Art. 10.

[44] As of 1 Feb. 2006, 155 states had acceded to the ICCPR, and 192 to the CRC.

[45] Human Rights Committee, General Comment 15 on the position of aliens under the Covenant (27th Session, 1986), reproduced in UN Doc. HRI/GEN/1/Rev.7 (12 May 2004) p. 140.

[46] Communication No. 169/2002, *Bakhtiyari*, UN Doc. CCPR/C/79/D/1069/2002 (6 Nov. 2003), para. 9.3: '... the continuation of immigration detention for Mrs Bakhtiyari and her children for the length of time... without appropriate justification, was arbitrary and contrary to Art. 9(1) ...'; *Concluding Observations of the Human Rights Committee on Australia*, UN Doc. A/55/40 (24 July 2000): '[T]he mandatory detention under the Migration Act of "unlawful non-citizens"... raises questions

Similar protection is provided by regional treaties such as the European Convention on Human Rights (ECHR).[47] Foreign nationals who had been detained in the United Kingdom on grounds of national security successfully challenged legislation allowing their indefinite detention without trial, on the ground that it applied to foreign but not to British nationals. The House of Lords held that while the rights of these two groups might differ in an immigration context, the ECHR did not permit discrimination between citizens and aliens in their right to liberty.[48]

The International Covenant on Economic, Social and Cultural Rights (ICESCR)[49] gives 'everyone' the right to the progressive realization of social, economic and cultural rights, including health, housing and education. It requires states to respect and protect the right to health by providing emergency health care to 'everyone', and equal access for 'all persons, including … minorities, asylum seekers and illegal immigrants' to health services. A state violates the ICESCR if it denies access to health facilities, goods and services to particular individuals or groups as a result of *de jure* or *de facto* discrimination.[50] The CRC entitles those under 18 to free health care, and basic social provision such as measures to reduce infant and child mortality. Despite these formal protections, however, most stranded migrants find it difficult in practice to claim and exercise their rights.

5. Obstacles to the Expulsion and Return of Stranded Migrants

International law recognizes the right of everyone to leave any country, including his or her own, and to return to their own country, as well as the obligation of states to receive back their own nationals. States may determine which non-nationals should enter and remain in their territory, and may remove those who do so in breach of domestic law. There may, however, be legal and practical obstacles to state action.

The return of irregular migrants – including those who have been stranded – increasingly takes place on the basis of bilateral and multilateral readmission agreements, which regulate the technical details arising from implementation of states' rights to control the entry of aliens and their international obligation to re-

of compliance with Art. 9(1) of the Covenant, which provides that no person shall be subjected to arbitrary detention'.

[47] Convention for the Protection of Human Rights and Fundamental Freedoms (ECHR), 4 Nov. 1950, *ETS* No. 5.

[48] *A(FC) and others (FC) (Appellants)* v. *Secretary of State for the Home Department (Respondents)* [2004] UKHL 56. See also *Ahmed* v. *Austria* [1997] 24 *EHRR* 278, ECtHR.

[49] International Covenant on Economic, Social and Cultural Rights, 16 Dec. 1996, 993 *UNTS* 3.

[50] UN, ECOSOC, Committee on Economic, Social and Cultural Rights, *General Comment No. 14 on the right to the highest attainable standard of health*, UN Doc. E/C.12/2000/4 (11 Aug. 2000), para. 50.

admit their own nationals.[51] Contracting Parties typically agree to re-admit without formality those of their citizens who are residing without authorization in another country or who have crossed its border illegally, including those whose asylum applications have been rejected. Agreements increasingly include an obligation to readmit third country nationals and stateless persons coming from or having resided in the country concerned.[52] Countries who accede to the Protocol against the Smuggling of Migrants to the UN Convention on Transnational Organized Crime undertake to accept without unreasonable delay the return of nationals or permanent residents.[53]

States may be barred from returning migrants where international law protects against *refoulement*, and they may find return difficult or impossible in a number of other situations.[54] These include situations where an individual is legally stateless; where he or she is unable to prove a nationality and there is no clear country of nationality or former residence; where the country of nationality does not cooperate in return; where there is no safe means of travel to that country; where the humanitarian situation makes return generally unsafe; where the country of nationality has no diplomatic representation;[55] or where – exceptionally – there is no government with whom to negotiate.[56] International law also restricts the means which may be used to enforce involuntary removal.

5.1 **Voluntary return**

Voluntary return implies 'an absence of any physical, psychological or material pressure',[57] and is also incompatible with coercive methods employed by the state to compel an individual to agree to leave. One emerging, and negative, trend in some European countries is coercion through the withdrawal of social benefits from irregular migrants in order to compel them to cooperate with return or to leave of their own accord.[58] This threat of destitution as an instrument for com-

[51] 15 agreements were concluded between 1950 and 1970, and 302 between 1990 and 2000. See Inter-Governmental Consultations for Asylum, Refugee and Migration Policies in Europe, North America and Australia (IGC), *IGC Report on Readmission Agreements* (Geneva, IGC 2002).

[52] See, e.g., Art. 5(3)(c) of the Partnership Agreement between members of the African Caribbean and Pacific Group of States of the one part, the European Community and its Member States of the other part, Cotonou, 23 June 2000, Cm 5882.

[53] Protocol against the Smuggling of Migrants by Land, Sea and Air, loc. cit. n. 38, Art. 18(1).

[54] See C. Phuong, 'The Removal of Failed Asylum Seekers', 25 *Legal Studies* (2005) p. 117.

[55] See European Council on Refugees and Exiles (ECRE), *The Way Forward: Europe's Role in the Global Refugee Protection System* (London, ECRE, June 2005) p. 18.

[56] E.g., Somalia.

[57] *Voluntary Repatriation: International Protection*, UNHCR 1996, para. 2.3.

[58] E.g., the UK's Asylum and Immigration (Treatment of Claimants, etc.) Act 2004, c. 19, s. 9. Vanda de Graca, a mother and her four year old child from Angola, were the first family to be evicted from their home under new legislation withdrawing all benefits from failed asylum seekers who do not leave Britain voluntarily. Previously, parents with children under 18 would qualify for state support until they were deported. Report in *Guardian Weekly*, 2-8 Sept. 2005.

pelling return has created 'acute tensions within host states between immigration laws and human rights protection'.[59]

The European Commission has stressed that irregular migrants 'are protected by universal human rights standards' and should enjoy basic rights such as 'emergency health care, and primary school education for their children'.[60] These may not be curtailed by the state. Where the removal of a failed asylum seeker is delayed through no fault of his or her own – in other words, although the term was not used, where she or he is stranded – it has been described as 'morally unacceptable for him [or her] to be rendered destitute'.[61]

5.2 Bars to involuntary return

Exceptions are made to the general rule that a state may return an alien to his country of nationality in the case of refugees, and where involuntary return would expose any person to torture or to 'irreparable harm'.[62] The ICCPR bar to *refoulement* covers both a first country of return, and also 'any country to which the person may subsequently be removed'.[63]

The European Court of Human Rights has applied the ECHR Article 3 prohibition[64] to situations in which a state seeks to deport or expel a non citizen. In the case of a Somali national whose refugee status in Austria had been withdrawn following his conviction for attempted robbery, the Court re-stated Austria's right to control entry, residence and expulsion of aliens, but found that deportation to Somalia would breach the Convention 'for as long as [the appellant] faces a seri-

---

[59] S. Da Lomba, 'Fundamental Social Rights for Irregular Migrants: the right to health care in France and England', in B. Bogusz, R. Cholewinski, A. Cygan and E. Szyszczak (eds.), *Irregular Migration and Human Rights* (Leiden, Martinus Niijhoff 2004) p. 363.

[60] European Commission, *Communication from the Committee to the Council, the European Parliament, the European Economic and Social Committee and the Committee on Regions on immigration, integration and employment* (COM (2003) 336, 3 June 2003) p. 26.

[61] UK, *Parliamentary Select Committee on Home Affairs*, Fourth Report, HC Session 2002-2003, para. 55.

[62] The 1951 Refugee Convention (Convention relating to the Status of Refugees, 28 July 1951, 189 *UNTS* 137) protects refugees against *refoulement* to a country where 'life or freedom' would be threatened (Art. 33); under Art. 3 of the Convention against Torture (Convention Against Torture and Other Cruel, Inhuman or Degrading Treatment or Punishment, 10 Dec. 1984, 1465 *UNTS* 85), no person may be returned to a country where there is a substantial risk of torture; the ICCPR, loc. cit. n. 35, protects 'all persons' within the state's territory or under its 'control' against 'extradition, deportation, expulsion or other removal' to a country in which there is a real risk of 'irreparable harm'; specific reference is made to the right to life, and freedom from torture. Human Rights Committee, General Comment No. 31, loc. cit. n. 36, para. 12.

[63] '... Article 2 [ICCPR] .... entails an obligation not to extradite, deport, expel or otherwise remove a person from their territory, where there are substantial grounds for believing that there is a real risk of irreparable harm... either in the country to which removal is to be effected or in any country to which the person may subsequently be removed'. Human Rights Committee, General Comment No. 31, loc. cit. n. 36, para. 12.

[64] ECHR, loc. cit. n. 47, Art. 3, which provides that '(n)o-one shall be subjected to torture or to inhuman or degrading treatment or punishment'.

ous risk of being subjected there to torture or inhuman or degrading treatment'.[65] In a case concerning the deportation of an Indian national from the United Kingdom on national security grounds, the Court noted 'the immense difficulties faced by States ... in protecting their communities from terrorist violence'. It nonetheless ruled that the Convention prohibits torture 'in absolute terms ... irrespective of the victim's conduct'. The prohibition 'is equally absolute in expulsion cases'.[66]

Where extradition is sought so that an individual may face trial in another country, rendition is sometimes made conditional on assurances that the prohibited conduct – for example the death penalty – will not be imposed.[67] Similarly, where the prohibited conduct is the infliction of torture in pre-trial detention, protective action such as visits by consular officials of the rendering state or by an inter-governmental human rights institution has sometimes been made a condition for rendition.[68]

However, the 'extraordinary rendition' of individuals to states where torture is known to be used, on the basis of diplomatic assurances that the individual would not be subject to ill treatment, has been held to violate the Convention against Torture. In a case where an Egyptian national, convicted in absentia for membership of a terrorist group, was refouled from Sweden to Egypt, the Committee against Torture found that

> 'it was known, or should have been known, to the State's authorities... that Egypt resorted to consistent and widespread use of torture against detainees, and that the risk of such treatment was particularly high in the cases of detainees held for political or security reasons'.

The Committee also found that 'the procurement of diplomatic assurances, which ... provided no mechanism for their enforcement', did not suffice to protect against the 'manifest risk' of torture.[69]

The UN High Commissioner for Human Rights has criticized the 'emerging practice' of seeking diplomatic assurances that transferred detainees would not be subjected to torture, and doubted that a post return monitoring system would be effective.[70]

---

[65] *Ahmed* v. *Austri*a, loc. cit. n. 48.

[66] *Chahal* v. *UK* (1996) 23 *EHRR* 413, paras. 79-80. See, too, *A (FC)* v. *SSHD* [2004] UKHL 56, para. 9.

[67] See *Soering* v. *UK* (1989) 11 *EHRR* 439; see also the discussion in J. Fitzpatrick, 'The Post Exclusion Phase', *International Journal of Refugee Law*, Special Supplementary Issue, loc. cit. n. 5, p. 291.

[68] See *Report to the Turkish Government on the visit to Turkey carried out by the European Committee for the Prevention of Torture and Inhuman or Degrading Treatment or Punishment (CPT), from 27 February to 3 March 1999*, Doc. CPT/Inf(2000) 17 <http://www.cpt.coe.int/documents/tur/2000-17-inf-eng.htm>.

[69] Communication No. 233/2003, *Agiza*, UN Doc. CAT/C/34/D/233/2003 (24 May 2005), para. 13.4.

[70] 'Based on the long experience of international monitoring bodies and experts, it is unlikely that a

5.3 Statelessness[71]

By definition, legal statelessness is incompatible with return, since there is no country of nationality to which return is possible. The 1954 Convention Relating to the Status of Stateless Persons prohibits expulsion where such an individual is lawfully on the territory,[72] but is silent on the key issue of admission: there is no obligation to admit a stateless person. This is a serious protection gap.

5.4 Unclear identity and nationality

The European Commission has described unclear identities and lack of valid travel documents as the 'main obstacle' to return, noting that establishing identity poses a number of difficult problems.[73]

Some rejected asylum seekers may lack identity papers because they were unable safely to obtain valid passports and visas from national authorities before leaving, or if it was only through the use of misleading entry visas – i.e., issued for a purpose other than asylum – that they were able to leave the country of feared persecution. Others may have used false passports provided by smuggling or trafficking operators. Many trafficked women have their documents stolen or destroyed either on arrival in a third country or prior to transfer.[74] Others may have deliberately destroyed their identify documents and claimed a false nationality in order to avoid removal. Difficulties also arise where countries of nationality

---

post return monitoring mechanism set up explicitly to prevent torture and ill treatment in a specific case would have the desired effect. These practices often occur in secret, with the perpetrators skilled at keeping such abuses from detection. The victims, fearing reprisal, often are reluctant to speak about their suffering, or are not believed if they do. Although efforts could be made to improve on the practice of seeking these assurances, in my view it is fundamentally flawed in several ways. First, we must acknowledge that diplomatic assurances would presumably only be sought after an assessment has been made that there is a risk of torture in the receiving state … Second, in most cases, assurances are concluded between states who are already parties to binding international and regional treaties which prohibit torture or inhuman or degrading treatment or punishment and *refoulement* to such practices. The system was devised by the community of states and they agreed to be bound by it. Ad hoc arrangements, such as assurances, concluded outside the system threaten to weaken its foundations and retard the progress that has been achieved over more than half a century to extend its ambit and protection to all …', Louise Arbour, UN High Commissioner for Human Rights, Address given at Chatham House and the British Institution of International and Civil Law, London, 15 Feb. 2006.

[71] See *Nationality and Statelessness: A Handbook for Parliamentarians* (Inter-Parliamentary Union with UNHCR 2005).

[72] Convention Relating to the Status of Stateless Persons, 28 Sept. 1954, 360 *UNTS* 117, Art. 31.

[73] See ECRE, *The Return of Asylum Seekers whose Applications have been rejected in Europe* (London, ECRE, June 2005) pp. 18-20. See also European Commission, *Communication to the Council and the European Parliament on a Community Return Policy on Illegal Residents* (COM (2002) 564, 14 Oct. 2002), para. 2.2.6.

[74] See UNHCR, *UNHCR's Activities in the Field of Statelessness: Progress Report*, Doc. EC/55/SC/CRP.13/Rev.1 (30 June 2005), para. 18.

refuse to issue documents or confirm nationality, or are unable to do so because they lack reliable registration or public records for their citizens.

5.4.1 *Mistaken nationality attribution*

In the absence of identity documents, some states have taken steps to identify, or attribute, nationality by other means, including language and dialect analysis. Some identification processes are crude, and criticized as unreliable, and are reported to have resulted in some people being sent to countries of which they are not nationals. The procedure used in one EU Member State has been described by Amnesty International:

> 'The interview is based on a nationality questionnaire with questions about the national flag or the principal cities. If the answers are inadequate, 'experts' are brought in; in many cases, these are foreign nationals who come from Africa and claim that they can quickly determine the nationality of an African by the skin, the shape of the face and the accent. Sometimes a representative from the embassy of the presumed country of origin... goes to a detention centre to speak directly with the detainees and confirm nationality. Identification is usually carried out through an 'opaque' mirror along one side of an interview room, apparently due to embassy staff fears of being recognized by detainees.'[75]

Use of techniques such as language and dialect analysis has been criticized on the grounds that they are not reliable in determining national origin, nationality or citizenship.[76] Such criticism reinforces anecdotal evidence of migrants who are stranded in one country, then sent or removed to another, including under readmission agreements, where they are again aliens and continue to be stranded because a mistaken nationality determination has been made; for example, where Jamaicans have been sent from a francophone African country to Nigeria because, as English speakers, they were assumed to be Nigerian.

5.4.2 *Ineffective protection by country of nationality*

Return may also become difficult where there is no consular representation, where states do not cooperate, or where the domestic bureaucratic process is complex and cumbersome. Some countries restrict the return of their own nation-

---

[75] See Amnesty International, *Spain: the Southern Border*, Doc. EUR 41/008/2005 (20 June 2005) <http://web.amnesty.org/library/index/engeur410082005>. In one case, the interviewee was given an expulsion order stating his nationality as Liberian, although he had told the authorities that he was from Sierra Leone.

[76] See 'Guidelines for the Use of Language Analysis in Relation to Questions of National Origin in Refugee Cases', 11 *International Journal of Speech, Language and the Law: Forensic Linguistics* (2004) p. 179, drafted by a group of linguists from Dutch, Belgian, US, Australian and UK universities. See also A. Reath, 'Language Analysis in the Context of the Asylum Process: procedures, validity and consequences', 1 *Language Assessment Quarterly* (2004) p. 209.

als, either outright or through laws and practices which effectively block expeditious returns.

In Mexico, the majority of migrants detained in migration facilities or holding centres have no access to consular assistance because of the lack of consular representatives.[77] Chinese irregular migrants are advised that

> 'only after the public security organ of your former domicile in China verifies and confirms your identity and your family members have paid for your return to China, can the relevant consular officer issue the home-bound travel document to you'.[78]

5.5 Prohibited means of removal[79]

International law limits the means which may be used to compel non-nationals to leave, where expulsion or deportation is ordered under national law and an individual physically resists removal. Where mandatory return takes place, it should be conducted in safety and dignity, consistent with human rights law.

Noting that Member States 'should be allowed to remove a person despite his or her (physical) resistance', the European Commission has called for EU standards to cover what it referred to as 'the intensity of coercion measures'. The Commission argues that 'removal ... should be subject to minimum standards safeguarding both the rights of the person concerned and the effectiveness of the removal'.[80] Safeguards are clearly necessary. Although the Council of Europe's 46 members are all bound by the ECHR's ban on inhuman and degrading treatment, deaths have resulted from methods used to enforce expulsion orders in its Member States:

> 'All too often, persons awaiting expulsion are subjected to ... dangerous methods of restraint and even violence and inhuman or degrading treatment. All too often, the officials...resort to an unjustified, improper or even dangerous use of force'.[81]

[77] UN, ECOSOC, Commission on Human Rights, *Report on Visit to Mexico by the UN Special Rapporteur on the Human Rights of Migrants*, UN Doc. E/CN.4/2003/85/Add.2 (30 Oct. 2002), para. 34.

[78] See *Guide to China's Consular Protection and Services Overseas* (2003 edn.): 'You should report truthfully to the Chinese diplomatic or consular mission in that country your authentic and detailed personal information, including your name, date of birth, place of birth, occupation, home address, telephone number, description about your illegal exit from China or illegal stay in the country concerned. Only after the public security organ of your former domicile in China verifies and confirms your identity and your family members have paid for your return to China, can the relevant consular officer issue the home-bound travel document to you'.

[79] See the report for the Medical Foundation for Care of Victims of Torture by C. Granville-Chapman, E. Smith and N. Moloney, *Harm on Removal: Excessive Force against Failed Asylum Seekers* (London, Medical Foundation for Care of Victims of Torture 2004).

[80] COM (2002) 564, loc. cit. n. 73, para. 2.3.2.

[81] Parliamentary Assembly of Council of Europe, Recommendation 1547 (2002), *Expulsion Procedures in Conformity with human rights and enforced with respect for safety and dignity*, para. 3.

The Council of Europe's Parliamentary Assembly has urged governments, *inter alia*, to forbid specific practices, including 'the use of poison gas or stun gas', the wearing of masks or hoods by security escorts, and 'partial or total obstruction of the respiratory tract'.[82] It also noted the difficulty of gathering reliable information:

> 'it is often only by chance that ill treatment suffered during deportation comes to light …[V]ery few people, on returning to their countries of origin, bring proceedings against those responsible for expelling them'.[83]

International codes of conduct already exist which apply generally to law enforcement operations, and which place strict limits on the use of force. They should apply equally to migration enforcement operations.[84] Where removal is delegated to private contractors, whether national or international, human rights law equally applies. States are required to respect human rights not only through the actions of their own agents, but also through those of private persons who are contracted to provide services, and who act on their behalf. Thus, when a state contracts 'private persons or entities' to execute removal programs, it has a duty to prevent, punish, investigate or redress any human rights violations by the non-state entity.[85]

6. Concluding Comments

Migrants may become stranded for reasons over which they have no control, or as a result of their own voluntary actions. In both situations they are entitled to the protection of their basic rights under international law.

A review of the stark but not exceptional situations referred to in this chapter illustrates – in Weissbrodt's phrase – the 'disjuncture' between the rights enjoyed in theory and the practical reality.[86] It underscores the need to reinforce international protection for migrants generally, and for this vulnerable group in particular, and to strengthen the international legal regime which decouples the right to have rights from one's nationality status. These situations also illustrate some of the dilemmas facing states seeking to 'manage' migration bilaterally in a world in which the forces which lead to the movement of people are global in nature, and are driven by international economic inequities.

Today the rights of legally stranded migrants lie at what may be seen as a jurisdictional intersection, between the diplomatic protection of their own states, protection under the domestic law of their 'host' state, and the emergent protection

---

82 Ibid., para. 13(ix)(g).

83 Ibid., para. 5.

84 See UN Code of Conduct for Law Enforcement Officials (UNGA Res. 34/169 of 17 Dec. 1979), which – e.g., in Art. 3 – sets criteria of strict necessity and proportionality.

85 Human Rights Committee, General Comment 31, loc. cit. n. 36, para. 8.

86 See the chapter by David Weissbrodt in this volume.

regime being created in international human rights law. In this situation, many stranded migrants find themselves outside any system of effective protection, and caught in a legal limbo.

At present, those who are legally stranded have no UN agency to which they can turn, because none has a mandate for migrants which is in any way comparable to the UNHCR's protection mandate for refugees. Except for those who are legally stateless, migrants fall outside the protection mandate of the UNHCR, and only if they are migrant workers do they come within that of the ILO. The protection of stranded migrants is clearly within the mandate of the High Commissioner for Human Rights, but the special rapporteurs of the Human Rights Commission – including the Special Rapporteur on the Human Rights of Migrants – have only a limited protection role, and the UN Treaty Bodies have as yet little effective oversight capacity. The IOM increasingly provides assistance to stranded migrants, at the request of governments.[87]

The Global Commission on International Migration has urged states to assist stranded migrants, and to find solutions for those who cannot be returned to their country of origin.[88] For those stranded migrants who have a country of nationality, it is important to strengthen consular protection. For migrants who have no nationality, and for those whose nationality does not provide effective protection and assistance, there is a need to review the concept of statelessness to protect those who are stateless *de facto* and to invigorate protection for those who are stateless *de jure*. In all situations, however, states have a responsibility under international law to protect the rights of those stranded on their territory.

Selected Bibliography

A Study of Statelessness, UN, Aug. 1949, UN Docs. E/1112; E/1112/Add.1.

Exclusion from Protection, Special Supplementary Issue of 12 *International Journal of Refugee Law* (2000).

Nationality and Statelessness: A Handbook for Parliamentarians (UNHCR/IPU, 2005).

Aleinikoff, T.A., and V. Chetail (eds.), *Migration and International Legal Norms* (T.M.C. Asser Press, The Hague 2003).

Benhabib, S., *The Rights of Others: aliens, residents and non citizens* (Cambridge, Cambridge University Press 2004).

Bogusz, B., R. Cholewinski, A. Cygan and E. Szyszczak (eds.), *Irregular Migration and Human Rights* (Leiden, Martinus Nijhoff 2004).

Global Commission on International Migration (GCIM), *Migration in an Interconnected World: New directions for action* (GCIM, Geneva, 2005).

Goodwin-Gill, G., *International Law and the Movement of Persons between States* (Oxford, Clarendon Press 1978).

[87] IOM, loc. cit. n. 13; IOM, *Migrants' Rights: IOM Policies and Activities*, Doc. MC/INF/259 (13 Nov. 2002) para. 5.

[88] GCIM Report, op. cit., n. 3, at p. 60.

Lillich, R., *The Human Rights of Aliens* (Manchester, Manchester University Press 1984).

Marks, S., and A. Clapham, *International Human Rights Lexicon* (Oxford, Oxford University Press 2005).

Special Rapporteur on Human Rights of Migrants, Reports to UN Commission of Human Rights 1999 <http://www.ohchr.org/english/issues/migration/rapporteur/>.

Weissbrodt, D., *Final Report on the Rights of Non-Citizens*, UN Doc. E/CN.4/Sub.2/2003/23 (26 May 2003).

Chapter 3
DETENTION OF IRREGULAR MIGRANTS AND ASYLUM SEEKERS

Shyla Vohra[*]

'Enslave the liberty of one human being and the liberties of the world are put in peril'.
William Lloyd Garrison (1804-1879)

1. INTRODUCTION

Liberty and security of the person is a fundamental human right enshrined in instruments at the global, regional and national levels. The term 'liberty of the person' in the context of the right is interpreted restrictively and is said to relate 'only to a very specific aspect of human liberty: the *freedom of bodily movement* in the narrowest sense. An interference with personal liberty results only from the forceful detention of a person at certain narrowly bound locations'.[1] Significantly, there is no prohibition under international law against detention *per se*, nor does the existence of the right aim at the abolition of deprivation of liberty.[2] Rather, the applicable principles are in the nature of procedural guarantees aimed at ensuring that deprivations of liberty are carried out fairly and correctly.

In the context of migration, states often detain migrants either for entering illegally, for not having correct documentation to stay, or pending deportation. More and more, states are also using detention against migrants in the name of national security, in order to validate identity or for questioning under anti-terrorism laws. There is also an increasing trend for states to use detention as a form of migration control; that is, states are using detention as a policy to maintain the 'integrity' of

[*] Master of Laws *Cum Laude* from Leiden University in the Netherlands, focusing on the law of international institutions, following completion of a Bachelor of Arts and a Bachelor of Laws degree from Monash University in Australia.

[1] M. Nowak, *UN Covenant on Civil and Political Rights: Commentary* (Strasbourg, N.P. Engel 1993) p. 160. The text continues to give examples of narrowly bounded locations 'such as a prison or some other detention facility, a psychiatric facility, a reeducation, concentration or workcamp, or a detoxification facility for alcoholics or drug addicts, as well as an order for house arrest … All less grievous restrictions on bodily movement such as limitations on domicile or residency, exile, confinement to an island or expulsion from State territory, do not fall within the scope of the right to personal liberty but instead under freedom of movement under Arts. 12 and 13' of the ICCPR.

[2] Unlike, for example, the prohibitions of torture or genocide.

R. Cholewinski, R. Perruchoud and E. MacDonald, eds., International Migration Law

their borders, and as a deterrent to future arrivals.[3] It is not disputed that national sovereignty means that a state has the power to control its borders, to determine the non-nationals it admits to its territory, in certain circumstances to remove non-nationals, and to take necessary steps to protect its security. However, this authority is mitigated by the fact that all migrants are human beings who possess fundamental and inalienable human rights and freedoms, which are protected under a range of international human rights instruments and customary international law. States do not have an unlimited or unfettered authority over migration issues. International law and the growth of international human rights law in particular, including treaties entered into on a bilateral, regional or international level, limits state authority over the issues of entry, stay and removal. Detention of migrants under the migration law of a state is therefore subject to provisions of international human rights law, which will determine its legality.

By their very nature of being 'behind closed doors', conditions of detention are often not open to public scrutiny, and there is much evidence that states regularly and consistently breach their obligations under international law, thus violating migrants' fundamental human rights.[4] This chapter seeks firstly to examine the international legal provisions regulating the authority to detain and the right of a detainee to challenge the detention: i.e., when are deprivations of liberty permissible under international law and what recourse do those who are wrongly deprived of their liberty have? It will secondly look at the international law regarding the conditions and standards of detention once a deprivation of liberty occurs. Lastly, the chapter seeks to appraise state practice in this area around the world today. For reasons of length, it will not explore detention of migrants in times of war, including the 'war on terror' and the associated international humanitarian law provisions.[5] Rather, it will focus on the provisions relevant to detention of irregular migrants and asylum seekers as part of the migration policy of a state.

2. The Definition of Detention

There are two types of detention – administrative and criminal. Criminal detention covers imprisonment, both pre- and post-trial, of persons charged under criminal laws. The term 'administrative detention' covers a range of situations

[3] Amnesty International, Open Letter to the incoming UK Presidency on the Occasion of World Refugee Day, *The Human Cost of 'Fortress Europe': Detention and expulsion of asylum seekers and migrants in the EU* (20 June 2005).

[4] Nowak, op. cit. n. 1, at p. 184, writes that 'experience has shown that precisely the situation of "special power relationships" within closed facilities often occasions massive violations of the most diverse of human rights'.

[5] For a comprehensive treatment of detention and international humanitarian law, see J. Pejic, 'Procedural principles and safeguards for internment/administrative detention in armed conflict and other situations of violence', 87 *International Review of the Red Cross*, No. 858 (June 2005) p. 375. On the issue of detention of IDPs in time of conflict, see Simon Bagshaw's contribution to this volume.

outside the process of police arresting suspects and bringing them into the criminal justice system. The detention of migrants and asylum seekers is therefore generally administrative detention. Such detention occurs by administrative order, or at the sole discretion of an administrative authority, without trial or charge.[6] In most cases, detained migrants will be held under the migration legislation of the country concerned, although it is of concern to note that the legislation of a number of countries criminalizes violations of immigration law, meaning that irregular migrants are detained and treated as criminals.[7]

A few international instruments have sought to define the concepts of deprivation of liberty and detention:[8] the Committee on the Rights of the Child has adopted the definition of detention outlined in the UN Rules for the Protection of Juveniles Deprived of their Liberty,[9] which states, in Rule 11(b), that

> '[d]eprivation of liberty means any form of detention or imprisonment or the placement of a person in another public or private custodial setting from which this person is not permitted to leave at will, by order of any judicial, administrative or other public authority'.

The 1999 UNHCR Revised Guidelines on Applicable Criteria and Standards Relating to the Detention of Asylum Seekers define detention as

> 'confinement within a narrowly bounded or restricted location, including prisons, closed camps, detention facilities or airport transit zones, where freedom of movement is substantially curtailed, and where the only opportunity to leave this limited area is to leave the territory'.[10]

---

[6] P. Williams, *Treatment of Detainees: Examination of Issues Relevant to Detention by the United Nations Human Rights Committee* (Geneva, Henri Dunant Institute 1990) p. 73.

[7] The Special Rapporteur on the human rights of migrants 'is concerned by the fact that under the legislation of a considerable number of countries violations of the immigration law constitute a criminal offence. Undocumented and irregular migrants therefore become particularly vulnerable to criminal detention, which is punitive in nature, for such infractions as irregularly crossing the State border, using false documents, leaving their residence without authorization, irregular stay, overstaying their or breaching conditions of stay. The Special Rapporteur notes with concern that criminalization of irregular migration is increasingly being used by Governments to discourage it'. UN, ECOSOC, Commission on Human Rights, 59th Session, *Report of the Special Rapporteur, Ms. Gabriela Rodríguez Pizarro, submitted pursuant to Commission on Human Rights resolution 2002/62*, UN Doc. E/CN.4/2003/85 (30 Dec. 2002) para. 17.

[8] The only international instrument which does not include post-trial imprisonment in its definition of detention is the Body of Principles for the Protection of All Persons under Any Form of Detention or Imprisonment, adopted by the General Assembly in Resolution 43/173 of 9 Dec. 1988. The UN Working Group on Arbitrary Detention has exhaustively analyzed the distinction made in the Body of Principles, and concluded that such a distinction would not be appropriate for carrying out its mandate. See UN, ECOSOC, Commission on Human Rights, 53rd Session, *Report of the Working Group on Arbitrary Detention*, UN Doc. E/CN.4/1997/4 (17 Dec. 1996) paras. 50-85.

[9] UNGA Res. 45/113 of 14 Dec. 1990, Annex.

[10] UNHCR Revised Guidelines on Applicable Criteria and Standards Relating to the Detention of Asylum-Seekers (Feb. 1999) <http://www.unhcr.org/cgi-bin/texis/vtx/protect/opendoc.pdf?tbl=

There is a distinction, therefore, between detention and other forms of restriction of movement, which may include, for example, limitations on residency or reporting requirements. The former, on which this paper focuses, entails a significant degree of confinement. The European Court of Human Rights has stated that

> '[i]n order to determine whether someone has been 'deprived of his liberty'... the starting-point must be his concrete situation, and account must be taken of a whole range of criteria such as the type, duration, effects and manner of implementation of the measure in question. The difference between deprivation of and restriction upon liberty is merely one of degree or intensity, and not one of nature or substance.'[11]

Migrants who are detained pending deportation or identity proceedings, or asylum seekers detained while their claims are processed, are often held in separate purpose-built detention facilities, or 'asylum centres'. However, the Special Rapporteur on the human rights of migrants has noticed in the course of her country visits that places such as schools, warehouses, airport terminals, and sports stadiums have been converted into centres for the administrative custody of migrants. Further, in some countries, where no such facilities exist, migrants are held in prisons.[12] The European Committee for the Prevention of Torture and Inhuman or Degrading Treatment or Punishment (CPT), which is the body responsible for monitoring the Council of Europe Convention of the same name,[13] has also expressed concern about the detention of irregular migrants and asylum seekers in the international zone of airports and point of entry holding facilities, noting that conditions are often makeshift and inadequate, particularly for lengthy stays.[14] The CPT has expressed the view that where deprivation of liberty is necessary for extended periods under migration legislation, persons should be 'accommodated in *centres specifically designed for that purpose*, offering material conditions and a regime appropriate to their legal situation and staffed by suitably qualified personnel'.[15]

PROTECTION&id=3bd036a74> Guideline 1. This definition in turn is based upon the Note of the Sub-Committee of the Whole on International Protection of 1986 (37th Session, UN Doc. EC/SCP/44 para. 25) which defined detention to mean 'confinement in prison, closed camp or other restricted area, on the assumption that there is a qualitative difference between detention and other restrictions on freedom of movement'.

[11] *Amuur* v. *France* (1996) 22 *EHRR* 533, para. 42.

[12] UN Doc. E/CN.4/2003/85, loc. cit. n. 7.

[13] European Convention for the Prevention of Torture and Inhuman or Degrading Treatment or Punishment, 26 Nov. 1987, *ETS* No. 126.

[14] *The CPT Standards*, Doc. CPT/Inf/E (2002) 1 - Rev. 2004.

[15] CPT, *7th General Report on the CPT's activities covering the period 1 January to 31 December 1996* (22 Aug. 1997), Doc. CPT/Inf (97) 10 <http://www.cpt.coe.int/en/annual/rep-07.htm> para. 29 (original emphasis).

3. Applicable Principles Regarding the Authority to Detain

> 'Wrongfully to deprive human beings of their freedom and to subject them to physical constraint in conditions of hardship is manifestly incompatible with the principles of the Charter of the United Nations as well as with the fundamental principles enunciated in the Universal Declaration of Human Rights'.[16]

The fundamental principle in international law regarding detention is stated in Article 9 of the Universal Declaration of Human Rights (UDHR):[17] 'No one shall be subject to arbitrary arrest, detention or exile'. This principle has been incorporated into the International Covenant on Civil and Political Rights (ICCPR)[18] whose Article 9(1) states that '[n]o one shall be subjected to arbitrary arrest or detention. No one shall be deprived of his liberty except on such grounds and in accordance with such procedures as are established by law'.

The Working Group on Arbitrary Detention[19] has noted that the above ICCPR provision reflects the principles of customary international law, and therefore is also binding on states which are not party to the Convention.[20]

The basic concepts contained in the provision above are therefore the prohibition against arbitrariness and the requirement of legality ('established by law'). These two concepts form the basis of the authority to detain – whether the detention itself is allowed by international law – and each will be examined below.

3.1 The prohibition against arbitrariness

Detention will violate international law if it is found to be arbitrary. When drafting the text of Article 9 of the ICCPR, the Commission on Human Rights first proposed to define all the grounds for which a person may be deprived of his or her liberty, e.g., mental illness, contagious disease, espionage, criminality, etc. However, it quickly became apparent that not only would such a list be unreasonably long, but also it would be impossible for states to agree on. A proposal to instead prohibit arrest or detention which was 'arbitrary' was unanimously adopted in 1949.[21] No clear definition of the word 'arbitrary' emerged, however, and both the jurisprudence of UN bodies and academic opinion need to be studied in order

---

[16] *Case concerning United States Diplomatic and Consular Staff in Tehran*, ICJ Rep. (1980) p. 3, at p. 42.

[17] UNGA Res. 217A (III), UN Doc A/810 at p. 71 (1948).

[18] UNGA Res. 2200A (XXI), 21 UN GAOR Supp. (No. 16) at 52, UN Doc. A/6316 (1966), 999 *UNTS* 171.

[19] Established by the UN Commission on Human Rights by its Resolution 1991/42.

[20] ECOSOC, Report of the Working Group on Arbitrary Detention, *Civil and Political Rights, Including the Question of Torture and Detention*, UN Doc. E/CN.4/2005/6 (1 Dec. 2004) para. 53 <http://daccessdds.un.org/doc/UNDOC/GEN/G04/167/19/PDF/G0416719.pdf?OpenElement>.

[21] Nowak, op. cit. n. 1 at p. 164. Ironically, given its mandatory detention regime for unlawful migrants and asylum seekers, it was Australia who proposed the use of the word 'arbitrary'.

to help clarify its meaning. It is apparent that it means more than 'unlawful'; it relates to the concepts of injustice, unpredictability, unreasonableness and capriciousness. The prohibition against arbitrariness should be interpreted broadly and assessed on a case-by-case basis.[22] Basically, it means that in a case where liberty is deprived, in situations of arrest or detention, there must be an applicable law which is not manifestly unjust or unpredictable. The Human Rights Committee has stated[23] that

> 'the drafting history of article 9, paragraph 1, confirms that 'arbitrariness' is not to be equated with against the law, but must be interpreted more broadly to include elements of inappropriateness, injustice and lack of predictability. This means that remand in custody pursuant to lawful arrest must not only be lawful but reasonable in all the circumstances. Further, remand in custody must be necessary in all the circumstances'.[24]

The Human Rights Committee has stressed that

> 'paragraph 1 is applicable to all deprivations of liberty, whether in criminal cases or in other cases such as, for example, mental illness, vagrancy, drug addiction, educational purposes, immigration control, etc.'[25]

The concepts of reasonableness and necessity therefore help define the prohibition against arbitrariness. The Australian Human Rights and Equal Opportunity Commission in its report on detention of unauthorized arrivals in Australia[26] adds that

> '[t]he question whether a particular restriction on liberty is necessary and reasonable or arbitrary for the purposes of the ICCPR is not a matter of purely subjective judgement. The jurisprudence of the Human Rights Committee indicates that, to avoid the taint of arbitrariness, detention must be a proportionate means to achieve a legitimate aim, having regard to whether there are alternative means available which are less restrictive of rights'.

---

[22] The Working Group on Arbitrary Detention considers that '[i]t is not possible, and in the view of the Working Group it is not necessary, to give an exhaustive list of arbitrary detention; arbitrariness must be assessed in the light of all the relevant circumstances of a given detention'. UN Doc. E/CN.4/2005/6, op. cit. n. 20, at para. 54.

[23] *Alphen* v. *the Netherlands*, Communication No. 305/1988, Human Rights Committee Report 1990, Vol. II, UN Doc. A/45/40 (4 Oct. 1990), para. 5.8.

[24] See also Nowak, op. cit. n. 1, at p. 173, who writes that '[c]ases of deprivation of liberty provided for by law must not be manifestly unproportional, unjust or unpredictable, and the specific manner in which an arrest is made must not be discriminatory and must be able to be deemed appropriate and proportional in view of the circumstances of the case'.

[25] Human Rights Committee, General Comment No. 8, reproduced in UN Doc. HRI/GEN/1/Rev.7 (12 May 2004).

[26] Australia Human Rights and Equal Opportunity Commission Inquiry Report, *Those who've come across the seas: Detention of unauthorized arrivals* (May 1998).

The Working Group on Arbitrary Detention has explicitly stated that detaining irregular migrants is not, in itself, arbitrary, and explained that

> '[i]n case of illegal entry the need for the immigration authorities for identity checks and the initial immigration screening may justify temporary detention of unlawful non-citizens, particularly if they are unwilling to cooperate with the authorities and if they are likely to abscond. But any deprivation of liberty must be proportionate to the aims pursued and a fair balance shall be struck between the conflicting interests: the interest of the State to implement its immigration policy and to protect the community against illegal immigration, on the one hand, and the fundamental right to liberty of the unlawful entrants, on the other hand'.[27]

Specifically with regards to asylum seekers, the Working Group has stated that if detention of asylum seekers results from exercising the right to seek asylum, such detention might be considered arbitrary.[28] This question will be addressed further in Section 3.3 below.

In practice today, the increasing use of detention as a deterrent to irregular entry means that this fair balance is not always struck. A policy of detention for unlawful entrants, including asylum seekers, means that individualized assessments as to whether the detention is proportionate and necessary in the circumstances are not made. In its observations of trends in EU countries for example, Amnesty International 'is concerned that the authorities are using the risk of absconding as justification for detention without a detailed and meaningful assessment of the risk posed by each individual'.[29] In its report on its visit to Australia, the Working Group on Arbitrary Detention raised 'several concerns about the mandatory detention of unauthorized arrivals in Australia because of its automatic and indiscriminate character', and found that detention is effected 'without a prior assessment of the particular circumstances of each individual case which would balance the conflicting interests'.[30]

3.2 Established by law

The second element of Article 9(1) is legality. Deprivation of liberty is prohibited 'except on such grounds and in accordance with such procedures as are established by law'. 'Law' in this sense refers to the domestic legal system, and means that deprivation of liberty must be allowed for by legislation. Nowak writes that

---

[27] UN, ECOSOC, Commission on Human Rights, 59th Session, *Report of the Working Group on Arbitrary Detention: Visit to Australia*, UN Doc. E/CN.4/2003/8/Add.2 (24 Oct. 2002) para. 12 <http://daccessdds.un.org/doc/UNDOC/GEN/G02/153/91/PDF/G0215391.pdf?OpenElement>.

[28] UNHCHR, *Fact Sheet No. 26, The Working Group on Arbitrary Detention* <http://www.unhchr.ch/html/menu6/2/fs26.htm#VI>.

[29] Amnesty International Open Letter, loc. cit. n. 3, which specifically refers to reports on detention conditions and deportation practice in the United Kingdom, Spain and Italy.

[30] UN Doc. E/CN.4/2003/8/Add.2, op. cit. n. 27, at pp. 2, 7.

> '[t]he term "law" is to be understood here in the strict sense of a general-abstract, parliamentary statute or an equivalent, unwritten norm of common law accessible to all individuals subject to the relevant jurisdiction'.[31]

Purely administrative provisions are insufficient. This means that arresting or detaining a person by an administrative act can only be allowed if it is enforcing a provision in legislation. The legislation itself must provide for the arrest or detention clearly, and must regulate the relevant procedures to be observed. The principle of legality will therefore be violated if somebody is arrested or detained on grounds which are not clearly established in a domestic law. The principle of legality goes hand in hand with the 'prohibition against arbitrariness', meaning that it is not enough if the arrest or detention is prescribed by law. The law itself must not be arbitrary, and the enforcement of the law must not take place arbitrarily.

The Working Group on Arbitrary Detention has further contended that even if the ICCPR, or any other international treaty, has not been incorporated into domestic law under the national system, a State Party cannot argue that it is not bound thereby and that its national laws do not therefore need to be in compliance with it.[32] Similarly, the European Court of Human Rights has found that 'the notion of lawfulness' requires that deprivations of liberty must not only conform to national law, but also to the relevant provisions of the European Convention on Human Rights (ECHR).[33]

3.3 Other relevant instruments

These basic requirements of detention – being established by law and not arbitrary – are reflected in other international instruments addressing particular groups of persons. At the international level, paragraphs 1 and 4 of Article 16 of the International Convention on the Protection of the Rights of All Migrant Workers and Members of Their Families (ICRMW)[34] almost mirror the wording of Article 9 of the ICCPR, referring to the right to liberty and security of person and the prohibition of arbitrary arrest or detention.

Further, the authority to detain refugees and asylum seekers has been specifically addressed by the UNHCR. Its Executive Committee[35] has stated that refugees and asylum seekers should not normally be detained, and, rather than referring to the general prohibition on arbitrariness, it has specified the grounds for which detention is permissible:

---

[31] Nowak, op. cit. n. 1, at p. 171.

[32] See UN Doc. E/CN.4/2003/8/Add.2, loc. cit. n. 27, para. 24.

[33] *Chahal* v. *UK* (1996) 23 *EHRR* 413, where the Court found, at para. 132, that 'neither the proceedings for habeas corpus and for judicial review of the decision to detain Mr Chahal before the domestic courts, nor the advisory panel procedure, satisfied the requirements of Article 5 para. 4'.

[34] UNGA Res. 45/158 of 18 Dec. 1990, 45 UN GAOR Supp. (No. 49A) at 262, UN Doc. A/45/49 (1990).

[35] EXCom Conclusion No. 44 (XXXVII) of the Executive Committee of UNHCR (GAOR, 41st Session, Supp. No. 12A (Doc. A/41/12/Add.1) para. 128; Doc. HCR/IP/2/Eng/REV.1991 (1992) p. 96, para. (b).

> 'To verify identity; to determine the elements on which the claim to refugee status or asylum was based; to deal with cases where refugees or asylum seekers had destroyed their travel and/or identification documents... in order to mislead the authorities of the State in which they intended to claim asylum; or to protect national security or public order'.

The UNHCR has emphatically stated that these are the only reasons that can be used to justify the detention of asylum seekers, and cautions states against using detention to deter future asylum seekers or to dissuade them from pursuing asylum claims. The concepts of proportionality and reasonableness are also fundamental in the detention of asylum seekers as elaborated in the UNHCR's Revised Guidelines, which in their Guideline 3 state that

> '[w]here detention of asylum seekers is considered necessary it should only be imposed where it is reasonable to do so and without discrimination. It should be proportional to the ends to be achieved (i.e., to ensure one of the above purposes) and for a minimal period'.

Beyond these specific limitations to detention of asylum seekers, there is a danger that the prohibition against penalizing refugees on account of their illegal entry or presence (Article 31 of the 1951 Convention relating to the Status of Refugees)[36] could be violated.[37]

The authority to detain children has been elaborated by the UN Convention on the Rights of the Child (CRC),[38] which requires that detention of a child be a measure of last resort and for the shortest appropriate period of time (Article 37(b)). In keeping with the general requirements regarding detention as stated above, Article 37 also specifies that no child should be deprived of his or her liberty unlawfully or arbitrarily.

The fundamental principle prohibiting arbitrary or unlawful detention in the ICCPR has also been incorporated into a number of human rights treaties at the regional level. Regional human rights instruments incorporating this principle include the 1981 African Charter on Human Rights and People's Rights (ACHRPR)[39] and the American Convention on Human Rights (ACHR).[40] The

---

[36] Convention relating to the Status of Refugees, 28 July 1951, 189 *UNTS* 137.

[37] For a comprehensive treatment of this issue under the 1951 Convention, see G. Goodwin-Gill, 'Article 31 of the 1951 Convention Relating to the Status of Refugees: Non-penalization, Detention and Protection', in E. Feller, V. Türk and F. Nicholson (eds.), *Refugee Protection in International Law* (Cambridge, Cambridge University Press 2003) p. 185.

[38] UN Convention on the Rights of the Child, 20 Nov. 1989, 1577 *UNTS* 3.

[39] OAU Doc. CAB/LEG/67/3 rev. 5, reprinted in 21 *International Legal Materials* (1982) p. 58. Article 6 proclaims that 'every individual shall have the right to liberty and to the security of his person. No one may be deprived of his freedom except for reasons and conditions previously laid down by law. In particular, no one may be arbitrarily arrested or detained'.

[40] OAS Treaty Series No. 36, 1144 *UNTS* 123. Article 7 stipulates that '[e]very person has the right to personal liberty and security of person. No one shall be deprived of his physical liberty except for the reasons and under the conditions established beforehand by the constitution of the State Party

ECHR provides that '[e]veryone has the right to liberty and security of person. No one shall be deprived of his liberty save in the following cases and in accordance with a procedure described by law'.[41] Rather than a generic prohibition of arbitrariness, the ECHR provides an exhaustive list of when detention may occur. Article 5(1)(f) refers specifically to migrants in detention, and states that detention is permissible in cases of 'the lawful arrest or detention of a person to prevent his effecting an unauthorized entry into the country or of a person against whom action is being taken with a view to deportation or extradition'.

3.4 Challenging the authority to detain

That deprivations of liberty must be lawful and must not be arbitrary is therefore a firmly established principle in both treaty and customary international law. Indeed, those deprived of their liberty have the fundamental right to challenge the lawfulness of the detention. Article 9(4) of the ICCPR states that

> '[a]nyone who is deprived of his liberty by arrest or detention shall be entitled to take proceedings before a court, in order that that court may decide without delay on the lawfulness of his detention and order his release if the detention is not lawful'.

This right is mirrored in the ICRMW,[42] whose Article 15(8) adds that, when migrant workers attend such court proceedings, they shall have the assistance, if necessary without cost to them, of an interpreter if they cannot speak or understand the language used. This right is also found in the CRC,[43] the regional instruments mentioned above, and is mentioned as a procedural safeguard in the UNHCR Guidelines in relation to the detention of asylum seekers.[44] The 1988 Body of Principles for the Protection of all Persons under Any Form of Detention or Imprisonment[45] also gives some practical guidance as to the implementation of the right to challenge the lawfulness of detention, and specify that all persons detained have the right:

- 'not to be kept in detention without being given an effective opportunity to be heard promptly by a judicial or other authority';[46]

---

concerned or by a law established pursuant thereto. No one shall be subject to arbitrary arrest or imprisonment'.

[41] Convention for the Protection of Human Rights and Fundamental Freedoms, 4 Nov. 1950, *ETS* No. 5, Art. 5(1).

[42] ICRMW, loc. cit. n. 34, Art. 15.

[43] CRC, loc. cit. n. 38, Art. 39.

[44] UNHCR Revised Guidelines, loc. cit. n. 10, Guideline 5(iii).

[45] UNGA Res. 43/173 of 9 Dec. 1988, Annex.

[46] Ibid., Principle 11(1).

- 'at any time to take proceedings according to domestic law before a judicial or other authority to challenge the lawfulness of their detention';[47]

- to do so through proceedings that are 'simple and expeditious and at no cost for detained persons without adequate means';[48]

- to have the assistance of legal counsel, to receive reasonable help in obtaining counsel, and to have adequate time and facilities to communicate with them;[49]

- to be given an explanation of all relevant rights, and the right to receive such information in a language the detainee understands and to have the assistance, free of charge if necessary, of an interpreter.[50]

That the right to challenge the lawfulness of detention extends to *all* persons deprived of their liberty and not just those in criminal detention has been affirmed by the Human Rights Committee. Further, the review must examine the merits of detention and must be 'in its effects, real and not merely formal'.[51] The European Court of Human Rights has also specified that judicial review must be 'effective' and that the obligation of effectiveness implies that a number of procedural rights have to be granted to the foreigner. Among those rights are the right to free linguistic assistance, the right of access to the case file and the right to legal aid.[52]

States must also provide an effective remedy where deprivation of liberty is found to be unlawful or arbitrary.[53] While such a remedy would include immediate release from detention, the ICCPR, the ICRMW and the ECHR also explicitly provide a right to compensation. Further, de Zayas writes that

> '[p]ursuant to the principle *ubi jus, ibi remedium*, compensation should also be granted, whether or not the universal and regional human rights conventions specifically envisage such compensation'.[54]

At times, the Human Rights Committee has made concrete recommendations that a State Party should pay compensation when it has found that detention has

---

[47] Ibid., Principle 32(1).

[48] Ibid., Principle 32(2).

[49] Ibid., Principle 17(1).

[50] Ibid., Principles 13 and 14.

[51] *A* v. *Australia,* Communication No. 560/1993, UN Doc. CCPR/C/59/D/560/1993 (30 April 1997) p. 24.

[52] *Amuur* v. *France*, loc. cit. n. 11. See also the discussion on the website of the Jesuit Refugee Service Europe, Caring for Detainees, at <http://www.detention-in-europe.org/mambo/index.php?option=content&task=view&id=23>.

[53] Human Rights Committee General Comment No. 8, loc. cit. n. 25, at para. 1.

[54] A. De Zayas, 'Human Rights and Indefinite Detention', 87 *International Review of the Red Cross* No. 857 (March 2005) p. 15 at p. 34.

been unlawful.[55] In Australia, it has further been asserted that when a court has determined that a migrant's detention was unlawful, the relevant Government department should have conducted an urgent audit to see if other, similar cases were also affected by the decision, meaning that others should be released following the Court's ruling.[56]

There is widespread evidence that, in the context of detention of irregular migrants and asylum seekers, this right to challenge the lawfulness of detention is widely violated. Serious repercussions flow from the violation of this right. For example, a lack of judicial review, particularly where national legislation does not provide for any maximum time limit for administrative detention, means that, in practice, detention can be prolonged and can even become indefinite.[57] Further, while some states insist that the right to challenge detention is allowed, if detainees are not given practical assistance to enjoy this right, such as access to free legal counsel, the enjoyment of the right remains academic. Amnesty International writes that

> '[u]nder international standards, detained asylum-seekers have the right to contact legal counsel, relatives and others. Yet in the USA detained asylum-seekers face problems with all forms of access, including access to legal counsel, access to other visitors, phone calls, ability to send and receive correspondence, access to newspapers and television, access by NGOs and by other caregivers. Many asylum-seekers in detention are cut off from their families, legal representation and the support of NGOs. The net result is that they are denied access to justice'.[58]

4. Applicable Principles Regarding Conditions of Detention

> 'Migrants subjected to administrative proceedings have in general far fewer guarantees and rights than those who are the subject of judicial proceedings… these elements re-

---

[55] See, e.g., *C* v. *Australia*, No. 900/1999, UN Doc. CCPR/C/76/D/900/1999 (13 Nov. 2002), and *Bakhtiyari* v. *Australia*, UN Doc. CCPR/C/79/D/1069/2002 (29 Oct. 2003). In neither case has Australia complied with the recommendation to provide compensation.

[56] 'Department "ignored" its duty', *The Age,* 27 Oct. 2005.

[57] The jurisprudence of the Human Rights Committee has established that even if the initial detention is not arbitrary, a subsequent period of detention may become arbitrary; for example, when one has regard to the length of the detention. (Human Rights Committee, *Spakmo* v. *Norway*, Communication No. 631/1995, UN Doc. CCPR/C/67/D/631/1995 (11 Nov. 1999); *A* v. *Australia*, loc. cit. n. 51; Human Rights Committee, *Concluding Observations: Switzerland*, UN Doc CCPR/C/79/Add.70 (8 Nov. 1996). Indeed, the prohibition against prolonged arbitrary detention has been listed in the American Law Institute's (ALI) Restatement of the Law (Third) as an action unlawful 'for a state to practice, encourage or condone', i.e., it has been recognized as a prohibition under international customary law (ALI Restatement (Third) of Foreign Relations Law of the United States (1987), Sec. 702, Comments and Reporters' Notes).

[58] Amnesty International, *USA: Lost in the Labyrinth: detention of asylum seekers* (New York, Amnesty International USA 1999) <http://www.amnestyusa.org/countries/usa/document.do?id=CCA1246D90686CB0802569000693482>.

sult in administrative detention being beyond any control, disproportionate powers being exercised by immigration authorities, and incidents of discrimination and abuse'.[59]

The fundamental principle which underpins standards of detention under international law is found in Article 10 of the ICCPR, which states that '[a]ll persons deprived of their liberty shall be treated with humanity and with respect for the inherent dignity of the human person'.

Case-law of the Human Rights Committee shows that breaches of this Article need not meet the standard of inhuman treatment within the meaning of Article 7 of the ICCPR, which prohibits torture, cruel, inhuman or degrading treatment or punishment. Incommunicado detention is one example of a practice which the Committee has found to breach Article 10, yet not violate the prohibition in Article 7.[60] Novak further elaborates the distinction as follows:

> '... Art. 7 principally accords a claim that State organs refrain from certain action (prohibition of mistreatment) while Art. 10 also covers *positive State duties to ensure* certain conduct: Regardless of economic difficulties, the State must establish a minimum standard for humane conditions of detention (*requirement of humane treatment*)'.[61]

However, specific elaboration of the standards or safeguards applicable to administrative detention is less internationally recognized at the treaty level, and many must be drawn from soft law. Non-binding texts[62] need to be examined in order to determine the actual conditions to be applied to deprivations of liberty.

The Standard Minimum Rules for the Treatment of Prisoners[63] were first adopted in 1955 and then extended in 1977 to enhance protection of persons detained without charge. When drafting these rules, UN delegates specifically emphasized that they should be considered when interpreting Article 10 of the ICCPR.[64] The Rules cover specific material needs of detainees such as clothing

[59] UN Doc. E/CN.4/2003/85, loc. cit. n. 7.

[60] See, e.g., *Penarrieta, Pura de Toro, et al.* v. *Bolivia*, Communication No. 176/1984, UN Doc. CCPR/C/31/D/176/1984 (2 Nov. 1987).

[61] Nowak, op. cit. n. 1, at p. 188.

[62] Standard Minimum Rules for the Treatment of Prisoners, ECOSOC Res. 663 C (XXIV) of 31 July 1957 and 2076 (LXII) of 13 May 1977 <http://www.unhchr.ch/html/menu3/b/h_comp34.htm>. The Body of Principles, loc. cit. n. 45, and the Rules for Juveniles, loc. cit. n. 9, were adopted by consensus by UN Member States, and therefore, although not strictly legally binding (except insofar as some of the rules they contain reflect customary international law), have a certain authoritative weight. See A-M. Tootell, J. Hughes and D. Petrasek, 'The Relevance of Key UN Instruments for Detained Asylum Seekers', in J. Hughes and F. Liebaut (eds.), *Detention of Asylum Seekers in Europe: Analysis and Perspectives* (The Hague, Martinus Nijhoff 1998) p. 183.

[63] *First United Nations Congress on the Prevention of Crime and the Treatment of Offenders: Report by the Secretariat*, (UN Publication Sales No. 1956.IV.4) Annex I.A.

[64] UN GAOR, 13th Session, Third Committee, 16 Sept. to 8 Dec. 1958, pp. 160-173 and 227-241. See also N. Poynder, 'The Incommunicado Detention of Boat People: A Recent Development in Australia's Refugee Policy', 3(2) *Australian Journal of Human Rights* (1997) <http://bar.austlii.edu.au/au/journals/AJHR/1997/4.html>.

and bedding, food, personal hygiene, medical services, exercise and sport, books and religious worship. They also specify that

- different categories of prisoners shall be kept in separate institutions (or parts of institutions), taking account of their sex, age, criminal record, the legal reason for their detention and the necessities of their treatment;[65]
- women should be held separately from men;[66]
- handcuffs, chains, irons and straitjackets should never be used as punishment;[67]
- people detained for civil or administrative reasons should be kept separately from people imprisoned for a criminal offence.[68]

The 1988 Principles for the Protection of all Persons under Any Form of Detention or Imprisonment[69] further provide authoritative guidance in the practical interpretation of Article 10. They stress the importance of detainees having access to the outside world and of independent supervision of detention conditions. They state that the basic rights of detained individuals include the following:[70]

- the right to promptly notify[71] and receive visits from family members;[72]
- the right to legal counsel;[73]
- the right to 'treatment appropriate to their unconvicted status', for those who are awaiting trial or detained for non-criminal reasons, meaning separation from convicted prisoners;[74]
- the right to be provided with a proper medical examination and free medical treatment and care;[75]
- the right to obtain, within the limits of available resources, educational, cultural and informational materials.[76]

---

[65] See the Standard Minimum Rules for the Treatment of Prisoners, loc. cit. n. 62, Rule 8.

[66] Ibid., Rule 8(a).

[67] Ibid., Rule 33.

[68] Ibid., Rule 8(c).

[69] Body of Principles, loc. cit. n. 45.

[70] The actual rights enumerated in the Body of Principles are too numerous to adequately reflect in this chapter.

[71] Body of Principles, loc. cit. n. 45, Principle 16.

[72] Ibid., Principle 19.

[73] Ibid., Principle 17.

[74] Ibid., Principle 8.

[75] Ibid., Principle 24.

[76] Ibid., Principle 28.

The UN Working Group on Arbitrary Detention considers that most of the provisions of the Body of Principles are declaratory of existing rights under international customary law.[77]

Similar standards and basic rights for children in detention are found in the 1990 Rules for Juveniles Deprived of Their Liberty.[78] These Rules regulate the management of facilities where juveniles are held (applying to persons under the age of 18 years), and cover detention for any purpose, including administrative detention. Further, the 1999 UNHCR Revised Guidelines on Applicable Criteria and Standards Relating to the Detention of Asylum Seekers, as its name suggests, provides the standards to be followed in the detention of asylum seekers.[79] Some regional instruments are also relevant; for example, the Twenty Guidelines on Forced Return, adopted in 2005 by the Committee of Ministers of the Council of Europe.[80]

5. The Gap Between Theory and Practice

> 'Expectations among governments are lowered when the traditional leaders in setting standards of due process and generosity lower their own standards ...'[81]

On paper, the international law regarding administrative detention which is relevant to irregular migrants and asylum seekers seems clear enough. Such detention must not be arbitrary; it must be lawful; detainees have a right to judicial review; conditions of detention must be humane; and minimum standards are well-documented. Basic provisions in international treaties are supplemented by numerous declarations and resolutions, as well as by regional and national case-law. Yet, this is an area of law where the gap between theory and practice seems to be ever-widening.

Regrettably, it is the 'standard setters', wealthy industrialized countries such as the United States, Australia and many European countries which have adopted particularly restrictive and hostile policies to all those entering their borders illegally or in search of asylum, and the practice of detention is on the rise. In the absence of official statistics, the precise scale of arbitrary, unlawful or inhumane detention is unknown. However, the reports of the Special Rapporteur on the

---

[77] UN, ECOSOC, Commission on Human Rights, 49th Session, *Report of the Working Group on Arbitrary Detention*, UN Doc. E/CN.4/1993/24 (12 Jan. 1993) p. 9 (Deliberation 02).

[78] Loc. cit. n. 9.

[79] Loc. cit. n 10.

[80] In this regard, see also the proposed standards on detention in the European Commission proposal for a Directive of the European Parliament and Council, *On common standards and procedures in Member States for returning illegally staying third-country nationals* (COM (2005) 391, 1 Sept. 2005).

[81] W. Frelick, 'The Year in Review', *World Refugee Survey* (1997), US Committee for Refugees, p. 14.

human rights of migrants, the Working Group on Arbitrary Detention, and organizations such as Amnesty International and Human Rights Watch, as well as information from the media, all point to the fact that detention practices, in the name of migration control, regularly violate fundamental rights, and that this is happening in all parts of the world.

Why do states ignore their international obligations in this area? There are larger questions of why countries which go to war in the name of democracy and human rights fail to provide such rights within their own borders. Such debate, while vital, is beyond the scope of this chapter. Nevertheless, the current global climate of insecurity, hostility and fear necessarily affects migrants to a great extent, as they are generally viewed with suspicion and mistrust. The United Kingdom, for example, following the events of 9/11, has declared a public emergency and derogated from Article 9 of the ICCPR in order to extend the power to arrest and detain in cases where a person is suspected of being a threat to national security.[82] At the time of writing, the Australian Parliament is debating new anti-terrorism measures, including preventative detention which would not be subject to effective judicial review, in clear violation of Article 9 of the ICCPR. The United States has enacted extensive legislation and administrative measures granting the Government wide powers regarding arrests on suspicion of terrorist activity, detention without trial, and forced deportation. As the Director of the American Civil Liberties Union remarked, '[i]mmigrants weren't the enemy. But the war on terror quickly became a war on immigrants'.[83]

The threat of terrorism[84] cannot, however, solely be blamed for the numerous detention systems around the world which fail to comply with the safeguards in international law. Lack of respect for the relevant international law in this area predates September 11 and the rise of tightened security regimes. There is a need also to consider current attitudes to non-citizens trying to gain entry and reside in another country. The increase in international migration itself, and emigration push factors in developing countries, mean that there is a growth in irregular migration and a perception that many asylum seekers are in fact 'economic migrants' seeking to abuse the international protection regime. Ghosh writes that

> '[r]ecent experiences in several western European countries such as Austria, Denmark and France have shown that once the negative perception of migration, including fears about cultural erosion and joblessness, takes hold and the anti-immigration issues are injected into the political agenda, parties across the political spectrum, including those

[82] See the chapters by Andrew Schoenholtz, Stefanie Grant and David Weissbrodt in this volume.

[83] 'US Report Faults the Round-up of Illegal Immigrants After 9/11', *The New York Times*, 17 June 2003.

[84] For a comprehensive treatment of the 'war on terror' on detention practices, see S. Borelli, 'Casting light on the legal black hole: International law and detentions abroad in the "war on terror"', 87 *International Review of the Red Cross* No. 857 (March 2005) p. 39.

> in power, find themselves on the defensive and react to the situation by demanding or implementing more stringent anti-immigration policies'.[85]

The Australian Government too has long attempted to justify its mandatory detention regime through 'scare politics', telling the public that 'whole villages' were preparing to go to Australia from the Middle East, and explicitly stating that those who arrived in Australia were 'people of dubious morals'; that they were 'queue jumpers',

> 'who stole places from the world's most vulnerable refugees, that they might be criminals, that they posed a threat to Australian culture and Australian way of life, and, even before the September 11 terrorist attacks on the United States, that they might be terrorists'.[86]

Further, it is evident that it is not only wealthy western countries where xenophobic politics mean that migrants are viewed with hostility and suspicion; rather, such practices are apparent in all parts of the world. Arguably, such attitudes translate into curtailing rights of non-citizens at best, and treating them as criminals at worst.

A fundamental challenge for policy makers therefore is to find the balance between the current international approach to migration based on a framework of control and the need to establish a migration management strategy in which human rights are a fundamental component. The IOM, for example, considers, in its work with governments on managing migration, that border control and state security do not need to be compromised in order to recognize and respect an individual's human rights – the two interests are not necessarily contradictory, and achieving one of these aims does not need to be at the expense of the other. What are some of the measures that can be taken to reach the necessary balance? There are 4 key concepts or themes to consider, in what is not an exhaustive list.

(i) *Knowledge*: Before rights can be respected, it is necessary to know exactly what they are. This helps us to understand how certain control or security measures can violate them. Knowledge of the correct standards is not something that should be the exclusive domain of a few senior officials. It is important that all people who enforce laws or who operate within the detention environment have this knowledge too. This is where training is an important tool which needs to be used as widely as possible. Arguably, when a state accepts international obligations by ratifying a treaty, or enacts national legislation, it has an affirmative obligation to disseminate information on the content of its own obligations under, and the rights accorded to individuals by, those laws. Such dissemination should

[85] B. Ghosh, *Elusive Protection, Uncertain Lands: Migrants' Access to Human Rights* (Geneva, IOM 2003) at p. 17.

[86] D. Corlett, *Following Them Home: The Fate of The Returned Asylum-Seekers* (Melbourne, Black Inc. Books 2005) p. 4.

target not only the general public, but also, importantly, the officials charged with implementing those particular laws. Civil society also has a role to play in the dissemination of information and the provision of training on international and national rights and obligations: in some countries, NGOs effectively enter into partnership with the state in implementing this role; in others, where the state fails in its dissemination obligation, it is civil society which steps in to keep the public informed.

(ii) *Incorporation*: The main applicable international standards should be adopted in national legislation to contribute to a framework for effective migration policy and administration. Governments at times need to be reminded that they themselves have determined the content and extent of their international obligations and voluntarily agreed to abide by them. Arguably, international standards are only truly effective in practical terms once they have been brought down to the national level and have become part of the national legal and policy framework.

(iii) *Accountability*: Once the main human rights instruments have been adopted and implemented, an independent body should be set up to monitor the implementation of laws and to seek remedies in cases of violations. This is not the same as enforcement; however, independent monitoring bodies are key players in a democracy. They ensure that the government can be held responsible for its actions, and that violations will be made public and analyzed. They can assist in ensuring that a government abides by its own laws, and that, if it does not, it must answer for it. At the international level, UN monitoring mechanisms such as the ICCPR's Human Rights Committee, the Working Group on Arbitrary Detention and the Special Rapporteur on the human rights of migrants are already established and work tirelessly on such issues as detention of irregular migrants and asylum seekers. The ICCPR obliges all States Parties to submit regular reports to the Human Rights Committee on the implementation of the rights found therein. Inter-state and individual complaint mechanisms are also in place. However, the importance of national monitoring bodies, such as national human rights commissions, needs also to be emphasized.[87] The value of public reports and media exposés can be immense, particularly in an area such as detention which is 'behind closed doors', and where violations can occur without the public being aware of what is happening in their own country. In Australia, two recent high level reports on detention have brought about important changes to the system.[88]

---

[87] Human Rights Watch writes that '... a national human rights commission may sometimes be able to obtain access to restricted information or locations, such as prisons or detention camps, that would otherwise be secret, and they may sometimes be able to demand a higher level of accountability from government forces or agencies than NGOs can do. And if a state-sponsored national human rights commission issues a hard-hitting statement or document, so officially acknowledging that a particular problem exists or abuse has taken place, it can be much more difficult for a government to dismiss than, say, a similar statement or report issued by a local or international NGO'. Human Rights Watch, *Protectors or Pretenders? Government Human Rights Commissions in Africa* (New York, Human Rights Watch 2001) p. 3.

[88] M. Palmer, *Inquiry into the circumstances of the Immigration detention of Cornelia Rau: Report*

(iv) *Transparency*: Government actions, decisions, laws and policies must be accessible to the public. Secret and closed government actions do not sit easily with the notion of democracy. Freedom of information is key to ensuring transparency. It also fits with the other themes mentioned, such as accountability: an open government whose actions can be seen will necessarily have to be accountable for them. It fits with the concept of knowledge as well: if the public are familiar with their rights and obligations in the context of national laws, this can firstly help ensure that they are respected, and secondly prevent the laws from being executed in an arbitrary manner. Further, in order to remain accountable and transparent, no one in government should have excessive, unreviewable powers of discretion. Rather, the grounds for releasing persons from detention, or to grant visas, should be clearly outlined in the relevant legislation.[89]

NGOs have an important role in helping governments to achieve these measures. They can provide training and information on applicable standards, they can lobby to ensure that relevant standards are incorporated into law and implemented, and they can help monitor the implementation of laws and publicize their violations. The media too have an important role to play in terms of both transparency and accountability, particularly in reporting violations committed by governmental officials. The media can also be a powerful tool in influencing the public's perception of asylum seekers and migrants, who can be portrayed in either a positive or negative light, and therefore it also needs to be held accountable to certain standards.

6. Conclusion

> 'It is often said that a society's moral strength is measured by how humanely it deals with the most vulnerable individuals living within its domain. The... detention centre, deliberately hidden from the public gaze, threatens to leave an indelible mark on our legacy, a stain that history will have difficulty erasing. Our political leaders need to be given a wake-up call to prevent us from sliding even further down the slope of divisiveness and recrimination on this issue. We need to reaffirm the inviolable dictum that human rights begin at home'.[90]

Commonwealth of Australia, Canberra, July 2005 <http://www.minister.immi.gov.au/media_releases/media05/palmer-report.pdf>; and Commonwealth Ombudsman, *Inquiry into the circumstances of the Vivian Alvarez Matter,* Report by the Commonwealth Ombudsman of an inquiry undertaken by Mr. Neil Comrie (Report No. 3 of 2005), Canberra, Oct. 2005 <http://www.ombudsman.gov.au/publications_information/Special_Reports/2005/alvarez_report03.pdf>.

[89] See further 'Asylum Seekers Resource Centre Briefing Paper on Detention Reforms' (June 2005) <http://asrc.ewock.com/images/ASRC_Briefing_Paper_on_Detention_Reforms_1_.doc>.

[90] D. Silove, Z. Steele and R. Mollica, 'Detention of Asylum-seekers: Assault on Health, Human Rights, and Social Development', 367 *The Lancet* (5 May 2001) p. 1436.

Detention of irregular migrants and asylum seekers is not, in itself, contrary to international law. Legally recognized principles and standards are in place to ensure that detention is carried out in a lawful, humane manner. Yet, as shown above, the practice of detention around the world today is commonly in violation of international legal norms, and states are ignoring their obligations in the name of border control or national security.

This chapter has largely addressed the issue of detention of asylum seekers and irregular migrants together, focusing on the concept and legality of detention itself. In practice, however, and in accordance with international law, the two groups need to be clearly distinguished in managing a detention regime, contrary to the current practices for all unauthorized arrivals in countries such as Australia. Detention pending deportation for irregular migrants who have been caught without required visas, or in breach of visa conditions (i.e., 'detention on the way out'), can be clearly justifiable and in most cases will be limited in time. The practice of detaining people due to the unauthorized manner of their arrival ('detention on the way in') seems, from an evaluation of current practice, to be where violations of international standards most commonly occur. This is particularly the case where such individuals claim asylum and are placed in detention, sometimes for years, while their claims are processed; and the potential for violations is exacerbated where detainees do not have proper access to legal representation, interpreters or systems of review.

Alternatives to detention in the asylum field do exist. Silove writes that

> '[a]lternative regimes to detention have been tested and are already in place in many recipient countries – systems that monitor asylum seekers living in the community; the lodging of financial bonds by families, friends or humanitarian agencies to ensure compliance of the refugee applicant with immigration procedures; and even temporary forms of asylum. Each provision, however imperfect, allows asylum seekers to live with dignity and a degree of freedom in the community. As yet, no recipient society has experienced anything approaching a breakdown in social order by virtue of allowing asylum seekers in our midst'.[91]

Such alternatives deserve close inspection by the number of countries who routinely detain all unauthorized arrivals. While some may contend, as above, that detention need not play any part in a state's migration policy, arguably it can serve a useful purpose. Key to balancing migration control or state security with human rights is ensuring that the procedural guarantees clearly elaborated by international law are observed. There is no hard evidence that treating asylum seekers or other authorized arrivals humanely will serve to attract further arrivals – this message of deterrence often being glibly offered as the justification for harsh detention policies.

In all cases of detention, it would seem that humanizing the system need not come at the expense of security or border control. The observance of the minimal

[91] Ibid.

safeguards and guarantees as elaborated in this chapter, which states themselves have agreed upon, need not threaten a state's national interest, and should be capable of being relatively easily achieved in practice.[92] Coupled with relevant training, sound national laws and governmental accountability and transparency, the observance of the international standards in place would only serve to protect the integrity of a state's admissions system, while respecting the rights to which all human beings are entitled.

Selected Bibliography

Borelli, S., 'Casting light on the legal black hole: International law and detentions abroad in the "war on terror"', 87 *International Review of the Red Cross* (March 2005) p. 39.

de Zayas, A., 'Human Rights and Indefinite Detention', 87 *International Review of the Red Cross* (March 2005) p. 15.

Ghosh, B., *Elusive Protection, Uncertain Lands: Migrants' Access to Human Rights* (Geneva, IOM 2003).

Nowak, M., *UN Covenant on Civil and Political Rights. Commentary* (Strasbourg, N.P. Engel 1993).

Office of the UN High Commissioner for Human Rights, 'Human Rights and Arrest, pre-Trial Detention and Administrative Detention', in OHCHR, *Human Rights in the Administration of Justice: A Manual on Human Rights for Judges, Prosecutors and Lawyers* (Professional Training Series, No. 9) (Geneva, OHCHR 2003) p. 159.

Pacurar, A., 'Smuggling, Detention and Expulsion of Irregular Migrants: A Study on International Legal Norms, Standards and Practices', 5 *European Journal of Migration and Law* (2003) p. 259.

Tootell, A-M., J. Hughes and D. Petrasek, 'The Relevance of Key UN Instruments for Detained Asylum Seekers', in J. Hughes and F. Liebaut (eds.), *Detention of Asylum Seekers in Europe: Analysis and Perspectives* (The Hague, Martinus Nijhoff 1998).

UN, ECOSOC, Commission of Human Rights, 59th Session, *Report of the Special Rapporteur, Ms. Gabriela Rodríguez Pizarro, submitted pursuant to Commission on Human Rights resolution 2002/62*, UN Doc. E/CN.4/2003/85 (30 Dec. 2002).

Williams, P., *Treatment of Detainees: Examination of issues relevant to detention by the United Nations Human Rights Committee* (Geneva, Henri Dunant Institute 1990).

Working Group on Arbitrary Detention, *Deliberation No. 5 concerning the situation regarding immigrants and asylum seekers*, UN Doc. E/CN.4/2000/4 (28 Dec. 1999).

[92] Following two public inquiries into abuses in the Australian detention system and large-scale media attention, for example, the Government has introduced a number of changes into the system, with the aim of addressing significant flaws which had been identified. See further the opening statement by A. Metcalfe (Secretary, Department of Immigration and Multicultural Affairs) to the Senate Legal and Constitutional Legislation Committee, Additional Estimates for the Immigration and Multicultural Affairs Portfolio for 2005-2006, *Official Committee Hansard* (13 Feb. 2006) at pp. 6 et seq. <http://www.aph.gov.au/Hansard/senate/commttee/S9093.pdf>.

Chapter 4
CONSULAR PROTECTION AND ASSISTANCE

Richard Perruchoud*

1. Introduction

The decision to leave one's own country to work abroad or to begin a new life elsewhere is one often fraught with difficulties. To migrate to another country may increase opportunities and result in a better standard of living, but it may also involve obstacles and hardships.

Migrants often have to face discrimination, collectively and individually, and may be subject to hostility and exploitation. With the growing awareness and recognition of the many problems that may arise in connection with migration, governments are increasingly interested and concerned to identify appropriate answers and solutions to these difficulties, in particular as migration is often viewed unfavourably by host governments and local communities alike. Such negative reactions may trigger further misconceptions and suspicion, which culminate in overt hostility towards and discrimination against migrants, and, in some cases, a denial of their human rights.[1]

In some societies, xenophobia, itself provoked by economic recession and unemployment, may exacerbate such hostile reactions against migrants and add to the difficulties they already face. The rise in the number of incidents involving violations of the rights of migrants continues to be a cause for concern, particularly as they occur in contravention of the standards enshrined in national and international legal instruments established to protect such rights.

Thus, the international community is confronted with a growing contradiction between its intentions as documented in various laws and international norms aimed at protecting the human rights of migrants, and the reality of their everyday violation. Migrants are still frequently viewed as not only inherently different but also as inherently exploitable, and are often treated as scapegoats for the ills

* Director of the International Migration Law and Legal Affairs Department at the IOM, in Geneva.

The author thanks Louis Channel Sindabona for his research assistance.

[1] See *Human Rights of Migrants*, Note by the Secretary-General, UN Doc. A/58/275 (12 Aug. 2003); see also Global Commission on International Migration (GCIM), *Migration in an Interconnected World: New Directions for Action* (Geneva, GCIM 2005) pp. 32-35.

R. Cholewinski, R. Perruchoud and E. MacDonald, eds., International Migration Law

of our societies. There is ample evidence of discrimination in employment, and in education and other services.[2]

The vulnerability affecting some categories of migrants should no longer be considered as an inevitable feature of migration, especially irregular migration. Protection of vulnerable migrants should be strengthened, through remedial and preventive mechanisms. The purpose of this paper is therefore to identify the current protection gap; highlight the contribution that an old institution of public international law – consular protection and assistance – can make to improve respect for migrants' rights; encourage states and other actors to make better use of this institution; and propose practical measures aimed at a more efficient use of consular protection and assistance.

2. The Protection Gap

An important issue is how to ensure the effective respect for migrants' rights, and the means to improve the compliance of individual countries with their international commitments in this regard.

There are various international mechanisms available to protect, and provide redress in the event of violation of, human rights, that may be activated once the claimant has exhausted all available local procedures. In many instances, the obligation to respect human rights is enshrined in national legislation, often even in the constitution or similar basic laws. Therefore, the violation of the human rights of migrants also often constitutes a violation of national laws. Domestic means of supervision and redress are thus available to migrants, and they fulfil an important role in ensuring respect for their rights, to the extent provided for in the national legislation.

A number of treaties that determine and protect the human rights of migrants have their own supervision and monitoring regimes. For example, the International Covenant on Civil and Political Rights (ICCPR)[3] and the International Covenant on Economic, Social and Cultural Rights[4] have instituted their own periodic reporting and monitoring systems, under which States Parties report on the measures taken, the progress made and the difficulties encountered in the implementation of their commitments entered into under those treaties. Individuals alleging the violation of their human rights may also file a complaint with the Sub-Commission on the Prevention of Discrimination and Protection of Minorities, which, if satisfied that there are reasonable grounds to support the allegations, will investigate it further and, if necessary, refer it to the Human Rights Commission. Individual communications may also be examined under the complaints procedure of the Optional Protocol to the ICCPR.

---

[2] R. Perruchoud, 'Normas legales para la protección de los trabajadores migrantes' [Legal norms on the protection of migrant workers], *Notas de Población* No. 73, CEPAL (2001) p. 273.

[3] 999 *UNTS* 171.

[4] 993 *UNTS* 3.

An individual complaints procedure is also provided for in the International Convention on the Elimination of All Forms of Racial Discrimination of 21 December 1965,[5] as well as in the Convention against Torture and Other Cruel, Inhuman and Degrading Treatment or Punishment of 10 December 1984.[6]

In relation to the rights of migrant workers, each ILO Member State is called upon to periodically report on the measures taken to apply, in law and in practice, the obligations under the particular labour convention to which it is a party. These reports are examined by the Committee of Experts on the Application of Conventions and Recommendations, whose observations may be published in a report submitted to the International Labour Conference. Furthermore, employers' and workers' organizations, as well as governments, can make representations to the International Labour Office regarding the non-respect by a Member State of its obligations under a labour convention to which it is a party.[7]

The 1990 UN International Convention on the Protection of the Rights of All Migrant Workers and Members of Their Families (ICRMW) provides for the establishment of a Committee on the Protection of the Rights of All Migrant Workers and Members of Their Families (Article 72).[8] This Committee will examine reports on the application of the Convention submitted by States Parties, and may receive complaints from states and individuals. Under Article 73(1), States Parties are obliged to submit reports on the 'legislative, judicial, administrative and other measures they have taken to give effect to the provisions of the ... Convention'. These reports must be submitted within one year after the entry into force of the Convention for the State Party concerned, and thereafter every five years or whenever the Committee so requests.

Article 76 foresees the possibility for one state to submit a communication to another if it considers that the other is failing in its obligations under the Convention. If the problem is not resolved within six months of the initial communication, either state may refer it to the Committee. The Committee provides its good offices with a view to reaching a friendly settlement. This procedure is optional and will become operational only after ten states have declared their agreement thereto, including the two parties to the disagreement concerned. Finally, Article 77 establishes an individual complaint procedure. The Committee can receive communications from, or on behalf of, individuals who allege that their rights as established under the Convention have been violated by a State Party. Communications must satisfy a set of requirements to be admissible, in particular the prior exhaustion of local remedies.[9]

---

[5] 660 *UNTS* 195.

[6] 1465 *UNTS* 85.

[7] See R. Perruchoud (ed.), *Migrations et protection des droits de l'homme* (Geneva, OIM, 2005) pp. 83-99.

[8] UNGA Res. 45/158 of 18 Dec. 1990, Annex. This Convention is considered in more detail in the contributions by Weissbrodt and Cholewinski to this volume.

[9] The Committee is required to bring any communication before it to the attention of the State Party concerned, which is then obliged, within six months, to submit to the Committee 'written explanations or statements clarifying the matter and the remedy, if any, that may have been taken by the

At first glance, therefore, the impression is one of ample means of recourse and redress. One may be tempted to conclude that, taken together, these mechanisms of implementation and supervision are more than adequate. And yet this impression is not a reflection of reality, or reflects only a partial, ideal world, not reality as it is experienced by many on a daily basis. We must therefore ask ourselves what went wrong, what is missing and, more importantly, how can the situation be improved? Looking at the mechanisms of implementation and supervision, we find that they are for the most part reactive, and come into play only once a violation is alleged, and then operate to remedy a wrongful situation. More attention has to be paid to preventive measures, to mechanisms able to ensure the respect for the rights and freedoms of migrants, and to prevent their violation.

One such mechanism – that of consular protection and assistance – seems to have been neglected both as a reactive and preventive measure. It may thus be useful to analyze its content, as well as its relevance in special situations, and to examine the possibilities for its more effective use as a means of safeguarding the respect of migrants' rights.

3. The Main Features of Consular Protection and Assistance

The Vienna Convention on Consular Relations (VCCR) of 24 April 1963[10] codified international consular law, which, until then, was contained mainly in numerous bilateral treaties,[11] some regional instruments, and general usages and customs. This Convention was a major step in determining the present state of international law in this field, and is considered as the cornerstone of international consular relations.

The main consular functions relevant to the protection and assistance of migrants are defined as follows in Article 5 of the VCCR:

> '(a) protecting in the receiving State the interests of the sending State and of its nationals, both individuals and bodies corporate, within the limits permitted by international law;
>
> …
>
> (d) issuing passports and travel documents to nationals of the sending state, and visas or appropriate documents to persons wishing to travel to the sending state;
>
> (e) helping and assisting nationals, both individuals and bodies corporate, of the sending State;

State'. The Committee then forwards its views to the State Party concerned and to the individual. This procedure is also optional and applies only to those States Parties that have made a declaration to this effect under Article 77; it will come into force when ten States Parties have made this declaration.

10 596 *UNTS* 261.

11 For a list, see L.T. Lee, *Consular Law and Practice*, 2nd edn. (Oxford, Oxford University Press 1991) Appendix I, pp. 646-657.

(f) acting as notary and civil registrar and in capacities of a similar kind, and performing certain functions of an administrative nature, provided that there is nothing contrary thereto in the laws and regulations of the receiving State;

(g) safeguarding the interest of nationals, both individuals and bodies corporate, of the sending State in cases of succession 'mortis causa' in the territory of the receiving State, in accordance with the laws and regulations of the receiving State;

(h) safeguarding, within the limits imposed by the laws and regulations of the receiving State, the interests of minors and other persons lacking full capacity who are nationals of the sending State, particularly where any guardianship or trusteeship is required with respect to such persons;

(i) subject to the practices and procedures obtaining in the receiving State, representing or arranging appropriate representation for nationals of the sending State before the tribunals and other authorities of the receiving State, for the purpose of obtaining, in accordance with the laws and regulations of the receiving State, provisional measures for the preservation of the rights and interests of these nationals, where, because of absence or any other reason, such nationals are unable at the proper time to assume the defence of their rights and interests;

(j) transmitting judicial and extra-judicial documents or executing letters rogatory or commissions to take evidence for the courts of the sending State in accordance with international agreements in force or, in the absence of such international agreements, in any other manner compatible with the laws and regulations of the receiving State;

…

(m) performing any other functions entrusted to a consular post by the sending State which are not prohibited by the laws and regulations of the receiving State or to which no objection is taken by the receiving State or which are referred to in the international agreements in force between the sending State and the receiving State'.[12]

As can be seen, consular functions are many and varied, and include the protection of the interests of the sending state and its nationals, the development of economic and cultural relations, the issuing of passports and visas, the administration of the property of nationals of the sending state, the registration of deaths, births,

[12] For a more succinct definition of consular functions, see Article 2 of the European Convention on Consular Functions (Paris, 11 Dec. 1967, *ETS* No. 61), which reads as follows:
'1. A consular officer shall be entitled to protect the nationals of the sending State and to defend their rights and interests.
2. He shall likewise be entitled to further the interests of the sending State, including its interests in relation to commercial, economic, social, professional, touristic, artistic, scientific, educational and maritime matters and civil aviation, and to promote and develop co-operation between the sending and the receiving States in these and other fields.
3. Upon notification to the receiving State, any Contracting Party is entitled to entrust the protection of its nationals and the defence of their rights and interests to consular officers of another Contracting Party'.

and the like. They are sufficiently broad and apply directly to the protection and assistance of migrants.[13]

Article 5 of the VCCR is a clear indication that the protection and assistance afforded to a migrant for the defence of his or her rights before the authorities of the receiving state constitutes one of the paramount functions of a consular officer.

Another relevant provision in a migration context is Article 65(2) of the ICRMW, which stipulates that

> 'States parties shall facilitate as appropriate the provision of adequate consular and other services that are necessary to meet the social, cultural and other needs of migrant workers and members of their families'.

Consular protection and assistance is considered as part of a state's foreign policy, aimed at safeguarding it national interests. Foreign policy objectives include the protection of the rights of nationals abroad, as well as safeguarding their other entitlements. Consular protection and assistance is also seen as a logical consequence of a state's duty to protect the human rights of its nationals, wherever they may reside, and of the migrants on its territory irrespective of their migratory status.

Various attempts have been made to define protection and assistance. Consular protection is usually understood as applying to cases concerning a claim against a governmental official for allegedly infringing the rights of a migrant. Consular assistance, on the other hand, is generally viewed as aimed not at redressing a wrong, but at responding to a state of necessity in which the migrants find themselves: assistance to sick persons, payment of alimony, information concerning detained migrants, return of destitute migrants, assistance in case of deportation, and similar activities. Very often, however, and rightly so, protection and assistance are used interchangeably or side by side, with no distinction being made between them.

Another distinction is occasionally made between active and passive consular protection and assistance. The former is that exercised in the receiving state by consular officers of the sending state, in accordance with the provisions of the VCCR, while the latter refers to that exercised by consular officers of other states in that same sending state. Thus, while active consular protection concerns a state's activities in respect of its own nationals on the territories of other states, the passive form refers to its allowing other states to do the same on its own territory. The difference here, then, is essentially one of perspective.

[13] For a detailed description of these functions, see Lee, op. cit. n. 11, at pp. 115-372.

4. The Relevance of Consular Protection and Assistance in Special Situations

The legal provisions governing consular protection and assistance in special situations – particularly any form of detention – are contained in the VCCR and the ICRMW.

Article 36 of the VCCR reads as follows:

'1. With a view to facilitating the exercise of consular functions relating to nationals of the sending State:

(a) consular officers shall be free to communicate with nationals of the sending State and to have access to them. Nationals of the sending State shall have the same freedom with respect to communication with and access to consular officers of the sending State;

(b) if he so requests, the competent authorities of the receiving State shall, without delay, inform the consular post of the sending State if, within its consular district, a national of that State is arrested or committed to prison or to custody pending trial or is detained in any other manner. Any communication addressed to the consular post by the person arrested, in prison, custody or detention shall also be forwarded by the said authorities without delay. The said authorities shall inform the person concerned without delay of his rights under this subparagraph;

(c) consular officers shall have the right to visit a national of the sending State who is in prison, custody or detention, to converse and correspond with him and to arrange for his legal representation. They shall also have the right to visit any national of the sending State who is in prison, custody or detention in their district in pursuance of a judgment. Nevertheless, consular officers shall refrain from taking action on behalf of a national who is in prison, custody or detention if he expressly opposes such action.

2. The rights referred to in paragraph 1 of this Article shall be exercised in conformity with the laws and regulations of the receiving State, subject to the proviso, however, that the said laws and regulations must enable full effect to be given to the purposes for which the rights accorded under this Article are intended'.

The ICRMW, in its Article 16(7) stipulates that:

'7. When a migrant worker or a member of his or her family is arrested or committed to prison or custody pending trial or is detained in any other manner:

(a) The consular or diplomatic authorities of his or her State of origin or of a State representing the interests of the State shall, if he or she so requests, be informed without delay of his or her arrest or detention and of the reasons therefor;

(b) The person concerned shall have the right to communicate with the said authorities. Any communication by the person concerned to the said authorities shall be forwarded without delay, and he or she shall also have the right to receive communications sent by the said authorities without delay;

(c) The person concerned shall be informed without delay of this right and of rights deriving from relevant treaties, if any, applicable between the States concerned, to correspond and to meet with representatives of the said authorities and to make arrangements with them for his or her legal representation'.

Article 23 of the ICRMW confirms the right of migrants to consular protection and assistance in the following terms:

> 'Migrant workers and members of their families shall have the right to have recourse to the protection and assistance of the consular or diplomatic authorities of their State of origin or of a State representing the interests of that State whenever the rights recognized in the present Convention are impaired. In particular, in case of expulsion, the person concerned shall be informed of this right without delay and the authorities of the expelling State shall facilitate the exercise of such right'.

A number of other international instruments contain provisions on consular protection and assistance, such as the 1984 Convention against Torture;[14] the 1963 Convention on Offences and Certain Other Acts Committed on Board Aircraft;[15] the 1997 International Convention for the Suppression of Terrorist Bombings;[16] the 2000 Protocol against the Smuggling of Migrants by Land, Sea and Air, supplementing the United Nations Convention against Transnational Organized Crime;[17] the 1988 Body of Principles for the Protection of All Persons under Any Form of Detention or Imprisonment;[18] and the 1985 Declaration on the Human Rights of Individuals Who are not Nationals of the Country in which They Live.[19]

It is generally agreed that the VCCR, while not a human rights treaty *stricto sensu*, contains provisions relevant to the protection of human rights and concerns such protection.[20] It is further not disputed that the ICRMW is a human right treaty. These instruments confer a number of rights both on states and on migrants: the right to information on consular protection and assistance; the right to consular notification; the right of consular assistance; and the right of consular communication.

---

[14] Loc. cit. n. 6.

[15] 704 *UNTS* 219.

[16] 2149 *UNTS* 284.

[17] UNGA Res. 55/25 of 15 Nov. 2000.

[18] UNGA Res. 43/173 of 9 Dec. 1988.

[19] UNGA Res. 40/144 of 13 Dec. 1985.

[20] See in particular *Advisory Opinion OC-16-99* of 1 Oct. 1999, delivered by the Inter-American Court of Human Rights on the 'Right to information on consular assistance in the framework of the guarantees of the due process of law'.

Notification of the right to consular protection and assistance to concerned migrants is of utmost importance,[21] and is viewed as an essential guarantee in offering those detained the opportunity to receive a fair trial; it is this right to information that gives the right to due process of law practical meaning. Migrants in detention, faced with a foreign social and legal environment and a language that they often do not master, are in a condition of particular vulnerability; in such cases, the right to information on consular protection and assistance takes on particular importance.

The right to consular notification allows migrants to request – and require – that the receiving state inform the relevant consular post that they have been arrested or otherwise detained. The bearer of this right is the migrant, and the right is contingent upon the wishes of the migrant concerned.[22] Thus, a migrant may expressly refuse that his national authorities be informed of his detention or, more generally, of his whereabouts. The right to address a communication to the consular post has to be implemented 'without delay', which is subject to interpretation: it is generally understood that such notification should be prompt, preferably at the time the migrant is deprived of his liberty, but at least prior to his having to make a first statement before the authorities.[23]

The right of consular assistance recognizes the right of a state to assist its nationals abroad, and the corresponding right of the national abroad to contact the consular officer to obtain such assistance.[24]

The right of consular communication defines the right of the consular authorities and nationals of the sending state to communicate with each other; this right represents one of the major protective functions of consular officers.[25] Its importance – as well as the close link between the rights of migrants to consular assistance and human rights – is also stressed by Article 10 of the UN Declaration on the Human Rights of Individuals Who are not Nationals of the Country in which They Live.[26]

---

[21] In the case *Avena and other Mexican nationals, Mexico* v. *United States of America*, the ICJ ruled that there is a duty to inform the arrested person 'as soon as it realized that the person is a foreign national, or once there are grounds to think that the person is probably a foreign national'. ICJ Rep. 2004, para. 88.

[22] In the *LaGrand* case, the ICJ concluded that Article 36(1) created 'individual rights' but did not feel it necessary to consider whether this individual right has assumed the character of a human right. *Germany* v. *United States of America*, ICJ Rep. 2001, paras. 77-78.

[23] See however L. Caflisch, 'La pratique suisse en matière de droit international public', *Revue suisse de droit international et de droit européen* (5/2004) p. 690.

[24] See in this respect the *International Agenda for Migration Management*, Berne, 16-17 Dec. 2004 (IOM, Swiss Federal Office for Migration, 2005) p. 42.

[25] Lee, op. cit. n. 11, at p. 133.

[26] Article 10 of the Declaration, loc. cit. n. 19, reads as follows: 'Any alien shall be free at any time to communicate with the consulate or diplomatic mission of the State of which he or she is a national or, in the absence thereof, with the consulate or diplomatic mission of any other State entrusted with the protection of the interests of the State of which he or she is a national in the State where he or she resides'.

In summary, a detained migrant has the following rights: to be informed without delay by the arresting authority of the right to consular notification and communication; to choose whether or not to have the consular post contacted; to have the consular post contacted promptly by the arresting authority and to obtain consular protection and assistance; to communicate freely with the consular post; and to accept or decline any consular protection and assistance offered.

The consular officer has corresponding rights and obligations: to be promptly informed of the detention, at the request of the national; to communicate with and have access to a detained national if he or she so desires, at all stages of the case; to visit and correspond with the detainee; to arrange for the detainee's legal representation; and to provide any other type of assistance with the agreement of the detainee.

The disregard by a state of its obligations under Article 36 VCCR, such as those related to consular notification, constitutes a breach of its international obligations and engages its responsibility. Remedies include *restitutio in integrum,* compensation, satisfaction and assurance of non-repetition, available either singly or in combination. The International Court of Justice has ruled that if a state fails in its obligation of consular notification, an apology is not sufficient in cases in which the individuals concerned have been subjected to prolonged detention or convicted and sentenced to severe penalties.[27] It has also ruled that the obligation to review and reconsider potential breaches of Article 36 of the VCCR must be fulfilled through a judicial process: in particular, executive clemency procedures would not be suited to that purpose.[28]

It is important to underline at this juncture one fundamental difference between diplomatic protection on the one hand, and consular protection and assistance on the other. The former is a discretionary prerogative of the state, which may decide to extend or not its diplomatic protection to its national; the latter includes rights and obligations of both states and nationals. It is sometimes suggested that both institutions are analogous and that the individual has the right to seek consular protection and assistance, but not to obtain it. This analogy is specious and contradicted by case-law. Article 36 of the VCCR makes it clear that the national of the sending state has rights deriving from the treaty, rights that can be invoked as human rights. As stated by the Inter-American Court of Human Rights,

> 'it is evident that the Vienna Convention on Consular Relations recognizes assistance to a national of the sending State for the defense of his rights before the authorities of the host State to be one of the paramount functions of a consular officer. Hence, the provision recognizing consular communication serves a dual purpose: that of recognizing a State's right to assist its nationals through the consular officer's actions and, correspondingly, that of recognizing the correlative right of the national of the sending State to contact the consular officer to obtain that assistance'.[29]

[27] See *LaGrand*, loc. cit. n. 22, at para. 123.

[28] See *Avena*, loc. cit. n. 21, at para. 143.

[29] *Advisory Opinion OC-16-99*, loc. cit. n. 20, at para. 80.

The Court therefore concluded that

> 'Article 36 of the Vienna Convention on Consular Relations endows a detained foreign national with individual rights that are the counterpart to the host state's correlative duties. This interpretation is supported by the article's legislative history'.[30]

The Court could have added that this conclusion was also supported by other treaties, customary law and national practice.[31] The International Court of Justice has also concluded that the VCCR creates individual rights which may be invoked before the Court by the national state of the detained person.[32]

A final remark refers to the nature of consular protection and assistance: its main features are contained not only in the VCCR, but also in numerous bilateral and some regional agreements. It is now generally accepted that the rights and obligations deriving from consular protection and assistance – whether applicable to states or individuals – are not only based on treaties but are also part of the *corpus* of customary international law.

5. Towards a Better Use of Consular Protection and Assistance

A number of means can be considered, at different levels and in regard to various actors, to improve the effectiveness of consular protection and assistance, and to ensure effective respect of migrants' rights.[33]

5.1 Measures to be taken by the receiving state

- Respect fully and effectively all migrants' rights instruments.

- Accord to consular officers of other countries the required facilities, privileges and immunities recognized under international law, so that they can adequately perform their functions.

- Make sure its officials, at all levels, are fully aware of the rights and obligations deriving from the exercise of consular protection and assistance by consular officers and migrants. Numerous cases illustrate that law enforcement officials are unaware that the VCCR exists; it has even

[30] Ibid., at para. 84.

[31] See, for instance, the position taken by the United States in the *Hostages (U.S. Diplomatic and Consular Staff) in Tehran* case, ICJ Rep. 1979, p. 174.

[32] *LaGrand*, loc. cit. n. 22, at para. 77.

[33] A general description of practical difficulties in the field of consular protection and assistance was given at a 'Seminar on Consular Protection and Assistance', organized in Guatemala City on 29-30 July 1999, in the framework of the Regional Conference on Migration (Puebla Process). Unpublished papers, on file with the author.

been suggested that the example from the *Miranda* judgment should be followed, through the development of a set of VCCR rights that enforcement officials would have to read to migrants under arrest.[34]

5.2 Measures to be taken locally by the sending state

- Disseminate information regarding the rights and duties of potential migrants, including the right to consular protection and assistance; inform potential migrants of the principal laws and regulations of importance to migrants in the prospective receiving states.
- Organize information campaigns on the risks of irregular migration, in particular as regards trafficking and smuggling.
- Draw up a 'protection map' identifying the problems most frequently encountered by migrants, in order to better define and refine the protection strategy.
- Conduct training and capacity building of consular officers, so that they have full knowledge of the provisions of the VCCR and related instruments, and migrants' rights generally.[35]
- Strengthen cooperation with civil society institutions and NGOs helping migrants abroad.

5.3 Measures to be taken abroad by the sending state

- Strengthen information programmes on rights available to migrants, including the right to consular protection and assistance.
- Increase consular staff.
- Improve and modernize the equipment of consular posts.
- Establish a network of lawyers to provide *pro bono* legal assistance to migrants.
- Inform migrants of their duty to respect the laws of the country in which they reside and implications of their breach.

[34] See E.L. Aralica, 'The Inherent Conflict – Vienna Convention on Consular Relations and United States Domestic Law', 11 *Across Borders International Law Journal* (2004) p. 12; see also UN, ECOSOC, Commission on Human Rights, 61st Session, *Report of the Special Rapporteur on the human rights of migrants, Ms. Gabriela Rodríguez Pizarro: Visit to Peru*, Doc. E/CN.4/2005/85/Add.4 (13 Jan. 2005).

[35] See Doc. A/58/275, loc. cit. n. 1, at paras. 25-27.

- Exchange best practices among consular posts.

- Develop collaboration and links with migrant communities abroad and request consular officers to regularly visit such communities.

- Strengthen cooperation with NGOs and civil society organizations active in the field of migrants' human rights.

- Systematize the registration of migrants abroad, especially undocumented migrants, and issue certificates of registration attesting to the identity of the migrants and enabling them to have unencumbered access to consular protection and assistance. A recent illustration of the usefulness of such measures was given in November 2005, in the wake of hurricane Stan, when the Government of Mexico agreed to accept the registration certificate (*matrícula consular*) of Guatemalan migrants as a valid identity document authorizing the holders to stay exceptionally for six months in the southeastern part of Mexico.

5.4 Measures to be taken collectively by sending and receiving states

- Authorize consular officers of a given state to provide consular protection and assistance to nationals of other states that have no consular representation in the receiving state.

- Make available to those sending states that are also developing countries the means to establish appropriate consular structures, as the lack of such structures indirectly contributes to the continued disregard for the human rights of migrants. This measure would best be discussed and put into practice in the framework of regional consultative processes.

5.5 A role for international organizations

Consular protection and assistance, as mentioned above, is a state responsibility and competence. It therefore sounds surprising to study the possible measures an international organization may take. A state may, however, delegate some of its competences to an international organization on a bilateral basis, or collectively through a mandate conferred upon the organization to ensure the respect of migrants' rights.

In addition, consular protection and assistance is generally exercised on behalf of individuals, but may also be applied to groups, to people in distress and victims of natural disasters, sometimes irrespective of nationality. As Lee has noted,

> 'the standard for consular protection of nationals has increasingly assumed human rights proportions, merging the minimum international standard with that of national treatment. Since human rights are, by definition, 'rights which attach to all human

> beings equally, whatever their nationality', a corollary of the adoption of the human rights standard is the growing concern of consuls with the well-being of not only their nationals, but also non-nationals. This is reflected in the expanding consular role in protecting and assisting refugees, stateless persons, permanent residents of the sending State, persons of designated third States, as well as individuals of humanitarian concern'.[36]

The case of the International Organization for Migration (IOM) deserves some attention, both with regard to its objectives and activities. Although one of the objectives conferred on the IOM by its Member States is to ensure effective respect for migrants' rights,[37] this global mandate cannot be interpreted as a general authorization to engage in consular protection and assistance. However, it does empower the Organization to offer its services in this field and, if the states concerned agree, to act as a *de facto* or independent consular post protecting migrants' rights in a given country.

One such IOM programme was recently implemented in Central Asia. The programme, titled 'Legal Assistance for Migrants in Kazakhstan and Central Asia', is aimed at providing legal assistance, free legal advice, counseling and assistance in administrative and judicial procedures to migrants in need, in addition to the capacity-building of local NGOs and government officials. The categories of persons included migrants from Central Asia, migrants from other developing countries, rejected asylum seekers, returnees, and victims of trafficking and smuggling. The IOM was authorized by the Government of Kazakhstan to implement this project, and, in many respects, to act as a consular post and to extend *de facto* consular protection and assistance to an undefined caseload of migrants in need coming from an undefined number of sending states; the latter very often had no consular post or no means of providing effective protection and assistance, and welcomed the offer of services provided by the IOM.

Such an approach could be further explored and expanded, at a time when some IOM Member States have invited the Organization to enhance their capacity to provide consular access and protection, in particular through technical and operational assistance, with the understanding that such a role would in no way absolve the states from their responsibility to protect their nationals abroad; equally, it does not absolve the territorial state from its duty to ensure effective respect for the human rights of all persons present on its territory. This IOM role would be particularly relevant in terms of stranded migrants,[38] victims of trafficking and smuggling, and other undocumented migrants or migrants in an irregular situation. In such circumstances, the IOM would perform quasi consular services and act as a 'Consul-at-Large'.

---

[36] Lee, op. cit. n. 11, at p. 643.

[37] See Resolution No. 923 (LXXI) adopted on 29 Nov. 1995 by the IOM Council on 'Future Activities of IOM', and document MC/1842 of 9 May 1995, entitled 'IOM Strategic Planning: Toward the Twenty-First Century'. See also Doc. MC/INF/259 of 13 Nov. 2002, 'Migrants' Rights: IOM Policy and Activities'.

[38] On this issue, see the chapter by Stefanie Grant in the present volume.

6. Conclusion

The international instruments on consular protection and assistance confer rights upon migrants: whether these are individual or human rights – provided this distinction is relevant to the case in question – is still debated.[39] Our conclusion is that the right to consular protection and assistance should be considered as a human right. This old institution could be a powerful tool for the protection of the human rights of migrants, provided states adopt measures more conducive to its efficient operation. At a time when human rights bodies and migrants' associations look for innovative schemes to better protect migrants' rights, a reminder of some existing institutions, not necessarily associated with traditional human rights instruments, should contribute to the attainment of a more robust protection of vulnerable migrants.

Selected Bibliography

Aralica, E.L., 'The Inherent Conflict – Vienna Convention on Consular Relations and United States Domestic Law', 11 *Across Borders International Law Journal* (2004) p. 12.

Ballard, L.A., *The Vienna Convention, Consular Access and Other Assistance Available to Foreign Nationals: A Guide for Criminal Defense and Immigration Attorneys* (New York, Columbia Law School 1998).

James, A., *A Universal Safeguard: Providing Consular Assistance to Nationals in Custody* (Woodbridge, International Justice Project 2003).

Kunzli, A., 'Case Concerning Mexican Nationals', 18 *Leiden Journal of International Law* (2005), p. 49.

Lee, L.T., *Consular Law and Practice*, 2nd edn. (Oxford, Oxford University Press 1991).

Tams, C.J., 'Consular Assistance: Rights, Remedies and Responsibility: Comments on the ICJ's Judgment in the LaGrand Case', 13 *European Journal of International Law* (2002) p. 1257.

Uribe, V., 'Consuls at Work: Universal Protection of Human Rights and Consular Protection in the Context of Criminal Justice', 19 *Houston Journal of International Law*, (1995) p. 375.

Warren, M., *Rights of Consul Information, Notification and Access for Detained Foreign Nationals* (Ottawa, Human Rights Research 2001) <http://www3.sympatico.ca/aiwarren/standards.htm>.

—, *Consular Rights of Foreign Nationals: International Norms* (Ottawa, Human Rights Research 2004) <http://www3.sympatico.ca/aiwarren/norms.htm>.

—, *Consular Notification and Assistance: A Guide for Defense Attorneys*, 11th edn. (Ottawa, Human Rights Research 2004) <http://www3.sympatico.ca/aiwarren/attorneys.htm>.

[39] See C.J. Tams, 'Consular Assistance: Rights, Remedies and Responsibility: Comments on the ICJ's Judgment in the LaGrand Case', 13 *European Journal of International Law* (2002) p. 1257; A. Kunzli, 'Case Concerning Mexican Nationals', 18 *Leiden Journal of International Law* (2005) p. 49.

Chapter 5
MULTIPLE NATIONALITY: THE PRACTICE OF GERMANY AND THE NETHERLANDS

Betty de Hart* **and Kees Groenendijk****

1. Introduction

Multiple nationality means the simultaneous possession of two or more nationalities. It arises from the sovereign power of states to determine their own nationality law. Academic literature has extensively discussed arguments for and against multiple nationality, ranging from loyalty conflicts, through rights and duties towards more than one state, to the question of whether multiple nationality either furthers or hinders integration in the country of residence.[1]

However, no treaty on the international level has ever dealt with the question of multiple nationality. The International Law Commission of the United Nations has concerned itself more with the problem of statelessness than that of multiple nationality.[2]

At the regional level, the Council of Europe addressed the issue in the Convention on the Reduction of Cases of Multiple Nationality and Military Obligations

* Senior Researcher at the Centre for Migration Law of the Radboud University Nijmegen.

** Professor of Sociology of Law at the Radboud University Nijmegen, Chairman of its Centre for Migration Law, Chairman of the Standing Committee of Experts on international immigration, refugee and criminal law, and Co-Director of the European Commission's Network on the Free Movement of Workers within the European Union.

[1] See, e.g., T.A. Aleinikoff, and D. Klusmeyer, 'Plural Nationality: Facing the Future in a Migratory World', in T.A. Aleinikoff and D. Klusmeyer (eds.), *Citizenship today. Global Perspectives* (Washington, Carnegie Endowment 2001) p. 63; M. Feldblum, 'Managing Membership: New Trends in Citizenship and Nationality Policy', in T.A. Aleinikoff and D. Klusmeyer (eds.), *From Migrants to Citizens* (Washington, Carnegie Endowment 2003) p. 475; R. Hansen and P. Weil (eds.), *Dual Nationality, Social Rights and Federal Citizenship in the US and Europe: The Reinvention of Citizenship* (New York/Oxford, Bergham Books 2002); D. Martin and K. Hailbronner (eds.), *Rights and Duties of Dual Nationals: Evolutions and Prospects* (The Hague, Kluwer Law International 2003); S.A. Renshon, 'Dual Citizenship and American Democracy: Patriotism, National Attachment and National Identity', 21 *Social Philosophy and Policy* (2004) p. 100; P.J. Spiro, *Embracing Dual Nationality* (Washington, International Migration Policy Program, Carnegie Endowment 1998); T. Faist and J. Gerdes, 'Dual Citizenship as a Path-Dependent Process', 38 *International Migration Review* (2004) p. 913.

[2] R. Donner, *The Regulation of Nationality in International Law* (New York, Transnational Publishers 1994) p. 207.

R. Cholewinski, R. Perruchoud and E. MacDonald, eds., International Migration Law

in Cases of Multiple Nationality of 1963 (hereafter, the Strasbourg Convention).[3] The Preamble stated that cases of multiple nationality were 'liable to cause difficulties', and set out the aim of 'joint action to reduce as far as possible the number of cases of multiple nationality'. However, the Strasbourg Convention does not contain a general exclusion of the possibility of multiple nationality; it only covers the case of voluntary acquisition of another nationality. In Chapter I, the Convention provides for the automatic loss of the nationality of one State Party in case of acquisition of the nationality of another. In Chapter II, it assumes that multiple nationality may occur, in preventing individuals in such situations from having multiple military obligations.

Since 1963, the Council of Europe's position towards multiple nationality has changed. Of particular interest are Resolutions 12 and 13 of the Committee of Ministers of 1977, and Parliamentary Assembly Recommendation 1081 of 1988.[4] The 1988 Parliamentary Assembly Recommendation held that it was desirable for each of the spouses of a mixed marriage to have the right to acquire the nationality of the other without losing their nationality of origin. Children born of mixed marriages should also be entitled to acquire and keep the nationality of each of their parents. In 1993, a Second Protocol amending the 1963 Convention was adopted, which allows State Parties not to enforce the general loss of nationality of origin in three cases: for second generation immigrants, spouses in mixed marriages and children with parents with different nationalities.[5] The guiding principles of this Second Protocol were both the unity of the family and the integration of immigrants.

A further step was taken in the European Convention on Nationality of 1997 (hereafter, the European Convention).[6] The European Convention was the first comprehensive approach on the international level to codify the main principles and rules applicable to nationality.[7] The Convention is a progressive consolidation of the obligations and ideas which have emerged as a result of developments in both international and domestic law. It is inspired by a range of international instruments, and aims to contribute to the progressive development of international law.[8] Although the European Convention leaves the Strasbourg Convention of 1963 untouched, it takes a totally different stance towards multiple nationality.

---

[3] Convention on the Reduction of Cases of Multiple Nationality and on Military Obligations in Cases of Multiple Nationality, Strasbourg, 6 May 1963, *ETS* No. 43.

[4] Council of Europe, Committee of Ministers, Resolution (77)12 on the nationality of spouses of different nationalities; Council of Europe, Committee of Ministers, Resolution (77)13 on the nationality of children born in wedlock. Council of Europe Parliamentary Assembly, Recommendation 1081 (1988).

[5] Second Protocol amending the Convention on the Reduction of Cases of Multiple Nationality and on Military Obligations in Cases of Multiple Nationality, Strasbourg, 2 Feb. 1993, *ETS* No. 149.

[6] European Convention on Nationality, Strasbourg, 6 Nov. 1997, *ETS* No.166.

[7] R. Schaerer, 'The European Convention on Nationality', 40 *German Yearbook of International Law* (1997) p. 438.

[8] G.R. de Groot, 'The European Convention on Nationality: a Step Towards a *Ius Commune* in the Field of Nationality Law', 7 *Maastricht Journal of European and Comparative Law* (2000) p. 117.

While the aim of the Strasbourg Convention was to prevent it from occurring, the European Convention is neutral on this issue. The Preamble notes

> '... the varied approach of States to the question of multiple nationality and recognising that each state is free to decide which consequences it attaches in its internal law to the fact that a national acquires or possesses another nationality'.

Article 15 provides the following:

> 'The provisions of this Convention shall not limit the right of a State Party to determine in its internal law whether:
> a. its nationals who acquire or possess the nationality of another State retain its nationality or lose it;
> b. the acquisition or retention of its nationality is subject to the renunciation or loss of another nationality'.

Both the Preamble and Article 15 are an expression of state sovereignty in designing rules concerning multiple nationality. However, other articles of the European Convention somewhat limit this sovereignty. Even states that attempt to avoid multiple nationality may not exclude it in general. Article 14 obliges State Parties to allow multiple nationality for children who acquired a different nationality automatically at birth, and for their nationals who have acquired another nationality automatically by marriage. Article 16 requires State Parties not to make renunciation or loss of another nationality a condition for the acquisition or retention of its nationality where such renunciation or loss is not possible or cannot reasonably be expected. Article 17 further determines that nationals holding multiple nationality shall have the same rights and duties as other nationals. For the purpose of this chapter, Article 7(3) is relevant, which provides that loss of nationality is not allowed if the person concerned would thereby become stateless, except in cases in which the nationality was acquired by means of fraudulent conduct, false information or concealment of any relevant fact attributable to the applicant, as provided in Article 7(1)(b). The Explanatory Report to the Convention explains that Article 7(1)(b) includes the case in which a person acquires the nationality of the State Party on condition that the nationality of origin would subsequently be renounced and the person chooses not to do so.[9] In such circumstances, the State Party would be entitled to revoke its grant of nationality, even if this leads to statelessness.

In this chapter, we discuss the practice of two states, the Netherlands and Germany. Both countries have ratified the European Convention on Nationality.[10]

---

[9] Explanatory Report on the Convention on Nationality, *ETS* No. 166, remark 61.

[10] Germany withdrew from the Strasbourg Convention of 1963 on 21 Dec. 2001. See the Announcement about the validity of the Convention, 7 Jan. 2002, BGBI, 2002, II, p. 171. The Netherlands ratified the Strasbourg Convention in 1985, *Tractatenblad* 1964, p. 4. It ratified the European Convention in 1998, *Tractatenblad* 1998, p. 10.

Moreover, both States have demonstrated a remarkable change of attitude towards multiple nationality. The Netherlands, which tolerated multiple nationality for a considerable period during the 1990s, recently adopted a new policy of fighting against it. Germany, which has been depicted as a country traditionally opposing multiple nationality, has begun accepting it in a limited number of cases. After a discussion of the political debates that instigated these remarkable policy changes, we will look at the practice of both countries. We will specifically examine the way both implement the renunciation requirement, the obligation of the individual to renounce his or her former nationality upon naturalization, as well as the practice of deprivation of nationality in cases in which the former nationality was not renounced. The main issue is whether the implementation of the renunciation requirement and deprivation of nationality are in compliance with the obligations of the European Convention on Nationality.

2. Political Debates on Multiple Nationality in the Netherlands and Germany[11]

For a considerable period, the Netherlands was one of the countries that tolerated multiple nationality. At the beginning of the 1980s, the first plea for the abolishment of the renunciation requirement by leftwing political parties was unsuccessful; however, in 1992, it was removed by the coalition Government of Christian Democrats (CDA) and Social Democrats (PvdA). The Government hoped that immigrants would naturalize more frequently and integration would be furthered. The new policy was successful and naturalization rates went up.[12]

However, some political parties observed this development with concern. The Christian Democrats, now in opposition, and the conservative-Liberals (VVD) in particular thought that the rising numbers of naturalization applications demonstrated that naturalization had become too easy. They wanted more emphasis on the value of Dutch nationality. In the political debates that followed, the central question was whether naturalization should be a means of integration, as advocated by the Social Democrats and Green Left, or the crowning of a completed integration process, as argued by the Christian Democrats, liberals and small orthodox-protestant parties. The debates resulted in the re-introduction of the renunciation requirement in October 1997. In the revised Dutch Nationality Law that came into effect in 2003, this starting point of renunciation was upheld, although

[11] More extensively on Dutch political debates on multiple nationality, see B. de Hart, 'Political Debates on Dual Nationality in the Netherlands (1990-2003)', *IMIS-Beitraege* (2004) p. 149. On the German political debates, see S. Green, *The Politics of Exclusion: Institutions and Immigration Policy in Contemporary Germany* (Manchester, Manchester University Press 2004).

[12] For a discussion of the effects of the abolishment of the renunciation requirement in 1992 and its re-introduction in 1997, see A. Böcker, K. Groenendijk and B. de Hart, 'De toegang tot het Nederlanderschap. Effecten van twintig jaar beleidswijzigingen' [Access to Dutch nationality. Effects of twenty years of policy changes], 80 *Nederlands Juristenblad* (2005) p. 157.

a number of exceptions were allowed (see Section 4). Political controversy was focused on the issue of first generation immigrants and naturalization. Until then, neither left- nor right-wing parties called into question the possibility of multiple nationality for second and third generation immigrants, or children from mixed marriages, who acquired multiple nationality at birth or by option.

The general debate was reopened even before the revised Nationality Law came into force in April 2003. After the Christian Democrats asked for a ban on multiple nationality for third generation immigrants, the Minister of Immigration and Integration promised a Memorandum on the issue of multiple nationality and renunciation. In the Memorandum, the Minister concluded that the Christian Democrats' wish could not be granted, due to the obligations under the European Convention. Instead, the Minister introduced a Bill in Parliament, in June 2005, which would abolish two of the existing exceptions to the renunciation requirement, those for second generation immigrants and spouses of Dutch nationals.[13] By abolishing these exceptions, the Minister hoped to prevent the transmission of multiple nationality by immigrants to subsequent generations. The Government has stated that multiple nationality is a hindrance to integration, without providing an explanation as to how this connection between the two should be perceived. A further proposal concerned allowing the withdrawal of Dutch nationality from dual nationals who have damaged 'essential interests of the Dutch state'; those who, in other words, have committed crimes of terrorism.[14] The Dutch Government further urged Morocco to revise its nationality law, in order to allow for the renunciation of Moroccan nationality.[15] After the murder of Dutch filmmaker Theo van Gogh on 2 November 2004, the same Bill was promoted in the context of the fight against terrorism.

In Germany, the debate on multiple nationality started at the beginning of the 1990s. Three circumstances created the opportunity to adopt a more liberal naturalization policy, including a general acceptance of multiple nationality. Firstly, German reunification removed the objections that amendment of the Nationality Law would include an acceptance of the existence of the DDR. Secondly, in 1990, the *Bundesverfassungsgericht* rejected awarding voting rights at the local level to foreigners, referring to nationality law as the way to include immigrants in the political community.[16] Lastly, in 1992, churches, immigrant organizations

[13] Bill to amend the Dutch Nationality Law in order to limit multiple nationality and to provide for loss of nationality in case of conduct seriously prejudicial to the vital interests of the Kingdom, Second Chamber 2004-2005, 30 166, No. 2, Article I B.

[14] The wording of this proposal is taken from Art. 7(1)(d) of the European Convention. See G.R. de Groot, 'Een onwenselijk wetsontwerp ter wijziging van de Rijkswet op het Nederlanderschap. Kritische beschouwingen over wetsontwerp nr. 30 166 (R 1795)' [An undesirable Bill to amend the Dutch Nationality Law: A Critical Consideration of Bill No. 30 166 (R 1795)], 4 *Journaal Vreemdelingenrecht* (2005) p. 439.

[15] The major immigrant groups in the Netherlands are Moroccans, Turks and Surinamese.

[16] Decisions of the Federal Constitutional Court, 26 June 1990 and 31 Oct. 1990, BVerfGE Vols. 83, 37, 59 ff.

and the Greens campaigned for multiple nationality after violent attacks on Turkish immigrants, collecting one million signatures. Political parties from left to right favoured a more liberal naturalization policy. Nevertheless, the revised Nationality Law of 1999 did not include acceptance of multiple nationality. In 1998, the red-green Government of Social Democrats and Greens agreed to put forward a Bill abolishing the renunciation requirement. However, even before the Government could formulate and present its Bill in Parliament, the leaders of CDU and CSU launched a petitioning campaign against multiple nationality. They collected 5 million signatures, and caused a wave of publicity and public debate,[17] which helped them win the elections in Hessen in February 1999. As a result, the red-green Government lost its majority in the *Bundesrat* and was forced to revise its plans. The Bill presented to Parliament no longer included abolishment of the renunciation requirement for naturalization, although it did extend the list of exceptions. The *ius soli* acquisition of German nationality for second generation immigrants only allowed for a temporary toleration of multiple nationality, as those concerned had to choose between the German and the foreign nationality between the ages of 18 and 23.

The amendment of the German Nationality Law did not end the controversy over multiple nationality. In 2004, it came to light that around 50,000 persons had automatically lost German citizenship because they had re-acquired their foreign nationality. This caused public and political upheaval, especially in the context of upcoming elections. The German Government has proposed a bilateral agreement to the Turkish Government on exchange of information on naturalizations, and demanded information on the Turkish immigrants who re-acquired their nationality of origin after 1 January 2000.[18]

In both countries under review here, the debate focused on distinct immigrant groups. In Germany it concentrated almost entirely on Turkish immigrants, while in the Netherlands it currently centres on Moroccans. Although in the Netherlands the debate was, at first, on first generation immigrants and naturalization, it now also includes objections to multiple nationality for the second and third generations. In Germany, this has always been the case. The German Christian Democrats persisted in their rejection of *ius soli* acquisition for the second generation, on the grounds that it would 'force' German nationality upon their parents. Hence, immigrant children were constructed as different from children of mixed marriages, whose right to retain multiple nationality was not questioned. Both countries allow multiple nationality for their emigrants in some cases, and for children of mixed marriages. Germany allows multiple nationality for *Aussiedler* and has granted German nationality to large numbers of Polish nationals living abroad.[19]

---

[17] A.H. Cooper, 'Party-Sponsored Protest and the Movement Society: the CDU/CSU Mobilises Against Citizenship Law Reform', 11 *German Politics* (2002) p. 88.

[18] German Parliament, 'Response of federal government to questions of FDP', 3 May 2005, Drucksache (Printed edition) 15/5419.

[19] *Aussiedler* are persons of German descent from the territory of the former Soviet Union; see

Efforts by leftwing parties to raise the issues of multiple or hybrid identities, transnational ties with both countries, or the *Lebensmittelpunkt* [principal centre of interests] in the country of residence, as arguments in favour of acceptance of multiple nationality were unsuccessful. This failure can be explained by the changing approach to integration policy. The Netherlands, for a long time viewed as a pacesetter of multicultural politics, has shifted towards a more assimilationist approach, demanding integration by legal measures.[20] In Germany, the issue of integration was explicitly linked to loyalty, thus requiring a univocal choice for German society and single German nationality.

3. The Renunciation Requirement in Law and Policy

The German Nationality Law of 1913 did not contain a renunciation requirement. Germany ratified the Strasbourg Convention of 1963 in 1969.[21] The renunciation requirement was introduced in law for the first time in that year, as part of the introduction of gender equality, which granted migrant men and women the same rights to German nationality after marrying a German. The naturalization guidelines of 1977 extended the renunciation requirement to all categories of naturalization.

In the Netherlands, renunciation has been required since 1860. It was codified in the first Dutch Nationality Law of 1892.[22] Although the wording of the law opens the possibility of waiving the requirement, renunciation was always required in practice. If the country of origin did not allow renunciation, naturalization was refused.[23] A revised Article 5a, introduced in 1977, stipulated that renunciation *could* be required. The current Nationality Law is both stricter and more lenient. On the one hand, it states that naturalization is refused if the foreign nationality is not renounced; on the other, it leaves room for exceptions to be made if renunciation 'cannot reasonably be expected'.[24]

Since the 1960s, both Germany and the Netherlands have developed a cautious policy of exceptions to the renunciation requirement. In particular, people from Eastern European countries were not required to renounce their foreign nationali-

K. Groenendijk, 'Regulating ethnic immigration: the case of the *Aussiedler*', 23 *New Community* (1997) p. 361.

[20] C. Joppke and E. Morawska, 'Integrating Immigrants in Liberal Nation-States: Policies and Practices', in C. Joppke and E. Morawska (eds.), *Towards Assimilation and Citizenship: Immigrants in Liberal Nation-States* (Basingstoke and New York, Palgrave MacMillan, 2003), p. 1.

[21] As noted, loc. cit. n. 10, Germany withdrew from the Strasbourg Convention on 21 Dec. 2001. The withdrawal took effect on 22 Dec. 2002.

[22] Art. 4 of the Dutch Nationality Law of 1892.

[23] E. Heijs, *Van Vreemdeling tot Nederlander. De verlening van het Nederlanderschap aan vreemdelingen 1813-1992* [From Alien to Dutch Citizen. Granting Dutch Nationality to Aliens 1813-1992] (Amsterdam, Het Spinhuis 1995) p. 74.

[24] Art. 9(1)(b) *Rijkswet op het Nederlanderschap* [Dutch Nationality Law].

ty. German authorities could grant naturalization if '*ernsthafter and nachhaltiger*' [serious and enduring] efforts to renounce the nationality during a considerable period of time were unsuccessful.

Today, Germany and the Netherlands allow several legal exceptions to the renunciation requirement. First of all, they do not require renunciation of the other nationality if this is either legally impossible or extremely difficult and routinely refused by foreign authorities.[25] This complies with the obligation imposed by Article 16 of the European Convention. Both States use lists of countries that routinely refuse renunciation. Comparing the lists, there appear to be remarkable differences, and only four countries (Algeria, Tunisia, Morocco and Syria) are mentioned on both. While Germany includes five more countries of which renunciation is not expected, the Netherlands specifies twelve (see Table 1).

Furthermore, neither state requires renunciation in cases involving refugees; if high fees are charged for renunciation; if military service is required before renunciation (in Germany only under certain conditions); and if renunciation has economic disadvantages, e.g., regarding inheritance or real estate.

Germany has a specific exception for EU nationals, on the basis of reciprocity: renunciation is not required if the other EU Member State does not require renunciation from Germans.[26] Multiple nationality can also be accepted if a request for renunciation has not been decided within a reasonable time period.[27] The Netherlands has specific exceptions for second generation immigrants and spouses of Dutch nationals.[28] However, as mentioned above, a Bill has been brought before Parliament to abolish these exceptions. A further exception is for nationals of states that have signed the Second Protocol of the Strasbourg Convention of 1993 (Italy and France). Besides these exceptions, waiving the renunciation requirement is possible in exceptional cases, after individual consideration for reasons of fairness (*billijkheid*). In Germany, it is also possible in case of '*unzumutbare Bedingungen*'[29] [unreasonable conditions].

---

[25] Art. 9(1)(b) Dutch Nationality Law; Arts. 12(1)(1) and 12(2)(2) *Staatsangehörigkeitsgesetz* [German Nationality Law]. The Netherlands publishes a regularly revised list in *Tussentijdse Berichten Nationaliteiten* [Interim Notice Nationality]. The information provided is based on the most recent one: TBN 2005/5 of 21 Aug. 2005. The list is based on information provided by the Ministry of Foreign Affairs. The information on Germany is based on *Vorläufige Anwendungshinweise zum StAG in der Fassung des Zuwanderungsgesetzes von 30 Juli 2001* [Preliminary instructions for implementing the Nationality Law as amended by the Immigration Law of 30 July 2001], 15 Feb. 2005, Ministry of Interior. The list is the result of regular meetings between representatives of the federal and the county level.

[26] Art. 12(2) German Nationality Law. This counts for 14 of the 25 EU Member States: Belgium, Finland, France, Greece, the United Kingdom, Ireland, Italy, Malta, Poland, Portugal, Sweden, Slovakia, Hungary and Cyprus. For Slovenia and the Netherlands, it only counts for specific groups, e.g., spouses of nationals.

[27] Art. 12(1)(3) German Nationality Law.

[28] Arts. 9(3)(c) and (d) Dutch Nationality Law.

[29] Art. 12(1)(3) German Nationality Law.

It is clear that many exceptions to the renunciation requirement are allowed. Both Dutch and German practice could be typified as a policy of 'renunciation, unless …'. How these exceptions work out in practice and how many naturalizations actually occur with multiple nationality will be dealt with in the following paragraphs.

Table 1. List of countries the nationality of which nationals are not required to renounce because it is legally impossible or impossible in practice

Country	*No renunciation required by Germany and the Netherlands*	*No renunciation required by Germany*	*No renunciation required by the Netherlands*
Afghanistan		X	
Algeria	X		
Argentina			X
Bangladesh			X
Colombia			X
Costa Rica			X
Cuba		X	
Dominican republic			X
Ecuador			X
Eritrea		X	
Greece			X
Iran		X	
Libya			X
Yemen			X
Lebanon		X	
Mexico			X
Morocco	X		
Rwanda			X
Syria	X		
Tunisia	X		
Uruguay			X
Total number of countries	*4*	*5*	*12*

Source for the Netherlands: Tussentijds Bericht Nationaliteiten (TBN 2005/5) [Interim Notice Nationalities].
Source for Germany: Vorläufige Anwendungshinweise zum StAG in der Fassung des Zuwanderungsgesetzes von 30 Juli 2001, 16 Feb. 2005, Ministry of Interior. [Preliminary instructions for implementing the Nationality Law as amended by the Immigration Law of 30 July 2001].

4. The Implementation of the Renunciation Requirement

The Committee of Experts on Nationality of the Council of Europe has noted the diverging practices of State Parties concerning the renunciation of previous nationality, and pointed out the practical problems that may arise.[30] The Netherlands and Germany are illustrative of these diverging practices.

In the Netherlands, naturalization is granted on the condition that renunciation is documented within a certain period of time afterwards. The applicant has to sign a statement declaring his willingness to renounce together with the request for naturalization. If the other conditions are met, Dutch nationality will be granted. The new Dutch citizen is required to provide proof of his renunciation within three months. If this is not produced, two reminders are sent. If no reaction follows, the Dutch nationality can be withdrawn. If the applicant informs the Dutch Immigration and Naturalization Service (hereafter, IND) that the renunciation procedure has started, the administration will await further information.

In Germany, applicants receive the written decision on naturalization only after they have documented their release from their former nationality. A provisional assurance of nationality can be granted if this is necessary for the renunciation of the other nationality to be accepted. The German procedure results in a higher barrier for naturalization than the Dutch. In Germany, in some cases the renunciation requirement leads to a considerable extension of the duration of the procedure, with some running longer than five years.[31] The question remains as to whether such a lengthy procedure meets with the state's obligation to process an application for naturalization within a reasonable time.[32]

It may also lead to (temporary) statelessness. If the conditions for acquisition of nationality are fulfilled and the new nationality is not acquired, while the foreign nationality has been renounced, it might even lead to permanent statelessness. The explanatory report to the European Convention explains that the state whose nationality has been renounced must allow the recovery of the nationality, or must consider it never lost, in order to prevent statelessness.[33] The Committee of Experts on Nationality favours the Dutch practice of requiring renunciation of existing citizenship not before the granting of the new one but within a specified period of time, with the possibility of withdrawal should the renunciation not be forthcoming.[34]

Administrative practice creates an impediment to naturalization if it has to be individually proved in each case that renunciation is not possible. The situation of Iranians in Germany is a case in point. Before 1999, Iranians had to prove individually that they tried to give up their Iranian nationality before German nationality could be granted, although it was well-known that it was virtually impos-

[30] *Report on Conditions for the Acquisition and Loss of Nationality*, 14 Jan. 2003, Committee of Experts on Nationality (2002) 1, p. 13.

[31] *Bericht der Beauftragten der Bundesregierung für Migration, Flüchtlinge und Integration über die Lage der Ausländerinnen und Ausländer in der Bundesrepublik Deutschland* [Report of the Representative of the Federal Government for Migration, Refugees and Integration on the Situation of Foreigners in Germany], Berlin, Aug. 2005, p. 347.

[32] Art. 10 of the European Convention, loc. cit. n. 6.

[33] Explanatory Report to the European Convention on Nationality, loc. cit. n. 9, on Art. 8, No. 79.

[34] Committee of Experts on Nationality, *Report on Conditions for the Acquisition and Loss of Nationality*, 14 Jan. 2003, CJ-NA (2002)1, p. 13.

sible to renounce Iranian nationality. Of 14,410 who attempted to do so, a mere 42 succeeded.[35] Although, in such cases, naturalization with multiple nationality could be accepted, it took individual Iranians a lot of effort for many years to get that far. Since 2001, Iranians in Germany no longer have to prove renunciation individually. Iran is now among the countries of which renunciation is no longer required. This made it possible to finally grant a large number of applications of Iranian immigrants. However, one of the *Länder* still requires Iranians to present a certificate of renunciation with the documents required by Iranian law.[36]

Against this background, it is remarkable that, in 2004, the Netherlands placed Iran on the list of countries of which renunciation can be required. Now, Iranian nationals have to provide a declaration of permission of naturalization from the Iranian authorities. The request for naturalization is not granted, but delayed until the document is presented, for a maximum period of one year. This considerably lengthens the procedure of naturalization for Iranian nationals, unless they are exempted from the renunciation requirement (as refugees).

Similar problems in Germany arise with Afghan nationals, who are required to renounce their nationality in several *Länder*, although this is very difficult because of the situation of the central administration in Afghanistan. Renunciation is also required of people from the former Yugoslavia, although in many cases this is not possible, as is illustrated by the high percentage of naturalizations with multiple nationality from this group (90.1% for Serbia and Montenegro).[37] It is questionable whether such practices are permissible under Article 16 of the European Convention. Upholding the renunciation requirement in such cases says less about the actual possibility for immigrants to renounce their nationality of origin than it does about the wish of German and Dutch authorities to have a lenient or strict policy of naturalization.

A final issue to be mentioned is the different consequences of the renunciation requirement for different groups of immigrants. The renunciation requirement works selectively. It does not affect immigrants who cannot renounce because the law of their country of origin does not allow it; nor does it affect immigrants who automatically lose their original nationality upon naturalization elsewhere. The requirement does not affect refugees, who do not have to renounce and generally have a high willingness to naturalize; and it hardly affects EU nationals, who have a low willingness to naturalize. In Germany, most EU nationals do not have to renounce their nationality. The group that is affected are immigrants from countries where multiple nationality is allowed. In the Netherlands, of the major

---

[35] *Die Beauftragte der Bundesregierung für Ausländerfragen über die Lage der Ausländer in der Bundesrepublik Deutschland*, Sept. 2002 [Report of the Representative of the Federal Government for Migration, Refugees and Integration on the Situation of Foreigners in Germany], Berlin und Bonn, p. 61.

[36] The report of the *Auslanderbeauftragte* [Representative for Foreigners] does not specify which Land; see ibid., p. 349.

[37] *Bericht der Beauftragten der Bundesregierung für Migration, Flüchtlinge und Integration 2005* [Report of the Representative of the Federal Government for Migration, Refugees and Integration] p. 352 and Table 43 in Appendix.

immigrant groups of Moroccans, Surinamese and Turks, only the latter is affected by the renunciation requirement, as Moroccans cannot renounce and Surinamese lose their nationality automatically upon naturalization abroad (see Table 2).[38]

Hence, the effects of the renunciation requirement are dependent not on the level of integration of the immigrant, but on the nationality law of the country of origin – a factor that the individual immigrant cannot influence. This puts into perspective the argument that multiple nationality hinders integration, which was put forward in both Dutch and German political debates on the issue.

Table 2. Naturalizations with retention of former nationality in Germany (2002) and the Netherlands (2001)

Nationality	**Germany: Naturalizations with retention of former nationality (2002)**	**Netherlands: Naturalizations with retention of former nationality (2001)**
No renunciation required by either country		
Morocco	99.4 %	100 %
Renunciation required by both countries		
Turkey	19.1	100
Former Yugoslavia	90.1	99
Iraq	23.8	7
Israel	92.2	96
Ukraine	77.4	45
No renunciation required by Germany		
Afghanistan	99.7	99
Average all nationalities	**41.5 %**	**76 %**

5. Deprivation of Nationality

Since 1985, Dutch Nationality Law has allowed for the withdrawal of Dutch nationality in cases in which an individual has not met the obligation to renounce the former nationality.[39] For a lengthy period, this provision remained without effect, even after the reintroduction of the renunciation requirement in 1997. It was not implemented because there was not enough qualified manpower to do so, and because it was not given political priority. Since 2002, the political attitude towards multiple nationality has changed, and the policy of withdrawing Dutch nationality in cases in which the foreign nationality has not been renounced has been tightened. However, in many cases this does not result in actual withdrawal. In 2002, 1,336 cases of possible withdrawal were considered, and in only 102

[38] A. Böcker, K. Groenendijk and B. de Hart, 'De toegang tot het Nederlanderschap. Effecten van twintig jaar beleidswijzigingen' [Access to Dutch Nationality. Effects of twenty years of policy changes], 80 *Nederlands Juristenblad* (2005) p. 157.

[39] Art. 15(1)(d) Dutch Nationality Law.

cases was this actually carried out (7.6%). In 2004, 1,197 cases were considered, and 17 actual withdrawals took place (1.4%).[40]

The result is a growing amount of Dutch case-law on the renunciation requirement. Two issues are addressed in this. The first concerns the efforts that the individual citizen is required to make in order to prove that he or she has done everything possible to renounce the foreign nationality. Dutch case-law shows that sending a request, or several requests, to the foreign authorities indicating the wish to renounce the nationality is not enough. If such requests remain unanswered, the applicant should retry on a regular basis. If not, Dutch nationality can be revoked.[41] The second issue is that of the limits set by the European Convention to the policy of withdrawal. The Afdeling Rechtspraak Raad van State [the highest Dutch administrative court] considered the case of an Egyptian national who had not renounced his Egyptian nationality, although the IND had urged him to do so several times. After its third letter requesting renunciation remained unanswered, the IND withdrew his Dutch nationality. They did so despite the fact that by then the applicant had provided proof of his renunciation of Egyptian nationality. The IND claimed that it was too late. The applicant had now lost both nationalities and had become stateless. In order to be readmitted as a foreign national, he had to return to Egypt to apply for a long-term visa, which was not possible because the applicant no longer had an Egyptian passport. The Court judged that the withdrawal occurred in breach of the obligation of the Dutch State to prevent statelessness, as laid down in the Dutch Nationality Law.[42] That the applicant had renounced his Egyptian nationality should have been taken into account at the moment of the decision.[43]

It is interesting in this case that, although the European Convention, contrary to the Strasbourg Convention, does not directly require the loss of nationality, the Highest Administrative Court concluded that Article 7 (on the loss of nationality) had direct effect. A further relevant issue is whether deprivation on the grounds of lack of willingness to give up the former nationality is actually allowed by Article 7, which provides an exhaustive enumeration of grounds for loss of nationality. Only if one of these grounds is present may loss resulting in statelessness be acceptable: in Article 7(1)(b), in cases of fraudulent conduct, false information or concealment of any relevant fact. The grounds of loss listed in Article 7 do not include refusal to renounce the former nationality. The explanatory report, however, does mention it under Article 7(1)(b). By way of comparison, it is interesting to note that the Austrian Nationality Law has a provision similar to Article 15(1)(d)

---

[40] Figures provided by the Immigration and Naturalization Service (IND).

[41] Afdeling Rechtspraak Raad van State 200410536/1, 10 Aug. 2005; Afdeling Rechtspraak Raad van State 200410550/1, 10 Aug. 2005 [Administrative Jurisdiction Department of the Council of State].

[42] Art. 14(4) Dutch Nationality Law. Art. 4(b) of the European Convention on Nationality, loc. cit. n. 6, determines the general principle that statelessness shall be avoided when formulating rules on nationality.

[43] Afdeling Rechtspraak Raad van State 200306971/1,18 Aug. 2002, *Jurisprudentie Vreemdelingenrecht* 2004/403, with note by G.R. de Groot.

of the Dutch Nationality Law (allowing for the withdrawal of Dutch nationality in cases in which an individual has not met the obligation to renounce the former nationality). Austria made a reservation to its ratification of the European Convention in order to be able to maintain this ground of loss of nationality.[44]

In Germany, large numbers of Turkish-German nationals have lost their German nationality in recent years. Until the coming into effect of the revised citizenship law on 1 January 2000, this did not occur as long as the individual lived in Germany (the so-called *Inlandsklausel*). This allowed immigrants to reapply for the foreign nationality after they had obtained German nationality, giving them multiple nationality. The Red-Green Government amended the law in order to allow for the withdrawal of German nationality from people living in Germany,[45] in order to prevent this practice by Turkish immigrants. This has resulted in the automatic loss of German nationality of around 50,000 immigrants.[46] If naturalization took place before the amendment of the law, the re-obtained Turkish nationality does not lead to loss of nationality; but if naturalization and re-acquisition of Turkish nationality took place after it came into force, German nationality is lost automatically, even if the re-acquired nationality has also been lost. Hence, in some cases it might result in statelessness. If naturalization and the application for re-acquisition of foreign nationality took place before 1 January 2000, but the foreign nationality was re-acquired after this date, German nationality is still lost.[47]

Although the abolishment of the *Inlandsklausel* has general effect, its purpose was to target a specific group: Turkish immigrants. The media attention and administrative practices also targeted Turkish immigrants. Six of the *Länder* have written letters specifically and only to immigrants of Turkish origin, ordering them to declare their nationality, sometimes under the threat of a fine if they do not comply.[48]

The question is whether this administrative practice, targeting a specific group, is in compliance with Article 5(1) of the European Convention, which prohibits discrimination in law and practice on the grounds of sex, religion, race, colour or national or ethnic origin. An administrative practice which specifically targets Turkish immigrants could be viewed as discrimination on the grounds of national or ethnic origin.

In Germany, the Convention was used as an argument in favour of introducing *ius soli* acquisition for second-generation immigrants. Article 14(1)(a) of the European Convention states that a State Party 'shall allow children having different nationalities acquired automatically at birth to retain these nationalities'. How-

---

[44] See note by G.R. de Groot, loc. cit. n. 43.

[45] Art. 25(1) German Nationality Law.

[46] *DGB Informationen zur Migrationspolitik* 21 July 2005 cites the higher number of 90,000 immigrants.

[47] S. Uslucan, 'Fataler Doppelpass ins Abseits? – Zum "tückischen" Rückerwerb der türkischen Staatsangehörigkeit' [Fatal Dual Passport at Stake? On 'Devious' Reacquisition of Turkish Nationality], *Zeitschrift für Ausländerrecht* (2005) p. 115.

[48] DGB *Informationen zur Migrationspolitik* 21 July 2005.

ever, the German Nationality Law requires the children to choose one or other nationality upon reaching the age of majority.[49] In the view of the German Government, this so-called 'optional model' required a reservation whereby Germany declared that loss of German nationality *ex lege* may be effected on the basis of a mandatory choice in cases in which a foreign national also acquires German nationality by virtue of having been born in Germany. Article 7 of the European Convention, which contains an exhaustive enumeration of grounds of loss, does not mention the 'optional model' as provided for in Article 29 of the German Nationality Law.[50]

If the young person does not opt for one or other nationality within the required period, German nationality is automatically lost. This provision has been much contested. It often results in the loss of the effective nationality of second generation immigrants born and brought up in Germany.

6. Conclusion

In political debates in Germany and the Netherlands multiple nationality was discussed in the context of the integration of immigrants. Some argued that multiple nationality hinders integration, others maintained the opposite stance. Which standpoint is adopted depends on the place attributed to naturalization in the integration process: is naturalization viewed as the crowning of a completed integration process, or as a step in that process itself?

The focus on integration is called into question by the fact of the selective working of the renunciation requirement. Some immigrants are required to renounce the former nationality, while others are not. This is determined by foreign nationality law on one hand, and the attitude of the state authorities of the country of residence on the other. The renunciation requirement does not apply to all immigrants equally. The relevant question is why different groups of immigrants should be treated differently, especially since the issue of whether they have to renounce their former nationality cannot be influenced by the individual immigrant, but is determined by the sovereignty of the foreign state. Hence, whether an applicant for naturalization renounces the former nationality or not often says little about his or her willingness to integrate, the 'completion' of the integration process, loyalty, or the willingness to make a clear choice.

The renunciation requirement works selectively on the basis of ethnicity, albeit indirectly. We have seen that political debates focus on specific immigrant groups. This cannot be explained by the size of these groups: in the Netherlands, Turkish immigrants form the largest group of dual nationals, but Moroccans are

---

[49] Art. 29 German Nationality Law.

[50] R. Göbel-Zimmermann, 'Das neue Staatsangehörigkeitsrecht – Erfahrungen und Reformvorschläge' [The New Nationality Law. Experiences and proposals for amendment], 22 *Zeitschrift für Ausländerrecht* (2003) p. 65.

the focus of debates. Can the different treatment of Turkish immigrants in Germany, who lost their German nationality after reapplying for Turkish nationality, be justified if this policy is not also enforced against other immigrants who have done the same? In view of the extension of the policy of withdrawal of nationality, multiple nationality has become a liability. A strict policy of withdrawal may erode the validity of citizenship both as an integrating factor and as a status providing complete legal security as the final stage in the integration process.

Germany and the Netherlands are among a minority of European countries that require renunciation. There is no indication that those states that do not do so have more problems with the integration of immigrants or other significant difficulties in relation to multiple nationality than those that do.

In spite of the renunciation requirement, multiple nationality is allowed in a considerable number of cases. The European Convention prevents the abolition of some of the exceptions. Hence, we estimate that the percentage of persons naturalizing while retaining the former nationality in Germany and the Netherlands is unlikely to fall below around 40 per cent. And every year tens of thousands of children with multiple nationality are born. It seems safe to conclude that cases of multiple nationality are unavoidable, even when legislation or treaties seek to reduce them.[51]

However, if countries like Germany, the Netherlands, and others choose to retain the renunciation requirement, they should at least be guided by the following principles. Firstly, the policy of prevention of multiple nationality should not lead to statelessness. The prevention of statelessness is a norm of customary international law, which should prevail above the prevention of multiple nationality. Secondly, administrative practices should not target specific national or ethnic groups, in order to prevent discrimination. Finally, the renunciation requirement should not result in administrative practices that form an effective barrier to naturalization, e.g., by extending the duration of naturalization procedures for an unreasonable period of time.[52]

Selected Bibliography

Aleinikoff, T.A., and D. Klusmeyer, 'Plural Nationality: Facing the Future in a Migratory World', in T.A. Aleinikoff and D. Klusmeyer (eds.), *Citizenship Today: Global Perspectives* (Washington, Carnegie Endowment 2001) p. 63.

Böcker, A., K. Groenendijk, and B. De Hart, 'De toegang tot het Nederlanderschap. Effecten van twintig jaar beleidswijzigingen' [Access to Dutch nationality. Effects of twenty years of policy changes], 80 *Nederlands Juristenblad* (2005) p. 157.

[51] Committee of Experts on Nationality, *Report on Multiple Nationality*, 20 Oct. 2000, CJ-NA (2000) 12, p. 4.

[52] Art. 10 of the European Convention, loc. cit. n. 6, requires State Parties to ensure that applications relating to acquisition, retention, loss and recovery or certification of their nationality are processed within a reasonable period of time.

Donner, R., *The Regulation of Nationality in International Law* (New York, Transnational Publishers 1994).

Faist, T. and J. Gerdes, 'Dual Citizenship as a Path-Dependent Process', 38 *International Migration Review* (2004) p. 913.

Feldblum, M., 'Managing Membership: New Trends in Citizenship and Nationality Policy', in T.A. Aleinikoff and D. Klusmeyer (eds.), *From Migrants to Citizens* (Washington, Carnegie Endowment 2003) p. 475.

Göbel-Zimmermann, R., 'Das neue Staatsangehörigkeitsrecht – Erfahrungen und Reformvorschläge' [The New Nationality Law: Experiences and Proposals for Amendment], 22 *Zeitschrift für Ausländerrecht* (2003) p. 65.

Green, S., *The Politics of Exclusion: Institutions and Immigration Policy in Contemporary Germany* (Manchester, Manchester University Press 2004).

Groenendijk, K., 'Regulating ethnic immigration: the case of the *Aussiedler*', 23 *New Community* (1997) p. 361.

Groot, G.R. de, 'The European Convention on Nationality: a Step Towards a *Ius Commune* in the Field of Nationality Law', 7 *Maastricht Journal of European and Comparative Law* (2000) p. 117.

Hansen, R., and P. Weil, 'Introduction: Dual Citizenship in a Changed World: Immigration, Gender and Social Rights', in R. Hansen and P. Weil, eds., *Dual Nationality, Social Rights and Federal Citizenship in the US and Europe: The Reinvention of Citizenship* (New York/Oxford, Bergham Books 2002) p. 1.

Hart, B. de, 'Political Debates on Dual Nationality in the Netherlands (1990-2003)', *IMIS-Beitraege* (2004) p. 149.

Heijs, E., *Van Vreemdeling tot Nederlander. De verlening van het Nederlanderschap aan vreemdelingen 1813-1992* [From Alien to Dutch Citizen. Granting Dutch Nationality to Aliens 1813-1992] (Amsterdam, Het Spinhuis 1995).

Legomski, S., 'Dual Nationality and Military Service: Strategy Number Two', in D. Martin and K. Hailbronner (eds.), *Rights and Duties of Dual Nationals: Evolutions and Prospects* (The Hague, Kluwer Law International 2003) p. 79.

Martin, D., and K. Hailbronner (eds.), *Rights and Duties of Dual Nationals: Evolution and Prospects* (The Hague, Kluwer Law International 2003).

Renshon, S.A., 'Dual Citizenship and American Democracy: Patriotism, National Attachment and National Identity', 21 *Social Philosophy and Policy* (2004) p. 100.

Schaerer, R., 'The European Convention on Nationality', 40 *German Yearbook of International Law* (1997) p. 438.

Schuck, P.H., 'Plural Citizenships', in R. Hansen and P. Weil (eds.), *Dual Nationality, Social Rights and Federal Citizenship in the US and Europe: The Reinvention of Citizenship* (New York/Oxford, Bergham Books 2002) p. 61.

Spiro, P.J. *Embracing Dual Nationality* (Washington, International Migration Policy Program, Carnegie Endowment 1998).

Uslucan, S., 'Fataler Doppelpass ins Abseits? - Zum "tückischen" Rückerwerb der türkischen. Staatsangehörigkeit' [Fatal Dual Passport at Stake? On 'Devious' Reacquisition of Turkish Nationality], *Zeitschrift für Ausländerrecht* (2005) p. 115.

Trade and Labour Migration

Chapter 6
GATS MODE 4 AND THE MOBILITY OF LABOUR

Michele Klein Solomon*

1. Introduction

Migration is on the rise and predicted to remain at current levels or increase in the decades to come, yet there is no comprehensive international legal framework governing the cross-border movement of people. Indeed, the only multilateral legal instrument of potential global applicability governing the mobility of labour is a trade instrument – the General Agreement on Trade in Services (GATS) of the World Trade Organization (WTO) – and it does so indirectly. While states have been willing to accept binding legal obligations on many other aspects of migration, as is clear from this volume, they have been reluctant to undertake formal multilateral commitments that limit their sovereign right to determine which non-nationals may enter and remain within their territories, and under what conditions.[1]

Nonetheless, many states are coming to recognize the need to facilitate certain kinds of international movement of persons, particularly for work, in today's mobile world and increasingly integrated global economy. Greater labour mobility is projected to result in substantial global economic gains. A recent World Bank study has predicted that, if carefully managed, a 3 per cent increase over the next 20 years in the share of migrants in the labour force of industrial countries would boost global real income by $356 billion, rivalling potential gains from global reform of merchandise trade.[2] Equally significantly, those gains would be shared by developed and developing countries. As developing countries are often rich in labour, and relatively poor in other resources, liberalization of movements of labour are of predominant interest for many. Indeed, some consider breaking down

* Director of the Migration Policy, Research and Communications Department at the IOM.

[1] Even in the pressing humanitarian case of refugees fleeing persecution, the principal legal instruments contain no obligation on a State Party to admit refugees to its territory, only an obligation not to send them back to a place where they have a well-founded fear of persecution. See the Convention Relating to the Status of Refugees, 28 July 1951, Arts. 1A, 33(1), 189 *UNTS* 150, and the Protocol Relating to the Status of Refugees, 31 Jan. 1967, 606 *UNTS* 267.

[2] World Bank, *Global Economic Prospects 2006: Economic Implications of Remittances and Migration* (Geneva/Washington DC, World Bank 2005).

R. Cholewinski, R. Perruchoud and E. MacDonald, eds., International Migration Law

barriers to global labour mobility as 'the unfinished business of globalization'.[3] While many observers suggest that the facilitation of labour mobility at the international level through a multilateral legal instrument is a long-term goal that is unlikely to yield significant results in the near term, particularly for lower-skilled workers, prospects for future developments in this area nevertheless warrant close attention.[4]

International trade liberalization negotiations have resulted in the substantial reduction of barriers to trade in goods and capital, which in turn has led to substantial global economic gains. Barriers to the movement of people, however, have been identified as a continuing and substantial impediment to further advances in this regard, the gains from which are predicted both to exceed those from further liberalization in other sectors and to benefit developing and developed economies alike. Against the backdrop of increasing international movement of people (precipitated by transportation and communication revolutions), demographic projections forecasting ageing and declining populations in much of the developed world, and persistent disparities in wages and access to economic opportunities, international attention is focused on whether and how the global trading system can contribute to progressively facilitating the movement of people in an orderly, predictable, and safe manner that benefits everybody.

This chapter looks at Mode 4 of the GATS[5] – governing the temporary provision of a service by a service supplier of one country in the territory of another – and its relevance for creating international rules governing the movement of people. Its point of departure is the article by Charnovitz entitled 'Trade Law Norms on International Migration' in *Migration and International Legal Norms*.[6] Charnovitz highlighted the relatively low level of obligations assumed by WTO Member States regarding entry of service providers, when compared to obligations concerning goods, technology, and other services.[7] However, he anticipated that governments would make deeper commitments in the former field in ensuing trade rounds, although he did note that even the marginal progress made during the Uruguay Round was further limited by the insertion of specific requirements

---

[3] World Commission on the Social Dimension of Globalization, *A Fair Globalization: Creating Opportunities for All* (Geneva, International Labour Office 2004) <http://www.ilo.org/public/english/wcsdg/docs/report.pdf>.

[4] In June 2004, the International Labour Conference 2004 adopted a Resolution concerning a Fair Deal for Migrant Workers in a Global Economy calling on the ILO to carry out a plan of action for migrant workers, which included the development of a non-binding multilateral framework for a rights-based approach to labour migration. The framework, approved by the Tripartite Meeting of Experts in November 2005, focuses more on the treatment to be afforded to labour migrants than on rules or principles to govern access to labour markets. For a brief overview of the framework, see the chapter by Ryszard Cholewinski in this volume.

[5] Final Act Embodying the Results of the Uruguay Round of Multilateral Trade Negotiations (1994), Annex 1B General Agreement on Trade in Services (GATS).

[6] S. Charnowitz, 'Trade Law Norms on International Migration', in T.A. Aleinikoff and V. Chetail (eds.), *Migration and International Legal Norms* (The Hague, T.M.C. Asser Press 2003) p. 241.

[7] Ibid., at pp. 246-247.

and prohibitions in national regulations.[8] Lastly, Charnovitz proposed several ways to liberalize barriers to human mobility, including a 'GATS visa', greater recognition of qualifications, more equitable social insurance taxation schemes, and elimination of economic needs tests, restrictions on internal mobility in host countries, and prevailing wage requirements.[9]

Since the publication of Charnovitz's piece in 2003, the Doha Round of trade negotiations has continued, and much work related to Mode 4 has been done, albeit without major breakthroughs at the time of writing of the present chapter. What has been accomplished, however, is a more in-depth exploration of the relationship between trade and migration, and the identification of a number of critical areas in which international cooperation regarding the movement of people could move forward, whether as part of Mode 4 or through complementary efforts. Consequently, this chapter focuses on developments since 2003 in international cooperation on the movement of people, with particular emphasis on Mode 4 and related work.

2. Situating Mode 4

The GATS is the multilaterally agreed framework for trade in services, and applies to all 150 WTO members.[10] Its goals are to progressively liberalize trade in services through negotiations, to thereby encourage economic growth and development, and to increase the participation of developing countries in world trade in services.

The GATS consists of (1) general obligations, and (2) specific commitments. The general obligations comprise a framework agreement on trade in services and include such requirements as the 'most favoured nation' (MFN) obligation on each WTO Member to treat all other Members as well as it does the most favourably treated among them;[11] the requirement to administer specific commitments in a reasonable, objective and impartial manner;[12] and certain transparency requirements to publish or make available at the national level all measures of general application pertaining to the Agreement.[13] The specific commitments are the means by which countries determine which service sectors they will permit foreign suppliers to enter and under what conditions. These specific commitments are contained in individual schedules of commitments, annexed to the GATS.

[8] Ibid., at p. 248.

[9] Ibid., at pp. 250-251.

[10] For an excellent overview of the GATS and Mode 4, see J. Nielson and D. Taglioni, 'A Quick Guide to the GATS and Mode 4', *OECD-World Bank-IOM Seminar in Trade and Migration* (2003) <http://www.iom.int/jahia/webdav/site/myjahiasite/shared/shared/mainsite/microsites/IDM/workshops/Trade_2004_04051004/related%20docs/quick_guide.pdf>.

[11] GATS, loc. cit. n. 5, Art II.

[12] Ibid., Art. VI.1.

[13] Ibid., Art. III.

Twelve service sectors and approximately 160 sub-sectors have been identified for the purpose of developing specific commitments.

In addition, the GATS sets out four possible modes for the trading of services between WTO Members. Mode 1 is 'cross-border supply', where the service itself crosses a border (e.g., editing or design services). Mode 2 is 'consumption abroad', where a service consumer of one country goes to another country and 'consumes' (receives) the service in the territory of the service supplier (e.g., a person going to another country to receive medical treatment or education). Mode 3 is 'commercial presence', where the service supplier establishes a commercial presence in another WTO Member in order to provide the service (e.g., a bank or other service firm that opens a branch in a foreign territory). Lastly, Mode 4 is defined in Article I.2(d) of the GATS as 'the supply of a service … by a service supplier of one member, through presence of natural persons of a member in the territory of another member' (e.g., a person who is a service supplier such as a banker or an architect is present in a foreign country to provide the service). A 'natural' person is a human being as opposed to a merely legal entity, such as a business.

Modes 3 and 4 are effectively counterparts to one another.[14] Commercial presence (Mode 3) was inserted into the GATS to accommodate the desire of many developed countries to include liberalization of investment in services, i.e., the movement of capital, within its scope; presence of natural persons (Mode 4) was included to accommodate the desire of many developing countries to provide similar treatment for the movement of labour. Indeed, as many developing and least developed countries are comparatively labour-rich, they have identified progress in terms of liberalization in Mode 4 as their predominant interest in the current trade round, so that they can export labour intensive services at all skills levels and, as a result, receive significant amounts of remittances sent back by workers, and other export earnings.[15] However, the use of Mode 4 to provide a service is often associated with the use of Mode 3 in Members' schedules, which lay out their individual commitments regarding market access and national treatment in specific sectors and which are distinct from general obligations imposed on all Members and sectors. This is reflected in the commitments scheduled for intra-corporate transferees, usually in connection with related commitments made under Mode 3. Liberalization of movements related to a commercial presence is not advantageous for developing countries, as they have neither extensive commercial presence in WTO Member States nor the resources to expand it. Addi-

[14] A. Mattoo and A. Carzaniga (eds.), *Moving People to Deliver Services* (New York/Washington DC, Oxford University Press and World Bank 2003).

[15] R. Chanda, 'Movement and Presence of Natural Persons and Developing Countries: Issues and Proposals for the GATS Negotiations', *Trade-Related Agenda, Development and Equity (TRADE) Working Paper 19*, South Centre (May 2004) <http://www.southcentre.org/publications/workingpapers/paper19/wp19.pdf>. On the subject of remittances and the regulatory frameworks governing them, see Manuel Orozco's contribution to the present volume.

tionally, restrictions on Mode 3 may also translate into barriers to the temporary movement of labour.

Further guidance on Mode 4 is provided in the GATS Annex on Movement of Natural Persons Supplying Services under the Agreement (hereafter, 'Annex').[16] The terms of Mode 4 make no reference to movement, to labour migration or indeed to employment. The Annex clarifies that Mode 4 is related to the movement of persons, and contains the following negative definition of particular relevance to migration: the GATS does not apply 'to measures affecting natural persons seeking access to the employment market of a Member, nor shall it apply to measures regarding citizenship, residence or employment on a permanent basis'.[17] The Annex also states that, regardless of their obligations under the Agreement, Members are free to regulate the entry and stay of individuals in their territories provided that such measures 'are not applied in such a manner as to nullify or impair the benefits accruing to any Member under the terms of a specific commitment'. In principle, therefore, visa requirements, work permits and other regulatory measures applied to some persons and not to others are not *per se* inconsistent with the requirements of the GATS.

What does this mean for migration? Conceptually, Mode 4 movement of natural persons is a small subset of overall migratory movements. Mode 4 movement can be seen as a subset of a subset of a subset of migration. While no one knows for sure how many people cross international borders annually, and how many of these are migrants (i.e., persons living outside their country of origin for at least one year, as opposed to tourists, students, business visitors, etc.), current estimates put the number of migrants at some 200 million persons.[18] Within that total, according to ILO estimates, a sizeable number are persons engaged in remunerative activity in the host country.[19] Within the realm of labour migrants, there are those who move permanently and those who move temporarily. It is as a subset of temporary labour migrants that one finds Mode 4 movers – service suppliers of one WTO Member who cross borders temporarily to supply a service in the territory of another. Many of these, however, are not captured within the estimate of 200 million migrants, as their stay is for less than one year. An inter-agency working group of the UN's Statistics Division is working to try to quantify Mode 4 movement – how much, from where to where, what the value of services supplied is, etc. – but the task is not easy as standard statistical indices do not contain a 'Mode 4' category, and neither do national statistics bureaus.

---

[16] GATS, loc. cit. n. 5, Annex on Movement of Natural Persons Supplying Services under the Agreement. See also WTO Council for Trade in Services, 'Presence of Natural Persons (Mode 4), Background Note by the Secretariat', WTO Doc. S/C/W/75 (8 Dec. 1998).

[17] GATS, loc. cit. n. 5, Annex on Movement of Natural Persons Supplying Services under the Agreement, para. 2.

[18] Global Commission on International Migration, *Migration in an Interconnected World: New Directions for Action* (Geneva, GCIM 2005).

[19] International Labour Office, *Towards a Fair Deal for Migrant Workers in the Global Economy* (Geneva, ILO 2004) <http://www.ilo.org/public/english/standards/relm/ilc/ilc92/pdf/rep-vi.pdf>. The report estimated the number of economically active migrants at 86 million adults.

The precise scope of Mode 4 is not clear at the international level, and its echo at the national level is even less so. While the Annex clarifies some issues, other important ones remain unsettled. For example, essential terms such as 'temporary', 'employment' and 'entering the labour market' are not defined in the relevant texts. The implication is that several important issues are either subjects for further clarification and negotiation amongst the WTO Members or left to national level discretion and interpretation: which persons are considered service suppliers, whether the proposed supply of a service constitutes employment and further whether it constitutes entering the labour market, and whether a stay is deemed temporary. At present, there is much discussion of which categories of service suppliers are covered by the GATS, such as self-employed or independent service suppliers, foreigners employed by host country companies, foreign employees of foreign firms established in another country, and others. There is also discussion of what constitutes the 'supply of a service'. For example, is a fruit-picker a temporary agricultural labourer or the supplier of fruit-picking services?[20] Similarly, certain manufacturing-related activities might be considered services, depending in part on the ownership of the other factors of production. For example, a factory which is contracted to sew shirts is a supplier of tailoring services, whereas a factory which owns the cloth and produces the shirts for sale under its own brand name is a textile manufacturer.[21] Moreover, individual Member schedules have defined temporary stay in ranges from a few months to up to 5 years. At present, there is no WTO jurisprudence on Mode 4, and consequently little guidance to states and other stakeholders such as the business community on how these terms should and will be interpreted.

Moreover, while Mode 4, by its own terms, is potentially applicable to service suppliers at all skills levels, to date the commitments of nearly all WTO Members under it are limited to the highly skilled, and within that group most often to intra-corporate transferees, managers, and executives.[22] A major concern of many developing countries with respect to Mode 4 is its current application predominantly to highly skilled persons, as many see their greatest gains, and the industrialized world's obvious needs, at the lower end of the skills spectrum, in such sectors as construction and hospitality. There is also the question of whether limiting Mode 4 to the movement of service providers is meaningful in view of current global economic trends, i.e., toward greater outsourcing of production to places where labour is less expensive and toward breaking the production cycle into discrete activities or 'services' that can be performed by separate companies in different countries to produce a final product. Moving away from or beyond the service rationale of Mode 4, however, would take the discussions beyond the

---

[20] Nielson and Taglioni, loc. cit. n. 10, at p. 8, para. 19.

[21] Ibid., at para. 20.

[22] See ibid., at pp. 12-13 for a breakdown of categories of commitments under Mode 4. See also J. Nielson, 'Trade and Migration: GATS Mode 4', in *World Migration 2005: Costs and Benefits of International Migration* (Geneva, IOM 2005) p. 185.

theory and jurisdiction of the GATS and raise legitimate concerns that an international migration forum or various regional fora may be more appropriate venues for this debate.

At the national level, Mode 4 concepts of service providers who move temporarily to provide a service in a foreign country are alien to most domestic immigration laws. Those countries that permit the entry of foreign nationals for work do so not by reference to 'service providers' but by the more commonly used categories of economic immigrants of either a temporary or permanent nature, or both, with temporary labour migration programmes significantly on the rise in many industrialized countries.[23] In addition to traditional business visitor and seasonal agricultural worker programmes, temporary admissions with some form of work attached are now available in many developed countries for students, trainees, working holiday makers, and the like. With the rise of interest in temporary labour migration, many countries are shifting the focus of activities and initiatives on labour migration to private employers and away from the government. Permanent labour migration remains a significant means by which the traditional immigration countries seek to rectify labour market shortages and address the need for certain specified skills, with focus on identified sectors and occupations changing over time. With respect to both temporary and permanent labour migration, labour market tests, which assess whether there are national workers or resident foreigners available to undertake vacant positions, continue to be a primary means of protecting the domestic labour market in many countries.

In brief, the trade law concepts developed in the GATS negotiations bear little resemblance to domestic immigration laws and regulations, and therein lies one of the principal challenges. For migration regulators, whether a person applying for a visa or a work permit is or is not a Mode 4 service supplier is not necessarily evident from the application itself, nor necessarily relevant to its success. The trade and business interest in predictable, efficient access to foreign markets is hampered by the lack of national regulatory systems designed to facilitate the movement of Mode 4 service suppliers.[24]

Notwithstanding the efforts of the negotiators of the GATS during the Uruguay Round, who created the definition of Mode 4 to exclude complex and controversial migration considerations from this services trade framework, the ability to effectively implement existing Mode 4 commitments suffers from the lack of

---

[23] For an interesting comparative analysis, see D. Papademetriou, 'Migration Management in the Traditional Countries of Immigration', in *World Migration 2003, Managing Migration: Challenges and Responses for People on the Move* (Geneva, IOM 2003) p. 142.

[24] See the presentation by E. Yost at the IOM/World Bank/WTO seminar on *Managing the Movement of People: What Can be Learned for Mode 4 of the GATS?* (4-5 Oct. 2004), noting that 'each government puts employees in different categories, but from a company perspective they are all just employees, and educating, training, recruiting and placing workers on a global basis is as important as manufacturing, investing and marketing on a global basis'. Documents relating to this workshop, including background papers, presentations and the final report, are available on the IOM website at <http://www.iom.int/en/know/idm/tms_200410.shtml> (hereafter, the '2004 seminar').

regulatory 'fit' with concepts familiar to domestic migration law, as do prospects for future liberalization. Whereas the Uruguay Round negotiators sought to define away the problem of migration law and practice, the Doha negotiators now recognize that migration regulators need to be brought to the table and inform the discussion, both to improve the ability to effectively implement existing Mode 4 commitments and to identify ways to further reduce barriers to services trade in a way that accommodates their legitimate concerns.

What are the principal concerns of migration regulators? Those most frequently cited can be summarized in the following five categories. First, as labour market, security and other national conditions fluctuate regularly, migration regulators place a high value on flexibility, the ability to adjust to changing needs and priorities; the GATS, on the other hand, is a permanent, binding and multilateral treaty commitment requiring equal access to service suppliers of all Member States in perpetuity. Second, related to this, migration regulators seek to ensure that foreign workers do not compete with or undermine the conditions of the local workforce with respect to such issues as wage parity, i.e., foreign workers should receive the same pay and benefits as domestic workers in the same industry. Third, regulators are concerned about a range of social, security and non-trade related matters, such as access to health care, education, social security, and other welfare benefits, as well as safety, security or health threats to the populace. Fourth, while Mode 4 is designed to address only temporary movement, a principal concern of migration regulators is the risk that temporary entry becomes a means of permanent stay, either by overstaying an authorized permit or by the capacity to switch to other visa categories which provide for a more secure residence status. Finally, for many developing countries, the emigration of skilled workers and the potential for this to lead to skills shortages, brain drain, and 'brain waste'[25] for the home economy remains a significant concern, particularly in such critical, high-emigration sectors as education and health care.

3. Developments Since 2003

Since the publication of the Charnovitz article, there has been much activity on Mode 4, including some of relevance to migration policy makers and practitioners. There have been developments both within and outside the context of the GATS negotiations.

[25] 'Brain waste' occurs when skilled migrants are unable to find jobs in the destination country in accordance with their qualifications and skills for a number of reasons, such as the absence of mechanisms that adequately recognize diplomas, qualifications and experience obtained in their home country or elsewhere, insufficient linguistic ability, or discrimination in employment. In these circumstances, the home economy is adversely affected because such workers are earning lower than expected salaries with the result that their remittances will also be reduced. Similarly, the extent of the knowledge and skills transferred back to their country of origin will not be of the quality that it could have been if migrants were able to find suitable employment in the destination country.

3.1 Outside the negotiations

It is now recognized that a key first step to realizing the potential that the movement of people might bring to global economic growth is to bring together trade and migration policy makers and practitioners, in order to explore the links between their two disciplines, to identify ways of improving the effectiveness of existing trade commitments regarding the movement of persons as providers of services, and to explore possibilities for further liberalization of trade in this field.

Since the April 2002 symposium on Movement of Persons Under GATS, sponsored by the WTO and the World Bank, two important seminars have been held to bring together trade and migration officials in a non-negotiating context. The first took place in November 2003, jointly organized by the Organization for Economic Cooperation and Development (OECD), the World Bank and the IOM.[26] It brought together for the first time trade and migration officials from 98 countries and from a wide range of international organizations, as well as representatives of business and civil society. For the OECD, this seminar was part of the annual series of OECD Services Experts Meetings organized by the organization's Trade Directorate. For the IOM, it was part of the series of inter-sessional workshops of the IOM Council's International Dialogue on Migration, in line with its goal of contributing to a better understanding of contemporary migration and facilitating inter-state cooperation in its management. The seminar addressed three main issues. First, it looked at the relationship between trade and migration, situating GATS Mode 4 in the broader context of temporary labour migration. It examined existing schemes intended to facilitate temporary movement at the national, bilateral and regional levels, and asked what lessons could be drawn from these schemes for GATS Mode 4. Second, it explored issues relating to the management of Mode 4, and temporary labour migration more generally, in both home and host countries. Lastly, it explored what progress could be achieved in the current GATS negotiations, and areas for possible further work.

Some of the key findings from the seminar include the following:

- Countries' limited use of Mode 4 is partly linked to the lack of flexibility of GATS commitments in a context of rapidly changing needs, the complexity of the Agreement, and the conceptual and terminological gap between GATS definitions and migration regimes.
- There is a need to better identify the range of complementary policies required to manage the potential costs and reap the benefits of increased Mode 4 liberalization. Such policies include incentives to turn brain drain into brain circulation; utilizing greater commitments under Mode 4 to increase other forms of trade; remittance management; and measures to manage the social and labour market impact of temporary foreign workers.

[26] For a full report on this seminar, see the OECD report on *Trade and Migration: Building Bridges for Global Labour Mobility* (Paris, OECD 2004).

– Given the political will and appropriate policy responses, concerns about the problem of overstaying are manageable. A number of countries are successfully combating it by mobilizing resources for monitoring the stay and departure of temporary migrants, and focusing on employer obligations in sponsored entry programs. Better management of remittances can also be crucial in establishing an enabling environment for return, by helping to create opportunities in countries of origin and enhance the welfare of receiving families.
– In promoting greater labour mobility, the possible consequences of increased labour supply, which may be unequally distributed among different sectors, need to be taken into account, as some groups in society may be negatively affected – for example, from a trade union perspective, Mode 4 liberalization is perceived as having the potential to open the door to unregulated migration, with consequent negative impacts on local employment, wages and conditions, especially for low skilled labour.
– There is a need for international cooperation in managing migration: while the WTO is not an appropriate forum for migration-related debate, international dialogue on this issue should be encouraged in forums such as the IOM's Council and, for issues involving labour and migration, the ILO as well.

As a follow up to the 2003 seminar, in October 2004, the IOM, the World Bank and the WTO co-hosted a seminar entitled 'What Can Be Learned from Existing Approaches to Managing Temporary Labour Migration for GATS Mode 4?'[27] This seminar, attended by trade and migration officials from 89 countries and representatives of international organizations, businesses and civil society, took the analysis of the 2003 seminar to a deeper level by examining case studies of practice at the national, bilateral and regional levels in managing temporary labour migration and regional trade regimes. A principal concern of trade negotiators is how to create a set of reciprocal obligations and liberalization incentives between countries home to and host of temporary service providers. In other words, what can the home countries of service providers seeking access to foreign markets bring to the negotiating table that is of sufficient interest to the receiving countries to encourage them to open their markets to foreign providers? Apart from offering needed skills and services, what non-trade measures might be available to increase the willingness of destination countries to open their markets to temporary workers from abroad? These questions informed the development of this seminar and the series of case studies that were presented. What emerged was a focus on ways to create greater confidence in migration managers that temporary workers do not pose a security threat, that they have the necessary qualifications to perform the specified service, that sufficient flexibility is retained to adjust to

[27] 2004 seminar, loc. cit. n. 24.

changes in the domestic economy and labour market, and that temporary labour migration remains truly temporary.

The case studies explored existing measures employed by states to address each of these concerns. For example, certain measures taken at the national level were examined, such as the multi-level work permit scheme of the United Kingdom, which seeks to balance the interests of employers in being able to recruit and transfer skilled people from abroad and the desire to safeguard the welfare of the domestic workforce, and the comprehensive programme developed by the Philippines to facilitate the overseas employment of Filipino workers, aimed at enhancing the competitiveness of labour, empowering the workforce, and ensuring workers' welfare and protection. The programme in the Philippines contains a variety of welfare initiatives for overseas workers which help ensure that they will return, and provides pre-departure skills training and testing targeted at labour demands in destination countries, and employer accreditation.

A series of bilateral agreements in which the country of origin is responsible for pre-departure screening, i.e., checking both the qualifications and criminal records of potential employees and the reliability of employers, were also analyzed. Similarly to the national measures, a number of these agreements contain provisions that seek to create an interest for both workers and employers to see the former return at the end of their contracts, for example through facilitated re-entry of the migrant in the work programme and re-hiring by the employer, providing for employer sanctions in case of breach, and making a worker ineligible for a future visa and/or employment if he/she fails to return to the country of origin at the end of the contract period. As a result, the record of return of migrants to their home countries under some of these agreements is high. Some bilateral agreements contain mechanisms to protect the domestic labour market by verifying that a domestic labour shortage exists before opening the market to overseas workers. Germany employs particularly interesting protective mechanisms in some bilateral agreements: it inserts a quota adjustment clause, making access quotas adjustable as a result of changes in the level of unemployment, and a regional market protection clause, which prevents labour migration into certain areas of Germany with very high unemployment rates. In addition, many bilateral agreements contain measures relating to the protection of migrant workers, such as designating liaison officers in destination countries to assist them, establishing standard employment contracts and regulations for the activities of private agencies, and providing migrants with information on their legal rights.

A variety of approaches to facilitating mobility through regional trade agreements was also explored during the seminar. Such agreements range on a spectrum from those that are similar to the GATS in being limited to the temporary movement of service providers, through those that facilitate movement for specified trade- or investment-related activity and those that provide for free movement of labour including entry to the labour market, to those that cover human mobility more generally, including migration that is permanent and/or for reasons other than work. Those at the more liberal end of the spectrum, facilitating the greatest degree of mobility, are generally related to broader economic integration arrangements.[28] Specific approaches to facilitating mobility that offer insights of potential relevance to Mode 4 include the pre-clearance mechanism employed through the Asia-Pacific Economic Cooperation (APEC) Business Travel Card, which facilitates entry but does not confer any rights of access, and the North American Free Trade Agreement (NAFTA) scheme, which confers rights of temporary entry to certain business persons.[29]

One session during the seminar devoted to consideration of national implementation of international trade obligations revealed that, while regulatory uniformity across all countries on Mode 4 – that is, common national definitions and legislation – is unlikely, the concepts and definitions it uses need to be better integrated into national regulatory schemes if its commitments are to be successfully implemented, as highlighted in the discussion above.

Employers and workers' representatives shared their perspectives on labour mobility and Mode 4. Not surprisingly, employers support predictable and liberalized rules for the admission of foreign workers, in order to have access to a larger pool of labour from which they can select employees, and to be able to quickly and efficiently transfer workers to other locations. Employers often experience time delays in hiring foreign workers and transferring employees, and are frustrated with the lack of transparency of many states' migration policies as well as lack of consistency between the migration policies of different states. The distinction in Mode 4 between the services and manufacturing sectors is meaningless when viewed from the interests of business in liberalizing both. In addition, the exclusive focus of Mode 4 on temporary movement is also frustrating as employers are often interested in longer term involvement with foreign workers, particularly the highly skilled.

In terms of workers' representatives, trade unions are focused primarily on protecting the interests of their members in their own countries, with particular emphasis on the lower-skilled – whom they see as relatively less well protected by legal, economic and social arrangements. Trade unions are concerned about any possible expansion of the scope of Mode 4 to include lower-skilled workers, particularly over the implications for payment into social security schemes from which they are unlikely to benefit, the lack of protection of rights such as the freedom to join trade unions, and the reluctance of the sending countries to pursue enforcement of their citizens' rights for fear of host country reprisals.

The dialogue at the 2004 seminar was highly constructive, and not only helped improve understanding between the trade and migration communities but also served to build confidence in the ability of these communities to work together to achieve mutual and/or complementary goals. As evidence of this, a number of participants suggested that a template be developed with the successful compo-

[28] J. Nielson, *Labour Mobility in Regional Trade Agreements* (Paris, OECD 2002) <http://www.olis.oecd.org/olis/2002doc.nsf/43bb6130e5e86e5fc12569fa005d004c/3fa47b23cfa41557c1256b96002af272/$FILE/JT00123956.PDF>.

[29] On NAFTA, see the chapter in this volume by Gustavo A. Flores-Macías.

nents of existing measures to manage temporary labour migration, and considered for use in Mode 4 negotiations.

Some of the key findings from the seminar include the following:

- Continued dialogue is the single most important means to create a better understanding and to build trust between the migration and trade communities, to develop confidence in their ability to work together, and to identify avenues and methods for making progress, whether within Mode 4 or in pursuit of a broader goal of more effective and productively managed migration for work.

- There is a particular need for progress in increasing transparency of information about national migration procedures with a bearing on trade in services, with specific reference to temporary movement under the GATS. In a related vein, there is a continuing need for bridging the conceptual and regulatory gaps between trade and migration by providing Mode 4 with an identity within domestic migration laws. At a minimum, it is necessary to clearly indicate where within existing national migration regulations Mode 4 movement can be and is covered.

- There is a need to establish a two-way set of commitments, as opposed to imposing obligations solely on the receiving countries to make Mode 4 workable. Greater exploration is required of what the countries seeking market access can bring to the negotiating table, such as commitments to verify the qualifications, identity and criminal records of potential service providers; to cooperate in efforts to reduce the incidence of irregular migration; to accept the return of nationals, etc.

- Lessons can be drawn from existing practice in domestic administrative procedures and national regulations, including existing bilateral and regional migration and trade agreements. Templates could be developed based on these lessons that identify regulatory policies and related measures that help make temporary labour mobility successful.

In order to draw upon the rich experiences of states in managing temporary labour migration through bilateral agreements, the IOM has, since the 2004 seminar and with the support of the World Bank, been undertaking a more in-depth study of bilateral mechanisms employed by states to regulate and facilitate temporary labour migration.

3.2 Within the negotiations

In recent months, a number of proposals have been put forward to help clarify the basis upon which the GATS negotiations may be able to achieve progress. These 'horizontal' proposals are distinct from offers in the form of sectoral commitments in individual Members' schedules in that they would apply to all sectors.

First, the Modalities for the Special Treatment for Least Developed Countries (LDCs) in the Negotiations on Trade in Services[30] were developed in recognition both of the particular interests of the LDCs in the Doha Development Agenda, and of the assistance required for such countries to be able to fulfil their objectives, in terms of increased trade and investment and the associated benefits. The Modalities highlight the important role that the services economy plays in achieving social and developmental objectives, including poverty reduction, human and sustainable development, as well as the specific developmental challenges LDCs face in this regard; further, they increase the level of flexibility accorded to LDCs through Articles IV and XIX of the GATS, and reiterate that Members shall make specific commitments in sectors and modes of supply that are of export interest to the LDCs.

Paragraph 6 of the Modalities states that

> 'Members shall, as provided for in Articles IV and XIX of the GATS, give special priority to providing effective market access in sectors and modes of supply of export interest to LDCs, through negotiated specific commitments pursuant to Parts III and IV of the GATS. LDCs should indicate those services sectors and modes of supply that represent priority in their development policies, so that Members take these priorities into account in the negotiations'.[31]

Paragraph 9 goes on to say,

> '[i]t is recognized that the temporary movement of natural persons supplying services (Mode 4) provides potential benefits to the sending and recipient Members. LDCs have indicated that this is one of the most important means of supplying services internationally. Members shall, to the extent possible, and consistently with Article XIX of the GATS, consider undertaking commitments to provide access in Mode 4, taking into account all categories of natural persons identified by LDCs in their requests.'[32]

The LDCs have had difficulty in identifying their specific sectors of export interest due to constraints such as limited technical and analytical resources to devote to exploring export opportunities, and a lack of targeted technical assistance to help them in this regard.[33] Nonetheless, they have consistently expressed their export interest in Mode 4 generally, in all types of occupations and categories of natural persons and specifically in such sectors as tourism, construction, and professional services – with a specific emphasis on non-professional service pro-

---

[30] WTO Doc. TN/S/13 (5 Sept. 2003) (hereafter, 'the Modalities').

[31] Ibid., at para. 6.

[32] Ibid., at para. 9.

[33] Communication of the LDC Group, 'Implementation of the Modalities for the Special Treatment for Least Developed Country Members in Trade in Services Negotiations', WTO Doc. JOB (05)/114 (17 June 2005).

viders (including semi- and low-skilled). The LDC Group has now posed a series of questions to Members designed to prompt discussion and facilitate implementation of these modalities in the interests of LDCs. For example, how can negotiations on future disciplines, or guidelines on domestic regulation, adequately incorporate LDCs' interests, particularly with respect to effectively implementing Mode 4 commitments?

Second, it is now recognized that one of the main impediments to further liberalization is the lack of regulatory transparency; in another words, the lack of adequate information on opportunities and conditions of entry for service providers. Regulations governing the entry and stay of foreign workers intending to provide services are not harmonized globally, but rather are adopted at the national level according to national priorities and as part of national immigration policies, legislation and administration. There is no general governing standard and no central repository for information on these requirements.

Transparency is key for several reasons: (a) for the business community, the lack of clear and readily-accessible information can be a major obstacle to mobility, and may particularly affect individual service suppliers (or small- and medium-size enterprises) as they lack the resources of large companies to learn about national regulatory requirements across a range of WTO Members; (b) improved information means better planning and business strategies; (c) transparency can help countries to better manage immigration issues because they can more readily obtain and exchange information; and (d) lack of transparency means that it is hard for trade negotiators to convince the business community and other stakeholders of the benefits of GATS, and of trade liberalization more generally.[34] Here, better information will increase the policy makers' understanding of the relationship between trade commitments and immigration requirements.

There are several transparency requirements included in the GATS. Article III requires Members to publish promptly all measures of general application that pertain to or affect the operation of the GATS. Members are also obliged to provide notification annually of any new or changed laws, regulations or administrative guidelines that significantly affect trade in services covered by specific commitments. Lastly, they are required to establish enquiry points to respond to requests for information from other WTO Members.[35]

Some negotiators have included in their GATS commitments themselves detailed information on how the promised access might be utilized. Some commentators, such as Chaudhuri et al.,[36] go a step further and recommend that a consolidated text, including all measures that pertain to the temporary admission

[34] I owe this insight to Paul Henry, Senior Policy Analyst, Economic Policy and Programs, Citizenship and Immigration, Canada.

[35] Transparency issues come up in other areas: for example, Art. VI.4 on domestic regulations refers to objective and transparent criteria related to qualifications requirements and procedures, technical standards and licensing requirements.

[36] S. Chaudhuri, A. Mattoo and R. Self, 'Liberalizing Mode 4: A Possible Approach', paper presented at the UNCTAD Expert Group Meeting on Movement of Natural Persons, Geneva, 29-31 July 2003.

of natural persons and information on the materials or evidence required of an applicant seeking temporary admission into their territories, be inserted as an additional commitment in Members' schedules. However, such approaches have been criticized by those who think that schedules are not the most appropriate vehicles for this kind of information,

> 'given that they represent binding legal commitments, and WTO members may be reluctant to bind administrative procedures, including undertakings regarding processing times for, or costs of, applications'.[37]

On 21 June 2005, Canada made its Proposal on Transparency of Horizontal Mode 4 Commitments,[38] in which it suggests that each Member should provide, 'voluntarily and separate from its specific commitments, all relevant information sources for each of its commitments'.[39] The idea is that listing the various laws, regulations, policies, practices or administrative guidelines would 'make more transparent the regulatory context of a particular commitment'.[40] This information should be made available not only to requesting Members, but to their trade officials and business people as well. Canada attached to the Proposal a template for the presentation of the relevant information. It also submitted a Communication entitled 'Mode 4 commitments and economic need tests' (ENTs), which encourages Members to increase transparency by exchanging information on their Mode 4 ENTs along the lines of a template attached to the Communication in an appendix.[41]

Australia, supporting the Canadian initiative, submitted on 25 June 2005 a version of its own revised Horizontal Mode 4 offer,[42] following the transparency template provided by Canada. In this document, Australia states that the information it provides is given for transparency purposes only and should not be considered as forming part of its specific commitments.[43]

The third proposal that has been made within the GATS negotiations concerns domestic regulations. Article VI.4 of the GATS calls for the development of any necessary disciplines which will ensure that 'measures relating to qualification requirements and procedures, technical standards and licensing requirements do not constitute unnecessary barriers to trade in services'. In particular, these disciplines will ensure that such requirements are based on objective and transparent criteria; that they are not more burdensome than necessary to ensure the quality of the service; and that licensing procedures do not in themselves constitute a restriction on the supply of services. Disciplines of this sort were developed in

[37] OECD, *Trade and Migration*, op. cit. n. 26, at p. 112.
[38] WTO Doc. TN/S/W/47 (21 June 2005).
[39] Ibid., at para. 7.
[40] Ibid., at para. 7, n. 3.
[41] WTO Doc. TN/S/W/46 (21 June 2005).
[42] WTO Doc. TN/S/W/48 (30 June 2005).
[43] Ibid., at para. 2.

1998 for accounting. The Working Party on Domestic Regulation has been entrusted with the mandate of GATS Article VI.4. Some outstanding issues relate to the scope and coverage of disciplines. For example, some Members are in favour of development of horizontally applicable disciplines and have submitted proposals to this end (Switzerland, the European Union, and Japan); others would prefer disciplines tailor-made to specific sectors. Another issue where the opinion of Members diverges is whether disciplines only apply to sectors where commitments have been made or to all measures of general application. Japan, in its proposal for a new GATS Annex on Domestic Regulations, submitted in May 2003,[44] includes both possibilities, with obligations on transparency applicable to all sectors whether or not commitments have been made, and obligations related to a 'necessity test'[45] (to determine whether a regulation was 'least burdensome' to trade in seeking to fulfil the regulatory objective) applicable only where commitments have been made.[46] In addition, it did not preclude the possibility of the adoption of disciplines in specific sectors.

Looking at the proposals that have been put forward in this area, it appears that the priority given to the five types of regulatory measures covered[47] varies from country to country.[48] Some are general in scope; for example, a group of developing countries, including Brazil, Colombia, and the Philippines, proposed in an informal 'room document' certain 'Elements for draft disciplines on domestic regulation',[49] including definitions of the different types of domestic regulations and transparency requirements for their promulgation and application.[50] Others focus on qualification requirements,[51] or on technical standards.[52] The most con-

[44] Communication from Japan, *Draft Annex on Domestic Regulation*, WTO Doc. JOB(03)/45/Rev.1 (2 May 2003).

[45] Already present in the Discipline for Accountancy.

[46] It covers also other issues, such as the availability of administrative and judicial reviews.

[47] General provisions, transparency requirements, licensing requirements and procedures, qualification requirements and procedures, and technical standards.

[48] The US informal paper on transparency with regard to domestic regulation, *Proposal for Transparency: Disciplines in Domestic Regulation* (WTO Doc. JOB(04)/128, 15 Sept. 2004), suggests introducing a 'prior comment period' before the entry into force of a proposed regulation, during which time stakeholders would be able to comment on it. It also proposes that Members should be required to clearly publish regulations and provide 'inquiry points' to which interested parties would be able to address questions about a particular regulatory measure.

[49] Communication from Brazil, Colombia, Dominican Republic and the Philippines, 'Elements for draft disciplines on domestic regulation', Room Document (18 Feb. 2005) <http://www.tradeobservatory.org/library.cfm?refid=60487>.

[50] Ibid., at paras. 11-17. The draft rules also reaffirmed each Member's right to regulate and to introduce new regulations (para. 5), as well as special and differential treatment for developing countries (e.g., longer time-frames for compliance and technical assistance support). Ibid., at paras. 18-22.

[51] Communication from Chile, India, Pakistan and Thailand, 'Proposed Elements for Disciplines on Qualification Requirements and Procedures', WTO Doc. JOB(05)/50 (30 March 2005).

[52] Communication from Mexico, 'Mexico's Experience of Disciplines on Technical Standards and Regulations in Services', WTO Doc. S/WPDR/W/30 (24 Sept. 2004); Communication from Switzerland, 'Proposal for Disciplines on Technical Standards in Services', WTO Doc. S/WPDR/W/32 (1 Feb. 2005).

troversial question may be whether the GATS covers measures related to visa and entry permits: Colombia, Peru and the Philippines, in a room document on 'Mode 4-regulatory issues', argued that they must in principle be deemed to be included in the term 'measures' as used in the Annex.

Other key issues remaining in the current round of the GATS negotiations on Mode 4 include the categories of persons to be covered and the removal of restrictive market access conditions.

As mentioned above, the categories of persons covered by WTO Members' commitments are often limited to service suppliers linked with commercial presence in the host country (such as intra-corporate transferees). This limitation is problematic for developing countries, which lack extensive commercial presence in WTO Member States and do not have the capital resources to establish such a presence. Developing countries are advocating for the expansion of commitments to include categories of natural persons who are not linked to commercial presence, notably 'contractual service suppliers' and 'independent professionals'.[53] Similarly, many developing countries are seeking deeper commitments in service sectors of particular export interest to them, such as tourism and construction. While the inclusion of these categories would provide more opportunities for developing countries to benefit from Mode 4 movement, the lack of corresponding categories in domestic immigration laws and regulations could continue to pose regulatory problems for migration managers.

Finally, the issue of removal of restrictive market access conditions attached to the various categories of natural persons (both those are linked to and those that are de-linked from commercial presence) is a continuing concern.[54] For example, proponents argue that ENTs or labour market tests should be limited to exceptional circumstances, and that any such application should be non-discriminatory and transparent. In addition, they propose that a minimum duration of stay could be specified for each category, in order to lessen unpredictability and the confusion between temporary and permanent stay. They also support the provision of possibilities for renewal of temporary stay, subject to the fulfilment of certain conditions, with renewal procedures clearly specified and less onerous than the initial process. In addition, they encourage the elimination of absolute wage parity as a pre-requisite for the entry of natural persons – in its place, minimum wages could be fixed for foreign service providers, and/or minimum salary benchmarks could be developed. Similarly, they argue that numerical quotas should be limited to exceptional circumstances; where they are used, the criteria for fixing such quotas should be clearly specified, as should the possibility for increases based on

[53] Communication from Bolivia, Chile, Colombia, Dominican Republic, Guatemala, India, Indonesia, Mexico, Pakistan, Peru, Philippines and Thailand, 'Assessment of Mode 4 offers of Members: Review of Progress as established in Paragraph 15 of the Guidelines and Procedures for the Negotiations on Trade in Services (S/L/93)', WTO Doc. JOB(05)/131 (30 June 2005) (hereafter, the 'Developing Country Communication') para. 3(a).

[54] Ibid., at para. 3(d).

changes in the market situation. Lastly, while rules requiring the recognition of qualifications cannot be eliminated, care should be taken to develop licensing and qualifications disciplines that do not block effective and meaningful market access.

4. The Hong Kong Ministerial Conference

At the Hong Kong Ministerial Conference on the Doha Work Programme, held on the 13-18 December 2005, ministers from the WTO's Member governments approved a 44-page Declaration.[55] The principal merit of the Declaration is to put the Doha round trade negotiations 'back on track'. With regard to services, the text in reality satisfies neither those WTO Member States who wanted the language in the Services Annex of the draft Declaration to be made more ambitious (e.g., the EU, in exchange for limited commitments on agriculture), nor those who sought to weaken the text.

Annex C on services was the most controversial part of the Declaration. Several developing countries opposed its inclusion on the grounds that it had not been agreed by Members (it was drafted by the Chair of the services' negotiations), and that it introduced qualitative objectives for each Mode and a requirement for Members to enter into plurilateral negotiations if requested to do so. The original text was, however, watered down, with the recommendations for achieving liberalization of trade in services rewritten in a less mandatory and prescriptive language (they are now to guide Members' actions to 'the maximum extent possible'). Article 7 of the final text still advocates the adoption of a plurilateral method of negotiation, in addition to the bilateral 'request and offer' approach used predominantly up to now. Under this method, supported by the EU and other developed countries, a Member or a group of Members can present a request in any specific sector or mode of supply, while those to whom the requests have been made shall consider them, with a view to entering into plurilateral negotiations. Developing countries consider this approach a threat to the existing flexibilities of the GATS, which allow them to choose freely which sectors to liberalize, and how far they should do so. They fear that the new provisions will place more pressure on them to engage in negotiations.[56]

More specifically on Mode 4, the text refers to 'new or improved commitments on the categories of Contractual Services Suppliers, Independent Professionals and Others, de-linked from commercial presence', and of 'Intra-corporate Transferees and Business Visitors, to reflect *inter alia* removal or substantial re-

[55] Declaration of the WTO Ministerial Conference, 6th Session, Hong Kong 13-18 Dec. 2005, WTO Doc. WT/MIN(05)/DEC (22 Dec. 2005).

[56] With a view to addressing the concerns of G-90 countries and some Association of Southeast Asian Nations (ASEAN) Members, an explicit reference was made to the fact that collective requests shall be considered in the context of paragraph 2 of Article XIX of the GATS, stipulating that liberalization should take account of countries' development levels.

duction of economic needs tests and indication of prescribed duration of stay and possibility of renewal, if any'.[57] This wording is not as strong as that suggested in the 'alternative annex C' advanced by the G 90 (including the group of African, Caribbean and Pacific countries, the LDC group and the African Union), which requested WTO Members to ensure that any negotiated commitments reflect 'improvements in all four modes of supply both in terms of *market access and national treatment* and in particular Mode 4 liberalization in categories de-linked from commercial presence'.[58] Some trade analysts consider that the positive gains from Mode 4 along these lines will be limited, and for most developing countries will actually be outweighed by pressures to open up their markets in Mode 3 (the text calls for 'enhanced foreign equity participation'[59] and for 'allowing greater flexibility on the types of legal entity permitted').[60]

A new-time frame for the services negotiations was adopted, with very tight deadlines. WTO Member States were supposed to have presented plurilateral requests to other Members by 28 February 2006, and to come up with a final draft schedule of commitments by 31 October of that year, with a view to reaching a final agreement and concluding the round by the end of the year. Such a tight time-frame for issues which have been discussed for many years in the WTO without much progress was motivated by the upcoming expiry, in July 2007, of the 'fast track' (trade promotion) authority given to the US Administration by its Congress.[61] Therefore, missing these deadlines might result in a substantial stalling of multilateral action.

5. Conclusion

In sum, there is much at stake in the current round of trade negotiations on Mode 4 of the GATS that is of direct relevance and concern to migration managers, and to the development of international migration law more generally. These negotiations are likely to have a significant impact on prospects for the development of an international legal framework for the movement of people, both within the context of the Mode 4 negotiations (with respect to the limited categories of service providers on which agreement is likely at this time), and by fostering

[57] WTO Ministerial Declaration, loc. cit. n. 55, Annex C, Arts. 1(d)(i) and (ii).

[58] Available at <www.tradeobservatory.org/library.cfm?refid=78019>.

[59] WTO Ministerial Declaration, loc. cit. n. 55, Annex C, Art. 1(c)(i).

[60] Ibid., Art. 1(c)(iii).

[61] This means that Congress must vote the deal as a whole, without the possibility of introducing any amendments (and thus preventing the United States from having to renegotiate the whole deal). Given the current political climate in the US Congress, it is unlikely to be extended, which will make it more difficult to have the United States on board after this date. Even before this happens, a supplementary difficulty might still arise in relation to Mode 4: after the United States-Chile and United States-Singapore trade agreements, the Senate and House judiciary committees reminded the Administration that immigration policies fall within the exclusive competence of Congress, and should no longer be part of bilateral or multilateral trade agreements.

spin-off efforts to create more coherent means of managing labour mobility at the regional and global levels. While great progress in Mode 4 is highly unlikely at this time, the pressure to conclude a trade agreement is usefully serving as a catalyst for the greater exploration of ways to create a more efficient, fair and safe approach to the management of global labour mobility.

Selected Bibliography

Chanda, R., 'Movement and Presence of Natural Persons and Developing Countries: Issues and Proposals for the GATS Negotiations', *Trade-Related Agenda, Development and Equity (TRADE) Working Paper 19*, South Centre (May 2004) <http://www.southcentre.org/publications/workingpapers/paper19/wp19.pdf>.

Charnowitz, S., 'Trade Law Norms on International Migration', in T.A. Aleinikoff and V. Chetail (eds.), *Migration and International Legal Norms* (The Hague, T.M.C. Asser Press 2003) p. 241.

Chaudhuri, S., A. Mattoo and R. Self, 'Liberalizing Mode 4: A Possible Approach', paper presented at the UNCTAD Expert Group Meeting on Movement of Natural Persons, Geneva, 29-31 July 2003.

International Labour Office, *Towards a Fair Deal for Migrant Workers in the Global Economy* (Geneva, ILO 2004) <http://www.ilo.org/public/english/standards/relm/ilc/ilc92/pdf/rep-vi.pdf>.

Mattoo, A., and A. Carzaniga (eds.), *Moving People to Deliver Services* (New York/Washington DC, Oxford University Press and World Bank 2003).

Nielson, J., 'Trade and Migration: GATS Mode 4', in *World Migration 2005: Costs and Benefits of International Migration* (Geneva, IOM 2005) p. 185.

—, *Labour Mobility in Regional Trade Agreements* (Paris, OECD 2002) <http://www.olis.oecd.org/olis/2002doc.nsf/43bb6130e5e86e5fc12569fa005d004c/3fa47b23cfa41557c1256b96002af272/$FILE/JT00123956.PDF>.

Nielson, J., and D. Taglioni, 'A Quick Guide to the GATS and Mode 4', *OECD – World Bank – IOM Seminar in Trade and Migration* (2003) <http://www.iom.int/jahia/webdav/site/myjahiasite/shared/shared/mainsite/microsites/IDM/workshops/Trade_2004_04051004/related%20docs/quick_guide.pdf>.

OECD, *Trade and Migration: Building Bridges for Global Labour Mobility* (Paris, OECD 2004).

Papademetriou, D., 'Migration Management in the Traditional Countries of Immigration', in *World Migration 2003, Managing Migration: Challenges and Responses for People on the Move* (Geneva, IOM 2003) p. 142.

Chapter 7
GLOBAL REMITTANCES AND THE LAW: A REVIEW OF REGIONAL TRENDS AND REGULATORY ISSUES

Manuel Orozco*

1. Introduction

The global context of international relations is inextricably associated with the movement of people, goods and services. Migrants, for example, have increasingly linked their home countries into the global economy through their economic relationships, and their remittances in particular. Globally, at least US$232 billion was sent home by around 200 million migrants to their families in 2005. These considerable financial flows are remittances, the money that labour migrants send home to their families and communities in their countries of origin.[1] Remittances generate large global capital flows that present significant opportunities for businesses and financial enterprises.

The process by which migrants send money is directly related to a market structure that involves a competitive environment, a range of players, and rules and regulations that define the terms of reference under which money can be sent. Within the context of the law, remittances are considered as a financial payment system that involves exchanges of foreign currency. The regulatory environments thus deal with the nature of the transactions, the ability to track the fund payment, and in some cases, the impact on foreign exchange.

One of the problems in remittance transfers stems from a lack of correspondence between rules imposed on transfers and people's (remitters and businesses) realistic capacity to comply with them. For example, remitters are often required to provide inaccessible forms of identification, or companies are required to police their clients. The end result is that people choose informal networks. It is thus important to find a balance between reality and the law in order to improve the ability to regulate these increasingly important economic practices.

The effect that the law has on these transfers in turn has consequences for development. In fact, if appropriate mechanisms are adapted to the needs of senders and recipients, remittance regulations can also serve as an engine to transform

* Director of Remittances and Development at the Inter-American Dialogue, where he also heads the Central America program.

[1] Remittances do occur domestically, typically from urban to rural areas, but these are not considered in this analysis.

informal transfers into formal flows. By creating a framework that encourages the use of formal channels, the impact that remittances have on development is increased. This chapter reviews and explores the various regulatory frameworks that exist across various regions of the world.

2. Remittance Intermediation and Regulatory Environments

In order to explain these money transfers, it is important to understand the behaviour of the remittance marketplace. The demand for remittance services is accompanied by a supply side that often is more complex and diffuse than imagined. Intermediaries of remittance transfers represent a complex array of large and small businesses, which includes both licensed and unlicensed corporations. However, the functioning of money transfers is dependent upon the extent to which a competitive environment exists, the types of regulatory frameworks in place and their attendant costs, and the preferences of remittance senders as to the kinds of players involved. Many factors may influence each element of market functioning; for example, banks potentially have greater opportunities in this regard because they can offer financial services 'bundles', linking remittance transfers to other banking products and thus adding value to the service for the consumer. These innovative products are an increasingly common feature of the marketplace.

Overall, there are three kinds of remittance sending intermediaries: non-bank financial intermediaries (NBFIs); banks (and credit unions) that provide remittance sending services; and informal intermediaries, such as non-formal couriers or even friends who take, or facilitate the sending of, money to the intended recipient. Depending on what part of the world one is focusing on, the proportion of sending via these three means varies.

The choice of which industry player will be used for transmission is an important part of the cost of sending remittances and the relative profits available to each party. In addition to this choice, the other two factors that dominate the functioning of the marketplace of transfers are competition and government regulation. Furthermore, these factors are relevant for both the sending and receiving markets.

The marketplace of both NFBIs and banks in remittance intermediation is shaped by numerous issues: the number and type of companies involved; the degree of competition; government regulations and policy environment; the type and number of remittance and related services that are provided; and the demand for remittance services from immigrants.

All businesses involved in remittance transfers are subject to local, national and international laws and regulations in the countries within which they operate. Regulatory frameworks help define and structure the ways in which private transactions take place. Countries regulate the kind of institution allowed to make international money transfers, and the conditions in which foreign currency transfers are permitted. Critical issues concerning regulatory environments include the number of regulatory bodies, the rules they establish for inbound and outbound transfers, and compliance with the rules on financial services. Other important factors are identification requirements of the sender or recipient; registration and licensing of the remitting company, bank, or distribution agent; and financial disclosure information. At least nine issues are commonly covered in the regulation of remittances, and include aspects relating to insurance, anti-money laundering, foreign exchange controls, and 'know your customer' rules. These issues are listed below, and most countries cover some if not all of these aspects:

1. the number of regulatory bodies (Central Banks, Ministries of Finance, supervisory agencies);

2. the number and type of businesses allowed (fully licensed banks, NBFIs, Post Offices, etc.);

3. insurance requirements to operate (bond, capital requirements, etc.);

4. types of documentation required from customers to perform a transaction;

5. the control of commissions, fees and other transaction costs;

6. the method of remittance transfer processing (bulk, batched or individual);

7. anti-money laundering programs and guidelines;

8. the amount limits set for 'know your customer' requirements;

9. enforcement and compliance issues.

In all, the complexity of legal arrangements in a globalized world tends to complicate the regulatory environment. Regulations can and often do increase costs and bar certain players and stakeholders from legal participation in the remittance market. For example, undocumented migrants may fear or be prevented from using officially sanctioned remitters because they lack the requisite local identification. Likewise, smaller transmitters may be prevented from growing because of legal requirements that they provide verifiable guarantees.

Regulations are not the only barriers to sending or, more often, receiving remittances. Other obstacles may include the small volume of remittance flows between particular countries, war or civil disruptions and disorganization in the recipient country, lack of technological sophistication, or cultural practices such as distrust of large institutions or a preference for person-to-person delivery.

However, legal instruments are important in preventing criminal activity that may go undetected by underground or informal networks, some of which are not criminal by nature, but yet need supervision and regulation. The group of 'unlicensed' or 'informal' businesses is made up by a variety of players, such as individual entrepreneurs; travel agents who, for example, have a license for airfare sales, but not for financial transfers; or retail outlet stores, whose agents offer 'alternative' transfers to licensed businesses, although they may also have a license to provide transfers. Informal businesses typically operate in countries where flows are not particularly attractive to licensed companies due to their small volume, where foreign currency transfers are highly regulated by the state, where technology is still inaccessible to individuals and businesses, or where customers have greater trust in and preference for person-to-person delivery. However, these unlicensed businesses and entrepreneurs remain aware of the presence of a regulatory environment. In many instances, they have matured and evolved into formally licensed and fully compliant business operations.

2.1 Regulatory frameworks in Europe

Regulations – laws and policies – are an extremely important aspect of remittances. Both countries of destination and origin may have regulations governing the sending and receiving of these sums of money. In practice, however, it is the sending countries that are more likely to have added extensive and/or stringent regulations which shape consumer and provider choices and prices.

2.1.1 *The European Union (EU)*

According to the European Parliamentary Financial Services Forum (EPFSF), the European Union has a 'fragmented payments landscape'[2] in which each Member State has its own standards and regulations when it comes to cross-border payments.

Minikin and Cignola argue that the United Kingdom and Sweden have among the most flexible regulatory environments in Europe.[3] Money transfer operators (MTOs)[4] have only to register and apply standard security assessments in both of these countries. In contrast, the EU in general, and specific countries within Europe, have far more stringent rules and laws that apply to remittances. For example, France requires money remitters to obtain full banking licenses, complete with conditions such as relatively high capital requirements.[5]

---

[2] European Parliamentary Financial Services Forum, 'Briefing: Payment Services Directive', 21 Feb. 2006. <http://www.epfsf.org/meetings/2006/briefings/briefing_21feb2006.pdf>.

[3] R. Minikin and F. Cignola, 'Obstacles and challenges to remittance flows from the EU to developing countries' (2005) (unpublished manuscript on file with the author).

[4] MTOs are typically money transfer companies that operate the transfer of money through remittance agents or their own outfits from the point of transfer to the distribution point on the receiving end. In some countries, such as the United States, an MTO is required to acquire a license also known as a Money Service Business license, which is a requirement for any business involved in financial transfers (check cashing, money transfers, prepaid cards, etc.).

[5] Facility for Euro-Mediterranean Investment and Partnership, *Study on improving the efficiency*

The EU's regulations that affect remittance transfers include anti-money laundering requirements, initially shaped by the Financial Action Task Force (FATF) of the Organization for Economic Cooperation and Development (OECD). In 1990, the FATF released forty recommendations for the fight against money laundering, in particular that associated with the illicit drug trade. After the terrorist attacks in the United States in September 2001, new recommendations aimed at preventing the financing of terrorism were added (further revisions had also occurred in 1996).[6] The crucial challenge for the EU has been to strike a balance between customer protection and anti-money laundering requirements on the one hand, and the costs for the industry on the other.[7]

Subsequent to the EU's 1991 introduction of policies aimed at combating money laundering, which were limited to the financial sector, new requirements came into effect in 2001 expanding those sectors required to comply to professions and businesses, such as lawyers and casinos. In October 2005, the EU adopted the Third Money Laundering Directive addressing identification verification, intended to deal with terrorist financing.[8] Importantly for the purposes of this chapter, MTOs are not included in this measure unless cash payments exceed 15,000 Euros, a bar which also applies to other institutions falling under this Directive. It is expected to be implemented by Member States by the end of 2007.[9]

The remittance market will be affected, however, if a new legislative proposal which has been issued by the European Commission is translated into European law and policy:

> '[The proposed EU regulation] will require payers' information to accompany credit transfers and transfers sent by money remitters and also set standards for the verification of ID... Whereas at present there is no legal obligation to identify customers making one-off payments of less than 15,000 Euros, there is no such exemption under the draft regulation. The identification obligations to which remittance providers are subject would therefore expand considerably'.[10]

---

of workers' remittances in Mediterranean countries (Rotterdam, European Investment Bank 2006) <http://www.eib.eu.int/Attachments/country/femip_workers_remittances_en.pdf>.

[6] 'The eight Special Recommendations call for the ratification of the UN resolution against the financing of terrorism, the criminalization of the financing of terrorism, the confiscation of terrorists' assets, the reporting of suspicious transactions, international cooperation, monitoring of remittance systems, monitoring of originator information for transactions, surveillance on NGOs as possible vectors for financing terrorism, and detection of physical cross-border transportation of currencies'. Ibid., at p. 10.

[7] European Parliamentary Financial Services Forum, 'Briefing: Payment Services Directive', 21 Feb. 2006 <http://www.epfsf.org/meetings/2006/briefings/briefing_21feb2006.pdf>.

[8] Directive 2005/60/EC of the European Parliament and of the Council of 26 Oct. 2005 on the prevention of the use of the financial system for the purpose of money laundering and terrorist financing, OJ 2005 L 309/15.

[9] UK Remittance Working Group, *UK Remittance Market* (London, Profile Business Intelligence 2005) <http://www.dfid.gov.uk/pubs/files/uk-remittances-report.pdf> at p. 16.

[10] Ibid.

EU directives need to be translated into national law if they are to be effective. Minikin and Cignola argue that this fourth proposed directive would loosen controls in the countries with the strictest regulations concerning remittance transfers, and tighten them for nations with less arduous restrictions. One solution to the inevitable tension between improving security and expanding and enhancing formal remittance transfers is the use of a waiver clause.[11] This clause would release 'smaller remittance businesses from compliance with authorisation requirements'. This exception is supported by the United Kingdom and opposed 'by countries, such as Germany, France, Spain and Italy, which support tighter security regulations'.[12]

Stricter regulations and procedures surrounding customer identification could make it more difficult for some migrants to open bank accounts. As a result, countries such as France, Belgium, the Netherlands and the United Kingdom have introduced 'basic bank accounts', which have limited features for people who do not meet the qualification criteria for a standard bank account and which are only intended for making payments, such as remittances. Germany, Ireland, Portugal and Sweden have also passed legislation in support of these types of 'basic' banking services.[13]

2.1.2 *The United Kingdom*

The United Kingdom has, in relative terms, less regulation governing remittance transfers than other European countries. Remittances are not considered to be a 'regulated' activity in the United Kingdom, as defined by the Financial Services and Markets Act of 2000.[14] Unlike France and Germany, for example, the United Kingdom does not require MTOs to hold a banking license in order to conduct business. Levels of regulation are determined by magnitude of financial risks involved in the business; and because MTOs do not lend money and have less systematic risks than banks, they are subject to fewer regulations. However, money transfers are considered to pose a risk in terms of money laundering, and for that reason MTOs are subject to regulation in relation to the procedures in place to combat that threat.

Two regulatory authorities oversee companies sending remittances in the United Kingdom. The Financial Services Authority (FSA) provides regulations for banks and Her Majesty's Revenue and Customs (HMRC) supervise MTOs. Minikin and Cignola argue that banks have far tougher regulatory requirements:

> 'Due to the more complex nature of banks as financial operators, FSA compliance requirements are more cumbersome and include prudential ratios, financial forecasts,

[11] Art. 11 of Directive 2005/60/EC, loc. cit. n. 8.
[12] Minikin and Cignola, loc. cit. n. 3, at p. 11.
[13] Facility for Euro-Mediterranean Investment and Partnership, op. cit. n. 5.
[14] Financial Services and Markets Act 2000, c. 8.

> complex anti-money laundering procedures as well as the payment of a consistent fee. On the other hand, [HMRC] regulations require [MTOs] to undergo a fairly simple registration process, to comply with basic anti-money laundering procedures and to pay a moderate annual fee'.[15]

Businesses such as banks, building societies, and other financial institutions that are already regulated by the FSA need not apply for registration with HMRC. According to the UK Remittances Working Group, there is 'a perception among some players in the industry that the FSA and HMRC do not always work in a coordinated manner and that a single regulator would be preferable'.[16]

Although customer identification is widely recognized as a central element in fighting money laundering, there is no legal requirement for how firms in the United Kingdom must verify their new customers' identities. As a result, the FSA has acknowledged that there can be a 'fear factor' with respect to legal enforcement of remittance activities which causes some operators to use conservative measures in accepting IDs, with an adverse affect on certain consumers. The FSA has been actively trying to resolve this issue since April 2004, and in March 2005 the Joint Money Laundering Steering Group published a draft of their new Guidance Notes which suggest steps for making compliance with ID requirements easier for consumers.[17]

2.2 Regulatory environments in the Americas

The rules governing money transfers in the Americas are similar to those of other regions in the world. The concern within the United States about inbound and outbound payments means that regulators pay particular attention to 'suspicious activities' and compliance with anti-money laundering provisions. They also, however, address consumer issues concerning the rights of money senders. In Latin America the approach is broader, seeking to develop and enforce rules that do not conflict with US regulations.

Most transfers to Latin America today take place through fully licensed businesses. However, informal businesses make up over 30 per cent of the total volume of remittances transferred to Haiti, Cuba and Nicaragua (see textbox). Regulatory procedures monitoring the US-Latin America corridor primarily occur in the United States. In order for a business to legally offer money transfers, the company has to comply with federal and state (and sometimes municipal) regulations regarding money laundering, suspicious activities, and day-to-day operations. The compliance process often requires that MTOs possess an insurance bond and conduct regular audits, as well as make information available about the transfers and the agents with whom the company operates.

[15] Minikin and Cignola, loc. cit. n. 3.

[16] UK Remittance Working Group, op. cit. n. 9, at p. 17.

[17] Ibid., at p. 15.

Textbox: Remittances to Cuba

In Cuba, remittances occur predominantly in an informal context. The majority of Cubans choose to send remittances through informal mechanisms, particularly through *mulas*.

Mulas are entrepreneurs – men and women, Cuban Americans and foreign nationals (Mexicans and Colombians among others) – who can and do travel with ease and frequency to the island. They carry both money and packages of goods to the sender's relatives in Cuba for relatively inexpensive fees. They are known through word of mouth, through the references of relatives, acquaintances, and friends who recommend them as 'reliable' people to send packages of any kind.

Mulas go to Cuba predominantly as tourists, as they are informal entrepreneurs without a license to operate as a business. However, they have a well-established network of contacts including Miami residents and businesses, customs officials in Cuba, and the distributors of goods.

There is no single type of *mula* and their numbers may run into the thousands. Some are salaried and employed by a particular entrepreneur who hires them to travel back and forth to Cuba. There are also *mulas* who are sole proprietors of their informal remittance businesses and who work with family networks in the United States and Cuba. Depending on the business size, some of these sole proprietorships have an informal financial infrastructure in Cuba which they utilize to have their distribution operations active at any time. Carrying a significant pool of thousands of dollars, and using a fax machine, these individuals transmit messages to their Cuban counterpart with the coordinates of where to deliver money and to whom. In other cases, the individuals who have less capital available travel with greater frequency and arrange for the money to be delivered by their relatives. In general, regular *mulas* tend to travel to Cuba twice a month.

Finally, *mulas* may be either sporadic or entrepreneurial travellers. The sporadic traveller is a person who is approached by an entrepreneur to arrange delivery of money. Instead of earning a salary for the operation, their trip is paid for in exchange for carrying money and in-kind remittances. There are many individuals, particularly low income Cubans and the elderly, who find this to be a practical and useful means to enable them to visit their relatives in Cuba. These sporadic or occasional *mulas* may only conduct such operations once a year.

It is also important to stress that many of the formal money transfer businesses make use of the *mulas* as their distribution network in Cuba. The main reason for this is that given the regulatory constraints, as well as the capital investment requirements to establish agencies in Cuba, it is more convenient for the licensed business to rely on the *mula* to deliver the money. In this sense, there is a semi-formal money transfer process in place.

Central to the existence of *mulas* is trust. People who send remittances to Cuba rely on *mulas* because of their reputation, low cost and relative efficiency in delivering the money within a reasonable amount of time (no more than three days following arrival to the country, unless outside Havana). The popular consensus on the good work performed by a *mula* is shared widely in the community, further reinforcing their reputation. Both *mulas* and sporadic travellers are intertwined in social networks of various kinds, from neighbourhood links to work connections to national ties.

Source: M. Orozco, 'Challenges and opportunities of marketing remittances to Cuba', *Inter-American Dialogue*, Washington DC (July 2002) <http://www.thedialogue.org/publications/country_studies/remittances/Cuba_remittances.pdf>.

Money transfer companies are regulated in more than 40 US States and municipalities as non-bank financial institutions (also known as money service businesses, MSBs), requiring both a license and a bond to operate. Federally, the regulatory environment of MSBs is managed by the Treasury Department through the Office of the Comptroller of the Currency, the Financial Crimes Enforcement Network (FinCEN), and the Office of Foreign Assets Control (OFAC), agencies that ensure compliance with the Bank Secrecy Act 1970 and the USA Patriot Act 2001.[18] The activities of the FinCEN focus on preventing money laundering practices, while the OFAC is involved in monitoring transfers from certain entities or countries of its choosing. In addition to the requirements to submit to audits by, and report to, these organizations, MSBs need to meet several procedural legal obligations, which include a written compliance handbook, employing the services of a compliance officer and implementing an anti-money laundering training program for staff. These regulations put MSBs on the same legal footing as that of banks and other financial institutions in the United States.

In order to ensure efficient reporting, companies have developed database records containing customer information, including data on recipients. Moreover, companies monitor transactions that exceed a typical amount sent by an immigrant, usually over US$10,000. The requirement that immigrants provide full identification and contact information for both the sender and the recipient, which puts the burden on the sender, is key to regulating transfers. Despite high levels of company compliance, there are still challenges in preventing money laundering. Because not all remittance companies are fully interconnected, an individual could visit different agencies to send money separately and above the $10,000 limit. In response to this situation, several US companies supported the creation of ECO, Enforcement Compliance Officer, which is a compliance company that shares and monitors information from nearly thirty businesses about daily transactions and spots suspicious activities, and then submit reports to the MTOs about trends in their transactions. The business operates independently from each company's own compliance system.

The regulatory environment in Latin America is minimal. In some countries, money transfer institutions and their counterpart distributors are required to hold a license. They are also often required to report transfers above US$10,000. However, because most transactions are below $300, little reporting occurs. Moreover, in some countries companies do not report any kind of information about their business, nor are they required to do so. This situation not only adds to uncertainty over the amounts received and recorded by the Central Bank, but also raises risks of potential illicit activities. A positive aspect in the money transfers system in Latin America and the Caribbean is that outbound transfers of foreign currency are allowed in most countries, thus facilitating intra-regional flows through licensed businesses. In many developing countries there exist substantive re-

[18] The Bank Secrecy Act 1971 (31 USC 1051); The Uniting and Strengthening America by Providing Appropriate Tools Required to Intercept and Obstruct Terrorism Act 2001 (115 Stat. 272).

strictions about international outbound payments based on fears of capital flight. However, such restrictions can motivate informal and underground transfers.

The regulatory system, particularly in the United States, has increased monitoring of transactions, but has also increased costs for companies that provide training for and implement oversight programs. Businesses are concerned not only about increased operating costs, but also that the stringent identification requirements for both senders and recipients will lead to greater utilization of informal services by individuals who would rather use an unlicensed business than provide extensive information.

A serious issue that has arisen in the past three years has been the closing of bank accounts of remittance companies as a result of pressure from the US Treasury regulators. After 11 September 2001, regulations have required that MTOs and financial institutions apply strict requirements such as tightened 'know your customer' guidelines, the Bank Secrecy Act and the Patriot Act.[19] These requirements have made the internal costs of regulatory compliance soar. It has been observed that MTOs and financial institutions often have to devote as much as 65 per cent of their time and personnel to compliance issues.

In addition to compliance pressures, within this post 9/11 context US Treasury Department regulators have pressed banking institutions to perceive MTOs as high-risk businesses and have encouraged them to close the bank accounts of many of these operators.[20] In this respect, one analyst has stressed that 'bankers are concluding that the best approach is to withdraw services, in some cases leaving these bank customers (and their customers) with no legitimate financial system alternatives'.[21] As a result, many businesses have been unable to fully operate because large banks in particular have been closing MTO accounts nationally. Early in 2006, the Bank of America decided to cancel all its accounts with MTOs, including those with MoneyGram or Western Union. In fact, between 2002 and 2004, ten businesses reported the closure of over sixty of their bank accounts.[22]

[19] After 9/11, Congress toughened requirements on banks to investigate their own customers: the 'know your customer' requirement became that of 'know your customer's customer', considerably tighter than before. The Bank Secrecy Act, loc. cit. n. 18, requires banks to keep basic data on account holders and report cash transactions larger than US$10,000 and file 'Suspicious Activity Reports'. The USA Patriot Act, loc. cit. n. 18, added new requirements for banks to scrutinize high-risk customers and fulfill special due diligence obligations with foreign financial firms, although it is unclear whether it is banks or MTOs that the Act refers to. As William Fox, the Director of the Treasury Department's Financial Crimes Enforcement Network, stated, '[i]t does no one any good if banks refuse to take these businesses – that just encourages them to go underground', G.R. Simpson, 'Did Ice Cream Shop Feed Al Qaeda?', *Wall Street Journal,* 30 Dec. 2004.

[20] In order for an MTO to operate it needs a bank account so that it can both store the money it collects from migrants' transactions and wire it to their partners in the recipient country. These partners, in turn, are in charge of disbursing the funds. Without a bank account an MTO would have to physically transport the money across borders.

[21] Legal Foundation, Jan. 2005.

[22] Interviews with businesses members of the National Money Transmitters Association (NMTA), 2005.

According to the National Money Transmitters Association because businesses are left with virtually no available accounts, some MTOs have been forced to sell their operations, or have considered doing so.

2.3 Regulatory frameworks in Africa

Regulatory frameworks vary widely in Africa, and discussion of these is usually limited to taxation and foreign exchange policies. However, financial and monetary policies and regulations in their home country substantially affect the availability and choice of remittance channels for migrants, as do other contextual factors such as staff that speak their language and share similar cultural backgrounds.[23]

Since 11 September 2001, money transfer services have been substantially affected by new requirements such as 'know your customer' rules, financial liberalization or control, the licensing and regulation of money transfer services, and government incentives for sending and investing remittances.[24]

In Africa, 'know your customer' requirements have increased, imposing greater compliance obligations for financial service providers in relation to client identification, verification and record-keeping. Furthermore, organizations are required to develop policies, protocols and training plans in keeping with the stricter environment. These requirements have not only reduced accessibility to the formal systems for illiterate, and sometimes illegal, migrants, but have also added user costs. Relationships between banks and MTOs have also changed, as banks have become less willing to establish the necessary links with small, unknown MTOs, whose practices may risk running afoul of the guidelines established by the FATF. An illustrative case is that of Somali remittances from the United States and Western Europe. Regulators discourage businesses from operating those corridors, and Somali MTOs are often the object of suspicion by banks by virtue of being Somali alone.

South Africa provides a good example of the difficulties of implementing the tighter control environment. The combination of costly exchange services and legal immigration status requirements have placed international transfers far outside of the reach of many migrants who have no previous experience with formal financial institutions (also known as 'unbanked migrants'). Genesis Analytics estimate that 95 per cent of remittances flow outside of the transfer controls systems in this context.[25] A further illustration of the impact of these regulations can be drawn from a case study of Western Union in South Africa. Western Union began operations there in 1995 through Union African Money Transfers (UAMT),

---

[23] C. Sander and S. Munzele Maimbo, 'Migrant Labor Remittances in Africa: Reducing Obstacles to Developmental Contributions', *Africa Region Working Paper Series No. 64* (Nov. 2003) p. 21 <http://www.worldbank.org/afr/wps/wp64.pdf>.

[24] Ibid., at p. 26.

[25] Genesis Analytics, *Supporting Remittances in Southern Africa. Estimating Market Potential and Assessing Regulatory Obstacles* (Johannesburg, Genesis Analytics 2005).

which covered 150 outlets. UAMT struggled to comply with the new legislation, and the costs of the stringent reporting requirements forced the business to reduce its operation to 17 outlets. The South African Reserve Bank's 2001 prohibition on the net settlement of foreign exchange transactions meant that UAMT was no longer able to pay out South African recipients with the money paid in by South African remitters. As a result, customers were forced to wait until the actual funds transferred reached South Africa, and Western Union was not able to fulfil its product guarantee of immediately accessible funds. Faced with the rising costs of exchange controls, poor customer satisfaction, and the requirement of increased credit exposure, Western Union ended its partnership with UAMT and withdrew services from South Africa.[26]

Ghana struggles with many of the same problems in dealing with its highly regulated exchange environment. Despite the fact that non-bank money transfer operators have been licensed and regulated by the Financial Institutions (Non-Banking) Law of 1993 (Provisional National Defense Council Law 328), the money transfer system remains weak, due to the absence of bank or non-bank financial branches in some parts of the country and delays in the transfer of remittances, especially between remittance service providers. Furthermore, a lack of innovation on the part of financial institutions due to regulatory constraints and the absence of effective competition in service provision have hampered attempts to strengthen the formal system.[27] These regulatory constraints include the current restriction against non-resident investments in Government treasury bills and bonds; the requirement of pre-approval from the Minister of Finance for non-residents wishing to invest in Ghanaian-registered securities; and the favouring of residents over non-residents in the tax regime relating to interest income on instruments issued by local financial institutions.[28]

Stringent regulatory controls are one obstacle to money transfers within West Africa. In most of the region, outbound cross border payments are not allowed unless banks are performing the transaction for the exclusive purpose of foreign trade. Moreover, Ghana only allows the exportation of the equivalent of c5,000 (US$0.54), and Nigeria only allows N1,000 (US$7.74). But even this type of permitted transaction may occur only as long as there is a market for West African currency, which outside of Francophone Africa is not the case. Francophone countries may freely circulate CFA Francs[29] in the WAEMU[30] region up to CFA F300,000 (US$542) without justification, but the banknotes may not be exported

[26] Ibid., at p. viii.

[27] Bruks Associates and Citizens International, *Improving the Developmental Impact of Private Remittance Flows to Ghana. Remittance Recipients, Intermediaries and Legal Review* (Ghana, Bruks Associates 2005).

[28] Ibid.

[29] Franc de la Communauté Financière d'Afrique.

[30] West African Economic and Monetary Union: Benin, Burkina Faso, Côte d'Ivoire, Guinea-Bissau, Mali, Niger, Senegal, and Togo.

to other ECOWAS countries. In practice this means that outbound transfers must be completed through a bank with supporting documentation.[31]

These situations in turn create an environment in which most remittance intermediaries are informal players. A survey conducted by this author of West African migrants living in Ghana showed that over eighty per cent of migrants use informal networks.

Table: Remittance Transfer Method of Choice among West Africans in Ghana

Remittance transfer methods	(%)
Bank branch	1.3
Money transfer company office	5.6
Internet (online banking/remittance service	0.3
Other company	3
Use friend, relative or other person	65.2
Send cash via a driver	10.5
Take cash home when visiting	12.5
Travel agency	1.6
Total	100

Source: Orozco, loc. cit. n. 31.

2.4 The regulatory environment in Asia[32]

Financial flows are always subject to a range of laws and policies: governments need to ensure, for example, that taxes are paid and criminal money is not laundered. These regulations directly and indirectly define and shape how remittance transfers (among other financial transactions) take place. Interestingly, India has become a regional leader in the development of policies designed to attract and manipulate the receipt of remittances through formal channels. There, until the 1990s, the Government focus was on the promotion of non-resident Indian (NRI) savings accounts. It was able to augment foreign currency reserves by encouraging NRI deposits to Indian banks through offers such as higher interest rates, exchange rate guarantees for foreign currency accounts, and certain tax exemptions on deposits. After a surge in NRI deposits in the 1980s, India began to see these as an important component of external debt and began to implement policies geared towards reducing the country's dependence on them. Indeed, a subsequent

[31] M. Orozco, *West African Financial Flows and Opportunities for People and Small Businesses*, report prepared for the United States Agency for International Development, March 2006 <http://www.watradehub.com/downloads/events/West%20African%20Financial%20Flows%20and%20Opportunities%20for%20SME%20v14.pdf>.

[32] Significant portions of the material used in this section are based on research led by the author for an extensive study of intra-regional Southeast Asian remittances sponsored by the Asian Development Bank. See M. Orozco and R. Fedewa, 'Regional Integration? Trends and Patterns of Remittance Flows within South East Asia', *TA 6212-REG Southeast Asia Workers Remittance Study* (Aug. 2005).

liberalization of foreign exchange rate management has contributed to a decline in NRI deposits and an increase in worker remittances since the 1990s. Although India is the world's largest recipient of worker remittances, other countries throughout Asia have also taken steps to manage remittance flows. International money transfers tend to be sources of additional, specifically targeted regulation in Asia, as in most of the rest of the world.

2.4.1 *Regulatory bodies*

Southeast Asian money transfers are governed by an array of regulations and government institutions. Notably, in most countries, the Minister of Finance has a key role to play in the regulatory bodies, indicating the seriousness with which these states take financial regulations. A second common feature across most countries is that two or more institutions share the obligations to oversee the rules regarding money transfers. Central banks are key institutions, such as the Bank Negara Malaysia (BNM), the Hong Kong Monetary Authority (HKMA), and the Bank of Indonesia. In all three cases, the banks report to the Ministers of Finance above them, and have authority over the banking sector below. The central banks also have jurisdiction over MTOs and other companies involved in the remittance business, where they are allowed to operate at all. Unusually, in Hong Kong, the police register MTOs and related business entities.

The Philippines seeks to give some independence to the Charter of the Central Bank (Bangko Sentral ng Pilipinas (BSP)) by not giving the Minister of Finance direct control and by having it dominated by private sector members. At the same time, to improve coordination between different Government institutions and functions, the Finance Minister is one of the members of the Monetary Board, the BSP's policy-making body; while the task of registering banks, remittance companies, and foreign exchange corporations is left to the Securities and Exchange Commission (SEC).[33] The Reserve Bank of India (RBI) is similar in that it is governed by a twenty member Board of Directors, with one seat reserved for a Government official from the Ministry of Finance. The RBI was granted the power to authorize and issue licenses to businesses and individuals handling remittance transfers by the Foreign Exchange Management Act (FEMA) of 1999.[34]

In Japan, the Financial Services Agency (FSA) is responsible for supervising and surveying securities transactions by financial institutions.

2.4.2 *Authorized remittance agents*

National policies vary in terms of which businesses may get licenses to remit money legally. It is exclusively up to banks to make wire transfers in Japan, Ma-

[33] Asian Development Bank (ADB), PHI: 4185, Technical Assistance Final Report, *Enhancing the Efficiency of Overseas Workers' Remittances* (Manila, ADB 2004) p. 27 <http://www.adb.org/Documents/TARs/PHI/tar-phi-4185.asp>.

[34] Foreign Exchange Management Act 1999 (Act No. 42 of 1999, 29 Dec. 1999).

laysia, and Indonesia, whereas the Philippines, Hong Kong, and Singapore allow greater latitude as to what institutions may do this. Post offices may also have the authority to send transfers directly, again with country-by-country differences in specifics.

Japan's control over remittance transfer businesses is particularly strict in that all transmitting companies must receive banking licenses. The basis for this rule is that remittances are considered to be 'exchange transactions' under the law. One exception is that, under a different legislative policy, the Post Office also has the right to transmit money abroad.

In many ways similar to Japan's regulatory environment, Indonesia and Malaysia also only allow banks to make money transfers, including for remittances. Again, the one exception to this policy concerns Post Offices, which are also allowed to engage in the business. Money transfer companies, such as Western Union or MoneyGram, have to enter into partnerships with licensed banks.

Malaysia allows both foreign and domestic banks to operate as agents of money transfer companies, whereby the MTO operates as the 'back end' processor of international transfers. Interestingly, a direct arrangement to assist the remittance of Nepalese migrants' money was made, allowing a private Nepalese company, Impex Sdn Bhd (IME), to perform this function. This arrangement was made bilaterally between the Nepali and Malaysian Governments. Otherwise, only domestic banks may engage in international money transfers.

Like Indonesia and Malaysia, India has promoted an innovative partnership scheme in order to expand access to authorized remittance transfers. At present, there are 91 banks and financial institutions in India licensed to deal in foreign currency. Additionally, under the money transfer service scheme (MTSS), authorized Indian agents can enter into partnerships with reputable foreign money transfer companies. Such partnership arrangements are also open to registered non-banking financial institutions and approved travel agents. However, under the MTSS there is a cap on each individual transaction, and a single person can only receive up to 12 remittances each year.

A far more liberal approach is that of Hong Kong, Singapore, and the Philippines, which do not restrict authorization to make remittances to banks. Indeed, businesses wanting to become licensed remittance agents (RAs) do not even need to possess a minimum level of capital. Already-licensed banks in Singapore are additionally allowed to open Limited Purpose Branches at a modest annual license fee of SGD 1,000.[35] Through such branches, Singapore appears to have encouraged more foreign bank branches with large migrant populations among their clients to establish remittance businesses, thereby making their presence more visible and more easily accessed by their country's migrant workers.

[35] AriSu Management Consultants, 'Country Report: Malaysia', *TA 6212-REG Southeast Asia Workers Remittance Study* (2005).

2.4.3 *Regulations affecting Filipino recipients*

Generally, private companies are free to set the cost of their transfer services with no government constraint. The Philippines, however, requires recipients obtaining their money at any bank to pay for expenses like the documentary stamp tax levied by the Philippine National Bank. This stamp tax is a standard price, but other bank charges can and do vary.[36]

2.4.4 *Preventing the use of transfers for money-laundering and other crime*

Governments in Asia have been concerned to prevent the use of international money transfers for the purposes of money-laundering and other illegal activities. Three general sets of practices serve to diminish this threat to *bona fide* remittance transfers, corridors, and routes. First, the standard 'know your customer' principles, established in December 1998 by the Basle Committee on Banking Regulations and Supervisory Practice, provide an international guide to aiding the prevention of money-laundering. These rules call for, at very minimum, the transferring business to obtain the name, date of birth, address, and valid identity document of the sender. Further information is also encouraged such as job, telephone number, visa validity, nationality, and so on.

Second, countries set points at which senders have to apply 'know your customer' rules. In practice, Japan, Singapore and India require such information for any international money transfer no matter how small. Malaysia does not have a minimum bar above which they apply, but the law does require that all transmitters identify themselves, and that the bank verifies this identity claim. There is, however, a threshold of MYR 50,000, after which special forms must be completed. Sending institutions in Malaysia are required to retain records of monies sent for at least six years. In Hong Kong, there are strict inspections for any remittances of HK 20,000 and higher.

Third, countries also may set guidelines for the receipt of remittances. In general, however, the guidelines for remittance recipients are less strict than for senders. Indonesia, for example, only requires a strict identity check for amounts exceeding IDR 100 million, and the Philippines requires companies to monitor those receiving remittances of more than PHP 500,000. Consistent with its lack of a minimum amount above which the 'know your customer' rules apply to senders, Malaysia does not have a limit beyond which companies are required to perform checks on recipients.

The prevention of money-laundering not only involves requiring that sending businesses check up on their customers, but also threshold levels beyond which businesses are required to report transactions to the government. As can be expected, different countries have different reporting requirements, and the

[36] I. Manalastas, 'Regulatory Framework', *Southeast Asia Workers' Remittances Study*, TAR: STU 38233, Aug. 2005.

threshold at which these come into play also varies. Japan's Foreign Currency and Foreign Trade Law requires banks to declare their customers' transfers of more than JPY2 million; and when more than JPY30 million is sent, it has to be reported to the Bank of Japan (for the purposes of compiling the data for its balance of payments). The Philippines requires that transaction amounts over PHP 500,000[37] are reported to the Anti-Money Laundering Council, while in Malaysia transfers of MYR50,000 or more must be reported to authorities. Hong Kong, Singapore, and Indonesia do not have fixed sums at which reporting requirements come into play; Indonesia does, however, require that transfers of IDR500 million or more are reported to the Center for Reporting and Analysis of Financial Institutions (PPATK). Finally, all of the Southeast Asian countries examined here are required to file reports of suspicious transactions, regardless of the amount believed to be suspect.

2.4.5 *Identification document checks*

Banks not only have to establish their *bona fides* directly with governments, but they are more often than not charged with determining the identity and, often implicitly, the legal status of their customers or those who would like to use their institution to transmit money. Providing legally mandated or legally acceptable forms of identity documents is often a precondition to sending remittances. 'The kind of identity required, however, varies across countries and thus may set limitations as to who is effectively allowed to remit through licensed businesses'.[38]

The Philippines, Japan, Malaysia, Indonesia, and Singapore all require current and valid passports as a means for non-nationals and non-citizens to set up accounts and transfer money to their home country. In some countries, however, a valid passport is insufficient and additional documentation may be necessary. Singapore requires a permanent resident card, Malaysia requires a work permit or employer's letter, and Japan and the Philippines require proof of being a legal alien, although in the latter State even such proof may not in itself suffice.

3. Conclusion

Regulatory issues matter, and today, as international politics pays increasing attention to matters of anti-terrorism and organized criminal activities, money transfers are highly scrutinized. The contemporary design and application of the law in this area takes place at the centre of the struggle between market globalization and global anti-terrorist rhetoric. Remittance transfers are subjected to stringent processes of legal regulation that are often asymmetrical to or incommensurable with the typical nature of these flows. The result is an increased re-

[37] Ibid., at p. 11.

[38] Orozco and Fedewa, loc. cit. n. 32, at p. 48.

treat to informal networks in parts of the world in which confidence-building is more easily achieved through greater legal liberalization than higher levels of regulation. Examples abound everywhere in the world: anti-Castro Cuban-Americans, for example, have resorted to informal mechanisms to send money to their relatives due to stringent legal restrictions. A similar trend can be observed in Africa and Asia. In the former, due to restrictions on foreign exchange controls and outbound money transfers that only allow banking institutions to perform these transactions, the average West African is placed beyond the legal framework, by virtue of their social status that prevents them from accessing, and therefore using, the formal financial system.

Selected Bibliography

Facility for Euro-Mediterranean Investment and Partnership, *Study on improving the efficiency of workers' remittances in Mediterranean countries* (Rotterdam, European Investment Bank 2006).

Genesis Analytics, *Supporting Remittances in Southern Africa. Estimating Market Potential and Assessing Regulatory Obstacles* (Johannesburg, Genesis Analytics 2005).

Orozco, M., 'Challenges and opportunities of marketing remittances to Cuba', *Inter-American Dialogue*, Washington DC (July 2002) <http://www.thedialogue.org/publications/country_studies/remittances/Cuba_remittances.pdf>.

—, *West African Financial Flows and Opportunities for People and Small Businesses*, Report prepared for the United States Agency for International Development (March 2006) <http://www.watradehub.com/downloads/events/West%20African%20Financial%20Flows%20and%20Opportunities%20for%20SME%20v14.pdf>.

Orozco, M. and R. Fedewa, 'Regional Integration? Trends and Patterns of Remittance Flows within South East Asia', *TA 6212-REG Southeast Asia Workers Remittance Study* (Aug. 2005).

UK Remittance Working Group, *UK Remittance Market* (London, Profile Business Intelligence 2005) <www.dfid.gov.uk/pubs/files/uk-remittances-report.pdf>.

Chapter 8
MIGRATION AND FREE TRADE AGREEMENTS: LESSONS FROM NAFTA AND PERSPECTIVES FOR CAFTA-DR

Gustavo A. Flores-Macías*

1. INTRODUCTION

When the North American Free Trade Agreement (hereafter, NAFTA)[1] was negotiated, it was envisioned as a development tool that would not only bring economic prosperity to the region but also narrow the income gap between Canada, Mexico, and the United States. When the Agreement entered into force in 1994, the difference in wealth among the three member countries was considerable, both in terms of the size of their economies and income per capita.[2] In addition to strengthening cooperation and fostering trade among the member countries, one of NAFTA's explicit objectives was to improve living standards by creating new employment opportunities in the region. However, there was no explicit mention of the regulation of migration as a goal in the text of the Agreement.[3]

The text of NAFTA included very little on migration – it only referred to the temporary entry of business persons – but the Agreement was expected to reduce considerably the unauthorized migratory flows between Mexico and the United States. According to classical international trade theory, trade would become a substitute for migration since Foreign Direct Investment (FDI) would flow into the labour intensive country – Mexico – and generate new, more competitive, and better-paid jobs that would deter people from migrating to search for employment opportunities in the United States. Thus, among the consequences of NAFTA were expected to be a reduction of the income differential in the region, a net in-

* Doctoral fellow in Government and Instructor of Globalization at Georgetown University.

1 North American Free Trade Agreement between the Government of Canada, the Government of the United Mexican States, and the Government of the United States of America, reprinted in 32 *International Legal Materials* (1993) p. 289 (Table of Contents, Preamble, Parts I-III) and 32 *International Legal Materials* (1993) p. 605 (Parts IV-VII, Annexes). The text of NAFTA is also available at <www.nafta-sec-alena.org>

2 In 1994, GDP per capita (constant 2000 US$) was $5,309 in Mexico, $19,460 in Canada, and $29,550 in the US; total GDP (constant 2000 US$) was $0.475 trillion in Mexico, $0.566 trillion in Canada, and $7.775 trillion in the United States. See World Bank, World Development Indicators (Online Resource) (Washington, DC: World Bank 2002).

3 NAFTA, loc. cit. n. 1, Preamble.

R. Cholewinski, R. Perruchoud and E. MacDonald, eds., International Migration Law

crease in the number of jobs, and, as a result, a rise in the living standards in the source country. In this sense, NAFTA became an ambitious roundabout way to reduce unauthorized migratory flows across the busiest border in the world.

However, the text of the Agreement did little to advance this goal. The only migration-related provision it contained addressed the temporary entry of business persons, with the objective of avoiding the undue impairment or delay of trade in goods or services and investment.[4] Moreover, the Member States deliberately included a clause stating that NAFTA would not impose any obligation on a Party to confer employment-related rights on citizens of another Party.[5] In a similar fashion, the labour side agreement signed as part of NAFTA did not specifically refer to the issue of migrants' rights. Instead, it appealed to the effective enforcement of domestic labour standards in each country. In short, the text of NAFTA did not intend to deal directly with migratory issues.

Evaluating NAFTA's migration record, there is a clear gap between actual migratory flows and the expectations that the countries' leaders had in mind when negotiating the treaty. The statistics show that migratory flows, both legal and illegal, between Mexico and the United States have increased considerably since the Agreement came into effect.[6] The expected result of the Agreement – a decrease in unauthorized migratory flows as a consequence of development – remains unfulfilled for several reasons. The generation of employment has proved to be insufficient, wages have remained depressed, and strong transnational migrant networks have emerged, to name only a few. More than ten years after it came into force, NAFTA has led to an unparalleled economic integration in the region, but it has also witnessed unprecedented levels of migration.

In light of the experience of NAFTA, the prospect of a decrease in unauthorized migration as a result of the Central America-Dominican Republic-United States of America Free Trade Agreement (hereafter, CAFTA-DR)[7] is remote. Increased economic integration and reticent migration provisions should lead to similar results as those of NAFTA. In both cases, labour migration was virtually neglected, except for NAFTA's creation of a non-immigrant visa, which has

---

[4] Ibid., Arts. 1601 and 1602.

[5] Ibid., Art. 1201.

[6] According to the US Census Bureau, the number of Mexicans living in the United States more than doubled, from 4.3 million in 1990 to 9.2 million in 2000. See N. Malone, et al., *The Foreign Born Population: 2000*, US Census Bureau C2KBR-34 (issued Dec. 2003) <http://www.census.gov/prod/2003pubs/c2kbr-34.pdf>.

[7] Central America-Dominican Republic-United States Free Trade Agreement between the Governments of Costa Rica, the Dominican Republic, El Salvador, Guatemala, Honduras, Nicaragua, and the United States of America. The text of CAFTA-DR is available at <http://www.ustr.gov/Trade_Agreements/Bilateral/CAFTA/CAFTA-DR_Final_Texts/Section_Index.html>. Strictly speaking, the acronym CAFTA refers to the free trade agreement between the US and Central American countries; the –DR was added when the Dominican Republic joined the negotiations in 2004. For the sake of accuracy, CAFTA-DR has been used throughout this chapter, although many simply refer to the contemporary Agreement as CAFTA, which is reflected in some of the quotations used here, e.g., *infra*, n. 47.

consistently been under-utilized. Today, after more than a decade of NAFTA, it is clear that much more than the roundabout approach adopted by both Agreements is needed to decrease the flows of migrants looking for employment opportunities in the United States.

This chapter presents an overview of the neglect of immigration provisions by the texts of NAFTA and CAFTA-DR. First, it reviews the Governments' high hopes for a reduction of labour migration as a consequence of NAFTA, as well as the theory on which these expectations were based. Second, it looks into the texts of NAFTA and CAFTA-DR to examine the provisions and objectives related to migration. Next, it explores NAFTA's migration record, along with the reasons why its results have not met expectations. Finally, this chapter argues that, based on the experience of NAFTA, labour migration is likely to increase instead of decrease as a result of CAFTA-DR.

2. Expectations and Theory

NAFTA was signed in December 1992 by Canada, Mexico and the United States, and came into effect on 1 January 1994. During its negotiation, the Agreement was conceived of as an important step towards reducing migration between Mexico and the United States. Government rhetoric on both sides of the border highlighted NAFTA's important contribution to decreasing migration flows as a result of the job opportunities it would generate in Mexico, and the increase in productivity that would raise wages and decrease the income differential between the two countries. The achievement of these two objectives was intended to reduce the incentives for Mexican workers to migrate north for economic reasons.[8]

These expectations were consistent with classical international trade theory. Theoretically, and in the absence of protectionism, trade among countries with different factor endowments becomes a substitute for migration.[9] By eliminating barriers to trade between Mexico, Canada, and the United States, the capital-intensive countries – Canada and the United States – would focus on producing capital-intensive goods, while the labour-intensive country – Mexico – would specialize in producing labour-intensive goods, each according to its comparative advantage. Consequently, FDI would both generate more jobs in Mexico and raise wages as productivity increased due to technology transfer and competition.

[8] For more on the neoclassical theory of migration, which explains international labour migration as a cost-benefit analysis, see M. Todaro and L. Maruzsko, 'Illegal Migration and US Immigration Reform: A Conceptual Framework', 13 *Population and Development Review* (1987) p. 101; and G. Borjas, 'Economic Theory and International Migration', 23 *International Migration Review* (1989) p. 457.

[9] D. Acevedo and T. Espenshade, 'Implications of a North American Free Trade Agreement for Mexican Migration into the United States', 18 *Population and Development Review* (1992) p. 729, at p. 730; P. Martin, 'Investment, Trade, and Migration', 29 *International Migration Review* (1995) p. 820.

In turn, migration would tend to decrease as a result of the latter country's focus on producing labour intensive goods.[10] In other words, NAFTA would contribute indirectly to decreasing labour migration flows between Mexico and the United States.

During negotiations, the Governments' perspective was that free trade agreements reduced migration because they bring employment to the source country, decreasing the need to migrate somewhere else for economic reasons.[11] Accordingly, the Agreement faced strong opposition from labour unions in the United States and Canada, which were afraid that NAFTA would result in 'a giant sucking sound' of jobs going south to Mexico.[12] In line with international trade theory, but without the Governments' optimism about rising living standards, blue-collar workers were afraid that entire manufacturing industries would go to Mexico, bringing down wages in the region.

In spite of opposition in all three countries, US President William Clinton and Mexican President Carlos Salinas led the myriad government voices that claimed the reduction of illegal migration as an explicit goal of NAFTA, by creating jobs through FDI, improving wages, reducing consumer prices, and raising living standards. On the Mexican side, President Salinas declared in a speech in the United States that

> '[f]ree trade is the way to increase growth and employment … and NAFTA is a migration-reduction agreement, because Mexicans will not have to migrate north looking for jobs in this country, but will be able to find them in my own'.[13]

On the US side, President Clinton declared in a press conference at the White House that

> '[e]verything people worried about in the 1980s will get worse if this thing is voted down, and will get better if it's voted up, so if you want to have the immigration problem eased, you must vote for NAFTA, not against it'.[14]

---

[10] The Commission for the Study of International Migration and Cooperative Economic Development concluded that trade liberalization would deter migration flows to the United States. See Commission for the Study of International Migration and Cooperative Economic Development, *Unauthorized Migration: An Economic Development Response* (Washington DC, Commission for the Study of International Migration and Cooperative Economic Development 1990), Executive Summary.

[11] For an overview of the Governments' rhetoric on NAFTA see R. Manning, 'Five Years after NAFTA', *Center for Immigration Studies Background Paper* (2001).

[12] In 1992, Presidential candidate Ross Perot warned in respect of NAFTA that we would hear 'a giant sucking sound of jobs' leaving the United States.

[13] 'Mexican Leader, at MIT, Hails Trade Pact', in *The Boston Globe*, 29 May 1993. Similarly, in an interview conducted by *The Journal of Commerce*, President Salinas declared, 'With the economic recovery that NAFTA will provide, migration will diminish dramatically because families will not have to leave Mexico looking for an opportunity in the US. Before NAFTA, growth in Mexico was concentrated on the northern states. With NAFTA we have the possibility to stimulate growth in the southern states of the country as well', *The Journal of Commerce*, 3 Dec. 1993.

[14] 'At "Trade Fair", Clinton Sells NAFTA with Specter of Illegal Immigrants', *The Washington Post,* 21 Oct. 1993. Likewise, at a meeting with business persons in California, Clinton remarked, 'My

To be sure, these statements clearly echoed the theoretical relationship between trade, development, and migration.[15]

3. Migration Provisions in NAFTA

In spite of the expectations generated as to NAFTA's indirect ability to reduce the flows of labour migrants from Mexico, the Agreement discretely included a section dealing with temporary migration for skilled labour. It omitted to deal extensively with migration issues, except for the temporary entrance of four categories of business persons:[16] business visitors, traders and investors, intra-company transferees, and professionals. According to the Agreement, the objectives of including this form of temporary migration were to

1) avoid unduly impairing or delaying trade in goods or services or conduct of investment activities under this Agreement;

2) further the preferential trading relationship between the three countries;

3) facilitate reciprocal temporary entry through transparent criteria and procedures;

4) foster border security; and

5) protect the domestic labour force and permanent employment in their respective territories.[17]

Notwithstanding these objectives, the Agreement was explicit as to the inexistence of obligations among the Parties concerning access to employment markets. In line with Article 1 of the World Trade Organization's (WTO) General Agreement on Trade in Services,[18] NAFTA's Part V, concerned with Investment, Ser-

---

friends in California are worried about the large influx of illegal immigrants. Over the period of the next few years, we will dramatically reduce pressures on illegal immigration from Mexico to the US. But if you beat NAFTA, it will increase pressure on people coming here', in 'NAFTA and California Business: Clinton Promises More Computer Sales, Fewer Illegal Immigrants', *The San Francisco Chronicle,* 21 Oct. 1993.

[15] Beyond what can be considered political rhetoric, the US International Trade Commission advised in 1990 that a Free Trade Agreement (FTA) between the United States and Mexico would decrease the real wage differential in the long run. US International Trade Commission, *The Likely Impact on the US of a Free Trade Agreement with Mexico* (Washington DC, USITC 1990), p. viii.

[16] Understood as 'a citizen of a Party who is engaged in trade in goods, the provision of services or the conduct of investment activities' (as defined in NAFTA, loc. cit. n. 1, Art. 1608).

[17] NAFTA, ibid., Ch. XVI: Temporary Entry for Business Persons, Arts. 1601 and 1602.

[18] WTO, Final Act Embodying the Results of the Uruguay Round of Multilateral Trade Negotiations (1994), Annex 1B: General Agreement on Trade in Services (GATS), Art. 1.

vices and Related Matters, explicitly states in Chapter 12, 'Cross-Border Trade in Services', that

> 'Nothing in this Chapter shall be construed to:
>
> (a) impose any obligation on a Party with respect to a national of another Party seeking access to its employment market, or employed on a permanent basis in its territory, or to confer any right on that national with respect to that access or employment'.[19]

The issue of migration was also excluded from the North American Agreement for Labor Cooperation (NAALC),[20] commonly known as the NAFTA labour side agreement. The NAALC did not seek to explicitly protect labour migrants' rights. Rather, it calls on the Parties to enforce their domestic labour standards effectively, establishes a cooperation mechanism between the Member States, and sets forth common labour goals. Among the most important objectives of the NAALC are to

> '1) improve working conditions and living standards in each Party's territory;
> 2) encourage cooperation to promote innovation and rising levels of productivity and quality;
> 3) encourage the publication and exchange of information, data development and coordination, and joint studies to enhance mutually beneficial understanding of the laws and institutions governing labor in each Party's territory;
> 4) promote compliance with, and effective enforcement by each Party of, its labor law; and
> 5) foster transparency in the administration of labor law'.[21]

4. Migration Provisions in CAFTA-DR

CAFTA-DR was signed on 5 August 2004 by Costa Rica, the Dominican Republic, El Salvador, Guatemala, Honduras, Nicaragua, and the United States. In many ways, it was modelled on NAFTA. Therefore, its migration-related provisions are very similar to, and in fact concede less than, than those of its predecessor.

In terms of the Parties' obligations regarding access to the employment market, CAFTA-DR Chapter 11, 'Cross-Border Trade in Services', mirrors NAFTA's Chapter 12 (cited above), establishing that CAFTA-DR does not impose any obligation on a Member State with respect to a national of another Party seeking access to its employment market, or employed on a permanent basis in its territory. Emulating NAFTA, CAFTA-DR does not confer any right on that national

[19] NAFTA, loc. cit. n. 1, Art. 1201: Scope and Coverage, Section 3.

[20] North American Agreement for Labor Cooperation between the Government of Canada, the Government of the United Mexican States, and the Government of the United States of America, reprinted in 32 *International Legal Materials* (1993) p. 1480. The text of NAALC is also available at <http://www.naalc.org/english/agreement.shtml>.

[21] NAALC, ibid., Art. 1.

with respect to that access or employment.[22] In fact, CAFTA-DR is even less expansive than NAFTA in addressing migration among its Member States. Unlike NAFTA, for instance, CAFTA-DR does not deal with the entry of business persons; instead, the Parties were very explicit in setting aside any restrictions to their existing immigration policies by signing an Understanding Regarding Immigration Measures. The Understanding's only clause is that 'no provision of the agreement shall be construed to impose any obligation on a Party regarding its immigration measures'.[23]

In contrast to NAFTA's labour side agreement, which created the NAALC, CAFTA-DR includes a chapter on labour that mentions migrant workers' rights, albeit *en passant*. Chapter 14 of CAFTA-DR creates a Labor Affairs Council at the cabinet level[24] as well as a Capacity Building Mechanism,[25] including among the functions of the latter cooperation concerning the 'dissemination of information regarding labor rights of migrant workers in each Party's territory'.[26]

In brief, NAFTA and CAFTA-DR both include minimal provisions regarding ac-cess to employment markets or migrant workers' rights. Arguably, the inclusion of any further provisions regarding these two issues would have guaranteed even stronger domestic opposition in the US, seriously jeopardizing the Agreements' chances of ratification in Congress. In light of this, the Governments of the Member States were hoping that the theory of international trade would take care of the rest.

5. NAFTA's Migration Record

In retrospect, NAFTA's migration record does not appear to have achieved the expected results. This is partly because the Agreement shied away from dealing with the large majority of migrants from Mexico to the United States – unskilled labour[27] – and partly because of the unanticipated social and economic consequences of NAFTA. In terms of skilled labour, the TN visa class was created in 1994 as a result of NAFTA's Chapter 16, 'Temporary Entry for Business Persons'. A temporary worker provision established in the US-Canada Free Trade Agreement and continued in NAFTA, the TN visa system established a cap of 5,500 annual issuances for Mexicans until 2004.[28] NAFTA's temporary visa provisions were intended to expedite temporary labour mobility for business visitors, traders and investors, intra-company transferees, and professionals.

Contrary to expectations, the number of temporary Mexican migrants under the TN visa class has been underwhelming in both absolute and relative terms. TN

[22] CAFTA-DR, loc. cit. n. 7, Art. 11.1: Scope and Coverage.

[23] CAFTA-DR, loc. cit. n. 7, Understanding Regarding Immigration Measures, 5 Aug. 2004.

[24] CAFTA-DR, ibid., Art. 16.4, Section 1.

[25] Ibid., Art. 16.5.

[26] Ibid., Annex 16.5, Section 3(h).

[27] US Commission on Immigration Reform, *Binational Study: Migration between Mexico and the United States* (1997) p. iv <http://www.utexas.edu/lbj/uscir/binational/full-report.pdf>.

[28] NAFTA, loc. cit. n. 1, Annex 1603.D.4.

visa issuances for Mexicans have never reached even half of the ceiling originally established. Only in fiscal years 2002 and 2004 did the number issued exceed the 2,000 mark.[29] Relatively speaking, migration under the TN visa class is extremely low when compared with other kinds of legal migration, and insignificant when contrasted against illegal migration. In 2004, for instance, the year in which the highest numbers of NAFTA visas were issued to date, the TN visa represented less than 3 per cent of the non-immigrant H visas, and less than 5 per cent of the immigrant visas issued to Mexicans.[30]

Regarding unskilled labour, NAFTA has failed to decrease labour migration between Mexico and the United States for several reasons. The two main development objectives that would contribute to the decline of migration flows, i.e., the creation of jobs and the reduction of the wage differential, have not materialized.[31] The most important factors that have played a role in complicating the Governments' original theoretical understanding of the relationship between trade and migration will now be reviewed.

During an initial adjustment period following the introduction of NAFTA, unauthorized migration was expected to increase in the short-term, but level off and decrease as living standards improved in Mexico.[32] As a result of opening to competition with more competitive firms, different industries in Mexico were affected in different ways. Some industries – furniture, for example – were severely damaged and eventually virtually disappeared due to their inability to compete with capital intensive international firms that sold goods and services at lower prices, while others – the banking and telecommunications industries – were strengthened.[33] In theory, unemployment resulting from affected industries would temporarily increase the flow of labour migrants to the United States until absorbed either by new competitive industries or by the existing ones once they adjusted.

The actual results, however, have been very different. The experience of NAFTA has shown that, as economies become more integrated, the tendency towards increased labour migration, which was expected in the early years, has remained in the long run.[34] The following factors have contributed to the disparity between expectations and reality:

---

[29] US Department of State, Bureau of Consular Affairs, *Reports of the Visa Office 2001* and *2004*. (Washington DC, 2001 and 2004) Table XVI.

[30] Ibid., Table XVI.

[31] J. Audley, et al., *NAFTA's Promise and Reality: Lessons from Mexico for the Hemisphere* (Washington DC, Carnegie Endowment for International Peace 2003) p. 4.

[32] D. Massey, 'Economic Development and International Migration in Comparative Perspective', 14 *Population and Development Review* (1988) p. 383; L. Young, 'Free Trade or Fair Trade: NAFTA and Agricultural Labor', 22 *Latin American Perspectives* (1995) p. 49.

[33] J. Hornbeck, *NAFTA at Ten*, Congressional Research Service Report for Congress RS21734, p. 4 (issued Feb. 2004) <http://digitalcommons.ilr.cornell.edu/key_workplace/41/>.

[34] International Organization for Migration (IOM), *World Migration 2005: Costs and Benefits of International Migration* (Geneva, IOM 2005) p. 393. For estimates on Mexico-US migration flows, see also J. Passel and R. Suro, *Rise, Peak, and Decline: Trends in US Migration 1992-2004*, Pew Hispanic Center Report, 27 Sept. 2005. Annex A, Table 1b.

a) *The number of jobs created since NAFTA came into effect has not met the growing demand for employment.* Insufficient employment is due to two main factors. First, jobs generated in the new industries did not necessarily compensate for the jobs lost in the industries that disappeared or were adversely affected. Second, population growth constituted an additional pressure as new people had to be incorporated into the labour market every year.[35] Therefore, the alternatives for displaced and newly incorporated workers are finding employment in the new industries, joining the informal labour market, or migrating to the United States. Unemployment has remained fairly constant in Mexico since 1994, but informality and migration, both legal and illegal, have increased since the Agreement came into effect.[36]

b) *The income gap between Mexico and the United States has increased as wages in Mexico remain depressed.* In spite of decreasing consumer prices, real wages have remained stagnant in Mexico throughout NAFTA's existence. When NAFTA was signed, the expectation was that the income differential between the US and the Mexican economies would narrow as a result of the Agreement, but the opposite has occurred. FDI arrived in Mexico in the form of export-oriented, labour-intensive, low-wage, manufacturing businesses, as in the case of the textile industry, establishing few inter-industry linkages.[37] The possibility of earning considerably higher wages in the United States overrides the prospect of finding a new job in Mexico.[38]

c) *Maquiladoras located along the border became a temporary station that facilitates labour migration to the United States.* Maquiladoras are foreign-owned factories where imported parts are assembled into products for export. Consequently, they are normally set up near the border in order to minimize transportation costs.[39] Maquiladoras employ mostly women with little or no labour security, thus depressing salaries, disrupting traditional family structures, and encouraging men to migrate to the United States.[40] This sector accounts for an increasingly higher percentage of total exports in Mexico.[41]

---

[35] S. Polaski estimates Mexico's annual growth in labour supply is about 1 million additional workers on average between 1994 and 2003; see S. Polaski, 'Jobs, Wages and Household Income', in J. Audley, et al., loc. cit. n. 31, at p. 14.

[36] Ibid., at p. 12. For an account of the increase of informality in Latin America, see also A. Portes and K. Hoffman, 'Latin American Class Structures: Their Composition and Change during the Neoliberal Era', 38 *Latin American Research Review* (2003) p. 41.

[37] P. Cooney, 'The Mexican Crisis and the Maquiladora Boom', 28 *Latin American Perspectives* (2001) p. 55.

[38] Manning, loc. cit. n. 11, at p. 10.

[39] In 2004, 74% of the maquiladoras were located in Mexico's border states. See Instituto Nacional de Estadística Geografía e Informática (INEGI), *Anuario de estadísticas por entidad federativa* (Mexico's Statistical Yearbook) (Mexico, INEGI 2005) <http://www.inegi.gob.mx/prod_serv/contenidos/espanol/bvinegi/productos/integracion/pais/aepef/2005/AEPEF_2005_Archivo1.pdf>.

[40] Manning, loc. cit. n. 11, at p. 13.

[41] See *supra* n. 39.

d) *Increasing integration between societies has multiplied the effects of migrant networks over time.* In spite of the economic benefits that job creation as a result of the Free Trade Agreements (FTAs) may bring, labour migration is unlikely to recede wherever kinship networks are present. Some studies have suggested that migration between Mexico and the United States has more to do with social capital and household considerations than it does with the cost-benefit analysis of the neoclassical theory.[42] Social capital is 'the sum of the resources, actual or virtual, that accrue to an individual or a group by virtue of possessing a durable network of more or less institutionalized relationships of mutual acquaintance and recognition'.[43] Information and assistance from people already living in the United States play a role in decreasing the costs of migration and raising the benefits of US employment. Over time, each act of migration tends to be self-perpetuating, since the network expands with every additional migrant. Consequently, the process of Mexicanization of the US agricultural workforce, combined with well-established networks, should continue to boost migration.[44]

e) *Even if living standards improve in migrant communities, people will continue to migrate due to tradition.* Migration to the United States is not simply an economic phenomenon, but also a social one. The longing for the way of life across the border has become part of the culture in some of the migrant communities. The way of life of *El Norte* continues to exert a strong cultural pull in migrant communities even when the costs outweigh the benefits in a rational analysis.[45]

As a consequence of these factors, migration between Mexico and the United States since NAFTA came into effect has increased considerably. Furthermore, unforeseen events at the time the Agreement was signed became additional hurdles for Mexican economic development. The economic crisis in 1994-95, for example, magnified the hardship that was expected in the first years after the Agreement came into effect. China's increasing role in the global marketplace also complicated the scene for Mexican reception of FDI. The Asian country's entry into the WTO has diverted some of the maquiladoras that would otherwise have been established in Mexico, because of the lower costs that China's abundant labour force and lower wages represent.

---

42 D. Massey and K. Espinosa, 'What's Driving Mexico-US Migration? A Theoretical, Empirical, and Policy Analysis', 102 *American Journal of Sociology* (1997) p. 940.

43 P. Bourdieu and L. Wacquant, *An Invitation to Reflexive Sociology* (Chicago, University of Chicago Press 1992) p. 119.

44 P. Martin, et al., 'Labor Migration and Economic Development,' paper prepared for the Commission for the Study of International Migration and Cooperative Economic Development (1989), cited in Acevedo and Espenshade, loc. cit. n. 9, at p. 734.

45 Massey, loc. cit. n. 32, at p. 398.

6. What Can Be Expected of CAFTA-DR?

The spirit of the text of CAFTA-DR was very similar to that of NAFTA in terms of development and migration.[46] The exclusion of stipulations related to the entry of business persons and the inclusion of the Understanding Regarding Immigration Measures made it clear that CAFTA-DR would stay away from addressing the issue directly. One indication that CAFTA-DR was seen through the same lens as NAFTA was given by President Bush's statement urging Congress to approve the Agreement:

> 'If you're concerned about immigration to this country, then you must understand that CAFTA and the benefits of CAFTA will help create new opportunity in Central American countries, which will mean someone will be able to find good work at home, somebody will be able to provide for their family at home, as opposed to having to make the long trip to the United States. CAFTA is good immigration policy, as well as good trade policy'.[47]

Notwithstanding this perspective, the outlook for CAFTA-DR in terms of alleviating migration pressures through development seems to be grimmer than that of NAFTA in 1994. The experience with the latter shows that CAFTA-DR could face similar obstacles to reducing labour migration flows. The Mexican experience points to three main problems:

1) Wages do not necessarily increase, since rising costs for maquiladoras causes them to relocate elsewhere.

2) Displaced workers laid off by affected industries seek employment elsewhere.

3) As the Central American and the US economies become more integrated and migrant networks expand and strengthen, the costs of migrating decreases and it becomes easier to enter and remain in the United States.

Two factors further complicate the scene. First, the Central American countries have to compete for FDI with Mexico's better infrastructure and proximity to the United States. Second, China's entrance into the world trade arena as a supplier of cheap manufactured products – through cheap labour – will complicate the creation of employment opportunities and the aim of raising wages in Central America and the Dominican Republic. China displaced Mexico in 2003 as the

---

[46] See, e.g., the Labor Advisory Committee on Trade Negotiations and Trade Policy Report on the US-Central America Free Trade Agreement (19 March 2004) <http://www.ustr.gov/assets/Trade_Agreements/Bilateral/CAFTA/CAFTA_Reports/asset_upload_file63_5935.pdf>.

[47] George W. Bush, 23 June 2005, *Statement of the President on the Central American and Dominican Republic Free Trade Agreement* <http://www.state.gov/e/eb/rls/rm/2005/48546.htm>.

number two supplier of goods and services to the US, and this trend is expected to continue.[48]

7. Conclusion and Key Challenges

This chapter has argued that neither NAFTA nor CAFTA-DR addresses the issue of migratory flows. The scope of both Agreements in their current form is limited, and their reach will not go beyond the limits of any free trade agreement's main objective: the removal of barriers to trade among states, such as quotas and tariffs, while maintaining the individual trade policy of each *vis-à-vis* non-members.

From the experience of NAFTA, it is evident that much more is needed to address migration, both legal and illegal, than what these Agreements include. As long as a demand for cheap labour in the United States, a significant wage differential between the United States and the source countries, and the need for remittances back home are present, labour migration to the United States will not decrease. Consequently, governments must go beyond indirect measures and deal with migration directly if any progress is to be made in regulating the thousands of migrants travelling to the United States every year searching for employment opportunities. In the words of a report by the Woodrow Wilson Center,

> 'The current status – a de facto guest worker program that lacks legal protection on the US side, and serves as a safety valve for the consequences of slow growth on the Mexican side – limits productivity, creates an underclass with few labor rights, and undermines the rule of law'.[49]

In addition to development efforts, migration has to be addressed explicitly both internationally and domestically. For instance, if a true goal of economic integration is to reduce migration through development, further forms of integration should be explored. A customs union, which establishes a common external trade policy, may be a feasible intermediate step between the existing free trade area and other solutions involving different degrees of labour mobility, such as a common market.[50] However, the outlook for such a measure is grim in the short- to

---

[48] US International Trade Administration, *Foreign Trade Highlights* (2005) Table 11: Top 50 Suppliers of US Imports <http://ita.doc.gov/td/industry/otea/usfth/aggregate/H04T11.html>.

[49] Woodrow Wilson International Center for Scholars and Consejo Mexicano de Asuntos Internacionales, *The United States and Mexico: Forging a Strategic Partnership* (Washington DC, 2005).

[50] The Caribbean Community and Common Market (CARICOM), for example, concerning the movement of community nationals, states the Member States' commitment to the 'the goal of free movement of their nationals within the Community' (Revised Treaty of the Chaguaramas Establishing the Caribbean Community Including the CARICOM Single Market and Economy, Art. 45). Consequently, Community nationals in the categories of university graduates, media workers, sportspersons, artists, and musicians have the right to seek employment in their jurisdictions (ibid., Art. 46). On CARICOM, see Sophie Nonnenmacher's chapter in this volume.

medium-term. The issue of migration remains a thorny one in the domestic arena in the United States, particularly when elections are near. In this context, it is necessary to look beyond short-term electoral gains and to understand the common benefits that regulating migration brings.

To be sure, the experience of CAFTA-DR will add another reference point to the analysis of the effects of FTAs in the region. If CAFTA-DR produces results similar to those of NAFTA, it may be time for the United States to reconsider the classical link between trade, development and migration. Consequently, a key issue is the search for feasible ways to address migration, both indirectly (through development) and directly (through international agreements), to complement the existing frameworks of NAFTA and CAFTA-DR. How to achieve this objective will remain an important challenge in the move towards the negotiation of a Free Trade Area of the Americas.

Selected Bibliography

Acevedo, D., and T.J. Espenshade, 'Implications of a North American Free Trade Agreement for Mexican Migration into the United States', 18 *Population and Development Review* (1992) p. 729.

Audley, J., et al., *NAFTA's Promise and Reality: Lessons from Mexico for the Hemisphere* (Washington DC, Carnegie Endowment for International Peace 2003).

International Organization for Migration, *World Migration 2005*: *Costs and Benefits of International Migration* (Geneva, IOM 2005).

Martin, P., 'Investment, Trade, and Migration', 29 *International Migration Review* (1995) p. 820.

Massey, D., 'Economic Development and International Migration in Comparative Perspective', 14 *Population and Development Review* (1998) p. 383.

Young, L., 'Free Trade or Fair Trade: NAFTA and Agricultural Labor', 22 *Latin American Perspectives* (1995) p. 49.

Forced Migration

Chapter 9
CHANGING PARADIGMS IN REFUGEE LAW

Rosemary Byrne*

1. Introduction

Just as the collapse of the Berlin Wall and the fall of the Twin Towers transformed migration patterns and immigration controls, so they have recast many of the dimensions of refugee and asylum law. This is not to say that the fundamental analytical axes for understanding refugee law and policy in the old world order of the 1980s are not enduring starting points for examining current developments in the field. The eternal tensions remain. Policies of migration control compete against refugee protection, and the objectives of normative protection under the 1951 Convention relating to the Status of Refugees[1] are balanced against available administrative resources (and the political will to allocate them). The battle between the strategies of states and counter-strategies of asylum seekers continues, as both engage in the dialectic process of adapting policies and practices to the fluctuations of 'the market place of protection.'[2] And as the legal framework for asylum seekers has adapted to the changing national and ideological terrains, so have these basic tensions within refugee law become more complex. It is tempting to attribute the direction – or acceleration – of core trends and developments in the field of asylum law to the processes unleashed by the events of 11/9 and 9/11;[3] the former hastening the construction of a common migration and asylum system within an expanding EU, and the latter securitizing approaches to human rights, asylum and extradition. Yet the powerful forces of globalization that drive and direct migration have also contributed to this period of unprecedented codification of refugee norms, practices and policies – within and beyond Europe. As transborder flows of information, expertise, and development of professional net-

* Teaches international and human rights law at Trinity College Dublin, where she is also a Research Fellow at the Institute of International Integration Studies.

[1] Convention relating to the Status of Refugees, 28 July 1951, 189 *UNTS* 137 (hereafter '1951 Convention').

[2] For a discussion of paradigm of the 'market place of protection' in the context of harmonizing European asylum policy, see G. Noll, *Negotiating Asylum* (The Hague, Kluwer 2000).

[3] These dates mark the fall of the Berlin Wall on 9 Nov. 1989 and the terrorist attack on the Twin Towers on 11 Sept. 2001.

R. Cholewinski, R. Perruchoud and E. MacDonald, eds., International Migration Law

works have transformed so many areas of legal and social policy,[4] the intensified interactions across borders between international, regional and national officials, policy makers, asylum adjudicators and non-governmental organizations have had a formative impact on the expansion and deepening of refugee law. This is the legal and sociological landscape in which contemporary refugee practice is developing.

The removal of frontiers and ideological divides with the fall of the Iron Curtain heightened the impetus to translate limited attempts at inter-governmental harmonization of asylum policy into wide-reaching, binding European law. As the Baltics and Central and Eastern Europe changed from sending states to transit and, increasingly, to host states for refugees and migrants, the dismantled exit barriers in the East became porous points of entry to Western Europe.[5] Although the European Union had successfully introduced Directives on Temporary Protection, Standards of Reception, and Family Reunification,[6] the March 2004 target date set for the completion of the definitional and procedural harmonization, envisioned under Part III, Title IV, Article 63 of the EC Treaty, [7] was not met. By the close of 2005, the two core Directives of European asylum law had been passed: the Directive for the Qualification and Status of Third Country Nationals and Stateless Persons as Refugees or who Otherwise Need International Protection; and the Directive for Minimum Standards for Procedures Granting and Withdrawing Refugee Status.[8]

In *Migration and International Legal Norms*, Guy Goodwin-Gill and Kathleen Newland emphasized how the absence of an international supervisory mechanism under the 1951 Convention has left the application of the treaty to domestic legal systems. This has produced a fragmented interpretation of international legal obligations towards refugees, with the result that many individuals are excluded from formal protection.[9] While this remains a defining feature of the international

[4] R. Holton, *Making Globalization* (New York, Palgrave MacMillan, 2005).

[5] R. Byrne, G. Noll, and J. Vedsted Hansen, 'Understanding Refugee Law in an Enlarged European Union', 15 *European Journal of International Law* 2 (2004) p. 357.

[6] Council Directive 2001/55/EC of 20 July 2001 on minimum standards for giving temporary protection in the event of a mass influx of displaced persons and on measures promoting a balance of efforts between Member States in receiving such persons and bearing the consequences thereof, OJ 2001 L 212/12 (hereafter 'Temporary Protection Directive'); Council Directive 2003/9/EC of 27 Jan. 2003 laying down minimum standards for the reception of asylum seekers (hereafter 'Standards for Reception Directive') OJ 2003 L 31/18; Council Directive 2003/86/EC of 22 Sept. 2003 on the right to family reunification, OJ 2003 L 251/12.

[7] Treaty Establishing the European Community, OJ 2002 L 325/33, Part III, Title IV, Art. 63.

[8] Council Directive 2004/83/EC of 29 April 2004 on minimum standards for the qualification and status of third country nationals and stateless persons as refugees or as persons who otherwise need international protection and the content of the protection granted, OJ 2004 L 304/12 (hereafter 'Qualification Directive'); Council Directive 2005/85/EC of 1 Dec. 2005 on minimum standards on procedures in Member States for granting and withdrawing refugee status, OJ 2005 L 326/13 (hereafter 'Procedures Directive').

[9] G. Goodwin-Gill and K. Newland, 'Forced Migration and International Law', in T.A. Aleinikoff and V. Chetail (eds.), *Migration and International Legal Norms* (The Hague, T.M.C. Asser Press, 2003) p. 123.

legal refugee regime, the recent adoption of the European asylum directives represents the most substantial move towards concretizing transnational legal norms and practices in refugee law since the entry into force of the 1951 Convention. Its significance goes beyond the complex process of harmonization and codification, however. The content of this legislation reflects the current – and will impact the future – development of refugee law within and beyond the twenty-seven states of the European Union.

2. Refugee and Subsidiary Protection

The long recognized legal limitations of the definition of refugee under Article 1A of the 1951 Convention has lead to three discernible trends across national systems. The first is towards a restrictive application of that definition. As restrictionist practices leave many outside of the traditional refugee protection framework, however, they have given rise to the second trend, which has been towards a re-examination of the legal interpretative frameworks that can expand the narrow criteria of the 1951 refugee definition. Among the developments of the substantive criteria for refugee status has been a movement towards recognizing 'persecution' perpetrated by non-state agents, as well as a broader interpretation of the most ambiguous of the five grounds of persecution, 'membership of a particular social group' under Article 1A(2). The third trend has been towards an increased reliance upon forms of 'subsidiary' or 'complementary' protection against *non-refoulement* for those individuals who do not meet the criteria of Article 1A of the 1951 Convention. While the term 'subsidiary' or 'complementary' protection is used generally, it encompasses various forms in national law and practice. It ranges from explicit guarantees based upon human rights treaties, such as the Convention against Torture (CAT),[10] the International Covenant on Civil and Political Rights (ICCPR),[11] and the European Convention on Human Rights and Fundamental Freedoms (ECHR),[12] to more discretionary forms of humanitarian and exceptional leave to remain.[13] Many 'subsidiary' forms of protection available in national jurisdictions often do not carry the same rights and entitlements as those that are set forth in the 1951 Convention, and that are thus attached to refugee status in domestic laws.[14]

These trends have lead to a transformation of the understanding of the fundamental conception of 'protection' that underlies international refugee law. In the

---

[10] Convention against Torture and Other Cruel, Inhuman or Degrading Treatment or Punishment, 10 Dec. 1984, 1465 *UNTS* 85, Arts. 3, 22.

[11] International Covenant on Civil and Political Rights, 16 Dec. 1966, 999 *UNTS* 171, Art. 7.

[12] Convention for the Protection of Human Rights and Fundamental Freedoms, 4 Nov. 1950, *ETS* No. 5.

[13] R. Mandal, 'Protection Mechanisms Outside of the 1951 Convention ("Complementary Protection")' (Geneva, UNHCR 2005) <www.unhcr.se/Pdf/Legal_protection_research_2005.pdf>.

[14] R. Piotrowicz and C. van Eck, 'Subsidiary Protection and Primary Rights', 53 *International and Comparative Law Quarterly* (2004) p. 193.

field of asylum, 'protection', as originally set out in the mandate for the United Nations High Commissioner for Refugees and incorporated into the UNHCR Handbook, is directly linked to ensuring that 'refugees' – as defined by the 1951 Convention – are treated in compliance with international human rights standards. With the restrictive application of the 1951 Convention, and increased recourse to alternative legal bases for *non-refoulement*, legal parlance has increasingly come to refer to asylum seekers as 'protection' seekers. This is illustrative of how the conception of protection in the area of refugee law has expanded beyond the narrow group of 1951 Convention refugees, to embrace those who may be entitled to protection from *non-refoulement* under other international human rights treaties.[15] The normative character of this conception was strengthened with the introduction of the Qualification Directive.[16] This Directive not only provides the first legal framework for 'subsidiary' protection in regional or international law, but it also defines 'international protection' as including both refugee and subsidiary protection status. Under Article 2(e) of the Directive, the eligibility of a person for subsidiary protection is defined as

> 'a third country national or a stateless person who does not qualify as a refugee but in respect of whom substantial grounds have been shown for believing that the person concerned, if returned to his or her country of origin ... would face a real risk of suffering serious harm ... and is unable, or owing to such risk, unwilling to avail himself or herself of the protection of that country'.

'Suffering serious harm' under Article 15 of the Directive is defined as the death penalty, 'torture or inhuman or degrading treatment or punishment' and 'serious and individual threat to a civilian's life or person by reason of indiscriminate violence and situations of international or internal armed conflict'.[17] The specification of the death penalty as a form of serious harm offers a more robust guarantee against *refoulement* in death penalty cases, as it must be interpreted in accordance with the 2003 Protocol No. 13 to the ECHR, Concerning the Abolition of the Death Penalty in All Circumstances.[18] Drawn from Article 3 of the ECHR and the CAT, the interpretation of 'torture or inhuman or degrading treatment or punishment' should follow the jurisprudence of both the European Court of Human Rights and the Committee against Torture.[19] The last criterion, which ap-

[15] See R. Plender and N. Mole, 'Beyond the Geneva Convention: constructing a de facto right of asylum from international human rights instruments', in F. Nicholson and P. Twomey (eds.), *Refugee Rights and Realities: Evolving International Concepts and Regimes* (Cambridge, Cambridge University Press 1999) p. 81.

[16] Qualification Directive, loc. cit. n. 8, Arts. 2(e), 5.

[17] Ibid., Art. 15

[18] Protocol No. 13 to the ECHR, Concerning the Abolition of the Death Penalty in all Circumstances, 3 May 2002, *ETS* No. 187.

[19] H. Battjes, 'A Balance between Fairness and Efficiency? The Directive on International Protection and the Dublin Regulation', 4 *European Journal of Migration and Law* (2002) p. 159 at p. 168.

plies to situations of indiscriminate violence and internal armed conflict, is drawn from the 2001 Temporary Protection Directive, which applies to situations of mass influx.[20] However, contrary to the Temporary Protection Directive, claimants seeking protection under the Qualification Directive must show a serious and individualized threat in order to fulfil the criteria for subsidiary protection.

The need to elaborate the definitional criteria in the Directive responds to the normative gaps in international refugee law, and highlights their impact on protection. This is illustrated by Article 6 of the Qualification Directive, which specifies that 'persecution or serious harm' includes that carried out by 'non-state actors'.[21] While Article 6 brings closure to the absence of protection for those suffering persecution from non-state actors within select Member States of the European Union, this issue still has significant implications for refugees in many non-EU jurisdictions. In the European context, the Dublin Convention, and now the Dublin II Regulation, made the failure of states such as Germany and France to recognize non-state agent 'persecution' particularly problematic. Under these regimes, which determine the state responsible for examining the asylum application, a claim could be transferred amongst EU Member States without any substantive consideration of its merits, and absent any explicit obligation to examine the standards of procedural and substantive protection in the receiving Member State.[22]

3. Membership of a Particular Social Group

Within the interpretative diversity of international refugee law, national jurisdictions have been moving towards an expanding conception of membership of a 'social group'. Aleinikoff observes that the national jurisprudence arising from 'social group' cases is pushing the boundaries of international refugee law, as adjudicators are confronted with persecution claims related to, *inter alia*, domestic abuse, female genital mutilation, coercive family planning policies, and discrimination against the disabled.[23] The rapid pace of normative evolution in this area

[20] Temporary Protection Directive, loc. cit. n. 6. Under Art. 2(c), 'displaced persons' who are entitled to temporary protection are defined as those who have 'fled areas of armed conflict or endemic violence' and 'persons at serious risk of or have been the victims of, systemic or generalized violence of their human rights'.

[21] 'Actors of persecution or serious harm include: ... non-State actors, if it can be demonstrated that the actors mentioned in (a) and (b), including international organizations, are unable or unwilling to provide protection against persecution or serious harm'. Art. 6, Qualification Directive, loc. cit. n. 8.

[22] Convention determining the State responsible for examining applications for asylum lodged in one of the Member States of the European Communities, 15 June 1990, OJ 1997 C 254/1 (hereafter, 'Dublin Convention'); Council Regulation 343/2003/EC of 18 Feb. 2003 establishing the criteria and mechanisms for determining the Member States responsible for examining an asylum application lodged in one of the Member States by a third-country national, OJ 2003 L 50/1 (hereafter, 'Dublin II').

[23] T.A. Aleinikoff, 'Protected Characteristics and Social Perceptions: An Analysis of the Meaning of "Membership of a Particular Social Group" Determination', in E. Feller, V. Türk and F. Nicholson

can be witnessed through the international and regional developments that followed Aleinikoff's analysis of state practice in 2001 for the UNHCR Global Consultations process. His examination of common law cases traces two dominant approaches to the definition of social group. The first, based upon 'protected' characteristics, requires that its members share immutable and innate characteristics. The second, based upon 'social perceptions', requires that the 'social group' merely be perceived as such by society. The selection by an asylum adjudicator of one interpretive approach to the exclusion of the other can result in opposite decisions. Following the scrutiny of this protection gap through the Global Consultations process, the UNHCR integrated both approaches into its guidelines on International Protection in 2002,[24] as did the Qualification Directive in 2004.[25]

This process of conceptual convergence moves towards a more consistent approach to the Convention criteria. It should be seen in the context of the unprecedented flow of information and jurisprudence across borders, and between decision makers and advocates, that did not exist a decade ago. Easy electronic access to UNHCR, NGO and academic position papers, alongside asylum jurisprudence from courts across many jurisdictions, has dramatically enhanced the technical expertise and the breadth of the community that is able to engage in the progressive development of refugee law.[26] A more integrated approach to the interpretation of the international refugee definition and attendant process obligations has also been furthered by the establishment of organizations such as the International Refugee Law Judges Association.[27] This cross-fertilization of ideas and principles is inevitable given the universal accessibility to information and expertise through the internet, and the existence of transjurisdictional professional networks.

4. Safe Third Country Practices

Parallel to developments in substantive protection, the diversity of procedural mechanisms remains strong in the industrial states of the North, with its resort to a phalanx of procedural barriers aimed at excluding, deterring or deflecting asylum seekers from entry into the jurisdiction and its variety of refugee status determination systems. These policies, which include, *inter alia*, carrier sanctions, visa lists, accelerated border procedures, readmission agreements with transit countries and countries of origin, safe third country practices, and detention, create a

(eds.), *Refugee Protection in International Law: UNHCR's Global Consultations on International Protection* (Cambridge, Cambridge University Press 2003) p. 263 at p. 264.

24 UNHCR, 'Guidelines on International Protection: "Membership of a Particular Social Group"', para. 11. See also V. Türk and F. Nicholson, 'Refugee Protection in International Law: An Overall Perspective', in E. Feller, V. Türk and F. Nicholson, loc. cit. n. 23, p. 3 at pp. 17-18.

25 Qualification Directive, loc. cit. n. 8, Art. 10(d).

26 See, e.g., <www.refugeecaselaw.org>; <www.unhcr.org>; and <www.refugeelawreader.org>.

27 See website of the International Association of Refugee Law Judges at <www.iarlj.nl>.

continuing challenge to the provision of access to fair determination procedures and hence protection.[28]

Safe third country policies have now come of age on an international scale. Considered a mere 'notion' by the UNHCR a decade ago, the 'safe third country' concept now gives rise to procedures used by a vast number of states for deflecting asylum claims onto other jurisdictions. These policies, in practice, are often implemented automatically on a similar basis to that under the Dublin regime. Hence removals of asylum seekers are carried out without a meaningful and individualized review of the protection standards in the receiving state, or even an explicit guarantee that the returned asylum seeker will be admitted into a determination system. Without parallel binding universal instruments that would eliminate the definitional diversity that impedes protection standards, or the procedural barriers that prevent their fair application, safe third country returns without adequate assessments of effective protection – as discussed in this volume by Legomsky – will continue to put sending states in potential breach of their obligation of *non-refoulement* under the 1951 Convention.

The adoption by the EU of a safe third country policy in the Procedures Directive is not surprising.[29] An interesting feature of the EU safe third country practice is its stated policy linkage with both capacity building and the transfer of cases back to new (at that time, future) Member States. The EU policy of transferring asylum seekers back to these new transit states required a commitment to strengthen refugee laws in the candidate countries, alongside the construction of barriers to entry. Characteristic of the attempt to deflect arrivals of asylum seekers was the proliferation of readmission agreements containing no explicit guarantees that asylum seekers would have their claims considered in the receiving state.[30] Yet the transfer of responsibility for the assessment of an asylum claim, and the asylum seeker, to another state through which he or she has transited to the West was attractive, not only to the old Members of the EU, but also to the then future, now new, Member States. These countries in turn incorporated the necessary legislation into their national systems to return asylum seekers back across their eastern frontiers.[31] These practices gave rise to critiques over the criteria for determining standards of safety in a third state, a controversy which has

---

[28] S. Legomsky, *Immigration and Refugee Law and Policy* (Eagen, MN, West Group 2004) ch. 11, section B. 7.

[29] C. Costello, 'The Asylum Procedures Directive and the Proliferation of Safe Third Country Practices, Deterrence, Deflection and the Dismantling of International Protection?', 7 *European Journal of Migration Law* (2005) p. 35.

[30] R. Cholewinski, *The Baltic States in the context of the Dublin Convention and Related Asylum Norms* (Helsinki, IOM 2001). See also N. Albuquerque Abell, 'The Compatibility of Readmission Agreements with the 1951 Convention relating to the Status of Refugees', 11 *International Journal of Refugee Law* (1999) p. 60.

[31] See R. Cholewinski, op. cit. n. 30; R. Byrne, G. Noll and J. Vedsted-Hansen, 'Western European Asylum Policies for Export: The Transfer of Protection and Deflection Formulas to Central Europe and the Baltics', in R. Byrne, G. Noll and J. Vedsted-Hansen (eds.), *New Asylum Countries? Migration Control and Refugee Protection in an Enlarged European Union* (The Hague, Kluwer 2002) p. 2.

continued with the adoption of the Procedures Directive. Under this legislation, the substantive criteria for designating safe third countries improve the standard of protection by requiring of receiving states 'observance', and no longer simply the ratification, of the 1951 Convention and the ECHR. These criteria, however, still fall well below the concept of 'effective protection' that was presented by the Commission in its discussion of the 'safe third country' concept, and that has developed within the broader context of international law. The Commission found that there was a 'general agreement' among states that 'effective protection' entailed physical security, protection against *refoulement* and access to UNHCR or national asylum procedures with sufficient safeguards.[32] In his review of international standards, Legomsky identifies a more expanded framework of protection norms, including the obligation on states not simply to confirm that a third country has asylum procedures in place, but also that an asylum seeker will be admitted into that procedure for a determination of his or her claim.[33]

Safe country practices have also been advanced further as a policy mechanism for limiting the substantive assessment of asylum claims through the adoption of the Safe Country of Origin concept in the Procedures Directive. Under the Directive, asylum seekers arriving from states appearing on an official list of 'safe countries' agreed upon by EU Member States would have their claims deemed 'unfounded'.[34] The compromises on standards of protection that could easily result from the rapid creation and implementation of such a list have been headed off by the enhanced capacity of non-governmental organizations to monitor not only national, but also regional and international refugee policy. The credibility of the safe country criteria adopted under EU legislation by Member States was seriously challenged when Statewatch produced documentation of the 'closed doors' negotiation process used in drawing up the EU safe country list. This publicly demonstrated an alarming absence of in-depth analysis of country conditions and the lack of consensus among states on human rights standards within the specified jurisdictions. Statewatch was able to document that of the seven African countries that are on the list (which claims 'unanimous' agreement by EU states) there was not one for which Member States' individual assessments were all in agreement regarding conditions of safety. Revealingly, upon review of country of origin conditions in each of the African countries on the list, the Commission clearly opposed their designation as 'safe' in every case.[35]

---

[32] European Commission, *Proposal for a Council Directive on Minimum standards on procedures in Member States for granting and withdrawing refugee status* (COM (2000) 578, 20 Sept. 2000) p. 6.

[33] S. Legomsky, 'Secondary Refugee Movements and the Return of Asylum Seekers to Third Countries: The Meaning of Effective Protection', 15 *International Journal of Refugee Law* 4 (2004) p. 567.

[34] Procedures Directive, loc. cit. n. 8, Arts. 23(4)(c), 30, 30A, 30B, Annex B to Annex 1.

[35] The African states that were listed are: Benin, Botswana, Cape Verde, Ghana, Mali, Mauritius, and Senegal. See Statewatch, 'EU divided over list of "safe countries of origin"' (Sept. 2004) <www.statewatch.org/news/2004/sep/safe-countries>.

5. Exclusion

The attacks of September 11, with aliens accessing a host state with the intention of carrying out violence, associated the right to asylum with the potential for terrorist activity that could threaten the life of the nation. Renewed interest in the provisions under Article 1F of the 1951 Convention, which exclude individuals from protection against *non-refoulement* based upon the commission of a 'crime against peace, a war crime, or a crime against humanity', followed the arrival of asylum seekers in flight from the Balkans and Rwanda.[36] The content of these crimes has evolved through the jurisprudence of the *ad hoc* International Criminal Tribunals for Rwanda and the Former Yugoslavia.[37] Yet with the potential for international crimes to be carried out within, and against, the receiving state, the events of September 11 recalibrated the equilibrium between national interests in controlling entry and the right to substantive and procedural protections in seeking refugee status. With the advent of the 'securitization' of human rights law, exclusion has been revisited by scholars, states and the UNHCR. Among the central protection concerns have been the threat to procedural safeguards in the application of the exclusion provisions of Article 1F, the risk that exclusion will provide an automatic bar to access to a refugee determination process, and the fear that national legislation will both expand the narrow list of grounds for which exclusion is permitted under Article 1F and restrict the broader range of protection offered to excluded individuals under the wider body of human rights law that addresses non-returnability.[38]

6. Cessation

This movement towards excluding individuals from protection under the 1951 Convention, and the official policies directed towards hosting refugees on a temporary, rather than permanent, basis, has invited a re-examination of the cessation clauses under Article 1C, whereby individuals lose their protection upon a change in conditions in their country of origin that removes the need for international protection. The process of the UNHCR's Global Consultations has illus-

---

[36] See M. Bliss, '"Serious Reasons for Considering": Minimum Standards of Procedural Fairness in the Application of the Article 1F Exclusion Clauses', 12 *International Journal of Refugee Law* (2000) p. 92.

[37] E. Møse, 'The Criminality Perspective', 15 *Georgetown Immigration Law Journal* (2001) p. 463; H. Storey and R. Wallace, 'War and Peace in Refugee Law Jurisprudence', 95 *American Journal of International Law* (2001) p. 349.

[38] UNHCR, 'Addressing Security Concerns without Undermining Refugee Protection, UNHCR's perspective', Position Paper 29, Nov. 2001 <www.unchr.ch>; UNHCR, 'Guidelines on International Protection: Application of the Exclusion Clauses: Article 1F of the 1951 Convention relating to the Status of Refugees', UN Doc. HCR/GIP/03/05, 4 Sept. 2003; G. Gilbert, 'Current issues in the application of the exclusion clauses', in E. Feller, V. Türk and F. Nicholson, loc. cit. n. 23, at p. 425.

trated the limited reliance upon these clauses in the past by the UNHCR, and the need for international criteria to be carefully adopted in the context of ending the protection afforded to individuals under the 1951 Convention. The risk that the operational flexibility required to implement the cessation clauses might be accompanied by a less rigorous application of the normative standards under Article 1C is of concern to experts in the field. More developed procedural protections to accompany the implementation of the cessation clauses are needed to ensure that cessation criteria are not applied in an overly-formalistic manner, and that adequate account is taken of factors including human security, sustainability of return, and human rights situations.[39]

7. Asylum Determination Procedures

These trends, which are pushing the progressive development of international refugee law, demonstrate the extent to which globalization not only affects the flows of forced and voluntary migration, but also contributes to the strengthening of government coordination in attempting to regulate migration, and the increasing role of civil society bodies concerned with the treatment and protection of migrants and asylum seekers. The result of this has been a movement towards the deepening of refugee principles and norms through the formal codification of procedures and practices under the participatory eye of civil society.

Accompanying this process of standard setting is the emergence of grassroots and refugee policy NGOs as vigilant, visible and vocal networks. The impact of this participation can be seen in the publication, in September 2005, by the UNHCR of its own refugee status determination procedures.[40] Given the Organization's extensive role in international determination processes in 80 countries, this movement towards accountability followed increasing pressure from NGOs. The UNHCR's public statements in the debates on minimal procedural guarantees in the process of the negotiations for the Procedures Directive included a range of submissions on the procedural prerequisites for an effective protection regime.[41] The need to proclaim publicly the right to legal representation and an effective remedy in regional standards left the institution somewhat exposed to criticism when these guarantees were found not to be present in the procedures of some of its regional and national branch offices engaged in refugee determination processes.[42] After the establishment of a web site monitoring UNHCR status

[39] UNHCR, 'The Cessation Clauses: Guidelines on their application,' 2004 <http://www.unhcr.org>; 'Summary Conclusions: Cessation of Refugee Status, Expert Roundtable, Lisbon, May 2001' in E. Feller, V. Türk and F. Nicholson, loc. cit. n. 23, p. 479 at p. 545.

[40] UNHCR, 'Procedural Standards for Refugee Status Determination under UNHCR's Mandate', (Geneva, UNHCR, 2005) <http://www.unhcr.org/cgi-bin/texis/vtx/publ>.

[41] UNHCR, 'Note on key issues of concern to UNHCR on the draft Asylum Procedures Directive', March 2004 <www.unhcr.org>.

[42] See 'Eight NGO's tell UNHCR that new procedures must not retreat from established standards of fairness', 9 Aug. 2005 <www.rsdwatch.org>.

determination procedures by concerned advocates, the international body moved towards more transparent decision-making by publishing in September 2005 its standards and procedures.

8. Warehousing

The 'warehousing' of refugees is another area of refugee law that has been pushed onto the international agenda by the intensive transnational efforts of NGOs. These North/South advocacy networks have highlighted the plight of refugees kept in camps for an extensive period with limited rights in their host country.[43] As a result of this global campaign, the anti-warehousing movement is also able to report grassroots initiatives targeting the rights to work, to a livelihood and to freedom of movement in countries as diverse as Kenya, Uruguay, Australia, Malaysia, Thailand, Pakistan, Namibia, the United Kingdom, Zambia and Zimbabwe.[44] Not long ago, NGOs in the area of refugee law and policy were relatively marginalized in the broader international dialogue on the evolving normative protection framework. In this era of intensive international integration, the anti-warehousing campaign shows how the capacity of networks to coordinate their agendas, access and transfer expertise, and publicize their work can influence the evolving direction of international standard setting in the field.

9. Conclusion

As the eternal tensions that frame the field of refugee and asylum law remain, so do the key challenges for ensuring that legal responses to migration provide effective protection of refugees. The changing context, in which international refugee law is rapidly evolving, however, poses new challenges. As this field enters an unprecedented period of development and codification, the need for effective criteria and procedures is heightened. As evidenced by the expansion of protection through the wider interpretation of core elements of the refugee definition, and the clearer exposition of the content of international crimes, the codification of refugee norms and standards provides the opportunity for best practice and current human rights law to serve as a rich resource for the interpretation of 1951 Convention standards, in light of procedurally complex risks of *refoulement*. In the highly politicized realm of refugee law, the consequence of codifying poorly framed criteria is a serious threat to protection. The refocus on cessation, exclusion, and safe country practices all point to a growing reliance upon selective cri-

---

[43] See for instance the global anti-warehousing campaign coordinated by the US Committee for Refugees at <www.refugees.org>.

[44] 'Anti-Warehousing Work Around the World', 26 *Refugee Reports* (Washington, US Committee for Refugees and Immigrants 2005).

teria as a means of circumventing a meaningful evaluation of claims for protection under the 1951 Convention. Faith in the legal formulas that curtail individual assessment has yet to offer the promised deliverance from the risk of *refoulement*. While motivations for, and patterns of, migration may change, as long as international refugee law remains committed to an individualized procedure to determine protection needs, the quest for robust criteria that effectively translate into national practice will remain. The challenge of this decade is to utilize the greater access to, and flow of, information on refugee policy and practice. With the expanded scope of informed participants across sectors, and an increase in transnational research on core legal issues and procedures, there is hope for a significantly stronger international refugee protection regime. The search for the necessary political will, however, remains a truly eternal quest.

Selected Bibliography

Albuquerque Abell, N., 'The Compatibility of Readmission Agreements with the 1951 Convention relating to the Status of Refugees', 11 *International Journal of Refugee Law* (1999) p. 60.

Aleinikoff, T.A., 'Protected Characteristics and Social Perceptions: An Analysis of the Meaning of "Membership of a Particular Social Group" Determination', in E. Feller, V. Türk, and F. Nicholson (eds.), *Refugee Protection in International Law: UNHCR's Global Consultations on International Protection* (Cambridge, Cambridge University Press 2003) p. 263.

Battjes, H., 'A Balance between Fairness and Efficiency? The Directive on International Protection and the Dublin Regulation', 4 *European Journal of Migration and Law* (2002) p. 159.

Bliss, M., '"Serious Reasons for Considering": Minimum Standards of Procedural Fairness in the Application of the Article 1F Exclusion Clauses', 12 *International Journal of Refugee Law* (2000) p. 92.

Byrne, R., G. Noll, and J. Vedsted Hansen, 'Understanding Refugee Law in an Enlarged European Union', 15 *European Journal of International Law* 2 (2004) p. 357.

—, 'Western European Asylum Policies for Export: The Transfer of Protection and Deflection Formulas to Central Europe and the Baltics', in R. Byrne, G. Noll and J. Vedsted Hansen (eds.), *New Asylum Countries? Migration Control and Refugee Protection in an Enlarged European Union* (The Hague, Kluwer 2002) p. 2.

Cholewinski, R., *The Baltic States in the context of the Dublin Convention and Related Asylum Norms* (Helsinki, IOM 2001).

Costello, C., 'The Asylum Procedures Directive and the Proliferation of Safe Third Country Practices, Deterrence, Deflection and the Dismantling of International Protection?', 7 *European Journal of Migration Law* (2005) p. 35.

Gilbert, G., 'Current issues in the application of the exclusion clauses', in E. Feller, V. Türk and F. Nicholson (eds.), *Refugee Protection in International Law: UNHCR's Global Consultations on International Protection* (Cambridge, Cambridge University Press 2003) p. 425.

Legomsky, S., 'Secondary Refugee Movements and the Return of Asylum Seekers to Third Countries: The Meaning of Effective Protection', 15 *International Journal of Refugee Law* 4 (2004) p. 567.

Mandal, R., 'Protection Mechanisms Outside of the 1951 Convention ("Complementary Protection")' <http://www.unhcr.se/Pdf/Legal_protection_research_2005.pdf>.

Møse, E., 'The Criminality Perspective', 15 *Georgetown Immigration Law Journal* (2001) p. 463.

Noll, G., *Negotiating Asylum* (The Hague, Kluwer 2000).

Piotrowicz, R., and C. van Eck, 'Subsidiary Protection and Primary Rights', 53 *International and Comparative Law Quarterly* (2004) p. 193.

Plender, R., and N. Mole, 'Beyond the Geneva Convention: Constructing a De Facto Right of Asylum from International Human Rights Instruments', in F. Nicholson and P. Twomey (eds.), *Refugee Rights and Realities: Evolving International Concepts and Regimes* (Cambridge, Cambridge University Press 1999) p. 81.

Storey, H., and R. Wallace, 'War and Peace in Refugee Law Jurisprudence', 95 *American Journal of International Law* (2001) p. 349.

Türk, V., and F. Nicholson, 'Refugee Protection in International Law: An Overall Perspective', in E. Feller, V. Türk, and F. Nicholson (eds.), *Refugee Protection in International Law: UNHCR's Global Consultations on International Protection* (Cambridge, Cambridge University Press 2003) p. 3.

UNHCR, 'Addressing Security Concerns without Undermining Refugee Protection, UNHCR's perspective', Position Paper 29, Nov. 2001 <www.unchr.org>.

Chapter 10
ADDRESSING SECONDARY REFUGEE MOVEMENTS

Stephen H. Legomsky*

1. INTRODUCTION[1]

Refugees today seldom travel directly from their countries of origin to the countries in which they intend to request asylum. For a variety of reasons, they are usually forced to travel circuitous routes to their ultimate intended destinations. The movement from the country of origin to one of the intermediate ('third') countries is often called a 'primary' movement. The subsequent movement from a third country to their ultimate destination, where they request asylum, is usually called a 'secondary' movement.

Secondary refugee movements occur for a variety of reasons. The third countries are often developing states, frequently in the regions of origin, in which the living conditions, personal freedoms, or physical safety levels fall far short of acceptable international standards or even basic subsistence requirements. Sometimes it is, or becomes, obvious that any protection the third country is able to offer will not be durable. The refugee recognition rates, reception arrangements or integration conditions might be more favourable in the destination country. In other cases, refugees might move on for the same reason that voluntary migrants move on – better life opportunities for themselves and their families, including employment and education.[2] Still other refugees might move on because they have family members in the destination country, or at least existing enclaves from their countries of origin.[3] In many cases, the decisions as to itinerary are in the

* Charles Nagel Professor of International Law at Washington University, St. Louis, and the founding Director of the Harris Institute for Global Legal Studies.

[1] Much of this analysis is distilled from a far more detailed consultant's report prepared for the UNHCR, and published in revised form as S.H. Legomsky, 'Secondary Refugee Movements and the Return of Asylum Seekers to Third Countries: The Meaning of Effective Protection', 15 *International Journal of Refugee Law* (2003) p. 567. I thank the participants at the November 2005 Geneva workshop convened by the IOM, and especially Michele Klein Solomon, for their helpful comments on an earlier draft.

[2] See, e.g., UNHCR, Executive Committee (EXCOM) Conclusion 58 (XL), 'Problem of Refugees and Asylum-Seekers Who Move in an Irregular Manner from a Country in Which They Had Already Found Protection' (1989), para. b.

[3] UNHCR Global Consultations in Budapest, Background Paper No. 2, 'The application of the "safe third country" notion and its impact on the management of flows and on the protection of refugees'

hands of professional smugglers or traffickers, and the refugees themselves have little or no say in the matter.[4]

Secondary refugee movements have engendered some fundamental questions of law and policy. From the standpoint of the individual, precisely how much legal freedom should one have to choose the country that will decide his or her asylum claim in substance? From the standpoints of countries of origin, third countries, ultimate destination countries, and the world community, how should the responsibility for protecting refugees be allocated?

In recent years the ultimate destination countries have displayed increasing reluctance to decide asylum claims filed by those who have arrived at their frontiers after secondary movements. The practice has been to return the person to the relevant third country for the latter to decide the asylum claim. They have employed two distinct but related devices for doing so. Under the so-called 'safe third country' approach, the state rejects asylum applications filed by individuals who have travelled through countries that are generally thought to be safe and in which, it is felt, the person *should have requested* protection. This restriction might be imposed unilaterally or it might be part of an agreement with one or more other countries. The other heading, which covers people who *in fact received* some kind of protection in a third country, is termed 'first country of asylum'. The precise requirements vary.

In Europe, both sorts of third country limitations – first country of asylum restrictions and safe third country restrictions – are now common. Typically, they entail regional agreements whereby states accept common rules for determining which of them should adjudicate the asylum claims of individuals whose flights have taken them through several signatory states. Those agreements normally contain language that purports to assure that asylum applicants are sent only to 'safe' countries for adjudication of their claims. But there is disagreement over the very concept of a 'safe third country' limitation, over the definition of 'safe', and over how that definition is applied in practice.[5] In North America, similar is-

(May 2001) p. 1; European Commission, Staff Working Paper, *Evaluation of the Dublin Convention* (SEC (2001) 756, 13 June 2001) p. 18.

[4] UNHCR, op. cit. n. 3, at p. 1; European Commission, Staff Working Paper, *Revisiting the Dublin Convention: Developing Community legislation for determining which Member State is responsible for considering an application for asylum submitted in one of the Member States* (SEC (2000) 522, 21 March 2000), para. 29.

[5] See, e.g., J. Bhabha, 'European Harmonisation of Asylum Policy: A Flawed Process', 35 *Virginia Journal of International Law* (1994) p. 101; R. Byrne and A. Shacknove, 'The Safe Country Notion in European Asylum Law', 9 *Harvard Human Rights Journal* (1996) p. 185; R. Byrne, G. Noll and J. Vested-Hansen (eds.), *New Asylum Countries? Migration Control and Refugee Protection in an Enlarged European Union* (The Hague, Kluwer 2002); M. Fullerton, 'Failing the Test: Germany Leads Europe in Dismantling Refugee Protection', 36 *Texas International Law Journal* (2001) p. 231 at pp. 243-250; K. Hailbronner, 'The Concept of "Safe" Country and Expeditious Asylum Procedures: A Western European Perspective', 5 *International Journal of Refugee Law* (1993) p. 31; A. Hurwitz, 'The Dublin Convention: A Comprehensive Assessment', 11 *International Journal of Refugee Law* (1999) p. 646; R. Marx and K. Lumpp, 'The German Constitutional Court's Decision of 14 May 1996 on the Concept of "Safe Third Countries" – A Basis for Burden-Sharing in Europe?', 8 *International Journal of Refugee Law* (1996) p. 419.

sues have arisen out of a 2002 agreement between Canada and the United States.[6] The agreement spells out the two countries' respective responsibilities for those asylum seekers who travel through the territory of one before applying for asylum at a land border port of entry in the other.

Countries that adopt such return policies are attempting to promote important national interests. These include reducing illegal immigration, assuring the smooth functioning of their asylum systems, and minimizing the fiscal impact of the asylum processing itself. Moreover, there are instances in which countries rightly regard particular asylum seekers as the primary responsibility of other countries. But the returns have also engendered major problems, both for the asylum seekers themselves and for the third countries to which the applicants are returned. In a nutshell,

> '[t]here is, first, the problem of "orbit" – refugees who have escaped from persecution or from other trauma, only to be shuttled consecutively from one country to another. There is the more serious problem of 'chain' refoulement, in which the third country in turn refoules the person to his or her persecutors in the country of origin. The third country might not have a fair refugee status determination procedure in place. The third country might not be a party to the 1951 Refugee Convention. The third country might not provide formal refugee or other lawful status or might not provide the kind of documentation that the person needs to procure the necessities of life or to travel. The protection afforded by the third country might not be durable. The third country might be unable to protect the person from discrimination, or persecution, or other human rights violations; indeed, the government of the third country might engage in those practices itself. There might be threats to the applicant's physical security or basic subsistence. The third country might practice indiscriminate or long-term detention or might otherwise inhibit essential freedom of movement. One recurring problem has been the return of asylum seekers to third countries to which they have no links or connections ...'[7]

Apart from those concerns about practices and conditions in third countries, there can be serious deficiencies in the procedures by which the *destination countries* themselves decide whether return is appropriate in a particular case. Finally, some of the more common destination state practices have the effect of distributing the responsibility for refugee protection inequitably, so that the obligations fall disproportionately on developing countries and on those whose frontiers are geographically the most accessible, usually within the region of origin.[8]

[6] Agreement Between the Government of Canada and the Government of the United States of America Regarding Asylum Claims Made at Land Borders (15 Dec. 2002), text reproduced in advance in 79 *Interpreter Releases* (23 Sept. 2002) p. 1446 et seq.; see generally B. Frelick, 'North America Considers Agreement to Deflect Asylum Seekers', 7 *Bender's Immigration Bulletin* (15 Nov. 2002) p. 1404; A. Macklin, 'Disappearing Refugees: Reflections on the Canada-US Safe Third Country Agreement', 36 *Columbia Human Rights Law Review* (2005) p. 101.

[7] Legomsky, loc. cit. n. 1, at p. 572. For more detailed descriptions of how these problems have manifested themselves in the various regions, see ibid., at pp. 574-598.

[8] Ibid., at p. 572.

These problems should be distinguished from the related problems associated with returns to *countries of origin*. The latter are explored in a useful paper by Gregor Noll, undertaken as part of the predecessor project to this book.[9] The purpose of the present chapter is to synthesize the possible strategies for addressing the problems associated with secondary refugee movements. Section 2 considers ways to reduce the need for secondary refugee movements in the first place. Section 3 examines after-the-fact responses.

2. Reducing the Need for Secondary Movements

The most obvious way to erase the need for secondary refugee movements is to erase the need for primary refugee movements. Without primary movements, there will never be secondary movements. The root causes of primary forced migration, in turn, include human rights violations, armed conflict, natural disasters, economic collapse, and other serious disturbances of public order. The commonly prescribed policy responses – peacemaking and peacekeeping efforts, development aid, disaster relief, and 'carrots and sticks' intended to curb human rights abuses – are equally well-known. The principal impediments to success have been finite international resources and lack of political will.

Once primary forced migration has occurred, the most viable tools for reducing irregular secondary movements include the three traditional durable solutions to refugee flows – voluntary repatriation to the country of origin when conditions permit, local integration in the first country of asylum, and orderly permanent resettlement elsewhere.[10] All three, of course, are problematic. Voluntary repatriation to the country of origin is ideal when conditions in the country of origin have sufficiently improved; the returning refugees are able to contribute to the rebuilding process, and the pressure on the third country is lessened. But if conditions have not sufficiently improved, or the refugees have forged close bonds elsewhere, or the country of origin has not yet recovered economically from the traumatic events that spawned the refugee flow and cannot support a large returning population, then the obstacles to voluntary repatriation are formidable. Invariably, moreover, there will often be real questions as to whether the repatriation is truly voluntary.

Local integration in the third country is another possible way to reduce secondary refugee movements, but it too can be highly problematic. Most first countries

[9] G. Noll, 'Return of Persons to States of Origin and Third States', in T.A. Aleinikoff and V. Chetail (eds.), *Migration and International Legal Norms* (The Hague, T.M.C. Asser Press 2003), ch. 4. The chapter focuses principally on the obligations of states to readmit their own nationals, though the issue of when states are obliged to readmit third country nationals is acknowledged on p. 72.

[10] See, e.g., UNHCR, Executive Committee Conclusion 22 (XXXII), 'Protection of Asylum-Seekers in Situations of Large-Scale Influx' (1981), para. 1.2 (concerned with large-scale influxes); 'UNHCR Executive Committee of the High Commissioner's Programme: Standing Committee, 21st meeting, "New Directions for Resettlement Policy and Practice"', UN Doc. EC/51/SC/INF.2 (June 2001)', 13 *International Journal of Refugee Law* (2001) p. 690 at p. 691.

of asylum are developing countries that lack the resources to support large refugee populations, have nonetheless displayed exceptional generosity in hosting a disproportionate share of the world's refugees already, and are growing increasingly exasperated with what they perceive as an inequitable allocation of the burdens associated with refugee flows. In recent years, consequently, they have become far less inclined to accept new refugees or maintain past levels of generosity.

For similar reasons, problems that surface in third countries often parallel those that had driven the refugees from their countries of origin – human rights violations, armed conflict, natural disaster, economic collapse, and other serious disturbances of public order. Thus, the same strategies that were mentioned above for erasing the need for primary forced migration from countries of origin can apply for the purpose of erasing the need for secondary refugee movements from third countries, thus facilitating local integration. The goal would be to strengthen the refugee protection capacities of third countries.

Expanded opportunities for orderly permanent resettlement in the ultimate destination countries might diminish (although admittedly not eliminate) the incentive or the need for irregular secondary movements. Such commitments could be embodied in international responsibility-sharing agreements or be purely unilateral. In recent years, efforts by the UNHCR and others along these lines have borne fruit.[11] The major issue has been the political will of the developed states to make those commitments on a significant scale.

Harmonization of the relevant countries' refugee and asylum laws, as has been the pattern in the European Union, is thought by some to have potential for diminishing the incentives for secondary refugee movements, provided the harmonized criteria conform to international refugee law and do not amount to reductions in protection.[12] No one believes that harmonization will eliminate all incentives for secondary refugee movements, but the theory is that refugees will have less reason for onward movement if one of the motives for it – differentials in the treatment of refugees – were eliminated. At most, of course, harmonization would decrease secondary refugee movements within the harmonized region, not movements into that region.

3. Responding to Secondary Movements After the Fact

But suppose all the preceding strategies fail, and large secondary movements occur. What responses are possible then? Again, voluntary repatriation to either the country of origin or the third country would be workable if all the components of a successful return are in place – but let us assume they are not. A fair and gen-

[11] For details, see Legomsky, loc. cit. n. 1, at p. 601 (n. 143).

[12] Ibid., at pp. 603-606.

erous process of responsibility-sharing for permanent resettlement would then become ideal, but, even with the successes of the last several years on that score, the number of refugees accepted for permanent resettlement by all the world's nations combined is still just a minute proportion of the world's refugee population. Clearly, whatever progress is made toward increasing permanent resettlement in the foreseeable future, it is imperative that the developed states both strengthen the protection capacities of the major third countries and refrain from returning asylum seekers to countries in which protection is inadequate.

Efforts to strengthen the protection capacities of third countries have been ongoing for some time.[13] Withholding return to those countries in appropriate cases raises a slightly different but fundamental question: exactly what conditions must be in place in a third country – either a first country of asylum or a safe third country – before the country in which the asylum claim is filed (a) may, under international law and (b) should, as a matter of policy, return an asylum seeker to that third country without a substantive determination of the claim? To answer those questions, and in the process to flesh out the content of the 'effective protection' requirement, the UNHCR commissioned the previously mentioned consultant's report and convened a roundtable in Lisbon in 2002 to forge consensus on the constraints imposed by international law.[14]

In order to formulate specific criteria for the permissibility of returning asylum seekers to third countries, it was first necessary to articulate some more general assumptions and premises. These are laid out in the consultant's report.[15] Three of them require emphasis here.

First, in contrast to the explicit right of *non-refoulement* in Article 33 of the 1951 Refugee Convention,[16] the Convention nowhere creates a right to receive asylum (despite a passing reference, in the Preamble, to 'international cooperation' with respect to asylum). Similarly, several other international human rights instruments refer to asylum but stop short of obligating states to grant it.[17] Cer-

---

[13] See, e.g., UNHCR, 'Strengthening Protection Capacities in Host Countries, Global Consultations on International Protection', Doc. EC/GC/01/19 (19 April 2002); UNHCR, 'Global Consultations on International Protection Follow-Up to the Third Meeting of the Third Track: Protection of Refugees in the Context of Individual Asylum Systems', Doc. EC/GC/02/3 (16 April 2002), section IV.

[14] Legomsky, loc. cit. n. 1. For the 'Summary Conclusions' of the 2002 UNHCR expert roundtable in Lisbon, see <http://www.unhcr.org/cgi-bin/texis/vtx/protect/opendoc.pdf?tbl=PROTECTION&id=3e5f323d7> (Lisbon, Dec. 2002) (hereafter, Summary Conclusions).

[15] Legomsky, loc. cit. n. 1, at pp. 612-626.

[16] Convention Relating to the Status of Refugees, 28 July 1951, 189 *UNTS* 137.

[17] E.g., Art. 2 of the Declaration on Territorial Asylum, adopted by the Committee of Ministers of the Council of Europe (278th meeting of the Ministers' Deputies, 18 Nov. 1977), referred to the right of Member States to grant asylum, but pointedly refrained from creating an obligation to do so. Article II(1) of the OAU Convention Governing the Specific Aspects of Refugee Problems in Africa (1001 *UNTS* 45), entitled 'Asylum', obliges OAU Member States to 'use their best endeavours … to receive refugees' but again imposes no obligation to grant asylum. Article III of the Principles concerning the Treatment of Refugees of the Asian-African Legal Consultative Committee (8th Sess., Bangkok, 1966), recognizes a state's 'sovereign right to grant or refuse asylum in its territory to a refugee'. See generally G.S. Goodwin-Gill, *The Refugee in International Law*, 2nd edn. (Oxford, Oxford University Press

tainly no international instrument establishes an absolute right to receive a decision on the substance of an asylum claim *by the country of one's choosing*.

At the same time, however, the 1951 Convention does not require refugees to apply for asylum in the first possible place; nor does it require 'direct' travel from the country of origin to the country in which durable protection is sought. Consequently, 'asylum should not be refused solely on the ground that it could be sought from another state'.[18]

Second, while consensus for the following assertion cannot be claimed, it is submitted that, taken together, a collection of specific international law rulings and opinions now add up to a principle of more general applicability: no state may knowingly assist another state to do what international law would forbid the first state from doing on its own. The assisting state would be an accomplice to the misdeed committed by the second state. As applied here, this 'complicity principle', as I shall call it, means that no country may return a refugee or asylum seeker to a third country knowing that the latter will do *anything* to that person that international law would prohibit the sending country from doing on its own.[19] The specific authorities that in my view support the complicity principle, in combination with the International Law Commission's Articles on State Responsibility (with which I argue this principle is compatible), are elaborated in the consultant's report. As that report also explains, acceptance of this principle will still require judgments as to what it means for a state to 'know' that the third country will breach its international legal obligations.[20]

Third, not all asylum seekers are refugees. Conversely, however, refugee rights attach the moment one *in fact* meets the refugee criteria; subsequent formal recognition is merely declaratory.[21] A country may not, therefore, *refoule* an asylum seeker or deny other Convention rights solely because the person has not yet been *determined* to be a refugee.

On those assumptions, the question boils down to this: under precisely what circumstances may a country refuse to decide the substance of an asylum claim that is filed in its territory and, instead, return the applicant to a third country? Over the years, the UNHCR has addressed selected components of this issue, not always with full consistency. The requirements most frequently stressed have

1996) p. 88. But cf., the Universal Declaration of Human Rights, Art. 14(1) ('Everyone has the right to seek *and to enjoy* in other countries asylum from persecution').

[18] EXCOM Conclusion 15 (XXX), 'Refugees Without an Asylum Country' (1979), para. h(iv). That view is shared by J.C. Hathaway, *The Law of Refugee Status* (Toronto, Butterworths 1991) p. 46.

[19] Another route to this result is to regard the second state as the agent of the first state. Admittedly, the choice of conceptualizations could affect outcomes in some cases, since the international legal obligations of the two states might differ. Thus, if the second state is not a party to a particular human rights treaty, then the complicity theory is arguably inapplicable to that extent; one cannot assist State X in the commission of a legal wrong if the actions of State X do not violate any of its legal obligations. For present purposes, it will be assumed that the two states' international legal obligations coincide in all relevant respects.

[20] Legomsky, loc. cit. n. 1, at pp. 618-626.

[21] Authorities for this proposition are cited ibid., at p. 612 and n. 191.

been the consent of the third country to readmit the person, protection against persecution and chain *refoulement*, respect for fundamental human rights, and the assurance of a fair refugee status determination. Agreement on a consistent, comprehensive set of legal prerequisites to returning an asylum seeker to a third country remains lacking.[22]

Combining the complicity principle with several pre-existing formulations, the consultant's report interpreted international law as imposing the following preconditions on the return of asylum seekers to third countries:

> 'Under certain circumstances, a destination country (i.e., a country in which an asylum application has been lodged) may decline to determine the application in substance and instead return the applicant to a third country (i.e. a country other than the destination country or the country of origin). Such returns are permissible, however, only if all of the following conditions, collectively referred to as effective protection, are met:
>
> 1. The third country has explicitly agreed (a) to readmit the particular individual; and (b) to accord him or her either a fair refugee status determination or effective protection without such a determination...
>
> 2. The applicant has no well-founded fear of being persecuted, in the third country, on any of the 1951 Convention grounds.
>
> 3. The applicant has no well-founded fear of being refouled by the third country, directly or indirectly, to a territory where his or her life or freedom would be threatened on any of the 1951 Refugee Convention grounds... If the third country is not a party to the 1951 Refugee Convention or the 1967 Refugee Protocol, that fact must be considered in determining whether this and the other minimum legal requirements for return have been met.
>
> 4. The destination country may not knowingly return the applicant to a third country that will violate any of the applicant's rights under the 1951 Refugee Convention (apart from *non-refoulement*, which is treated separately in criterion 3 above)... The destination country may shift to the applicant the burden of identifying any particular Convention provisions that he or she believes the third country will violate, as well as the burden of producing some evidence of the prospective violations, but once those burdens are met, the government of the destination country retains the ultimate burden of proving that the third country will not violate those provisions.
>
> 5. The destination country may not knowingly return the applicant to a third country that will breach any of the applicant's rights under any human rights agreement to which the destination country is a party... Depending on the circumstances of the case, knowingly sending the applicant to a third country where he or she will lack either physical security or basic subsistence can be 'cruel, inhuman or degrading treatment' for purposes of the various human rights agreements that use that term.

[22] Ibid., at pp. 626-629.

6. The third country will either provide a fair refugee status determination or provide effective protection without such a determination... Many first countries of asylum provide no formal refugee status determination but nonetheless provide some form of *de facto* protection. Such arrangements are not adequate substitutes for refugee status determinations, unless in the particular case the lack of formal status or documentation does not impair the other requirements of effective protection enumerated here. A fair refugee status determination also requires respect for the privacy interests of the applicant and his or her family, as well as consideration of any special vulnerabilities of the applicant. Specially vulnerable groups include, but are not limited to, torture victims, women, subcategories of women (for example victims of rape or other sexual violence, pregnant women, and women who are single heads of households), children (especially unaccompanied children), the elderly, the physically or mentally disabled, and stateless persons.

7. The third country is willing and able to provide effective protection for as long as the person remains a refugee or until another source of durable effective protection can be found.

8. Even when the third country will otherwise provide effective protection, return is prohibited if, in the light of the applicant's comparative family ties to the destination country and the third country, return would violate the applicant's internationally recognized right to family unity.

9. The destination country must apply each of the above criteria on an individual, case-by-case basis. The applicant may not be returned involuntarily to the third country until this procedure, including appeal, has been completed'.[23]

The legal analysis on which these conclusions rest occupied more than 60 pages of the consultant's report. Rather than attempt to summarize that analysis in this short chapter, I take the liberty of referring the reader to the original report.[24]

The participants at the 2002 Lisbon roundtable included representatives of the UNHCR, NGOs, and the governments of countries of origin, third countries, and ultimate destination countries, as well as academics, lawyers, and judges. After two days of intense discussion, the participants adopted a consensus document that incorporated the vast bulk of the above conclusions.[25] The most significant difference was that, rather than call these criteria 'prerequisites' or 'requirements', the consensus document referred to them as 'critical factors'.[26] In addition, rather than preclude return to a third country whenever there is a real risk of that country violating *any* rights conferred by human rights treaties to which it is a party, the consensus document referred to violations of '*fundamental* human rights ..., *including but not limited to* the following' [emphasis added];[27] it

[23] Ibid., at pp. 673-675.

[24] Ibid., at pp. 612-673.

[25] Summary Conclusions, loc. cit. n. 14, at paras. 9, 14, and 15.

[26] Ibid., at para. 15.

[27] Ibid., at para. 15(b).

proceeded to list freedom from torture or 'cruel, inhuman or degrading treatment or punishment', the right to life, and the right not to be deprived of liberty without due process.[28]

4. Conclusion

Since Lisbon, progress has been modest. On 11 March 2004, as part of its Convention Plus initiative, the UNHCR established the Core Group on Addressing Irregular Secondary Movements of Asylum Seekers and Refugees, consisting of several states, international organizations, and NGOs. Its charge was to develop frameworks concerning irregular secondary movements, based on 'international solidarity and burden-sharing'. The Core Group discussed a draft of a multilateral framework prepared by the Co-Chairs (Switzerland and South Africa).[29] There was consensus on the need to address the problems of irregular secondary movements at the international level, especially through responsibility-sharing agreements.[30] There was disagreement, however, on such fundamental issues as whether to emphasize strengthening the protection capacities of third countries; whether to focus on specific groups of refugees (such as Somalis) rather than attempt a more ambitious generic framework; whether to limit the framework to those asylum seekers and refugees who had already found protection in third countries rather than include also those who merely 'could have found' protection elsewhere; whether 'effective protection' should even be defined in a multilateral framework, or at least in an authoritative UNHCR statement; what the role of readmission should be; and whether the framework should address the repatriation of rejected asylum seekers to their countries of origin (as distinguished from returns to third countries).[31] On 11 July 2005, the deliberations on the draft multilateral framework were suspended.[32]

In the end, I remain of the belief that the Lisbon principles offer a realistic starting point for a future multilateral framework.[33] Despite the large ideological differences among the various states, international organizations and NGOs represented in Lisbon, the participants reached broad consensus on the major principles that should govern the return of asylum seekers to third countries. Obtaining broader worldwide agreement and operationalizing those understandings are the next, and perhaps the most challenging, steps. In the interests of refugee protec-

[28] Ibid.

[29] Joint Statement by the Co-Chairs, Convention Plus Core Group on Addressing Irregular Secondary Movements of Refugees and Asylum-Seekers, High Commissioner's Forum, Forum/2005/7 (8 Nov. 2005), Annex 1, paras. 1-3.

[30] Ibid., at p. 2 of main statement ('points of convergence').

[31] Ibid., at para. 4 and pp. 4-5 (diplomatically entitled 'points for further reflection').

[32] Ibid., at para. 1.

[33] Following roughly similar lines is a recent report by the European Council on Refugees and Exiles (ECRE), *Guarding Refugee Protection Standards in Regions of Origin* (London, ECRE, Dec. 2005).

tion, fair responsibility-sharing among the world's nations, and regional stability, one hopes that future progress will be swift and meaningful.

SELECTED BIBLIOGRAPHY

Aleinikoff, T.A., and V. Chetail (eds.), *Migration and International Legal Norms* (The Hague, T.M.C. Asser Press 2003).

Frelick, B., 'North America Considers Agreement to Deflect Asylum Seekers', 7 *Bender's Immigration Bulletin* (15 Nov. 2002) p. 1404.

Goodwin-Gill, G.S., *The Refugee in International Law*, 2nd edn. (Oxford, Oxford University Press 1996).

Hathaway, J.C., *The Rights of Refugees Under International Law* (Cambridge, Cambridge University Press 2005).

Legomsky, S.H., 'Secondary Refugee Movements and the Return of Asylum Seekers to Third Countries: The Meaning of Effective Protection', 15 *International Journal of Refugee Law* (2003) p. 567.

Macklin, A., 'Disappearing Refugees: Reflections on the Canada-U.S. Safe Third Country Agreement', 36 *Columbia Human Rights Law Review* (2005) p. 101.

Noll, G., 'Return of Persons to States of Origin and Third States', in T.A. Aleinikoff and V. Chetail (eds.), *Migration and International Legal Norms* (The Hague, T.M.C. Asser Press 2003) ch. 4.

Summary Conclusions of the 2002 UNHCR expert roundtable in Lisbon, Protecting Refugees, Legal and Protection Policy Research Series, Expert Meetings, Effective Protection (Lisbon, Dec. 2002) <http://www.unhcr.org/cgi-bin/texis/vtx/protect/opendoc.pdf?tbl=PROTECTION&id=3e5f323d7>.

UNHCR, Executive Committee Conclusion 58 (XL), 'Problem of Refugees and Asylum-Seekers Who Move in an Irregular Manner from a Country in Which They Had Already Found Protection' (1989) <http://www.unhcr.org/cgi-bin/texis/vtx/excom/opendoc.htm?tbl=EXCOM&id=3ae68c4380>.

Chapter 11
RESPONDING TO THE CHALLENGE OF INTERNAL FORCED MIGRATION: THE GUIDING PRINCIPLES ON INTERNAL DISPLACEMENT

Simon Bagshaw[*]

1. Introduction

Contrary to the hopes and aspirations of many, the bi-polar world of Cold War confrontation has not been replaced by a 'new world order' where 'diverse nations are drawn together in common cause, to achieve the universal aspirations of mankind: peace, security, freedom and the rule of law'.[1] True, authoritarian regimes have given way to democratic alternatives in a number of regions, and, in the absence of superpower rivalry, several long-standing conflicts in places such as Namibia, Nicaragua, El Salvador, Cambodia and Mozambique have wound down. On the downside, however, the post-Cold War era and later periods have witnessed a broad range of humanitarian crises affecting all regions of the globe, stemming for the most part from internal armed conflict and associated human rights violations. Among the critical issues to arise against this backdrop of conflict and crises has been the need to respond to the plight of an estimated 25 million persons[2] forcibly displaced within the borders of their own countries, often in acute need of physical protection and humanitarian assistance.[3]

---

[*] Protection Officer in the Inter-Agency Internal Displacement Division of the UN Office for the Coordination of Humanitarian Affairs in Geneva. The present chapter is based on S. Bagshaw, *Developing a Normative Framework for the Protection of Internally Displaced Persons* (New York, Transnational Publishers 2005). The views herein, and any errors or omissions, should be attributed solely to the author and not the United Nations.

[1] US President George Bush, 'State of the Union Address', 29 Jan. 1991, reproduced in *Keesings Record of World Events: News Digest for January 1991*, p. 37940.

[2] Norwegian Refugee Council/Global IDP Project, *Internal Displacement – A Global Overview of Trends and Developments in 2004* (Geneva, Norwegian Refugee Council 2005) p. 4.

[3] See for example, R. Cohen and F. Deng, *Masses in Flight: The Global Crisis of Internal Displacement* (Washington DC, Brookings Institution Press 1998) p. 2: 'Of the world's populations at risk, internally displaced persons tend to be among the most desperate. They may be forcibly resettled on political or ethnic grounds or find themselves trapped in the midst of conflicts and in the direct path of armed attack and physical violence. On the run without documents, they are easy targets for roundups, arbitrary detention, forced conscription, and sexual assaults. Uprooted from their homes and deprived of their resource base, many suffer from profound physical and psychological trauma. They are more often deprived of shelter, food and health services than other members of the population'.

R. Cholewinski, R. Perruchoud and E. MacDonald, eds., International Migration Law

In 1992, in response to the increasing international concern at the large number of 'internally displaced persons'[4] throughout the world and their need for protection and assistance, the UN Secretary-General, at the request of the Commission on Human Rights, appointed a Representative on Internally Displaced Persons, a position that was held by Francis Deng until July 2004.[5] During this time, Deng focused his efforts on three main areas of work: visiting countries affected by internal displacement; promoting a more effective institutional framework at both the international and regional levels; and, last but not least, developing a normative framework to meet the protection, assistance and development needs of internally displaced persons.[6]

Although each of these areas are of interest in their own right, the present chapter is concerned primarily with Deng's efforts to develop the normative framework, a significant feature of which has been the avoidance of the tradition-

[4] In line with the Guiding Principles on Internal Displacement, internally displaced persons are 'persons or groups of persons who have been forced or obliged to flee or to leave their homes or places of habitual residence, in particular as a result of or in order to avoid the effects of armed conflict, situations of generalized violence, violations of human rights or natural or human-made disasters, and who have not crossed an internationally recognized State border'. *Report of the Representative of the Secretary-General, Mr. Francis M. Deng, submitted pursuant to Commission on Human Rights Resolution 1997/39. Addendum. Guiding Principles on Internal Displacement*, UN Doc. E/CN.4/1998/53/Add.2 (11 Feb. 1998).

[5] Commission on Human Rights Res. 1992/73 UN Doc. E/CN.4/RES/1992/73. While the mandate of the Representative came to an end in July 2004, the Commission had earlier requested the Secretary-General, in building upon the work of the Representative, to establish a mechanism that will 'work for the strengthening of the international response to the complex problem of situations of internal displacement, and engage in coordinated international advocacy and action for improving protection and respect of the human rights of the internally displaced, while continuing and enhancing dialogues with Governments, as well as non-governmental organizations and other relevant actors' (Commission on Human Rights Res. 2004/55, UN Doc. E/CN.4/RES/2004/55, para. 24). The Secretary-General subsequently appointed a Representative of the Secretary-General on the Human Rights of Internally Displaced Persons, a position currently held by Walter Kälin.

[6] The Representative's efforts in these respects were detailed in his reports to the Commission on Human Rights and the General Assembly, available at <www.ohchr.org>. For more information on the international response to internal displacement, see Cohen and Deng, op. cit. n. 3, and, by the same authors, *The Foresaken People – Case Studies of the Internally Displaced* (Washington DC, Brookings Institution Press 1998); F. Deng, *Protecting the Dispossessed – A Challenge for the International Community* (Washington DC, Brookings Institution Press 1993); D.A. Korn, *Exodus Within Borders – An Introduction to the Crisis of Internal Displacement* (Washington DC, Brookings Institution Press 1999); Internal Displacement Unit, Office for the Coordination of Humanitarian Affairs, *No Refuge: The Challenge of Internal Displacement* (Geneva, United Nations 2003); S. Bagshaw and D. Paul, *Protect or Neglect? Towards a More Effective United Nations Approach to the Protection of Internally Displaced Persons* (Washington DC, Brookings Institution Project on Internal Displacement 2004); S. Bagshaw, *Developing a Normative Framework for the Protection of Internally Displaced Persons* (New York, Transnational Publishers 2005); *Protecting and Assisting the Internally Displaced: The Way Forward* supplement to *Forced Migration Review* (Oct. 2005). Comprehensive web-based resources on internal displacement can be found at the Brookings-Bern Project on Internal Displacement <www.brook.edu/fp/projects/idp/idp.htm> and the Internal Displacement Monitoring Centre <www.internal-displacement.org>.

al intergovernmental law-making process of negotiating, drafting and adopting a 'hard' treaty in favour of a more flexible and nuanced approach, which resulted in the 'soft' restatement of existing international norms in the form of the Guiding Principles on Internal Displacement, as presented to the Commission on Human Rights in 1998.

2. Developing the Normative Framework

From the outset, the question of the extent to which existing international law addressed the needs of the internally displaced was identified as a critical area of focus for Deng. Prior even to his appointment, a report of the Secretary-General noted that, although the problems and needs of the internally displaced can be defined in terms of already-recognized rights, the situation in which they find themselves differs significantly from that of the general population.[7] It therefore called for the elaboration of more specific principles or guidelines on the treatment that should be accorded to the internally displaced in order to ensure the effective protection of their human rights.[8]

In his first report to the Commission on Human Rights in 1993, Deng noted a tension between those for whom existing law provided adequate coverage for the rights of the internally displaced and those who advocated a new regime: '[b]oth are motivated by the same policy considerations. Those who consider the present law adequate want to strengthen its protection by reaffirming it and focusing attention on implementation and enforcement mechanisms'. Those advocating a new regime 'are particularly concerned that the internally displaced often suffer unusual hardships, deprivations and gross violations of human rights which require special attention and remedial measures'. Navigating between the two, Deng concluded that it would be useful to prepare a compilation and analysis of relevant international standards that would include a commentary on the implications of these standards, and the extent to which they address the problems faced by internally displaced persons, and practical proposals for their implementation. Once completed, the question of what additional standards specifically concerning internally displaced persons are needed could then be addressed.[9]

---

[7] According to the report, '[i]nternally displaced persons typically have suffered from a series of human rights violations which add up to a characteristic and distinctive syndrome. The cumulative effect of these violations, together with the fact of having been forced to flee their home and the difficulties, risks and deprivations invariably associated with their new situation, make their needs qualitatively different from those of other persons'. *Internally Displaced Persons: Analytical report of the Secretary-General*, UN Doc. E/CN.4/1992/23 (14 Feb. 1992) para. 91.

[8] Ibid., at para. 92.

[9] *Comprehensive study prepared by Mr. Francis M. Deng, Representative of the Secretary-General on the human rights issues related to internally displaced persons, pursuant to Commission on Human Rights Resolution 1992/73*, UN Doc. E/CN.4/1993/35 (21 Jan. 1993) paras. 55-88.

2.1 The compilation and analysis of legal norms

The following year, Deng assembled a team of experts in international law who, working under his direction, embarked upon the preparation of a two-part compilation and analysis of legal norms (hereafter 'compilation and analysis report') that was to form the basis for the Guiding Principles.

The first part examined the relevant provisions of international law applicable once people have been displaced.[10] On the basis of information acquired from field reports, other relevant studies, and discussions with experts, the compilation and analysis report identified a broad spectrum of needs of internally displaced persons in regard to equality and non-discrimination, life and personal security, subsistence, movement, personal identification, documentation and registration, property, family and community values, self-reliance, and humanitarian assistance, and analysed the extent to which these needs are met by international human rights law, international humanitarian law and, by analogy, refugee law.

The compilation and analysis report found that while existing law covers many aspects of relevance to the situation of the internally displaced, there nonetheless remain gaps and grey areas where the law fails to provide sufficient protection. It concluded, therefore, that where the needs of the displaced are not sufficiently protected by international law, it is important 'to restate general principles of protection in more specific detail', and address the gaps in 'a future international instrument on the protection of internally displaced persons'.[11]

While the primary focus of the first part of the compilation and analysis report was on those guarantees relevant both to situations of internal displacement and return, it acknowledged that, 'in order to achieve comprehensiveness in the elaboration of the legal framework that relates to displacement', it was necessary to examine also the legal norms relevant to protection *from* displacement and to a right not to be displaced.[12] Thus, a separate study on the legal aspects relating to protection against arbitrary displacement was undertaken in 1996. This study, which constitutes the second part of the compilation and analysis report, found that although many provisions in international law point to a general rule according to which forced displacement may be undertaken only exceptionally, and be neither discriminatory nor arbitrarily imposed, this protection is largely implicit. It concluded, therefore, that the legal basis for providing protection prior to displacement could be strengthened significantly by articulating a right not to be arbitrarily displaced.[13]

[10] *Report of the Representative of the Secretary-General, Mr. Francis M. Deng, submitted pursuant to Commission on Human Rights Resolution 1995/57. Compilation and analysis of legal norms*, UN Doc. E/CN.4/1996/52/Add.2 (5 Dec. 1995).

[11] Ibid., at para. 413.

[12] Ibid., at para. 11.

[13] *Report of the Representative of the Secretary-General, Mr. Francis M. Deng, submitted pursuant to Commission on Human Rights Resolution 1997/39. Addendum. Compilation and Analysis of Legal Norms, Part II: Legal Aspects Relating to the Protection against Arbitrary Displacement*, UN Doc. E/CN.4/1998/53/Add.1 (11 Feb. 1998) paras. 84-88.

2.2 The Guiding Principles on Internal Displacement

Following submission of the first part of the compilation and analysis report to the Commission in 1996, the Representative and the legal team began to develop a comprehensive normative framework of protection and assistance for the internally displaced. This resulted in the elaboration of a set of guiding principles that were finalized at an expert consultation in January 1998, and submitted to the Commission later that year as the Guiding Principles on Internal Displacement.[14]

The 30 principles aim to 'address the specific needs of internally displaced persons worldwide by identifying rights and guarantees relevant to their protection'.[15] They are organized into five sections and apply to the different phases of displacement. Following a section of general principles, there are sections relating to protection from arbitrary displacement, protection and assistance during displacement, humanitarian assistance, and return or resettlement and reintegration.

The stated scope and purpose of the Principles is to provide guidance to the Representative of the Secretary-General in implementing his mandate; to states when confronting situations of displacement; to all other authorities, groups and persons in their relations with the internally displaced; and, finally, to inter- and non-governmental organizations when addressing internal displacement.[16] In essence, the Principles are intended as a 'persuasive statement that should provide not only practical guidance, but also an instrument for public policy education and consciousness-raising', as well as having the potential to perform a preventive function.[17]

3. The Guiding Principles in Context

A key feature of Deng's approach to developing the normative framework is that it was essentially an exercise in what might be termed soft law-making through restatement. That is to say that the rationale behind the Guiding Principles was not the creation of 'brand new' law, but the application of existing general principles and norms to the specific context of internal displacement. As Walter Kälin has observed, the Principles

> 'restate in more detail many of those existing legal provisions which respond to the specific needs of internally displaced persons and spell them out in order to facilitate their application in situations of internal displacement. They also clarify aspects of the protection of internally displaced persons where present international law contains certain grey areas or even gaps. For these reasons the introductory part of the Guiding

[14] E/CN.4/1998/53/Add.2, loc. cit., n. 4.

[15] Ibid., at para. 9.

[16] Ibid., 'Introduction: Scope and Purpose', para. 3.

[17] Ibid.

Principles stresses that they reflect and are consistent with international human rights and humanitarian law'.[18]

The outcome of this approach is a broad and progressive restatement of international law which details more precisely, and, importantly, in a more accessible and readable format, the relevant provisions of human rights and humanitarian law as they apply to the internally displaced.

3.1 Clarifying the grey areas

As indicated, the compilation and analysis report demonstrated that, while existing law covers many aspects of relevance to the situation of internally displaced persons, there nonetheless remain two areas where the law fails to provide sufficient protection.[19] The first concerns situations where a general norm exists, but a corollary, more specific right has not been articulated that would ensure implementation of the general norm in areas of particular need to internally displaced persons. In this regard, the compilation and analysis report notes that although it is possible to infer specific legal rights from existing general norms, the protection of internally displaced persons would be strengthened by spelling out these guarantees in the context of internal displacement.[20] It recommended the restatement of existing general norms in relation to discrimination, the protection of life, gender-specific violence, detention, shielding, forced recruitment, subsistence needs, medical care, free movement, family related needs, the use of one's own language, religion, work, education, association, political participation, and the need for access to international assistance – all of which are duly provided for in the Guiding Principles.

With respect to discrimination, for example, the compilation and analysis report observes that internally displaced persons, 'often living in alien surroundings, deprived of their security, property and social status, are particularly exposed and vulnerable to discriminatory treatment'.[21] However, an explicit prohibition of discrimination against the internally displaced on the sole basis of their displacement does not exist in human rights law.[22] The compilation and analysis report notes that several international and regional human rights treaties have clauses requiring States Parties to respect and ensure the rights and freedoms provided for in those instruments without discrimination. Of these, Article 26 of the International Covenant on Civil and Political Rights (ICCPR)[23] is held to be the most

[18] W. Kälin, 'Introduction to the Guiding Principles on Internal Displacement', paper presented at the Regional Workshop on Internal Displacement in the South Caucasus, 10-12 May 2000, on file with the author.

[19] E/CN.4/1996/52/Add.2, loc. cit. n. 10, at para. 410.

[20] Ibid., at para. 411.

[21] Ibid., at para. 48.

[22] Ibid., at para. 49.

[23] UNGA Res. 2200A (XXI), 21 UN GAOR Supp. (No. 16) at p. 52, UN Doc. A/6316 (1966), 999 *UNTS* 171.

far-reaching guarantee, providing that the law shall prohibit any discrimination and guarantee to all persons equal and effective protection against discrimination on any ground such as race, colour, sex, language, religion, political or other opinion, national or social origin, property, birth or other status.

According to the compilation and analysis report, the term 'other status' was meant to be interpreted broadly, and has come to include 'nationality and disability and reasonably includes youth and old-age'.[24] Consequently, it asserts that '[n]on-discrimination clauses thus appear to ban discrimination against internally displaced persons based on their status as such',[25] and calls for an explicit statement to this effect in a future international instrument on internally displaced persons.[26] Thus, according to Principle 1(1),

> '[i]nternally displaced persons shall enjoy, in full equality, the same rights and freedoms under international and domestic law as do other persons in their country. They shall not be discriminated against in the enjoyment of any rights and freedoms on the ground that they are internally displaced'.

This is clearly a necessary assumption given that the internally displaced are often at risk of discriminatory treatment on account of their being displaced.[27] However, it might be argued that applying the term 'other status' to the internally displaced is a progressive step. The *travaux préparatoires* of the ICCPR suggest a broad interpretation of the term 'other status',[28] and the Human Rights Committee considers the term to include nationality.[29] However, this is the only ground that the Committee has specifically enumerated as constituting 'other status', and violations of the prohibition of discrimination have been found primarily with regard to gender-specific distinctions. Distinctions between married and unmarried couples, between conscripted soldiers and civilians, between soldiers and conscientious objectors or between pupils in public and private schools were not considered to be discriminatory in the relevant cases.[30] However, as Nowak ob-

---

[24] E/CN.4/1996/52/Add.2, loc. cit. n. 10, at para. 52.

[25] Ibid.

[26] Ibid., at para. 65.

[27] For example, see S. Bagshaw, *Internally Displaced Persons and Political Participation – The OSCE Region* (Washington DC, Brookings Institution Project on Internal Displacement, Sept. 2000), detailing discriminatory practices against the internally displaced in the exercise of voting rights in a number of OSCE states.

[28] According to Marc Bossuyt, proposals to add 'association with minority groups', 'economic or other opinion' and 'educational attainment' to the enumerated grounds of discrimination were thought to be unnecessary since they were deemed adequately covered by the expressions 'discrimination on any ground' and 'other status'. M. Bossuyt, *Guide to the Travaux Préparatoires of the International Covenant on Civil and Political Rights* (Dordrecht, Martinus Nijhoff 1986) p. 486.

[29] See *Gueye et al.* v. *France, Decision of the Human Rights Committee under article 5(4) of the Optional Protocol to the International Covenant on Civil and Political Rights - Thirty-fifth session concerning Communication No. 196/1985*, UN Doc. CCPR/C/35/D/196/1985 (6 April 1989) paras. 9.4, 9.5 and 10.

[30] M. Nowak, *CCPR Commentary* (Strasbourg, NP Engel 1993) p. 473.

serves, the decisive question, which is ultimately subject to resolution only on a case-by-case basis, is

> 'whether a specific distinction between various persons or groups of persons [in this case, between internally and non-displaced persons] is to be considered discriminatory. This is the case only when the Parties concerned find themselves in a comparable situation and when the distinction is based on unreasonable and subjective criteria'.[31]

3.2 Addressing the gaps

In addition to situations where a general norm exists but a corollary, more specific right has not been articulated that would ensure implementation of the general norm in areas of particular need to internally displaced persons, the compilation and analysis report also found that international law failed to provide sufficient protection to the internally displaced in cases where no explicit norms exist to address their needs. It may be, for example, that a norm exists in human rights law but not in humanitarian law and vice versa, as will be illustrated below.

The compilation and analysis report brought to light several such cases, notably in regard to disappearances; the missing and the dead; the use of landmines and like devices; detention, particularly in 'closed camps'; needs for personal identification, documentation and registration; property-related needs; and relief workers and organizations.[32] According to the report, in such cases it is only possible to articulate rights by 'analogising' from existing provisions of law that apply only in limited situations or to certain categories of persons.[33] It recommended that such 'clear protection gaps' be addressed in a future international instrument.[34] Consequently there are several provisions contained in the Principles which seek to do just this.

With regard to detention, for example, as the compilation and analysis report observes, while civilians in general may be at risk of arbitrary detention, especially in situations of armed conflict, it can be a particular problem for the internally displaced, who face arrest and detention often without judicial warrant or other legal safeguards, and sometimes as a means of collective punishment. Moreover,

> 'relocation frequently involves internment in a compound or camp with no freedom to leave ... [I]n some cases, internally displaced persons are considered as part of the political opposition or counter-insurgency simply because they are on the run, have left their homes, or have been detained by warring forces in a situation of armed conflict.'[35]

---

[31] Ibid., at pp. 473-474. See Bagshaw, loc. cit. n. 27, for cases of discrimination against displaced persons in the exercise of voting rights that would meet Nowak's test of 'unreasonable and subjective criteria'.

[32] E/CN.4/1996/52/Add.2, loc. cit. n. 10, at para. 416.

[33] Ibid.

[34] Ibid., at para. 413.

[35] Ibid., at para. 144. See for example, Human Rights Watch, *Emptying the Hills – Regroupement in Burundi* (New York, Human Rights Watch June 2000).

While the right of everyone to be free from arbitrary arrest or detention is recognized in several international and regional human rights instruments, the compilation and analysis report observes that there are no precedents as regards the question of whether the detention of internally displaced persons in closed camps is permissible. That said, it notes that the act of holding someone in a closed camp constitutes detention under Article 9(1) of the ICCPR. The Human Rights Committee has stressed that

> 'paragraph 1 is applicable to all deprivations of liberty, whether in criminal cases or in other cases such as, for example, mental illness, vagrancy, drug addiction, educational purposes, immigration control, etc.'.[36]

In accordance with Article 9(1), detention in closed camps is only permissible if it is imposed 'on such grounds and in accordance with such procedures as established' by domestic legislation. Without a legal basis, therefore, internally displaced persons cannot be detained in a closed camp, and any such detention must not be arbitrary, i.e., 'it has to be reasonable and necessary in all circumstances'.[37]

The foregoing provisions of international and regional human rights law may, however, be derogated from in situations of armed conflict, and international humanitarian law as applicable to non-international armed conflict does not provide standards concerning when persons may be deprived of their liberty or the associated legal safeguards, such as the right to an effective remedy. In fact, the compilation and analysis report observes that Article 5 of Additional Protocol II to the Geneva Conventions[38] provides a regime for the treatment of persons who are 'deprived of their liberty for reasons related to the armed conflict', implicitly allowing, therefore, for the internment or detention of internally displaced persons. As regards international armed conflict, the Fourth Geneva Convention[39] provides in Article 42 that aliens who are protected civilians may be interned or placed in assigned housing only if the security of the Detaining Power absolutely requires such a step, and, in accordance with Article 43, such decisions must be periodically reviewed by a court or administrative board. Also, Articles 79-135 contain a complete regime for the treatment of internees, whilst Article 75 of Additional Protocol I[40] requires that persons arrested, detained or interned for actions related

[36] Human Rights Committee, *General Comment No. 8*, reproduced in UN Doc. HRI/GEN/1/Rev.7 (12 May 2004).

[37] E/CN.4/1996/52/Add.2, loc. cit. n. 10, at para. 151, citing *Alphen* v. *Netherlands, Views of the Human Rights Committee under article 5, paragraph 4, of the Optional Protocol to the International Covenant on Civil and Political Rights - Thirty-ninth session concerning Communication No. 305/1988*, UN Doc. CCPR/C/39/D/305/1988 (15 Aug. 1990) para. 5.8, and Nowak, op. cit. n. 30, at pp. 172-173.

[38] Protocol Additional to the Geneva Conventions of 12 Aug. 1949, and Relating to the Protection of Victims of Non-International Armed Conflicts (Protocol II), 8 June 1977, 1125 *UNTS* 609.

[39] Geneva Convention relative to the Protection of Civilian Persons in Time of War, 12 Aug. 1949, 75 *UNTS* 287.

[40] Protocol Additional to the Geneva Conventions of 12 Aug. 1949, and Relating to the Protection of Victims of International Armed Conflicts (Protocol I), 8 June 1977, 1125 *UNTS* 3.

to the hostilities be promptly informed of the reasons for the measures, and requires that they be released as soon as the circumstances justifying the detention have ceased to exist, unless the detention is for a penal offence.

The compilation and analysis report concludes that the preconditions of lawful detention of internally displaced persons in closed camps 'remain unclear', and that there is a 'clear gap in international law concerning detention in situations of non-international armed conflict' that should be addressed in a future international instrument.[41] Thus, Principle 12 seeks to provide some guidance by stating that:

> '1. Every human being has the right to liberty and security of person. No one shall be subjected to arbitrary arrest or detention.
> 2. To give effect to this right for internally displaced persons, they shall not be interned in or confined to a camp. If in exceptional circumstances such internment or confinement is absolutely necessary, it shall not last longer than required by the circumstances.
> 3. Internally displaced persons shall be protected from discriminatory arrest and detention as a result of their displacement'.

Also, Principle 14 provides that internally displaced persons have the right to liberty of movement and freedom to choose their own residence and, '[i]n particular ... the right to move freely in and out of camps and other settlements'.

4. Taking the Guiding Principles Seriously

Deng's approach to developing the Principles represents a clear departure from the more traditional intergovernmental approach to human rights law-making, in particular treaty-making, one driven by an appreciation of the fact that the problem of protection of and assistance for the internally displaced required an immediate response from the international community. As Deng remarked in 1993, whilst it would be favourable to develop a legal instrument specifically addressing the problem of internal displacement, the preparation of such an instrument 'takes time and can only be conceived in a long-term perspective. Meanwhile, the compelling conditions and urgent needs of the internally displaced call for a speedy remedy'.[42]

For Deng, the most suitable strategy for attaining a 'speedy remedy' was to restate existing law, thereby avoiding 'some of the pitfalls in the process of law-making', not least of all the need for consensus among states on the object and purpose and text of the proposed instrument – a pertinent consideration when it comes to standard-setting on an issue such as internal displacement. Indeed, it is by no means certain that states would reach broad agreement on the need for

[41] E/CN.4/1996/52/Add.2, loc. cit. n. 10, at para. 156.
[42] E/CN.4/1993/35, loc. cit. n. 9, at para. 282.

legislative action in this context or the form that this should take, let alone on its specific content. As already indicated, from the outset, Deng acknowledged the tension between those who believe that the existing law provides adequate coverage for the rights of the internally displaced and those who advocate a new legal regime.[43]

By avoiding the traditional intergovernmental treaty-making route, Deng achieved, in the relatively short period of four years, the elaboration of a broad and progressive set of non-binding principles that restate more precisely the range of human rights protection available to the internally displaced. However, precisely because of their non-binding nature and their formulation outside of the traditional intergovernmental standard-setting process, we must ask: to what extent have states taken the Guiding Principles seriously, and to what extent do the Principles have genuine meaning and practical effect for the protection of the rights of the displaced?

Notwithstanding their lack of binding force and formal governmental endorsement – and the reservations of some states in these respects[44] – the short answer to these questions is that, since their presentation to the Commission on Human Rights in 1998, the Guiding Principles have been well-received; they are being widely – and increasingly – used. Prior even to their presentation to the Commission, the Principles had already been endorsed by the international humanitarian, human rights and development organizations and consortia of NGOs that make up the UN's Inter-Agency Standing Committee (IASC).[45] They have since become the established framework within which these different agencies and organizations implement assistance and protection activities on behalf of the internally displaced.

In 1998, the Commission on Human Rights took note of the Principles, of their endorsement by the IASC and of Deng's intention to use them in his work.[46] The General Assembly subsequently followed suit,[47] and since then the resolutions of both these bodies have become stronger and increasingly supportive. In unanimously adopted resolutions, both bodies have welcomed Deng's use of the Principles, expressed appreciation that UN agencies, regional organizations and NGOs are also using them in their work, and encouraged their further dissemination and application. Since 2001, and reflecting developments on the ground,

---

[43] Ibid., at para. 71.

[44] Egypt, India and Sudan in particular expressed concerns about standard-setting by non-governmental actors, even though these states have also joined the consensus on resolutions calling for the dissemination of the Principles. See further, R. Cohen, 'The Guiding Principles on Internal Displacement: An Innovation in International Standard Setting', 10 *Global Governance* (2004) p. 459 at pp. 472-475.

[45] *Report of the Representative of the Secretary-General, Mr. Francis M. Deng, submitted pursuant to Commission on Human Rights Resolution 1998/50*, UN Doc. E/CN.4/1999/79 (25 Jan. 1999) para. 13.

[46] Commission on Human Rights Res. 1998/50, UN Doc. E/CN.4/RES/1998/50.

[47] UNGA Res. 54/167 of 17 Dec. 1999, UN Doc. A/RES/54/167 (25 Feb. 2000).

resolutions of both bodies have noted with appreciation that an increasing number of states are also making use of the Principles.[48]

Indeed, in terms of measuring the support for and utility of the Principles, of perhaps greater importance than pronouncements by UN bodies is the fact that an increasing number of governments have begun to use them. In Colombia, government departments refer to the Principles in their published materials and use them in their public awareness campaigns. Moreover, the Constitutional Court has delivered judgments that cite the Principles in support of actions in favour of the internally displaced on the grounds that they clarify the gaps and grey areas in existing international law, and have been widely accepted by international human rights organizations, and should, therefore, be used as the parameters for the creation of rules and for the interpretation of Colombia's national law on forced displacement.[49]

In Angola, the Principles have been incorporated into national law as a decree on the minimum standards that apply in the resettlement of internally displaced persons.[50] In Burundi, they provide the framework for the joint Government-UN protection strategy for internally displaced persons.[51] The Government of Uganda has adopted a national policy on internal displacement based on the Principles[52] and a similar initiative is under consideration in Nigeria.[53] In November 2004, the chairman of the National Transitional Government of Liberia signed an 'instrument of adoption', adopting the Principles 'to serve as a source of ongoing guidance and reference for the protection, dignity and rights of internally displaced persons'.[54] In the Americas, in May 2004, the Government and the Congress of Peru passed a national law on internal displacement based on the Principles[55] and the Government of Mexico is reportedly seeking a constitutional amendment and the development of a policy and legislation on internal displacement on the same basis.[56]

---

[48] For example, see Commission on Human Rights Res. 2003/51, UN Doc. E/CN.4/RES/2003/51, and UNGA Res. 58/177 of 22 Dec. 2003, UN Doc. A/RES/58/177 (12 March 2004).

[49] See the Court's judgments in cases T-227/97 and T-186589/T-201615/T-2459. Cited in *Report of the Representative of the Secretary-General on internally displaced persons, Mr. Francis M. Deng, submitted pursuant to Commission on Human Rights Resolution 2000/53*, UN Doc. E/CN.4/2001/5 (17 Jan. 2001) para. 29.

[50] See *Report of the Representative of the Secretary-General on internally displaced persons, Francis M. Deng, submitted pursuant to Commission on Human Rights Resolution 2002/56*, UN Doc. E/CN.4/2003/86 (21 Jan. 2003) para. 23.

[51] Ibid.

[52] See Internal Displacement Monitoring Centre, *Uganda – Overview* (Aug. 2005), available at <www.internal-displacement.org>.

[53] *Report of the Representative of the Secretary-General on internally displaced persons, Francis M. Deng*, UN Doc. E/CN.4/2004/77 (4 March 2004) para. 17.

[54] *The Guiding Principles on Internally Displaced Persons – Instrument of Adoption* (8 Nov. 2004). On file with the author.

[55] Ley No. 28223, *Ley sobre los desplazamientos internos*. Published in *El Peruano* (20 May 2004) 268725.

[56] E/CN.4/2004/77 (2004), loc. cit. n. 53, at para. 18.

5. The Future

Such developments notwithstanding, one question that remains is whether the Guiding Principles are essentially a pre-cursor to an international treaty on internally displaced persons. This option was never expressly ruled out by Deng, and it will be recalled that when he embarked upon developing the normative framework the possibility of preparing a treaty was not excluded. Rather, the concern was that the development of such an instrument would take time and could only be conceived in a long-term perspective. There have since been moves on the African continent towards developing an instrument of a more binding nature. For instance, the Executive Council of the African Union has adopted a decision to the effect that the specific needs of internally displaced persons should be addressed through a 'legal instrument', presumed to be a protocol to the Union's 1969 Convention Governing Specific Aspects of Refugee Problems in Africa, though the precise details of this are yet to be worked out.[57]

At the same time, it is perhaps more pertinent to focus on the likelihood of the Guiding Principles gaining binding force at the national (and possibly the African regional) rather than the international level. Indeed, the use of the Principles by the Governments of Angola, Burundi, Uganda, Liberia and Peru, and their incorporation into domestic law and policy, are all important examples of the potential that exists for the Principles to become hard law at the national level while remaining soft at the international level – a potential that the current Secretary-General acknowledged in his report entitled *In Larger Freedom*, in which he urged Member States

> 'to accept the Guiding Principles … as the basic international norm for the protection of [internally displaced persons], and to commit themselves to promote the adoption of these principles through national legislation'.[58]

Selected Bibliography

Bagshaw, S., *Developing a Normative Framework for the Protection of Internally Displaced Persons* (New York, Transnational Publishers 2005).

Bagshaw, S., and D. Paul, *Protect or Neglect? Towards a More Effective United Nations Approach to the Protection of Internally Displaced Persons* (Washington DC, Brookings Institution Project on Internal Displacement 2004).

Cohen, R., and F. Deng, *Masses in Flight: The Global Crisis of Internal Displacement* (Washington DC, Brookings Institution Press 1998).

[57] See EX.CL/Dec.129 (V), *Decision on the Meeting of Experts on the Review of OAU/AU Treaties Doc. EX/CL/95 (V)*, on file with the author. See further, P. Tigere and R. Amukhobu, 'The African Union's Institutional Framework for Responding to Forced Displacement in Africa', *Conflict Trends*, No. 3 (2005) p. 48.

[58] *In larger freedom: towards development, security and human rights for all. Report of the Secretary-General*, UN Doc. A/59/2005 (21 March 2005) para. 210.

—, *The Forsaken People – Case Studies of the Internally Displaced* (Washington DC, Brookings Institution Press 1998).

Deng, F., *Protecting the Dispossessed – A Challenge for the International Community* (Washington DC, Brookings Institution Press 1993).

Forbes-Martin, S., *Handbook for Applying the Guiding Principles on Internal Displacement* (New York, OCHA and the Brookings Institution Project on Internal Displacement 1999).

Inter-Agency Standing Committee, *Implementing the Collaborative Response to Situations of Internal Displacement – Guidance for United Nations Humanitarian and/or Resident Coordinators and Country Teams* (Geneva, UN 2004).

Internal Displacement Unit, Office for the Coordination of Humanitarian Affairs, *No Refuge: The Challenge of Internal Displacement* (Geneva, UN 2003).

International Committee of the Red Cross, *Internally Displaced Persons: The Mandate and Role of the International Committee of the Red Cross* (Geneva, ICRC 2000).

Kälin, W., *Guiding Principles on Internal Displacement: Annotations*, Studies in Transnational Legal Policy, No. 32 (Washington DC, American Society of International Law/Brookings Institution Project on Internal Displacement 2000).

—, 'Introduction to the Guiding Principles on Internal Displacement', 10 *International Journal of Refugee Law* (1998) p. 557.

Korn, D.A., *Exodus Within Borders – An Introduction to the Crisis of Internal Displacement* (Washington DC, Brookings Institution Press, 1999)

UN Commission on Human Rights, *Report of the Representative of the Secretary-General, Mr. Francis M. Deng, submitted pursuant to Commission on Human Rights resolution 1997/39, Addendum, Guiding Principles on Internal Displacement*, UN Doc. E/CN.4/1998/53/Add.2 (11 Feb. 1998).

Various Authors, *Protecting and Assisting the Internally Displaced: The Way Forward*, Supplement to *Forced Migration Review* (Oct. 2005).

Chapter 12
CLAIMS FOR RESTITUTION AND COMPENSATION

Norbert Wühler*

1. Introduction

Commissions and tribunals set up to deal with reparation claims are not a new phenomenon. As early as 1794, the Jay Treaty set up two commissions to address large numbers of claims by British and US citizens that still existed at the end of the American War of Independence. By 1918, around 100 mixed claims commissions of this sort had been created, but although they continued to be established for a time after the First World War, the period following the Second World War then saw a radical decline in their number.[1]

The last two decades, however, have witnessed a new proliferation of institutions and mechanisms set up to resolve, and provide remedies for, increasing numbers of claims in a variety of situations and circumstances.[2] They all have their distinct features, which stem, of course, from the contexts in which they have arisen, and which have implications for the legal basis of their establishment, the manner in which they have been established, and the issues of who can bring claims before them and for what losses. Other differences relate to what remedies are available; what law is applicable; what procedures are used; how decisions are made; how the institutions are funded; and how their decisions are implemented and enforced.

There are, on the other hand, many similarities that these claims tribunals share, and they are often faced with the same issues and challenges. The most important common feature is that they have to deal with large – sometimes very

* Director of Claims and Compensation Programmes at the IOM in Geneva.

[1] For a review of the 'larger tapestry of historic international claims settlement', see D.J. Bederman, 'The United Nations Compensation Commission and the Tradition of International Claims Settlement', 27 *New York University Journal of International Law and Politics* (1994) p. 1, in which he examines international claims practice during the last 200 years.

[2] See K. Oellers-Frahm and A. Zimmermann (eds.), *Dispute Settlement in Public International Law – Texts and Materials,* 2nd rev. and updated edn. (Berlin and Heidelberg, Springer Verlag 2001); P. Sands, R. Mackenzie, and Y. Shany (eds.), *Manual on International Courts and Tribunals* (London, Butterworths 1999). The most comprehensive recent overview is provided by the International Centre for Transitional Justice in P. de Greiff (ed.), *The Handbook of Reparations* (Oxford, Oxford University Press 2006).

R. Cholewinski, R. Perruchoud and E. MacDonald, eds., International Migration Law

large – numbers of claims, and this is true as much for mechanisms at the national level as it is for those at the international level.[3] They often have limited time and resources available to complete their task, and typically expectations are high from both the claimants and the sponsors of the institutions. As a consequence, there is always a tension between the search for individual justice and fairness and the need for an expedient process that resolves all the claims within a reasonable time period, and which can therefore only provide 'rough justice' for the claimants as a whole.[4]

In the context of the present volume, it is important to note that the types of situations giving rise to claims for restitution and compensation, and the commissions and tribunals set up for their resolution, were previously not linked to migration issues, but rather operated in the traditional framework of state responsibility. Recently, however, more and more mechanisms have been established, both at the international and the national levels, to deal with claims of, and provide remedies for, victims of conflicts who have lost their homes and property in the course of displacement; such commissions are thus an important part of increasing efforts to address the consequences of forced migration.

2. Contexts and Types of Claims

The mechanisms set up in the last two decades have two main fields of application. They either provide a process through which an individual may seek the restitution of a right (typically one related to real property or housing), sometimes combined with the possibility to claim for compensation for the loss of that right in lieu of restitution; or they aim at rehabilitating victims of large-scale human rights violations through the payment of compensation. Restitution and compensation claims have most often arisen as a result of widespread violence or conflict that inflicted losses of personal or real property on large groups of victims. Claims programmes are not only needed to provide redress to individual victims, but also to address large-scale losses and rights violations at a more general level, to assist with the processes of rebuilding and social reconciliation within the affected societies. In this regard, the restitution of land and other property rights is of particular importance, as it is one major requirement for the successful and sustainable return and reintegration of refugees and internally displaced persons (IDPs).[5]

---

[3] The numbers range from a few thousand to more than 2.6 million in the case of the UN Compensation Commission. These systems are therefore also referred to as 'mass claims processes'.

[4] Within this context, the process goals which mass claims programmes are expected to meet are speed, economy and consistency; see H. Das, 'The Concept of Mass Claims and the Specificity of Mass Claims Resolution', in Permanent Court of Arbitration (ed.), *Redressing Injustices Through Mass Claims Processes: Innovative Responses to Unique Challenges* (Oxford, Oxford University Press 2006) p. 3 at p. 10.

[5] For a recent overview see S. Leckie (ed.), *Returning Home: Housing and Property Restitution Rights of Refugees and Displaced Persons* (New York, Transnational Publishers 2003).

The need to resolve land and property issues has also become apparent recently in reconstruction efforts following natural disasters. One of the challenges for the governments whose countries were affected by the tsunami will be the restitution of real property rights, and the reconstruction of property records and land registers in the coastal regions. This enormous endeavour may well involve some form of individual claims process for tsunami victims. Pakistan faces a similar challenge in the areas worst hit by the earthquake at the end of 2005.

Finally, the provision of compensation for large-scale human rights violations and the creation of processes for the resolution of property issues that arise from these are increasingly seen as an integral part of transitional justice programmes. Compensating victims on an individual level may constitute an important step in a reconciliation process, complementing other measures such as the reform of the judicial system and the prosecution of those responsible for atrocities and injustices.

Affected governments, international organizations and international peace-'brokers' have all included claims mechanisms in their peace-building, reconciliation and reconstruction efforts, recognizing the important role that individual compensation or restitution may play in ensuring sustainable peace after an armed conflict, or as a means of distancing themselves from the injustices of past regimes. The Dayton Peace Agreement, which ended the war in the former Yugoslavia, included an Annex that provided for the creation of the Commission for Real Property Claims of Displaced Persons and Refugees in Bosnia (CRPC).[6] The UN Security Council gave the Special Representative of the Secretary-General in Kosovo the authority to establish institutions for the restitution of property in that region, which led to the creation of the Housing and Property Claims Commission (HPCC) and the Housing and Property Directorate (HPD).[7] The Iraq Property Claims Commission (IPCC) was established after the end of the second Iraq war, during the transition period in which the governing powers were handed over from the US Civil Administrator of the Coalition Provisional Authority to the Interim Iraqi Governing Council.[8] Furthermore, the property provisions in the proposed agreement for a comprehensive settlement of the Cyprus problem (the 'Annan Plan') contained an elaborate individual claims process for the resolution of questions of land and property rights on the island.

Depending on the circumstances giving rise to the claims and the political context and specific competencies of a given process, restitution and compensa-

[6] On the CRPC, see, e.g., H. van Houtte, 'The Property Claims Commission in Bosnia-Herzegovina: A New Path to Restore Real Estate Rights in Post-War Societies?', in K. Wellens (ed.), *International Law: Theory and Practice: Essays in Honour of Eric Suy* (The Hague, Martinus Nijhoff 1998) p. 549.

[7] On the HPCC, see, e.g., A. Dodson and V. Heiskanen, 'Housing and Property Restitution in Kosovo', in Leckie, op. cit. n. 5, at p. 225.

[8] The IPCC was re-named as the Commission for the Resolution of Real Property Disputes (CRRPD) in the Iraqi statute that modified its jurisdiction and procedure in 2005. The IOM provides expert advice and technical assistance to this Commission.

tion claims can involve a number of different remedies. They may provide for return to the land or property in question; for confirmation of title to property, enabling the claimant to sell or otherwise dispose of the property; or, if restoration of property or confirmation of title is not possible, for financial or other compensation, such as alternative housing. The programmes mentioned in the preceding paragraph all provide for one or several of these remedies.

Apart from real property rights, claims programmes may also address the loss of personal or business property, or they may provide compensation for detention, injury, torture or death. International mechanisms of this kind include the Iran-United States Claims Tribunal,[9] the UN Compensation Commission (UNCC),[10] the Eritrea Ethiopia Claims Commission (EECC),[11] and a number of processes relating to the Holocaust.[12] Several countries that have suffered sustained internal violence or large-scale human rights violations have created domestic reparations and/or reconciliation and truth commissions.[13] As is apparent from their names, these commissions had wider goals than providing pure financial compensation to the victims.[14]

---

[9] On the Tribunal, see, e.g., D.D. Caron and J.R. Crook, *The Iran-United States Claims Tribunal and the Process of International Claims Resolution* (New York, Transnational Publishers 2000).

[10] On the UNCC, see, e.g., V. Heiskanen, 'The United Nations Compensation Commission', 296 *Recueil des Cours* (2003) p. 255.

[11] On the EECC, see, e.g., G.H. Aldrich, 'The Work of the Eritrea-Ethiopia Claims Commission', 6 *Yearbook of International Humanitarian Law* (2006) p. 435.

[12] On the Claims Resolution Tribunal that deals with claims to Swiss bank accounts which had been dormant since the Second World War, see, e.g., S. Beauchamp, 'The New Claims Resolution Tribunal for Dormant Accounts in Switzerland: Distribution Organ, Mass Claims Adjudicative Body or Sui Generis?', 3 *The Journal of World Investment* (2002) p. 999. On the German Forced Labour Compensation Programme (GFLCP) that the IOM is implementing on behalf of the German Foundation 'Remembrance, Responsibility and Future', see, e.g., R. Bank, 'The New Programs for Payments to Victims of National Socialist Injustice', 44 *German Yearbook of International Law* (2001) p. 307; on the personal injury claims under this programme, see, E. Kristjánsdóttir and B. Simerova, 'Processing Claims for "Other Personal Injury" Under the German Forced Labour Compensation Programme', in Permanent Court of Arbitration, op. cit. cit. n. 4, at 109. Slave labour and refugee claims are also dealt with in the Holocaust Victim Assets Programme (Swiss Banks) (HVAP) that the IOM is implementing as part of the Swiss Banks settlement under the District Court of the Eastern District of New York; see, e.g., P. van der Auweraert, 'Holocaust Reparation Claims Fifty Years After: The Swiss Banks Litigation', 71 *Nordic Journal of International Law* (2002) p. 557.

[13] See, e.g., P.B. Hayner, *Unspeakable Truths: Facing the Challenge of Truth Commissions* (London, Routledge 2002).

[14] The most ambitious and comprehensive attempt in this respect is the newly created National Reconciliation and Reparations Commission in Colombia, to which the IOM provides expert advice; see Law 975 on Justice and Peace of 2005, which foresees the demobilization and prosecution of members of guerrilla groups, paramilitaries and drug cartels; the release of illegally obtained assets; the return of property or compensation; the establishing of historic truth; and the reconciliation of parties to the conflicts in the country.

3. The Right to Restitution and/or Compensation

The above overview shows that there are an increasing number of cases in which bodies have been set up in specific situations to deal with restitution and/or compensation claims of individuals, both at the national and the international level. There are also many international instruments that provide for or make reference to a duty of states to afford remedies for gross violations of human rights or international crimes. Most recently, the Draft Basic Principles and Guidelines on the Right to a Remedy and Reparation for Victims of Violations of International Human Rights and Humanitarian Law were adopted by the UN Commission on Human Rights (the so-called van Boven/Bassiouni principles),[15] and the Principles on Housing and Property Restitution for Refugees and Displaced Persons were adopted by the Sub-Commission on the Promotion and Protection of Human Rights (the so-called Pinheiro principles).[16] The Guiding Principles on Internal Displacement lay down the responsibility of competent authorities to assist IDPs 'to recover, to the extent possible, their property and possessions which they left behind or were dispossessed of upon their displacement'. When this is not possible, they shall 'provide or assist these persons in obtaining appropriate compensation or another form of just reparation'.[17]

One issue, however, remains undecided, set out by Tomuschat in the following manner:

> 'Notwithstanding the many beneficial effects which attach to compensation, the question that cannot be avoided is whether the granting of compensation to individuals, in particular to the nationals of an author state, is an obligation with its roots in positive international law or whether it merely constitutes a recipe of political expediency'.[18]

In contrast to the International Commission of Inquiry on Darfur, with whose report[19] he disagrees in this respect, Tomuschat, like the majority of commentators, still sees no individual right to restitution or compensation under current

[15] UN, ECOSOC, Commission on Human Rights, 55th Session, *Draft Basic Principles and Guidelines on the Right to a Remedy and Reparation for Victims of Violations of International Human Rights and Humanitarian Law*, UN Doc. E/CN.4/2003/63 (revised as of 5 Aug. 2004).

[16] UN, ECOSOC, Commission on Human Rights, Sub-Commission on the Promotion and Protection of Human Rights, 56th Session, *Final Report of the Special Rapporteur, Paulo Sérgio Pinheiro. Principles on housing and property restitution for refugees and displaced persons*, UN Doc. E/CN.4/Sub.2/2005/17 (28 June 2005).

[17] UN, ECOSOC, Commission on Human Rights, 54th Session, *Report of the Representative of the Secretary-General, Mr. Francis M. Deng, submitted pursuant to Commission resolution 1997/39. Addendum: Guiding Principles on Internal Displacement*, UN Doc. E/CN.4/1998/53/Add.2 (11 Feb. 1998) Principle 29(2). For a general assessment of the Guiding Principles on Internal Displacement, see Simon Bagshaw's contribution to this volume.

[18] C. Tomuschat, 'Darfur – Compensation for the Victims', 3 *Journal of International Criminal Justice* (2005) p. 579, at p. 582.

[19] UN, Security Council, *Report of the International Commission of Inquiry on Dafur to the Secretary-General*, UN Doc. S/2005/60 (1 Feb. 2005).

customary international law.[20] In his view, the difficulties that would be raised by individual reparation claims based on general international law,[21] coupled with the need to adapt compensation to the societal context of the relevant events, are the main reasons why this remains the current state of the law. Efforts to ensure appropriate reparation are indeed likely to be more successful if they are concentrated on claims mechanisms, developed with specific conflicts in mind, that are established to respond to the requirements and particularities of a particular situation.

4. Characteristics of and Challenges Facing Recent Claims Mechanisms

Each claims mechanism has of necessity its own characteristics and challenges, given the particular historic and factual circumstances which gave rise to its creation, the specific violations and losses it is set up to address, and the political and legal framework within which it is established. It is striking, on the other hand, how many of the same issues these mechanisms face and how many features they share, particularly in terms of the implementation of their mandate, the organization of their work and the enforcement of their decisions.[22] This section summarizes the main areas of this 'unity in diversity', and it begins by setting out the key features that determine what structures have been set up, and what procedures and methods they use in order to accomplish their tasks.

The four main parameters that determine the working of a claims mechanism are the number and types of claims before it; the resources, both financial and human, that are available to it; the methods that it uses to process and resolve the claims; and the time that this takes. These factors are all inter-related and affect each other, but the single most important one is the volume of claims that a commission or tribunal has to deal with. When a mechanism is faced with tens or hundreds of thousands of claims, it is practically impossible that one commis-

[20] For recent assessments of the status of the law, see L. Zegveld, 'Remedies for Victims of Violations of International Humanitarian Law', 85 *International Review of the Red Cross* (2003) p. 497; E-C. Gillard, 'Reparation for Violations of International Humanitarian Law', ibid., at p. 529; and S. Bagshaw, 'Property Restitution for Internally Displaced Persons: Developments in the Normative Framework', in Leckie, op. cit. n. 5, at p. 375. The International Law Association has established a Committee on Compensation for Victims of War that will look at this topic and issue reports over the next three years.

[21] See also UN Security Council, *Report of the Secretary-General on the Rule of Law and Transitional Justice in Conflict and Post-Conflict Societies*, UN Doc. S/2004/616 (3 Aug. 2004) p. 18, para. 55: 'Difficult questions include who is included among the victims to be compensated, how much compensation is to be awarded, what kinds of harm are to be covered, how harm is to be quantified, how different kinds of harm are to be compared and compensated and how compensation is to be distributed'.

[22] See N. Wühler, 'The Different Contexts in which International Arbitration is Being Used: International Claims Tribunals and Commissions', 4 *The Journal of World Investment* (2003) p. 379.

sion or panel, or even several such bodies, can review all claims individually and decide them on a case-by-case basis,[23] at least not within a reasonable time and at acceptable cost. It is therefore not surprising that virtually all recent international claims commissions have applied, to a greater or lesser extent, what have become known as 'mass claims processing techniques', which rely heavily on the support of a substantial secretariat, including in particular the use of modern information technology.[24]

The typical structure of a claims mechanism includes a decision-making body (sometimes more than one, and usually called the 'commission' or 'panel'), a secretariat that supports it, and a supervisory or policy organ. While the latter is not always present, in particular in national commissions, the first two always are. Differences exist as to how much is left to the discretion of the implementing organs in shaping the programme during the claims resolution process itself. In post-conflict environments, for example, where a claims programme often plays an important role in securing a newly-found, and often still-fragile, peace, the provision of a larger role to the international community (through the participation of international members in a commission) is frequently more readily accepted, as is one that leaves the details of the organization's structures and processes to be developed by those charged with the implementation of its programme. The role of the policy organ is normally to set out a programme's main political goals, and to ensure that it is properly embedded in the general framework of a country's reconciliation or reconstruction agenda. Issues such as evidentiary standards or evaluation criteria are more often left to be developed by the decision-making bodies themselves, particularly in the case of international claims mechanisms. Organizing the practicalities of the processing of the claims and ensuring the efficient and smooth running of the resolution process typically falls to the executive head of the secretariat, who has to coordinate cooperation between its different departments.

---

[23] Domestic courts, which deal with cases one by one and which render individual decisions, have also adapted their procedures when dealing with large numbers of similar cases arising out of the same circumstances. The prime example concerns the rules developed in the United States for class action suits. Indeed, the techniques used to implement judgements or settlements in such cases have to a very significant degree informed the organization and working methods of modern international mass claims mechanisms; see, for instance F.E. McGovern, 'The Intellectual Heritage of Claims Processing at the UNCC', in R. Lillich (ed.), *The United Nations Compensation Commission: Thirteenth Sokol Colloquium* (New York, Transnational Publishers 1995) p. 191.

[24] Hans Das summarizes his experiences with the CRPC and the HPCC as follows: 'Court-driven models, with elaborate adversarial proceedings and full procedural guarantees for all the parties with an interest in the claimed property are not appropriate if the process is aimed at providing effective remedies to hundreds of thousands of claimants within a reasonable time period. Administrative models are arguably better equipped to efficiently resolve mass claims, especially in the highly chaotic conditions in the wake of an armed conflict. While judicial models offer more elaborate procedural rights for the parties, the need for such elaborate procedural rights needs to be balanced against the right of masses of claimants to a speedy and effective remedy'. H. Das, 'Restoring Property Rights in the Aftermath of War', 53 *International and Comparative Law Quarterly* (2004) p. 429 at p. 437.

While the final decision on the claims rests, in most cases, with a commission or a panel, claims programmes are usually 'secretariat-heavy', with the size of secretariats invariably exceeding that of their counterparts in domestic courts.[25] This is not only because of the large numbers of claims that these mechanisms must resolve, and all of the logistical, clerical and administrative functions that go with this, but also due to the involvement of the secretariat staff in the review of the claims, and the preparation of the decisions rendered on each. The more standardized the decision-making process, the more the relevant secretariat is involved in these functions.

Often the first task of a secretariat is to reach out to potential claimants, and to inform the public about the claims programme. This is an important stage of the process, which contributes significantly to its fairness and transparency. Potential claimants need to know what claims they can make and how they should submit them; but it should also be made very clear which situations the particular claims programme is *not* addressing, and which claims are ineligible. Clarity over a commission's mandate is crucial for the management of expectations, and a failure in this respect is likely to have a significant impact not only on the workload of a mechanism, but ultimately on its acceptance, and its ability to bring closure to a conflict or to the other issues it is supposed to resolve.[26] The breadth and depth of an information campaign depends on the available resources and the choice of the right media,[27] but often the even greater challenge is to deal with the expectations, hope, frustration and anger of claimants in a manner that is at once efficient and humane, and that takes into account the often-desperate situation of those seeking redress. The same considerations apply to the information and assistance that claimants should be provided with during the claims procedure. This begins with an explanation of the requirements of the process and assistance with the filling out of the claim form, and it continues through the provision of ongoing information on the status of the claim to the implementation of the decision.

[25] For instance, at the peak of the UNCC's operation, almost 300 Secretariat staff supported some 15 commissioner panels. At the beginning of 2006, more than 1,200 staff of the Commission for the Resolution of Real Property Disputes in Iraq processed claims for submission to 38 regional commissions.

[26] In the GFLCP, for example, it was not made clear at the inception of the programme whether the 'Italian Military Internees' of the Second World War were eligible for compensation under the German Foundation Act. By the time the German Government and the Foundation decided that they were ineligible, the IOM had received around 120,000 such claims. Most of them had to be rejected (these constituted almost half of all rejections); more than 15% appealed, most without success (these constituted more than half of all appeals), and a number of these claimants brought lawsuits against the German Government, the Foundation, German companies and the IOM in the Italian and German courts.

[27] The public information campaign for a national programme is normally easier to manage and less costly than one that needs to reach potential claimants in many countries. However, even for national programmes it can become more complex and expensive when larger numbers of potential claimants live outside the country. The international notice for the Swiss Banks settlement, for example, cost more than USD 20 million. In the case of the GFLCP and the HVAP, the IOM was able to reach large numbers of claimants through outreach activities supported by its world-wide net of field offices, including free public service announcements.

Providing general information to, and seeking the assistance of, victims associations and others who are willing to help potential and actual claimants has often proved beneficial to both sides.[28]

The collection and registration of claims often pose considerable organizational and logistical challenges, particularly in international programmes where the claimants reside in many different countries and the claims can be filed in a number of languages.[29] De-centralized intake in the countries in which the claimants live is more claimant-friendly, but it makes it harder to ensure consistency in the registration process and the initial review of the claims. Centralized intake in one or only a few locations, normally through mail, is more streamlined, but fewer claimants have the opportunity to file their claims in person.[30] Claims programmes use standard forms to collect information in a consistent way that facilitates the efficient processing of the claims. Modern programmes rely heavily on information technology, with a central database and various software applications supporting the different stages of the claims processing.[31] The data must be entered into the database, and, if the various stages in the review, verification and decision of the claims are properly recorded, it will provide the basis for a range of support functions, such as status tracking, workflow management, reporting, auditing, generation of notifications to claimants, and management of compensation payments.

Beyond these, information technology can also be used directly in the review, verification and evaluation of the claims. As a result of the circumstances which caused the losses or injuries in question, it will in many cases be impossible for the claimants to provide documentary evidence to support their claims. Those who seek the return of property that they lost in wars or other conflicts will have fled from their houses and abandoned their belongings in very difficult and chaotic circumstances. Documents proving their property rights will have been lost, stolen or destroyed. After conclusion of hostilities, restrictions on movement and security risks often prevent claimants from travelling to their previous homes in order to search for records in cadastres[32] and other property archives. In other cases in which the events causing the losses took place many years before the establishment of the claims programme, the lapse of time itself can create significant evidentiary difficulties.

---

[28] For the GFLCP, this worked well through a steering group of most affected victims associations organized by the IOM in the early stages of the programme. Sometimes, on the other hand, a programme has to try to protect (potential) claimants from self-appointed representatives who provide incorrect information, raise false expectations and in some cases even take money from people for their supposedly 'good services'.

[29] In the GFLCP and the HVAP, the IOM received claims from over 70 countries in 27 languages.

[30] Where the required connectivity is available, a web-based system would today allow on-line registration of claims even directly into a central database. The issues of the verification of the claimant's identity and the submission of documents supporting the claim would, however, still remain.

[31] See, e.g., V. Heiskanen, 'Virtue Out of Necessity: International Mass Claims and New Uses of Information Technology', in Permanent Court of Arbitration, op. cit. n. 4, at p. 25.

[32] A cadastre is a public record of the ownership of land for the purposes of calculating taxation.

In order to address these problems, claims commissions have developed several techniques. For example, all recent international commissions and tribunals have applied a relaxed standard of proof. Different terms have been used to describe this standard, such as reference to a requirement of 'available', 'reasonable' or 'credible' evidence, but they have all been interpreted in similar ways. In addition, many commissions use presumptions in certain instances.[33] The loss of property was, for instance, presumed by the Property Claims Commission under the GFLCP if it occurred in certain areas and during certain periods of German occupation in the Second World War.[34]

The founding instruments or the procedural rules of a number of claims commissions also require them to actively assist claimants in the procurement of evidence for and the verification of their claims.[35] Such a fact-finding role has led the secretariats of these commissions to organize extensive searches for claim- or claimant-related information in external archives and registers, and to cooperate with national authorities such as cadastres and other offices holding real property records. In a number of cases, large amounts of information were either loaded into databases that the commission secretariats created for this purpose, and which they then matched against information in claims databases,[36] or the matching was done from the claims database against an external database.[37]

Another technique that is widely used in mass claims processing is the identification and grouping of claims with similar factual or legal characteristics, again through the use of the information in the claims database. Its purpose is to in-

---

[33] See, for a comprehensive overview, H. Das, *Resolving Mass Claims: New Approaches to Evidence and Claims Resolution in International Mass Claims Processes*, Ph.D. Dissertation (University of Leuven, 2004), to be published in 2006.

[34] The Property Claims Commission under the GFLCP was to base its decisions on compensability 'on relaxed standards of proof taking into account the lapse of time between the date the loss occurred and the date the claim was made; the circumstances in which the specific loss or types of losses occurred; the information available from other cases; and the background information available to the Commission regarding the circumstances prevailing during the National Socialist era and the Second World War and the participation of German enterprises in the commitment of National Socialist wrongs'. Section 22 of the Supplemental Principles and Rules of Procedure of the Property Claims Commission <http://www.compensation-for-forced-labour.org>.

[35] Art. 33 of the CRPC's Book of Regulations states, for instance, that 'if no evidence is available to a claimant or if the evidence presented is of doubtful credibility, the Commission will initiate evidence collection or evidence verification procedures', using, *inter alia*, 'the bodies and services where records on real property are kept'. CRPC Book of Regulations on the Conditions and Decision-Making Procedure for Claims for Return of Real Property of Displaced Persons and Refugees (4 March 1999) <http://www.crpc.org.ba>.

[36] The CRPC collected all existing cadastral and census records and entered them into a separate database against which it matched the data in its claims database. The UNCC collected information on the departure of persons from Kuwait and Iraq during the jurisdictional period from a multitude of Government and private sources and entered them into a separate database against which it matched the data in its claims database.

[37] The IOM matched the data in its GFLCP claims database against electronic records of the International Tracing Service in Germany, the largest archive of WWII personal data with 40 million records of 12 million people.

crease the efficiency and fairness of the process by reviewing and deciding similar claims in a coordinated and consistent way.[38] Some commissions have taken this further, by first deciding samples from claims groups and then instructing their secretariat to apply the criteria and rules from these sample decisions to the remaining claims in the group, limiting themselves to quality control checks before adopting the results of the secretariat's reviews.[39]

Once a decision is rendered by a commission or tribunal, the question of its finality remains. There is much debate over the extent to which such decisions should be subject to appeal or reconsideration. Commentators not involved closely with the context of claims mechanisms generally argue that an independent legal remedy should be foreseen to guarantee the claimants' rights of due process. The practice of the international mechanisms in particular tends to grant only rather more limited remedies, if any; such practice is determined more by what is deemed to be feasible than by the strict application of formal concepts. A key factor is again the number of claims to be addressed, and consequently of decisions that would be subject to appeal, given the delay that large numbers of appeals would mean for the completion of the process. The tendency is to provide such an independent legal remedy in cases of claims for restitution of real property, whereas the position is less consistent with respect to pure monetary claims, regardless, for example, of the size of the claims or whether the first instance process is more judicial or more administrative in nature.

Requests for reconsideration of decisions on property restitution can be brought to the same commission that rendered the decision in the first instance in both the CRPC and the HPCC. A request can be based on new evidence or on the grounds that there was a 'material' error in the first decision.[40] A much more limited mechanism was established in the UNCC for the correction of 'computational, clerical, typographical or other errors',[41] although in certain categories the claims were for billions of US dollars. Even with this limited standard, and leaving aside the hundreds of thousands of individual claims in the smaller categories,

---

[38] Cf., e.g., van Houtte's description of the use of this technique by the CRPC: 'The computer should be able to select (for decision-making) all claims which belong to the same class, *inter alia*, by locating property, type of claim and evidence submitted. The claim forms contain all the information which may be encoded by computer, so that computer-selection of a particular category of claims is possible'. Van Houtte, loc. cit. n. 6, at p. 557.

[39] See P.A. Karrer, 'Innovation to Speed Mass Claims: The Work of the Property Claims Commission of the German Foundation "Remembrance, Responsibility and Future"', 5 *Journal of World Investment & Trade* (2004) p. 57 at p. 60.

[40] Claimants before the Property Claims Commission under the GFLCP had to show a 'manifest' error in the first decision for a request for reconsideration to be admissible. It must be remembered that the Commission could only award compensation, that the amount of the funds available for compensation was pre-determined, and that the payment of compensation could only start after all claims and reconsideration requests had been decided. Supplemental Principles and Rules of Procedure of the Property Claims Commission, loc. cit. n. 34.

[41] UNCC, *Provisional Rules of Claims Procedure*, UN Doc. S/AC.26/1992/10 (26 June 1992), Art. 41 <http://www2.unog.ch/uncc>.

the UNCC had to develop 'fast track' procedures to be able to process the correction requests brought in the larger categories within a reasonable time-frame.[42]

The last phase of the claims process is the implementation and enforcement of the decisions. This is a crucial stage, not only for the satisfaction of the individual claimants, but for the effectiveness and ultimate success of the programme as a whole. Even in the case of purely monetary compensation, problems often arise at this stage as the payments are dependent on timely and sufficient funding, and this is not always guaranteed.[43] In fact, a regular funding mechanism that provides the financial means for the payment of all accepted claims is the exception rather than the rule, and future programmes will need to confront this requirement at an early stage.[44]

While the payment of compensation may at times be technically challenging,[45] the enforcement of decisions that involve the return of successful claimants into the properties that were taken from them, or that they had to abandon, is invariably more complex in political and human terms, particularly when such properties are occupied by others at the time the enforcement is to take place. The first set of issues concerns the enforcement power of the claims mechanism. Even where it is formally entrusted with this task, it requires the assistance of domestic organs, including law enforcement authorities, in cases in which occupants of the property have to be evicted. An international commission in a post-conflict situation needs the cooperation of the local authorities even more than would a national body, and, where this is not forthcoming, more robust implementation and monitoring mechanisms must be put in place.[46]

---

[42] Correction requests were submitted in approximately 20% of the almost 10,000 large individual claims in Category 'D' (individual claims for damages of over USD 100,000 each). In the absence of such a streamlined procedure, the Iraq Commission for the Resolution of Real Property Disputes, for instance, is faced with a real bottleneck: there is only one Appellate Division for the decisions of 38 regional commissions (soon to be increased to 50), and there is no limitation on the grounds for appeal; it is thus not surprising that the Appellate Division has only resolved a small portion of the appeals pending.

[43] For instance, by early 2006, the Iraq Commission for the Resolution of Real Property Disputes had issued thousands of decisions awarding the claimants compensation without funds being available to it to make the payments (USD 200 million were ostensibly earmarked by the Ministry of Finance for the purpose, but the Commission had no access to this). The Dayton Peace Agreement had envisaged the creation of a compensation fund and compensation awards to be determined by the CRPC; no contributions were made to the fund and the contemplated income-generating activities could not be sustained, therefore the fund was never created and the CRPC issued no compensation awards.

[44] In some cases, the lack of funding has even threatened the existence of the mechanism itself. The HPCC in Kosovo, for instance, was for a number of years lacking adequate funds to function, and at one point it was forced to reduce staff to such an extent that its operation was significantly slowed down. The CRPC management also had to spend a lot of energy on fund-raising activities.

[45] In the GFLCP, for instance, the IOM had to make payments of more than EUR 450 million in several instalments to beneficiaries in over 70 countries, including to thousands of heirs and legal successors of beneficiaries who became deceased during the process, involving a multitude of banking arrangements and sophisticated payment controls.

[46] In the case of the CRPC, for instance, the Dayton Peace Agreement did not specify a particular implementation procedure, and local authorities were often unwilling or unable to take the necessary measures to allow those in whose favour it had decided to regain possession of their property.

The second issue related to the enforcement of restitution decisions is the fact that the needs of the occupants who have to vacate properties as a result frequently compete with equally or more compelling needs of other sectors of the population, and a transitional government will often not have the means to satisfy all of these needs adequately. Again, Iraq provides a typical example, where in many cases secondary displacement will result from decisions of the CRRPD, as long as the provisions in the new statute that are intended to address this issue have not been implemented. International assistance to countries in transition or emerging from periods of conflict should include alternative housing or other rehabilitation facilities, in order to avoid the creation of new instances of displacement as a result of the decisions of claims mechanisms.

5. Conclusion

Claims for restitution and compensation, and mechanisms to address them, are here to stay. There have at some point been discussions or proposals for some form of claims or reparations programme in relation to the following countries or situations, in alphabetical order: Chad (victims of ex-dictator Habré); comfort women (rape of Philippine women during the Second World War); Darfur (proposal by the International Commission of Inquiry on Darfur); Guam (crimes during the Second World War); Georgia/South Ossetia (property restitution and/or compensation); Hereros (extermination by Germany between 1904 and 1908); Kenya (IDPs as a result of inter-ethnic violence in the 1990s); Rwanda (draft law on reparation for survivors of genocide); and Zimbabwe (detainees from liberation war).

To this list must be added Cyprus, where any solution to the property issues will have to include a restitution and compensation mechanism; and, in the Middle East, any comprehensive agreement resolving the issues between Israel and the Palestinians will likely include a mechanism for claims by Palestinian refugees for return and/or compensation.

In view of the proliferation of claims mechanisms in recent years, and considering the list of potential new mechanisms, the question has been raised of whether the time has come for a permanent international claims mechanism, or at least a 'Permanent War Damage Compensation Commission'.[47] Reference is often made in these discussions to the International Criminal Court, which was the culmination of a similar trend and which consolidates relevant activities in the areas of its jurisdiction. The differences between this and the field of restitution

Eventually, the High Representative in Bosnia and Herzegovina had to impose specific laws on the enforcement of CRPC decisions. 'However, the lack of a credible enforcement procedure has created severe problems for CRPC certificate holders, and has caused frustrations both among the claimant population and the international community'. H. Das, loc. cit. n. 24, at p. 441.

[47] This was the topic of one panel of the 7th Hague Joint Conference of the American and Dutch Societies of International Law in 2005.

and compensation claims are, however, so large that a permanent institution is not the best way forward. The following considerations support this conclusion: that international law does not yet provide a sufficient basis for the right of individuals to restitution or compensation; that the specifics of the remedies must be adapted to the particular situation in question, and should not be made uniform by a permanent statute; that the acceptability of a claims mechanism depends to a large extent on the degree to which it is 'embedded' in the environment in which the claimants live, and on the participation in the decision-making body of representatives of the affected groups; and that the procedural rules, methodologies and techniques should not be predetermined, but should be adjusted to the needs of the particular process.[48]

These differences on the one hand, and the common features shared by claims mechanisms on the other, suggest the adoption of an approach that would seek to build upon the experience and expertise developed by previous claims commissions and tribunals rather than the establishment of a permanent body. Analyzing the practice of the earlier commissions, identifying lessons learned by and the best practices of the various professions involved, and developing a 'toolbox' of claims processing methodologies and techniques would make available valuable know-how that could be deployed to kick-start new programmes. This would be general enough to be adapted to the particular circumstances in question; it would not pre-set the organization and procedures of future programmes and would ensure the necessary flexibility, but would at the same time avoid the problem of every new mechanism having to 're-invent the wheel' – very much still an issue today. In this way, precious time could be gained at the beginning of a programme, and the capacity of its staff could be built while the process is in operation. An intuitive version of such an approach has operated in the heads of a small number of specialists who have in the past moved from one mechanism to the other, but it is hoped that a small core facility attracting and maintaining this expertise would eliminate the subjectivity and uncertainty from the current situation, and would make it predictable and reliable for the benefit both of those who need to implement claims programmes, and, ultimately, of those for whom they are established.

Selected Bibliography

Bank, R., 'The New Programs for Payments to Victims of National Socialist Injustice', 44 *German Yearbook of International Law* (2001) p. 307.

Bederman, D.J., 'The United Nations Compensation Commission and the Tradition of Interna-

[48] In addition, as how often or seldom such an institution would be mandated to address a particular situation cannot be foreseen, a permanent commission could be 'idle' for long periods of time, incurring significant costs that would need to be covered outwith specific 'programmes'. If, on the other hand, it had to deal with several 'mass claims programmes' at the same time, such a commission could easily get overwhelmed by the magnitude and complexity of the cumulative tasks.

tional Claims Settlement', 27 *New York University Journal of International Law and Politics* (1994) p. 1.

Caron, D.D., and J.R. Crook, *The Iran-United States Claims Tribunal and the Process of International Claims Resolution* (New York, Transnational Publishers 2000).

Das, H., 'The Concept of Mass Claims and the Specificity of Mass Claims Resolution', in Permanent Court of Arbitration (ed.), *Redressing Injustices Through Mass Claims Processes: Innovative Responses to Unique Challenges* (Oxford, Oxford University Press 2006) p. 3.

Dodson, A., and V. Heiskanen, 'Housing and Property Restitution in Kosovo', in S. Leckie (ed.), *Returning Home: Housing and Property Restitution Rights of Refugees and Displaced Persons* (New York, Transnational Publishers 2003) p. 225.

Gillard, E-C., 'Reparation for Violations of International Humanitarian Law', 85 *International Review of the Red Cross* (2003) p. 529.

Heiskanen, V., 'The United Nations Compensation Commission', 296 *Recueil des Cours* (2003) p. 255.

—, 'Virtue Out of Necessity: International Mass Claims and New Uses of Information Technology', in Permanent Court of Arbitration, ed., *Redressing Injustices Through Mass Claims Processes: Innovative Responses to Unique Challenges* (Oxford, Oxford University Press 2006) p. 25.

Karrer, P.A., 'Innovation to Speed Mass Claims: The Work of the Property Claims Commission of the German Foundation "Remembrance, Responsibility and Future"', 5 *Journal of World Investment & Trade* (2004) p. 57.

Leckie, S. (ed.), *Returning Home: Housing and Property Restitution Rights of Refugees and Displaced Persons* (New York, Transnational Publishers 2003).

Permanent Court of Arbitration (ed.), *Redressing Injustices Through Mass Claims Processes: Innovative Responses to Unique Challenges* (Oxford, Oxford University Press 2006).

Sands, P., R. Mackenzie, and Y. Shany (eds.), *Manual on International Courts and Tribunals* (London, Butterworth's 1999).

van der Auweraert, P., 'Holocaust Reparation Claims Fifty Years After: The Swiss Banks Litigation', 71 *Nordic Journal of International Law* (2002) p. 557.

van Houtte, H., 'The Property Claims Commission in Bosnia-Herzegovina: A New Path to Restore Real Estate Rights in Post-War Societies?', in K. Wellens (ed.), *International Law: Theory and Practice: Essays in Honour of Eric Suy* (Leiden, Martinus Nijhoff 1998) p. 549.

Wühler, N., 'The Different Contexts in which International Arbitration is Being Used: International Claims Tribunals and Commissions', 4 *The Journal of World Investment* (2003) p. 379.

Human Rights of Specific Migrant Groups

Chapter 13
THE PROTECTION OF NON-CITIZENS IN INTERNATIONAL HUMAN RIGHTS LAW

David Weissbrodt[*]

1. Introduction

Globalization and the growth of the world economy have increased international trade in goods and services as well as facilitated international financial transfers. While Adam Smith prescribed the free movement of goods, capital, and people as the hallmark of the market system,[1] nations have been far less receptive to the last of these three than to the first two. Despite this unease, the population in developed nations is aging and there is an increased need for workers – many of whom must come from other countries. Modern forms of transportation have made travel much easier. Persistent unemployment, underemployment, poverty, and economic insecurity in developing countries have impelled millions to seek work in developed nations. They arrive through regular migration procedures, irregular methods, or trafficking. Also, armed conflicts, human rights abuses, and environmental disasters cause more people to leave their homes in search of safer places to live. From 1975 to 2000 the number of migrants in the world increased, under the various different pressures of globalization, from 75 million to 175 million.[2] Accordingly, countries must come to terms with having many non-citizens on their territory.

[*] Regents Professor of Law and the Fredrikson & Byron Professor of Law at the University of Minnesota Law School.

[1] See generally A. Smith, *The Wealth of Nations* (1776) (Homewood, Illinois, R.D. Irwin 1963). The Internet revolution has made it much less necessary for individuals to travel in order to make productive contributions to the world economy and to seek a better way of life. One can be inventive and well compensated in Bangalore or in Shanghai these days without traveling to Berlin, Chicago, or Tokyo. Despite the implications of these new economic and technical developments, however, skilled and unskilled migrants continue to move from nation to nation in search of prosperity.

[2] P.A. Taran, 'Events in the international community', Briefing for UN General Assembly delegates, 11 Nov. 2003, p. 2.

R. Cholewinski, R. Perruchoud and E. MacDonald, eds., International Migration Law

2. WHO IS A NON-CITIZEN?

Approximately 175 million individuals – or three per cent of the world's population – currently reside in a country other than the one in which they were born.[3] They include migrants, that is, individuals who are engaged in a remunerated activity in a state of which they are not a national.[4] Non-citizens also include refugees, asylum seekers, and immigrants who have entered a new country for reasons of family reunification.[5] There are also non-immigrants, that is, individuals who enter the country without the intent to remain on a permanent basis. For example, foreign workers, who have temporary permission to remain, foreign students, business visitors, tourists, and unsuccessful asylum seekers. In many countries there are individuals who entered or remained without permission, have been subjected to trafficking, or who otherwise lack the requisite documentation to remain.[6] Not all non-citizens, however, are born abroad. A large number are stateless persons – those who either never acquired citizenship of the country of their birth or lost their citizenship, and have no claim to that of another state.[7] Such persons include individuals native to the country of their residence who failed to register for citizenship during a specified period and have been since denied it.[8] There are also persons who lost their citizenship after acquiring the nationality of their non-citizen spouses, only to lose their adopted citizenship upon divorce; and children born in states that recognize only the *jus sanguinis* principle (under which children acquire their parents' citizenship) to non-citizen nationals

[3] UN, ECOSOC, Commission on Population and Development, *World Demographic Trends: Report of the Secretary-General*, UN Doc. E/CN.9/2003/5 (2003) p. 16. This figure of 175 million is indicative of the number of individuals who may be in this situation; it may include persons who have become naturalized citizens of their new countries, but may not include individuals whose nationalities have not been recognized in their countries of origin.

[4] International Convention on the Protection of the Rights of All Migrant Workers and Members of Their Families, UNGA Res. 45/158, Annex, 45 GAOR Supp. (No. 49A) p. 262, UN Doc. A/45/49 (1990), entered into force 1 July 2003, Art. 2(1).

[5] See, e.g., European Commission against Racism and Intolerance (ECRI), *Second Report on Denmark*, adopted on 16 June 2000, paras. 18-25.

[6] See, e.g., P. Anderson, 'In a Twilight World – Undocumented Migrants in the United Kingdom' (1999) <http://www.geocities.com/jrsuk/Twilight.html>; M.J. Gibney, 'Outside the Protection of the Law: The Situation of Irregular Migrants in Europe', *Oxford University Refugee Studies Centre Working Paper No. 6* (2000); UN, ECOSOC, Commission on Human Rights, Sub-Commission on the Promotion and Protection of Human Rights, *The Rights of Non-citizens: Progress Report of the Special Rapporteur*, UN Doc. E/CN.4/Sub.2/2002/25/Add. 3 (3 June 2002) para. 3.

[7] See, e.g., UNHCR, *Contribution to the OSCE Implementation Meeting on Human Dimension Issues* (2002) paras. 11-12; UN, ECOSOC, Commission on Human Rights, Sub-Commission on the Promotion and Protection of Human Rights, *The Rights of Non-citizens: Examples of Practices in Regard to Non-citizens*, UN Doc. E/CN.4/Sub.2/2003/23/Add. 3 (26 May 2003) para. 7.

[8] See, e.g., Human Rights Watch, *The Bedoons of Kuwait: Citizens Without Citizenship* (New York, Human Rights WatchuHH 1995) <http://www.hrw.org/reports/1995/Kuwait.htm>; *Beldjoudi* v. *France* (1992) 14 *EHRR* 801.

of states that recognize only *jus soli* (in which children acquire the citizenship of their country of birth).[9]

3. Synthesis of the Rights of Non-Citizens

International human rights law is grounded upon the premise that all persons, by virtue of their humanity, have fundamental rights.[10] Accordingly, international human rights law generally requires the equal treatment of citizens and non-citizens.[11] Exceptions may be made to this general principle only if they are to serve a legitimate state objective[12] and are proportional to the achievement of that objective.[13]

With regard to civil and political rights, the Human Rights Committee – which is responsible for monitoring the implementation of the International Covenant on Civil and Political Rights[14] (ICCPR) – explained in its General Comment 15 that almost all rights protected by the Covenant must be guaranteed without discrimination between citizens and non-citizens.[15] Among these rights are freedom from

---

[9] See, e.g., Concluding Observations of the Committee on the Elimination of Discrimination Against Women: Guinea, UN Doc. A/56/38 (31 July 2001) paras. 97-144; European Convention on Nationality, *ETS* No. 166, entered into force 1 March 2000 (Art. 6: 'Each Party shall provide in its internal law for its nationality to be acquired by children born on its territory who do not acquire at birth another nationality'). The issue of stateless persons is dealt with in detail by Gelazis in her contribution to this volume.

[10] See Universal Declaration of Human Rights (UDHR), Art. 2(1), UNGA Res. 217A (III), UN Doc A/810 (1948) p. 71.

[11] See, e.g., International Covenant on Civil and Political Rights (ICCPR), Arts. 2(1), 4, UNGA Res. 2200A (XXI), 21 GAOR Supp. (No. 16) p. 52, UN Doc. A/6316 (1966), 999 *UNTS* 171, entered into force 23 March 1976.

[12] See Committee on the Elimination of Racial Discrimination, General Recommendation XIV on the Definition of Discrimination (Art. 1(1)) (22 March 1993) UN Doc. A/48/18 (15 Sept. 1993) p. 115, para. 2: 'The Committee observes that a differentiation of treatment will not constitute discrimination if the criteria for such differentiation, judged against the objectives and purposes of the Convention, are legitimate or fall within the scope of article 1, paragraph 4 [relating to special measures], of the Convention. In considering the criteria that may have been employed, the Committee will acknowledge that particular actions may have varied purposes. In seeking to determine whether an action has an effect contrary to the Convention, it will look to see whether that action has an unjustifiable disparate impact upon a group distinguished by race, colour, descent, or national or ethnic origin'. The Human Rights Committee has similarly observed that differences in treatment may be permissible under the Covenant 'if the criteria for such differentiation are reasonable and objective and if the aim is to achieve a purpose which is legitimate under the Covenant'. Human Rights Committee, General Comment 18 on Non-discrimination (10 Nov. 1989) para. 13, reproduced in UN Doc. HRI/GEN/1/Rev.6 (2003) p. 146.

[13] See J. Fitzpatrick, 'The Human Rights of Migrants', in T.A. Aleinikoff and V. Chetail (eds.), *Migration and International Legal Norms* (The Hague, T.M.C. Asser Press 2003) p. 169 at p. 172. See also, e.g., *Berrehab* v. *The Netherlands* (1988) 11 *EHRR* 322.

[14] ICCPR, loc. cit. n. 11.

[15] Human Rights Committee, General Comment 15 on The position of aliens under the Covenant (11 April 1986) para. 1, reproduced in UN Doc. HRI\GEN\1\Rev.1 (1994) p. 18.

arbitrary killing and detention; freedom from torture or cruel, inhuman or degrading treatment or punishment; equality before courts and tribunals; and freedom of thought, conscience and religion.[16] Furthermore, non-citizens should have the right to marry; to receive protection as minors; and to peaceful association and assembly.[17] The ICCPR contains a narrow exception to the general principle of equality for non-citizens with respect to two categories of rights – political rights that are explicitly guaranteed to citizens, such as the right to vote; and freedom of movement, such as the right to choose one's place of residence, which may be denied to undocumented immigrants.[18]

The International Covenant on Economic, Social and Cultural Rights (ICESCR) establishes that states shall, in general, protect the rights of all individuals – regardless of citizenship – to work; just and favourable working conditions; an adequate standard of living; good health; education; and other economic, social and cultural rights.[19] Article 2(3) of the ICESCR allows developing countries, 'with due regard to human rights and their national economy', to 'determine to what extent they would guarantee the *economic* rights recognized in the [ICESCR] to non-nationals'.[20] This exception may be made only with respect to economic rights and not to social and cultural rights.[21] Further, like all exceptions, those provisos must be narrowly construed so as to maintain the overall thrust of the human rights protections.[22]

Under Article 1(3) of the International Convention on the Elimination of All Forms of Racial Discrimination (ICERD), states may not discriminate against persons of any particular nationality.[23] The Committee on the Elimination of Racial Discrimination, tasked with monitoring the implementation of this Convention, has indicated that states may draw distinctions between citizens and non-citizens as long as such distinctions do not have the effect of limiting non-citizens' enjoyment of rights enshrined in other instruments, such as the Universal Declaration of Human Rights (UDHR), the ICCPR and the ICESCR, and all non-citizens are treated equally.[24] The Committee has also determined that differential treatment

---

[16] Ibid., at para. 7.

[17] Ibid.

[18] ICCPR, loc. cit. n. 11, Arts. 12(1), 25.

[19] International Covenant on Economic, Social and Cultural Rights (ICESCR), UNGA Res. 2200A (XXI), 21 GAOR Supp. (No. 16) p. 49, UN Doc. A/6316 (1966), 993 *UNTS* 3, entered into force 3 Jan. 1976.

[20] Ibid. (emphasis added).

[21] See C. Tiburcio, *The Human Rights of Aliens under International and Comparative Law* (Leiden, Martinus Nijhoff 2001) pp. 145-147.

[22] Measures adopted by states to protect their citizens and economies from non-citizens should not lead to the detriment of the enjoyment of human rights. *Federation Internationale des Ligues des Droits de L'Homme* v. *Angola*, African Commission on Human and Peoples' Rights, Communication No. 71/92 (Oct. 1997) para. 16; see also Tiburcio, op. cit. n. 21, at pp. 96-97, 147.

[23] International Convention on the Elimination of All Forms of Racial Discrimination (ICERD), 660 *UNTS* 195, entered into force 4 Jan. 1969.

[24] Committee on the Elimination of Racial Discrimination, General Recommendation XI on Non-citizens (19 March 1993), reproduced in UN Doc. HRI\GEN\1\Rev.1 (1994) p. 66.

based on citizenship or immigration status will constitute discrimination if the criteria for such differentiation are inconsistent with the objectives and purposes of the Convention; are not proportional to the achievement of those objectives and purposes; or do not fall within the scope of Article 1(4) of the Convention relating to special measures, that is, what is popularly known as 'affirmative action'.[25]

There are several major treaties specifically protecting the rights of migrant workers, including the International Convention on the Protection of the Rights of All Migrant Workers and Members of Their Families (ICRMW)[26] – which came into force in July 2003 and has been ratified by 34 nations – and ILO Conventions 97[27] and 143,[28] which have been ratified by 43 and 18 nations respectively.[29]

The ICRMW provides for the following list of rights and liberties for all migrant workers and their families, regardless of immigration status: non-discrimination;[30] freedom to leave any country and to enter their country of origin;[31] the right to life;[32] freedom from torture and ill-treatment;[33] freedom from slavery or forced labour;[34] freedom of thought, conscience, and religion;[35] freedom of opinion and expression;[36] freedom from arbitrary or unlawful interference with privacy, family, home, correspondence, or other communications;[37] property rights;[38] liberty and security of person;[39] the right of migrants deprived of their liberty to be treated with humanity;[40] the right to a fair and public hearing by a competent, independent, and impartial tribunal;[41] prohibition of retroactive application of criminal laws;[42] no imprisonment for failure to fulfil a contract;[43] no destruction of travel or identity documents;[44] no expulsion on a collective basis or without

[25] Committee on the Elimination of Racial Discrimination, General Recommendation XIV, loc. cit. n. 12, at para. 2.

[26] Loc. cit. n. 4.

[27] ILO Convention No. 97 concerning Migration for Employment (Revised 1949), entered into force 22 Jan. 1952.

[28] ILO Convention No. 143 concerning Migrations in Abusive Conditions and the Promotion of Equality of Opportunity and Treatment of Migrant Workers, entered into force 9 Dec. 1978.

[29] For the ratification information on these two conventions, see <http://www.ilo.org/ilolex/cgi-lex/ratifce.pl?C097> and <http://www.ilo.org/ilolex/cgi-lex/ratifce.pl?C143>.

[30] ICRMW, loc. cit. n. 4, Art. 7.

[31] Ibid., Art. 8.

[32] Ibid., Art. 9.

[33] Ibid., Art. 10.

[34] Ibid., Art. 11.

[35] Ibid., Art. 12.

[36] Ibid., Art. 13.

[37] Ibid., Art. 14.

[38] Ibid., Art. 15.

[39] Ibid., Art. 16.

[40] Ibid., Art. 17.

[41] Ibid., Art. 18.

[42] Ibid., Art. 19.

[43] Ibid., Art. 20.

[44] Ibid., Art. 21.

fair procedures;[45] the right to consular or diplomatic assistance;[46] the right to recognition as a person before the law;[47] equality of treatment between nationals and migrant workers as to work conditions and pay;[48] the right to participate in trade unions;[49] equal access to social security;[50] the right to emergency medical care;[51] the right of a child to a name, birth registration, and nationality;[52] and equality of access to public education.[53] In addition, States Parties must ensure respect for migrants' cultural identity;[54] the right to repatriate earnings, savings, and belongings;[55] and the right to information about rights under the ICRMW.[56]

In an attempt to discourage irregular migration,[57] the ICRMW provides additional rights to migrant workers who are documented or in a regular situation. Indeed, for migrant workers and their families in a documented or regular situation, the ICRMW provides for the right to liberty of movement in the territory of the state of employment;[58] equal access to education, vocational guidance, housing, social and health services, and cultural rights;[59] equality of treatment with nationals in respect of protection against dismissal and access to unemployment benefits;[60] the right to vote, be elected, and participate in the public affairs of the state of origin;[61] and the right to have a family.[62]

In general, the ICRMW does not create new rights for migrants, but instead reaffirms basic human rights norms found in existing treaties and embodies them in an instrument applicable to migrant workers and their families. The Convention takes into account relevant international labour standards such as ILO Conventions 97[63] and 143,[64] as well as the Slavery Conventions.[65] The Convention

[45] Ibid., Art. 22.
[46] Ibid., Art. 23.
[47] Ibid., Art. 24.
[48] Ibid., Art. 25.
[49] Ibid., Art. 26.
[50] Ibid., Art. 27.
[51] Ibid., Art. 28.
[52] Ibid., Art. 29.
[53] Ibid., Art. 30.
[54] Ibid., Art. 31.
[55] Ibid., Art. 32.
[56] Ibid., Art. 33.
[57] Ibid., Preamble, Recital 15.
[58] Ibid., Art. 39.
[59] Ibid., Arts. 43, 45.
[60] Ibid., Art. 54.
[61] Ibid., Art. 41.
[62] Ibid., Art. 44.
[63] ILO Convention 97, loc. cit. n. 27.
[64] ILO Convention 143, loc. cit. n. 28.
[65] Slavery, Servitude, Forced Labour and Similar Institutions and Practices Convention of 1926 (Slavery Convention of 1926), 60 *LNTS* 253, entered into force 9 March 1927; Protocol amending the Slavery Convention, 182 *UNTS* 51, entered into force 7 Dec. 1953; Supplementary Convention on the Abolition of Slavery, the Slave Trade, and Institutions and Practices Similar to Slavery (7 Sept. 1956), 226 *UNTS* 3, entered into force 30 April 1957; Convention for the Suppression of the Traffic

also refers to other instruments, such as the ICESCR,[66] the ICCPR,[67] UNESCO's Convention against Discrimination in Education,[68] and the Convention on the Rights of the Child (CRC).[69]

The ICRMW innovates by defining the rights that apply to specific categories of migrant workers and their families, and presents a division of migrant workers into sub-categories: 'frontier workers'; seasonal workers; seafarers employed on vessels registered in a state other than their own; workers on offshore installations which are under the jurisdiction of a state other then their own; itinerant workers; migrants employed for a specific project, and self-employed workers.

In an Opinion of 17 September 2003, the Inter-American Court of Human Rights[70] issued one of the most important international judicial reaffirmations of the rights of migrants when it declared

> 'that non-discrimination and the right of equality are *jus cogens* [that is, peremptory norms of international law] applicable to all residents regardless of immigration status... The Court acknowledged that governments have the right (within the bounds of other applicable human rights norms) to deport individuals and to refuse to offer jobs to people without employment documents. However, the Court said, once the employment relationship is initiated, unauthorized workers become rights holders entitled to the full panoply of labor and employment rights available to authorized workers.'[71]

For the 192 nations that have ratified the CRC,[72] children of non-citizens shall have the right to a name and to acquire a nationality, and should not be excluded from schools – even if they lack legal status.[73] In general, children should have the right to acquire citizenship of the country in which they are born – particularly where they would otherwise be stateless.[74] Similar provisions ensuring ac-

---

in Persons and of the Exploitation of the Prostitution of Others (2 Dec. 1949), 96 *UNTS* 271, entered into force 25 July 1951; International Agreement for the Suppression of the 'White Slave Traffic' (18 May 1904), 35 Stat. 1979, 1 *LNTS* 83, entered into force 10 July 1905; International Convention for the Suppression of the 'White Slave Traffic' (4 May 1910), 211 Consol. T.S. 45, 103 BFSP 244, entered into force 5 July 1920.

[66] ICESCR, loc. cit. n. 19.

[67] ICCPR, loc. cit. n. 11.

[68] Convention against Discrimination in Education (4 Dec. 1960), 429 *UNTS* 93, entered into force 22 May 1962.

[69] UN Convention on the Rights of the Child (CRC) (20 Nov. 1989), UNGA Res. 44/25, Annex, 44 GAOR Supp. (No. 49), UN Doc. A/44/49 (1989) p. 167, entered into force 2 Sept. 1990.

[70] IACtHR, Juridical Condition and Rights of Undocumented Migrants, Advisory Opinion OC-18/03 of 17 Sept. 2003, requested by Mexico.

[71] P.A. Taran, 'The Key Role of International Labour Standards in Defending Rights of Non-Nationals' (unpublished paper, 9-10 Nov. 2003) pp. 5-6, quoting B. Lyon, 'Press Release: Interamerican Court Condemns Discrimination on the Job against Undocumented Workers', National Employment Law Project (28 Sept. 2003) <http://www.nelp.org/news/pressreleases/interamctopress09300.cfm>.

[72] CRC, loc. cit. n. 69.

[73] Committee on Economic, Social and Cultural Rights, General Comment 13, UN Doc. E/C.12/1999/10 (1999) para. 34.

[74] See A. Eide, 'Citizenship and International Human Rights Law: Status, Evolution, and Chal-

quisition of citizenship at birth, protecting against statelessness, and protecting the rights of stateless persons can be found in the Convention on the Reduction of Statelessness[75] and the Convention relating to the Status of Stateless Persons,[76] which have only been ratified by 29 and 57 nations respectively.

In at least 143 countries, based on their accession to the Convention relating to the Status of Refugees, the standards that govern the treatment of refugees and asylum seekers should be applied without distinction as to nationality.[77] Eligibility for asylum should not depend on the ethnic or national origin of applicants.[78] Refugees should be entitled to treatment that is at least as favourable as that accorded to citizens in areas such as freedom of religion, access to courts and legal assistance, elementary education, and public assistance.[79] Furthermore, they should also be accorded treatment no less favourable than that given to non-citizens generally in regard to acquisition of property, access to professions, housing, post-secondary education, and so on.[80] Conditions in refugee shelters and conditions of detention of undocumented immigrants and asylum seekers should meet international standards.[81]

4. Common Problems with Regard to the Rights of Non-Citizens

Despite the existence of such an extensive framework for the protection of non-citizens, there remains a disjuncture between those prescribed rights and the realities that non-citizens must face. There are institutional and endemic problems facing them in many countries. Xenophobia and racism – at times reflected in a country's legislation – prevail, and serve to deny non-citizens the rights they are guaranteed by international law, leaving them subject to harassment and abuse by political parties, officials, the media, and by society at large.[82]

---

lenges', in N. Butenschon, U. Davis and M. Hassassian (eds.), *Citizenship and the State in the Middle East* (Syracuse, Syracuse University Press 2000) p. 88; A. Eide, 'Working paper on citizenship and the minority rights of non-citizens', UN Doc. E/CN.4/Sub.2/AC.5/1999/WP.3 (5 April 1999); see also CRC, loc. cit. n. 69, Art. 8.

75 Convention on the Reduction of Statelessness (30 Aug. 1961), 989 *UNTS* 175, entered into force 13 Dec. 1975.

76 Convention relating to the Status of Stateless Persons (28 Sept. 1954), 360 *UNTS* 117, entered into force 6 June 1960.

77 The Convention relating to the Status of Refugees (28 July 1951), 189 *UNTS* 150, entered into force 22 April 1954, for example, has been ratified by 143 countries. See <http://untreaty.un.org/ENGLISH/bible/englishinternetbible/partI/chapterV/treaty2.asp>.

78 See the Concluding Observations of the Committee on the Elimination of All Forms of Racial Discrimination: Italy, UN Doc. A/50/18 (22 Sept. 1995) para. 83.

79 Convention relating to the Status of Refugees, loc. cit. n. 77.

80 See ibid.

81 See Concluding Observations of the Committee on the Elimination of Racial Discrimination: Hungary, UN Doc. CERD/C/61/CO/6 (23 Aug. 2002) para. 14.

82 See, e.g., ECRI, *Second Report on Austria*, paras. 16–21, adopted on 16 June 2000; Conclud-

Non-citizens continue to suffer discrimination. For example, the Committee on the Elimination of Racial Discrimination found that, in Norway, a list of housing accommodation contained discriminatory requirements such as 'no foreigners desired', 'whites only' and 'Norwegians with permanent jobs' only.[83] A study in South Africa found that people were being detained on suspicion of being illegal immigrants simply because of the colour of their skins and their accents.[84] Because non-citizens are often of both a different race and a different culture, they become the victims of both racism and xenophobia.

In addition to discrimination, non-citizens often face outright abuse.[85] For example, those women of Asian origin working as domestic servants in Kuwait were frequently subjected to debt bondage, passport deprivation, illegal confinement, rape, and other physical assault.[86]

At the same time, it is usually the case that non-citizens cannot assert their rights for fear of retribution,[87] and have no way of participating in the political process[88] so as to assure legal protection. As a result, they are left without the effective means to challenge or have remedied violations of their human rights.

Two particularly vulnerable groups of non-citizens are undocumented, or 'illegal', immigrants[89] and irregular migrants.[90] Undocumented immigrants are individuals who enter without following the required immigration procedures or who enter as non-immigrants and then remain beyond the limits of their permission to remain. Irregular migrants are smuggled or trafficked into the country or otherwise enter through irregular means. Undocumented immigrants may live under substandard conditions, and face raids on homes and workplaces, and interrogations in which they may be subjected to abuse, inhumane or degrading treatment, and violations of their right to privacy.[91] Their encounters with the police may not

---

ing Observations of the Committee on the Elimination of Racial Discrimination: Ukraine, UN Doc. A/56/18 (16 Aug. 2001) para. 375.

[83] *F.A.* v. *Norway*, Communication No. 18/2000: Norway, 17 April 2001, UN Doc. CERD/C/58/D/18/2000 (17 April 2001).

[84] See P. Sebolao, 'Human Rights Body Calls for Guidelines on Arrest of Aliens', *Business Day*, 23 March 1999, p. 2.

[85] See, e.g., Human Rights Watch, *'Hidden in the Home': Abuse of Domestic Workers with Special Visas in the United States* (New York, Human Rights Watch 2001) <http://www.hrw.org/reports/2001/usadom/>.

[86] Concluding Observations of the Committee on the Elimination of Racial Discrimination: Kuwait, UN Doc. A/48/18, (15 Sept. 1993) paras. 359-381.

[87] See, e.g., P. Anderson, loc. cit. n. 6; M.J. Gibney, loc. cit. n. 6; see also the website of the NGO GISTI (Groupe d'information et de soutien des immigrés) at <http://www.gisti.org/doc/publications/2002/sans-papiers/.>; *The Rights of Non-citizens: Progress Report of the Special Rapporteur*, loc. cit. n. 6, at para. 3.

[88] See *supra* n. 18 and accompanying text.

[89] See, e.g., the authorities quoted at *supra* n. 87.

[90] See, e.g., UN, ECOSOC, Commission on Human Rights, *Report of the Special Rapporteur on the Human Rights of Migrants*, UN Doc. E/CN.4/2002/94 (15 Feb. 2002); and the same report of the previous year, UN Doc. E/CN.4/2001/83 (9 Jan. 2001).

[91] *The Rights of Non-citizens: Progress Report of the Special Rapporteur*, loc. cit. n. 6, at para. 3.

be noticed because they have no relatives close by to raise questions about their detention or even death.[92] Even when they suffer violations of their human rights, they may not seek judicial remedies because they fear deportation.[93] If they can find work, they are often employed in the informal economy, in which their employers exploit their fear of being reported to the authorities and may subject them to conditions that resemble slavery.[94] Without documentation, they also cannot obtain basic government services like health care and education.[95]

Persons who emigrate through irregular channels – such as smuggling and trafficking networks – risk dying of suffocation in containers or drowning when an overloaded ship sinks.[96] There have been cases where sexual favours have been demanded of trafficked women in order to let them continue on their way, as well as cases of rape.[97] Where they are intercepted by the authorities, irregular migrants are vulnerable to excessive use of force and cruel or degrading treatment, and are at times accused of being smugglers and traffickers themselves.[98] Unfortunately, countries of origin are often unwilling to acknowledge the nationality of their citizens who have been trafficked and then try to return home; as a result, they also refuse to represent such trafficked persons or act on their behalf.[99]

Non-citizens are frequently caught in the mesh of differing rules on determining nationality, and have been rendered stateless as a result. In 2005, the Inter-American Court of Human Rights issued its landmark decision in *Bosico* v. *Dominican Republic*,[100] forbidding racial discrimination in the granting of citizenship and thus diminishing the likelihood of statelessness.[101] This case was brought by two children of Haitian descent, who were born and had resided in the Dominican Republic their entire lives, but who had nonetheless been denied birth certificates, barred from acquiring Dominican nationality, and exposed to possible expulsion.[102] The Inter-American Court found that the Dominican Republic's discriminatory application of birth registration and nationality laws rendered children of Haitian descent stateless and effectively deprived them of a number of essential human rights, such as the right to a name, the right to equal protection before the law, and the right to education. The Court determined that the Dominican Government

[92] Ibid.

[93] Ibid.

[94] Ibid.; see also Human Rights Watch, op. cit. n. 85.

[95] *The Rights of Non-citizens: Progress Report of the Special Rapporteur*, loc. cit. n. 6, at para. 3.

[96] Ibid., at para. 4.

[97] Ibid.

[98] Ibid.

[99] Ibid.

[100] *Dilcia Yean and Violeta Bosico* v. *Dominican Republic*, Judgment of 8 Sept. 2005, IACtHR (Ser. C) No. 134 (2005).

[101] Justice Initiative, Open Society, *Inter-American Court of Human Rights Affirms the Human Right to Nationality and Upholds the International Prohibition on Racial Discrimination in Access to Nationality* (17 Oct. 2005) <http://www.justiceinitiative.org/db/resource2?res_id=103001>.

[102] Ibid.

should create an effective procedure to ensure that all children born on the territory of the State were granted birth certificates regardless of parental citizenship or migratory status, and that they had equal access to State education. Furthermore, the Court ruled that the Government should compensate the parties and their families for the injuries they had suffered.

A major problem that non-citizens continue to face is arbitrary detention, even though it is prohibited by the ICCPR.[103] For example, in *A* v. *Australia*,[104] the Human Rights Committee found that Australia's practice of detaining Southeast Asian 'boat people' violated the Covenant. In 1989, a Cambodian national arrived in Australia by boat, applied for refugee status, and was kept in detention for four years. The Human Rights Committee found that his detention violated Article 9(1) of the ICCPR (prohibiting arbitrary detention), because there were no specific grounds justifying detention for that length of time. The Committee further noted that detention of immigrants must be open to periodic review. In addition, the Committee found that Australia had violated Article 9(4) of the ICCPR (guaranteeing access to a court), because Australian law did not allow courts to order the release of 'boat people'.[105]

Nonetheless, non-citizens – especially asylum seekers, undocumented immigrants, and victims of trafficking – continue to be placed in detention[106] for indefinite periods.[107] These persons, who have often been traumatized by experiences of persecution or abuse, are detained side-by-side with criminals in the same prison facilities, which are frequently overcrowded and unhygienic.[108] They are denied contact with their families and access to legal assistance,[109] and the opportunity to challenge their detention. Even unaccompanied children and families are placed in arbitrary detention,[110] and, in the case of families, children are separated from their parents and taken to other facilities.[111] Detained children are deprived of the

[103] ICCPR, loc. cit. n. 11, Art. 9(1). See also the chapter by Shyla Vohra in this volume.

[104] Communication No. 560/1993, *A* v. *Australia*, UN Doc. CCPR/C/59/D/560/1993 (30 April 1997).

[105] In Australia itself the decision has had limited impact. See Report of Amnesty International, *Refuge! Asia: Ethnicity and Nationality. Refugees in Asia*, AI Index: ASA 01/01/97 <http://web.amnesty.org/library/pdf/ASA010011997ENGLISH/$File/ASA0100197.pdf>. In contrast to US and UK decisions, recent Australian decisions have permitted the indefinite detention of immigration detainees. See *Minister for Immigration and Multicultural and Indigenous Affairs* v. *Al Khafaji* [2004] HCA 38, 208 ALR 201; *Al-Kateb* v. *Godwin* [2004] HCA 37, 208 ALR 124.

[106] See ECRI, *Second Report on Belgium* (18 June 1999) paras. 11–15; ECRI, *Second Report on Croatia* (15 Dec. 2000) para. 31. See also the chapter by Vohra in this volume.

[107] See, e.g., Human Rights Watch, *'Locked Away': Immigration Detainees in Jails in the United States* (New York, Human Rights Watch 1998) <http://www.hrw.org/reports98/us-immig/>.

[108] See ibid.

[109] See ibid.

[110] See, e.g., ECRI, *Second Report on Malta* (14 Dec. 2001).

[111] See, e.g., Concluding Observations of the Committee on the Rights of the Child: Lebanon, UN Doc. CRC/C/15/Add.169 (1 Feb. 2002) para. 52.

special care they require,[112] and are not afforded the right to education.[113] A pregnant woman in detention in Australia complained to the authorities for a fortnight about pain and bleeding she was experiencing:[114] when she was finally admitted to hospital, she was found to have miscarried.[115]

This situation has worsened since 11 September 2001, as several countries have invoked anti-terrorism measures in order to justify indefinite detention or otherwise violate the rights of non-citizens, on the basis of unspecified allegations related to terrorism or national security.[116] The Government of the United States has detained and summarily deported thousands of immigrants and non-immigrants who were from certain Middle Eastern and Asian nations.[117]

Where non-citizens face expulsion orders, they are frequently denied the right to challenge those orders in court.[118] They may also be faced with *refoulement*[119] – expulsion to countries of origin where they may be subjected to persecution or abuse.[120]

5. Recommendations for the Protection of Non-Citizens

The continuing discriminatory treatment of non-citizens in contravention of relevant human rights instruments demonstrates the need for clear, comprehensive standards governing the rights of non-citizens, their implementation by states, and more effective monitoring of compliance.

Since the seven core human rights treaties[121] deal with many of the problems encountered by non-citizens, states should push for the universal ratification

[112] See, e.g., Concluding Observations of the Committee of the Rights of the Child: Czech Republic, UN Doc. CRC/C/15/Add.201 (31 Jan. 2003) para. 56.

[113] See, e.g., Concluding Observations of the Committee on the Rights of the Child: Italy, UN Doc. CRC/C/15/Add.198 (31 Jan. 2003) para. 21.

[114] M. Saunders, 'Illegals Drugged Then Deported', *Australasian Business Intelligence*, 14 March 2000.

[115] Ibid.

[116] See, e.g., UN, ECOSOC, Commission on Human Rights, *Report of the Special Rapporteur on the Rights of Migrants*, UN Doc. E/CN.4/2003/85 (30 Dec. 2002).

[117] See, e.g., Human Rights Watch, *World Report 2002: United States* <http://hrw.org/wr2k2/us.html>; Human Rights Watch, *World Report 2003: United States* <http://www.hrw.org/wr2k3/us.html>.

[118] See, e.g., Concluding Observations of the Human Rights Committee: Syrian Arab Republic, UN Doc. CCPR/CO/71/SYR (5 April 2001) para. 22.

[119] See, e.g., Convention relating to the Status of Refugees, loc. cit. n. 77, Art. 33(1); Convention Against Torture, and Other Cruel, Inhuman, or Degrading Treatment or Punishment, 10 Dec. 1984, UNGA Res. 39/46, Annex, 39, GAOR Supp. (No. 51) p. 197, UN Doc. A/39/51 (1984), entered into force 26 June 1987, Art. 3; ICCPR, loc. cit. n. 11, Art. 7; Convention for the Protection of Human Rights and Fundamental Freedoms (ECHR), 4 Nov. 1950, *ETS* No. 5, entered into force 3 Sept. 1953, Art. 3.

[120] See, e.g., Concluding Observations of the Human Rights Committee: Yemen, UN Doc. CPR/CO/75/YEM (26 July 2002).

[121] These treaties are listed on the website of the Office of the UN High Commissioner for Human Rights at <http://www.ohchr.org/english/law/>.

and implementation of those treaties, including the ICRMW. In addition, states should be encouraged to ratify the additional international agreements addressing the problems of non-citizens, including the Protocol Relating to the Status of Refugees;[122] the Conventions on the Reduction of Statelessness and relating to the Status of Stateless Persons;[123] the Convention against Transnational Organized Crime;[124] the Protocol to Prevent, Suppress and Punish Trafficking in Persons, Especially Women and Children,[125] and the Protocol against the smuggling of Migrants by Land, Sea and Air,[126] which supplement the Convention; and the Vienna Convention on Consular Relations and its Protocols.[127] States should further ratify, as appropriate, Protocol Nos. 4 and 7 to the European Convention on Human Rights (ECHR)[128] and the European Framework Convention for the Protection of National Minorities.[129] Moreover, they should also be encouraged to abide by the Declaration on the Human Rights of Individuals Who Are Not Nationals of the Country in Which They Live.[130]

Since many problems frequently faced by non-citizens are covered by more than one treaty, it would be desirable for each of the treaty bodies to take into account the jurisprudence of their counterparts, in order to establish a consistent, structured approach to the protection of the rights of non-citizens. At a minimum, this should be done by those treaty bodies that have adopted specific standards, following the example of the Committee on the Elimination of Racial Discrimination, which has updated its General Recommendation providing interpretive guidance relating to non-citizens in such a way as to establish a comprehensive and integrated approach to the rights of non-citizens.[131] In addition, treaty bodies should intensify their dialogues with States Parties regarding the rights accorded to, and the actual situation faced by, non-citizens.

---

[122] Protocol relating to the Status of Refugees, 606 *UNTS* 267, entered into force 4 Oct. 1967.

[123] Loc. cit. nn. 75 and 76.

[124] UN Convention against Transnational Organized Crime, UNGA Res. 55/25 of 15 Nov. 2000, Annex I, GAOR, 55th Sess., Supp. No. 49 p. 44, UN Doc. A/45/49 (Vol. I) (2001), entered into force 29 Dec. 2003.

[125] Protocol to Prevent, Suppress and Punish Trafficking in Persons, Especially Women and Children, supplementing the UN Convention against Transnational Organized Crime, ibid., entered into force 25 Dec. 2003.

[126] Protocol against the smuggling of Migrants by Land, Sea and Air, supplementing the UN Convention against Transnational Organized Crime, ibid., entered into force 28 Jan. 2004.

[127] Vienna Convention on Consular Relations and Optional Protocols (24 April 1963), 596 *UNTS* 8638.

[128] Protocol No. 4 to the ECHR (16 Sept. 1963), *ETS* No. 46, entered into force 2 May 1968; Protocol No. 7 to the ECHR (22 Nov. 1984), *ETS* No. 117, entered into force 1 Nov. 1988.

[129] Framework Convention for the Protection of National Minorities (1 Feb. 1995), *ETS* No. 157, entered into force 1 Feb. 1998.

[130] Declaration on the Human Rights of Individuals Who Are Not Nationals of the Country in Which They Live, UNGA Res. 44/144 of 13 Dec. 1985.

[131] Committee on the Elimination of Racial Discrimination, General Recommendation 30 on Discrimination against non-citizens, UN Doc. CERD/C/64/Misc.11/rev.3 (2004).

The UN Special Rapporteurs on the human rights of migrants and on trafficking in persons, appointed by the Commission on Human Rights, play important roles in continuing their reviews of the situations facing migrants and trafficked persons throughout the world, visiting countries of particular concern, receiving communications about human rights problems, and reporting to the Commission on Human Rights.[132] Governments, NGOs, representatives of non-citizens, and others should be encouraged to support the work of the Special Rapporteurs and to submit relevant information to them.

States should take actions to counter any tendency to target, stigmatize, stereotype, or profile, on the basis of race, members of particular population groups such as non-citizens – both by officials and by the media and society at large. They should ensure that all officials dealing with so-called 'irregular migrants' receive special training, including education in human rights obligations, and do not engage in discriminatory behaviour. Racist or xenophobic propaganda by political parties against non-citizens should be discouraged. Complaints made against officials, notably those concerning discriminatory or racist behaviour, should be subject to independent and effective scrutiny.

One of the most impressive advances in this regard was evident when the UK House of Lords, in December 2004, forbade discrimination against non-citizens who were detained because they were suspected of terrorism.[133] The House of Lords examined the Anti-Terrorism, Crime and Security Act 2001, adopted by the United Kingdom after 11 September 2001, which provided that non-UK nationals suspected of terrorism could be indefinitely detained if they could not be deported. In *A (FC) and Others* v. *Secretary of State for the Home Department*,[134] nine terrorism suspects successfully challenged their detention under the Act, alleging that the UK had violated Article 5 (the right to liberty and security) of the ECHR.[135] In its judgment, the House of Lords relied predominantly upon European human rights law, and upon General Recommendation 30 issued by the Committee on the Elimination of Racial Discrimination.

6. Conclusion

While non-citizens may have different reasons for leaving their countries of birth and living abroad, and even though there are different legal regimes for migrants,

[132] In March 2006, the UN General Assembly passed a resolution to replace the Commission on Human Rights by a reformed body, the Human Rights Council. UNGA Res. 60/251 of 15 March 2006, UN Doc. A/RES/60/251 (3 April 2006). The Council held its first session in June 2006 <http://www.ohchr.org/english/bodies/hrcouncil/1session/index.htm>.

[133] *A and Others* v. *Secretary of State for the Home Department* [2004] UKHL 56, [2005] 2 WLR 87 <http://www.publications.parliament.uk/pa/ld200405/ldjudgmt/jd041216/a&oth-4.htm>.

[134] Ibid.

[135] The House of Lords also found that indefinite detention constituted a disproportionate derogation under Art. 15 from the right to liberty and security of person in Art. 5. See ibid., e.g., paras. 124-134.

refugees, stateless persons, and others, they all share common experiences of discrimination and abuse that must be addressed. Unfortunately, different communities of non-citizens often do not see their common interests. Intergovernmental and non-governmental organizations focus narrowly on distinct groups, without perceiving the need for global responses that might benefit all those concerned in general. Although international human rights law offers some protection for the rights of non-citizens, much needs to be done to define more broadly the relevant rights, and to implement those rights in practice.

Selected Bibliography

Anderson, A., 'In a Twilight World – Undocumented Migrants in the United Kingdom' (1999) <http://www.geocities.com/jrsuk/Twilight.html>.

Committee on the Elimination of Racial Discrimination, General Recommendation 30, Discrimination against Non-citizens (64th Session, 2004), UN Doc. CERD/C/64/Misc.11/rev.3 (2004).

Eide, A., 'Citizenship and International Human Rights Law: Status, Evolution, and Challenges', in N. Butenschon, U. Davis and M. Hassassian (eds.), *Citizenship and the State in the Middle East* (Syracuse, Syracuse University Press 2000).

Fitzpatrick, J., 'The Human Rights of Migrants', in T.A. Aleinikoff and V. Chetail (eds.), *Migration and International Legal Norms* (The Hague, T.M.C. Asser Press 2003) p. 169.

Gibney, M.J., 'Outside the Protection of the Law: The Situation of Irregular Migrants in Europe', *Oxford University Refugee Studies Centre Working Paper No. 6* (2000).

Human Rights Committee, General Comment 15, The position of aliens under the Covenant (27th Session, 1986), *Compilation of General Comments and General Recommendations Adopted by Human Rights Treaty Bodies*, UN Doc. HRI\GEN\1\Rev.1 (1994) p. 18.

Lillich, R., *The Human Rights of Aliens in Contemporary International Law* (New York, William S. Hein & Co. 1984).

Tiburcio, C., *The Human Rights of Aliens under International and Comparative Law* (Leiden, Martinus Nijhoff 2001).

UN, ECOSOC, Commission on Human Rights, Sub-Commission on the Promotion and Protection of Human Rights, *The Rights of Non-citizens: Progress Report of the Special Rapporteur*, UN Doc. E/CN.4/Sub.2/2002/25/Add. 3 (3 June 2002).

Chapter 14
MIGRANT WOMEN

Nicola Piper*[*] and Margaret Satterthwaite[**]

1. Introduction

International human rights law has always protected migrant women: through general norms of non-discrimination and equality; substantive rights such as freedom of movement, labour rights, and the right to be free from debt bondage; and through identity-based rights for specific groups, such as women's rights and refugee rights. Until recently, however, these general standards have not been carefully examined for their application to women migrants. As reports of human rights violations against women migrants have gained attention, there has been a new focus on uncovering existing norms and progressively developing new standards to respond to gaps in the protection of migrant women.

These developments in the legal standards and practices are taking place alongside the evolution of new frameworks for creating gender-sensitive and rights-based migration policies. The latest World Survey on the Role of Women in Development by the UN Division for the Advancement of Women (UNDAW) is devoted to the issue of 'women and international migration'.[1] The March 2005 report, 'Gender Equality: Striving for Justice in an Unequal World' by the UN Research Institute for Social Development (UNRISD) discusses a number of subject areas from an explicit gender perspective, and one chapter is devoted to the issue of labour migration.[2] The ILO Multilateral Framework on Labour Migration[3] integrates gender throughout. In addition, the report by the Global Commis-

[*] Senior Research Fellow at the Asia Research Institute, National University of Singapore.

[**] Assistant Professor of Clinical Law at New York University School of Law, where she teaches international human rights and is Faculty Director of the Center for Human Rights and Global Justice.

[1] UN Department of Economic and Social Affairs, Division for the Advancement of Women (UNDAW), *2004 World Survey on the Role of Women in Development: Women and International Migration* (New York, UN 2005) <http://www.un.org/womenwatch/daw/Review/documents/press-releases/WorldSurvey-Women&Migration.pdf>.

[2] UNRISD, *Gender Equality: Striving for Justice in an Unequal World* (Geneva, UNRISD 2005) ch. 5, p. 57 <http://www.unrisd.org/80256B3C005BCCF9/(httpPublications)/1FF4AC64C1894EAAC1256FA3005E7201?OpenDocument>.

[3] *ILO Multilateral Framework on Labour Migration: Non-binding principles and guidelines for a rights-based approach to labour migration*, Tripartite Meeting of Experts on the ILO Multilateral

R. Cholewinski, R. Perruchoud and E. MacDonald, eds., International Migration Law

sion on International Migration (GCIM) that was launched in October 2005 refers to migrant women as among the most vulnerable groups of migrants, especially those working as domestic helpers.[4]

2. Background on Women's Migration and Human Rights Concerns

Women have participated in cross-border and international migration streams in their capacity as refugees, as family migrants, and as primary labour migrants in the skilled and unskilled categories. Global estimates suggest that, for more than 40 years, the proportion of migrants who are female has been increasing steadily, and has now reached almost 50 per cent. In 1960, female migrants accounted for nearly 47 out of every 100 migrants living outside their countries of birth. Since then, the share of females among international migrants has been rising steadily, reaching 48 per cent in 1990 and nearly 49 per cent in 2000. By 2000, female migrants constituted nearly 51 per cent of all migrants in the developed world and about 46 per cent of those in developing countries.[5] Similarly, about 49 per cent of refugees in the world are women.[6] The UNHCR reports that the proportion of women among refugee groups varies a great deal: although, in general, there are many fewer female asylum seekers, mass refugee flows in some regions or at specific times include more women than men.[7]

2.1 Women migrant workers

As foreign workers, women are mainly channeled into gender-specific jobs or female-dominated sectors. As skilled migrants, women have globally tended to go into what can be broadly classified as the welfare and social professions (education, health, social work) – traditionally female jobs. Nursing is the most female-dominated skilled sector, with 90 per cent or more of the nursing workforce being comprised of women.[8] As unskilled migrants, most women around the world

Framework on Labour Migration, Geneva, 31 Oct. – 2 Nov. 2005, Doc. TMMFLM/2005/1(Rev.) <http://www.ilo.org/public/english/protection/migrant/download/tmmflm-en.pdf>.

[4] GCIM, *Migration in an Interconnected World: New Directions for Action* (Geneva, GCIM 2005) p. 49 <http://www.gcim.org/attachements/gcim-complete-report-2005.pdf>.

[5] ILO, *Preventing Discrimination, Exploitation and Abuse of Women Migrant Workers: An Information Guide – Booklet 1: Why the Focus on Women International Migrant Workers* (Geneva, ILO 2003) p. 9.

[6] UNHCR, *2004 Global Refugee Trends: Overview of Refugee Populations, New Arrivals, Durable Solutions, Asylum-Seekers, Stateless and Other Persons of Concern to UNHCR* (Geneva, UNHCR 2005) p. 5.

[7] Ibid.

[8] J. Buchan and L. Calman, *The Global Shortage of Registered Nurses: An Overview of Issues and Actions* (Geneva, International Council of Nurses 2004) p. 7 <http://www.icn.ch/global/shortage.pdf>.

move as domestic or care workers, so-called 'entertainers',[9] or as unskilled workers in the manufacturing sector (especially the garment sector) and to a lesser degree in the agricultural sector (in manufacturing, male migrants are often part of higher management levels and women concentrated at low levels).[10] In France and Italy, more than 50 per cent of migrant women are believed to be engaged in domestic work,[11] and in Spain domestic service is the main and almost obligatory gateway for 63 per cent of non-EU foreign women.[12] The situation is not so different in Canada, which has a 'live-in-caregiver' programme.[13] Domestic work is also the single most important category of employment among women migrants to the Gulf States, as well as to Lebanon and Jordan.[14]

Globally, most women migrant workers generate income through jobs which are considered unskilled, are poorly paid and often performed in the domestic domain or related to the expansion of the service industry – all jobs that tend to be socially stigmatized and devalued economically.[15] It is common that destination countries focus on foreign workers' migration status by treating them as a special group not deserving of protection (i.e., as 'non-citizens' not eligible for equal treatment under labour laws – especially those who are irregular migrants). Another problem for women migrant workers is that the sectors or occupations in which they predominate – especially domestic work or certain forms of entertainment – may not count as 'work' for the purpose of labour law protections. In such circumstances, the rights of states clearly prevail over those of migrants, with states retaining not only the right to set the conditions under which foreign-

---

[9] In Japan, entertainers from the Philippines are actually classified as 'professionals' in terms of visa category.

[10] M. Dias and L. Wanasundera, *Sri Lankan Migrant Garment Factory Workers: Mauritius and Sultanate of Oman*, Study Series No. 27 (Colombo, Centre for Women's Research 2002).

[11] ILO, op. cit. n. 5, at p. 11.

[12] Colectivo Ioé, 'The Integration of Immigrant Women into the Spanish Labour Market', in J. Freedman (ed.), *Gender and Insecurity – Migrant Women in Europe* (Aldershot, Ashgate 2003) p. 91.

[13] D. McKay, 'Filipinas in Canada – De-Skilling as a Push Towards Marriage', in N. Piper and M. Roces (eds.), *Wife or Worker? Asian Women and Migration* (Lanham, Rowman and Littlefield 2003) p. 23.

[14] S. Esim and M. Smith (eds.), *Gender & Migration in Arab States – The Case of Domestic Workers* (Geneva, ILO 2004) p. 15 <http://www.ilo.org/dyn/gender/docs/RES/477/F2008148367/Gender%20-%20Migration%20in%20Arab%20States%20PDF%20File%20Revis.pdf>.

[15] Focusing on domestic work, Margaret Satterthwaite has identified the following forms of discrimination and abuse as prevalent among women migrant workers: (1) exploitative terms of work: pay, hours and contracts; (2) restrictions on the freedom of movement; (3) labour market discrimination against women – at home and abroad (the gender wage gap; the 'glass ceiling'; and labour market segregation); (4) dangerous and degrading working conditions: safety and health; (5) gender-based violence in the workplace; (6) gendered forms of racism and xenophobia against women migrant workers (at home and abroad); and (7) restrictions on migrant women's ability to organize for their rights (at home and abroad). M. Satterthwaite, 'Crossing Borders, Claiming Rights: Using Human Rights Law to Empower Women Migrant Workers', 8 *Yale Human Rights and Development Law Journal* (2005) p. 1 at pp. 22-62 <http://islandia.law.yale.edu/yhrdlj/PDF/Vol%208/satterthwaite.pdf>.

ers may enter, reside, and work, but also whether or not migrants will enjoy equal protection within their territory.

2.2 Women family migrants

The UN reports that women predominate among those officially crossing borders to unite their families.[16] This is true in part because guest worker programmes historically favoured men, with women eligible to join their husbands through reunification policies, if not independently.[17] Currently, women's migration for marriage is common, and, in the last few decades, businesses offering 'match-making' services have flourished.[18] Global statistics are very difficult to compile concerning this practice. Migration for marriage can tend to make women vulnerable, since their legal status is linked to that of their husbands; some countries have attempted to mitigate this vulnerability by extending independent status to women who suffer domestic violence or abuse by their husbands.[19]

2.3 Female forced migrants

Most women migrants cross borders voluntarily for work or family reasons.[20] A smaller number flee persecution, human rights violations, and conflict each year.[21] Women make up almost half of all 'persons of concern' to the UNHCR, a category that includes individuals categorized as refugees, asylum seekers, internally displaced persons (IDPs), stateless persons, and those who have returned after having been refugees or IDPs.[22] In addition to these categories, women also form significant proportions of other groups considered to be 'forced migrants' – a category that includes the UNHCR's 'persons of concern' as well as trafficked and smuggled people and those displaced by development projects or by environmental or natural disasters.

2.3.1 *Women refugees and asylum seekers*

The category 'women and children' constitutes the majority of all those displaced and made refugees;[23] in recent years, attention has been paid to disaggregating the two elements making up this category and attending to the specific concerns of displaced women. As members of the civilian population, women suffer both

[16] UNDAW, op. cit. n. 1, at pp. 11, 27.
[17] Ibid., at p. 27.
[18] Ibid., at p. 29.
[19] Ibid., at p. 30.
[20] Ibid., at p. 43.
[21] Ibid.
[22] UNHCR 2005, op. cit. n. 6, at p. 2, n. 1.
[23] C. Lindsey, 'Women and War', 839 *International Review of the Red Cross* (2000) p. 561 <http://www.icrc.ch/Web/eng/siteeng0.nsf/iwpList179/5BD0956E8C9593CFC1256B66005EFEE9>.

directly and indirectly from armed conflict. They are often victims of direct attacks by combatants, who may use sexual violence systematically against female members of the 'enemy' population.[24] In addition, when men are taken away by war (as combatants, internees, detainees, or exiles), women are left behind with children and the elderly and must take on additional responsibilities.[25] For these reasons, women often flee within or across borders, seeking assistance and safety.

According to the UNHCR, 49 per cent of the world's refugee population is female.[26] However, women tend to be under-represented among asylum seekers, though this varies greatly by region.[27] In Europe, on average, women make up only 29 per cent of asylum seekers, though there are many more women who are included on the applications of male relatives or spouses.[28]

2.3.2 *Internally displaced women*

Although the exact proportions are currently unknown, it is widely accepted that women make up a large portion of those displaced within their own countries. Roberta Cohen reports that 'women and children' account for 70 per cent of the IDP population.[29] IDPs often face difficulties accessing adequate assistance, since most humanitarian assistance is aimed at refugees – those who have crossed international borders.[30] For women, these difficulties are exacerbated by the heavy burdens of childcare, elder care, and the common shift of responsibilities for the household to women when conflict breaks out.[31]

2.3.3 *Smuggled women*

Like men, women sometimes provide monetary or other material incentives to intermediaries who help them cross borders. There is comparatively little research available on the phenomenon of migrant smuggling, in part because of the illicit nature of the activity, and in part because of its close relationship to the phenomenon of human trafficking.[32] As opportunities for legal migration become more

[24] Ibid.

[25] S. Gururaja, 'Gender Dimensions of Displacement', 9 *Forced Migration Review* (2000) p. 13.

[26] UNHCR 2005, op. cit. n. 6, at p. 5.

[27] Ibid.

[28] UNDAW, op. cit. n. 1, at p. 43.

[29] R. Cohen, 'Protecting Internally Displaced Women and Children', in W. Davies (ed.), *Rights Have No Borders: Internal Displacement Worldwide* (Oslo, Norwegian Refugee Council/Global IDP Survey 1998) <http://www.nrc.no/global_idp_survey/rights_have_no_borders/cohen.htm#Protecting%20Internally%20Displaced%20Women%20and%20Children>.

[30] F. Deng, 'Flocks without Shepherds: The International Dilemma of Internal Displacement', in Davies, op. cit. n. 29 <http://www.nrc.no/global_idp_survey/rights_have_no_borders/deng.htm#Flocks%20Without%20Shepherds>.

[31] Lindsey, loc. cit. n. 23.

[32] J. Bhabha, 'Trafficking, Smuggling, and Human Rights', *Migration Information Source* (2005) <http://www.migrationinformation.org/Feature/display.cfm?id=294>.

scarce, and economic opportunities are increasingly globalized, women may find themselves resorting to the services of smugglers at an increasing rate.[33]

2.3.4 *Trafficked women*

It is generally accepted that women and girls make up the majority of those who suffer from human trafficking, though global statistics are almost impossible to obtain given the illicit nature of the practice and poor reporting by governments in many parts of the world. Women and girls who are trafficked are often placed into domestic work, farm work, forced prostitution, or forced marriage.[34]

2.3.5 *Women displaced by development projects or natural disasters*

Millions of persons are displaced each year by large-scale development projects such as dams, power stations, or mines,[35] while many millions more are forced to flee from natural disasters such as tsunamis, earthquakes, or floods. Gender-differentiated impacts of these phenomena have been observed and are generally attributed to women's reproductive roles, their resulting restricted mobility, and comparatively limited education and employment opportunities.[36] In the Asian tsunami of 2004, for example, Oxfam found that more women died than men because they stayed in impacted areas to find their children or missing relatives, and because they were less likely to be able to swim or climb trees than men.[37]

3. Locating Migrant Women's Rights in International Human Rights Law

Migrants' human rights are at stake in countries of origin, transit and destination. Taken together, existing UN and ILO conventions provide extensive protection for women migrants, but they operate in a fragmented and scattered manner; moreover, it is sometimes not obvious that they could be fruitfully applied to women migrants when the focus is on the single variable of 'migration status'

---

[33] N. Piper, 'A Problem by a Different Name? A Review of Research on Trafficking in Southeast Asia and Oceania', 43 *International Migration* (2005) p. 203.

[34] See M. Wijers and L. Lap-Chew, *Trafficking in Women, Forced Labour and Slavery-like Practices in Marriage, Domestic Labour and Prostitution* (Utrecht, Foundation Against Trafficking in Women 1997).

[35] B. Pettersson, 'Development-Induced Displacement: Internal Affair or International Human Rights Issue?', 12 *Forced Migration Review* (2002) p. 16.

[36] A.B. Torres, *FMO Thematic Guide: Gender and Forced Migration* (Forced Migration Online 2002) <http://www.forcedmigration.org/guides/fmo007/default.htm>.

[37] Oxfam International, *Gender and the Tsunami* (Oxfam International 2005) <http://www.oxfamamerica.org/newsandpublications/publications/briefing_papers/briefing_note.2005-03-30.6547801151>.

rather than on the multiple variables that are relevant to women and men who migrate – including race or ethnicity, occupation, and gender.[38] By focusing on a single aspect of experience – e.g., that of being a migrant, a woman or a member of a racial minority – human rights professionals may fail to examine the ways in which rights standards can provide protection for individuals who experience multi-layered forms of discrimination.[39] The application of the methodology of intersectionality to human rights law has thus been suggested as a means of offering a more robust set of standards relating to women migrant workers.[40]

Briefly, intersectionality is an approach to combating discrimination in which the various forms of subordination that people face are taken into consideration in terms of how they act together. Instead of conceiving of a Filipina domestic worker, for example, as separately or consecutively disadvantaged by gender and racial discrimination in the United States, intersectionality calls attention to the ways in which race and gender interact – or intersect – to create specific forms of discrimination and oppression. A female Filipina migrant's experience of racism in the United States will be different from the racism experienced by a male Filipino migrant in the same location, and her experience of gender discrimination will differ from that of a native-born American woman of any race; these differences are seen as crucially important by those using intersectional analysis, since they may require different remedial and preventive actions. Further, by focusing on the dynamics of multiple forms of discrimination, intersectionality emphasizes society's responses to variously situated individuals and groups rather than the characteristics of disparate sets of people.[41]

Using this approach, the following human rights treaties have been found to include protective norms that are applicable to the exploitation of women migrants: the International Convention on the Elimination of All Forms of Racial Discrimination (ICERD),[42] the Convention on the Elimination of All Forms of Discrimination against Women (CEDAW),[43] the International Covenant on Civil and Political Rights (ICCPR),[44] the International Covenant on Economic, Social and Cultural Rights (ICESCR),[45] and the UN Convention on the Protection of the Rights of All Migrant Workers and Members of Their Families (ICRMW).[46]

---

[38] Satterthwaite, loc. cit. n. 15 at pp. 2-3.

[39] Ibid., at p. 3.

[40] Ibid., at pp. 3, 11-12.

[41] Ibid., at pp. 8-9.

[42] 660 *UNTS* 195, entered into force 4 Jan. 1969.

[43] UNGA Res. 34/180, 34 UN GAOR Supp. (No. 46) at p. 193, UN Doc. A/34/46, entered into force 3 Sept. 1981.

[44] UNGA Res. 2200A (XXI), 21 UN GAOR Supp. (No. 16) at p. 52, UN Doc. A/6316 (1966), 999 *UNTS* 171, entered into force 23 March 1976.

[45] UNGA Res. 2200A (XXI), 21 U.N.GAOR Supp. (No. 16) at p. 49, UN Doc. A/6316 (1966), 993 *UNTS* 3, entered into force 3 Jan. 1976.

[46] UNGA Res. 45/158, Annex, 45 UN GAOR Supp. (No. 49A) at p. 262, UN Doc. A/45/49 (1990), entered into force 1 July 2003. See also Satterthwaite, loc. cit. n. 15 at pp. 14-59.

The last of these Conventions, the ICRMW, entered into force in July 2003, having finally reached the required minimum number of ratifications. Although it is unusual among its fellow conventions in its usage of the male and female forms of personal and possessive pronouns (he/she, his/hers, etc.) thus making all rights provided specifically applicable to men and women, it does not address gender-specific needs in any way.[47] In her discussion of protective mechanisms for female migrant workers, Truong has observed that the ICRMW has recognized female migrant workers, but not in their role as 'reproductive workers' – a term with which she refers to jobs in 'sex-affective services' and the 'care-taking economy'.[48] Further, while much of the effort to combat these violations focuses on urging states to ratify the ICRMW, this singular focus is misplaced, and could be counterproductive as it is highly unlikely that the ICRMW will be ratified in the near future by a broad range of states that are hosting significant numbers of migrant workers.[49]

3.1 Labour exploitation and labour rights

In general, unskilled workers, who form the majority of migrants, are more vulnerable to rights violations than are their skilled counterparts, as they tend to work in the informal sectors of the labour market, or in sectors where labour standards are not applied or not applicable even for local workers. There are common problems affecting both male and female migrants, such as non- or under-payment of wages, unfair dismissal, debt bondage, withholding of travel documents, long working hours, and precarious working conditions. It has been noted, however, that, on the whole, abusive and exploitative practices in male-dominated sectors are better documented and more visible, since men usually work in groups in construction and agriculture and often in sectors that are organized by trade unions. Abuses against unskilled women migrants are less well-known, as they are likely to occur in a less visible situation. Since women migrant workers often go into individualized and unregulated work environments (e.g., domestic service or entertainment), data on migrant women in such 'invisible' occupations are not readily available.[50] This results in cases of exploitation, violence and harassment of, for instance, domestic workers, who have very low, if any, public visibility.[51]

---

[47] UNDAW, op. cit. n. 1, at p. 38; R. Cholewinski, *Migrant Workers in International Human Rights Law: Their Protection in Countries of Employment* (Oxford, Clarendon Press 1997).

[48] T-D. Truong, 'Gender, International Migration, and Social Reproduction: Implications for Theory, Policy, Research and Networking', 5 *Asian and Pacific Migration Journal* (1996) p. 27 at p. 32. Truong notes that the Vienna Declaration and Programme of Action of the 1993 World Conference on Human Rights, on the other hand, recognizes sexual violence and trafficking in women as an aspect of violation of human rights, but does not give prominence to female migrants as reproductive workers.

[49] Ibid.

[50] Esim and Smith, op. cit. n. 14, at p. 8.

[51] See, e.g., F. Scrinzi, 'The Globalisation of Domestic Work: Women Migrants and Neo-Domesticity', in Freedman, op. cit. n. 12, at p. 77 (discussing the case of Italy).

The specific situation of domestic workers has been highlighted by the UN Special Rapporteur for the human rights of migrants,[52] the ILO and the UN Development Fund for Women (UNIFEM) as well as a number of NGOs (e.g., Coordination of Action Research on AIDS and Mobility (CARAM) Asia, Migrants Rights International, and Human Rights Watch). Some of the UN treaty bodies (most notably the CEDAW and ICERD Committees), which are charged with monitoring the implementation of human rights conventions, have also called attention to human rights violations against foreign domestic workers.[53] There are differences between countries as to whether they recognize the domestic sector as an area of employment. In East and Southeast Asia, some countries and territories, such as Hong Kong, Singapore, Malaysia, and Taiwan, recognize domestic work for visa purposes, while others do not (e.g., Korea and Japan). However, legal status (such as a work permit) does not necessarily guarantee protection under labour laws. In fact, domestic work is widely excluded from national labour legislation; in the United States, for example, some federal labour laws apply (such as those governing the minimum wage), but not others (such as those requiring the provision of overtime supplemental wages). This is true in some other countries as well (such as Costa Rica). In Singapore, foreign domestic workers do not fall under the Employment Act,[54] not because they are non-citizens, but because of the nature of the work they perform. As in Singapore, foreign workers in industries such as construction and manufacturing in Taiwan are covered by industrial relations legislation (the Taiwan Labour Standards Law), but women working as domestic helpers or carers are not.[55]

One very complex and highly controversial issue is the human rights of migrant women in the sex industry. Feminists are broadly divided into two camps: (1) the abolitionists, who argue that all prostitution and other forms of sexual commerce are violations of women's human rights; and (2) the protagonists of 'sex workers' rights'. This is an ideologically charged and in many ways older debate, which often overlooks the multi-layered structure of this 'industry'[56] and silences the voices of those most directly affected.[57]

---

[52] See the Special Rapporteur's 2004 report on migrant domestic workers (UN Doc. E/CN.4/2004/76), and her report on her visit to Canada in 2001 (UN Doc. E/CN.4/2001/83/Add.1).

[53] See generally Satterthwaite, loc. cit. n. 15, e.g., at p. 35, n. 149, and pp. 38-39.

[54] B. Yeoh, S. Huang, and T. Devasahayam, 'Diasporic Subjects in the Nation: Foreign Domestic Workers, the Reach of the Law and Civil Society in Singapore', 28 *Asian Studies Review* (2004) p. 7.

[55] A. Loveband, 'Nationality Matters: SARS and Foreign Domestic Workers' Rights in Taiwan Province of China', 42 *International Migration* (2004) p. 121.

[56] The issue of work in this area could be approached from the viewpoint of a short-/medium-term versus long-term solution, advocating for minimum work standards to provide some level of immediate protection and some kind of regulation that workers in this 'sector' and NGO advocates can hold onto. Unlike in the case of domestic workers (see, e.g., <http://caramasia.gn.apc.org/page.php?page=home> under 'campaigns'), however, activists have not produced many concrete ideas how to go about this.

[57] L. Agustín, 'Migrants in the Mistress's House: Other Voices in the Trafficking Debate', 96 *Social Politics: International Studies in Gender, State and Society* (2005) p. 96.

Through provisions on equal rights in employment, just and favorable working conditions, and equal protection of the law, the major human rights conventions offer forceful protections for women migrant workers against exploitative terms of work.[58] The CEDAW guarantees women equal rights in employment, including the same employment opportunities as men, the free choice of profession, and the right to promotion. The Convention also extends to women the right to equal remuneration, including benefits, and equal treatment in respect of work of equal value. The ICESCR recognizes the right to fair wages – defined in the Covenant as wages that, at a minimum, provide a decent living for the worker and her family – and includes the specific right to equal pay for equal work. The ICESCR also guarantees workers rest, leisure, and reasonable limitations on working hours and periodic holidays with pay, as well as remuneration for public holidays. These rights must be extended to women and men without discrimination. The ICERD prohibits discrimination on the basis of race, colour, or national or ethnic origin in work, and provides for the rights to free choice of employment, and just and favorable working conditions. Under the ICCPR, all individuals – including women and men, non-citizens and citizens – are guaranteed equality before the law, and non-citizens and women may not be treated differently in court based on their non-citizen status or gender. This guarantee of equality is amplified in the ICRMW, which clearly requires states to ensure that migrant workers benefit from the same terms of work as nationals, including remuneration, hours of work, overtime pay, weekly rest, and holidays with pay. It also provides that migrant workers must have equal access to the authorities to vindicate their contract rights, and may claim their wages and other entitlements owed to them even if they have been expelled from the state of employment. The ICCPR and the ICRMW include protections against debt bondage or slavery-like practices.

Neither of the ILO's migrant worker-specific conventions (Nos. 97 and 143)[59] mentions the feminization of migration or the specific vulnerabilities of female migrants in certain jobs such as domestic work.[60] Despite this, a wide range of ILO conventions – including those concerning remuneration (Nos. 95, 100 and 131), discrimination (No. 111), occupational health and safety (No. 155), and freedom of association and the right to organize (Nos. 87 and 98) – are relevant for women migrant workers.

[58] For an expanded discussion of the protection of women migrant workers' rights under human rights treaties, see generally Satterthwaite, loc. cit. n. 15.

[59] Convention No. 97 of 1949 concerning Migration for Employment; Convention No. 143 of 1975 concerning Migrations in Abusive Conditions and the Promotion of Equality of Opportunity and Treatment of Migrant Workers.

[60] There is an increasing demand (coming mainly from NGOs) for the inclusion of domestic workers into national labour standards. As a general matter, trade unions (somewhat like many states) still seem to be at loss as to how to grapple with the organization, and extension of protection to, domestic workers, and thus how to treat them as 'proper' workers.

3.2 **Trafficking as a human rights issue**

Trafficking also involves human rights issues, as can be seen in the Recommended Principles and Guidelines on Human Rights and Human Trafficking set out by the Office of the UN High Commissioner for Human Rights.[61] In this document, governments are called upon to address trafficking not only from a 'crime prevention' approach, but also to design national policies that protect the rights of trafficked persons.

With most of the trafficking research taking the 'sexual violence' approach as its starting point, the focus is invariably on women and children, and it is the specific set of human rights addressing this type of violence that are seen as mostly at stake. Policy makers are influenced by this also.[62] Trafficking discourse has its origins in political activism by feminists, and in fact predates its designation as a migration phenomenon.[63] This framework emphasizes the sexual exploitation and abuse of women in the larger context of women's socio-economic disadvantage. Thus, this perspective of 'trafficking as a women's rights issue' highlights the persisting gender inequalities in the source countries making women more vulnerable to trafficking for the purpose of sexual exploitation. In recent years, a number of sociologists[64] and legal scholars[65] have called for an enlarged perspective on trafficking – one that examines the entire range of exploitative circumstances into which women are trafficked, not only sexual exploitation – which includes the perspectives of women themselves. Such a shift would also allow for greater reliance on the broad array of human rights instruments relevant to such exploitation, instead of limiting the focus to trafficking-specific instruments and provisions. While the CEDAW contains an anti-trafficking provision and norms in other treaties have also been recognized as requiring states to respond to the problem, the whole range of human rights treaties contain provisions concerning labor exploitation and servitude, for example, which could be usefully brought to bear in the trafficking arena.

---

[61] UN Doc. E/2002/68/Add.1 (20 May 2002).

[62] An alternative would be the 'migration' approach. See R. Skeldon, 'Trafficking: A Perspective from Asia', 38 *International Migration* (2000) p. 7; and Piper, loc. cit. n. 33.

[63] E.M. Ucarer, 'Trafficking in Women: Alternative Migration or Modern Slave Trade?', in M. Meyer and E. Prügl (eds.), *Gender Politics in Global Governance* (Boulder, Rowman and Littlefield 1999) p. 230.

[64] Agustín, loc. cit. n. 57.

[65] J. Chuang, 'Redirecting the Debate Over Trafficking in Women: Definitions, Paradigms, and Contexts', 11 *Harvard Human Rights Journal* (1998) p. 65; S.C. Inglis, 'Expanding International and National Protections against Trafficking for Forced Labor Using a Human Rights Framework', 7 *Buffalo Human Rights Law Review* (2001) p. 55; E.M. Bruch, 'Models Wanted: The Search for an Effective Response to Human Trafficking', 40 *Stanford Journal of International Law* (2004) p. 1; R. Kapur, 'Travel Plans: Border Crossings and the Rights of Transnational Migrants', 18 *Harvard Human Rights Journal* (2005) p. 107.

In the context of children, the UN Convention on the Rights of the Child[66] – which entered into force in 1990 and has achieved the largest numbers of ratifications of all UN conventions – can be invoked to protect the rights of trafficked children. There are also two ILO conventions of relevance in addressing children's rights issues which have implications for trafficking: the Minimum Age Convention of 1973 (No. 138), which requires states to pursue national policies which will effectively abolish child labour; and the Worst Forms of Child Labour Convention of 1999 (No. 182), which defines as the worst forms of child labour such practices as child slavery, forced labour, debt bondage, trafficking, serfdom, prostitution, pornography, and various forms of work that is hazardous to a child's health, safety and morals.

3.3 Gender discrimination and women's rights

Existing international instruments specifically providing protections to migrant workers in general lack gender-specific clauses, such as references to female migrants being prone to sexual harassment or sexual violence. The lack of explicit mention of women in the major human rights treaties does not mean that they are not covered by the protections afforded by those texts, but may reinforce the invisibility of gender-specific violations. In this context, women-specific instruments have an important role to play in addressing these lacunae. A recent position paper published by UNIFEM outlines the usefulness of the CEDAW in addressing problem areas specific to female migrants, especially for those working in the informal economy and private households.[67]

3.4 Refugee rights and the rights of the internally displaced

3.4.1 *Refugee rights*

In terms of refugees, one of the key subjects of debate in Europe as well as North America and Australia is the extent to which women have access to asylum protection, and are subsequently able to gain recognition as refugees under the 1951 UN Convention Relating to the Status of Refugees[68] (hereafter, 'Refugee Convention') and its 1967 Protocol,[69] or to find protection through a secondary status or some even less secure form of humanitarian protection. In relation to access, it is clear that women are less able to reach western countries as principal asylum applicants due to their lesser resources. The under-representation of women asylum seekers also reflects the gendered nature of the definition of 'refugee' associated

[66] UNGA Res. 44/25, Annex, 44 UN GAOR Supp. (No. 49) at p. 167, UN Doc. A/44/49 (1989), entered into force 2 Sept. 1990.

[67] M. Satterthwaite, *Human Rights Protections Applicable to Women Migrant Workers* (Bangkok, UNIFEM 2004).

[68] Convention relating to the Status of Refugees, 28 July 1951, 189 *UNTS* 137, entered into force 22 April 1954.

[69] Protocol relating to the Status of Refugees, 606 *UNTS* 267, entered into force 4 Oct. 1967.

with the Refugee Convention.[70] To obtain refugee status under the that Convention, an individual must demonstrate a history or fear of persecution based on race, religion, nationality, membership in a particular social group, or political opinion. In the past, women asylum seekers have encountered two major problems when seeking protection under the Refugee Convention. First, even when they encountered persecution on the basis of one of the protected categories, the *forms* of abuse they suffered – such as rape or sexual assault – were sometimes discounted as not rising to the level of acts qualifying as persecutory. Second, women who were persecuted because they dissented from gender norms were not understood to be suffering persecution on the basis of any of the five protected grounds. Significant progress has been made, however, in the last two decades, on both of these fronts.[71]

In 1985, the Executive Committee of the UNHCR (EXCOM) found that 'women asylum seekers who face harsh or inhuman treatment due to their having transgressed the social mores of the society in which they live may be considered as members of a "particular social group"'.[72] In 1991, the UNHCR adopted a set of Guidelines on the Protection of Refugee Women, which called for the integration of gender into all aspects of refugee programming and protection activities.[73] Between 1988 and 2002, the EXCOM made numerous recommendations to states concerning the need for more gender-sensitive handling of women refugees.[74] In 2002, the UNHCR published guidelines on gender-related persecution, in which the agency recommended that gender-related abuses should be recognized as persecution under the Refugee Convention.[75] A number of states, including Austra-

[70] M. Boyd and E. M. Grieco, *Women and Migration: Incorporating Gender into International Migration Theory*, Working Paper Series 98-138 (Tallahassee, Florida State University Center for the Study of Population 1998); M. Boyd and J. Pikkov, *Gendering Migration, Livelihood and Entitlements: Migration Women in Canada and the United States* (Geneva, UNRISD 2004) (Unpublished Background Paper); E. Kofman, *Gendered Migrations, Livelihoods and Entitlements in European Welfare Regimes* (Geneva, UNRISD 2004) (Unpublished Background Paper); S.E. Khoo, E. Ho and C. Voigt-Graf, *Gendered Migration, Livelihood and Entitlements in Australia, New Zealand, and Pacific Island Countries* (Geneva, UNRISD 2005) (Unpublished Background Paper).

[71] See generally N. Kelley, 'The Convention Refugee Definition and Gender-Based Persecution: A Decade's Progress', 13 *International Journal of Refugee Law* (2001) p. 559.

[72] EXCOM Conclusion No. 39 (XXXVI), 1985, on refugee women and international protection.

[73] UNHCR, Guidelines on the Protection of Refugee Women (July 1991) <http://www.unhcr.org/cgi-bin/texis/vtx/publ/opendoc.pdf?tbl=PUBL&id=3d4f915e4>.

[74] EXCOM Conclusion No. 54 (XXXIX), 1988, on refugee women; EXCOM Conclusion No. 60 (XL), 1989, on refugee women; EXCOM Conclusion No. 64 (XLI), 1990, on refugee women and international protection; UNHCR 1991, loc. cit. n. 73; EXCOM Conclusion No. 73 (XLIV), 1993, on refugee protection and sexual violence; EXCOM Conclusion No. 79 (XLVII), 1996, on international protection; EXCOM Conclusion No. 81 (XLVIII), 1997, on international protection; EXCOM Conclusion No. 87 (L), 1999, on international protection; A. Edwards, 'Age and Gender Dimensions in International Refugee Law', in E. Feller, et al. (eds.), *Refugee Protection in International Law* (Cambridge, Cambridge University Press 2003) p. 46.

[75] UNHCR, *Guidelines on International Protection: Gender-Related Persecution within the context of Article 1A(2) of the 1951 Convention and/or its 1967 Protocol relating to the Status of Refugees*, Doc. HCR/GIP/02/01 (7 May 2002) <http://www.unhcr.org/cgi-bin/texis/vtx/publ/opendoc.pdf?tbl=PUBL&id=3d58ddef4>.

lia, Canada, Ireland, the Netherlands, Norway, South Africa, Sweden, the United Kingdom, and the United States, have developed guidelines for the processing of gender-related asylum applications within their domestic legal systems.[76]

These changes and increasing awareness of gender-specific abuses have led to the recognition that gendered forms of violence can amount to persecution when inflicted on the basis of one of the protected grounds. In addition, a variety of gender-based persecution claims have been recognized as legitimate grounds for refugee protection. For instance, in some circumstances, women who oppose or dissent from cultural, religious, or state-imposed codes concerning their role, dress, or appropriate behaviour have successfully framed these abuses as persecution on the basis of political opinion or membership in a particular social group.[77] More complicated are claims that women who suffer domestic violence are eligible for refugee status because the abuse is aimed against them as members of a particular social group – women. In some countries, these claims have been accepted, while other countries have rejected the conceptualization of women as a group protected by the Refugee Convention.[78]

3.4.2 *Rights of the internally displaced*

Unlike refugees, IDPs do not benefit from a special set of legal norms. Instead, they are entitled to the same range of human rights protections as the firmly rooted population. In practice, however, a gap in norms has been identified, resulting from the vulnerability of IDPs and their significant humanitarian needs.[79] The former Special Representative of the UN Secretary-General on Internally Displaced Persons, Francis Deng, has explained that 'while existing law provides substantial coverage for the internally displaced, there are significant areas in which it fails to provide an adequate basis for their protection and assistance'.[80] For this reason, and because '[n]early always they suffer from severe deprivation, hardship and discrimination', Deng presented a set of 'Guiding Principles on Internal Displacement' to the UN Human Rights Commission in 1998; these principles have since been used to guide UN and NGO activities in the field of IDP assistance.[81] Some attention is paid in the Principles to the particular vulnerabilities of women IDPs, including the special needs of pregnant women, women with young children, and women heads of household.[82]

---

76 UNDAW, op. cit. n. 1, at p. 81 (n. 12).

77 Kelley, loc. cit. n. 71, at pp. 563-565.

78 Ibid, at p. 565.

79 UN Office for the Coordination of Humanitarian Affairs (OCHA), Guiding Principles on Internal Displacement (2000) <http://ochaonline.un.org/DocView.asp?DocID=575>. For more detail on the Guiding Principles, see the contribution by Bagshaw to the present volume.

80 Ibid.

81 Ibid.

82 Ibid., Principle 4(2).

4. Emerging Issues

4.1 Rights consciousness

Many women migrants do not know what their rights are because of a lack of education and/or information. As strangers to the destination society, migrants may be unfamiliar with the national language, laws, and practices, and so may be less able than others to know and assert their rights. Lack of a rights consciousness is also sometimes related to the attitude of migrants that exploitation is 'normal treatment' because treatment at home is the same or even worse. A study on Bolivian women migrants, for instance, has shown that the lack of a rights consciousness is not the same among all migrant women from the same country of origin: those of rural origins typically do not recognize the pattern of discrimination in the host state because it is reminiscent of the conditions that they left behind in Bolivia; it is women of urban origins, with a higher degree of education and knowledge of their rights, who tend to recognize the discriminatory nature of their treatment.[83] There is also another angle to this issue, to do with 'de-skilling' or social downward mobility: according to a trade union leader in Southern Europe, those migrant workers who were highly qualified workers in their own countries often do not perceive themselves identity-wise as 'labourers' in the destination country, despite working as such, and thus do not claim the rights due to them.[84]

A number of recent papers have consistently found that migrant women in general have a low level of awareness of their rights (see the ILO's Gender Promotion Programme (GENPROM) series).[85] This is to a large extent related to patriarchal systems in the countries of origin, where women have low status, low educational attainment, and low skill levels. ILO GENPROM studies suggest that traditions and cultures in which gender discrimination is widespread discourage the exercise of women's rights and self-will. In the countries of employment, migrant women then enter sex-segregated labour markets which generally place them at the bottom.[86]

A new trend reported in Asia is the tendency for increasingly 'rights-conscious' and militant cohorts of migrant domestic workers to join together seeking improved conditions. Unfortunately, this often is accompanied by another trend: of being replaced by those perceived to be less rights-conscious, less expensive, and more docile – attributes generalized to entire nationalities in many settings. A good example of this is that of Filipino domestics in Hong Kong and Taiwan

---

[83] I.H. Farah and C.G. Sánchez, *Bolivia: An Assessment of the International Labour Migration Situation – The Case of Female Labour Migrants*, Gender Promotion Programme (GENPROM) Working Paper No. 1 (Geneva, ILO 2002) p. 26 <http://www.ilo.org/public/english/employment/gems/download/swmbol.pdf>.

[84] F. Scrinzi, loc. cit. n. 51, at p. 83.

[85] Available at <http://www.ilo.org/public/english/employment/gems/publ/index.htm>.

[86] N. Piper, *Gender and Migration*, Background Paper (Geneva, GCIM 2005) <http://www.gender.gcim.org/mm/File/TP10.pdf>.

who are said to have been partially replaced by Indonesians and Sri Lankans, seen by the local community as less organized and thus less vocal and assertive. To address the lack of knowledge of rights, especially pronounced among some nationalities, NGOs have developed empowerment programmes.[87] Collaborative efforts with trade unions have also begun to emerge – an important development that might lead to increasing awareness among female (migrant and non-migrant) workers in the otherwise historically male-dominated sphere of trade unionism.[88]

4.2 The rights of returnees and the rights of emigrants

The issue of social rights and the question of their 'portability' across borders needs more detailed exploration.[89] A large number of migrants (typically the older generation) have accrued social rights and are beginning to raise issues of transferability upon returning to their countries of origin. A few existing analyses have shown that some rights, such as pensions, are reduced if accessed outside the country in which they were built up. The gender implications of these problems have not yet been explored in studies on such issues.

Most of the recent research focusing on state obligations toward migrant women has focused on the responsibilities of host states/states of employment. Also of crucial importance and growing prominence, however, are the obligations of migrants' states of nationality. Some of these obligations are being identified through analyses of existing human rights standards. Fitzpatrick and Kelly have examined the gendered aspects of these duties, which could be applied to invalidate the discriminatory practices of certain home states such as 'protective' restrictions placed on women seeking to migrate for work.[90] Others are increasingly attending to rights' claims being made by 'emigrant citizens' in relation to their home countries. Recent work by sociologists[91] and legal scholars[92] has focused attention on the rights that migrants have *vis-à-vis* their states of nationality while they are living abroad. These emerging discussions focus on issues such as voting and taxation, and do not take a specifically gendered perspective; there is, however, a great potential for such work, since women are likely to have different requirements and demands toward their state of nationality than men, given their position within the global economy.

---

[87] See generally N. Piper, 'Rights of Foreign Workers and the Politics of Migration in Southeast and East Asia', 42 *International Migration* (2004) p. 71.

[88] N. Piper, 'Transnational Politics and the Organising of Migrant Labour in Southeast Asia – NGO and Trade Union Perspectives', 20 *Asia-Pacific Population Journal* (2005) p. 87.

[89] K. Tamas, *Mapping Study on International Migration* (Stockholm, Institute for Futures Studies 2003).

[90] J. Fitzpatrick and K.R. Kelly, 'Gendered Aspects of Migration: Law and the Female Migrant', 22 *Hastings International and Comparative Law Review* (1998) p. 47.

[91] D. Fitzgerald, 'Rethinking Emigrant Citizenship', 81 *New York University Law Review* (2006) p. 90.

[92] K. Barry, 'Home and Away: The Construction of Citizenship in an Emigration Context', 81 *New York University Law Review* (2006) p. 11.

5. Concluding Remarks

Arguments that migrants do not have rights, or that the existing human rights framework is inadequate, should be countered with clear analyses and insistence on enforcing and monitoring the full breadth of international norms pertaining to migrant workers, female and male; gaps, however, must also be attended to.[93] Women migrants have long been situated at the crossroads of three major sets of norms: human rights standards pertaining to women (mostly strong, protective standards); the human rights of workers (clearly articulated and robust); and human rights rules concerning migrants (rules that remain in development, but which currently offer less protection than the rules pertaining to women and to workers).[94] This poses a clear but not insurmountable challenge to building an analytical approach to women migrant workers' rights that will encompass all aspects of their experiences. The methodology of intersectionality can be used 'to uncover empowering norms for migrant women … within the corpus of human rights law'.[95]

What remains an enormous problem – one common to human rights in general – is the gap between theory and practice, i.e., actual implementation by states. A number of recent studies have shown that possibly the most important root cause of non-ratification or non-implementation is lack of political will.[96] Analyses that identify the myriad protections that states have already agreed to extend to migrant women will serve as a tool for advocates seeking to increase the political will to implement those standards.

Selected Bibliography

Agustín, L., 'Migrants in the Mistress's House: Other Voices in the "Trafficking" Debate', 96 *Social Politics: International Studies in Gender, State and Society* (2005) p. 96.

Boyd, M., and E.M. Grieco, *Women and Migration: Incorporating Gender into International Migration Theory*, Working Paper Series 98-138 (Tallahassee, Florida State University Center for the Study of Population 1998).

Bruch, E.M., 'Models Wanted: The Search for an Effective Response to Human Trafficking', 40 *Stanford Journal of International Law* (2004) p. 1.

Chuang, J., 'Redirecting the Debate Over Trafficking in Women: Definitions, Paradigms, and Contexts', 11 *Harvard Human Rights Journal* (1998) p. 65.

---

[93] See generally Satterthwaite, loc. cit. n. 15.

[94] Ibid., at p. 14.

[95] Ibid., at p. 32.

[96] N. Piper and R. Iredale, *Identification of the Obstacles to the Signing and Ratification of the UN Convention on the Protection of the Rights of All Migrant Workers 1990: The Asia Pacific Perspective*, APMRN Working Paper No. 14 (Canberra, Asia Pacific Migration Research Network 2003); A. Pécoud and P. de Guchteneire, *Migration, Human Rights and the United Nations: An Investigation into the Low Ratification Record of the UN Migrant Workers Convention*, Global Migration Perspectives No. 3 (Geneva, GCIM 2004).

Cohen, R., 'Protecting Internally Displaced Women and Children', in W. Davies (ed.), *Rights Have No Borders: Internal Displacement Worldwide* (Oslo, Norwegian Refugee Council/Global IDP Survey 1998).

Edwards, A., 'Age and Gender Dimensions in International Refugee Law', in E. Feller, et al. (eds.), *Refugee Protection in International Law* (Cambridge, Cambridge University Press 2003) p. 46.

Fitzpatrick, J., and K.R. Kelly, 'Gendered Aspects of Migration: Law and the Female Migrant', 22 *Hastings International and Comparative Law Review* (1998) p. 47.

Inglis, S.C., 'Expanding International and National Protections against Trafficking for Forced Labor Using a Human Rights Framework', 7 *Buffalo Human Rights Law Review* (2001) p. 55.

Kelley, N., 'The Convention Refugee Definition and Gender-Based Persecution: A Decade's Progress', 13 *International Journal of Refugee Law* (2001) p. 559.

Piper, N., 'A Problem by a Different Name? A Review of Research on Trafficking in Southeast Asia and Oceania', 43 *International Migration* (2005) p. 203.

—, *Gender and Migration*, Background Paper (Geneva, Global Commission on International Migration 2005) <http://www.gcim.org/en/ir_experts.html>.

Satterthwaite, M., 'Crossing Borders, Claiming Rights: Using Human Rights Law to Empower Women Migrant Workers', 8 *Yale Human Rights and Development Law Journal* (2005) p. 1 <http://islandia.law.yale.edu/yhrdlj/PDF/Vol%208/satterthwaite.pdf>.

—, 'Women Migrants' Rights Under International Human Rights Law', 77 *Feminist Review* (2004) p. 167.

Truong, T-D., 'Gender, International Migration, and Social Reproduction: Implications for Theory, Policy, Research and Networking', 5 *Asian and Pacific Migration Journal* (1996) p. 27.

UN Department of Economic and Social Affairs, Division for the Advancement of Women (UNDAW), *2004 World Survey on the Role of Women in Development: Women and International Migration* (New York, UN 2005) <http://www.un.org/womenwatch/daw/Review/documents/press-releases/WorldSurvey-Women&Migration.pdf>.

Chapter 15
THE RIGHTS OF MIGRANT WORKERS

Ryszard Cholewinski*

1. Introduction

Globalization presents a number of challenges for the protection of migrant workers, and indeed all persons in their working environment. Growing economic interdependence among states is a well-recognized feature of globalization,[1] as is the freer flow of information, ideas and human values.[2] In the economic sphere, this phenomenon is also characterized by the liberalization of trade, services, investment and capital. Although the processes of globalization have contributed to growing labour migration pressures in countries of origin and the greater demand for such labour in destination countries, the movement of workers (the most abundant factor of production in labour-sending countries) has not been facilitated in the same way as the flow of capital, goods and services, with the exception, perhaps, of persons with specific skills.[3] Barriers to the flow of human capital are much harder to overcome given that admission to the territory remains a central characteristic of national sovereignty, which has been underpinned in recent times by increasing security concerns. Despite these barriers, however, migrants continue to leave their countries in search of employment opportunities elsewhere, either with a view to settlement or, as is more frequently the case

---

* Migration Policy, Research and Communications, IOM, Geneva. The views expressed in this article are the author's alone and do not necessarily reflect the position of IOM. This contribution also draws on a chapter entitled 'International Labour Law and the Protection of Migrant Workers: Revitalizing the Agenda in the Era of Globalization', in J.D.R. Craig and S.M. Lynk (eds.), *Globalization and the Future of Labour Law* (Cambridge, Cambridge University Press 2006) p. 409. A succinct version of this chapter, 'Protecting Migrant Workers in a Globalized World', has been published on the web by *Migration Information Source* (March 2005). See <http://www.migrationinformation.org/Feature/display.cfm?id=293>.

[1] P. Taran and E. Geronimi, *Globalization, Labour and Migration: Protection is Paramount*, Perspectives on Labour Migration 3E (Geneva, International Labour Office 2003) <http://www.ilo.org/public/english/protection/migrant/download/pom/pom3e.pdf> p. 2.

[2] B. Ghosh, *Elusive Protection, Uncertain Lands: Migrants' Access to Human Rights* (Geneva, IOM 2003) p. 12.

[3] E.g., information technology specialists, senior academics, health professionals, teachers, and sports stars. See Global Commission on International Migration (GCIM), *Migration in an Interconnected World: New Directions for Action* (Geneva, GCIM 2005) (hereafter *GCIM Report*) p. 15, para. 22.

R. Cholewinski, R. Perruchoud and E. MacDonald, eds., International Migration Law

today, to the improvement of their own situation and that of their families back home through temporary work and the transfer of earnings and savings.

The intense competition for workers generated by globalization has resulted in a profound restructuring of employment in both developed industrialized countries and developing countries. In the economies of developed countries, more jobs are usually available at the high-skilled and lower-skilled ends of the labour market. Unemployed national workers, however, are unwilling to fill low-status jobs because of poor pay, difficult and dangerous working conditions, and the availability of alternative social welfare provision. Given the absence of a willing domestic labour force, developed countries are increasingly looking outside their borders for lower-skilled workers in such sectors as agriculture, food-processing, construction, and manufacturing, and low-wage services such as domestic work and care of the elderly or children.[4] Moreover, employers and companies operating in these labour-intensive sectors are unable to relocate abroad, either because of the costs involved or because some of the services require face-to-face contact in the home country, and have therefore introduced alternative measures to remain competitive, which include downgrading manufacturing processes, deregulation, and the introduction of flexibility into their labour force, with a greater emphasis on cutting costs and sub-contracting.[5] This situation is exacerbated by the unprecedented expansion in many richer countries of an informal sector or 'underground economy'.[6] While both national workers and migrant workers can be found in the informal economy, its very existence is a source of great attraction for those migrants without legal status.

In this intensely competitive economic climate engendered by globalization, claims have surfaced, on the one hand, that it is no longer possible to afford workers the elaborate labour protections they once enjoyed, and to which they remain formally entitled to under national legislation and international labour standards. Increasing deregulation and flexible employment practices impact adversely on migrant workers employed in lower-skilled sectors, where their labour rights are most likely to be sacrificed by employers on the altar of maintaining competitiveness.[7] Moreover, these migrants are also less able to complain about their work conditions, particularly if they are in an irregular situation. However, on the other hand, proponents of decent work for all persons contend that the protection of the labour and human rights of migrant workers, both those lawfully resident and those in an irregular situation, who are more likely to find themselves in flexible, temporary and low-paid jobs, is more necessary than ever before.

Despite the existence of an international legal framework, many vulnerable migrant workers remain without protection. In addition to those NGOs traditionally preoccupied with the protection of the human rights of migrants,[8] major hu-

---

[4] Taran and Geronimi, op. cit. n. 1, at pp. 3-4.

[5] Ibid., at p. 4; Cf. *GCIM Report*, op. cit. n. 3, at p. 15, paras. 24-25 and p. 61, para. 47.

[6] Ghosh, op. cit. n. 2, at pp. 13-14; Cf. *GCIM Report*, op. cit. n. 3, at 61, para. 47.

[7] Cf., Taran and Geronimi, op. cit. n. 1, at p. 6.

[8] E.g., Migrants Rights International (MRI) <http://www.migrantwatch.org/>; December 18

man rights NGOs, such as Amnesty International and Human Rights Watch, have also begun to devote more attention to their treatment. Moreover, international organizations are undertaking innovative efforts to protect migrant workers, which focus less on the adoption of formal legal standards, and more on the development of cooperation and partnerships among the governments of all the countries involved in the labour migration process, together with social partners (employers and trade unions) and members of civil society, to ensure that migrant workers can properly prepare for departure and be safeguarded from unscrupulous recruitment agents; can move in humane conditions; can be protected fairly in the destination country; and are treated adequately on their return home.

2. International Legal Framework for the Protection of Migrant Workers

As David Weissbrodt argues eloquently in his contribution to this volume and in his previous capacity as Special Rapporteur on the human rights of non-citizens,[9] and as confirmed by the treaty bodies monitoring state implementation of international human rights law,[10] non-citizens, including migrant workers, are entitled, with few exceptions, to the same human rights protections as nationals. However, the difficult plight of non-citizens in many countries of the world in terms of the protection of their basic human and labour rights and their limited access to legal remedies, exacerbated often by their non-citizen and/or unauthorized status, reflects the gulf between rhetoric and reality in guaranteeing these rights to all persons.[11] To a great extent, this gulf is also manifested in the low acceptance by states of the specific international legal standards developed by the international community to protect migrant workers.

The ILO is the specialized UN agency concerned with the protection of persons in their working environment. In addition to the adoption of a large body of international labour law, which generally does not make any distinctions between

---

<http://www.december18.net/>; International Catholic Migration Commission (ICMC) <http://www.icmc.net/docs/en>; Migrant Forum in Asia <http://www.mfasia.org/>.

[9] UN Economic and Social Council, Commission on Human Rights, Sub-Commission on the Promotion and Protection of Human Rights, 55th Session, Item 5 of the Provisional Agenda, *The rights of non-citizens*, Final report of the Special Rapporteur, Mr. David Weissbrodt, submitted in accordance with Sub-Commission Decision 2000/103, Commission Resolution 2000/104 and Economic and Social Council Decision 2000/283, Doc. E/CN.4/Sub.2/2003/23 (26 May 2003) p. 2 (Executive Summary).

[10] See, e.g., Committee on the Elimination of Racial Discrimination (CERD), *General Recommendation No. 30: Discrimination Against Non-Citizens: 1/10/2004* <http://www.unhchr.ch/tbs/doc.nsf/(Symbol)/e3980a673769e229c1256f8d0057cd3d?Opendocument> paras. 2 and 3.

[11] *GCIM Report*, op. cit. n. 3, at p. 58, para. 24: '[T]here is an urgent need to fill the gap that currently exists between the principles found in the legal and normative framework affecting international migrants and the way in which legislation, policies and practices are interpreted and implemented at the national level'.

workers based on their nationality or legal status, the legislative arm of the ILO, the International Labour Conference, has also adopted two legally binding instruments relating specifically to the protection of migrant workers: Convention No. 97 of 1949 (C97) and Convention No. 143 of 1975 (C143),[12] which are both complemented by non-binding Recommendations, Nos. 86 and 151 respectively.

C97, which applies to the whole labour migration continuum from entry to return, covers the conditions governing the orderly recruitment of migrant workers. It also articulates the principle of equal treatment of lawfully resident migrant workers with national workers in respect of working conditions, trade union membership and enjoyment of the benefits of collective bargaining, accommodation, social security, employment taxes and legal proceedings relating to matters outlined in the Convention. However, it does not afford protection to irregular migrant workers.

The scope of C143 is broader. Adopted at a time when particular migration abuses, such as the smuggling of migrant workers, were attracting the attention of the international community, this instrument devotes a whole section (Part I) to the abuses associated with irregular migration, and underscores the need for inter-state cooperation and collaborative measures to prevent this phenomenon. It also imposes an obligation on States Parties 'to respect the basic human rights of *all* migrant workers',[13] thus confirming the applicability of this Part to irregular migrants. More specifically, Part I of C143 also protects irregular migrant workers and their families, on equal terms with regular migrants, in respect of rights which arise out of past employment as regards remuneration (i.e., unpaid wages), social security and other benefits.[14] Part II of C143 is concerned with the equal treatment of lawfully resident migrant workers with national workers on a more general basis and includes some liberal provisions, such as the right of migrant workers to free choice of employment after a prescribed period of up to two years of lawful residence for the purpose of employment or, if the laws or regulations of the State Party only provide for fixed-term contracts of less than two years, after completion of the first work contract.[15]

In the context of its broader human rights mandate, the UN, after 10 years of negotiations, adopted in 1990 the International Convention on the Protection of the Rights of All Migrant Workers and Members of Their Families (ICRMW),[16] which came into force on 1 July 2003 after having obtained its twentieth ratifica-

---

[12] Convention No. 97 of 1949 concerning Migration for Employment; Convention No. 143 of 1975 concerning Migrations in Abusive Conditions and the Promotion of Equality of Opportunity and Treatment of Migrant Workers. C143 is also known as the Migrant Workers (Supplementary Provisions) Convention. For the texts of these instruments, see <http://www.ilo.org/public/english/standards/norm/index.htm>.

[13] C143, loc. cit. n. 12, Art. 1. Emphasis added.

[14] Ibid., Art. 9(1).

[15] Ibid., Art. 14(a).

[16] UNGA Res. 45/158 of 18 Dec. 1990. For an analysis of the origins of the Convention, the drafting history and its provisions, see R. Cholewinski, *Migrant Workers in International Human Rights Law: Their Protection in Countries of Employment* (Oxford, Clarendon Press 1997) ch. 4.

tion. As with the ILO instruments, it covers the entire labour migration process, although its scope is considerably broader and the provisions are more detailed. The ICRMW is by far the lengthiest core international human rights instrument, containing 93 articles. To date, however, only 34 States Parties have ratified the Convention, none of them major receiving countries.[17]

In addition to underlining in explicit terms that most of the civil and political rights found in other more general human rights instruments apply to all persons, including migrant workers and members of their families, irrespective of their legal status, the ICRMW also clarifies, in Part III, that basic economic, social and cultural rights apply to both regular and irregular migrant workers. Part IV, on the other hand, only applies to regular migrant workers and affords them more rights, such as family reunion; this is worded, however, as a rather weak obligation on States Parties

> 'to take measures that they deem appropriate … to facilitate the reunification of migrant workers with their spouses or [common law partners] …, as well as with their minor dependent unmarried children'.[18]

In Part V, the ICRMW permits States Parties to limit the rights of particular categories of migrant workers, including temporary migrants such as seasonal workers, project-tied workers or specified-employment workers (see Section 3 below on temporary migrant workers). Part VI of the ICRMW is particularly important because it addresses the need for consultation and cooperation among all States Parties to ensure that international labour migration takes place in sound, equitable, humane and lawful conditions. Consequently, it includes state obligations to collaborate with a view to preventing and eliminating irregular migration, including the imposition of sanctions on those who exploit irregular migrants, such as traffickers, smugglers and employers.[19] This Part, therefore, dispels the myth that the ICRMW somehow promotes irregular migration. On the contrary, it sees the implementation of the provisions relating to the protection of all migrant workers, including irregular migrants, as a means to the elimination of this phenomenon.[20] Moreover, the ICRMW also underlines, in Article 79, that it does not affect the sovereign right of states to decide on the admission of foreigners into their territory.

Despite their comprehensive nature, these instruments provide incomplete protection for the rights of migrant workers, arguably because the international and regional backdrop to labour migration has changed significantly since they were first adopted. These changes include:

---

[17] See Annex.

[18] ICRMW, loc. cit. n. 16, Art. 44(2).

[19] Ibid., Art. 68(1).

[20] Ibid., Preamble, Recital 14: 'Considering also that recourse to the employment of migrant workers who are in an irregular situation will be discouraged if the fundamental human rights of all migrant workers are more widely recognized and, moreover, that granting certain additional rights to migrant workers and members of their families in a regular situation will encourage all migrants and employers to respect and comply with the laws and procedures established by the States concerned'.

- the decreasing significance of state agencies in recruiting migrant labour, and the increasing importance of private recruitment agencies and employment intermediaries;[21]
- the feminization of migrant labour, with the predominance of women migrant workers in non-regulated lower-skilled sectors, such as domestic work, care of children and elderly persons, and commercial sex work – areas characterized by a strong bond of subordination between the employer and employee, irregular employment (often facilitated by criminal trafficking networks) and usually being beyond the protection of national labour laws;
- the increasingly short-term or temporary nature of labour migration; and
- the considerable growth in irregular migration, and the need to balance control mechanisms in countries of employment with measures that facilitate labour migration and protect migrant workers.[22]

The difficulties of adequately protecting the rights of migrant workers in the context of increasing resort to temporary labour and the growth in irregular migration are considered below. The feminization of the migrant labour force and the rights of women migrants is addressed in the chapter by Nicola Piper and Margaret Satterthwaite in this volume. While the ILO and UN Conventions contain specific provisions combating abuses such as trafficking, which predominantly affects women, they do not instruct Contracting Parties to devote particular attention to the types of employment in which women are predominantly found (e.g., domestic and care work).

3. Temporary Migrant Workers

Globalization has fuelled the growth in temporary migrant worker programmes in many receiving industrialized countries,[23] which is one of the consequences

[21] The ILO is attempting to regulate private recruitment agencies, including their activities relating to migrant workers. See in particular Convention No. 181 of 1997 concerning Private Employment Agencies, which obliges States Parties, in consultation with the social partners and, where appropriate, in collaboration with other ILO Member States, 'to provide adequate protection for and prevent abuses of migrant workers recruited or placed in its territory by private employment agencies' (Art. 8(1)). Convention No. 181 revises an earlier instrument (Convention No. 96 of 1949 concerning Fee-Charging Employment Agencies) and has been ratified by 20 States Parties.

[22] Cf., International Labour Conference, 87th Session, Geneva, June 1999, Report III (1B), *Migrant Workers: General Survey on the Reports of the Migration for Employment Convention (Revised) (No. 97), and Recommendation (Revised) (No. 86), 1949, and the Migrant Workers (Supplementary Provisions) Convention (No. 143), and Recommendation (No. 151), 1975* (Geneva, International Labour Office 1999) (hereafter *General Survey 1999*) paras. 657-662.

[23] See P. Martin, *Managing Labor Migration: Temporary Worker Programs for the 21st Century* (Geneva, International Institute for Labour Studies 2003).

of 'flexible' labour markets. Given the increasing dependence of employers on temporary migrant labour, particularly in lower-skilled sectors such as agriculture, construction, the food industry and services, these programmes are likely to grow as policy makers devise new ways to channel the lawful admission of migrant workers, on a short-term basis, into the sectors concerned. There is also a renewed interest in the concept of temporary and circular migration,[24] considered a 'win-win' formula (if carefully designed and properly managed) for destination countries seeking to meet labour market needs and avoid the economic and societal problems connected with the integration of longer term migrants, and for countries of origin to address 'brain drain', promote the transfer of know-how, and gain from remittances.[25] These developments, however, pose a number of difficulties for the protection of the rights of this particular group of migrant workers.

In many countries with temporary labour migration programmes, migrant workers can find it difficult or even impossible to change their employers or employment, be reunited with their families, gain secure residence status, and access the full range of social security protections in the country of employment.[26] Moreover, temporary migrant workers are vulnerable to certain abuses in the recruitment process. In particular, less-skilled workers are more likely to use the services of private recruitment agents, who compete intensely for the sale of their labour to employers in the destination country. Such abuses include deliberate misinformation about working and living conditions in the country of employment and the charging of excessive fees.[27] The requirement in some countries that employers sponsor migrant workers may also result in exploitative practices, such as late payment of wages, the substitution of the original employment contract with one containing fewer safeguards for the migrant worker, restrictions on freedom of movement, and, in some cases, physical or sexual intimidation.[28]

---

[24] See, e.g., *GCIM Report*, op. cit. n. 3, at p. 17, para. 33 and p. 31, para. 42.

[25] See also ibid., at p. 16, para. 25. The World Bank underlined the importance of remittances for developing sending countries in the 2006 Global Economic Prospects Report. See World Bank, *Global Economic Prospects 2006: Economic Implications of Remittances and Migration* (Washington DC, The International Bank for Reconstruction and Development/World Bank Nov. 2005). Circular temporary migration may also benefit migrants especially if their reintegration back home and re-entry into the destination country is facilitated.

[26] M. Ruhs, *Temporary Foreign Worker Programmes: Policies, Adverse Consequences, and the Need to Make them Work*, Perspectives on Labour Migration 6 (Geneva, International Labour Office 2003) <http://www.ilo.org/public/english/protection/migrant/download/pom/pom6e.pdf> pp. 8-9, with reference to six programmes in five countries (Germany, Kuwait, Singapore, Switzerland, and the United States). See also R. Cholewinski, *The Legal Status of Migrants Admitted for Employment: A Comparative Study of Law and Practice in Selected European States* (Strasbourg, Council of Europe July 2004) pp. 82-84.

[27] ILO Convention No. 181, loc. cit. n. 21, prohibits private employment agencies from charging 'directly or indirectly, in whole or in part, any fees or costs to workers', although the competent authority, in the interests of the workers concerned and after consulting the social partners, may authorize exceptions in respect of certain categories of workers as well as types of services provided by private employment agencies (Art. 7).

[28] Ruhs, op. cit. n. 26, at pp. 13-15; *International Labour Migration Survey* (Geneva, International

Importantly, the ILO's specific conventions protecting migrant workers, C97 and C143, and the ICRMW do not generally differentiate between migrant workers admitted for settlement and those admitted for temporary employment in terms of their protection, although some adjustments have been made to address particular categories of temporary work. Students and trainees are excluded explicitly from the equal treatment part of C143 and the whole of the ICRMW, while Part V of the ICRMW, applicable to particular categories of migrant workers, removes certain rights protections from project-tied workers and specified-employment workers, in particular access to vocational guidance and placement services, vocational training, social housing, and free choice of employment.[29] While limitations are also possible in respect of the rights to be enjoyed by seasonal workers, the pertinent provision is not mandatory.[30] Indeed, with regard to seasonal workers who have been in their territory for a significant period of time, the ICRMW urges States Parties to treat them more favourably by facilitating their access to other forms of employment and to give them priority over other workers seeking admission.[31] With the exception of permissible minor adjustments, therefore, rights safeguards for temporary migrant workers and those migrants with a more secure residence status should be equivalent in principle. Moreover, recent policy proposals for making temporary labour migration programmes operate more effectively are not incompatible with ensuring adequate protection for the rights of migrant workers.[32] However, the rapid growth in temporary migrant worker programmes and their potentially adverse impact on the protection of migrants' rights were not anticipated by the instruments, and therefore these questions are not addressed with sufficient clarity or detail.[33] On the regional level, it is note-

Labour Office 2003) <http://www.ilo.org/public/english/protection/migrant/projects/survey/index.htm> p. 8.

[29] ICRMW, loc. cit. n. 16, Arts. 61 and 62.

[30] Ibid., Art. 59(1). See also R. Böhning, 'The Protection of Temporary Migrants by Conventions of the ILO and the UN', paper presented to the International Institute for Labour Studies Workshop on Temporary Migration – Assessment and Practical Proposals for Overcoming Protection Gaps, Geneva, 18-19 Sept. 2003 <http://www.ilo.org/public/english/bureau/inst/download/bohning.pdf> p. 6.

[31] ICRMW, loc. cit. n. 16, Art. 59(2).

[32] E.g., the *GCIM Report*, op. cit. n. 3, at p. 18, para. 34, recommends, *inter alia,* that, in the effective design of such programmes, careful consideration should be given to informing temporary migrants about their rights and conditions; ensuring that migrants are treated equally with nationals with respect to their employment rights; affording temporary migrants the right to change their employer during the period of their work permit; and monitoring the implementation of the work permits and contracts provided to such migrants with a view to blacklisting countries and employers that violate the provisions of such documents. See also Ruhs, op. cit. n. 26, at pp. 26-31, and more generally M. Ruhs and H-J. Chang, 'The Ethics of Labour Immigration Policy', 58 *International Organization* (2004) pp. 69-102.

[33] Indeed, the ILO report to the June 2004 International Labour Conference observes that 'current ILO standards were not drafted with the protection of temporary workers in mind and the provisions applicable to other lawfully admitted migrant workers may not always be well suited to their situation'. International Labour Conference, 92nd Session, 2004, Report VI, *Towards a Fair Deal for Migrant Workers in a Global Economy* (Geneva, International Labour Office 2004) p. 89, para. 282,

worthy, however, that while the European Commission's Green Paper on an EU Approach to Managing Economic Migration does raise the possibility of differentiated rights for temporary migrant workers,[34] the subsequent Policy Plan on Legal Migration, which sets out a road-map for policy-making in this field until 2009, proposes the adoption of a general framework directive guaranteeing a common framework of rights to all non-EU or third-country nationals in legal employment in EU Member States without reference to their length of stay, although the level of the rights that would be protected has not been specified at this stage.[35]

4. Irregular Migrant Workers

ILO C143 and particularly the ICRMW are significant because they explicitly purport to protect migrant workers in an irregular situation. Although international human rights law is generally applicable to all persons without distinction as to nationality or legal status, there are no express provisions to this effect in the other core human rights instruments.

In contrast, some of the equivalent regional arrangements, namely relevant Council of Europe instruments such as the European Convention on the Legal Status of Migrant Workers[36] and the European Social Charter (and Revised Charter),[37] are considerably more limited in personal scope. The Charter and the Revised Charter are applicable to 'foreigners only insofar as they are nationals of other Contracting Parties lawfully resident or working regularly within the territory of the Contracting Party concerned'.[38] Nonetheless, this formal position has been questioned recently by the European Committee of Social Rights, which monitors the application of the Charter and Revised Charter and administers the Collective Complaints Protocol,[39] and under which certain trade unions and NGOs can bring complaints against those Contracting Parties accepting the procedure under the Protocol. In a case against France, decided in September

with reference to the *Guidelines on Special Protective Measures for Migrant Workers in Time-bound Activities* (Doc. MEIM/1997/D.4, Annex I), adopted by the Tripartite Meeting of Experts on Future ILO Activities in the Field of Migration (21-25 April 1997).

[34] European Commission, *Green Paper on an EU Approach to Managing Economic Migration* (COM (2004) 811, 11 Jan. 2005). The Commission, ibid., at p. 10, asks whether the 'enjoyment of certain rights [should] be conditioned to a minimum stay' and, if so, 'which rights and for how long?'

[35] European Commission, *Policy Plan on Legal Migration* (COM (2005) 669, 21 Dec. 2005) p. 6. The Policy Plan, ibid., at pp. 6-8, also proposes the adoption of four specific directives governing the conditions of entry and residence of highly skilled workers, seasonal workers, Intra-Corporate Transferees (ICTs) and remunerated trainees.

[36] European Convention on the Legal Status of Migrant Workers (24 Nov. 1977; *ETS* No. 93).

[37] European Social Charter (18 Oct. 1961; *ETS* No. 35) and the Revised Social Charter (3 May 1996; *ETS* No. 163).

[38] Appendix to the European Social Charter, ibid., and the Revised Social Charter, ibid.

[39] Additional Protocol to the European Social Charter Providing for a System of Collective Complaints (9 Nov. 1995; *ETS* No. 158).

2004,[40] the Committee found a violation of Article 17 of the European Social Charter concerning protection and assistance to children and young persons in respect of national measures limiting the access of the children of irregular migrants to health care provision. The Committee found it difficult to apply the restrictive personal scope of the Charter to a situation which involved the denial of the fundamental right to health care to a particularly vulnerable group of persons, such as children. The Committee reasoned that it was necessary to interpret limitations on rights restrictively in order to preserve the essence of the right and to achieve the overall purpose of the Charter. The restriction in this case went to the very dignity of the human being, and impacted adversely on children who were exposed to the risk of having no medical treatment. Given that medical care is a prerequisite to the preservation of human dignity, any legislation or practice denying entitlement to such treatment to foreign nationals within the territory of a State Party, even if they are unlawfully present there, cannot be justified under the Charter.[41] The controversial nature of this opinion was reflected in the slim majority that voted in its favour, although a subsequent Resolution of the Council of Europe's political body, the Committee of Ministers, took note of a measure passed by the French Government in response to the decision.[42] The opinion constitutes a rare example of how non-nationals, regardless of status, can be afforded tangible protection by an international (regional) human rights instrument.

Another particularly important development at the regional level is the landmark Advisory Opinion on the juridical condition and rights of undocumented migrants, issued by the Inter-American Court of Human Rights in September 2003 in response to a request by Mexico. The Court ruled, *inter alia*, that the migratory status of persons can never constitute a justification in depriving them of the enjoyment and exercise of their human rights, including those related to work, and that migrants, upon taking up a work-related role, acquire rights by virtue of being workers that should be recognized and guaranteed independently of their regular or irregular situation in the state of employment.[43]

Despite the increasingly overt recognition that irregular migrant workers are entitled to the full range of human rights, and the recent regional developments applying these rights to the health care and employment fields, the challenge remains to ensure the enjoyment by irregular migrants of such rights at the national

---

[40] Complaint No. 14/2003, *International Federation of Human Rights (FIDH)* v. *France* <http://www.coe.int/T/E/Human_Rights/Esc/4_Collective_complaints/List_of_collective_complaints/RC14_on_merits.pdf>.

[41] Ibid., paras. 29-32.

[42] See Committee of Ministers Resolution ResChS(2005)6 – Collective complaint No. 14/2003 by the International Federation of Human Rights Leagues (FIDH) against France (4 May 2005) <http://wcd.coe.int/rsi/common/renderers/source_file.jsp?id=856639&SourceFile=1>, which 'takes note of the circular DHOS/DSS/DGAS No. 141 of 16 March 2005 on the implementation of urgent care delivered to foreigners resident in France in an illegal manner and non-beneficiaries of State Medical Assistance'.

[43] IACtHR, Advisory Opinion OC-18/03 of 17 Sept. 2003, Series A No. 18 <http://www.corteidh.or.cr/serieapdf_ing/seriea_18_ing.pdf> pp. 105-106, paras. 133-136.

level without exposing them to the threat of immediate detection and expulsion. According to a recent study on obstacles to effective access of irregular migrants to minimum social rights, undertaken on behalf of the Council of Europe, considerable attention still needs to be devoted to this area:

> '[N]ational laws in [Council of Europe] Member States make access to many of these rights very difficult if not impossible. Moreover, even where such access is not prohibited by the law and should be available, the very illegality of migrants' stay creates further legal and practical obstacles to the enjoyment of these rights'.[44]

Legal obstacles include the invalidity of employment contracts involving irregular migrants, denial of trade union rights, the imposition of formal obligations on those employed in the public service to denounce irregular migrants to the authorities, measures criminalizing irregular migration, and the unavailability of legal aid before employment tribunals. Practical obstacles encompass the difficulties irregular migrants experience in accessing the health care system in view of the absence of information about their rights, compounded by onerous bureaucratic conditions, and in providing adequate schooling for their children, despite the existence of compulsory education requirements in most countries; a position that is also exacerbated by the higher mobility of irregular migrants and their overall vulnerability.[45]

5. Obstacles to the Ratification of Multilateral Standards

As observed above, many states remain unwilling to ratify legally binding, multilateral instruments regulating international labour migration and protecting the rights of migrant workers. Indeed, there is a similar reluctance to enter into more liberal commitments in the international trade law field under Mode 4 of the General Agreement on Trade in Services (GATS), which is concerned with the supply of a service 'by a service supplier of one Member, through presence of natural persons of a Member in the territory of any other Member'.[46] While Mode 4 specifically excludes access to the domestic labour market on a permanent basis,[47] it clearly advocates a form of 'labour migration' (though not explicitly referred to as such), and therefore engages similar sensitivities among receiving and sending

---

[44] R. Cholewinski, *Study on Obstacles to Effective Access of Irregular Migrants to Minimum Social Rights* (Strasbourg, Council of Europe Dec. 2005) p. 58.

[45] Ibid.

[46] Final Act Embodying the Results of the Uruguay Round of Multilateral Trade Negotiations (1994), Annex 1B General Agreement on Trade in Services (GATS), Art. I(2)(d). See also the contribution by Michele Klein Solomon to this volume.

[47] GATS, ibid., Annex on Movement of Natural Persons Supplying Services under the Agreement, para. 2.

countries as those international instruments concerning the protection of migrant workers.[48]

In conducting the General Survey in 1999 on the ILO's migrant workers instruments, the ILO Committee of Experts on the Application of Conventions and Recommendations identified the following principal obstacles to their ratification:[49]

- the incompatibility of national legislation with the instruments' provisions in many sending and receiving countries;
- national labour administrations' lack of financial resources to implement the instruments;
- the existence of difficult economic situations and high unemployment rates in some countries, with the result that preference is given to national over foreign labour;
- the relative novelty of international labour migration for a number of countries,[50] and the need to develop appropriate national measures;
- the specific conditions of labour markets in certain countries;[51]
- the view of some major sending countries[52] that the instruments are primarily concerned with addressing labour shortages in countries of employment rather than the needs of sending countries.

Some of these obstacles also apply to the non-ratification of the ICRMW, such as its incompatibility with national legislation in many countries; the technical and financial challenges it poses for domestic administrations to implement it, given its ambitious provisions; its complexity; and the fact that the protection of migrant workers is usually the responsibility of several governmental departments, thus requiring coherence, cooperation and coordination within government itself. Other obstacles to ratification of the ICRMW relate to a chronic lack of aware-

[48] While current GATS Mode 4 commitments, in respect of which most countries provide for wage and labour standard parity, demonstrate that the World Trade Organization (WTO) can protect the rights of migrant workers, the WTO does not formally have a labour protection mandate. Moreover, Mode 4 does not specifically address the human dimension of labour migration or the social costs associated with it. See C. Dommen, 'Migrants' Human Rights: Could GATS help?', *Migration Information Source*, 1 March 2005 <http://www.migrationinformation.org/Feature/display.cfm?id=290>.

[49] *General Survey 1999*, op. cit. n. 22, paras. 629-635.

[50] E.g., Azerbaijan, China, Romania and Tajikistan.

[51] E.g., the high proportion of foreigners in the labour force in such countries as Bahrain and Luxembourg.

[52] E.g., Mexico and Pakistan.

ness and knowledge of the Convention, the absence of adequate promotional activity, particularly on the part of governments, and, above all, a general lack of political will.[53] That the ICRMW does not differentiate to a more significant degree between regular and irregular migrant workers, and between temporary migrant workers and others, has also been cited as an obstacle to ratification.[54]

A UNESCO-sponsored study in 2003 investigated the obstacles to the ratification of the ICRMW in seven countries in the Asia-Pacific region. It identified two major hurdles, applicable to sending and receiving countries respectively. First, there was a view among some sending countries that ratification may result in the loss of access by their workers to labour markets in destination countries at the expense of their non-ratifying competitors. Second, receiving countries in the region foresaw sensitive political issues because of the protections the ICRMW provides to irregular migrants, and the perception that it requires the admission of migrant workers' family members, even though, as noted in Section 2 above, it merely obliges States Parties to 'facilitate family reunion'. The study concluded that efforts should focus on changing domestic laws and policies in receiving countries, which could then be complemented by the drafting of a non-binding recommendation or declaration.[55]

6. Protecting Migrant Workers: Supplementing Legally binding standards

The relatively low rate of ratification of the ICRMW and the other international labour instruments relating to migrant workers,[56] together with their piecemeal and less than adequate implementation in those countries that have ratified, has coincided with the development of supplementary approaches to the protection of the rights of migrant workers at the international level.

In June 2004, the ILO's International Labour Conference adopted Conclusions on a fair deal for migrant workers in the global economy, as well as a plan of action for such workers. Rather than asking states to agree to a set of legally binding principles, this plan seeks to work with the social partners and other international

[53] See A. Pécoud and P. de Guchteneire, 'Migration, Human Rights and the United Nations: An Investigation into the Low Ratification Record of the UN Migrant Workers Convention', *GCIM Global Migration Perspectives* No. 3, Oct. 2004 <http://www.gcim.org/gmp/Global%20Migration%20 Perspectives%20No%203.pdf>.

[54] *GCIM Report*, op. cit. n. 3, at p. 57, para. 20.

[55] N. Piper and R. Iredale, *Identification of the Obstacles to the Signing and Ratification of the UN Convention on the Protection of the Rights of all Migrant Workers 1990: The Asia Pacific Perspective* (Paris, UNESCO Oct. 2003) <http://unesdoc.unesco.org/images/0013/001395/139528E.pdf>.

[56] However, as Patrick Taran argues, considerably more countries (76 – see Annex) have now ratified one or more of the three international instruments protecting migrant workers (C97, C143 and the ICRMW). See P. Taran, 'The Key Role of International Labour Standards in Defending Rights of Non-nationals', paper presented to the Expert Meeting on Clarifying and Expanding the Rights of Non-nationals, Open Society Initiative, New York, 9-10 Nov. 2003, p. 3.

organizations to develop 'a non-binding multilateral framework for a rights-based approach to labour migration, which takes account of labour market needs'.[57] The ILO Multilateral Framework on Labour Migration has now been developed and comprises a set of principles and guidelines in a broad range of areas, such as decent work; means for international cooperation on migration; effective management of labour migration; protection of migrant workers; prevention of and protection against abusive migration practices; and social integration and inclusion.[58] With reference to the June 2004 Conclusions, the Multilateral Framework urges the ILO Governing Body 'to periodically review the progress made in the implementation of the multilateral framework', and also contains examples of best practices relating to the areas identified.[59] The Multilateral Framework was discussed and adopted at a tripartite meeting of experts in October/November 2005, and the ILO Governing Body took note of the Framework at its meeting in March 2006 and agreed to its wider promotion and dissemination.

The UN's Special Rapporteur on the human rights of migrants[60] has issued seven general reports, all of which examine the situation of migrant workers.[61] The Special Rapporteur has also visited and reported on Burkina Faso, Canada, Ecuador, Iran, Italy, Mexico, the border between Mexico and the United States, Morocco, Peru, the Philippines, and Spain.[62] The ICRMW figures prominently in a number of these reports, which the Special Rapporteur has used to encourage Canada, the United States, Iran, Peru (which has since ratified), and Spain to ratify the Convention. A complementary approach at the regional level is the Special Rapporteurship on Migrant Workers and Members of Their Families, established in 1997 by the Inter-American Commission on Human Rights with a view to promoting the human rights of this vulnerable group in the Americas.[63] To date, the

---

[57] International Labour Conference, 92nd Session, 2004, *Report of the Committee on Migrant Workers*, Conclusions on a fair deal for migrant workers in a global economy – ILO plan of action for migrant workers <http://www.ilo.org/public/english/protection/migrant/download/ilcmig_res-eng.pdf> paras. 21 and 23.

[58] *ILO Multilateral Framework on Labour Migration: Non-binding principles and guidelines for a rights-based approach to labour migration*, Tripartite Meeting of Experts on the ILO Multilateral Framework on Labour Migration, Geneva, 31 Oct. – 2 Nov. 2005, Doc. TMMFLM/2005/1(Rev.) <http://www.ilo.org/public/english/protection/migrant/download/tmmflm-en.pdf>. Principles and guidelines are also proposed under the headings of global knowledge base, migration process, and migration and development.

[59] Ibid., at p. 18 and Annex II respectively.

[60] Gabriela Rodríguez Pizarro, Costa Rica (1999-2005); Jorge Bustamante, Mexico (2005-). For the Special Rapporteur's website, see <http://www.ohchr.org/english/issues/migration/rapporteur/index.htm>

[61] E/CN.4/2000/82 (6 Jan. 2000), E/CN.4/2001/83 (9 Jan. 2001), E/CN.4/2002/94 (15 Feb. 2002), E/CN.4/2003/85 (30 Dec. 2002), E/CN.4/2004/76 (12 Jan. 2004), E/CN.4/2005/85 (27 Dec. 2004), and E/CN.4/2006/73 (30 Dec. 2005).

[62] The country reports are available at <http://www.ohchr.org/english/issues/migration/rapporteur/visits.htm>.

[63] For the website of the Special Rapporteurship, see <http://www.cidh.org/Migrantes/defaultmigrants.htm>. The Special Rapporteur is a member of the Inter-American Commission on

Special Rapporteur has visited and reported on the situation of migrant workers in Costa Rica, Guatemala, Mexico and the United States.[64]

The International Organization for Migration (IOM) has also been active in facilitating and assisting closer cooperation on migration among governments, which also involves, *inter alia*, cooperation on labour migration and the protection of migrant workers. An exemplar of such activities is the 'Colombo process', known formally as the Ministerial Consultations on Overseas Employment and Contractual Labour for Countries of Origin in Asia, which began in Colombo, Sri Lanka in 2003 on the basis of cooperation among ten countries,[65] and which continued in Manila, the Philippines in 2004. At the recent Third Ministerial Consultations, held in Bali, Indonesia in September 2005, receiving countries for migrant workers from this region participated for the first time.[66] Important thematic areas addressed by the consultations concern action to ensure the welfare and well-being of vulnerable migrant workers, particularly women, during recruitment and employment, and providing valuable services to migrant workers, such as pre-departure information and orientation, support services during their stay abroad, and reintegration assistance. Recommendations in this area include the development of regulatory frameworks and related measures to prevent malpractices and abuses in recruitment (e.g., by the close supervision and monitoring of recruitment agencies); the establishment and operation of Migrant Welfare Funds; and close collaboration with receiving countries to set minimum wage levels and ensure safe and decent employment conditions for contract workers, particularly women, in low-skill and low wage sectors.[67] The IOM also recently facilitated the elaboration of the International Agenda for Migration Management

Human Rights and the current incumbent is Professor Gutiérrez Trejo from Venezuela, who was appointed for a four-year term in February 2004.

[64] See <http://www.cidh.org/Migrantes/migrants.countryreports.htm>. These reports contain considerable factual information on labour migration in the region, the conditions of migrant workers and their families, the national regulatory framework pertaining to labour migration, as well as the pertinent international and regional instruments accepted by the countries in question.

[65] Bangladesh, China, India, Indonesia, Nepal, Pakistan, the Philippines, Sri Lanka, Thailand, and Vietnam. Afghanistan, which participated as an observer in 2004, became a member of the group in 2005. While individual sending countries alone can do much to protect their workers abroad, and one model approach often cited is that of the Philippines (see T.D. Achacoso (former Administrator of the Philippine Overseas Employment Administration – POEA), 'The Role of the State in Managing an Overseas Employment Programme', unpublished paper (Oct. 2003) – on file with the author), clearly, concerted dialogue and action at the regional level, particularly with the participation of receiving countries, is more likely to lead to the desired results.

[66] Bahrain, Italy, Kuwait, Malaysia, Qatar, Republic of Korea, Saudi Arabia and the United Arab Emirates. The following regional and international organizations also participated in the process: Association of Southeast Asian Nations (ASEAN), EU, Gulf Cooperation Council (GCC), ILO, UN Development Fund for Women (UNIFEM) and the World Bank.

[67] Third Ministerial Consultations on Overseas Employment and Contractual Labour for Countries of Origin in Asia, Bali, 20-21 Sept. 2005, Summary of Statements and Recommendations of the Ministers. On file with the author.

(IAMM),[68] which is a product of another state-owned consultative process, the Berne Initiative, for which the IOM provided a Secretariat. This document sets out a number of common understandings and effective practices for a planned, balanced and comprehensive approach to the management of migration, including labour migration and the human rights of migrants, underlining that 'respect for and protection of the human rights and dignity of migrants is fundamental to effective migration management'.[69] While the IAMM represents the views of migration officials and experts from all regions of the world, it remains a unique document because it has not been adopted on the basis of formal negotiations between states. Rather, it has been designed as a practical tool for state administrators to assist them in the development of coherent migration policies.

7. Conclusion

Clearly, particularly vulnerable groups of migrant workers, such as female domestic workers, temporary and irregular labour migrants, are denied 'an adequate level of protection',[70] and continue to suffer abuses and malpractices at the hands of recruitment agents, employers, government officials and the population at large in receiving countries. These abuses and malpractices persist despite the standards that have been painstakingly devised to enable migrant workers to lead a dignified existence when resident and employed abroad. A 'protection gap', therefore, exists between the fine rhetoric of international human rights and labour standards and their enjoyment and implementation in practice. However, international organizations and other stakeholders, particularly NGOs, are seeking supplementary strategies to develop solutions that are not necessarily dependent on the ratification by the world's major receiving countries of specific legally binding instruments like the ICRMW.

It remains to be seen, however, whether these strategies can yield positive outcomes in terms of the necessary protections for migrant workers, which to date the legally binding standards, largely because of their relatively low acceptance rate and poor implementation, have been unable to deliver with any significant and lasting effect. While the ratification and effective implementation of binding

[68] *International Agenda for Migration Management*, Berne, 16-17 Dec. 2004 (IOM, Swiss Federal Office for Migration, 2005).

[69] Ibid., at p. 45. The IAMM, ibid., at p. 46, emphasizes also that 'migrants in an irregular situation are entitled to protection of their human rights', although it recognizes that they 'are particularly vulnerable in practice to discrimination and to exploitation and do not enjoy access to a range of social services and other forms of protection of the host society'. With regard to the principle of non-discrimination, the IAMM, ibid., at p. 47, recommends, as an effective practice, the 'implementation of measures to ensure the appropriate treatment of migrants, regardless of their status, and to prevent racist or xenophobic actions and policies and to eliminate discriminatory practices against migrants'.

[70] *Towards a Fair Deal for Migrant Workers in a Global Economy*, op. cit. n. 33, at p. 95, para. 312.

legal rules arguably still afford the best guarantee against the abuses and exploitation suffered by migrant workers, the growth in activities relating to migration generally and a greater willingness of governments to come together and cooperate with one another, *inter alia*, on labour migration, increasingly viewed (if properly managed) as having benefits for all involved in the process, may well yet bear fruit in the development of a greater confidence in, and inclination to adopt and implement, such rules in the future.

Selected Bibliography

Cholewinski, R., *Migrant Workers in International Human Rights Law: Their Protection in Countries of Employment* (Oxford, Clarendon Press 1997).

—, *The Legal Status of Migrants Admitted for Employment: A Comparative Study of Law and Practice in Selected European States* (Strasbourg, Council of Europe July 2004).

—, *Study on Obstacles to Effective Access of Irregular Migrants to Minimum Social Rights* (Strasbourg, Council of Europe Dec. 2005).

—, 'International Labour Law and the Protection of Migrant Workers: Revitalizing the Agenda in the Era of Globalization', in J.D.R. Craig and S.M. Lynk (eds.), *Globalization and the Future of Labour Law* (Cambridge, Cambridge University Press 2006) p. 409.

Fitzpatrick, J., 'The Human Rights of Migrants' in T.A. Aleinikoff and V. Chetail (eds.), *Migration and International Legal Norms* (The Hague, T.M.C. Asser Press 2003) p. 169.

Ghosh, B., *Elusive Protection, Uncertain Lands: Migrants' Access to Human Rights* (Geneva, IOM 2003).

International Labour Conference, 87th Session, Geneva, June 1999, Report III (1B), *Migrant Workers: General Survey on the Reports of the Migration for Employment Convention (Revised) (No. 97), and Recommendation (Revised) (No. 86), 1949, and the Migrant Workers (Supplementary Provisions) Convention (No. 143), and Recommendation (No. 151), 1975* (Geneva, International Labour Office 1999).

International Labour Conference, 92nd Session, 2004, Report VI, *Towards a fair deal for migrant workers in a global economy* (Geneva, International Labour Office 2004).

ILO, *Multilateral Framework on Labour Migration: Non-binding principles and guidelines for a rights-based approach to labour migration*, Tripartite Meeting of Experts on the ILO Multilateral Framework on Labour Migration, Geneva, 31 Oct. – 2 Nov. 2005, Doc. TMMFLM/2005/1(Rev.) <http://www.ilo.org/public/english/protection/migrant/download/tmmflm-en.pdf>.

Leary, V., 'Labour Migration' in T.A. Aleinikoff and V. Chetail (eds.), *Migration and International Legal Norms* (The Hague, T.M.C. Asser Press 2003) p. 227.

Piper, N. and R. Iredale, *Identification of the Obstacles to the Signing and Ratification of the UN Convention on the Protection of the Rights of all Migrant Workers 1990: The Asia Pacific Perspective* (Paris, UNESCO Oct. 2003) <http://unesdoc.unesco.org/images/0013/001395/139528E.pdf>.

Ruhs, M., *Temporary Foreign Worker Programmes: Policies, Adverse Consequences, and the Need to Make them Work*, Perspectives on Labour Migration 6 (Geneva, International Labour Office 2003) <http://www.ilo.org/public/english/protection/migrant/download/pom/pom6e.pdf>.

Taran, P., 'Human Rights of Migrants: Challenges of the New Decade' 38 *International Migration* (2000) p. 7.

Taran, P. and E. Geronimi, *Globalization, Labour and Migration: Protection is Paramount*, Perspectives on Labour Migration 3E (Geneva, International Labour Office 2003) <http://www.ilo.org/public/english/protection/migrant/download/pom/pom3e.pdf>.

UN, Economic and Social Council, Commission on Human Rights, Sub-Commission on the Promotion and Protection of Human Rights, 55th Session, Item 5 of the Provisional Agenda, *The rights of non-citizens*, Final report of the Special Rapporteur, Mr. David Weissbrodt, submitted in accordance with Sub-Commission Decision 2000/103, Commission Resolution 2000/104 and Economic and Social Council Decision 2000/283, UN Doc. E/CN.4/Sub.2/2003/23 (26 May 2003).

ANNEX

Ratifications of International Conventions for the Protection of the Rights of Migrant Workers

	States Parties	C97	C143	UN Convention
1	Albania	■	■	
2	Algeria	■		■
3	Armenia		■	
4	Azerbaijan			■
5	Bahamas	■		
6	Barbados	■		
7	Belgium	■		
8	Belize	■		■
9	Benin		■	
10	Bolivia			■
11	Bosnia and Herzegovina	■	■	■
12	Brazil	■		
13	Burkina Faso	■	■	■
14	Cameroon	■	■	
15	Cape Verde			■
16	Chile			■
17	Colombia			■
18	Cuba	■		
19	Cyprus	■	■	
20	Dominica	■		
21	Ecuador	■		■
22	Egypt			■
23	El Salvador			■
24	France	■		
25	Germany	■		
26	Ghana			■
27	Grenada	■		
28	Guatemala	■		■
29	Guinea		■	■
30	Guyana	■		
31	Honduras			■
32	Israel	■		
33	Italy	■	■	
34	Jamaica	■		
35	Kenya	■	■	
36	Kyrgyzstan			■
37	Lesotho			■
38	Libya			■
39	Madagascar	■		
40	Malawi	■		
41	Malaysia (Sabah)	■		
42	Mali			■
43	Mauritius	■		

	States Parties	C97	C143	UN Convention
44	Mexico			
45	Morocco			
46	Moldova			
47	Netherlands			
48	New Zealand			
49	Nicaragua			
50	Nigeria			
51	Norway			
52	Peru			
53	Philippines			
54	Portugal			
55	Saint Lucia			
56	San Marino			
57	Senegal			
58	Serbia and Montenegro			
59	Seychelles			
60	Slovenia			
61	Spain			
62	Sri Lanka			
63	Sweden			
64	Syria			
65	Tanzania (Zanzibar)			
66	Tajikistan			
67	Timor-Leste			
68	The Former Yugoslav Republic of Macedonia			
69	Togo			
70	Trinidad and Tobago			
71	Turkey			
72	Uganda			
73	United Kingdom			
74	Uruguay			
75	Venezuela			
76	Zambia			
	Total Number of Ratifications	**45**	**21**	**34**

	Ratification
	No ratification

Sources:
ILO, International Labour Standards <http://www.ilo.org/public/english/standards/norm/index.htm>.
UN High Commissioner for Human Rights <http://www.ohchr.org/english/countries/ratification/13.htm>.

Chapter 16
TRAFFICKING OF HUMAN BEINGS AND THEIR HUMAN RIGHTS IN THE MIGRATION CONTEXT

Ryszard Piotrowicz*

1. INTRODUCTION

Trafficking in human beings (THB) is widely regarded as constituting a most serious breach of the human rights of the victims. By its nature THB is clandestine; it is therefore difficult to secure reliable estimates of the numbers affected.[1] However, what is well-known is the nature of the experiences of victims of THB and the gravity of the breaches of their most basic rights and interests.

Victims of THB are usually taken from one country to another (although it is possible to be trafficked within one country). They are, accordingly, migrants of a kind. Some will have consented to travel to another country but not to the conditions of living and work to which they are exposed. Some may not even have consented to travel at all. Many will have been deceived about the nature of the work they will be required to perform. Generally, they will receive little or no payment for their work.

Victims of THB are exploited by their traffickers for their labour. They are furthermore exploited through the conditions of work and living they are forced to endure. Their hours of work are generally imposed on them. Their freedom of movement is restricted. Frequently, their passports or identity documents will have been confiscated. They are often subjected to sexual, physical and/or psychological abuse, all of which may be employed as means to establish and maintain control over them.

Most notoriously, victims of THB are women and children who have been trafficked for the sex trade, but the practice extends well beyond enforced prostitution. THB may also supply workers for sweat shops, domestic labour, agricul-

* Professor of Law at the University of Wales, Aberystwyth since 1999. I would like to thank Prof. Chris Harding, Dr. Uta Kohl, Jillyanne Redpath, Prof. Ivan Shearer, Natalia Szablewska and Prof. Colin Warbrick for their comments and suggestions. Responsibility for faults and errors remains mine alone.

[1] US State Department, *Trafficking in Persons Report 2005* suggests 600,000-800,000 persons annually, of whom approximately 80% are women and girls and up to 50% are minors. The majority of transnational victims appear to be trafficked into commercial sexual exploitation. The report is available at <http://www.state.gov/g/tip/rls/tiprpt/2005/46606.htm>.

R. Cholewinski, R. Perruchoud and E. MacDonald, eds., International Migration Law

tural labour and sports, notably boys used as jockeys for camel racing. Additionally, THB has been used to secure forced marriage (frequently linked to enforced prostitution), as well as in the procurement of children for adoption and even of organs for transplants.

2. Challenges to the Human Rights of Victims of THB

The essence of THB is that the victim is removed from their home environment, under the effective control of another, and exploited for the gain of others. The victim may, on the face of it, have breached local immigration laws through illegal crossing of the frontier or having lied about the reasons for entry. By working, the victim may also have breached local employment laws, and, in some cases, where work in the sex trade is concerned, there may be a breach of local vice laws. These factors make victims vulnerable to the local law enforcement authorities, and traffickers may exploit that vulnerability as a means of establishing and maintaining control over them.

The act of trafficking and the exploitation of their labour expose victims to a variety of criminal acts including deprivation of liberty, theft of identity documents, sexual, physical and psychological abuse and blackmail (threats to inform relatives or police about the victims' activities). THB is itself a breach of the laws of many, if not most, states. It has been described by the Commission of the European Communities as '… a serious crime against persons'.[2] Under certain circumstances, as discussed in Section 5.4 below, it is also recognized as a war crime and crime against humanity in the Statute of the International Criminal Court.[3]

Human rights issues may also arise in the treatment of victims by the traffickers. Those who have been required to perform forced labour, detained against their will and subjected to various kinds of abuse are clearly victims of crime. However, those crimes are generally committed not by the state but by private individuals, acting either alone or in organized criminal groups. The question therefore arises: do people traffickers owe human rights obligations towards their victims, or are such obligations owed only by the state? Arguably, a failure by the state in this context to guarantee human rights may arise through the failure to run its affairs sufficiently well, such that THB can flourish effectively unchecked. However, states have also assumed certain obligations of protection with regard to victims, and potential victims, of crime.

---

[2] European Commission, *Communication to the European Parliament and the Council, 'Fighting Trafficking in Human Beings – An Integrated Approach and Proposals for an Action Plan'* (COM (2005) 514, 18 Oct. 2005), since adopted: EU plan on best practices, standards and procedures for combating and preventing trafficking in human beings, OJ 2005 C 311/1.

[3] Rome Statute of the International Criminal Court 1998, 2187 *UNTS* 90, entry into force 1 July 2002. See in particular Arts. 8(2)(b)(viii), 8(2)(b)(xxi), 8(2)(b)(xxii), 8(2)(c)(vi) (war crimes) and Arts. 7(1)(c), 7(1)(d) and 7(1)(g) (crimes against humanity).

3. Definition of THB under International Law

There is a substantial regime of both hard and soft law pertaining to THB, much of which addresses human rights aspects. This framework is by no means all new, but there have been significant developments since 2000. The prevalence of THB has increased since the collapse of socialism in East-Central Europe and the consequent relaxation of border controls. This has provided much of the impetus for the legal regime that exists today.

The most widely accepted definition of THB is found in the Palermo Protocol to the UN Convention against Transnational Organized Crime (UNCTOC) of 2000.[4] Article 3(a) of the Protocol provides that

> '"[t]rafficking in persons" shall mean the recruitment, transportation, transfer, harbouring or receipt of persons, by means of the threat or use of force or other forms of coercion, of abduction, of fraud, of deception, of the abuse of power or of a position of vulnerability or of the giving or receiving of payments or benefits to achieve the consent of a person having control over another person, for the purpose of exploitation. Exploitation shall include, at a minimum, the exploitation of the prostitution of others or other forms of sexual exploitation, forced labour or services, slavery or practices similar to slavery, servitude or the removal of organs'.

There are therefore three elements to transnational THB: the act (recruitment, transportation, transfer, harbouring or receipt of persons); the method (threat or use of force or other forms of coercion, of abduction, of fraud, of deception, of the abuse of power or of a position of vulnerability, or of the giving or receiving of payments or benefits to achieve the consent of a person having control over another person); and the purpose (exploitation).

These elements indicate that THB includes a number of actors, each of whom may play a role in 'creating' a victim of trafficking, from the acquaintance in the victim's village who knows someone who can organize a job or a visa, to the individual who facilitates illegal crossing of the frontier, to the person who supplies rooms to accommodate victims in transit and the bar owner who eventually 'buys' the victim. THB does not therefore require that just one person carries out all the acts involved, from recruitment through to exploitation. The process involves several acts, each of which may be crimes against the victim. The state is not generally involved in these, although it may be through the activity of corrupt law enforcement and border officials, who facilitate or ignore the work of the traffickers. This may occur in source, transit or destination states. The primary threat to victims, however, is clearly one of criminal acts at the hands of private

[4] Protocol to Prevent, Suppress and Punish Trafficking in Persons, Especially Women and Children, supplementing the UN Convention against Transnational Organized Crime (UNCTOC), UNGA Res. A/RES/55/25 of 15 Nov. 2000, UN Doc. A/55/383; entered into force 25 Dec. 2003; 101 parties (July 2006) (hereafter 'Palermo Protocol'). UNCTOC entered into force on 29 Sept. 2003 and has been ratified by 122 parties (July 2006).

individuals. Such acts, however serious, are not necessarily human rights violations on the part of a state.

The legal regime for THB may be said both to reflect this reality but also to shape it, in that it addresses the rights and duties of the state, on the one hand, by making THB a crime and attempting to address its prevention, and, on the other, by acknowledging a human rights dimension to the issue. Two crucial matters require elaboration: the human rights and criminal law dimensions of THB; and the legal regime set up to combat it.

4. The Human Rights and Criminal Law Dimensions

All recent instruments on THB, as outlined in Section 5 below, refer to the human rights dimension of this issue. They also, to a greater or lesser extent, outline specific obligations undertaken by the state which may be considered human rights obligations, either because they reflect existing requirements, such as the duty not to return an individual to a territory where her life is under threat, or else constitute new positive duties voluntarily assumed by the state towards those within its jurisdiction.

However, several major instruments on THB also refer to it as, in itself, a violation of human rights. In other words, an essentially criminal activity, in which the state has no formal involvement, is said to be a human rights violation. This is significant because the discussion then turns to either state responsibility for criminal acts of private individuals, and/or private and individual responsibility for human rights violations. In fact it is clear that the relevant instruments treat THB as the latter: those who traffic in human beings are not merely engaging in a criminal act, they are also violating the human rights of their victims.

But why should this be so? If a person is kidnapped or raped, then that is a criminal act that may be prosecuted. The victim may also be able (at least in theory) to bring an action in tort/delict to secure compensation for the breach of her interests. But these acts are not generally regarded as breaches of human rights unless the state is in some way complicit or responsible. Clearly, this may be the case with THB where officials facilitate the work of traffickers. However, in these cases we are dealing with dishonest officials whose own criminal activities facilitate THB: the involvement of the state through these officials translates what is a criminal act into a breach of the human rights of the victim. In many cases, however, there is no such state involvement. Why, in such situations, should such THB, however heinous for the victim, be a breach of her human rights?

In fact there has been substantial discussion on whether human rights may be owed directly by one individual to another.[5] The obligation frequently found in

[5] See, for example, S. McInerney, 'The European Convention on Human Rights and the Evolution of Fundamental Rights in the Private Domain', in C. Harding and C.L. Lim (eds.), *Renegotiating Westphalia* (The Hague, Martinus Nijhoff 1999) p. 277 at pp. 307-315.

human rights instruments for states, not only to respect the relevant rights but to *ensure* their protection, suggests that they may be breached by non-state actors. But even so, the consequences for breach lie with the state rather than the perpetrator, whose accountability remains confined to criminal law and, sometimes, to tort/delict. What, in other words, does it mean to say that one non-state actor is responsible under international law for acts committed against another non-state actor? It certainly does not mean that the victim can pursue a remedy against the perpetrator under human rights law.[6]

The Council of Europe Convention on Action against Trafficking in Human Beings[7] (hereafter, 'European Convention') refers to THB as 'a violation of human rights and an offence to the dignity and the integrity of the human being'.[8] There is little or no legal difficulty in considering THB an offence. Most, if not all, of the aspects of the treatment of victims are criminal. The human rights dimension is addressed in the Explanatory Report accompanying the Convention,[9] which points out that the recognition of THB as a human rights violation is already apparent from a number of important instruments.[10] The explanation for so qualifying THB, and therefore for its treatment as such in the European Convention, is that human rights obligations may be owed horizontally as well as vertically: that is, they may be owed by individuals towards each other, not just by the state. The Report considers horizontal application in the context of the European Convention on Human Rights (ECHR),[11] and reaches the following conclusion:

> '[T]he case law of the European Court of Human Rights contains clear indications in favour of the applicability of the ECHR to relations between private individuals in the sense that the Court has recognized the liability of contracting States for acts committed by individuals or group of individuals *when these States failed to take appropriate measures of protection*'.[12]

---

[6] This notion of horizontal application is found to some extent in the Geneva Conventions of 1949 relating to the Protection of Victims of International and Non-International Armed Conflicts (75 *UNTS* 31, 75 *UNTS* 85, 75 *UNTS* 135 and 75 *UNTS* 287 respectively). Whilst the Conventions establish an obligation on states to ensure that the protections contained therein are guaranteed, and failure to achieve this gives rise to state responsibility, there is also individual responsibility for serious ('grave') breaches of the Conventions, though not enforceable by the victims of breaches. The notion of individual criminal responsibility for breaches of basic rights during armed conflicts is well-established in the founding statutes and case-law of the *ad hoc* international criminal tribunals, as well as the Statute of the International Criminal Court. Even in such cases, however, the language used is that of criminal accountability for criminal acts, not individual competence to achieve redress for breaches of human rights.

[7] 16 May 2005, *ETS* No. 197.

[8] Ibid., Preamble Recital 2.

[9] CM(2005)32 Addendum 2 final, 3 May 2005.

[10] Ibid., para. 42.

[11] Convention for the Protection of Human Rights and Fundamental Freedoms, 4 Nov. 1950, *ETS* No. 5, entry into force 3 Sept. 1953.

[12] Explanatory Report, op. cit. n. 9, at para. 44 (emphasis added). See, e.g., *Z and others* v. *United Kingdom*, judgment of 10 May 2001, Application No. 29392/95, para. 73: 'The Court reiterates that

In fact, this appears still to rely on vertical application because it insists on the liability of the state for failure to ensure protection. The issue is therefore the extent to which states have taken appropriate protection measures. It is nowhere expected that the state owes an absolute obligation of protection. Such a goal is unattainable. However, states must provide effective means of protection in order for this kind of obligation to be fulfilled. In the context of THB, this would include the enactment of appropriate legislation, that is, legislation that effectively criminalizes the practice and provides for necessary protections for the victims. As the Report states,

> '… if a violation of one of these rights and freedoms [contained in the ECHR] is the result of non-observance of … [an] obligation in the enactment of domestic legislation, the responsibility of the state for that violation is engaged'.[13]

Horizontal application, in other words, does not necessarily mean that the state is in breach of its human rights obligations just because a person has been trafficked. There must also be some failure on the part of the state to secure the rights and freedoms that are guaranteed. With THB, this might include the exposure of the victim to inhuman or degrading treatment or punishment by traffickers, where the state lacks legislation capable of addressing that threat, or perhaps where, even having such legislation in place, it is not in fact effectively implemented. Additional obligations of protection may also have been assumed unilaterally by the state, and the failure to observe these may constitute a breach of the beneficiaries' human rights.

The issue of who actually owes human rights obligations has also been considered by the UN Human Rights Committee, which monitors compliance with the International Covenant on Civil and Political Rights (ICCPR).[14] Its General

---

Article 3 enshrines one of the most fundamental values of democratic society. It prohibits in absolute terms torture or inhuman or degrading treatment or punishment. *The obligation on High Contracting Parties under Article 1 of the Convention to secure to everyone within their jurisdiction the rights and freedoms defined in the Convention, taken in conjunction with Article 3, requires States to take measures designed to ensure that individuals within their jurisdiction are not subjected to torture or inhuman or degrading treatment, including such ill-treatment administered by private individuals.* These measures should provide effective protection, in particular, of children and other vulnerable persons and include reasonable steps to prevent ill-treatment of which the authorities had or ought to have had knowledge' (emphasis added). In other words, the breach by the state, if any, lies in the failure to provide effective protection. Whether protection is effective will depend on the circumstances, but does not extend to an absolute obligation. More recently, in *M.C.* v. *Bulgaria*, the Court has held that the failure of Bulgaria to establish and apply effectively a criminal law system punishing all forms of rape and sexual abuse was a violation of its obligations under Articles 3 and 8: judgment of 4 Dec. 2003, Application No. 39272/98, para. 185. Nevertheless, the actual rape itself was not claimed by the applicant to be a breach of her human rights.

[13] Explanatory Report, op. cit. n. 9, at para. 44.

[14] UN, ICCPR, Human Rights Committee, *General Comment No. 31 [80], The Nature of the General Legal Obligation Imposed on States Parties to the Covenant*, UN Doc. CCPR/C/21/Rev.1/Add.13 (26 May 2004).

Comment No. 31 supports the notion that human rights are owed only by the state, though the state's obligations may be breached by failure to ensure adequate protection:

> 'The ... obligations are binding on States [Parties] and do not, as such, have direct horizontal effect as a matter of international law... However the positive obligations on States Parties to ensure Covenant rights will only be fully discharged if individuals are protected by the State, not just against violations of Covenant rights by its agents, but also against acts committed by private persons or entities that would impair the enjoyment of Covenant rights in so far as they are amenable to application between private persons or entities'.[15]

This perhaps begs the question of whether such rights are in fact ever amenable to application between private persons and entities. It might be argued that, if they are thus amenable, then there is an element of horizontal effect. However, the Committee makes clear that this is not really the case, seeing the matter rather in terms of the obligation of the state to 'take appropriate measures or to exercise due diligence to prevent, punish, investigate or redress the harm caused by such acts by private persons or entities'.[16] Thus, states must, for example, 'take positive measures to ensure that private persons or entities do not inflict torture or cruel, inhuman or degrading treatment or punishment on others within their power'.[17] Thus it is the failure of the state, not the criminal act of the trafficker, that brings about the breach of the victim's human rights.

It is important to identify exactly what is happening when THB occurs. Not all aspects of this practice are necessarily violations of victims' human rights. To refer to THB as a human rights violation without further justification is undesirable for two reasons. Firstly, it obscures our understanding of what is actually happening; and secondly – and from the victim's perspective more importantly – by obscuring what precisely is taking place we run the risk of failing to provide the best possible assistance and protection to victims. It does not necessarily help victims to assert that their human rights have been breached just because they have suffered as a result of serious criminal offences, if there is no failure of state protection.

---

[15] Ibid., at para. 8.

[16] Ibid. A similar assessment has been made by the Inter-American Court of Human Rights in the *Velásquez Rodríguez* case, Judgment of 29 July 1988, 9 *Human Rights Law Journal* (1988) p. 212, para. 172:

'[A]n illegal act which violates human rights and which is initially not directly imputable to a State (for example, because it is the act of a private person or because the person responsible has not been identified) can lead to international responsibility of the State, not because of the act itself, but because of the lack of due diligence to prevent the violation or to respond to it as required by the Convention'. The point is that the state is responsible for the human rights violation. Indeed one may query even the accuracy of referring to the illegal act as a human rights violation at all, because the Court is clearly assessing the responsibility of the state rather than that of the individual.

[17] General Comment No. 31, loc. cit. n. 14, at para. 8.

5. The Legal Regime

The legal regime relating to THB consists of both hard and soft law.[18] The hard law, principally treaties, is made up of trafficking-specific instruments, as well as more general instruments that have a bearing on THB. The same may be said for the soft law, although in that field there has been perhaps a greater emphasis on trafficking-specific measures. The law may be divided into the following, not always mutually exclusive, categories:

- the international law regime on THB – hard and soft law;
- the European Union regime on THB;
- the international protection regime;
- international criminal law.

5.1 The international law regime

There are in fact many treaties, some decades old, that address THB.[19] However, the contemporary regime has evolved rapidly in recent times, and it consists of two main elements. The first is the indirect promotion of victims' rights through the development of obligations of criminalization. In this scenario, the rights of the victim, if considered at all, are to some extent simply a function of their usefulness to the state as an instrument in the prosecution of traffickers, rather than an acknowledged value in themselves. The second, more direct, aspect is through the recognition of particular rights of victims in the process of criminal proceedings against traffickers, and then through states' acceptance of victims' rights, entailing obligations towards them outside criminal proceedings. Thus there has been recognition of the need to provide at least some level of support and assistance to victims, to assist rehabilitation and reintegration. Moreover, it is

[18] For an earlier treatment of this aspect with, however, more emphasis on Asian developments, see V. Muntarbhorn, 'Combating Migrant Smuggling and Trafficking in Persons, Especially Women: The Normative Framework Re-appraised', in T.A. Aleinikoff and V. Chetail (eds.), *Migration and International Legal Norms* (The Hague, T.M.C. Asser Press 2003) p. 151.

[19] See, for example: Convention Concerning Slavery (1926), 60 *LNTS* 253; ILO Convention No. 29 concerning Forced or Compulsory Labour (1930), 39 *UNTS* 55; Convention for the Suppression of the Traffic in Persons and of the Exploitation of the Prostitution of Others (1949), 96 *UNTS* 271; Convention on the Elimination of All Forms of Discrimination Against Women (1979), 1249 *UNTS* 13; ILO Convention No. 182 on Worst Forms of Child Labour (1989), reproduced in 38 *International Legal Materials* (1999) p. 1207; Convention on the Rights of the Child (1989), 1577 *UNTS* 3 and its Optional Protocol on the Sale of Children, Child Prostitution and Child Pornography (2000), UN Doc. A/54/49; Convention on the Protection of the Rights of All Migrant Workers and Members of Their Families (1990), UNGA Res. 45/158 of 18 Dec. 1990.

acknowledged that some victims may have an entitlement to international protection because of risks they face should they return to their home states.

The Palermo Protocol[20] is not primarily a human rights instrument; it is about international cooperation in the fight against transnational organized crime. As such, it contains obligations to criminalize THB,[21] as well as provisions on information exchange and training, border measures, and security and control of documents.[22] The Protocol does not disregard the human rights aspect, but the provisions in this regard are generally more aspirational than obligatory. While Article 9(b) does require parties to 'establish comprehensive policies, programmes and other measures … [t]o protect victims of trafficking in persons, especially women and children, from revictimisation', other provisions are less demanding. Thus protection of the privacy and identity of victims is required 'to the extent possible'.[23] Each Party must 'consider implementing measures to provide for the physical, psychological and social recovery of victims'.[24] Parties shall also 'consider adopting legislative or other appropriate measures' that would allow victims to remain in their territory.[25] That said, there is a saving clause which stresses the continued application of general international law, including human rights obligations.[26]

The protection regime is developed by the Optional Protocol to the Convention on the Rights of the Child on the Sale of Children, Child Prostitution and Child Pornography 2000.[27] This recognizes several activities as offences that must be punishable under domestic criminal law, whether committed domestically or transnationally, including child prostitution[28] and the sale of children for sexual exploitation, organ transfer or forced labour.[29] This instrument functions by seeking to eliminate the sale of children, child prostitution and child pornography through criminalization measures. As such, it does not directly create rights for individuals other than in Article 8, which requires the parties to 'adopt appropriate measures to protect the rights and interests of child victims of the practices prohibited under the … Protocol at all stages of the criminal process'.

While the definition of THB in the Palermo Protocol has achieved widespread acceptance, not all developments have been consistent with it. The South Asian Association for Regional Cooperation (SAARC) adopted a regional instrument on 5 January 2002 on Preventing and Combating Trafficking in Women and Chil-

20 Loc. cit. n. 4.
21 Ibid., Art. 5.
22 Ibid., Arts. 10 and 11.
23 Ibid., Art. 6(1).
24 Ibid., Art. 6(3).
25 Ibid., Art. 7(1).
26 Ibid., Art. 14.
27 Optional Protocol to the Convention on the Rights of the Child, loc. cit. n. 19.
28 Ibid., Art. 1.
29 Ibid., Art. 3.

dren for Prostitution.[30] As its title makes clear, this treaty is narrower in scope, in that it deals only with trafficking of women and children for the sex trade, although it is not limited to transnational trafficking.

The most recent major international instrument on the subject is the Council of Europe Convention on Action against Trafficking in Human Beings.[31] This takes the same definition as the Palermo Protocol, but places a clearer emphasis on the human rights dimension of THB, while nevertheless addressing also the need to take action to combat the practice. The tenor of this instrument is clear from its Preamble and Article 1. The Preamble states bluntly that THB is 'a violation of human rights and an offence to the dignity and the integrity of the human being';[32] that 'respect for victims' rights, protection of victims and action to combat trafficking in human beings must be the paramount objectives' of the Treaty.[33] Article 1 provides that the purposes of the Convention include the prevention and combating of THB, the protection of the human rights of the victims, and the designing of a comprehensive framework for the protection and assistance of victims and witnesses. The dual emphasis on human rights and action to combat THB is clear, but again the question arises: what exactly are the human rights involved? Do we mean human rights only *vis-à-vis* the state, or also with regard to the traffickers? The Explanatory Report accompanying the Convention suggests that there can indeed be horizontal breaches of human rights, but nevertheless stresses that any responsibility lies with the state.[34]

Notwithstanding possible doubts over the extent to which the act of trafficking in itself breaches the human rights of victims (and that is not to deny that THB may involve grave criminal acts), the Convention does impose human rights obligations on the Parties. Article 5(3) stipulates the promotion of 'a Human Rights-based approach' in the development and implementation of policies and programmes that states are obliged to establish in order to prevent THB. Chapter III, on measures to protect and promote the rights of victims, sets out minimum standards for the provision of assistance to victims to promote physical, psychological and social recovery: these include a reflection period of at least 30 days, during which a victim may have time to recover without having to make any de-

[30] SAARC Convention on Preventing and Combating Trafficking in Women and Children for Prostitution. The text of this Convention is available from the SAARC web site at <http://www.saarc-sec.org/old/freepubs/conv-traffiking.pdf>.

[31] Loc. cit. n. 7.

[32] Ibid., Recital 2.

[33] Ibid., Recital 4.

[34] In fact, the wording of the Explanatory Report, op. cit. n. 9, is ambiguous. Para. 44 provides, in part, that '[t]he liability of Contracting states for acts committed by individuals or groups of individuals in violation of the ECHR has been recognized'. If individuals are violating the rights contained in the ECHR, why should the state be responsible (assuming it has not been negligent or complicit)? The state is not deemed responsible for a breach of human rights every time that someone is murdered. The wording of para. 44 seems still to suggest that the responsibility of the state subsists for human rights violations in certain cases where individuals have committed crimes against others. It does not, however, clarify why this should be so.

cisions about her immediate future;[35] and a residence permit, either because this is considered necessary in light of the victim's personal situation, or because it is necessary to enable the victim's cooperation with the authorities in criminal proceedings. In fact this last provision neatly encapsulates the two main aspects of anti-trafficking measures: that of seeking to protect the victim and prosecute the traffickers.

Inasmuch as the European Convention and other instruments make provision for the welfare of victims of THB they may be said to be human rights instruments. However, such rights are limited. It must be borne in mind that we are generally dealing with non-nationals, many of whom may be on the territory of the host state illegally. Of course, the state has human rights obligations towards all persons within its jurisdiction, not only its own citizens; however, the rights created in these instruments are limited, albeit without prejudice to other rights which exist independently.

The soft law on THB is extensive and generally more emphatic in stressing the human rights dimension. In the years 2000-2005, there were initiatives by, amongst others, the UN High Commissioner for Human Rights (UNHCHR),[36] the European Union and the International Organization for Migration,[37] the Association of Southeast Asian Nations (ASEAN),[38] the Council of Europe,[39] the Organization for Security and Cooperation in Europe (OSCE),[40] the Stability Pact for South Eastern Europe,[41] and the UN High Commissioner for Refugees (UNHCR).[42] The contribution of the UNHCHR is striking for its insistence on the pri-

[35] European Convention, loc. cit. n. 7, Art. 13.

[36] Office of the UN High Commissioner for Human Rights (OHCHR), *Recommended Principles and Guidelines on Human Rights and Human Trafficking*, UN Doc. E/2002/68/Add.1 (2002) <http://www.ohchr.org/english/about/publications/docs/trafficking.doc>.

[37] Brussels Declaration on Preventing and Combating Trafficking in Human Beings (20 Sept. 2002) <http://europa.eu.int/comm/justice_home/news/forum_crimen/2002/workshop/brusels_decl_en.htm> and <http://www.belgium.iom.int/StopConference/Conference%20Papers/brudeclaration.pdf>.

[38] ASEAN Declaration Against Trafficking in Persons Particularly Women and Children (29 Nov. 2004) <http://www.aseansec.org/16793.htm>.

[39] Explanatory Report, op. cit. n. 9, at paras. 10-27.

[40] OSCE, Permanent Council, 462nd Plenary Meeting, Decision No. 557 – OSCE Action Plan to Combat Trafficking in Human Beings, Doc. PC.DEC/557 (24 July 2003) <http://www.osce.org/press_rel/2003/pdf_documents/07-3447-pc1.pdf>.

[41] Statement on Commitments, 11 Dec. 2002; Stability Pact for South Eastern Europe, Task Force on Trafficking in Human Beings, *Special Protection Measures for Trafficking Victims Acting as Witnesses*, Outcome document of the Working Group Meeting on 'Victims/Witness Protection', Portoroz, Slovenia, 26-27 March 2003.

[42] UNHCR, *Guidelines on International Protection: 'Membership of a Particular Social Group' within the Context of Article 1A(2) of the 1951 Convention and/or its 1967 Protocol relating to the Status of Refugees*, Doc. HCR/GIP/02/02 (7 May 2002) <http://www.unhcr.org/cgi-bin/texis/vtx/publ/opendoc.pdf?tbl=PUBL&id=3d58de2da>, Point 12; UNHCR, *Guidelines on International Protection: Gender-Related Persecution within the Context of Article 1A(2) of the 1951 Convention and/or its 1967 Protocol relating to the Status of Refugees*, Doc. HCR/GIP/02/01 (10 May 2002) <http://www.unhcr.org/cgi-bin/texis/vtx/publ/opendoc.pdf?tbl=PUBL&id=3d58ddef4>, Point 18; UNHCR,

macy of human rights, especially in the way that the state treats victims of THB on its territory.[43] This emphasis highlights the fact that, although victims of THB are, of course, migrants, and frequently irregular ones, nevertheless they have human rights entitlements in the destination state, irrespective of how they arrived there, even if in breach of immigration laws.

5.2 The European Union regime

THB is well recognized as one of the major challenges facing the EU in the context of the development of its immigration and asylum regimes.[44] The EU has adopted legally binding measures in this field, most notably a Council Framework Decision of 2002[45] and a Council Directive in 2004.[46] More recently, a Commission proposal for an action plan to address THB[47] has been adopted by the Council.[48] Like the European Convention, the Framework Decision asserts that THB comprises 'serious violations of fundamental human rights and human dignity'.[49] The language used here clearly suggests an acceptance that the practices of traffickers are not only very serious crimes against the victims but also breaches of their human rights. It is certainly not suggesting that the state response (or lack of it) is the major human rights abuse. The language even seems to go beyond an assertion that it is the state that is guilty of a human rights violation (for example, for failure to act), to one of direct responsibility of the traffickers (against which states may have a human-rights-based obligation to act). Yet this characterization of THB is subject to the same criticisms voiced above, unless what we are

---

Guidelines on International Protection: The Application of Article 1A(2) of the 1951 Convention and/or 1967 Protocol relating to the Status of Refugees to victims of trafficking and persons at risk of being trafficked, Doc. HCR/GIP/06/07 (7 April 2006) <http://www.unhcr.org/cgi-bin/texis/vtx/home/opendoc.pdf?tbl=RSDLEGAL&id=443679fa4>.

[43] OHCHR, Recommended Principles, loc. cit. n. 36, Principle 3: 'Anti-trafficking measures shall not adversely affect the human rights and dignity of persons, in particular the rights of those who have been trafficked, and of migrants, internally displaced persons, refugees and asylum-seekers'.

[44] See, for example, the *Presidency Conclusions*, Tampere European Council, 15-16 Oct. 1999, *Bulletin EU* 10-99, Points I.2-I.16, Conclusions No. 23 (1999); *Presidency Conclusions: Laeken European Council*, 14-15 Dec. 2001, *Bulletin EU* 12-2001, points I.2-I.29, Conclusions No. 42; and *Presidency Conclusions: Seville European Council*, 21-22 June 2002, *Bulletin EU* 6-2002, points I.2-I.33, Conclusions No. 28, as well as the Proposal for a Comprehensive Plan to Combat Illegal Immigration and Trafficking of Human Beings in the European Union (OJ 2002 C 142/23). The Hague Programme, 13 Dec. 2004 (OJ 2005 C 53/1), makes brief reference to THB in its Introduction, but it is clearly a part of the wider agenda on migration.

[45] Council Framework Decision 2002/629/JHA of 19 July 2002 on Combating Trafficking in Human Beings, OJ 2002 L 203/1.

[46] Council Directive 2004/81/EC of 29 April 2004 on the residence permit issued to third-country nationals who are victims of trafficking in human beings or who have been the subject of an action to facilitate illegal immigration, who cooperate with the competent authorities, OJ 2004 L 261/19.

[47] Loc. cit. n. 2.

[48] Loc. cit. n. 2.

[49] Council Framework Decision, loc. cit. n. 45, Preamble, Recital 3.

witnessing is the emergence of some kind of direct individual responsibility for human rights abuses, at least in the context of THB. Most of the Framework Decision, however, is concerned with tackling THB as a crime, with very little reference to the victims, viz. Article 7, which offers very limited measures on protection and assistance.

The 2004 Directive on the issue of short-term residence permits basically establishes a system whereby victims of THB may stay in the destination state while they remain of value to the authorities in the prosecution of traffickers (or smugglers). While some provision is made for the protection of the victims, there is no guarantee that they will be permitted to remain after their usefulness to the authorities has elapsed, although by giving evidence a victim may of course have made herself more vulnerable to revenge or retribution by a trafficker. This instrument is not intended to be a human rights instrument, but it is debatable, given the limited nature of the concessions offered to witnesses, whether it will achieve its purpose of securing their cooperation in prosecutions.[50]

5.3 The international protection regime

Whatever doubts may exist about the THB as a violation of human rights rather than a crime, victims may nevertheless have entitlements under the law of international protection. In other words, should a victim present in a destination or transit state be able to demonstrate that her life or safety is at serious risk should she return to her home state, she may be entitled to refugee status or subsidiary/complementary protection. In this scenario, we are moving away from the area of specific human rights guarantees aimed at victims of THB, to the application of general human rights law, most particularly the obligation to respect, and ensure respect for, the prohibition of torture and inhuman or degrading treatment or punishment. This obligation may require the state to permit a victim to remain on its territory where there is a real risk of her being exposed to such treatment in her home state.

Victims of THB have no special entitlement to remain in the destination state, but there is little doubt that, given the types of threat to which they may be exposed, there may be occasions when repatriation is not a safe option. In some cases a victim may be entitled to refugee status; moreover, the law of subsidiary protection, particularly as developed through the case-law of the European Court of Human Rights and as reflected in the Refugee Qualification Directive[51] of the European Union, certainly establishes an entitlement for the victim to remain in

[50] For a detailed discussion of this Directive, see R. Piotrowicz, 'European Initiatives in the Protection of Victims of Trafficking who Give Evidence Against Their Traffickers', 14 *International Journal of Refugee Law* (2002) p. 263.

[51] Council Directive 8043/04/EC of 27 April 2004 on minimum standards for the qualification and status of third country nationals and stateless persons as refugees or as persons who otherwise need international protection and content of the protection granted, OJ 2004 L 304/12.

the destination state in some circumstances.[52] The 1951 Refugee Convention[53] and the Qualification Directive (as well as other national or regional measures providing similar protection) may in fact offer a fundamental if limited guarantee to victims against enforced repatriation. Most of the hard and soft law instruments on THB also refer to the possible applicability of other instruments, some specifically mentioning the Refugee Convention.

5.4 International criminal law

The Palermo Protocol, in conjunction with its mother Convention, the UN Convention on Transnational Organized Crime, requires parties to establish their jurisdiction over THB and various related practices,[54] including the laundering of the proceeds of crime, corruption, and obstruction of justice.

The gravity of THB is, however, perhaps best exemplified by its inclusion as both a war crime and a crime against humanity in the Statute of the International Criminal Court (ICC). Clearly, not all THB occurs during armed conflicts, and that which does not cannot be a war crime. Nevertheless, the increased vulnerability to such practices that may arise in the chaos of war is recognized by the ICC Statute. Thus, a number of offences that may be linked to THB are stated to be war crimes, including deportation of the population,[55] outrages upon personal dignity,[56] rape, sexual slavery and enforced prostitution.[57]

THB may also be prosecuted as a crime against humanity. This is significant because a crime against humanity may also take place outside an armed conflict. A crime against humanity must be part of a widespread or systematic attack against a civilian population. The crime does not have to be transnational, nor does the state have to be involved in the offence. Again, most cases of THB are very unlikely to meet these criteria. Even if THB is an inhumane crime, that is insufficient to make it a crime against humanity. However, THB was actually envisaged as one offence that could be such a crime. Article 7 includes, as

[52] See also R. Piotrowicz, 'Victims of People Trafficking and Entitlement to International Protection', 24 *Australian Year Book of International Law* (2005) p. 159; R. Piotrowicz and C. van Eck, 'Subsidiary Protection and Primary Rights', 53 *International and Comparative Law Quarterly* (2004) p. 107, esp. at pp. 125-127. Possible entitlement of victims to refugee status has been suggested by the UNHCR in its *Guidelines on International Protection – Gender-Related Persecution* 2002, loc. cit. n. 42, Point 18; *Guidelines on International Protection – Membership of a Particular Social Group* 2002, loc. cit. n. 42, Point 12. Most recently, the UNHCR's *Guidelines on International Protection: The Application of Article 1A(2) of the 1951 Convention and/or 1967 Protocol relating to the Status of Refugees to victims of trafficking and persons at risk of being trafficked* (2006), loc. cit. n. 42, offer extensive analysis of the relevance of the Refugee Convention (see *infra* n. 53).

[53] Convention relating to the Status of Refugees, 189 *UNTS* 150; 28 July 1951; entered into force 22 April 1954 (hereafter 'Refugee Convention').

[54] Palermo Protocol, loc. cit. n. 4, Arts. 5 and 9; UNCTOC, loc. cit. n. 4, Art. 15.

[55] ICC Statute, loc. cit. n. 3, Art. (8)(2)(b)(viii).

[56] Ibid., Art. 8(2)(b)(xxi).

[57] Ibid., Art. 8(2)(b)(xxii); Art. 8(2)(c)(vi).

possible acts included in this category of crimes, enslavement,[58] deportation or forcible transfer,[59] and rape, sexual slavery and enforced prostitution.[60] Article 7(2)(c) stresses that enslavement may include THB: it means 'the exercise of any or all of the powers attaching to the right of ownership over a person and includes the exercise of such power in the course of trafficking in persons, in particular women and children'.

In this scenario, we have individual accountability for the breach of what are described in the Statute as serious crimes against individuals – but not breaches of their human rights as such, though clearly to the extent that a state is actively involved, complicit or negligent, one may make out a case that human rights have been breached.

6. Trends

There are two distinct but related trends in the modern development of the law relating to THB: on the one hand the legitimate interest of the state in controlling migration and crime, on the other the recognition of the human rights dimension, and there is sometimes a tension between the two. The interest of the state in combating trafficking arises because the practice threatens stability and security through encouraging irregular migration and violation of national laws on migration, employment and, perhaps, prostitution. On the other hand, THB entails often serious crimes being committed against the victims, who should not be held responsible for apparent breaches of national laws. Human rights issues arise because the state may sometimes be unwilling or unable to take and enforce the measures necessary to protect the basic interests of victims. These interests are recognized in several international instruments. There is, furthermore, a clear tendency to treat THB as a human rights issue, despite difficulties in attributing responsibility to the state for apparent breaches.

Selected Bibliography

Aleinikoff, T.A., 'Protected Characteristics and Social Perceptions: An Analysis of the Meaning of "Membership of a Particular Social Group"', in E. Feller, V. Türk and F. Nicholson (eds.), *Refugee Protection in International Law* (Cambridge, Cambridge University Press 2003) p. 263.

Gallagher, A., 'Human Rights and the New UN Protocols on Trafficking and Migrant Smuggling: A Preliminary Analysis', 23 *Human Rights Quarterly* (2001) p. 975.

Haines, R., 'Gender-related Persecution', in E. Feller, V. Türk and F. Nicholson (eds.), *Refugee Protection in International Law* (Cambridge, Cambridge University Press 2003) p. 319.

[58] Ibid., Art. 7(1)(c).

[59] Ibid., Art. 7(1)(d).

[60] Ibid., Art. 7(1)(g).

Muntarbhorn, V., 'Combating Migrant Smuggling and Trafficking in Persons, Especially Women: The Normative Framework Reappraised', in T.A. Aleinikoff and V. Chetail (eds.), *Migration and International Legal Norms* (The Hague, T.M.C. Asser Press 2003) p. 151.

Obokata, T., 'Trafficking of Human Beings as a Crime against Humanity: Some Implications for the International Legal System', 54 *International and Comparative Law Quarterly* (2005) p. 445.

Piotrowicz, R., 'European Initiatives in the Protection of Victims of Trafficking who Give Evidence Against Their Traffickers', 14 *International Journal of Refugee Law* (2002) p. 263.

—, 'Victims of People Trafficking and Entitlement to International Protection', 24 *Australian Year Book of International Law* (2005) p. 159.

Rijken, C., *Trafficking in Persons: Prosecution from a European Perspective* (The Hague, T.M.C. Asser Press 2003).

Chapter 17
AN EVALUATION OF INTERNATIONAL INSTRUMENTS THAT ADDRESS THE CONDITION OF STATELESSNESS: A CASE STUDY OF ESTONIA AND LATVIA

Nida Gelazis*

1. Introduction

The condition of statelessness creates a situation in which people do not have access to the protections and benefits that states provide their citizens. Although stateless people are certainly eligible for protection under international law, the absence of citizenship is a clear disadvantage, since it often puts the burden on them to find a legal remedy at the international level, rather than enabling them to depend on national institutions and laws. Furthermore, if no country claims them as citizens, they are often beyond the reach of state intervention on their behalf. Statelessness, therefore, is clearly abhorrent to the international system; yet this condition persists around the world, despite international conventions and norms that attempt to limit it.

Stateless people are not necessarily without citizenship of any kind and in some cases they are eligible for citizenship of one country or another. However, the direct link between a citizen and a state can be severed under a variety of conditions that occur quite often around the world, and, indeed, migration is often a factor in that process.

The Universal Declaration on Human Rights[1] includes the right to nationality in its Article 15, which is further elaborated in the Convention on the Reduction of Statelessness[2] and in the Convention on the Rights of the Child.[3] Although international law cannot be blamed for states' bad behaviour, this chapter argues that these Conventions inadequately address the complexity of the problems related to the condition of statelessness, which almost always arises from extraordinary circumstances that compel states to reject claims of citizenship by residents on their territories, or that compel individuals to forsake citizenship when it interferes with their safety, welfare or cultural identity.

* Program Associate and Editor of the East European Studies Program at the Woodrow Wilson International Center for Scholars in Washington DC.

1 UNGA Res. 217 A (III) of 10 Dec. 1948, UN Doc A/810 at 71 (1948).

2 Convention on the Reduction of Statelessness (CRS), 30 Aug. 1961, 989 *UNTS* 175.

3 Convention on the Rights of the Child, 20 Nov. 1989, 1577 *UNTS* 3.

R. Cholewinski, R. Perruchoud and E. MacDonald, eds., International Migration Law

Migration may contribute to the creation of statelessness. And, while a state cannot be seen as contributing to the increased incidence of statelessness due to its citizens leaving its territory, it may be viewed as doing so if it makes it difficult for migrants to gain citizenship. Here, I offer the examples of Estonia and Latvia, which, after breaking free from the Soviet Union, adopted restrictive citizenship policies in an effort to counteract the effects of 50 years of Soviet-era migration, which had radically changed the countries' ethnic compositions. Due to these policies, a large group of residents became stateless. Nevertheless, both countries were relatively successful in defending their policies and the international community had surprisingly little power to interfere on behalf of the stateless. Although it may be argued that this case is a historical and legal anomaly, the fear driving the policy – that migrants spoil cultural and linguistic homogeneity, which is detrimental to social cohesion – is by no means unique. Therefore, it is important to ensure that good precedents are created in the international community to help combat nationalism and xenophobia everywhere.[4]

The outcomes in both situations show that international legal standards can be rather easily evaded because of the vast diversity of naturalization procedures. States wanting to restrict access to citizenship can pick and choose among the great variety of such procedures available and argue that they are following established and accepted precedents. Although the international community can do little to change naturalization laws, international pressure, as well as the countries' small size and weak bargaining power, made it impossible for Estonia and Latvia to pursue policies that would lead to mass deportation or worse outcomes.

The Convention Relating to the Status of Stateless Persons provided guiding principles for Estonia and Latvia for the adoption of policies that granted stateless residents citizen-like rights and privileges, including limited voting rights. Yet, in delivering these rights, the policies may have prolonged the stateless condition of many, since the most pressing reasons for acquiring citizenship, namely freedom of movement and the ability to participate in politics, had already been met. Therefore, any attempts to improve the international legal remedies for the condition of statelessness should seek to balance the need to deliver rights to stateless people without destroying incentives that encourage stateless residents to actively pursue acquisition of citizenship.

The European Union accession process had by far the biggest impact on ameliorating the situation of statelessness in Estonia and Latvia. The EU alone had the ability to persuade both countries to repeal discriminatory laws and simplify naturalization procedures, not because it had clear legal standards to which the countries needed to adhere, but because of the strong leverage it had through the threat that Estonian and Latvian accession to the EU would be delayed. However, in the absence of clear legal norms, the political pressure of EU conditionality

[4] For instance, international consensus seems to be growing on the creation of an independent State of Kosovo. Without prohibitions in international law, Kosovo might restrict citizenship, to the exclusion of ethnic Serbs, particularly those currently living outside Kosovo's borders as refugees.

was unable to persuade the countries to eliminate the problem by granting citizenship to all stateless residents. Nor could it address the problem of encouraging stateless residents to apply for naturalization. As a result, the stateless population had still not been significantly reduced by the time Estonia and Latvia became Member States on 1 May 2004. The new hope is that stateless residents will be encouraged to apply for citizenship because it is linked with EU citizenship: citizenship applications in both countries have risen sharply over the last year and a half.

2. Reducing the Condition of Statelessness

Citizenship is the vehicle through which states grant social and political rights to the people, and the people bestow power on their states. For this reason, jurisdiction over nationality has been carefully guarded by many states, in the belief that it should be kept beyond the reach of international law. Due to the difficulties posed by bringing nationality into international legal structures, and thereby also associated issues such as sovereignty, social cohesion and self-determination, the issue of statelessness was dealt with at the international level not as one problem, but as a series of problems of how to deal with different types of stateless people, and laws were adopted in order of priority. The large stateless refugee populations that confronted the international community after World War II compelled states to begin negotiating a compromise for how to deal with this most vulnerable group first. Thus, international consensus was reached on the group of stateless people most in need of protection with the adoption of the Convention Relating to the Status of Refugees in 1951 (hereafter 'Refugee Convention').[5] However, the Protocol on Statelessness (originally drafted as an addendum to the Refugee Convention) was delayed and brought back to life only after the Convention came into force in 1954.

At that time, debates on the issue of statelessness focused on two separate goals: the elimination of statelessness on the one hand, and the reduction of statelessness on the other. After several draft conventions and numerous meetings, there was a general consensus that 'it was not feasible to suggest measures for the total and immediate elimination of present statelessness'.[6] Thus the focus shifted completely to those drafts dealing with the reduction of statelessness rather than the elimination of it.

The 1954 Convention Relating to the Status of Stateless Persons (CRSSP)[7] and the 1961 Convention on the Reduction of Statelessness (CRS)[8] address a

---

[5] Convention Relating to the Status of Refugees, 28 July 1951, 189 *UNTS* 150.

[6] Yearbook of the United Nations 1954, Chapter III 'Statelessness', p. 417.

[7] Convention Relating to the Status of Stateless Persons (CRSSP), 28 Sept. 1954, 360 *UNTS* 117.

[8] CRS, loc. cit. n. 2.

wide category of people who are not refugees, but who nevertheless, through no fault of their own, have become or have always been stateless. The Conventions do not specify how one might become stateless, but Article 1 of the CRSSP defines a stateless person as someone 'who is not considered as a national by any state under the operation of its law'. The status of 'stateless persons' is denied by the same Article to people who are considered to be refugees; 'to persons who are recognized by the competent authorities of the country in which they have taken residence as having the rights and obligations which are attached to the possession of the nationality of that country'; and to people who have committed crimes as defined by international instruments, serious non-political crimes, or 'have been guilty of acts contrary to the purposes and principles of the United Nations'.

For those who do fall within this category of 'stateless persons', the CRSSP grants certain rights, protections and obligations. Stateless persons are obliged to conform to the laws and regulations of the country of their residence.[9] The Convention prohibits states from arbitrarily deporting or displacing stateless persons,[10] and obliges states to treat them as they would other non-citizens.[11] It further compels states to provide them with a variety of public goods, including protection under the law and access to courts,[12] access to gainful employment[13] and state-sponsored welfare,[14] and administrative assistance, including identity papers and travel documents to facilitate their free movement, transfer of assets and eventual naturalization.[15]

The CRS goes a step further in defining situations in which states must automatically offer citizenship to certain stateless people, or at least ease naturalization requirements to better accommodate them. It particularly encourages states to grant citizenship to children born on their territory who would otherwise be stateless.[16] It also prohibits them from revoking citizenship arbitrarily, especially when depriving citizenship would render the individual stateless. The Convention strictly prohibits states from revoking citizenship due to a person's race, ethnicity, religion or political affiliation.[17]

While the CRS requires states to grant citizenship to people who would otherwise be stateless, it also gives states the discretion to determine the conditions that must be met by stateless people in order to qualify for naturalization. One such condition mentioned in the articles of the Convention is 'that the person concerned has always been stateless'.[18] States, therefore, might decide that they

[9] CRSSP, loc. cit. n. 7, Art. 2.

[10] Ibid., Art. 31

[11] Ibid., Art. 7.

[12] Ibid., Chapter II.

[13] Ibid., Chapter III.

[14] Ibid., Chapter IV.

[15] Ibid., Chapter V.

[16] CRS, loc. cit. n. 2, Arts. 1-4.

[17] Ibid., Art. 9.

[18] Ibid. This phrase appears as a possible limiting condition in Arts. 1(2)(d) and (5)(c), and Art. 4 (2)(d).

are under no obligation to grant citizenship to individuals who were once citizens elsewhere. Similarly, the Convention allows states to deny citizenship to people who could claim it in another state. However, long-term residents who have spent at least seven consecutive years in another state and lose their citizenship as a result of their prolonged absence from their native country can claim citizenship of the state in which they reside, and that state is obliged by the Convention to create conditions to facilitate their naturalization.[19] But for stateless migrants who have not lost their citizenship as a result of residing abroad, the Convention does not provide a remedy. When looked at from a certain perspective, the CRS does a better job of protecting states from excessive claims for citizenship than protecting individuals from the condition of statelessness. *Reducing* statelessness, after all, was the goal of the Convention, not eliminating it.

3. State-Building in Estonia and Latvia

This distinction between reducing the condition of statelessness and eliminating it entirely becomes important when applied to the case of the stateless residents of Estonia and Latvia. These two cases illustrate the weakness of the international legal framework, particularly when faced with the unusual circumstances brought about by the collapse of the Soviet Union. In re-establishing their nations, Estonia and Latvia granted citizenship automatically only to pre-war citizens and their descendants (who were, for the most part, ethnic Estonians and Latvians). Although the Russian Federation offered automatic citizenship to all citizens of the USSR, residents in the Baltic States chose to remain stateless rather than face possible deportation from Estonia and Latvia upon becoming Russian citizens. The result was that thousands of Soviet-era migrants, wanting to remain where they lived, became stateless.

Soviet-era migration was not insignificant. Soviet ideology strongly supported the creation of cosmopolitan societies. State policies were developed and implemented largely according to these aspirations.[20] The Russian language was the basic administrative language of the USSR, and while families in the Soviet Republics could choose to send their children to Russian and native language schools, graduates of Russian schools (in combination with Communist Party membership) had a clear advantage in terms of securing good jobs or a university education. Moreover, Russian was a requisite course in all native-language schools.

More stringent measures were also taken to manufacture cosmopolitan cities through forced migration within the USSR. Policies under Stalin were the most brutal, in the sense that force was clearly used to strip the 'bourgeoisie' of their property and to send them far from their native republics. The fortunate were able

[19] Ibid., Art. 7(4).

[20] See G. Smith, 'Nationalities Policy from Lenin to Gorbachev', in G. Smith (ed.), *The Nationalities Question in the Soviet Union* (New York, Longman Publishing Group 1990) p. 1.

to emigrate to the West, but thousands of people were killed or forced to migrate within Soviet territory. The Baltic States were particularly targeted as anti-Soviet, with the result that tens of thousands of ethnic Estonians, Latvians and Lithuanians were made to leave their homes. At the same time, incentives were given to ethnic Russians, Ukrainians, Georgians, and other groups to migrate to the Baltic States, as Soviet-era industrialization in the region demanded a large work force. The consequence was that the number of ethnic Estonians, Latvians, and Lithuanians dropped tremendously between 1934 and 1959 in their respective countries: 100,000 Estonians, 169,000 Latvians, and 267,000 Lithuanians vanished from census data in the region within the space of 25 years.[21] As a result, the percentage of ethnic Latvians in Latvia dropped from 75.5 per cent in 1935 to 55.1 per cent in 1995. Similarly, in 1934, the ethnic Estonians residing in Estonia made up 88 per cent of the population; in 1989, the percentage was 61.5.[22]

Repression of culture, language and religion in addition to forced migration policies were among the human rights-based arguments that the Baltic States used to make their case for secession from the USSR. The legal argument was that they became part of the Soviet Union through the secret protocols of the 1939 Ribbentrop-Molotov pact. Thus, the Baltic States appealed to those countries, such as the United States, that had continued to recognize their existence throughout the Cold War, considering them to have been illegally annexed to the Soviet Union. With Glasnost, Lithuania, Latvia and Estonia worked through diplomatic channels to reclaim their independent status on that legal basis. Although these countries were able, through international law, to deny the legitimacy of the Soviet occupation and reinstate themselves within the community of independent states, they obviously could not wipe away the demographic changes that had taken place over the course of the previous 50 years. However, all three countries were concerned that Soviet-era migrants would resist their efforts at democratic state-building. This concern, in combination with significant feelings of resentment against their involuntary inclusion in the Soviet Union and all the subsequent changes that ensued, prompted Estonia and Latvia to cling to the principle of legal continuity. This policy resulted in the creation of large stateless populations in both countries.

Once Latvia regained its independence, the democratically-elected Parliament reinstated the 1922 Constitution, in order to establish legal continuity with the inter-war Republic. All three Baltic States claimed that, despite 50 years of Soviet annexation, within the context of international law, the inter-war Republics

---

[21] See Appendix 2, Table I in M. Lauristin and P. Vihalemm (eds.), *Return to the Western World: Cultural and Political Perspectives on the Estonian Post-Communist Transition* (Tartu, Tartu University Press 1997) pp. 305-306. This table also indicates an even greater loss suffered by the Jewish populations in the region: between 1934 and 1959, 56,000 Jews and an astounding 204,000 Jews 'disappeared' from Latvia and Lithuania respectively.

[22] Data on ethnic composition of the Baltic States is found in I. Ziemele, 'The Role of State Continuity and Human Rights in Matters of Nationality of the Baltic States', in T. Jundzis (ed.), *The Baltic States at Historical Crossroads* (Riga, Academy of Sciences 1998) p. 248, at p. 260.

had never ceased to exist. This was a myth, to be sure, but one with international backing, since the United States and other countries never recognized the illegal act that allowed the Baltic States to be incorporated into the USSR.

In the spirit of the principle of state continuity, in 1991 Latvian leaders reinstated the 1919 Citizenship Law (as amended in 1927),[23] which granted individuals who had possessed Latvian citizenship prior to 1940 automatic citizenship in the restored Latvian State. The Resolution on the Renewal of the Republic of Latvia, Citizens' Rights and Fundamental Principles of Naturalization stated that the restored State considered the 1940 USSR law on citizenship null and void,[24] thus rendering thousands of residents of Latvian territory stateless. Only those who were citizens of the inter-war State and their descendants had the right to participate in the first elections of the restored State. As a result of this policy, only 64 per cent of the resident population was eligible to participate in the 1993 elections.[25]

On 22 July 1994 the Latvian Parliament, the *Saeima*, adopted a new law on citizenship.[26] This law reiterated the fact that pre-1940 citizens and their descendants are entitled to citizenship and laid down the ground rules for naturalization, but it also granted citizenship to individuals who were permanent residents of pre-1919 Latvia (the date of the creation of the inter-war Latvian State). Latvia adopted special provisions to encourage its *émigrés* to repatriate. The 'Transitional Provisions' of the 1994 law allowed inter-war citizens of the Republic to gain citizenship without renouncing that which they already held. Citizenship was also granted upon registration to Soviet-era immigrants of Estonian and Lithuanian ethnicity, to non-ethnic Latvians who finished Latvian language secondary schools and to spouses (for at least 10 years) of Latvian citizens.[27]

Article 10 of the 1994 law prohibits the naturalization of people who have 'turned against the Republic of Latvia's independence, its democratic parliamentary state system or the existing state authority in Latvia, if such has been established by a court decree'; people who, since 4 May 1990, have stirred ethnic hatred or racial discord through the propagation of fascist, chauvinist, national-socialist, communist, or other totalitarian ideas; officials of foreign states and those who have served in the armed forces or police of a foreign state (including the USSR) who were not permanent residents of Latvia prior to their conscription; those who have been employees, informants, or agents of the KGB or any other foreign security service; those who have been convicted of a crime and imprisoned for more than one year; and those who participated in the attempts to

---

[23] The Law on Citizenship of the Republic of Latvia (23 Aug. 1919).

[24] The Republic of Latvia Supreme Council and Government Reporter, No. 43, 1991. See also Ziemele, loc. cit. n. 22, at p. 260.

[25] See 'Constitution Watch: Latvia', *East European Constitutional Review* Vol. 2, No. 3 (Summer 1993) p. 11.

[26] Law on Citizenship of the Republic of Latvia, Republic of Latvia Saeima and the Cabinet of Ministers Zinotejs, 1994, No. 17.

[27] Ibid., Art. 13.

stop the independence movement after 13 January 1991 through their participation in the Latvian Communist Party, the Working Peoples' International Front of the Latvian SSR, the United Council of Labour Collectives, the Organization of War and Labour Veterans, or the All-Latvia Salvation Committee and its regional committees.

The new naturalization procedures required establishing permanent residence in Latvia for five years beginning from 4 May 1990, having command of the Latvian language, history and national anthem, and knowing the basic principles of the Constitution and the constitutional law on 'Rights and Obligations of a Citizen and a Person'.[28] Chapter III of the law describes the language exam, which includes testing the applicant on his or her ability to read, speak and write in Latvian on topics from everyday life. It also states that the disabled and the elderly are exempt from taking this exam. Applicants must also show proof of a legal source of income and renounce their former citizenship.[29]

To prevent what Latvian parliamentarians believed would be a run on the naturalization office, the 1994 law also instituted a 'windows' system for naturalization.[30] This law distinguished applicants for citizenship by age and by whether or not they were born in Latvia and separated them into eight groups accordingly. The first group (those born in Latvia who were 16-20 years of age at the time of their application) were scheduled to begin naturalization procedures on 1 January 1996. The eighth set of applicants (those born outside Latvia and over 30 years of age) could not begin the naturalization process until 1 January 2003.

Unsurprisingly, due to the strict new citizenship law, the number of registered Latvian residents who gained citizenship between 1995 and 1997 rose by only 1.4 per cent, leaving at least 28 per cent of registered residents stateless.[31] In the face of international pressure to end the condition of statelessness within its borders, Latvia stood by its citizenship policy and asserted its legality due to the principle of state continuity. Instead of amending its citizenship policies, the Latvian Parliament adopted a special Law on the Status of Former USSR Citizens Who are Not Citizens of Latvia or Any Other State.[32] This law applies to only those resident non-citizens who qualify for citizenship through naturalization, thus excluding former Soviet army personnel and their families. It stipulates in its Article 2 that stateless persons who have registered with the Government enjoy the same rights as Latvian citizens according to the Constitutional Law on Rights and Ob-

[28] Ibid., Art. 12.

[29] Ibid.

[30] Ibid., Art. 14.

[31] These percentages were calculated from the 1997 official Population Register of the Latvian Citizenship and Immigration Board, as reported in the UN Development Programme's *Latvia: Human Development Report 1997* (Riga, UNDP 1997) p. 49. Since these numbers only include residents who have actually registered with the Government, this figure reflects the minimum possible number of stateless persons residing in Latvia.

[32] The Law of the Republic of Latvia on the Status of Former USSR Citizens Who are Not Citizens of Latvia or Any Other State (12 April 1995).

ligations of a Person and a Citizen.[33] Moreover, the law confirms that resident non-citizens have the right to travel freely, are able to bring their spouses and dependents to Latvia, can maintain their native language and culture and are entitled to receive translation services in court proceedings. The law also stipulates that resident non-citizens will not be exiled or expelled from the territory of Latvia except according to law or when a foreign state agrees to receive them.

Like Latvia, Estonia followed the principle of continuity in re-establishing its democratic state, albeit to a lesser extent. After the 1991 Moscow putsch and the quick adoption of the Resolution on the National Independence of Estonia,[34] the Estonian Parliament immediately began working on a new Constitution. Moreover, as in Latvia and Lithuania, the struggle for independence was linked to pro-democratic forces and guarantees that no attempts would be made to restrict citizenship of the independent Republic on the basis of ethnic origin.[35] However, the new Constitution betrayed these initial intentions. The Estonian Constitution, adopted by referendum in 1992, included guarantees for the protection of minorities, but also guaranteed social rights to resident non-citizens. Article 28 of the Estonian Constitution stipulates that

> 'All persons shall have the right to health care. Estonian citizens shall be entitled to state assistance in the case of old age, inability to work, loss of a provider, and need... [T]his right shall exist equally for Estonian citizens, and citizens of foreign states and stateless persons who are sojourning in Estonia. The state shall encourage voluntary and local government social care. Families with many children and the disabled shall be entitled to special care by state and local authorities'.

The Constitution also stipulated that resident non-citizens would have the right to participate in local elections.[36] These policies implied that the political consensus on the citizenship question was to enforce a restrictive policy, and foreshadowed a protracted period of transition in which many residents would be left stateless. But they also show that the framers of the Constitution were aware of the 1960

---

[33] Constitutional Law of the Republic of Latvia on the Rights and Obligations of Citizens and Persons (10 Dec. 1991).

[34] Resolution by the Supreme Council of the Republic of Estonia on the National Independence of Estonia (20 Aug. 1991).

[35] See A. Semjonov 'Citizenship Legislation, Minority Rights and Integration in Estonia', paper presented for the Legal Information Centre for Human Rights (Tallinn), European Centre for Minority Issues (Flensburg) and Norwegian Institute of Human Rights (Oslo) Baltic Seminar on 'Minorities and Majorities in Estonia: Problems of Integration at the Threshold of the EU' (Tallinn, 8-9 Jan. 1998) p. 5.

[36] Although the Constitution drafters assumed that this would also give resident non-citizens the right to run for elected office in local councils and for mayor, the electoral law of 19 May 1993 denied non-citizens this right. David Laitin explains that '[m]ost delegates of the Riigikogu knew that they were breaking the spirit, if not the letter, of the Constitution, but the political goal of undermining the power of the current city councils in the northeastern cities proved of greater importance to them'. See D. Laitin, 'The Russian-Speaking Nationality in Estonia: Two Quasi-Constitutional Elections', *East European Constitutional Review* Vol. 2-3, No. 4-1 (Fall 1993-Winter 1994) p. 25.

CRSSP, which obliges states to provide public benefits to stateless people on their territory.

Upon the re-establishment of the Republic of Estonia, the *Riikigoku* (Parliament) re-instated the 1938 Law on Citizenship, as amended in 1940,[37] according to which citizenship was extended only to those residents who had Estonian citizenship prior to 16 June 1940 and their descendants.[38] An opportunity to gain citizenship automatically was also given to Soviet-era citizens who could prove that they supported the national independence movement by presenting their Congress of Estonia membership cards.[39] This citizenship law was still in place for the 1993 national elections, therefore severely restricting the number of eligible voters.[40] Estonia adopted the Law of the Republic of Estonia on Aliens on 8 July 1993,[41] which was very similar to the Latvian law on resident non-citizens in terms of granting constitutional rights protection to aliens. However, unlike the Latvian law, which guarantees resident non-citizens will not be deported, the Estonian law includes a negative incentive for non-citizens to register with the local immigration offices within the established time limit: do so or face possible expulsion from the territory of Estonia.[42] The 1993 elections resulted in the creation of a predictably right-of-centre and nationalistic government, dominated by the Fatherland Party. And it was this parliamentary majority that designed the new citizenship law adopted on 19 January 1995.

The 1995 Law of the Republic of Estonia on Citizenship[43] sets out nearly identical provisions for naturalization as the Latvian citizenship law. Two notable differences are that there were no special provisions regarding the repatriation of Estonian *émigrés*, as was the case in Latvia, and no special privileges were given to Latvian or Lithuanian residents. Moreover, the Estonian law does not follow the 'windows' system, therefore naturalization procedures were open to all permanent residents from the date the law came into force (1 April 1995). Nevertheless, naturalization proceeded at a snail's pace: by 1997 only 1060 applicants had managed to fulfill all the requirements to gain citizenship.[44]

---

[37] The Republic of Estonia's Law on Citizenship 1938, as amended in 1940, Riigi Teataja, 1938, No. 39, pos. 357. The 1940 amendments to this law dramatically changed what had originally been (in 1938) a relatively liberal law, in that it that simplified naturalization procedures for those who had permanently resided in the territory of Estonia for at least ten years, did not envisage any formal exam for knowledge of the Estonian language, and gave automatic citizenship to children born in Estonia to stateless parents. See Semjonov, loc. cit. n. 35, at p. 7.

[38] See Ziemele, loc. cit. n. 22, at p. 257.

[39] As much as 27.4% of the 1992 electorate had gained citizenship on this basis. See Semjonov, loc. cit. n. 35, at p. 7.

[40] Figures during the 1992 constitutional referendum show that only around 60% of the 1990 electorate was able to participate. See Semjonov, loc. cit. n. 35, at p. 6.

[41] The Republic of Estonia's Law on Aliens (8 July 1993), in *Legal Acts of Estonia*, 3, 27 Aug. 1993, pp. 59-66.

[42] Ibid., Art. 21.7-8.

[43] The Republic of Estonia's Law on Citizenship (31 Jan. 1995).

[44] See Semjonov, loc. cit. n. 35, at p. 7.

Estonia and Latvia issued stateless residents non-citizens' passports in order to facilitate free movement, as stipulated in the CRSSP. Social and political rights have been bestowed on these groups by the State, even to the extent that non-citizens in Estonia may vote in local elections. But, given the animosity felt by the Estonians and Latvians towards the Russian-speaking residents, it is doubtful that either country was following the spirit of the Convention, but simply looked to it as a guide for how to create an ethnocracy within the (not particularly restrictive) confines of international law.

4. International Laws and Practices Constraining State Nationality Policy

The Report on the Consequences of State Succession for Nationality[45] initially invokes the Hague Convention on Certain Questions Relating to the Conflict of Nationality Laws of 12 April 1930, which stipulates in Article 1 that it is 'for each State to determine under its own law who are its nationals'.[46] Yet, international law and state practice do indeed provide limits to this right. The Report outlines several general principles that should be taken into consideration when faced with the problem of citizenship in successor states. The principles relevant to the Baltic cases include a prohibition on discrimination on the basis of ethnicity or language, the creation of effective links between potential citizens and the state, the avoidance of the creation of statelessness, and the right of option for residents of successor states to choose their country of citizenship. Although it should be understood that adherence to one of these should never be a defense against ignoring one or all of the other principles delimiting a state's nationality policy, it is useful to show the ways in which one principle may indeed limit another, and how the standard of application of each principle is determined by the particular context and values of each state. The Baltic States, in the end, managed to defend their citizenship policies by clearly defining their status as re-established states as opposed to successor states.

The prohibition of discrimination on the basis of ethnic origin, colour, religion, language, or political opinions is a well-recognized limitation on a state's right to determine conditions for acquisition of citizenship. Article 1(3) of the International Convention on the Elimination of All Forms of Racial Discrimination[47] stipulates that

---

[45] Council of Europe, *On the Consequences of State Succession for Nationality*, Report adopted by the European Commission for Democracy through Law at its 28th Plenary Meeting, Venice, 13-14 Sept. 1996, Science and Technique of Democracy Collection, No. 23 (Strasbourg, Council of Europe 1998) pp. 19-52.

[46] Hague Convention on Certain Questions Relating to the Conflict of Nationality Laws, 12 April 1930, *LNTS* Vol. 179, p. 89, as cited in ibid., at p. 21.

[47] International Convention on the Elimination of All Forms of Racial Discrimination, 21 Dec. 1965, 660 *UNTS* 195.

> 'nothing in the Convention may be interpreted as affecting in any way the legal provisions of States Parties concerning nationality, citizenship or naturalization, provided that such provisions do not discriminate against any particular nationality'.

Moreover, Article 9 of the CRS prohibits states from depriving 'any person or group of persons of their nationality on racial, ethnic, religious or political grounds'. Thus, the citizenship legislation of all three Baltic States becomes suspect due to their stiff language requirements and firm stances on not granting citizenship to former Soviet military personnel. The Latvian law in particular seems to single out the ethnic Russian population as unsuitable to gain citizenship, whereas the Soviet era migrants of Estonian and Lithuanian ethnicity enjoy it automatically.

The discrimination on the basis of language common to these approaches was criticized by the Organization for Security and Cooperation in Europe (OSCE) High Commissioner on National Minorities, and recommendations for exempting the elderly and disabled from taking language examinations were adopted into the citizenship laws of the Baltic States, even if the recommendations that the language examinations be simplified were deemed unnecessary by Latvia and Estonia.[48] Moreover, attempts were made to grant non-citizens equality under the law, in terms of granting resident aliens protection under the constitution, social protection, and limited voting rights (the last of these in Estonia only).

One argument offered in defense of Latvian and Estonian discriminatory policies towards resident populations of ethnic Russians is that they serve to 'correct' 50 years of discrimination of ethnic Estonians and Latvians by Russia. Ziemele asserts that

> 'the measures which were undertaken by the independent governments of the Baltic States were measures of special protection in the sense of Article 26 of the ICCPR aimed at re-establishing *de facto* equality for discriminated groups in the respective societies which also involved the attribution of the status of State language to local languages'.[49]

In response to the allegations that the citizenship laws of Latvia and Estonia discriminate on the basis of ethnicity and language, the effective link principle may be invoked. This principle is derived from the recognition that there must be some kind of link between the state and an individual requesting citizenship. These links are very often birth, domicile and residence in the country in question.[50] Yet other criteria could be included as well, particularly in terms of the

[48] UN, ECOSOC, Commission on Human Rights, 54th Session, 31 March 1998, Agenda item 16: Rights of Persons Belonging to National or Ethnic, Religious, and Linguistic Minorities, 'Statement by Romans Baumanis, head of the delegation of Latvia', Appendix.

[49] Ziemele, loc. cit. n. 22, at p. 264.

[50] Council of Europe, *On the Consequences of State Succession for Nationality*, op. cit. n. 45, at p. 22.

state's responsibility to defend its citizens against the actions of other states.[51] For these reasons, successor states often choose not to grant automatic citizenship to individuals who had served in political or military capacities in the previous state.[52] According to this argument, former Soviet army, State, or KGB personnel were prohibited from gaining citizenship in the newly restored States of Lithuania, Latvia, and Estonia.[53] In the specific case of ethnic Russians' claims to be granted citizenship of Latvia and Estonia, knowledge of the native language, history, and Constitution are additional requirements for naturalization. The assumption is that Russians feel a stronger allegiance to Russia than the Baltic States, even if they have chosen not to live in the former for economic reasons. Russia has certainly shown concern over the status of Russian minorities living in the Baltic States, and its constitutionalized commitment to promote its interests in the 'near abroad' far surpasses any other state's claims on foreign territories and the resident ethnic populations there. So-called 'kin-state' policies recently adopted, such as the Law on the State Policy of the Russian Federation in Respect to Compatriots Abroad of 24 May 1999,[54] extend Russia's reach to countries like the Baltic States by offering links to Russia to people resident outside its borders. Given the history of Russian aggression in the region, Estonia and Latvia may be justified in demanding that ethnic Russians not only break their political ties to Russia, but also demonstrate a commitment to their adoptive countries.

Moreover, the Baltic States were not the first to use language as a determinant for citizenship. The Treaty of Peace between the Allied and Associated Powers and Italy (1947) dealt with the problem of citizenship and large-scale migration during World War II by determining the citizenship of inhabitants of territories acquired by Italy by language. It deemed that the 'inhabitants of the transferred territories "whose customary language is Italian" should be entitled to opt for the Italian nationality', while 'Italian nationals residing in Italy but who used habitually the Serbian, Croatian or Slovene language could opt for the Yugoslav nationality', with the requirement that if Italian citizens chose Yugoslav citizenship, they would be required to move there.[55]

The principle of avoiding conditions of statelessness has become hard law since the adoption of the CRS. In reference to citizenship laws, Article 8 of the

[51] *Nottebohm* case (Second Phase), judgment of 6 April 1955, ICJ Reports 1955, p. 23.

[52] Council of Europe, *On the Consequences of State Succession for Nationality*, op. cit. n. 45, at p. 14.

[53] Although international law and practice allows states to deny citizenship to military and government personnel of foreign states, this has become an excuse for Estonia to deny residence permits and even deport (formerly Soviet) Russian soldiers who are married to Estonian citizens. Certainly, the international community should demand that the right of families to stay together be protected at a higher standard than the right of states to deny citizenship on the basis of the effective links principle. See 'Estonia to Expel Eight Russian Reserve Officers', RFE/RL Newsline, 11 June 1997.

[54] Russian Federation Federal Law on the State Policy of the Russian Federation in Respect of Compatriots Abroad (17 March 1999) <http://www.venice.coe.int/docs/2002/CDL(2002)076-e.asp>.

[55] Council of Europe, *On the Consequences of State Succession for Nationality*, op. cit. n. 45, at p. 34.

Convention stipulates that State Parties 'shall not deprive a person of his/her nationality if such deprivation would render him/her stateless'. The fact that, in 1999, 13 per cent of residents in Estonia and 28 per cent in Latvia remained stateless offered little evidence that these two countries were trying their best to meet this requirement. Moreover, in line with the Convention on the Rights of the Child[56] and Article 24 of the ICCPR, states must grant citizenship to children born in their territories who would otherwise be rendered stateless.[57] This requirement was fulfilled in Latvia after its referendum on the status of children born to stateless parents in October 1998.[58] Estonia followed shortly thereafter, when the Parliament passed an amendment to the Law on Citizenship in December 1999.

The right of option gives residents the right to choose between taking citizenship in one of the two (or more) successor states or between the successor state and the predecessor state.[59] In cases where the option of taking the citizenship of the predecessor state is chosen, it is usually coupled with the obligation to leave the successor state.[60] All citizens of the USSR had the option of gaining automatic citizenship in the Russian Federation.[61] And, though restrictive, the citizenship laws of Estonia and Latvia do offer an option to most residents to become citizens through naturalization. Thus, it might be argued that the resident non-citizen populations actively chose the condition of statelessness because it was preferable to gaining Russian citizenship with the risk that they would need to emigrate. This is a problem that hard international law is ineffective in addressing, since it requires states to create conditions in which people can gain citizenship, but has no power over the individual preferences that determine how people will act.

The practice of granting citizenship to the resident population, that is, that the 'population goes with the territory', is said to be an international practice, but in the early 1990s there was no binding rule 'prescribing the automatic acquisition

---

[56] Convention on the Rights of the Child, loc. cit. n. 3.

[57] See Ziemele, loc. cit. n. 22, at p. 262.

[58] Ibid., at p. 263.

[59] See P. Weis, *Nationality and Statelessness in International Law* (Alphen aan den Rijn, Sijthoff & Noordhoff 1979) p. 43.

[60] Council of Europe, *On the Consequences of State Succession for Nationality*, op. cit. n. 45, at p. 45.

[61] Art. 13(2) of the Russian Law on Federation Citizenship, adopted 28 Nov. 1991, stated that 'Persons born on December 30, 1922, and thereafter, who lost the citizenship of the former USSR shall be deemed to have Russian Federation citizenship by birth, where they were born on the territory of the Russian Federation, or where either parent at the moment of their birth was a citizen of the USSR and was in permanent residence on the territory of the Russian Federation'. The Law on Citizenship of the Russian Federation (1 July 2002) has changed this policy, stipulating that former USSR citizens can gain Russian citizenship after they have resided for five years in Russia after having been issued permanent resident status. However, another law, the 1999 Law on State Policy of the Russian Federation in Respect of Compatriots Abroad, loc. cit. n. 54, makes a special case for citizens of the former USSR. Art. 11 states that '[i]ndividuals who are resident abroad and who were stripped of citizenship of the Russian Soviet Federated Socialist Republic (RSFSR) or the Russian Federation or who have lost this citizenship against their will, shall be considered to have had their citizenship of the Russian Federation restored unless they formally object to this decision'.

of the nationality of the successor state'.[62] When there is a successor state and a predecessor state, the rule has been that the successor state confers its citizenship on former nationals of the predecessor state habitually residing in the former; in almost all cases, this citizenship is conferred automatically,[63] though the right of option and effective links principles should also be considered. When the predecessor state ceases to exist, as happened with the USSR, successor states are even more strongly compelled to offer automatic citizenship to residents of their territories. Article 10 of the CRS gives effect to this obligation by providing that

> 'Every treaty between Contracting States providing for the transfer of territory shall include provisions to secure that no person shall become stateless as a result of the transfer... In the absence of such provisions a Contracting State to which territory is transferred or which otherwise acquires territory shall confer its nationality on such persons as would otherwise become stateless as a result of the transfer or acquisition'.

The automatic conferment of citizenship on permanent residents of the territory of the successor state was followed only by Lithuania. Why did Estonia and Latvia diverge from this practice and how did they get away with it? To answer this question it is necessary to return to the Baltic 'path of independence', and examine more closely the principle of state continuity embraced by the two States. If Estonia's original path of formally seceding from the USSR had been successful, the Baltic States would have had to sign a treaty with the USSR and thus be subject to the CRS, with all its implications for allocating citizenship. However, by asserting their status as continuous states, the Baltic States subverted the need to base their independence on a secession pact with the USSR, and progressed instead on the basis of international recognition of the illegality of their annexation. Following their re-assertions of independent statehood, inter-war national laws and international treaties were again recognized.[64] And, as a consequence, the Baltic States reinstated their inter-war citizenship laws, with all the ramifications they had for Soviet-era migrants. Thus, 'these states represent a special case since their claim to be identical with the three Baltic States annexed by the Soviet Union in 1940 was accepted by the international community'.[65]

---

[62] Council of Europe, *On the Consequences of State Succession for Nationality*, op. cit. n. 45, at p. 39.

[63] Ibid., at p. 14.

[64] Ziemele cites different acts on the part of the international community which support the Baltic States' claim that they had re-established their independent statehood. For instance, the fact that some countries withheld formal recognition of the Baltic States' independence due to the pre-existing recognition granted to the inter-war democracies, and the act of British and French banks in returning gold reserves deposited by the inter-war republics based on *restitutio ad integrum*, were both indicators that the international community accepted the Baltic States' actions. See Ziemele, loc. cit. n. 22, at pp. 255-256.

[65] Council of Europe, *On the Consequences of State Succession for Nationality*, op. cit. n. 45, at p. 38.

As a 'special case', Latvia and Estonia have been able to forestall disciplinary measures being taken by the international community. Moreover, clear attempts were made to bestow special status to stateless residents. These States offered protection and responsibility for aliens traveling abroad through the issue of non-citizens' passports. Social and limited political rights were given to these groups as well, even to the extent that non-citizens in Estonia may vote in local elections. Indeed, these measures were taken to soften the blow (to both the resident non-citizens and to the disapproving international community) of their restrictive policies. Yet they are merely a smoke-screen for clear discrimination against the Russian minority. However, with no support from international law, the hands of the international community were tied.

In 1997, the Council of Europe drew up the European Convention on Nationality in order to give hard-law status to the general principles and international practices concerning nationality, which entered into force on 3 January 2000.[66] The Convention provides important new limitations to states' nationality laws. Interestingly, Estonian and Latvian policies towards stateless residents have created an important benchmark for citizenship law, which was incorporated into the Convention. Article 20 requires that, in cases of state succession, nationals of the predecessor state habitually resident in the territory over which sovereignty is transferred to the successor state and who have not acquired its nationality shall have the right to remain in that state, and those persons shall enjoy equality of treatment with nationals of the successor state in relation to social and economic rights. Moreover, resident non-citizens may not be excluded from employment in the public sphere.

5. THE IMPACT OF EU ENLARGEMENT

As described above, international law was unable to compel Latvia and Estonia to grant their resident stateless populations citizenship. Moreover, there is no international legal basis for inducing the stateless residents either to apply for Russian citizenship or to go through the process of naturalization in their country of residence. To end this apparent standoff, the international community needed to rely on diplomacy and negotiation, and the most effective agent was the European Union.

The European Commission's Agenda 2000 opinions on the applicant countries[67] identified the extremely restrictive right to citizenship and discrimination against non-citizens in Latvia and Estonia as obstacles to membership. The EU encouraged both countries to simplify naturalization procedures for stateless residents (particularly children), to improve the delivery of language instruction in an

[66] European Convention on Nationality, 6 Nov. 1997, *ETS* No. 166.

[67] European Commission, *Agenda 2000 - Summary and Conclusions of the Opinions of the Commission concerning the Applications for Membership to the European Union presented by the Candidate Countries*, DOC/97/8 (Strasbourg/Brussels, European Commission 15 July 1997).

effort to remove one of the main barriers to citizenship, to delete discriminatory articles from the language laws, and to ratify the Framework Convention for the Protection of National Minorities (FCNM).[68]

The EU's strong leverage position was evident in the quick pace of reforms in Latvia. In 1998, the Latvian Parliament adopted a new citizenship law, which was subsequently upheld in a national referendum. As a result, the 'window system' was abandoned and the naturalization process was opened to all resident aliens. Further, the new law enabled children born in Latvia to stateless parents to be granted citizenship, and simplified the procedures for naturalization for people over the age of 65. Estonia followed suit in 1999 regarding stateless children, and in 2002 exempted children who had passed upper secondary school exams in civics from the corresponding exam in the naturalization process. Moreover, the Latvian government responded to the Commission's criticism of its discriminatory policies towards non-nationals by eliminating restrictions preventing non-citizens from working as fire-fighters, airline staff, pharmacists, and veterinary pharmacists and unemployment benefits are now available to non-citizens without their having to present certificates that they know the Latvian language. Estonia has yet to respond to similar criticism over its policy to exclude non-citizens from certain private sector jobs.

Despite changes in legislation, it has been difficult for both countries to raise the numbers of applications from among the residents eligible for citizenship. The most significant barrier to citizenship in both countries is the requirement of competence in the national language. The EU targeted substantial funds to language programs in both countries, as well as to social integration projects, so that Russian speakers could study the languages at no cost. These courses continue to be overburdened with students, and waiting lists are long. EU pressure also prompted Latvia to substantially lower naturalization fees in an effort to boost applicant numbers.

Perhaps the most powerful tool the EU has to resolve the problem of statelessness in the Baltic States is the desirability of EU citizenship. One hypothesis for why non-citizens had not applied for naturalization in great numbers was that Latvian or Estonian citizenship was not particularly desirable, both because it does not reflect the non-citizens' identity and because Estonian and Latvian citizenship was not seen as a great benefit, in terms of the rights and privileges that it might confer. The fact that the number of naturalization applications submitted nearly doubled the year that Latvia became an EU Member State[69] suggests that the prospect of gaining EU citizenship, and the real or imagined benefits that it confers, may have been the incentive stateless residents needed in order to take action towards gaining Latvian and Estonian citizenship.

---

68 Framework Convention for the Protection of National Minorities, 1 Feb. 1995, *ETS* No. 157.

69 In 2003, the Latvian Naturalization Board received 11,268 applications. In 2004, that number jumped to 21,297 and, in 2005, the number was 19,807. These and other statistics can be found at <http://www.np.gov.lv/en/faili_en/stat_angl.xls>.

EU law provides yet another remedy to the stateless residents in the Baltic States through the Tampere European Council's decision to improve the situation of third-country nationals. In 2003, the Council adopted Directive 2003/109/EC concerning the status of third-country nationals who are long-term residents,[70] which requires Member States to extend rights closely resembling the rights of citizens to third-country nationals who have lived in the territory for at least five years. The Directive specifically addresses equal treatment in terms of access to employment, education, social security and tax benefits, access to goods and services (particularly housing), freedom of association, free movement within the country of residence, and protection from expulsion. Most notably, the Directive offers third-country nationals that hold long-time residence permits and their families limited free movement rights to other EU Member States. Thus, as long-term third-country nationals, Estonia's and Latvia's stateless residents have access to certain rights and protections offered by the EU.[71] It should be noted that free movement and other rights would not be automatically transferred to long-term residents, but are contingent upon an application procedure to be determined by the Member State in accordance with the criteria set down in the Directive.

Of course, there will certainly be more restrictions to free movement placed on third-country nationals than on citizens, which still creates disparity. Thus, although it alleviates the problem to some degree, it certainly does not resolve the difficulties surrounding statelessness. So far, the EU has taken steps to integrate third-country nationals into its labour market and to extend social rights to them. Political rights, however, are limited to freedom of association, and non-citizens from third countries continue to be excluded from voting or other forms of political participation. Therefore, even though Estonia's and Latvia's resident alien populations are treated as long-term resident third-country nationals, the measures taken by the EU to date still represent no solution to their stateless status.

6. Conclusion

The case of post-Soviet state building in the Baltic States reflects a reality in which an unjust condition – the illegal occupation of the Baltic States by the USSR – resulted in an unjust outcome, as thousands of Soviet-era residents were rendered stateless by the re-established, independent Estonia and Latvia. The Baltic States' retaliatory measures against the Soviet-era migrants were carefully

[70] Council Directive 2003/109/EC of 25 Nov. 2003 concerning the status of third-country nationals who are long-term residents, OJ 2003 L 16/44. I am indebted to Mark Bell (Faculty of Law, University of Leicester, UK) for drawing my attention to this directive.

[71] Even though they are not technically citizens of a 'third country', resident aliens qualify as third-country nationals according to the Commission's definition. See R. Danelsons, 'Latvia', in I. Higgins (ed.), and K. Hailbronner, gen. rapp., *Migration and Asylum Law and Policy in the European Union: FIDE 2004 Reports* (Cambridge, Cambridge University Press 2004) p. 221 at pp. 228-229. Thanks and credit for finding this go to Bernard Ryan (School of Law, University of Kent, UK).

engineered in response to international criticism. These policy changes reflected their unwillingness to abandon their goal of creating ethnocracies, rather than build modern, multi-ethnic democracies. But it also reflects the relative weakness of international conventions on the prevention of statelessness; and the diversity of precedents for different forms of naturalization were used by the Baltic States as guidelines for how to create restrictive naturalization policies within the international legal framework. In the end, international conditionality related to EU and NATO accession were important mechanisms for coercing compliance.

As migration becomes more prevalent in our increasingly globalized world, it is important that the international community reinforce the legal rights of migrants to citizenship in their countries of residence. The impulse to create or maintain homogeneous societies is strong worldwide, and states may be easily tempted to violate human rights to do so. Currently, as these cases show, the international legal standards in place to prohibit discrimination on the basis of language and ethnicity are insufficient to prevent states from indulging in this impulse.

Selected Bibliography

Council of Europe, *On the Consequences of State Succession for Nationality*, Report adopted by the European Commission for Democracy through Law at its 28th Plenary Meeting, Venice 13-14 Sept. 1996, Science and Technique of Democracy Collection, No. 23 (Strasbourg, Council of Europe 1998).

European Commission, *Agenda 2000 – Summary and Conclusions of the Opinions of the Commission concerning the Applications for Membership to the European Union presented by the Candidate Countries* (Strasbourg/Brussels, European Commission 15 July 1997) DOC/97/8.

Jundzis, T. (ed.), *The Baltic States at Historical Crossroads* (Riga, Academy of Sciences 1998).

Lauristin, M., and P. Vihalemm (eds.), *Return to the Western World: Cultural and Political Perspectives on the Estonian Post-Communist Transition* (Tartu, Tartu University Press 1997).

Smith, G., 'Nationalities Policy from Lenin to Gorbachev', in G. Smith (ed.), *The Nationalities Question in the Soviet Union* (New York, Longman Publishing Group 1990).

Free Movement Regimes and Other Regional Developments

Chapter 18
FREE MOVEMENT OF EU NATIONALS AND UNION CITIZENSHIP

Kay Hailbronner*

1. Introduction

The right to free movement of EU nationals among the Member States has long been recognized as a fundamental component of the project of European integration, introduced for workers as early as 1968 in order to encourage the creation of a common labour market.[1] It has never, of course, been absolutely unlimited; and this, coupled with the fact that it has implications not merely for crossing international frontiers but for a whole host of different matters concerning life in the host nation, resulted in the development of a significant and complex body of Community law on the issue.

In comparison, the notion of 'Union citizenship' is a relative newcomer to the scene, laid out in the Treaty of Maastricht of 1992. Article 17 of the Treaty Establishing the European Community[2] (hereafter, the EC Treaty) provides that

> 'Citizenship of the Union is hereby established. Every person holding the nationality of a Member State shall be a citizen of the Union. Citizenship of the Union shall complement and not replace national citizenship'.

The Treaty, however, does little more than introduce this concept in the short section devoted to it, providing very little substance on how, if at all, it will impact on the law of the European Union – despite its obvious relations to, and implications for, the law pertaining to freedom of movement. It has been left largely to other institutions, and in particular to the Court of Justice, to flesh out the precise content and legal implications of Union citizenship.

The purpose of this chapter is to carry out a critical analysis of the impact of Union citizenship on freedom of movement within the EU, and in particular how

---

* Director of the Centre for International and European Law on Immigration and Asylum at the University of Konstanz.

[1] See Council Regulation 1612/68/EEC of 15 Oct. 1968 on freedom of movement for workers within the Community, OJ 1968 L 257/2.

[2] OJ 2002 C 325/33.

R. Cholewinski, R. Perruchoud and E. MacDonald, eds., International Migration Law

the former has been developed in the jurisprudence of the Court of Justice and in Community legislation. It begins by outlining the main features of the concept of Union citizenship as interpreted by the Court, particularly in terms of the finding that it represents the 'fundamental status' of nationals of Member States. The second section deals in more detail with the jurisprudence of the Court with regard to the expansion of social rights granted by individual Member States to cover all Union citizens on their territory, while the third analyses the residence rights of the latter as laid down by the Union Citizens Directive of 2004. The chapter then examines, given the developments referred to in the preceding sections, whether the traditional notion of nationality is still of any relevance within the European Union today. It concludes by outlining some of the risks inherent in the Court's apparent enthusiasm for extending the scope of Union citizenship, using as an example the recent controversy in the German Federal Constitutional Court over the European Arrest Warrant.

2. The Impact of Citizenship on Freedom of Movement

When the Treaty of Maastricht introduced the new concept of Union citizenship into EC law, there were conflicting views as to whether Union citizenship has only symbolic value or whether it implies additional legal content.[3] If one looks at Article 18 of the EC Treaty,[4] describing the right of Union citizens to move freely, it seems to contain not much that is new. Freedom of movement and residence is explicitly made subject to the limitations and conditions laid down in the Treaty and by the measures adopted to give it effect. A literal interpretation, based on the wording of the Treaty, indicates that the concept of Union citizenship as such will not change the legal content of the existing rights of free movement of Union citizens, as laid down in the various regulations and directives on workers, self-employed persons, students and non-economically active persons. The idea of Union citizenship thus seems to be concerned with nothing more than legislating itself into existence.

The European Court of Justice, however, made clear very early on that it is not willing to accept a *de lege lata* description of Union citizenship as a mere restatement of existing rights. In a series of decisions, starting with *Sala*[5] and *Grzelczyk*,[6] the Court declared that 'Union citizenship is destined to be the fundamental status of nationals of the Member States', implying that, in its opinion, the principle of equal treatment extends to all citizens of the Union, subject only to such exceptions that are expressly provided for.[7] Similarly, in *Sala*, a Portuguese national,

[3] Cf., C. Hilson, 'What's in a Right? The Relationship between Community, Fundamental and Citizenship Rights in EU Law', 29 *European Law Review* (2004) p. 636 at p. 650.

[4] Loc. cit. n. 2.

[5] *Martinez Sala* v. *Freistaat Bayern*, Case C-85/96 [1998] ECR I-2691.

[6] *Grzelczyk* v. *Centre Public d'Aide Social*, Case C-184/99 [2002] ECR I-6153.

[7] Ibid., at para. 31.

who neither qualified as a worker nor as a person entitled to free movement under the 1990 Directives on the free movement of non-economically active Union citizens[8] due to the lack of sufficient resources, was nevertheless declared to be entitled to social benefits such as a child benefit.[9] The Court not only overruled its previous case-law on the subject, but, in deviation from the explicit provisions of secondary Community law, stated that all Union citizens 'lawfully' resident in the territory of the host state could rely on the non-discrimination clause of Article 12 EC (ex-Article 6);[10] this entitles them to social benefits, including benefits reserved to workers under Regulations Nos. 1408/71 and 1612/68. Before *Sala*, the Court had always carefully examined whether the conditions required for the application of secondary Community law had been fulfilled.[11]

The weak methodological approach of the Court, particularly in dealing with the relationship between primary and secondary Community law,[12] and the rudimentary reasoning it employed in introducing a new judicial approach destined not only to overturn its previous jurisprudence, but also to serve as a landmark for its future decisions, make it difficult to analyse the manner in which it has interpreted the concept of Union citizenship.

A primary reason for the new approach to free movement could be seen in the very fact that the right of residence of all Union citizens, regardless of its economic underpinnings, had been conferred by the EC Treaty on all Union citizens. As Advocate General La Pergola argued, Article 18(1) EC was granted independently as a fundamental right regardless of whether or not 'it has been made subject to limitations under other provisions of Community law, including secondary legislation'.[13] Remarkably, neither the Court nor the Advocate General have devoted any attention to the fact that Article 18 EC refers to limitations *and* conditions. In making reference to the latter, Article 18 EC is unlike any other Treaty provision on free movement. The term 'conditions' denotes, in its ordinary legal sense, that certain requirements have to be fulfilled before a right comes into existence. Limitation, on the other hand, means that an existing right can be restricted if certain requirements (such as public order exceptions) are met. Therefore, one would have expected that the Court, in such a fundamental judgment, would devote some effort to declaring this distinction irrelevant in the present context, and to justifying this decision.

---

[8] Council Directive 90/364/EEC of 28 June 1990 on the right of residence, OJ 1990 L 180/26; Council Directive 90/365/EEC of 28 June 1990 on the right of residence for employees and self-employed persons who have ceased their occupational activity, OJ 1990 L 180/28; Council Directive 93/96/EEC of 29 Oct. 1993 on the right of residence for students, OJ 1993 L 317/59 (replacing Directive 90/366/EEC of 28 June 1990, OJ 1990 L 180/30). These Directives are no longer in force.

[9] See *Sala*, loc. cit. n. 5.

[10] Ibid., at para. 63.

[11] See C. Jacqueson, 'Union Citizenship and the Court of Justice: Something New under the Sun? Towards Social Citizenship', 27 *European Law Review* (2002) p. 260 at p. 265.

[12] See K. Hailbronner, 'Union Citizenship and Access to Social Benefits', 42 *Common Market Law Review* (2005) p. 1245.

[13] See the Opinion of the Advocate General in the *Sala* case, loc. cit. n. 5, at para. 18.

A second major feature of the 'fundamental status' reasoning of the Court concerns the use of the prohibition of discrimination on grounds of nationality in close connection with Union citizenship. When the Court, in *Sala* and elsewhere, argues that the introduction of the new status of 'citizen of the Union' implies that such citizens enjoy the right, laid down in Article 12 EC, not to suffer discrimination on grounds of nationality within the scope *ratione materiae* of the EC Treaty,[14] not much seems to have been added to the existing interpretation of that Article. The true meaning of the statement, however, only becomes clear upon examination of the somewhat sparse reasoning in the Court's judgments on the scope of application of the non-discrimination principle. An analysis shows that Union citizenship as a 'fundamental status' is used to expand the scope of application of Article 12 EC. That such an expansion is justified, however, is by no means self-evident. There is nothing in the Treaty that provides, for example, for enlarged access to social benefits. There is nothing in either primary or secondary Community law to support the assumption that equal access to social benefits for non-economically active Union citizens forms an integral part of Union citizenship. This may well be the reason why the Court in *Grzelczyk* did not only rely upon Union citizenship to explain its deviation from its previous jurisprudence but also referred to the development of Community law on the issues of educational and vocational training, although that reference is hardly convincing. The Community was not granted legislative competence in these matters by the Maastricht Treaty;[15] quite on the contrary, that Treaty explicitly ruled out harmonization and integration in this field.[16] If Union citizenship as such does not change anything in terms of the responsibility of Member States for the basic welfare needs of 'their' populations, one has to ask why that same citizenship, coupled with the right to move freely from one Member State to the other, is to be recognized as a valid argument for extending the scope of the non-discrimination principle beyond the limits drawn by secondary Community law on economically and non-economically active Union citizens.

An analysis of the Court's jurisprudence reveals a third element of Union citizenship. With the exception of *Garcia Avello*,[17] the Court has used the new concept of citizenship primarily to justify access to social benefits, also indicating that it would be willing to use it as a means of enforcing the obligation of Member States to grant entry and residence rights to non-economically active Union citizens, as laid down in the three Directives of 1990. In *Grzelczyk* the Court, although not even asked to rule on the topic, stated that an expulsion measure shall not be the 'automatic' consequence of dependence of a Union citizen or his/her family member upon the social assistance system of the host Member

[14] *Sala*, loc. cit. n. 5, at para. 62.

[15] OJ 1992 C 191/1.

[16] *Jacqueson*, loc. cit. n. 11, at p. 272.

[17] *Garcia Avello* v. *État belge*, Case C-148/02 [2003] ECR I-11613 (dealing with the conflict of laws relating to the names of Union citizens of dual nationality).

State. This statement has been taken up in Article 14(3) of the new Citizens Directive 2004/38/EC,[18] although what it actually means is far from clear. Recourse to the principle of proportionality is hardly sufficient to develop criteria for the circumstances under which a Union citizen becomes an 'unreasonable burden' on the social system of the host Member State, or for deciding whether a termination of residence rights can be considered to be 'automatic'. The conclusion that, in all cases, the individual's interests have to be weighed against the public interest is hardly of much help. The Court's criteria, developed in *Grzelczyk* and subsequent decisions on social assistance for job seekers and focusing on the existence of a 'genuine link' between the person seeking work and the labour market of the Member State concerned, may be obediently taken up by the Community legislator. Whether the concept of Union citizenship is itself sufficient to ground the development of detailed criteria in this regard, as the Court has suggested, is, however, far from certain.

3. From *Grzelczyk* to *Bidar* – Equal Social Rights for Union Citizens?

One of the most important implications of the dynamic approach to the concept of freedom of movement has been the development of 'social citizenship', hitherto unknown in European Community law. Together with Article 12 EC, which prohibits any discrimination on grounds of nationality 'within the scope of application of this Treaty', and without prejudice to any special provisions contained therein, the Court has used the law on free movement to develop a concept of 'social citizenship', characterized by the right of all Union citizens, regardless of their economic activity, to take advantage of the social systems of the Member State in which they are resident. Such rights are subject to the limitations of secondary Community law (such as having sufficient means of subsistence and health insurance); these, however, have been interpreted in a restrictive manner by the Court. In a sequence of judgments, the Court relied upon Union citizenship as a means of overcoming the distinction between economically active and non-economically active citizens. In *Grzelczyk*,[19] and more recently in *Bidar*,[20] the Court awarded assistance for students, in the form of a minimum income under Belgian law and a subsidized loan under British law, to cover maintenance costs. In *Trojani*, the Court decided that a French national residing in Belgium for some time at a campsite and subsequently in a Salvation Army hostel was entitled to the Belgium *minimex*, a kind of social welfare payment, although his work for the

[18] Directive 2004/38/EC of the European Parliament and of the Council of 29 April 2004 on the right of citizens of the Union and their family members to move and reside freely within the territory of the Member States, OJ 2004 L 158/1; corrected OJ 2004 L 229/35.

[19] *Grzelczyk*, loc. cit. n. 6.

[20] *Bidar* v. *London Borough of Ealing*, Case C-209/03 [2005] ECR I-2119.

Salvation Army could clearly not be considered as work in the sense of Article 39 EC.[21] Finally, in *Collins* the Court decided that an Irish-American dual national was entitled to claim job-seekers allowance according to British law 'in view of the establishment of a citizenship of the Union and the interpretation in the case-law of the right to equal treatment enjoyed by citizens of the Union'. This entitlement was, however, made subject to the fulfilment of a residence requirement.[22] In *Ioannidis*,[23] the Court awarded unemployment benefit to a Greek looking for employment in Belgium, whose application had been refused by the Belgian authorities for the sole reason that he had carried out his professional training not in Belgium, but in Greece.

The reasoning of the Court always progresses along the same basic lines. Union citizenship is declared to be the fundamental status of nationals of the Member States, enabling those who migrate to another EU country to enjoy the same treatment in law as the nationals of that country, irrespective of their own nationality.[24] For the Court, it follows from the fundamental status of citizenship that a citizen lawfully resident in the territory of a host Member State can rely on the non-discrimination clause of the Treaty in all situations which fall within the scope *ratione materiae* of Community law. It then usually goes on to point to some provisions in the EC Treaty which illustrate that the activity in question in the case does in fact fall within that scope; with regard to students, for example, the Court referred to those measures aimed at harmonizing laws and regulations in order to encourage the mobility of students and teachers. It thus argues that the situation of such persons is within the scope of application of the Treaty (in the case of students, for the purpose of obtaining assistance in the form of a subsidized loan or a grant intended to cover maintenance costs).[25] Similarly, in the case of job-seekers, the Court argued in *Collins* that, in view of the establishment of citizenship of the Union,

> 'it is no longer possible to exclude from the scope of Article 39(2) EC – which expresses the fundamental principle of equal treatment, guaranteed by Article 6 of the Treaty – a benefit of a financial nature intended to facilitate access to employment in the labour market of a Member States'.[26]

In *Trojani*, although briefly referring to the limitations under secondary Community law, the Court held that a social assistance benefit, such as the Belgian subsistence allowance, falls within the scope of application of the non-discrimination

---

[21] *Trojani* v. *Centre public d'aide sociale de Bruxelles*, Case C-456/02 [2004] ECR I-7573.

[22] *Collins* v. *Secretary of State for Work and Pensions*, Case C-138/02 [2004] ECR I-2703.

[23] *Office national de l'emploi* v. *Ioannidis*, Case C-258/04, Europäische Zeitschrift für Wirtschaftsrecht, *EuZW* 2005 p. 663.

[24] See *Grzelczyk*, loc. cit. n. 6, at para. 31.

[25] *Bidar*, loc. cit. n. 20, at para. 42.

[26] *Collins*, loc. cit. n. 22, at para. 63.

clause of the Treaty.[27] Therefore, a citizen of the Union who is not economically active may rely on Article 12 EC when he has been lawfully resident in the host Member State for a certain time, or possesses a residence permit. In *Ioannidis*, the Court referred to the *Collins* judgment, arguing that social benefits for persons looking for employment are covered by the provisions on the free movement of workers.[28]

In the decisions mentioned, the Court has not gone as far as to declare all limitations on the principle of equal treatment to be non-existent. It has also avoided a finding that secondary Community law provisions requiring sufficient means of subsistence are void or not in accordance with Article 18 EC. Starting from the basic assumption of equal treatment, however, new limitations and conditions have been drawn, which are not necessarily identical with those already laid down by the Member States in secondary Community law.

In *Collins*, the Court points to the right of a Member State to make the grant of a job-seekers allowance dependent upon a 'genuine link' existing between the person seeking work and the employment market of that state.[29] In the case of students, a 'certain degree of integration into the society of that state' was considered as a legitimate condition before granting assistance with maintenance costs.[30] Although Belgium in *Ioannidis* was allowed to limit its social benefits on the basis of the existence of a factual connection between the host state and the Union citizen, the Court considered it inadmissible to differentiate on the basis of where a secondary education diploma had been obtained. This criterion could not, on its own, be considered as a basis for deciding the issue of whether a real and effective connection exists between a Union citizen and the labour market of the relevant host country.[31]

The most remarkable feature of the Court's reasoning is that it seems to have no hesitation in attributing to Community law a different meaning from the one that would follow from an interpretation on the basis of the objective wording of the provision, its systemic context and its purpose.[32] Union citizenship and the principle of proportionality are used to promote something that looks rather like a postulate of migration policy instead of an interpretation of relevant primary and

---

[27] *Trojani*, loc. cit. n. 21, at para. 42.

[28] *Ioannidis*, loc. cit. n. 23, at para. 22.

[29] *Collins*, loc. cit. n. 22, at para. 69.

[30] *Bidar*, loc. cit. n. 20, at para. 57.

[31] *Ioannidis*, loc. cit. n. 23, at para. 31.

[32] For a criticism of the methodology of the Court, see K. Hailbronner, 'Die Unionsbürgerschaft und das Ende rationaler Jurisprudenz durch den EuGH?' [Union citizenship and the end of a rational jurisprudence by the European Court of Justice?], *Neue Juristische Wochenschrift* (2004) p. 2185; I. Niemann, 'Von der Unionsbürgerschaft zur Sozialunion?' [From Union citizenship to a social Union?], *Europarecht* (2004) p. 946; D. Martin and K. Hailbronner, *Rights and Duties of Dual Nationals – Evolution and Prospects* (The Hague, Kluwer 2003) p. 141 et seq.; S. Bode, 'Unterhaltsbeihilfen für ausländische Studenten ohne Daueraufenthaltserlaubnis' [Subsistence benefits for foreign students without permanent right of residence], *Europäische Zeitschrift für Wirtschaftsrecht* (2005) p. 279.

secondary Community law.[33] The reasons given for the disregard of secondary Community law are frequently unconvincing. In *Grzelczyk*, the Court relied on the Preamble of Council Directive 93/96/EEC of 29 October 1993 on the right of residence for students (hereafter, the Students Directive),[34] which explicitly made reference to the previous Court's jurisprudence in order to clarify that maintenance grants for students do not fall within the scope of application of the Treaty.[35] Nonetheless, the Court took the acknowledgement in the Preamble that beneficiaries of a right to residence must not be an 'unnecessary burden' on the host state[36] as an acceptance of a 'certain degree of financial solidarity between nationals of a host Member State and nationals of another Member State'.[37]

4. The Union Citizenship Directive 2004/38/EC

Directive 2004/38/EC[38] establishes, for the first time, a single legal instrument for all Union citizens regardless of their economic activity. However, the Directive still distinguishes economically active from non-economically active Union citizens, this distinction not having been fully abandoned in favour of a uniform status of 'Union citizen'. For a period of up to three months, all Union citizens have the right of residence in any Member State, subject only to the duty to have a valid passport or identity document. However, after three months for non-economically active Union citizens, residence rights can be made dependent upon proof of sufficient means of subsistence and health insurance. The previous EU-residence permit, however, has been abolished by the right of Member States to provide for an obligatory registration of Union citizens with the competent authority of the host state, attested by a registration certificate issued to that effect.[39] For third country family relatives, the Directive allows Member States to impose an obligation to obtain a residence card for periods of residence of longer than three months.

A new provision grants a special right of permanent residence for Union citizens who have resided legally for a continuous period of five years in the host Member State.[40] This right is not subject to the general conditions laid down in Chapter III for a right of residence for more than three months (in the case of non-economically active citizens particularly, sufficient resources for themselves and their family members not to become a burden on the social assistance system). No

[33] For a more detailed analysis of the Court's jurisprudence on student maintenance grants, see Bode, loc. cit. n. 32, at p. 326.

[34] Council Directive 93/96/EEC, loc. cit. n. 8.

[35] Ibid., Preamble, Recital 7.

[36] Ibid., Recital 6.

[37] *Grzelczyk*, loc. cit. n. 6, at para. 44.

[38] Directive 2004/38/EC, loc. cit. n. 18.

[39] Ibid., Preamble, Recital 12 and Art. 8.

[40] Ibid., Art. 16(1).

agreement, however, could be reached on granting complete equality with nationals concerning protection against expulsion. Host Member States may not take an expulsion decision against Union citizens or their family members who have a right to permanent residence on their territory except on 'serious grounds of public policy or public security'.[41] One wonders what this provision means in comparison to the general requirements for the expulsion of Union citizens, whereby a person can only be expelled if his personal conduct represents a genuine, present and sufficiently serious threat to one of the fundamental interests of society.[42] The legal situation becomes even more complex if a Union citizen who has resided for the previous ten years in a host state or with a minor is expelled. In case of ten-years' previous residence there must be 'imperative grounds of public security, as defined by Member States'. In cases involving minors, the expulsion must be considered as necessary in the best interest of the child, as provided for in the UN Convention on the Rights of the Child of 20 November 1989.[43] The Member States will have to implement these provisions. Most likely they will simply copy the relevant provisions of the Directive, leaving it to their national courts to interpret these various stages of protection against expulsion, which, however, taken literally, are very similar.

With regard to residence rights of family members, the Directive provides for an option to include in this group registered partners if the legislation of the host Member State treats registered partnership as equivalent to marriage.[44] There is, however, no obligation to grant such persons free movement if the registered partners of nationals are not granted that right. As to family members in the broader sense, the Directive again does not alter greatly the existing legal situation. Member States shall, in accordance with their national legislation, facilitate entry and residence for family members, irrespective of their nationality, who, in the country from which they have come, are dependents or members of the household of the Union citizen having the primary right of residence, or where serious health grounds strictly require that the Union citizen take personal care of the family member.[45] The same rule applies with respect to partners with whom the Union citizen has a durable relationship, duly attested.[46]

Visa requirements may still be imposed upon third country family members entitled to freedom of movement. In accordance with the Court of Justice's jurisprudence in the *MRAX* case,[47] however, in the absence of the relevant visa, Member States must give such persons every reasonable opportunity to obtain the

[41] Ibid., Art. 28(2).

[42] Ibid., Art 27(2).

[43] Convention on the Rights of the Child, UNGA Res. 44/25 of 20 Nov. 1989, 1577 *UNTS* 3.

[44] Directive 2004/38/EC, loc. cit. n. 18, Preamble, Recital 5; Art. 2(2)(b); Art. 3(1).

[45] Ibid., Art. 3(2)(a).

[46] Ibid., Art. 3(2)(b).

[47] *Mouvement contre le racisme, l'antisémitisme et la xénophobie ASBL (MRAX)* v. *État belge*, Case C-459/99 [2002] ECR I-6591.

necessary documents or have them brought to them within a reasonable period of time, or to prove by other means that they are covered by the rights of free movement and residence.[48]

The Member States have tried to include the most recent jurisprudence of the Court of Justice on Union citizenship into the Directive. The Preamble repeats that Union citizenship should be the fundamental status of nationals of the Member States when they exercise their right of free movement and residence.[49] Frequently, the phraseology of the Court is taken up or repeated verbatim in the text of the Directive, regardless of the fact that a statement of a court in a particular decision is not necessarily well suited to the formulation of an abstract restatement of the law, appropriate for an unlimited number of future cases. This is particularly evident in the Directive's provisions on the access of Union citizens to social benefits.

Directive 2004/38/EC explicitly deals with the right of Union citizens to be granted social benefits under the equal treatment clause in Article 24. Member States are not, however, obliged to extend social assistance during the first three months of residence generally, or, where appropriate, for the longer period in which those seeking employment are entitled to remain, as long as they are continuing to look for work and have a genuine chance of being engaged.[50] Neither are they obliged to provide maintenance grants for studies, including student loans, prior to the acquisition of a right of permanent residence, to any Union citizens other than – according to the established jurisprudence of the Court[51] – workers, self-employed persons, persons who retain such status and members of their families.[52]

It would be premature, however, to conclude that this implies a right to terminate the residence of any non-national Union citizens who become dependent upon social welfare. Article 14 of the Directive provides that the right of residence for up to three months is retained as long as they do not become an 'unreasonable burden' on the social assistance system of the host Member State. The Preamble of the Directive provides little guidance as to the interpretation of this provision; it simply stipulates that it is left to the individual Member States to decide whether or not they will grant assistance. In reality, however, a Member State may frequently have only limited discretion in this regard, as a situation constituting an 'unreasonable burden' on the social system will be difficult to show. Under national law, Member States will generally have to provide social assistance.

---

[48] See Directive 2004/38/EC, loc. cit. n. 18, Art. 5(4).

[49] Ibid., Preamble, Recital 3.

[50] Ibid., Art. 24(2). The extension of the three month limit for those seeking employment is contained in Art. 14(4)(b).

[51] For a survey of the jurisprudence see K. Hailbronner and H. Wilms, *Recht der Europäischen Union* [The Law of the European Union], 12/2004, Art. 39 EC, No. 144-166.

[52] Directive 2004/38/EC, loc. cit. n. 18, Art. 24(2).

What criteria could be used to determine the unreasonableness of a burden? In any individual case it will hardly ever be possible to demonstrate this. The social system as such cannot be substantially affected by one additional beneficiary. 'Unreasonableness' indicates a requirement to draw a balance between private and public interests. In case of disputes, courts, however, are unlikely to have many choices other then granting a residence right to a Union citizen who is for one reason or another dependent upon social welfare.

Regarding the residence rights for Union citizens beyond the initial period of three months, Article 14 makes the 'retention' of the right dependent upon fulfilment of the conditions contained in Articles 7, 12 and 13. Again, however, this does not mean that residence may immediately be terminated if non-economically active Union citizens no longer fulfil the requirements of Article 7: an expulsion measure shall not be the 'automatic consequence' if a Union citizen or his/her family members are compelled to have recourse to the social assistance system of the host Member State.[53]

The phrase 'automatic consequence', lifted directly from the *Grzelczyk* judgment,[54] is not explained further. The Preamble uses the phrase in connection with the 'unreasonable burden' test.[55] The host Member State, therefore, should examine whether it is a case of temporary difficulties and take into account the duration of the residence, the personal circumstances and the amount of aid granted in order to consider whether the beneficiary has become an unreasonable burden on its social assistance system.

In summary, the Directive has taken up some of the ECJ's decisions concerning the consequences of Union citizenship for access to social benefits. Article 24 states that all Union citizens residing on the basis of the Directive in the territory of a host Member State shall enjoy equal treatment with the nationals of that state 'within the scope of the EC Treaty'. Notwithstanding the repetition of this limitation in terms of the scope of the EC Treaty, which is laid down in Article 12 EC, the Directive to that extent is based upon the Court's assumption that access to all social benefits, including welfare grants and maintenance grants for students, in principle falls within the scope of application of the non-discrimination clause of the EC Treaty. However, in contrast to the Court of Justice's jurisprudence, the Directive tries to maintain the traditional distinction between economically and non-economically active Union citizens, making the residence right of the latter category dependent upon proof of sufficient means of subsistence and comprehensive sickness insurance. In addition, Union citizens for the first three months of residence, and job-seekers even for a longer period, are excluded from access to social assistance. Students are not entitled to maintenance aid for studies before they acquire a right of permanent residence. These provisions will have to be interpreted in the light of the Court's jurisprudence on a 'genuine link' to the

---

[53] Ibid., Art. 14(3).

[54] *Grzelczyk*, loc. cit. n. 6, at para. 43.

[55] Directive 2004/38/EC, loc. cit. n. 18, Preamble, Recital 16.

labour market, which alone can justify different treatment of Union citizens and members of their families.

5. Unlimited Equality for Union Citizens – Is Nationality Still Relevant?

Article 12 EC prohibits discrimination on grounds of nationality of Union citizens only 'within the scope of application of this Treaty, and without prejudice to any special provisions contained therein'. While the Court has used Union citizenship to state that access to social benefits, including welfare benefits, are within the scope of application even for non-economically active persons, this does not mean that nationality has become totally irrelevant and that there is unlimited equality in the area of social rights. Secondary Community law provides for a complex system of access to social insurance benefits. Whether the 'fundamental status' of Union citizenship may be used in the future to invalidate measures providing for differential treatment remains an open question. In *Baldinger*, the exclusion of a former Austrian national from an Austrian compensation scheme for ex-prisoners of war was held to be justified.[56] The claimant had been excluded from the scheme for the sole reason that after being employed in Austria he had acquired Swedish citizenship and moved to Sweden. The Court did not even consider the issue of Union citizenship, stating categorically that the exclusion rule of Regulation 1408/71/EEC justified the differential treatment.[57]

Nationality also still determines substantially the content of the right to free movement. Article 18 EC does not require that Union citizens be granted unlimited rights of entry and residence as are nationals. Therefore, the Court's jurisprudence thus far has not challenged the differential treatment of nationals and Union citizens with regard to removal on public order grounds.[58]

The close connection between non-discrimination and Union citizenship may give rise to new questions as to whether the differential treatment of Union citizens and nationals with regard to the former's basic status as (privileged) foreigners as compared to the latter can still be maintained. In spite of the Directive 2004/38/EC rules on an EU residence permit, Union citizens are still treated differently. Whether, for example, they may be registered in a national aliens' register is an open question. The fourth European Commission report on the citizenship of the Union,[59] in 2004, identifies a number of rights of Union citizens. The

[56] *Baldinger* v. *Pensionsversicherungsanstalt der Arbeiter*, Case C-386/02 [2004] ECR I-8411.

[57] Ibid., at para. 16. See also Council Regulation 1408/71/EEC of 14 June 1971 on the application of social security schemes to employed persons and their families moving within the Community, OJ 1971 L 71/2, Art. 4(4).

[58] See *Calfa*, Case C-348/96 [1999] ECR I-11; *Orfanopoulos* v. *Baden-Württemberg* and *Oliveri* v. *Baden-Württemberg*, Cases C-482/01 and C-493/01 [2004] ECR I-5257.

[59] European Commission, *Fourth Report on Citizenship of the Union* (COM (2004) 695, 10 June 2004).

Commission notes some gaps and suggests the development of the concept of equal rights in certain non-EU countries (including Switzerland, Norway, Iceland, etc.), such as the right to vote and stand as a candidate in local elections, through agreements between the Member States and the third countries concerned.[60] In addition, Union citizens should be entitled to participate in national or regional elections of Member States in which they are resident.[61] Member States currently do not grant electoral rights at national or regional levels to nationals of other Member States residing in their territory. The Commission, however, has come to the conclusion that the problems it has identified are mostly due to bad application and incorrect practice rather than to failure of national legislation to comply with Community rules.[62]

The response of the European Parliament's Committee on Civil Liberties, Justice and Home Affairs of 15 December 2005[63] goes considerably beyond the Commission's report. It emphasizes that EU citizenship is linked, regardless of the country of birth or origin, to the granting of social rights, including the right to work and to study and the right to social protection (such as health, retirement and other benefits).[64] Therefore, all EU citizens should enjoy the same rights whether their place of residence is located within the EU or in a non-Community country.[65] In addition, EU citizenship based on residence should be the ultimate goal of a dynamic process which will make the EU a genuine political community.[66] The Committee on Constitutional Affairs adds that the great disparities between the provisions governing access to nationality in different Member States may constitute 'a source of discrimination between residents who are third country nationals or stateless on the basis of their Member State of residence'.[67]

Further questions can be raised as to the development of Union citizenship. In spite of the provision in the EC Treaty that such citizenship is not replacing but supplementing nationality, the latter will gradually lose its importance as a basis for particular political and social rights. In the absence of a clear political consensus on the future of the EU, Union citizenship may well be considered as a useful tool for the promotion of the dynamic development of the Union, about which no consensus could be reached in the cumbersome traditional treaty-amendment process.

[60] Ibid., at p. 8.

[61] Ibid., at pp. 8-9.

[62] Ibid., at p. 10.

[63] European Parliament, Committee on Civil Liberties, Justice and Home Affairs, *Report on the Commission's Fourth Report on Citizenship of the Union* (the 'Catania Report'), Doc. A 6-0411/2005. However, this report was rejected by the Parliament, by 347 votes to 276, on 17 Jan. 2006.

[64] Ibid., at p. 8, para. 23.

[65] Ibid., at p. 8, para. 24.

[66] Ibid., at p. 8, para. 28.

[67] Ibid., at p. 12, suggestion 8.

6. Free Movement and Its Risks – The Example of the European Arrest Warrant

The Council Framework Decision of 13 June 2003 on the European arrest warrant and the surrender procedures between Member States[68] describes one of its major purposes as the replacement of traditional cooperation relations by a system of free movement of judicial decisions in criminal matters covering both pre-sentence and final decisions, within an area of freedom, security and justice.[69] Citizenship, although not explicitly mentioned anywhere in the actual text, clearly forms the basis of the whole Framework Decision. With free movement of citizens within the entire territory of the EU, it seems almost a logical conclusion to abolish formal extradition procedures among the Member States in respect of persons who are fleeing from justice after having been sentenced, and arrested persons suspected of having committed an offence. One major feature of the European arrest warrant is the new procedure for the surrender of Union citizens to any other EU Member State, subject only to a number of formal requirements. The arrest warrant, according to Article 2 of the Framework Decision, may be issued for acts punishable by the law of the issuing Member State by a custodial sentence or a detention order for a maximum period of at least twelve months, or, where a sentence has been passed or a detention order has been made, for sentences of at least four months. A number of offences, if they are punishable in the issuing Member State by a custodial sentence or a detention order for a maximum period of at least three years, shall 'without verification of the double criminality of the act' give rise to surrender pursuant to a European arrest warrant. Included among the offences are

- fraud;
- computer-related crimes;
- environmental crimes;
- facilitation of unauthorized entry and residence;
- racism and xenophobia;
- swindling, counterfeiting and piracy of products, and many other crimes such as participation in a criminal organization or terrorism.

---

[68] Council Framework Decision 2002/854/JHA of 13 June 2003 on the European arrest warrant and the surrender procedures between Member States, OJ 2002 L 190/1.

[69] Ibid., Preamble, Recital 5.

The German Federal Constitutional Court, in a decision of 18 July 2005,[70] decided, on the basis of a constitutional complaint of a German-Syrian dual national subject to extradition to Spain for participation in a terrorist organization, that the German law implementing the European arrest warrant violates the fundamental rights of the Basic Law and must therefore be declared void. In the context of Union citizenship, it is worth noting that the Constitutional Court is clearly concerned about the risks involved in a Union-wide system of enforcement of judicial decisions by arrest warrants. Although the Court does not challenge the fact that German nationals may be extradited to EU Member States based on a previous constitutional amendment, it emphasizes that German nationality as laid down in Article 16 of the German Basic Law does still grant a fundamental right of protection against extradition to a foreign state. Citizenship of the EU does not justify an unlimited restriction or abolition of the duty to protect German nationals. Therefore, the Court has imposed limits on the German implementing legislation, particularly when a European arrest warrant is issued against a German national on the basis of offences committed primarily in Germany. In addition, the German legislator has to take account of the principle of proportionality in deciding whether to institute criminal proceedings in Germany or to extradite a German national to an EU Member State on the basis of a European arrest warrant.

7. Conclusion

Leaving aside the constitutional subtleties of the German implementation law, the Constitutional Court decision reveals a hitherto unknown aspect of Union citizenship. Union citizenship has been always considered as a vehicle for the ever-increasing rights of nationals of EU Member States. However, it is crucial to understand that there is no set of rights without corresponding obligations. This is most evident in the context of social rights. The attribution of social rights requires the obligation to pay a corresponding amount of taxes to maintain that system. Therefore, expanding the concept of social rights to all Union citizens regardless of any connection to a Member State, justified solely on the basis of Union citizenship, inevitably raises the question of resulting obligations. As long as Member States may freely raise or lower their own taxes and attribute the money received to social welfare, education or promotion of the labour market, it is highly doubtful whether there is in fact something like financial solidarity between the Member States as a general principle of Community law, as claimed by the Court of Justice.[71]

In addition, the risks inherent in the concept of Union citizenship, through the loss of the traditional elements of national protection, have become obvious for the first time with the European arrest warrant. The risk of being extradited on

[70] BVerfG, decision of 18 July 2005, 2 BvR 2236/04.

[71] See *supra* n. 37.

the basis of the fulfilment of certain formalities, without any further verification and subject only to the criteria that every Member State is obliged to respect fundamental rights and fundamental legal principles as enshrined in Article 6 of the Treaty on the European Union, severely restricts the traditional protection Member States have granted their own nationals against extradition requests by foreign states. There is no question that there are criminal offences that are of a transnational nature and that must be prosecuted under the same procedural and substantive rules in every EU Member State; however, the list of punishable offences in the Framework Decision, outlined above, goes far beyond this category of cases. It includes offences that may well be interpreted and defined in very different ways in different Member States. It would not even be desirable to harmonize the penal law of the EU Member States with respect to all of the offences mentioned in Article 2(2) of the Framework Decision. Thus, under traditional concepts of nationality, it would seem to be a minimum requirement of the protection owed to an EU national that there will be no extradition if the offence can be tried within the individual's own state. Whether the European Union's idea of a common space of freedom, security and justice has materialized to such an extent that the traditional elements of protection inherent in nationality have become obsolete remains yet to be seen.

To sum up, therefore, free movement of Union citizens is not for free. It has its price, and it is to the credit of the German Federal Constitutional Court that it realized that the content of Union citizenship cannot be extended without corresponding effects upon the traditional benefits bestowed by the notion of nationality.

Selected Bibliography

Bode, S., 'Unterhaltsbeihilfen für ausländische Studenten ohne Dauer-aufenthaltserlaubnis' [Subsistence benefits for foreign students without permanent right of residence], *Europäische Zeitschrift für Wirtschaftsrecht* (2005) p. 279.

Hailbronner, K., 'Die Unionsbürgerschaft und das Ende rationaler Jurisprudenz durch den EuGH?' [Union citizenship and the end of a rational jurisprudence by the European Court of Justice?], *Neue Juristische Wochenschrift* (2004) p. 2185.

—, 'Union Citizenship and Access to Social Benefits', 42 *Common Market Law Review* (2005) p. 1245.

Hailbronner, K. and H. Wilms, *Recht der Europäischen Union* [The Law of the European Union], Kommentar, Vol. I-III (Stuttgart, Kohlhammer 2006).

Hilson, C., 'What's in a Right? The Relationship between Community, Fundamental and Citizenship Rights in EU law', 29 *European Law Review* (2004) p. 636.

Jacqueson, C., 'Union Citizenship and the Court of Justice: Something New under the Sun? Towards Social Citizenship', 27 *European Law Review* (2002) p. 260.

Martin D. and K. Hailbronner, *Rights and Duties of Dual Nationals – Evolution and Prospects* (The Hague, Kluwer 2003).

Niemann, I., 'Von der Unionsbürgerschaft zur Sozialunion?' [From Union citizenship to a social Union?], 39 *Europarecht* (2004) p. 946.

Chapter 19
LEGISLATIVE HARMONIZATION IN EUROPEAN IMMIGRATION POLICY

Philippe De Bruycker*

1. Introduction

As the area of freedom, security and justice was to have come into existence on 1 May 2004, as envisaged by the Treaty of Amsterdam and the conclusions of the Tampere Summit,[1] the time for assessment has come. There are nine principal texts[2] that have been adopted in the field of immigration (seven directives, one regulation and one decision):

1. Directive 2003/86/EC of 22 September 2003 on the right to family reunification;[3]
2. Directive 2003/109/EC of 25 November 2003 concerning the status of third-country nationals who are long-term residents;[4]
3. Directive 2004/114/EC of 13 December 2004 on the conditions of admission of third-country nationals for the purposes of studies, pupil exchange, unremunerated training or voluntary service;[5]

---

* Professor and Researcher at the Institute for European Studies and the Law Faculty of the Université Libre de Bruxelles in Belgium. I wish to thank warmly Elizabeth Warn from IOM Geneva for the help she provided by revising the English language of this article. All errors remain my own.

[1] The Tampere Summit (named after the Finnish city during the Finnish Presidency of the EU) was a special meeting of the EU Heads of State and of Government entirely devoted to Justice and Home Affairs. The aim of the political conclusions was to pave the way for the implementation of the legal provisions introduced in the Treaty on the European Community by the Treaty of Amsterdam. They can be easily found on the internet <http://ue.eu.int/ueDocs/cms_Data/docs/pressData/en/ec/00200-r1.en9.htm>.

[2] See a complete list in the Commission staff working paper entitled 'The Area of Freedom, Security and Justice: assessment of the Tampere programme and future orientations – List of the most important instruments adopted'. This document available only in English (SEC (2004) 680, 2 June 2004) is unfortunately accessible at the Commission only by request from its register of documents <http://europa.eu.int/comm/secretariat_general/regdoc/recherche.cfm?CL=fr>.

[3] OJ 2003 L 251/12.

[4] OJ 2004 L 16/44.

[5] OJ 2004 L 375/12.

4. Directive 2004/81/EC of 29 April 2004 on the residence permits issued to third-country nationals who are victims of trafficking in human beings or who have been the subject of an action to facilitate illegal immigration, who cooperate with competent authorities;[6]

5. Directive 2001/40/EC of 28 May 2001 on the mutual recognition of decisions on the expulsion of third-country nationals;[7]

6. Directive 2003/110/EC of 25 November 2003 on assistance in case of transit for the purposes of removal by air;[8]

7. Decision 2004/573/EC of 29 April 2004 on the organisation of joint flights for removals from the territory of two or more Member States of third-country nationals who are subjects of individual removal orders;[9]

8. Regulation 377/2004/EC of 19 February 2004 on the creation of an immigration liaison officers network;[10]

9. Directive 2005/71/EC of 12 October 2005 on a specific procedure for admitting third-country nationals for the purposes of scientific research.[11]

The results seem significant from a *quantitative* perspective. The only failure concerns the proposed Directive on the conditions of entry and residence of third-country nationals for the purpose of paid employment and self-employment economic activities, proposed by the Commission in 2001,[12] which will no longer be considered for adoption by the Council.

It is obvious, however, that a study on the level of legislative harmonization achieved cannot be based only on a purely quantitative dimension. Hence, the first part of this contribution is dedicated to a qualitative analysis of the content of these norms. The focus of the chapter is on the domain of immigration rather than that of borders and visas, in which the legislative activity has until now been less important than the operational cooperation between the Member States. It should be recognized, however, that this situation is changing with the adoption of the Regulation establishing a Community code on the rules governing the movement of persons across borders,[13] and that a future analysis of the common consular

[6] OJ 2004 L 261/19.
[7] OJ 2001 L 149/34.
[8] OJ 2003 L 321/26.
[9] OJ 2004 L 261/28.
[10] OJ 2004 L 64/1.
[11] OJ 2005 L 289/15.
[12] COM (2001) 386, 11 July 2001.
[13] Regulation 562/2006/EC of 15 March 2006 establishing a Community Code governing the movement of persons across borders (Schengen Borders Code), OJ 2006 L 103/1.

instructions on visas for the diplomatic missions and consular posts,[14] which form the intergovernmental inheritance of the Schengen system of cooperation which still governs visa policy, could also be of interest in this regard.

The dominant opinion is that the European immigration (and asylum) policy has been a failure as far as it concerns the harmonization of Member State laws. We want to measure the extent to which this opinion can be effectively confirmed by a legal analysis of the adopted rules, so as to ensure that it is founded on a rigorous scientific analysis of their content. A general study going beyond specific commentaries dedicated to one text or another is, to our knowledge, for the moment lacking. The first part of this contribution attempts to support the widely-held view by demonstrating the different techniques utilized by the Member States in the Council of Ministers to water down the content of the Commission's proposals. The second part illustrates that the adopted norms nevertheless represent a certain degree of progress, and that they could create a few surprises for those who exaggeratedly underestimate their significance. The intention is not to undertake a detailed analysis, as this would require an exhaustive and in-depth study of a considerable number of complex texts, which goes beyond the scope of the present contribution. Instead, our goal here is more modest, namely to conduct a general review based on a list of precise examples taken from the texts, while trying to avoid generalisations which usually risk being excessive.

2. A Legislative Framework of Little Substance

Before demonstrating how the content of the Commission's proposals has been watered down by the Council of Ministers, the data presented in the introduction need some clarification as to the various legislative techniques that have been used by the Council in the absence of explicit provisions in the treaty.

2.1 The legislative techniques

2.1.1 *The lack of guidance in the Treaty*

The Treaty of Amsterdam is not explicit regarding the objective that subsequent legislative action should seek to achieve. The idea of harmonization that originally appeared in the text presented by the Irish Presidency[15] in December 1996, in the course of the Intergovernmental Conference, and also in the Commission's

[14] OJ 2003 C 310/1.

[15] See the text 'The European Union today and tomorrow: adapting the European Union for the benefit of its people and preparing it for the future, general framework for a revision of the treaties', published by the General Secretariat of the Council under the title *Intergovernmental conference in view of revision of the treaties, Semester of Irish presidency*, Collection of texts (Luxembourg, Office of Official Publications of the European Communities 1997).

proposal of October 1996 on an area of freedom, security and justice,[16] was eventually dropped. Article 63 of the Treaty Establishing the European Community[17] makes use on several occasions of the notion of 'minimum standards' concerning asylum and refugees, which evokes the idea of a legislative approximation of limited significance. The nature of the measures envisaged in Article 63 concerning immigration is not defined at all. Despite the strong political will to build a 'Common European Asylum System', which is in contradiction to the actual text of the Treaty, which refers only to minimum standards, the conclusions of the Tampere Summit of October 1999 make mention of nothing other than approximation. This is the case in point 14 concerning the rules on the recognition and content of refugee status, and in point 20 regarding national legislation on the conditions for admission and residence of third-country nationals. There is thus no evidence of any political will to harmonize the internal laws of the Member States.

The Treaty Establishing a Constitution for Europe[18] does not give any additional indication regarding the significance of the norms to adopt. The method to follow is not explicit, except in Article III-267(4), which excludes harmonization of the laws and regulations of Member State regarding the integration of third-country nationals. This is not surprising, as it represents one of the rare areas in which Member States have agreed to coordinate their action outside the context of the fight against illegal immigration.[19] The significance of this can be seen, for example, in the controversy that has surrounded the adoption of the proposal for a directive on the right to family reunification of third-country nationals, where the Council rejected the Commission's harmonization-based approach. One might be tempted to deduce from this that the harmonization of the internal laws of Member States remains the objective in the other areas of the common immigration policy. This, however, is only an *a contrario* interpretation, which is not corroborated by Article I-42 (a) of the Constitution, which states that European laws and framework laws in the area of freedom, security and justice should be adopted with the objective of approximating the laws and regulations of the Member States. It is true that the notion of approximation, which is not defined by the Treaty, is particularly vague and can in theory cover harmonization as well as other, less ambitious notions. However, the explicit rejection of harmonization in some fields, and the fact that this term is never used unless to explicitly exclude the idea, allows us to conclude that the approximation of legislation refers to a lesser ambition than that of harmonization in the area of freedom, security and justice.

[16] Unpublished Doc. CONF 3912/96, made public on 18 Sept. 1996, that was annexed to Doc. SEC (96) 2004, 29 Oct. 1996.

[17] OJ 2002 C 235/1.

[18] OJ 2004 C 310/1.

[19] See P. De Bruycker, 'L'émergence d'une politique européenne d'immigration', in P. De Bruycker (ed.), *The Emergence of a European Immigration Policy* (Brussels, Bruylant, 2003) p. 48.

2.1.2 *The instruments used in practice*

The assessment above shows clearly that the regulation is the preferred instrument in the context of borders[20] and visa policy, while the directive is used for implementing immigration policy. This is hardly surprising, as directives effectively constitute the most appropriate instrument for bringing about the approximation of legislation called for in the conclusions of Tampere. The technique of mutual recognition, which is the cornerstone of judicial cooperation, is rarely used in the field of immigration. A directive on the mutual recognition of decisions on the expulsion of third-country nationals has been adopted, but it has thus far been inoperative in practice.[21] Mutual recognition was also used in the context of short-stay visa policy on the basis of Article 10(3) of the Schengen Convention, until the introduction of the uniform visa for the territories of the State Parties.

2.2 The 'watering down' of the Commission's proposals by the Member States

An analysis of the main directives adopted in the field of immigration is instructive in this regard, especially if we compare the texts actually adopted by the Council with the Commission's original proposals (and the same could be said for the measures on asylum). The techniques used by Member States to escape from the approximation of legislation are so obvious that specialists of European law commonly consider the insertion of certain provisions as a means of undermining the legal nature of the proposed instrument. To compile a complete inventory of the techniques used by Member States in seeking to avoid possible obligations is a difficult task, as they are as numerous as they are diverse. There are, in our view, three different types of techniques, of which there are six variants, which weaken the strength of the commitments contained in the relevant directives, or even, in some cases, empty them more or less completely of their content.

2.2.1 *Techniques affecting the meaning and significance of the directives with the adoption of ambiguous or even contradictory provisions*

The Directive on the right to family reunification offers a typical example of a provision that leaves room for interpretation even concerning the identity of the holder of the right that it intends to recognize. According to Article 3(1),

[20] It is particularly worth noting that the Commission proposed a regulation and not a directive in order to establish the Community Borders Code, loc.cit. n. 13.

[21] See K. Groenendijk, 'Synthesis Report on the Transposition of the Directive on the Mutual Recognition of Decisions on the Expulsion of Third Country Nationals in the Fifteen Member States of the European Union', in J-Y. Carlier and P. De Bruycker (eds.), *Immigration and Asylum Law of the EU: Current Debates* (Brussels, Bruylant 2005) p. 181.

> 'This directive shall apply where the sponsor is holding a residence permit issued by a Member State for a period of validity of one year or more who has reasonable prospects of obtaining the right of permanent residence'.

Thus, the significance of a clear and objective criterion (the possession of a residence permit for at least one year) is immediately qualified and obscured by a subjective issue: what constitutes a 'reasonable prospect' of a right of permanent residence, bearing in mind that the directive does not intend to limit the benefits of family reunification to persons falling under the Directive on long-term residents?

2.2.2 *Techniques that weaken the significance of the directive by allowing Member States to maintain their internal law as it stands*

a) The insertion of derogations 'made to measure' for certain Member States

These provisions create the possibility for the Member States concerned to derogate from the directive, and are part of the 'optional clauses' which create the potential, rather than the obligation, to act. There are many such provisions in certain directives, to the extent that one privileged observer has detected the existence of a 'market of optional clauses' taking place during the negotiations between Member States in the Council of Ministers. He managed to count in the Directive on asylum procedures approximately fifty possible exemptions for a text of around forty articles![22] Some of these provisions, such as that which allowed Member States to refuse family reunification[23] in cases involving children of above twelve or fifteen years of age, have become famous due to the action for annulment for violation of the right to family life that the European Parliament introduced against them before the European Court of Justice.[24] It goes without saying that such clauses open up possibilities for derogation without creating any obligation for Member States, the choice between alternative courses of action being a question of political expediency.

b) A reference to national law that weakens the substance of a provision

This technique concerns provisions that remain partially legally binding, but that leave to Member States the task of specifying part of their meaning, with a margin of discretion which varies according to each case. The best examples in rela-

[22] G. Elkahim, 'Quelques remarques du point de vue du négociateur', in F. Julien-Laferrière, H. Labayle and O. Edstrom (eds.), *Bilan critique de la politique européenne d'immigration et d'asile cinq années après Amsterdam/The European Immigration and Asylum Policy: Critical Assessment Five Years After Amsterdam* (Brussels, Bruylant 2005) p. 85.

[23] See Art. 4(1), last indent, and (6).

[24] Case 540/03 (OJ 2004 C 47/21).

tion to immigration are without doubt the articles relating to access to employment[25] for family members,[26] students,[27] and long-term residents in other Member States.[28] We can find other examples in the Directive on the residence permits issued to third-country nationals who are victims of trafficking, regarding the starting point and the length of the period of reflection granted to the concerned persons to decide whether or not to cooperate with the police and judicial authorities;[29] or in the Directive concerning the status of third-country nationals who are long-term residents, regarding the consequences of delay in case of the absence of a decision on the acquisition of long-term resident status.[30]

c) The authorization given to Member States to maintain or adopt more favourable national provisions than those of the directives

While the derogations can be considered as less favourable national provisions having been judged acceptable on certain points, all the directives offer equally to Member States the possibility to adopt or to maintain national conditions or provisions that are more favourable for the persons they concern. Such provisions, which have a long pedigree in Community Law, acquire specific meaning in the field of immigration policy. On the one hand, their existence can be easily understood, since the directives adopted in this area are sometimes relatively restrictive or minimalist, it is normal that those Member States that wish to be less severe or more generous can be so; this avoids an automatic harmonization at the level of the lowest common denominator, which is much feared and denounced by NGOs and the defenders of the rights of non-citizens and refugees. On the other hand, these provisions obviously contribute to the further dismantling of the directives in which they were introduced: the impossibility of achieving an 'upwards' harmonization, combined with the will to avoid its 'downwards' counterpart, must, of course, lead to doubt as to the reality of the harmonization process itself.

2.2.3 *Techniques that distort the directive as a legal norm*

a) The deflection of certain provisions outside the operative text of the directive

Point 18 of the Preamble to the Directive on the admission of students is a good example of this technique, as it more clearly expresses the principle and the ex-

[25] See especially K. Groenendijk, 'Access of Third-Country Nationals to Employment under the New EC Migration Law', in F. Julien-Laferrière, H. Labayle and O. Edstrom, op. cit. n. 22, at p. 141.

[26] Art. 14(2) of the Directive on the right to family reunification, loc. cit. n. 3.

[27] Art. 18 of the Directive on the conditions of admission of third-country nationals for the purposes of studies, loc. cit. n. 5.

[28] Art. 14(3) of the Directive concerning the status of third-country nationals who are long-term residents, loc. cit. n. 4.

[29] Loc. cit. n. 6. See Art. 6(1), second indent, according to which 'The duration and starting point of the period referred to in the first paragraph shall be determined according to national law'.

[30] Loc. cit. n. 4. See Art. 7(2), last indent.

ception concerning the access of students to paid jobs[31] than Article 17(1) of the text, which comprises two sentences that are somewhat contradictory.[32] Likewise, the notion of 'core benefits' of assistance and social protection regarding equality of treatment in Article 11(4) of the Directive on long-term residents is defined in point 13 of the Preamble.

The Decision on the organisation of joint flights for removals of third-country nationals by two or more Member States[33] is even more interesting: the 'common guidelines on security provisions for joint removals by air' appear in an annex to the Decision, and, although Article 7 stipulates that the Member States 'shall take them into account', the Preamble specifies in its point 10 that they are 'non-binding' and 'should provide useful guidance in the implementation of this Decision'. This is one of the worst legislative techniques imaginable, because the very core of a decision that is in principle compulsory is relegated to an annex, the legal status of which is more than ambiguous. The Decision deals with some very delicate issues for states, such as the measures of coercion that can be used to remove the individuals it concerns, and this is without doubt the explanation for the weakness of its content.

b) The inclusion of non-binding provisions in the text of directives

These are certainly among the most pernicious of provisions, with many lawyers even questioning whether it is appropriate to include them in the text of directives at all, defined by Article 249 of the Treaty on the European Community as binding as to the result to be achieved but leaving to the national authorities the choice of forms and methods of implementation. Indeed, these provisions simply open up for Member States a possibility that would have existed independently anyway had they not been mentioned. Policy makers will answer that they show the road to follow, and so could have a positive effect on the Member States in the future. Even if we can understand this political perspective, lawyers will continue to be disturbed by the introduction into a legally binding text of optional provisions representing mere wishes or hopes. As a legislative technique, it is disastrous; it makes the legal significance of the text difficult to understand, and will plunge the majority of readers, who have not followed closely the process of its elaboration, into an abyss of perplexity. In fact, it is indicative of the disagreement of the Member States over the text that they have adopted.

[31] Loc. cit. n. 5. It reads 'In order to allow students who are third-country nationals to cover part of the cost of their studies, they should be given access to the labour market under the conditions set out in this directive. The principle of access for students to the labour market under the conditions set out in this directive should be a general rule; however, in exceptional circumstances Member States should be able to take into account the situation of their national labour markets'.

[32] Ibid. 'Students shall be entitled to be employed … The situation of the labour market in the host Member State may be taken into account'.

[33] Council Decision on the organisation of joint flights for removals from the territory of two or more Member States, of third-country nationals who are subjects of individual removal orders, loc. cit. n. 9.

One of the best examples comes once more from the Directive on the right to family reunification, and deals with the definition of 'family members' with whom a third-country national can reunify. According to Article 4, the 'nuclear' family comprises the spouse and the minor children, who logically benefit from the right to family reunification by virtue of paragraph 1, while the Member States *may* authorize the stay of parents and adult unmarried children unable to support themselves, or the unmarried partner of the sponsor, by virtue of paragraphs 2 and 3. We find another example in the Directive on the conditions of admission of third-country nationals for the purposes of studies, pupil exchange, unremunerated training or voluntary service, in which the compulsory provisions are limited, contrary to what the title of the Directive suggests, to students; Article 3(1) second indent specifies that 'Member States *may* also decide to apply this directive to third-country nationals who apply to be admitted for the purposes of pupil exchange, unremunerated training or voluntary service'.

The consequence of the failure of Member States to agree on the conditions that must be fulfilled in order to benefit from the right to family reunification is that they all became optional: thus, according to Article 7 of the Directive, Member States *may* require proof that the sponsor has accommodation, medical insurance and resources for his or her family. In terms of the authorization given to Member States to maintain or adopt more favourable national standards than the directives, we may well congratulate ourselves that this technique enabled us to avoid alignment on the most restrictive standards. However, the consequence of this is a complete lack of harmonization of the conditions for family reunification. The Directive pretends to set out the conditions for the exercise of the right to family reunification, but the problem is that the harmonization of these conditions is essential to any determination of whether or not such a right exists. The same applies to the mobility of long-term residents.[34]

One final example may be particularly edifying in this regard. Article 7(4) of the Directive on the residence permit issued to third-country nationals who are victims of trafficking reads as follows: 'The Member States *may* provide the third-country nationals concerned with free legal aid, *if established and under the conditions set by national law*'. This is an example of a non-binding text referring twice to national law for its implementation.

3. A Failure to Moderate

Confronted with the break-up of the Commission's proposals by Member States in the Council of Ministers as described above, the Community institutions have reacted by trying to preserve the substance of the immigration policy as much as possible. However, if it is the failure, rather than the success, of the harmoniza-

[34] See Art. 15 of the Directive concerning the status of third-country nationals who are long-term residents, loc. cit. n. 4.

tion process that must be measured, this is not the consequence of these quite desperate efforts, but rather of the unexpected consequences that the adopted directives will have.

3.1 Attempts at remedial action by Community institutions

Confronted with the blocking tactics of the Justice and Home Affairs Ministers, the European Council has been forced to intervene in order to preserve the political dynamic of the programme that it adopted at the Tampere Summit of December 1999; the Commission itself tried to limit as much as possible the potentially perverse effects that the most restrictive provisions of the directives could have, and to put in place a mechanism aimed at restarting the debate over the desired level of harmonization in the future.

3.1.1 *Intervention by the European Council in the decision-making process*

Since the Tampere summit, which was especially devoted to Justice and Home Affairs matters and underlined from the outset the important role of the European Council in this field, the Council has continued to fundamentally direct immigration policy. It has successively adopted a number of conclusions, in particular during its meetings in Laeken of December 2001, Seville of June 2002 and Thessaloniki of June 2003, in which it went into greater detail regarding the direction that it intends to pursue.

The European Council felt that it had to intervene to fix a deadline for the Council of Ministers regarding the adoption of texts regarding asylum,[35] and even to urge the Commission to present a modified proposal for the Directives on asylum procedures and on family reunification, and for the 'Dublin II' Regulation.[36] Regarding family reunification, the aim was to unblock a text upon which the Council of Ministers could not reach an agreement. The Commission was therefore politically obliged, despite its legal independence, to draft a compromise text on the issue. This underlines its central role in the decision-making process, even in cases in which the Council of Ministers decides on the basis of unanimity. The decision by the European Parliament to challenge the Directive on the right to family reunification before the Court may have raised some issues of 'paternity' in this regard, the question being whether or not the Commission was obliged or not to support the position of the Council. Even if these interventions by the European Council do not directly influence the content of the text adopted, they deserve mention because of their importance in the process of adopting directives. When the directives come to be interpreted, an analysis of the different versions

[35] See point 37 of the Seville Conclusions (21-22 June 2002; *Bulletin EU* 6-2002).

[36] See point 41 of the Laeken Conclusions (14-15 Dec. 2001; *Bulletin EU* 12-2001). For discussion of the Directive on asylum procedures and the 'Dublin II' Regulation, see the chapter by Byrne in this volume.

of the text (the original proposal from the Commission, possibly a modified proposal and the text finally adopted by the Council) can therefore be illuminating.

3.1.2 *The introduction of stand-still clauses*

The introduction by Member States of derogations allowing them to clearly maintain less favourable national provisions than the general rule has created the risk of perverse effects, in that certain Member States could be tempted to align their legislation with the lowest standard. Thus, the adoption of the directives could, paradoxically, have the effect of increasing the disparity between the laws of Member States rather than bringing them closer together.

The Commission was, for the first time, confronted by this situation during the negotiations over the proposal for a Directive on the right to family reunification. Taking a position opposite to the one it adopted in the context of the amendments proposed by the European Parliament,[37] it suggested, in its second modified proposal, following a new approach based on flexibility, the introduction of limited derogations combined with a standstill clause to ensure that Member States would not abuse the possibility to derogate.[38] The Member States not only limited the scope of the standstill clause, but also changed the date for its entry into force. The Commission had proposed that it should take effect from the date of adoption of the Directive by the Council; the Member States, however, decided that it should do so only from the later date of the Directive's transposition. A standstill clause has also been introduced in the Directive on the status of third-country nationals who are long-term residents.[39]

3.1.3 *Provisions requiring the Commission to report on the implementation of directives ('appointment' or 'rendez-vous' clauses)*

Directives generally contain, among their final clauses, a provision envisaging that the Commission will report to the Council and the Parliament on their application by Member States and propose the necessary modifications should difficulties appear. When it became clear that the right to family reunification would not be harmonized, the Commission projected itself into the future, with the hope that harmonization would be possible at a later stage with the adoption of a new Directive. It is in this perspective that the Commission envisaged using the report on the application of the adopted directive, to be presented at the latest on 3 October 2007, as an 'appointment clause'; the idea is that the proposals for changes that could be formulated in that report will, as a priority, target the provisions affording Member States maximum flexibility.

---

[37] See the first modified proposal for a Directive on the right to family reunification (COM (2000) 624, 10 Oct. 2000) p. 4.

[38] COM (2002) 225, 2 May 2002, p. 3. The proposed standstill clause appears in Art. 3(6).

[39] Loc. cit. n. 4. See Art. 14(4).

3.2 Directives as vectors for change

The failure of the process of harmonization must be evaluated within a general context where different factors can intervene. Apart from the fact that the directives will automatically have an effect on political debate due to the necessity of transposing their content into national law, and that they were adopted into an enlarged European Union more diverse than we are yet fully aware of, they include, after all, some rather important innovations, and, moreover, risk producing some somewhat unexpected effects.

3.2.1 *The effect of boosting or releasing political debate at the national level*

The transposition of the directives adopted in the field of immigration can be seen as a mid-term process. Looking only to the more important texts, this process began with the obligation for Member States to transpose the Directive on the right to family reunification by October 2005, will continue with the Directive on the status of third-country nationals who are long-term residents (which was to be transposed by January 2006), and end in January 2007 with the Directive on the conditions of admission of third-country nationals for the purposes of studies. While the European agenda has been curiously influenced during the negotiation of the Directives by the continuous new developments in the endless debate over reform of the law on immigration in Germany, the governmental and parliamentary agenda regarding immigration at the national level will be largely dictated by the European Union in the next two years. This natural consequence of the progressive emergence of a common immigration policy should not be underestimated, because it will influence the political debate on the question of admission, which remains effectively taboo in certain Member States.

3.2.2 *The limitation effect of the growing diversity of Member States' internal legal order*

It is a very obvious fact that the European Union has become even more diverse[40] with the admission of ten new Member States on 1 May 2004, and that this diversity will grow in the coming years with the continuation of the process of enlargement. Nobody can today really evaluate the importance of the legal changes that the adoption of the new Directives has already brought about, or will imply, for the new Member States in the field of immigration. None of the Directives concerned were part of the Community *acquis* that the ten new Member States had to have transposed into their national legal systems as a whole by the date of their

[40] See on this subject J. Monar, 'Maintaining the Justice and Home Affairs Acquis in an Enlarged Europe', in J. Apap, *Justice and Home Affairs in the EU, Liberty and Security after Enlargement* (Cheltenham, Elgar Publishing 2004) p. 37.

entry. Even those norms that are apparently minimal for the 'old' Member States can require substantial changes from those that have just joined the European Union, which are not yet countries of immigration and where the legal framework in the field is sometimes limited, for obvious reasons.

3.2.3 *The effect of deepening 'legalization' of immigration issues*

Furthermore, the emergence of a common policy for immigration creates, at the European level, a new series of norms that did not exist before. It will not escape the notice of lawyers specialized in migration that these norms cover matters that were previously only subject to jurisprudence, administrative circulars or even practices. This development gives rise to what may be called a process of increasing 'legalization' of the question of immigration.

Article 17 of the Directive on the right to family reunification offers a good example of this phenomenon. This provision integrates into the text the jurisprudence developed by the European Court of Human Rights on the right to family life by specifying its scope of application. According to this provision,

> 'Member States shall take due account of the nature and solidity of the person's family relationships and the duration of his residence in the Member State and the existence of family, cultural and social ties with his/her country of origin where they reject an application, withdraw or refuse to renew a residence permit or decide to order the removal of the sponsor or members of his family'.

It is noteworthy that Member States will, on the basis of this text, have to take into account those criteria for the rejection of an application for family reunification, even though there are still some doubts about the application of the jurisprudence of the European Court of Human Rights, which deals mainly with expulsion cases, to the question of admission.

3.2.4 *Innovations in the framework of harmonization*

The idea of harmonization hides a series of new elements that cannot be neglected if the significance of the adopted Directives is to be objectively evaluated.

The Directive on a specific procedure for admitting third-country nationals for the purposes of scientific research is certainly the most remarkable. It creates a special procedure of admission for researchers based on collaboration between the state authorities in charge of immigration and the relevant research institutions, in order to facilitate and accelerate their admission with a view to helping to fill the gaps in scientific personnel, which will be needed if the Lisbon agenda is to be realized. The Directive on the residence permit issued to third-country nationals who are victims of trafficking in human beings or who have been the subject of an action to facilitate illegal immigration, who cooperate with the competent authorities is also worth noting. Despite the justified criticism that will certainly be raised as to its content, this Directive has its merits in that it provides a mechanism for 22[41] EU Members to fight organized crime by helping victims, originally based on experiences with similar, limited schemes in some Member States. Further, the new possibilities of mobility that the Directive concerning the status of third-country nationals who are long-term residents offers to those it concerns in the whole EU cannot be ignored. The same applies for students under Article 7 of the Directive on the conditions of admission of third-country nationals for the purpose of studies. The critics may rightly argue against these overly restrictive provisions, which are on certain essential points[42] in contradiction with the objectives of the EU regarding mobility, but they should not make us forget that these are the first steps of a possibly progressive extension of the right to free movement from European citizens to third-country nationals. Even the Directive on the right to family reunification, which became the emblematic text for illustrating the difficulties in the process of harmonization of the law on non-nationals at the European level, includes provisions that will have concrete repercussions in favour of third-country nationals. Article 5(4) fixes a maximum time limit of nine months for the response to an application for family reunification; while this may seem rather lengthy, it must be taken into account that this provision covers also the delivery of long-term visas for the first entry into the territory, for which, in some Member States, no deadlines currently apply.

Certain innovations are not compulsory, and are based on the technique of reference to the national law of the Member States. Two examples can be found in the Directive on the conditions of admission for the purpose of studies. Firstly, it introduces at the European level a legal basis for the admission of third-country nationals for the purpose of voluntary service, which is very often lacking in the internal law of Member States, and the absence of which can create problems for volunteers who find themselves assimilated under categories of people (workers or trainees) for whom the conditions of admission are not appropriate to their special case. Secondly, it seeks, in Article 19, to spread as widely as possible the best practices of certain Member States that aim to accelerate the procedure of admission for students and pupils, by creating a legal basis in Community law for collaboration agreements to be concluded between the authority of the Member State competent for migration and education institutions or organizations operating pupil exchange schemes.

[41] Denmark, the United Kingdom and Ireland in principle do not participate, because of the existing differentiation in the area of freedom, security and justice in the application of Title IV of Part 3 of the EC Treaty.

[42] As, for example, the right of long-term residents to reside in the other Member States as workers, recognized in Art. 14 of the Directive (loc. cit. n. 4), does not seem to have any real added value in comparison to the current rules that Member States apply to ordinary non-citizens.

3.2.5 *Unexpected legal effects in a system in the process of complete communitarization*

While it is true that Member States have tried to limit as much as possible the significance of the Directives adopted by using the techniques we have listed above, it should nevertheless not be concluded that they have been entirely emptied of all content. On the contrary, the necessity of reaching a compromise between certain Member States seeking harmonization without changes and others trying to promote a text with a certain European added value resulted, as emphasized above, in the ambiguous wording of certain provisions. Moreover, as is usually the case in such contexts, the Directives sometimes contain highly detailed provisions and prove to be, in the end, extremely complicated texts. The probability is high that such directives, leaving much open to interpretation, will generate a number of legal conflicts. The curious techniques of drafting legislation privileged by the Member States in certain cases risk introducing unexpected consequences and undesired effects when transposed to and implemented at the national level. Such an eventuality is more likely since the institutional framework in which these directives are adopted has entered into a process of increasing 'communitarization', which means that the Europeans norms can be the object of legal actions at the Community level, which has proved to be effective in the hands of the Commission, litigants, and, finally, the judge.

4. Conclusion

The European Commission, in its Communication on the assessment of the Tampere programme, concluded that

> 'it is clear that the successes that have been achieved are considerable. However, the original ambition was limited by institutional constraints, and sometimes also by a lack of sufficient political consensus. The step by step approach was often the only possible way of moving forward'.[43]

In a complementary working document annexed to this Communication, the Commission noted that Member States are sometimes reluctant to cooperate in this new European field, and, when their interests are concerned, they do not hesitate to use their veto to lower the level of ambition of the Commission's proposals and to reject the views of the European Parliament.[44] More specifically concerning immigration, the Commission considered that the 'progress has fallen short of initial ambitions and the assessment must be qualified'.[45] It is regrettable

43 COM (2004) 401, 2 June 2004, p. 5.

44 Working Document SEC (2004) 693 attached to the specified communication, p. 9.

45 Ibid., at p. 14.

that this 'qualified assessment' concerning 'considerable successes' tainted by a 'limited ambition' was not accompanied by a thorough evaluation of the whole community *acquis* in the field. Nonetheless, the qualitative analysis carried out in this chapter corroborates the Commission's conclusion.

The failure to harmonize is blatant, even to the point where the primacy of Community law over national law in the field of immigration can be questioned. Due to the multiple techniques used by Member States to empty the directives of their content on key points, this basic principle of Community law in fact proves to be extremely relative in this area. This result should not, however, come as a surprise, given that Member States did not accept in the Treaty of Amsterdam the objective of legislative harmonization, and that it also does not appear in the project for a Constitutional Treaty, despite the remarkably more ambitious objectives fixed for the European Union therein.

The nature of European immigration policy may be called into question due to the weakness of the legislative framework, which leads us to ask whether, and to what extent, that policy can be considered at all 'common'. The directives that have been adopted risk becoming part of a legislative decor for a European scene from which Member States, faced with a public awaiting action on one of the more politically sensitive areas, will hypocritically try to benefit from the 'merits' of a common policy devoid of any real substance. Such judgment must, however, be qualified, as other means of action exist at the European level, especially the operational coordination between Member States in the Council of Ministers regarding the fight against illegal immigration, the management of external borders and the return of third country nationals staying illegally.[46] Coordination is precisely one of the techniques which can be used to endow a policy with a certain content. It is crucial to recall that the European Commission proposed to make use of the open method of coordination in the field of immigration, in a Communication[47] that the Member States have, until now, ignored. The result is that the area of legal immigration is characterized by a weak legislative framework without coordination, with the exception of the field of integration of third country nationals (where the Commission's suggestion was even endorsed by the project for a Constitutional Treaty)[48] and the fields of the fight against illegal immigration and border management in which it predominates, albeit following a model different to that proposed by the Commission. The simultaneous rejection of both a substantial legislative harmonization, and the coordination that could partly compensate for its weaknesses, finally calls into question the genuine intent of Member States to develop a common policy on legal immigration, despite the strong expressions of political will evident in the European Council's Conclusions, which now appear more and more as mere pious wishes or incantatory formulas. It is, however, too early to gauge these emergent policies; these

[46] See P. De Bruycker, loc. cit. n. 19, at pp. 59-79.

[47] COM (2001) 387, 11 July 2001.

[48] Loc. cit. n. 18, Art. 267(4).

should be evaluated in the long-term, in particular on the basis of the boost that the new multi-annual programme, The Hague Programme (adopted by the European Council in November 2004),[49] could give them, even if the failure of the Constitution will deprive it of some of the legal bases it needs to develop fully. It is nevertheless clear that a gulf often separates the somewhat ambitious Conclusions of the European Council and their concrete implementation by the Council of Ministers in the field of Justice and Home Affairs.

How to explain this loss of substance that the policy suffers between these two bodies? The requirement of unanimity, often presented as the main cause, does not seem to be the only factor. One can wonder whether there are not deeper reasons, linked to the justifications of legislative harmonization, which do not always appear clearly. We cannot avoid being struck by the weakness of the arguments developed by the Commission in support of its main legislative proposals to justify its harmonizing ambitions. As far as family reunification is concerned, the Commission has indicated that its first proposal for a directive sought to harmonize the laws of Member States for two main reasons:

> 'Third-country nationals are to be eligible for broadly the same family reunification conditions, irrespective of the Member State in which they are admitted for residence purposes. And the possibility that the choice of the Member State in which a third-country national decides to reside will be based on the more generous terms offered there must be restricted'.[50]

Apart from the fact that the first argument does not demonstrate anything, it is doubtful whether migrants really choose their destination Member State because of the benefits that its internal legal framework could later offer them in terms of the reunification of their family. It can even be questioned whether the basic idea of the necessity of a common migration policy as a measure to compensate for the suppression of internal border controls, which has justified the progressive allocation of competences to the European Community since the adoption of the European Single Act in 1986,[51] should not be re-evaluated with regard to the realities of the mobility of third-country nationals in Europe. It could thus be that the fact that the usefulness of legislative harmonization in the field of legal immigration is not immediately apparent could constitute one supplementary element explaining the relative failure of the process. Contrast the success of operational coordination in the fight against illegal immigration, which meets the governments' more immediate concerns, and finds a more concrete justification with less costs and more benefits in terms of more efficiency and the necessary solidarity regarding the unequal burdens borne by Member States according to their geographical position.

[49] OJ 2005 C 53/1.

[50] COM (1999) 638, 1 Dec. 1999, point 7.4.

[51] OJ 1987 L 169/1.

It is possible to predict, as the Commission has done, that a second generation of rules will be adopted in the future to give more substance to the common policy. Indeed, a new generation of texts has been planned since very early on in the field of asylum, meaning that the Treaty of Amsterdam, which authorized only the adoption of 'minimum standards', was overtaken as soon as it had entered into force by the ambition of the Tampere conclusions to build not only a common asylum policy but also a 'Common European Asylum System'. Despite the fact that Member States will only have started to apply the first generation of directives, the Hague Programme has effectively planned the adoption of the second phase instruments and measures before the end of 2010. A similar evolution is not, however, planned regarding immigration. On the contrary, as noted at the beginning of this chapter, the Commission's proposal for a directive regarding economic immigration has not been adopted by the Council. The EU appears, at present, to be not yet ready to accept binding rules regarding the most sensitive form of immigration. In trying to resolve this deadlock, and after having published a Green Paper on an EU approach to managing economic migration,[52] the Commission was invited by the Hague Programme to present 'a policy plan on legal migration including admission procedures capable of responding promptly to fluctuating demands for migrant labour in the labour market before the end of 2005'.[53] Even if it will be necessary to carefully assess what the Commission has proposed, it seems that the European project nurtures fewer ambitions in the field of immigration in comparison with that of asylum. One can only speculate as to whether the Member States will easily withdraw from the somewhat minimalist choices that they have succeeded in imposing thanks to the requirement of unanimity for the adoption of the first directives.

Independently from this future political process, whose outcome it is impossible to predict, it appears that the legal dynamic launched with the adoption of the first directives will be more important than anticipated. Firstly, because the directives will have a greater impact than foreseen on certain Member States, it is necessary to take into account some of the innovations that they contain. Secondly, they contribute to a deeper 'legalization' of immigration issues; and some of their provisions will have consequences all the more unexpected because they will intervene within a legal framework in the process of complete 'communitarization', in which the rule of law and the judge will play a more important role. The hope is that this legal process will develop in interaction with the political process, and prevent the common immigration policy from falling into a debate tainted by litigation before courts and tribunals. If the latter is nevertheless to be the case, this situation will be largely due to the procrastination and hesitation of the political actors in the process of elaboration of the directives.

---

[52] COM (2004) 811, 11 Jan. 2005.

[53] Hague Programme, loc. cit. n. 49, Point 1.4. The Policy Plan was published in December 2005. See European Commission, *Policy Plan on Legal Migration* (COM (2005) 669, 21 Dec. 2005).

Selected Bibliography

Carlier, J-Y. and P. De Bruycker (eds.), *Immigration and Asylum Law of the EU: Current Debates* (Brussels, Bruylant 2005).

De Bruycker, P. (ed.), *The Emergence of a European Immigration Policy* (Brussels, Bruylant 2003).

Guild, E. and C. Harlow, *Implementing Amsterdam: Immigration and Asylum Rights in EC Law* (Oxford, Hart Publishing 2001).

Hailbronner, K., *Immigration and Asylum Law and Policy of the European Union* (The Hague, Kluwer Law International 2000).

Julien-Laferrière, F., H. Labayle and Ö. Edström (eds.), *La politique européenne d'immigration et d'asile: bilan critique cinq ans après le traité d'Amsterdam/The European Immigration and Asylum Policy: Critical Assessment Five Years After the Amsterdam Treaty* (Brussels, Bruylant 2005).

Chapter 20
MOVING FREELY ON THE AFRICAN CONTINENT: THE EXPERIENCES OF ECOWAS AND SADC WITH FREE MOVEMENT PROTOCOLS

Jonathan Martens*

1. Introduction

Sub-regional and regional integration, and the free movement of people as a means of achieving these, have been features of the contemporary political landscape in Africa since 1957, when Ghana became the first African country to achieve independence from colonial rule. Today, the continent hosts 14 sub-regional integration schemes and, of these, the Common Market for East and Southern Africa (COMESA), the East African Community (EAC), the Economic Community of Central African States (ECCAS), the Economic Community of West African States (ECOWAS), the Southern African Development Community (SADC), and the West African Economic and Monetary Union (UEMOA) have protocols, articles or objectives in their treaties promoting visa-free movement, and the corresponding rights of residence and establishment.[1] In its 2004 report, *Accelerating Regional Integration in Africa*, the UN Economic Commission for Africa (UNECA) identified ECOWAS and SADC as two of Africa's most promising sub-regional organizations, which, together with UEMOA, had achieved an 'above average' integration rating of at least 6 per cent between 1994 and 1999.[2] Both ECOWAS and SADC have also experimented with protocols on free movement, and the corresponding rights of residence and establishment. Despite their relative success with the integration process, however, neither has completely succeeded in realizing the common objective of free movement. The purpose of this chapter, then, is to offer a comparative analysis of the progress made towards the free movement of persons within Africa from the perspective of these two key sub-regional organizations.[3]

* Graduated from the University of Winnipeg (1996) and the Faculty of Law at McGill University in Montreal (2000) before joining the IOM in Bosnia as Legal Programme Development Officer.

[1] UN Economic Commission for Africa (UNECA), *Accelerating Regional Integration in Africa* (Addis Ababa, UNECA 2004) p. 198 <www.uneca.org/aria>.

[2] Ibid., at p. 231.

[3] ECOWAS and SADC have been designated as two of the five regional pillars of the African

R. Cholewinski, R. Perruchoud and E. MacDonald, eds., International Migration Law

2. Sub-regional Building Blocks of the Pan-African Vision

Whether moving in pursuit of greater opportunity, or as the result of catastrophe, Africans have moved throughout the continent with considerable freedom even after the fixed boundaries of nation-states were imposed by European colonial powers in the late 1800s. The colonial borders were largely arbitrary, dividing families, clans and ethnic groups, but they were not policed with particular effectiveness in most places, and it was colonial industrialization more than its artificial frontiers that changed traditional patterns of human movement in Africa for much of the following century. Independence brought with it new notions of an African identity, and competing visions for the future of the continent. Ghana was the first African country to achieve independence from European colonial rule and its President, Kwame Nkrumah, championed a 'United States of Africa' version of pan-African unity:

> 'If we are to remain free, if we are to enjoy the full benefits of Africa's rich resources, we must unite to plan for our total defence and the full exploitation of our material and human means in the full interests of our peoples. To go it alone will limit our horizons, curtail our expectations, and threaten our liberty'.[4]

While supportive of the pan-African ideal, other influential leaders, such as Tanzanian President Julius Nyerere, argued that African unity would be more sustainably achieved in stages, and that viable sub-regional economic groups were the necessary building blocks. The Organization for African Unity (OAU), which was established in 1963, would come to reflect this latter view, and incorporate as an objective the principle of economic cooperation as a strategy for development.[5] By the 1970s, regional integration was well under way with the formation of Africa's first sub-regional economic groups, including ECOWAS in 1975. In 1980, Nyerere's vision found expression in the Lagos Plan of Action,[6] in which OAU Member States committed themselves to reinforcing existing sub-regional economic groupings, and supporting the establishment of new ones, as the building blocks for their eventual assembly as the African Economic Community (AEC). Despite this initiative, the pace of integration was slower than expected, with the sub-regional schemes evolving at different speeds. In 1991, in Abuja, Nigeria, the OAU Heads of State and Government signed the Treaty Establishing the African Economic Community (hereafter, the Abuja Treaty) in hopes of spurring integra-

Economic Community (AEC). The remaining three pillars are COMESA, ECCAS, and the Inter-Governmental Authority on Development (IGAD). See <http://www.sec.ecowas.int>.

4 Kwame Nkrumah, quoted in M. Nyirabu, 'Appraising Regional Integration in Southern Africa', 13(1) *African Security Review* (2004) p. 21.

5 Ibid., at p. 22.

6 OAU, Lagos Plan of Action for the Economic Development of Africa 1988-2000 <http://www.uneca.org/itca/ariportal/docs/lagos_plan.pdf>.

tion by setting the targets of 2014 as the year by which each of the sub-regional organizations would meet the requirements of a free trade area, and 2025 as the year for the creation of the AEC.[7]

ECOWAS and SADC are two of the sub-regional building blocks considered key to the assembly of the AEC. Both ECOWAS, with 15 Member States, and SADC, which has 14, have experimented with free movement protocols as means to advance sub-regional integration, but historical, political and economic differences and disparities between the Member States of these sub-regional groups have yielded mixed results.

3. Free Movement and ECOWAS

3.1 Migration patterns in West Africa

According to Adepoju, 'migrants have always considered West Africa as an economic unit within which people, trade in goods and services flowed freely',[8] and while the political borders imposed by European colonial powers did little to interrupt these flows, colonialism did transform West African migration patterns. Historically, human movements within the sub-region were most consistent between areas with social or cultural similarities, and where geography made for easier passage. While colonial powers imposed borders that generally favoured European political and economic interests rather than reflecting African social and cultural realities, they were difficult to police. More disruptive to West African migration patterns than these borders were the colonial industrial projects that required significant amounts of cheap labour. Since then, migrant workers have been drawn generally from the interior of the sub-region, from countries such as Burkina Faso and Mali, to the industrial centres along the coast, particularly to Ghana, Côte d'Ivoire, Senegal and, most notably in the post-independence era, Nigeria. Much of this movement has been undocumented and, when economic conditions in these receiving countries were favourable, largely unnoticed. But as these economic hubs suffered post-independence setbacks – Ghana in the 1960s, Nigeria in the 1980s, and Côte d'Ivoire in the 1990s – governments of migrant receiving states often responded to public sentiment by attempting to protect their labour markets from non-citizens.[9]

---

[7] Treaty Establishing the African Economic Community, 3 June 1991, reprinted in 30 *International Legal Materials* (1991) p. 1241, Art. 6(2)(c).

[8] A. Adepoju, 'Creating a Borderless West Africa: Constraints and Prospects for Intra-Regional Migration', Draft Article of the *Migration Without Borders* Series (UNESCO, 1 Jan. 2005) Doc. SHS/2005/MWB/1 at p. 1 <http://unesdoc.unesco.org/images/0013/001391/139142e.pdf>.

[9] A. Adepoju, 'Fostering Free Movement of Persons in West Africa: Achievements, Pitfalls and Prospects for Intra-Regional Migration', 40 *International Migration* (2002) p. 12.

Migration patterns continue to change in West Africa, and where they were once described accurately as 'short-term, male dominated and over long distances',[10] they have begun to assume a more diverse character. In the globalized era, West African migrants are not all 'labour migrants'; many may be better described as 'commercial migrants' because of their tendency to be self-employed in the informal sector, instead of wage earners in the formal one.[11] Among the more noticeable trends, and one that is in line with global patterns, is the feminization of migration, with West African women more on the move as both professionals and low-skilled workers than previously. West Africans are also migrating well beyond the borders of the sub-region, where the traditional receiving countries have become source and transit countries for those moving to Europe and North America, as well as to post-apartheid South Africa.

3.2 The ECOWAS free movement protocol

ECOWAS was formed with the signing of the ECOWAS Treaty in Lagos, Nigeria, on the 28 May 1975,[12] and was one of the earliest sub-regional integration schemes in West Africa. The *Communauté économique de l'Afrique de l'Ouest* (CEDEAO) preceded ECOWAS, having been established in 1973, and counted as Member States much of French-speaking West Africa, but for Benin and Guinea. The CEDEAO underscored the divide between Francophone and Anglophone West Africa, and was thought at the time to present a significant obstacle to the formation of a broader, more inclusive configuration. This concern, however, proved unfounded as 15 states, including Côte d'Ivoire, as well as Benin and Guinea, supported the establishment of ECOWAS. [13]

The 1975 Treaty establishing the Economic Community of West African States (hereafter, the ECOWAS Treaty) sought

> 'to promote cooperation and development in all fields of economic activity, particularly in the fields of industry, transport, telecommunications, energy, agriculture, natural resources, commerce, monetary and financial questions and in social and cultural matters for the purpose of raising the standard of living of its peoples, of increasing and maintaining economic stability, of fostering closer relations among its members and of contributing to the progress and development of the African continent'.[14]

The ECOWAS Treaty also identified as an objective the abolition of any obstacles to the free movement of, *inter alia*, people between Member States[15] and,

---

[10] Adepoju, loc. cit. n. 8.

[11] Ibid.

[12] Treaty establishing the Economic Community of West African States, 28 May 1975, 1010 *UNTS* 17.

[13] A. Richardson, 'ECOWAS After Nearly 28 Years', *Daily Graphic* (4 March 2004) at pp. 1-2.

[14] ECOWAS Treaty, loc. cit. n. 12, Art. 2(1).

[15] Ibid., Art. 2(2)(d).

in Article 27, it reinforced this ambition by identifying automatic Community citizenship for all nationals of Member States as a goal.

By May 1979, as a result of the momentum created by the ECOWAS Treaty, the Community had negotiated its Protocol Relating to Free Movement of Persons and the Right of Residence and Establishment (hereafter, the 1979 Protocol).[16] The 1979 Protocol identified a phased approach through which free movement in the sub-region should be achieved, and committed State Parties to complete the process over a 'maximum transitional period of fifteen (15) years from the definitive entry into force of this Protocol'.[17] During Phase I, Parties were to drop visa requirements, allowing Community citizens to enter and stay in any Member State for up to 90 days provided they were in possession of valid travel documents and an international health certificate.[18] Member States nonetheless retained their sovereign right to deny entry to Community citizens determined to be inadmissible under existing national law.[19] They also retained their sovereign right of expulsion, but were required to notify both the government of which the person to be expelled was a citizen and the ECOWAS Executive Secretary, and they committed themselves to protecting the security of the person involved, and his or her family and property.[20] A further condition was the requirement that a Community citizen seek permission if he or she wishes to extend his or her stay in another Member State beyond 90 days.[21]

The 1979 Protocol was ratified in 1980, and national committees were established in a majority of Member States to monitor implementation of ECOWAS decisions and protocols on the free movement of persons and vehicles. Since then, several concrete measures have been implemented to further ease free movement in the sub-region. In 1982, ECOWAS established the Brown Card Motor Vehicle Insurance Scheme, to provide motor vehicles travelling between participating Member States with insurance coverage ensuring 'at least the same guarantees as those required by the laws in force in the territory of each of the parties'.[22] Perhaps even more significant has been the introduction of the ECOWAS travel certificate in 1985, which was intended to exempt its bearers from the requirement of completing immigration and emigration forms when travelling

[16] ECOWAS Protocol A/P.1/5/79 Relating to Free Movement of Persons, Residence and Establishment, 29 May 1979 <http://www.sec.ecowas.int/sitecedeao/english/ap010579.htm>.

[17] Ibid., Art. 2(2).

[18] Ibid., Art. 3(1) and (2).

[19] Ibid., Art. 4.

[20] Ibid., Art. 11(1), (2) and (3). See also the ECOWAS Supplementary Protocol A/SP.1/7/85 on the Code of Conduct for the Implementation of the Protocol on Free Movement of Persons, the Right of Residence and Establishment, 6 July 1985 <http://www.sec.ecowas.int/sitecedeao/english/asp010785.htm>, Art. 3.

[21] 1979 ECOWAS Protocol, loc. cit. n. 16, Art. 3(2).

[22] ECOWAS Protocol A/P1/5/82 on the Establishment of an ECOWAS Brown Card Relating to Motor Vehicle Third Party Liability Insurance, 29 May 1982 <http://www.sec.ecowas.int/sitecedeao/english/ap020582.htm>, Preamble, Recital 8.

between ECOWAS Member States.[23] While the travel certificate was a welcome development, it has been the printing of the document that has proved the biggest challenge. Participating Member States have issued it in different colours and formats, while those that have yet to make the certificate available to their citizens complain of high printing costs.[24] The travel certificate was followed by the adoption of the ECOWAS passport at the Heads of State and Government Summit in May 2000, which to date has only been issued by a minority of Member States.[25] Supplementary protocols regarding the rights of Residence and Establishment were proposed in 1986 and 1990 respectively, but only the former has been ratified by the ECOWAS Members.[26]

With the only visa-free sub-regional scheme in Africa, ECOWAS can claim a major achievement in pursuit of the objective of free movement of persons, but this undoubted success may belie the fact that implementation of the 1979 Protocol has proved a significant challenge. In addition to the costs of some measures, such as the printing of the travel certificates, which have been a deterrent for some states, 'nearly all the States still maintain numerous check-points, and ECOWAS citizens are subjected to administrative harassment and extortion'.[27] Furthermore, a number of Member States have retained or, at times, enacted national legislation that is at odds with the objective of the 1979 Protocol. In 1980, for example, at the time the Member States ratified the Protocol's first phase, the Nigerian oil industry was booming and the country had attracted large numbers of skilled and less skilled migrants from across West and Central Africa. The oil boom was short lived and, as revenues declined and employment opportunities receded, the Nigerian Government looked to protect its home grown workforce and considered suspending the 1979 Protocol.[28] By 1985, Nigeria had revoked Article 4 of the Protocol, and had expelled approximately 1.2 million undocumented migrant workers, most of them Community citizens.[29]

Mass expulsions of foreign nationals are not a new phenomenon in West Africa. The Governments of Côte d'Ivoire, Sierra Leone, Ghana, Guinea and Senegal had all conducted them prior to the formation of ECOWAS and the ratification of the 1979 Protocol. In the years following ratification, the Governments of Liberia (in 1983), Nigeria (in 1983 and again in 1985), Senegal (in 1990), Benin (in 1998), and Côte d'Ivoire (in 1999) all expelled large numbers of Community

[23] The ECOWAS travel certificate is in circulation in Burkina Faso, Gambia, Ghana, Guinea, Niger, Nigeria, and Sierra Leone. See <http://www.sec.ecowas.int/sitecedeao/english/achievements-1.htm> (Achievements of ECOWAS).

[24] See the ECOWAS website, ibid.

[25] UNECA, op. cit. n. 1, at p. 199; Adepoju, loc. cit. n. 8, at p. 15.

[26] Supplementary Protocol A/SP.1/7/86 on the Implementation of the Second Phase (Right of Residence) of the Protocol on Free Movement of Persons, Right of Residence and Establishment, 1 July 1986.

[27] See the ECOWAS website, loc. cit. n. 23.

[28] Richardson, loc. cit. n. 13, at p. 3.

[29] Adepoju, loc. cit. n. 8, at p. 6.

citizens.[30] More recently, some of these states, including Ghana in 1999, Nigeria in 2003, and Côte d'Ivoire[31] in 2005, have introduced processes to attempt to register immigrants and provide them with identity cards, which some fear may trigger more expulsions.[32] Yet, despite these countervailing influences, ECOWAS continues to pursue its interest in the free movement of persons, and reaffirmed its intent in the revised ECOWAS Treaty in 1993:

> '… the Community shall, by stages, ensure … the removal between Member States, of obstacles to the free movement of persons … and to the right of residence and establishment'.[33]

4. Free Movement and SADC

4.1 Migration patterns in Southern Africa

Southern Africa has a lengthy tradition of migration, and, over the past 150 years, much of it has been directed south, towards South Africa. Recent studies suggest that 42 per cent of the adult populations of Lesotho, Mozambique, and Zimbabwe have travelled to South Africa, and that 50 per cent of these have parents and 34 per cent have grandparents that worked there.[34] So while these figures indicate that southward migration is increasing, they may also suggest that the general intent of the movement remains temporary migration, rather than immigration, to South Africa.[35]

From the 1840s onwards, migrants travelled to South Africa to work in the mines and on the farms and, as in West Africa, were relatively unhindered by colonial borders. By 1920, however, South Africa's booming mining industry had already formed a joint recruitment centre to regulate the hiring of migrant labour, and otherwise avoid competition for labour between mining companies.[36] These migrants were recruited on fixed term contracts, and were required to return home when these came to an end. Migrants were further prohibited from bringing their families with them for fear that they might otherwise remain in

---

30 Adepoju, loc. cit. n. 9, at p. 12.

31 See T. Pitman, 'Citizenship at Heart of Ivorian Conflict', *Independent Online, South Africa*, (14 July 2005) <http://www.globalpolicy.org/nations/sovereign/citizen/2005/0714ivorian.htm>.

32 A. Adepoju, 'Migration in West Africa', paper prepared for the Policy Analysis and Research Programme of the Global Commission on International Migration (Sept. 2005) at p. 11.

33 Art. 3(2)(d)(iii) of the Economic Community of West African States (ECOWAS) Revised Treaty, 24 July 1993, reprinted in 35 *International Legal Materials* (1996) p. 660.

34 J. Crush, 'Migrations Past: An Historical Overview of Cross-Border Movement in Southern Africa', in D.A. McDonald (ed.), *On Borders: Perspectives on International Migration in Southern Africa* (New York, St. Martin's Press 2000) p. 12.

35 Ibid., at p. 22.

36 Ibid., at p. 14.

South Africa indefinitely.[37] With the emergence of independent neighbouring states in the 1960s, South Africa's apartheid Government began to police the country's borders for the first time, and migrants to South Africa were increasingly caught up in the dragnet of apartheid legislation.[38] South African censuses conducted during this time show a gradual increase in foreign-born Africans in South Africa, but most of these were temporary migrants, not immigrants, and eventually went home.[39] By the 1980s, most of the newly independent governments in the sub-region were discouraging their nationals from working in South Africa's mines, but migrant workers continued to come from Mozambique, Lesotho, Swaziland and Botswana. Most of them were able to return home only once a year, but this did not imply that they wished to settle in South Africa permanently. In 1995, only a year after the advent of South Africa's democracy, the South African Government offered permanent residency to migrants who had worked in the country for more than 10 years. Of those who were eligible, less than half applied for permanent residency.[40] More recent studies indicate that

> '[f]ew want to stay permanently in South Africa and almost none wish to become South African citizens. Foreign miners seem to want to remain migrants, as long as South Africa will have them'.[41]

4.2 The SADC draft free movement protocols

The SADC has as its predecessor the Southern African Development Coordination Conference (SADCC), which was an informal, *de facto* organization that was formed to support the liberation struggles in what were then Rhodesia, South West Africa, and South Africa. In April 1980, Angola, Botswana, Lesotho, Malawi, Mozambique, Swaziland, Tanzania, Zambia, and Zimbabwe signed the Lusaka Declaration to formally establish SADCC. Having had experience of being the frontline states in the fight against apartheid in South Africa, the Parties to the Lusaka Declaration cited the first objective of the new organization as the reduction of economic dependence on South Africa so as to present a united front to South Africa's apartheid Government.[42] With the achievement of liberation in Zimbabwe (formerly Rhodesia), Namibia (formerly South West Africa), and finally South Africa, SADCC welcomed these new states as members, and began to focus on economic cooperation and sub-regional integration. Namibia became party to the Lusaka Declaration in 1990, but with the impending admission of a democratic South Africa, Member States decided to formalize the Conference to prevent it from being dominated by the sub-region's political and economic

[37] Ibid.

[38] Ibid., at pp. 17-18.

[39] Ibid., at p. 17.

[40] Ibid., at p. 16.

[41] Ibid.

[42] See <http://www.africa-union.org/root/au/RECs/sadc.htm/>.

powerhouse.[43] South Africa became a SADC Member State in 1994, and was followed by Mauritius in 1995, the Democratic Republic of Congo and Seychelles in 1997, and Madagascar in 2005.

The SADCC formally became SADC in Windhoek, Namibia in August 1992. In support of its main objectives, which include the enhancement of 'the standard and quality of life of the people of Southern Africa … through regional integration',[44] Article 5(2)(d) of the Declaration and Treaty of the Southern African Development Community (hereafter, the SADC Treaty) requires the Community to 'develop polices aimed at the progressive elimination of obstacles to the free movement of … the people of the Region generally, among Member States …'.[45]

4.2.1 *The 1995 Draft Protocol on the Free Movement of Persons in SADC*[46]

In June 1995, only a year after South Africa's admission to SADC, the Community Secretariat circulated the Draft Protocol on the Free Movement of Persons in the Southern African Development Community (hereafter, the 1995 Draft Protocol) among its Member States, referring to Article 5 of the SADC Treaty as the motivation for its drafting. The 1995 Draft Protocol had as its main objective

> 'the progressive elimination of controls on movements of citizens of a Member State at an internal border with another Member State… within ten years of the Protocol's entry into force'.[47]

As with ECOWAS's 1979 Protocol, SADC's 1995 Draft Protocol proposed a phased approach for the achievement of free movement of persons within the sub-region. During the first phase, citizens of SADC Member States were to have the right to enter the territory of any other Member State freely and without a visa for a short visit not exceeding 6 months.[48] In phase II, they were to acquire the right to live in the territory of any other Member State, and 'to apply for, and accept offers of employment'.[49] In phase III, they would be accorded, *inter alia*,

---

[43] S. Mengelkoch, *The Right to Work in SADC Countries: Towards Free Movement of Labour in Southern Africa* (Baden-Baden, Nomos 2001) p. 31.

[44] The Declaration and Treaty establishing the Southern African Development Community (SADC), 17 Aug. 1992, reprinted in 32 *International Legal Materials* (1993) p. 116. <http://www.sadc.int/english/documents/legal/treaties/declaration_and_treaty_of_sadc.php> Art. 5(1)(a).

[45] Ibid., Art. 5(2)(d).

[46] The Draft Protocol on the Free Movement of Persons in the Southern African Development Community, SADC Secretariat, Gaborone (15 March 1996) <http://www.queensu.ca/samp/sampresources/migrationdocuments/documents/1996/draftprotocol.htm>. The Draft Protocol was drafted in 1995, but only formally tabled at an SADC Council of Ministers in March 1996; it is, however, most commonly referred to as the '1995 Protocol', and this usage has been retained here for the avoidance of confusion.

[47] Ibid., Arts. 3 and 4.

[48] Ibid., Art. 15(2)(a).

[49] Ibid., Art. 19(a) and (b).

the right to establish, manage and/or practice a profession, trade or business in the territory of another Member State.[50] In the final phase, Member States would eliminate SADC's internal national borders.[51]

The 1995 Draft Protocol inspired little enthusiasm – particularly in the sub-region's main migrant receiving countries. The South African Government (and, to a lesser extent, the Governments of Botswana and Namibia) had concerns that a policy of free movement in a sub-region with such significant economic disparity would encourage millions of low skilled workers to immigrate to South Africa to compete as equals in the country's labour market with millions of low skilled South Africans.[52] It was feared that such a mass influx of labour would place a considerable strain on the health and educational facilities in South Africa, and that it would exacerbate the rising levels of xenophobia directed towards African immigrants.[53] In addition to the doubts expressed by the South African Government, some of SADC's traditional migrant sending countries wondered about the extent to which they would be deprived of their skilled and professional labour force that may prefer the higher wages and standard of living to be had in South Africa.[54] Others speculated that the 1995 Draft Protocol would only serve to facilitate the activities of organized criminal groups, of which there were estimated to be approximately 500 operating on SADC territory, including those that were already involved in migrant smuggling and human trafficking operations.[55] In response to the 1995 Draft Protocol, the South African Government prepared a more cautious alternative, from which the SADC Secretariat borrowed the title for its own redraft of the 1995 Draft Protocol that same year: the SADC Protocol on the Facilitation of Movement of Persons in the Southern African Development Community. In sum, the 1995 Draft Protocol did not survive long, and was replaced in January 1997 by the Draft Protocol on the Facilitation of Movement of Persons in the Southern African Development Community (hereafter, the 1997 Draft Protocol).

---

[50] Ibid., Art. 25(a) and (b).

[51] Ibid., Art. 36.

[52] J.O. Oucho and J. Crush, 'Contra Free Movement: South Africa and the SADC Migration Protocols', 48(3) *Africa Today* (2001) p. 139 at p. 146.

[53] Ibid., at p. 147; J. Crush, et al., 'Migration in Southern Africa', Paper prepared for the Policy Analysis and Research Programme of the Global Commission on International Migration (Sept. 2005) p. 23; H. Solomon, 'Towards the Free Movement of People in Southern Africa?' *Occasional Paper No. 18, Institute for Security Studies (ISS)* (March 1997) <http://www.issafrica.org/Pubs/PAPERS/18/Paper18.html> p. 1.

[54] Solomon, loc. cit. n. 53.

[55] IOM, *Seduction, Sale and Slavery: Trafficking in Women and Children for Sexual Exploitation in Southern Africa,* 3rd edn. (Pretoria, IOM 2003) p. 16; Solomon, loc. cit. n. 53.

4.2.2 *The 1997 Draft Protocol on the Facilitation of Movement of Persons in SADC*[56]

The Preamble of the 1997 Draft Protocol mirrors precisely that of the 1995 draft, and includes the statement that the Heads of State or Government

> 'recognis[e] that full popular participation in the process of building the Region into a Community is only possible where the citizens of the Community enjoy freedom of movement of persons, namely: visa-free entry, residence and establishment in the territories of Member States',

and that this should be carried out

> '[p]ursuant to Article 5(2)(d) of the Treaty which requires SADC to develop policies aimed at the progressive elimination of obstacles to the free movement of... people of the Region generally...'.

The content of the 1997 Draft Protocol, however, is far more reticent than that of its predecessor, and the means by which these aims are to be achieved differ notably. The 1997 Draft Protocol

a. eliminates any mention of a citizen's 'right to entry, residence and establishment', and refers instead to the commitment of State Parties to 'facilitate' entry, residence and establishment;[57]

b. replaces references to 'free movement' in the 1995 Draft Protocol with references only to 'movement';[58]

c. promises sub-regional cooperation to prevent 'illegal movement of persons into and within the Region',[59] and eliminates the commitment to harmonize employment policies and labour relations found in the 1995 Draft Protocol;[60]

d. reduces visa-free entry from a six-month stay to a three month stay,[61] and requires that visa-free admission is conditional on the 'visitor possess[ing] a valid travel document' and having or producing 'evidence of sufficient means of support for the duration of the visit';[62]

---

[56] The 1997 Draft Protocol on the Facilitation of Movement of Persons in the Southern African Development Community, SADC Secretariat, Gaborone (Jan. 1997) <http://www.sadc.int/english/documents/legal/protocols/facilitation_of_movement.php>.

[57] Ibid., Art. 3.

[58] Ibid.; see, e.g., Art. 2.

[59] Ibid., Art. 11(e).

[60] See the 1995 Draft Protocol, loc. cit. n. 46, Art. 10(3)(g).

[61] 1997 Draft Protocol, loc. cit. n. 56, Art. 3(a).

[62] Ibid., Art. 14(2)(b) and (c).

e. reserves the right of State Parties to conclude bilateral agreements with other states on conditions of entry.[63]

In addition, the 1997 Draft Protocol curtails any preferential 'right' of residence and establishment for Community citizens in Articles 17(1) and 19 by requiring compliance with the application-for-residence process that is standard in most countries in the case of the former, and referring to national legislation, with no obligation on State Parties to adjust their national legislation to facilitate 'establishment', in terms of the latter.[64]

Despite the significant strides towards sub-regional integration that have been made in other areas, such as trade, SADC Member States have shown a reluctance to support the free movement ideal, described as an objective of the Community in Article 5 of the SADC Treaty. Having taken a step towards this goal with the 1995 Draft Protocol, SADC appears to have taken several steps backwards, replacing that progressive document with the much more cautious 1997 Draft Protocol.

5. Conclusion

ECOWAS and SADC are two of Africa's most promising sub-regional economic schemes, and have achieved 'above average' levels of success when measured against the continent's remaining twelve such organizations. However, despite achieving significant levels of economic integration, and recognizing the importance of free movement of persons to the integration effort in their respective treaties, both sub-regional organizations have found the implementation of this aim challenging. Of the two, ECOWAS appears to have been the more successful, having achieved a major success with the abolition of entry visas in the sub-region, and the introductions of the ECOWAS travel certificate and passport.[65] SADC is the younger organization by 17 years, and faces the additional challenge of a more dramatic economic disparity between its Member States; however, the 1997 Draft Protocol is not the bold move that is suggested by its Preamble, and seems likely to do little more than reinforce the status quo.

In West and Southern Africa, Africans are moving, often irrespective of political borders and national immigration laws. Free movement of persons' protocols recognize this reality; and, despite the concerns they engender and the challenges they present, they are the first step towards cooperative management of mobile populations, and real regional integration as envisaged by Kwame Nkrumah, Julius Nyerere, and others.

[63] Ibid., Art. 14(3).

[64] Oucho and Crush, loc. cit. n. 52, at pp. 152-153.

[65] UNECA, op. cit. n. 1, at p. 199.

Selected Bibliography

Adepoju, A., 'Migration in West Africa', paper prepared for the Policy Analysis and Research Programme of the Global Commission on International Migration (Sept. 2005).

—, 'Creating a Borderless West Africa: Constraints and Prospects for Intra-Regional Migration', (Jan. 2005) Draft Article of the *Migration Without Borders* Series (UNESCO) SHS/2005/MWB/1 <http://unesdoc.unesco.org/images/0013/001391/139142e.pdf>.

—, 'Changing Configuration of Migration in Africa', *Migration Information Source* (1 Sept. 2004) p. 1 <http://www.migrationinformation.org/feature/display.cfm?ID=251>.

—, 'Fostering Free Movement of Persons in West Africa: Achievements, Pitfalls and Prospects for Intra-Regional Migration', 40 *International Migration* (2002) p. 3 <http://www.iussp.org/Brazil2001/s20/S26_P03_Adepoju.pdf>.

Crush, J., 'Migrations Past: An Historical Overview of Cross-Border Movement in Southern Africa', in D.A. McDonald (ed.), *On Borders: Perspectives on International Migration in Southern Africa* (New York, St. Martin's Press 2000) p. 12.

Crush, J., et al., 'Migration in Southern Africa', paper prepared for the Policy Analysis and Research Programme of the Global Commission on International Migration (Sept. 2005).

IOM, *Seduction, Sale and Slavery: Trafficking in Women and Children for Sexual Exploitation in Southern Africa,* 3rd edn. (Pretoria, IOM 2003).

Mengelkoch, S., *The Right to Work in SADC Countries: Towards Free Movement of Labour in Southern Africa* (Baden-Baden, Nomos 2001).

McDonald, D.A. (ed.), *On Borders: Perspectives on International Migration in Southern Africa* (New York, St. Martin's Press 2000).

Nyirabu, M., 'Appraising Regional Integration in Southern Africa', 13(1) *African Security Review* (2004) p. 21.

Oucho, J.O. and J. Crush, 'Contra Free Movement: South Africa and he SADC Migration Protocols', 48(3) *Africa Today* (2001) p. 139.

Pitman, T., 'Citizenship at Heart of Ivorian Conflict', *Independent Online South Africa* (14 July 2005) <http://www.globalpolicy.org/nations/sovereign/citizen/2005/0714ivorian.htm>.

Richardson, A., 'ECOWAS After Nearly 28 Years', *Daily Graphic* (4 March 2004).

Solomon, H., 'Towards the Free Movement of People in Southern Africa?', *Occasional Paper No. 18, Institute for Security Studies (ISS)* (March 1997) <www.iss.co.za/Pubs/PAPERS/18/Paper18.html>.

UN Economic Commission for Africa (UNECA), *Accelerating Regional Integration in Africa*, (Addis Ababa, UNECA 2004) <http://www.eneca.org/aria/>.

Chapter 21
FREE MOVEMENT REGIMES IN SOUTH AMERICA: THE EXPERIENCE OF THE MERCOSUR AND THE ANDEAN COMMUNITY

Ana María Santestevan*

1. INTRODUCTION

It is quite evident that the phenomenon of migration, and labour migration in particular, constitutes a fundamental component of the social dimension of integration between countries; it is therefore not surprising that almost every process of regional integration has attempted to regulate it, either direct or indirectly. The main goal of this chapter is to identify the advances in the field of free movement of persons that have occurred in the processes of regional integration of the MERCOSUR and the Andean Community, in order to draw some lessons for the study of international legislation on labour migration more generally. It will focus on the body of norms and agreements in force among the countries of each regional bloc that seek to regulate the movement of persons, and the conditions for their entry into and exit from the territory of participating states.

2. MIGRATION IN SOUTH AMERICA

Latin American countries are distinguished by the frequency with which human displacements across national frontiers occur, a phenomenon that has its roots in the economic and social heterogeneity of the nations in the region. Facilitated by the geographical vicinity and the cultural proximity of destination states, intra-regional migratory flows move towards those countries whose economic structures

* Legal Consultant of the Office of Planning and Budget of the Presidency of the Republic of Uruguay and Professor of Labour Law at the Law School of the University of the Republic (Uruguay). The opinions expressed in this article are the exclusive responsibility of the author and do not necessarily reflect the views of the above-mentioned institutions. The information in this chapter is based on a report written by the author as a consultant for the International Organization for Migration (IOM), entitled 'The Migratory Variable in the MERCOSUR', Documents of the South American Meeting about Migration, Integration and Development, Lima, 13-14 July 1999 (unpublished report, on file with the author).

R. Cholewinski, R. Perruchoud and E. MacDonald, eds., International Migration Law

are more favorable to the generation of employment and that, usually, provide for greater levels of social equity. Besides these structural factors, the evolution of migratory patterns in the region have been influenced not only by the circumstances of economic 'boom and bust', but also by contingent social and economic factors. Therefore, for example, the instances of overthrow and re-establishment of democratic forms of government have had their impact on the creation of waves of migratory movements between nations with common borders.

However, despite changes in national social, economical and political contexts, the origins and destinations of the migratory flows within South America have not changed noticeably. In terms of the identification of the countries of destination, it is interesting to note that two thirds of Latin Americans who, in 1990, lived in countries of the region other than those of their birth were concentrated in Argentina and Venezuela.

The geographical and historical proximity that exists among the nationals of Latin American countries has given rise to an identifiable 'regional culture', which in turn has meant that relationships between populations have not been characterized by migration-based conflicts. Generally speaking, with minimal exceptions, it can be said that the prevalent environment is one of relaxed informality in the sub-regional movement of persons, helped by bilateral agreements that facilitate border crossings and the traditional goodwill of the authorities regarding the nationals of neighbouring countries.

Beginning in the second half of the 20th century, and continuing in the early years of the 21st century, extra-regional movements of people have begun to assume a more central role in overall migratory patterns. Although such migrants emigrate to a wide variety of destinations, with a notable presence of Latin Americans in many European and some Asian states (e.g., the Brazilian community in Japan), most go to the United States and, to a lesser extent, Canada. In general terms, then, this kind of movement is a case of 'south-north migration', which entails multiple repercussions for Latin American countries: most importantly, the loss of human resources and the risk that emigrants may not be effectively integrated into their chosen countries of destination. Furthermore, migration of this type implies the creation of transnational communities of migrants, which can in themselves serve to encourage further migration.

3. The Movement of Persons in the MERCOSUR

The formal birth of the MERCOSUR took place on 26 March 1991, when the Presidents of the Federal Republic of Brazil, the Republic of Argentina, the Republic of Paraguay and the Oriental Republic of Uruguay met in Asunción, Paraguay, to sign the integration treaty that began the process of the construction of the Common Market of the South (MERCOSUR).

3.1 The social content of the Asunción Treaty[1]

Although it has been said that the Asunción Treaty contains almost no references to social objectives, or to topics such as employment, labour conditions, movement of people or social security, it is possible, through a more attentive reading, to perceive that these issues were taken into consideration by the negotiators. For example, the first paragraph of the Treaty's Preamble alludes to the concept of 'social justice' as a goal of all the economic development processes in the region. The mere reference to social justice in connection with economic development itself implies the elaboration of a programme that will condition the entire integration process. As is known, the importance of the Preamble lies in its effect on the interpretation of the substantive provisions of the Treaty proper, providing the parameters and basic guidelines in terms of which the objectives and goals of the agreement are to be understood. It is commonly agreed that every process that seeks to achieve an advanced level of integration, as does the MERCOSUR, although born from a markedly economics-oriented perspective, will in time come to constitute an authentic common labour market.

3.2 Institutional structure of the MERCOSUR

In the almost fifteen years since the MERCOSUR began, its migration-related dimension has been considered many times and in many different contexts. From its beginnings in the Asunción Treaty, and in particular on the basis of the structure provided by the Protocol of Ouro Preto of 1994,[2] the MERCOSUR now comprises nine permanent organs, which oversee the work of a number of others that make proposals of a non-binding and consultative character:

a) the Council of the Common Market (CMC),[3] which oversees the Meetings of Ministers of the MERCOSUR Members;

b) the Common Market Group (GMC),[4] which oversees the working subgroups specialized in different technical subjects, the MERCOSUR Social-Labour Commission, and the Group of Services (among other auxiliary organs);

[1] *Tratado para la constitución de un Mercado Común entre la República Argentina, la República Federativa del Brasil, la República del Paraguay y la República Oriental del Uruguay*, [Treaty for the Constitution of a Common Market between the Republic of Argentina, the Federal Republic of Brazil, the Republic of Paraguay and the Oriental Republic of Uruguay] 26 March 1991.

[2] *El Protocolo Adicional al Tratado de Asunción sobre la Estructura Institucional del MERCOSUR*, [Additional Protocol to the Asunción Treaty on the Institutional Structure of MERCOSUR] known as the Protocol of Ouro Preto, was signed by the Presidents of the Member States in the city of Ouro Preto (Brazil) on 17 Dec. 1994.

[3] *Consejo del Mercado Común.*

[4] *Grupo Mercado Común.*

c) the MERCOSUR Trade Commission;[5]

d) the Joint Parliamentary Commission (CPC);[6]

e) the Economic-Social Consultative Forum;[7]

f) the MERCOSUR Administrative Secretariat;[8]

g) the Permanent Review Court of MERCOSUR;[9]

h) the Administrative Labour Court;[10]

i) the Consultative Forum of City Councils, Federal States, Provinces and Departments of MERCOSUR.[11]

3.3 Main advances of the MERCOSUR in the field of the free movement of persons

Starting with the institutional structure of the MERCOSUR, this chapter seeks to provide a systematic account of the most significant advances in terms of facilitating the movement of persons within the integrated territory.

3.3.1 *Working Subgroup No. 10 on Labour Relations, Employment and Social Security (SGT 10)*[12]

Since the very early stages of the MERCOSUR, the issue of the free movement of the labour force has been present in the agenda of the different organs, among which Working Subgroup No. 11 has been especially relevant. This group was replaced in 1995 by Working Subgroup No. 10.[13] SGT 10 has three thematic commissions:

[5] *Comisión de Comercio del MERCOSUR.*

[6] *Comisión Parlamentaria Conjunta.*

[7] *Foro Consultivo Económico y Social.*

[8] *Secretaría del MERCOSUR.*

[9] *Tribunal Permanente de Revisión del MERCOSUR.*

[10] *Tribunal Administrativo-Laboral del MERCOSUR.*

[11] *Foro Consultivo de Municipios, Estados Federados, Provincias y Departamentos del MERCOSUR.*

[12] *Subgrupo de Trabajo No. 10 sobre Relaciones Laborales, Empleo y Seguridad Social.*

[13] SGT 10 on Labour Relations, Employment and Social Security was created by Resolution No. 20/95. It is an auxiliary organ of the Common Market Group (GMC). Like its predecessor SGT 11, it has the peculiarity of having a tripartite character. Although workers and employers participate in a consultative capacity and the final decision is reserved to governments, in practice it has functioned through a search for consensus.

Commission II has been assigned the issue of labour migration, together with such matters as employment and professional training.

Initially, the consideration of migration-related topics was focused on three basic aspects: a) carrying out comparative studies of the legislation in force affecting migration in the four countries; b) coordinating with other related areas of the MERCOSUR project; and c) analyzing the current state of affairs in MERCOSUR State Parties, in terms of the 'mobility of the labour force'[14] and the possible 'harmonization of norms governing the free movement of workers'.[15]

After an active initial phase in terms of promoting the free movement of persons within the territory of the MERCOSUR, the pace of negotiations on this topic in SGT 10 slowed somewhat, particularly after the signing of the Protocol of Ouro Preto in December 1994; this instrument redefined the MERCOSUR project, limiting the ambition of the integration process to the construction of what is often referred to as an 'imperfect customs union'.

Faced with the need to adjust to these new guidelines, the States Parties chose to rethink their approach to the main labour issues, giving priority in the context of SGT 10 to the adoption of a framework of minimum rights for the workers of the region, the creation of a database and the encouragement of information exchanges regarding the labour policies applied by each Member. This resulted in the creation of two instruments that can be considered as the most important advances in the social dimension of the MERCOSUR integration process: the MERCOSUR Social-Labour Declaration,[16] approved in December 1998, and the Labour Market Observatory.[17]

In both texts, the issue of labour migration is especially pertinent: Article 1 of the Social-Labour Declaration contains the general principle of non-discrimination, while Article 4 establishes equality between the rights of migrant and frontier workers, on the one hand, and national workers on the other. These provisions also compel the Member countries to develop common norms and proce-

[14] The research on the mobility of the labour force within the MERCOSUR countries sought to detect the main obstacles for the free movement of workers in the region, taking into consideration the possible scenarios that the extended territory could present to its inhabitants. In particular, the problem of competitiveness, the labour market and the level of trade unionization were thoroughly treated, focusing on the commercial sector in the border areas, the building industry and the textile industry.

[15] The consultation on the 'Harmonization of norms governing the free movement of workers' examined the migration regulations in the four countries and the main aspects of labour law in each of them, in relation to the citizenship rights of workers. On this basis, a 'Project on the regulation of movements for reasons of work in the MERCOSUR' was proposed, but this was never approved by the competent organs.

[16] *Declaración Sociolaboral del MERCOSUR.*

[17] The *Observatorio de Mercado de Trabajo del MERCOSUR* [MERCOSUR Labour Market Observatory] was created in the framework of the SGT 10 with the objective of facilitating the decision-making process in MERCOSUR through the collection, analysis and diffusion of information on labour, labour migration, professional development, and the social security and labour norms of the Member States. For further information, see the Observatory's website at <www.observatorio.net>.

dures concerning the free movement of labour within the territories of the MERCOSUR States.

Another important product of the MERCOSUR labour organs is the signing of the Multilateral Agreement on Social Security, approved by the GMC in December 1997, and submitted to the national parliaments for consideration. The last of these took place on 5 May 2005, meaning that the Agreement is now in force in all four Member States. It represents a significant advance in this area, and constitutes an important instrument for sustaining the intra-regional mobility of workers.

In parallel fashion, the Ad Hoc Commission on Labour Migration[18] deserves to be mentioned as a specialized body within the structure of SGT 10. It was created in 1997 to carry out research on the situation of migrant workers from the border regions of the MERCOSUR Member States, with the intention of elaborating a unique body of norms to be applied by all four countries. Although the Commission has been able to rely on the support of the International Organization for Migration (IOM) in terms of the elaboration of technical instruments and the development of pilot projects in many frontier areas of the region, it has not yet been able to achieve its proposed goal.

Intimately related to the subject of the movement of workers in the MERCOSUR are the issues of professional training and the certification of qualifications in the countries of the region. This has been dealt with by SGT 10: the GMC recommended, in its Resolution No. 59/01, that State Parties should move 'towards the construction of an integral and systematic view on vocational training',[19] an idea taken up by the CMC in Resolution 01/03,[20] to which was annexed an 'Index of Practical Recommendations on Vocational Training',[21] the text of which will be promoted with the support of the Inter-American Research and Documentation Centre on Vocational Training (CINTERFOR/OIT). In fact, in the May 2005 meeting of the MERCOSUR organs, it was agreed that each country needed to elaborate a detailed report on this issue.

Lastly, it is important to point out that, in the context of an eventual restructuring of the work of SGT 10, the delegations agreed to give priority in the Working Programme for 2004 to issues related to employment, the eradication of child labour and the free movement of workers. In this regard, at the meeting held in May 2005, different initiatives were presented, each suggesting the adoption of concrete measures in order to facilitate the movement of workers within the region.

---

18 *Comisión Ad Hoc sobre Migraciones Laborales.*

19 MERCOSUR/GMC/RES No. 59/01, Art. 1. The texts of the Resolutions of the GMC, and other documents relating to the MERCOSUR, can be found (in Spanish and Portuguese) at <http://www.sice.oas.org/agreemts/Mercin_e.asp#MERCOSUR>.

20 MERCOSUR/CMC/REC No. 01/03.

21 Ibid., Annex [*Repertorio de Recomendaciones Prácticas sobre Formación Profesional*].

3.3.2 *The Social-Labour Commission of the MERCOSUR*

The Social-Labour Commission of the MERCOSUR (CSL) is a tripartite organ[22] within the framework of the GMC, operating at both the national and the regional levels, and created to assist with and promote the application of the MERCOSUR Social-Labour Declaration.

Among the functions that the regional CSL has is the elaboration of reports, or 'memoranda', on the level of progress made in each one of the rights contained in the Social-Labour Declaration. The monitoring procedure followed in the MERCOSUR is based on the control system used by the ILO in order to determine the degree to which international labour norms are being respected.

At a meeting in May 2003, the CSL examined reports submitted by all four countries on the fulfillment of Article 4 of the Social-Labour Declaration, relating to the rights of migrant and border workers. These reports, presented by the Governments and mostly written with the assistance of different social actors, represent an important addition to the information available on labour migration in the region, in that they deal not only with normative issues, but also with issues such as the implementation of migrants' rights, the institutional practices in the Member States, and the main obstacles that they face in seeking to promote the free movement of workers within the territory of the MERCOSUR.

3.3.3 *The Economic and Social Consultative Forum*

The Economic and Social Consultative Forum is the organ in which the economic and social sectors of the State Parties are represented; it was created by the Protocol of Ouro Preto as part of its redefinition of the nature and aims of the MERCOSUR project. Unlike SGT 10 and the CSL, it excludes government officials, being made up rather of delegates from trade unions and companies, with representatives of NGOs, research centres and other social organizations also present.

The contribution of the Consultative Forum to the migration-related dimension of MERCOSUR originated in a consultation carried out by the GMC in 1999 on the movement of workers in frontier regions. Since then, the Consultative Forum has analyzed and debated the economic, commercial and social-labour difficulties that frontier migrant workers have to face, making a very valuable contribution to the elaboration of the normative regime governing the movement of workers.

3.3.4 *The Meetings of MERCOSUR Internal Affairs Ministers*

Although not formally part of the institutional structure of the MERCOSUR, the meetings of the Internal Affairs Ministers of the State Parties have enthusiasti-

[22] Unlike in SGT 10, where tripartism is consultative, in the CSL the decision-making process requires the consensus of the three sectors, which means that each one of them has power of veto over all decisions.

cally promoted legislative harmonization, in particular on the issue of the movement of persons, and have elaborated proposals that, once approved by the CMC, have become decisions of great importance in the process of regional integration. It is quite surprising that it is precisely in the framework of these meetings that the most substantial advances in the field of the free movement of persons within the MERCOSUR have taken place.

In this manner, under the influence of the Internal Affairs Ministers, the CMC adopted its Decisions Nos. 18/99 and 14/00, by which it approved the Agreement on Movement Across Neighbouring Borders.[23] At the same time, the Technical Committee of the Meeting of the Internal Affairs Ministers began to analyze the possibility of perfecting the Agreement and its implementation, with a view to providing better benefits to the citizens of the Member States who live in the areas close to a border, furnishing them with documentation that enables them to pursue remunerative activities and to have access to education on either side of the border.

Likewise, by Decision No. 48/00, the CMC approved the Agreement on Visa Exemptions,[24] applicable to those who belong to particular categories of migrants native to one of the State Parties, such as artists, scientists, sportspersons, journalists, specialized technicians and professionals, who seek entry into the territory of another Member in order to pursue that activity. Such persons do not require a visa to enter into the territories of the other State Parties for a period of up to 90 consecutive days; further, their stay can be extended for an equivalent period, with a limit of 180 days per year. However, the Agreement does not apply to self-employed workers or workers with an employment relationship who are remunerated in the destination country.

Finally, it is important to mention Decision No. 28/02, adopted by the CMC, which endorsed the Agreement on the Regularization of Internal Migration for MERCOSUR Citizens,[25] and also the Agreement on Residence for State Party Nationals,[26] which were approved by the MERCOSUR Presidential Summit of 6 December 2002, and should be incorporated into the national law of the Member States.[27]

---

[23] Agreement on Movement Across Neighbouring Borders between the Member States of the MERCOSUR [*Acuerdo sobre Tránsito Vecinal Fronterizo entre los Estados parte del MERCOSUR*], MERCOSUR/CMC/DEC No. 18/99 and MERCOSUR/CMC/DEC No. 14/00.

[24] Agreement on Visa Exemptions between the Member Status of the MERCOSUR [*Acuerdo sobre Exensión de Visas entre los Estados parte del MERCOSUR*], MERCOSUR/CMC/DEC No. 48/00.

[25] Agreement No. 11/02 on the Regularization of Internal Migration for MERCOSUR Citizens [*Regularización Migratoria Interna de Ciudadanos del MERCOSUR*], approved by MERCOSUR/CMC/DEC No. 28/02.

[26] Agreement No. 13/02 on Residence for MERCOSUR State Party Nationals [*Residencia para Nacionales de los Estados Partes del MERCOSUR*], approved by MERCOSUR/CMC/DEC No. 28/02.

[27] These Agreements, even though they have not yet been incorporated into the national legislation of the Member States, doubtless constitute one of the most significant advances in the field of free movement of persons in the region.

3.3.5 *The Meetings of MERCOSUR Employment Ministers*

Given the conviction that the main motivation behind movements of people at the international level is the search for better employment opportunities, it is quite evident that migration-related issues have not been absent from the commitments assumed by the Employment Ministers of the MERCOSUR Member States. Furthermore, successive meetings between these Ministers have consistently reaffirmed the centrality of migration to the MERCOSUR project, emphasizing the need to promote concrete measures to ensure that migrant workers enjoy dignified working conditions and respect for their labour and social security rights, as provided for in national legislation.[28]

The MERCOSUR Employment Ministers, in the framework of the Regional Conference on Employment in Buenos Aires on 16 April 2004, adopted a Declaration reaffirming and reinforcing the commitments already assumed by the Member States.[29] Of particular relevance to the present chapter is Article 4 of this Declaration, which acknowledges the need to

> '[p]romote actions to harmonize the policies and the processes of integration in the labour markets of the region, in order to guarantee the free movement of workers, deepening the guidelines introduced by the Agreement on Residence for Nationals of the MERCOSUR and the Agreement on Migratory Regulation of the MERCOSUR's Citizens... [and] to ensure decent jobs for the workers who migrate within the region, coordinating specific programmes which guarantee the fulfillment of these goals in the frontier areas'.[30]

3.3.6 *The Meetings of MERCOSUR Education Ministers*

Another of the advances that can be identified in the consolidation of the social dimension of the MERCOSUR is the progress that has been made in terms of the

[28] The agreements of the Meetings of MERCOSUR Ministers are recorded in the respective Acts of each regional meeting. This commitment to labour and social rights comes from Act No. 1/96 of the Meeting of MERCOSUR Employment Ministers in Punta del Este (Uruguay) on 5 February 1996. Similarly, Act No. 1/98 of the Meeting of MERCOSUR Employment Ministers, and those of Bolivia and Chile, in Buenos Aires on 11 May 1998, confirms 'the need to include agreements on labour relations, employment, labour migration and social security'.

[29] *Declaración de los Ministros de Trabajo del MERCOSUR en la Conferencia Regional de Empleo*, Buenos Aires, 16 April 2004 <http://www.trabajo.gov.ar/crem/conferencia/files/declaracionfinal.doc>. Although the Declaration is not included in any formal MERCOSUR norm, and therefore is not compulsory for the Member States, it is an important political instrument demonstrating the priority that all of the Governments assign to labour topics in the integration process.

[30] [*Promover acciones conjuntas para armonizar las políticas y los procesos de integración de los mercados de trabajo de la región, a fin de garantizar la libre circulación de los trabajadores, profundizando los lineamientos planteados en el Acuerdo sobre Residencias para Nacionales del MERCOSUR y el Acuerdo de Regularización Migratoria de los Ciudadanos del MERCOSUR. Asegurar el trabajo decente para los trabajadores migrantes al interior de la región, coordinando programas específicos que garanticen el cumplimiento de estos objetivos en las zonas fronterizas*].

recognition of degrees and professional qualifications at different levels, in the framework of the Meetings of the Education and Culture Ministers of the MERCOSUR Members.

In this regard, the Education Ministers have developed three noteworthy Educational Integration Protocols, which were later submitted for ratification to the Member States, and which have an impact on the facilitation of employment and trans-frontier mobility of people: a) the Educational Integration Protocol on the Recognition of Certificates, Degrees, and Primary- and Non-Technical Secondary-Level Studies (1994);[31] b) the Educational Integration Protocol on the Revalidation of Diplomas, Certificates and Degrees, and the Recognition of Secondary-Level Technical Studies (1995);[32] and c) the Educational Integration Protocol on the Recognition of University Degrees for the Pursuit of Postgraduate Studies at the Universities of MERCOSUR Countries (1995).[33]

3.3.7 *The Joint Parliamentary Commission*

The Joint Parliamentary Commission (CPC), the legislative organ of the MERCOSUR,[34] has also considered the issue of the movement of persons within the integrated territory, developing a Project on the Status of Migrant Workers[35] and adopting different Recommendations, basically aimed at strengthening the ties between Argentina, Brazil and Paraguay in the region where the three borders meet.[36]

---

[31] Educational Integration Protocol on the Recognition of Certificates, Degrees, and Primary- and Non-Technical Secondary-Level Studies [*Protocolo de Integración Educativa y Reconocimiento de Certificados, Títulos y Estudios de nivel primario y medio no técnico*], MERCOSUR/CMC/DEC No. 4/94.

[32] Educational Integration Protocol on the Revalidation of Diplomas, Certificates and Degrees, and the Recognition of Secondary-Level Technical Studies [*Protocolo di Integración Educativa y Revalida de Diplomas, Certificados, Títulos y Reconocimiento de Estudios de Nivel Medio Técnico*], MERCOSUR/CMC/DEC No. 7/95.

[33] Educational Integration Protocol on the Recognition of University Degrees for the Pursuit of Postgraduate Studies in the Universities of MERCOSUR Countries [*Protocolo di Integración Educativa sobre Reconocimiento de Títulos Universitarios para la Prosecución de Post-grado en las Universidades de los Países del MERCOSUR*], MERCOSUR/CMC/DEC No. 4/95.

[34] The CPC does not have any actual legislative competences at a regional level; at present, however, the MERCOSUR Member States are considering the possibility of implementing a profound institutional re-structuring that would include the transformation of the CPC into a real regional Parliament.

[35] The Project on the Status of Migrant Workers [*Proyecto de Estatuto de los Trabajadores Migrantes*] was created by the CPC and was under consideration by the CMC. However, it was not incorporated into MERCOSUR law.

[36] MERCOSUR/CPC/REC No. 20/02 proposes the creation and regulation of a frontier area that includes the three borders in the Iguazú region; MERCOSUR/CPC/REC No. 27/02 proposes the elaboration of research on the common normative framework for the treatment of the needs of frontier workers; and MERCOSUR/CPC/REC No. 29/02 proposes that the Iguazú region be considered and treated as a 'laboratory for the integration issues of the MERCOSUR', among others.

Although the Recommendations are not of a legally binding nature, they nonetheless serve to influence and guide the action taken in terms of frontier workers, particularly by the auxiliary organs to the MERCOSUR Common Market Group.

3.3.8 *The MERCOSUR Group on Services*

As was agreed in the original Treaty, the MERCOSUR countries are committed to gradually liberalizing the movement of goods, services and factors of production; the Ad Hoc Group of Services was created, according to the terms of the agreement, with the aim of elaborating an Additional Protocol to the Asunción Treaty to regulate the relationship between Member States in terms of the provision of services in the MERCOSUR.

The MERCOSUR Protocol of Montevideo on Trade in Services was approved by Decision No. 13/97 of the CMC[37] and, after its approval, the incorporation of Annexes to the Protocol was negotiated by the same Ad Hoc Group. As a result, on 23 July 1998, the CMC approved the inclusion of specific provisions on the movement of persons who provide services that facilitate the movement of certain categories of worker within the MERCOSUR.[38]

The previously named 'Ad Hoc Group on Services' was subsequently transformed into 'The Group on Services' as an auxiliary organ of the Common Market Group, which, in order to implement GMC Resolution No. 36/00, elaborated the Agreement on the Creation of a MERCOSUR Visa.[39] This Agreement establishes common rules for the temporary movement of suppliers of services among the States Parties. The granting of the MERCOSUR Visa is not subject to proof of economic necessity or any previous work authorization, and it is exempt from all quota requirements regarding nationality.[40] This agreement was approved by the CMC in its Decision No. 16/03;[41] however, it is not yet in force, as it requires the ratification of all four Member States.

3.3.9 *The MERCOSUR Forum for Political Consultation and Agreement*[42]

Two initiatives of the Forum for Political Consultation and Agreement stand out in relation to the free movement of persons: a) the creation of the Ad-hoc Group on Border Integration, which mainly seeks to promote the integration of border

[37] *Protocolo de Montevideo sobre el Comercio de Servicios del MERCOSUR*, MERCOSUR/CMC/DEC No. 13/97.

[38] MERCOSUR/CMC/DEC No. 9/98.

[39] *Acuerdo para la Creación de la Visa MERCOSUR*, MERCOSUR/CMC/DEC. No. 16/03.

[40] Some MERCOSUR countries currently run a quota system in favour of nationals; e.g., in Brazilian law, foreigners cannot make up more than one third of the personnel of any one company.

[41] The Agreement was approved by the CMC by Decision No. 16/03, loc. cit. n. 39, and its objective is to facilitate the temporary movement of physical persons who provide services in MERCOSUR.

[42] MERCOSUR/CMC/DEC. No. 18/98 [*Foro de Consulta y Concertación Politica*].

regions in order to improve the quality of life of those living in such areas;[43] and b) the creation of the MERCOSUR Provisional Travel Document,[44] which can be issued by any of the Members' Consulates to nationals of other States Parties abroad, in order to allow them to return to their country of origin, when those other states do not have consular representation capable of issuing the National Travel Document in the country in question.

4. The Movement of Persons in the Andean Community

With a much longer pedigree than the MERCOSUR, the Andean Community of Nations (CAN) began with the signing of the Cartagena Agreement, on 26 May 1969.[45] Its goal of creating an integrated regional bloc of Andean countries sprang from the failure of the Latin American Free Trade Association, which was founded in 1960 with the purpose of harmonizing the interests of all the countries of the region. The Cartagena Agreement was initially signed by Bolivia, Colombia, Chile, Ecuador and Peru. Venezuela joined the project in 1973, while Chile abandoned it in 1976.

4.1 The social content of the Cartagena Agreement

The objective of the Agreement, according to its Article 1, is to promote the balanced and harmonic development of the Member Countries, to accelerate their growth through economic integration, to facilitate their participation in the process of regional integration as provided for by the Montevideo Treaty,[46] and to establish the conditions necessary for the transformation of the Latin American Free Trade Association into a common market, all with a view to achieving an enduring improvement in the standard of living of the population of the region.

From the very beginning, the Andean integration project looked to achieve goals that went beyond the strictly economic and commercial, working more on

[43] MERCOSUR/CMC/DEC No. 5/02 [*Grupo Ad Hoc sobre Integración Fronteriza*].

[44] MERCOSUR/CMC/DOC No. 38/04 [*Documento de Viaje Provisorio del MERCOSUR*].

[45] After the European Union, the Andean Community is the longest-running regional integration process. The Agreement on Andean Sub-regional Integration, known as the Cartagena Agreement, reprinted in 8 *International Legal Materials* (1969) p. 910, was signed on 26 May 1969 by the Presidents of Bolivia, Colombia, Ecuador, Peru and Venezuela in the city of Cartagena de Indias, Colombia, with the aim of creating the Andean Community.

[46] The Treaty of Montevideo Establishing the Latin American Free Trade Association, 18 Feb. 1960, 2 MIGO 1575, created the Latin American Free Trade Association [*Asociación Latinoamericana de Libre Comercio*], which was then changed to the Latin American Integration Association [*Asociación Latinoamericana de Integración*] by a new agreement signed in Montevideo in August 1980 between the Governments of the Republic of Argentina, the Republic of Bolivia, the Federal Republic of Brazil, the Republic of Colombia, the Republic of Chile, the Republic of Ecuador, the United States of Mexico, the Republic of Paraguay, the Republic of Peru, the Republic of Venezuela and the Oriental Republic of Uruguay. See Treaty of Montevideo Establishing the Latin American Integration Association, 12 Aug. 1980, reprinted in 20 *International Legal Materials* (1981) p. 672.

communitarian, social and cultural aspects. This element derived from certain legal instruments which have become the historical pillars of the social dimension of the Andean Community, such as the Andrés Bello Agreement on Education, Science and Culture;[47] the Hipólito Unanue Agreement on Cooperation in Health Issues;[48] and the Simón Rodríguez Agreement on Social-Labour Integration.[49]

4.2 The institutional structure of the Andean Community

The Andean System of Integration is the set of closely related organs and institutions that work together to deepen the level of Andean sub-regional integration and to promote the process globally. The organs and institutions that constitute the Andean System of Integration are the following:

a) The Andean Presidential Council.[50]

b) The Andean Council of Foreign Affairs Ministers.[51]

c) The Andean Commission.[52]

---

[47] The Andrés Bello Agreement on educational, scientific and cultural integration [*Convenio Andrés Bello de integración educativa, científica y cultural*] was signed by the State Parties of the Andean Community on 31 January 1970, with the main objective of improving efforts in the fields of education, science, technology and culture. This Agreement was then changed by the new Agreement of the same name signed on 27 November 1990.

[48] On 29 November 1974, the Ministers of Health of the Andean countries (Bolivia, Colombia, Chile, Ecuador, Peru and Venezuela) signed an agreement concerning healthcare, which is known as the Hipólito Unanue Agreement [*Convenio Hipólito Unanue*]. Its main objective is to improve the levels of human health in the countries of the Andean region, and it compels the states involved to initiate coordinated actions to promote, in this regard, the balanced development of the member countries and to improve the standard of living of their inhabitants. The Hipólito Unanue Agreement was adopted into the Andean Integration System by Decision 445 of the Council of Foreign Ministers; and through Decision 449, the Council of Foreign Ministers approved the terms of the Hipólito Unanue's incorporation into the Andean Integration System and also approved new Organizational and Operational Regulations for the Hipólito Unanue Agreement. Finally, the Ministers of Health of the member countries adopted Resolution REMSAA XXIII/372 of 10 December 2001, by which they agreed to rename the Agreement as 'the Health Body – Hipólito Unanue Agreement' [*Organismo Andino de Salud - Convenio Hipólito Unanue*], affirmed by the Council of Foreign Ministers in its Decision 528 of 7 July 2002. Most Decisions and other documents pertaining to the CAN are available at <http://www.comunidadandina.org/ingles/treaties.htm>. A more comprehensive listing of documents in Spanish can be found at <http://www.comunidadandina.org/documentos.asp>.

[49] One of the most important institutional actions in the social field was the Simón Rodríguez Agreement on Social-Labour Integration [*Convenio Simón Rodríguez de integración sociolaboral*] signed by the Labour Ministers of Bolivia, Colombia, Chile, Ecuador and Venezuela on 26 October 1973. This agreement draws special attention to the harmonization of legal and social security norms, professional training, and the participation of both employers and employees in the development of the sub-regional integration process.

[50] *El Consejo Presidencial Andino.*

[51] *El Consejo Andino de Ministros de Relaciones Exteriores.*

[52] *La Comisión.*

d) The Andean Parliament.[53]

e) The Andean Development Corporation.[54]

f) The Latin American Reserve Fund.[55]

g) The Business Consultative Council.[56]

h) The Labour Consultative Council.[57]

i) The Simón Bolivar Andean University.[58]

j) The Agreements.[59]

k) The Court of Justice of the Andean Community.[60]

l) The General Secretariat.[61]

4.3 Free movement of persons in the Andean Community

Although the Constitution of the Andean Community did not have a direct effect on the movement of persons within the integrated territory – which has basically retained its historical characteristics since the Community was created – it is possible to distinguish two distinct phases, characterized by differing levels of political will to implement the legal instruments adopted to promote the free movement of the citizens of the CAN Member States.

4.3.1 *First phase: Difficulties of building a genuine common trade community*

The Simón Rodríguez Agreement on Social-Labour Integration, signed in 1973 with the intention of creating a common market, stated that its main objectives were to harmonize the levels of labour protection by means of specific labour norms; to improve the use of human resources; to solve the problems of employment and unemployment; to apply common measures of social security; to improve and coordinate professional training systems; to ensure the participation of employers and employees in the integration process; and to establish a regime

[53] *El Parlamento Andino.*
[54] *La Corporación Andina de Fomento.*
[55] *El Fondo Latinoamericano de Reservas.*
[56] *El Consejo Consultivo Empresarial.*
[57] *El Consejo Consultivo Labora.*
[58] *La Universidad Antina Simón Bolivar.*
[59] *Los Convenios.*
[60] *El Tribunal de Justicia.*
[61] *La Secretaría General.*

to facilitate the mobility of the work force. In the context of these objectives, the issue of labour migration was addressed in a concrete and specific way, through Decisions Nos. 113 and 116 of the Cartagena Agreement Commission in 1977, which created the Andean Social Security Instrument and the Andean Labour Migration Instrument (IAML) respectively.[62]

From a legal point of view, the second of these Instruments (the IAML) dealt with every aspect of the regulation of the field of labour migration: the basic definitions of migration regulation; the mechanisms to ensure the implementation of the Instrument; the procedures for hiring employees; the measures to be taken in case of non-observance by any of the Member States; the protection of migrant workers and their families (including workers without the necessary documents); and the obligation on the Member States to punish employers who hire migrants in an abusive or irregular way. Everything was taken into account, constituting a complete regulatory framework for labour migration. However, despite the formal perfection of the IAML, it could not take precedence over national legislation, and was thus unable to become a real communitarian instrument with binding legal effect in the Member States.

Until the mid-90s, the issue of migration was one of the main topics of disagreement between the Andean States, basically due to the impossibility of fulfilling, in an equitable way, the commitments assumed with regard to social protection and recognition of the labour rights of migrant workers. These disputes resulted in the total deactivation of the Simón Rodríguez Agreement, and in repeated violations of the provisions of Cartagena Agreement Commission Decisions Nos. 113 on social security and 116 on labour migration.

4.3.2 *Second phase: Strategic re-definition of the Andean Community*

The structural changes that have occurred in each of the CAN Member States during the last twenty years, and the challenges that have emerged in the international context, have forced a rethink of the doctrinal foundations and the strategic direction of the integration process. This period of reflection of all Members aims to provide more coherent answers to the demands of the 21st century, updating the framework on which the project of Andean integration is built.

The change in the conceptual and political path of the CAN became evident with the approval of the document entitled 'New Strategic Design',[63] on 5 Sep-

[62] In the 27th Period of Extraordinary Sessions of the Cartagena Agreement Commission, held in the city of Lima (Peru) from 14-17 February 1977, the above-mentioned instruments were approved. The Andean Instrument of Social Security [*Instrumento Andino de Seguridad Social*] was created by Decision 113, while Decision 116 approved the Andean Instrument of Labour Migration [*Instrumento Andino de Migración Laboral*].

[63] The document called 'New Strategic Design' [*Nuevo Diseño Estratégico*] is not a legal instrument binding on the Member States, but rather a political document that comes from the Andean Presidential Council. This Council was created in 1990 to evaluate, drive and guide the integration process, meeting every six months. Between 1989 and 1991 six presidential meetings were held. After a suspension of approximately four years, the meetings were held again in Quito in September 1995, where the new strategy of the Andean integration process was approved.

tember 1995, when the 7th Meeting of the Andean Presidential Council took place in Quito, Ecuador. On this occasion, the Presidents agreed to 'deepen the process of Andean integration, enhancing the achievements made in the trade field, and using them to help realize the objectives of social and economic development'.[64]

On this basis, the Presidential Council set in motion actions geared towards the formulation of an Andean Social Agenda, and approved in 1996 a Protocol[65] to amend the institutional structure of the sub-regional integration process. This modification of the original Agreement allowed the Presidents and Foreign Affairs Ministers to assume, in a clearer and more structured manner, their leading role in the integration process.

The Amending Protocol explicitly provided that Member States should engage in

> 'updating the objectives and strengthening the implementation of the Andrés Bello, Hipólito Unanue and Simón Rodríguez Conventions and the José Celestino Mutis Programme [on agriculture, food safety, and environmental protection] to adapt them to the goals and purposes of the Andean Integration System'.[66]

From the institutional point of view, overall responsibility for the social dimension of the integration process was assumed by the Andean Council of Foreign Affairs, which in turn receives support of the ministerial groups that have direct responsibility for the different aspects of the social policy. In the specific case of the movement of persons within the integrated territory, the Foreign Affairs Ministers rely on the Andean Committee of Migration Authorities,[67] which was constituted in 1993.

Confirming the political will to make progress in the field of the free movement of persons within the territory of the sub-region, the Andean Presidential Council, in its 1998 meeting, instructed the Andean Council of Foreign Affairs to take steps to facilitate the freedom of movement among the Member States. To this end, it also established, under the coordination of the Ministers of Foreign Affairs, 'an integrated High Level Expert Group for national migration, labour, security, and integration authorities'.[68]

---

[64] [*Profundizar el proceso de integración andina elevando los logros obtenidos en el campo comercial, y ponerlo al servicio de los objetivos de un desarrollo económico social*]. See the Quito Act, 7th Meeting of the Andean Presidential Council, Quito, Ecuador, 5 Sept. 1995.

[65] The Amending Protocol [*Protocolo Modificatorio del Acuerdo de Integración Subregional Andino*], better known as the Trujillo Protocol [*Protocolo de Trujillo*], was signed in Trujillo (Bolivia) on 10 March 1996 by the Presidents of Bolivia, Colombia, Ecuador, Peru and Venezuela, and replaces Chapter II of the Cartagena Agreement, creating the current institutional structure of the CAN.

[66] See the Trujillo Act, 8th Meeting of the Andean Presidential Council, Trujillo, Bolivia, 10 March 1996, reproduced in UN Doc. A/51/87 (25 March 1996), Annex.

[67] The Andean Committee of Migration Authorities [*Comité Andino de Autoridades de Migración*] comprises ministers of the Member States responsible for migration, and is a consultative organ of the Council of Foreign Affairs Ministers.

[68] [*un Grupo de Expertos de Alto Nivel integrado por las autoridades nacionales migratorias,*

4.4 Main advances in the field of free movement of persons within the Andean Community

Undoubtedly, the most important advances aimed at promoting the free movement of persons within the Andean Community are basically introduced through the Decisions that emanate from the Andean Council of Foreign Affairs Ministers. It is useful to analyze the issue of labour migration from the viewpoint of the legal instruments that seek to encourage or regulate it. To this end, this section will seek to summarize the content of the relevant decisions.[69]

4.4.1 *The Protocol of Substitution of the Simón Rodríguez Agreement*

The Protocol of Substitution of the Simón Rodríguez Agreement of Social Labour Integration was adopted by Andean Council of Foreign Affairs Ministers, on 24 June 2001;[70] it is, at present, going through the process of ratification by the Member States. Among its objectives, the new text foresees the possibility of proposing and debating initiatives on topics related to the social-labour field, which can make a meaningful and effective contribution to the development of the Social Agenda of the sub-region (Article 1). Its content in general seeks to advance the definition and coordination of the Community's policies in terms of employment, vocational and professional training, health and security at work, social security, and labour migration. Its organs are composed in such a manner as to provide for the tripartite participation of Government representatives, employers and employees.

4.4.2 *The Andean Labour Migration Instrument (Decision No. 545)*[71]

In fulfillment of the mandate of the Andean Presidential Council, and with the support of the IOM, a modification of Decision No. 116, which had originally created the IAML, was proposed, which was introduced for consideration at the 3rd Meeting of the Advisory Council of Employment Ministers in May 2002, and approved by the Andean Council of Foreign Affairs Ministers, on 25 June 2003, in its Decision No. 545.

laborales, de seguridad y de integración] Guayaquil Act, 10th Andean Presidential Council, Guayaquil, Ecuador, 6 April 1998, para. 28.

[69] The methodology in this section differs from that used above in examining the case of the MERCOSUR, in that here it is not necessary to begin an analysis of the provisions related to free movement of persons with an examination of the institutional structure of the integration project.

[70] The Protocol of Substitution of the Simón Rodríguez Agreement [*Protocolo Sustitutorio del Convenio Simón Rodríguez*] replaced the previous Agreement (the Simón Rodríguez Agreement) and was signed by the Governments of Bolivia, Colombia, Ecuador, Peru and Venezuela in Valencia, Venezuela, on 24 June 2001 <http://www.comunidadandina.org/ingles/normativa/convention.htm>.

[71] Andean Council of Foreign Affairs Ministers, Dec. No. 545 of 25 June 2003, which approved the Andean Labour Migration Instrument [*Instrumento Andino de Migración Laboral*] replacing Dec. No. 116 of the Cartagena Agreement Commission, loc. cit. n. 62.

This Decision, which replaces Decision No. 116, sets as its objective '… to establish provisions that will progressively and gradually permit the unhampered movement and temporary residence of Andean nationals in the sub-region as wage workers'.[72]

The new Andean Labour Migration Instrument was formulated on the basis of a model of full regional integration, and, apart from recognizing a series of fundamental rights which promote the protection of migrant workers and their families,[73] it contains a programme of different levels of liberalization which obliges the Member States to adopt concrete measures and to adjust their internal normative orders in favour of the free movement of persons in accordance with the agreed schedule. However, it is important to point out that the IAML will not be in force until a Regulation has been formally adopted, the text of which is currently being formulated by the Advisory Council of Employment Ministers.

4.4.3 *The Andean Social Security Instrument (Decision No. 583)*[74]

Inspired by the aim of achieving a common market, and in order to make the regional normative regime capable of dealing with changes in the social security systems of the Andean countries, the Andean Council of Foreign Affairs Ministers elaborated and approved a new Andean Social Security Instrument (Decision No. 583), which replaces its previous version. As with the IAML, this Instrument requires the elaboration of a specific Regulation which, as yet, has not been adopted.[75]

4.4.4 *The Andean Instrument on Health and Safety at Work (Decision No. 584)*[76]

This Instrument, approved by the Andean Council of Foreign Affairs Ministers on 7 May 2004, replaces Decision No. 547. It contains basic norms that are to act as a foundation for the gradual and progressive harmonization of the laws and regulations governing labour activities in each of the Member States. According to the

[72] Ibid., Art. 1.

[73] The text reflects to a very high degree the provisions of the 1990 International Convention on the Protection of the Rights of All Migrant Workers and Members of Their Families, UNGA Res. 45/158 of 18 Dec. 1990, Annex, 45 GAOR Supp. (No. 49A) p. 262, UN Doc. A/45/49 (1990).

[74] Andean Council of Foreign Affairs Ministers, Dec. No. 583 of 7 May 2004, approved the Andean Instrument of Social Security [*Instrumento Andino de Seguridad Social*], replacing both its own earlier Dec. No. 546, and Dec. No. 113 of the Cartagena Agreement Commission, loc. cit. n. 62.

[75] During the 16th Meeting of the Andean Presidential Council, in Lima, on 18 July 2005, the Advisory Council of Employment Ministers were instructed to conclude as soon as possible the technical coordination necessary for the formulation of the Regulations implementing the Andean Labour Migration and Social Security Instruments.

[76] Andean Council of Foreign Affairs Ministers, Dec. No. 584 of 7 May 2004, approved the Andean Instrument on Health and Safety at Work [*Instrumento Andino de Seguridad y Salud en el Trabajo*], replacing its earlier Dec. No. 547.

text of the Decision, this Instrument should be useful not only for promoting the adoption of guidelines on systems of safety and health management at work in the CAN, but also for establishing a preventive policy of risk management at work.

4.4.5 *Travel documentation*

The approval of Decision No. 503,[77] in June 2001, represented a very important step towards the free movement of persons within the sub-region. This Decision affirms that national identification documents are the only requirement for nationals and foreigners resident in the Member States to travel within the integrated territory as tourists.

Other norms related to travel documentation are contained in Decisions No. 504[78] (on the creation of an Andean Passport), No. 525[79] (on minimum specific technical characteristics of Andean Passport nomenclature and security), and No. 526[80] (on airport immigration formality booths for incoming nationals and foreign residents of Member States).

An additional element that should be mentioned is that of the Andean Migration Card, contained in Decision No. 397,[81] which was conceived as a unique instrument for gathering rich and useful information for all the countries; it has, however, never been put into practice.

4.4.6 *General Framework of Principles and Rules for Liberalizing the Trade in Services in the Andean Community*

In order to regulate the services market in the CAN, the Member States have signed a General Framework of Principles and Rules for Liberalizing the Trade in Services in the Andean Community (Decision No. 439),[82] which establishes a set of economic, social and legal conditions on the basis of which Community norms

[77] Andean Council of Foreign Affairs Ministers, Dec. No. 503 of 22 June 2001, on Recognition of national identity documents [*Reconocimiento de documentos nacionales de identificación*], published by La Gaceta Oficial No. 680.

[78] Andean Council of Foreign Affairs Ministers, Dec. No. 504 of 22 June 2001, on the Creation of the Andean Passport [*Creación del Pasaporte Andino*], published by La Gaceta Oficial No. 680.

[79] Andean Council of Foreign Affairs Ministers, Dec. No. 525 of 7 July 2002, on Minimum specific technical characteristics of Andean Passport nomenclature and security [*Características técnicas específicas mínimas de nomenclatura y seguridad del Pasaporte Andino*].

[80] Andean Council of Foreign Affairs Ministers, Dec. No. 526 of 7 July 2002, on Airport incoming immigration formality booths for nationals and foreign residents of Member Countries [*Ventanillas de entrada en aeropuertos para nacionales y extranjeros residentes en los Países Miembros*].

[81] Cartagena Agreement Commission, Dec. No. 397 of 16 Sept. 1996 on the Andean Migration Card [*Tarjeta Andina de Migración*].

[82] Commission of the Andean Community, Dec. No. 439 of 11 June 1998, on the General Framework of Principles and Rules and for Liberalizing the Trade in Services in the Andean Community [*Marco General de Principios y Normas para la Liberalización del Comercio de Servicios en la Comunidad Andina*].

in this field will be elaborated, resulting in the progressive liberalization of the regime governing the offer and provision of services.

In this context, the need to regulate the practice of professionals and technicians is seen as one of the main challenges. In order to respond to this, a High-Level Working Group was created, with the participation of Ministries of Foreign Trade, Migration Offices and some professional associations.

4.4.7 *The Community Policy for Border Integration and Development*

One of the areas in which the political will to make progress in terms of the free movement of persons is readily evident is with regard to the border or frontier areas of the Community. In this regard, the adoption of Decision No. 459 in 1999 should be highlighted,[83] which sets out the so-called Community Policy for Border Integration and Development, and creates a High-Level Working Group on the same issue. Subsequently, in its June 2001 meeting, the Andean Council of Foreign Affairs Ministers adopted Decision No. 501, which promotes the free movement of persons, vehicles, goods and services in the Border Integration Zones of the Andean Community.[84] To the same end, Bi-national Border Service Centres were set up,[85] and a Border Integration and Development Projects bank of the Andean Community has been established.[86]

5. Relations between MERCOSUR and the Andean Community

Although the history of the integration process among South American countries finds its deepest roots in the 19th century with the integrationist proposal of 'Libertador' Simón Bolívar, beginning with the struggle for independence from the Kingdom of Spain, one more recent link between the countries that are now integrating in the CAN and the MERCOSUR is the Latin American Integration As-

[83] Andean Council of Foreign Affairs Ministers, Dec. No. 459 of 25 May 1999, on Communitarian Policy on Border Integration and Development [*Política Comunitaria para la Integración y el Desarrollo Fronterizo*].

[84] Andean Council of Foreign Affairs Ministers, Dec. No. 501 of 22 June 2001, on Border Integration Zones in the Andean Community [*Zonas de Integración Fronteriza (ZIF) en la Comunidad Andina*]. Art. 4(e) states that Member States must promote the free transit of persons, goods and services in the Border Integration Zones, and simplify immigration, customs, and plant and animal health formalities.

[85] Andean Council of Foreign Affairs Ministers, Dec. No. 502 of 22 June 2001, on Bi-national Border Service Centres in the Andean Community [*Centros Binacionales de Atención en Frontera (CEBAF) en la Comunidad Andina*].

[86] Art. 10 of Dec. No. 501, loc. cit. n. 84, states that 'The Border Integration and Development Projects bank is hereby established in the General Secretariat of the Andean Community, with the assistance of the Inter-American Development Bank … and the Andean Development Corporation …, among other bodies'.

sociation, created by the Montevideo Treaty in 1980, with the aim of establishing a common market in the entire region.[87]

In parallel fashion, some Member States of the Andean Community of Nations are also integrating into the MERCOSUR bloc. This is the case for Bolivia, Chile and Peru, which, although not full members of the MERCOSUR, have incorporated into it as 'Associated States'. On the other hand, Venezuela has recently signed a Framework Agreement[88] in which it requests that it be incorporated into the MERCOSUR as a full Member. In the same way, Argentina, Brazil, Paraguay and Uruguay are Associated Members of the Andean Community, according to Decision No. 613 adopted on 7 July 2005.[89] Notwithstanding these initiatives, however, which confer on states different levels of participation in the processes of integration in South America, the two sub-regional blocs maintain negotiations on commercial matters (as they do with other regional blocs).

The Framework Agreement on Regional Energy Complementarity, signed by the States Parties and Associated States of the MERCOSUR on 8 December 2005, also deserves mention here,[90] due to the potential effect that it may have on the development of an integrated South American region. According to the text of this Agreement, its objective is to

> 'advance regional energy integration in terms of the systems of production, transport, distribution and commercialization of energy in the States Parties, in order to guarantee the supply of energy and to establish the conditions for minimizing the transaction costs of energy exchange between those States, ensuring a just and reasonable valuation of such resources, strengthening the development processes in a sustainable manner, and respecting the international obligations in force and the regulatory frameworks extant in each State Party'.[91]

[87] Treaty of Montevideo (1980), Instrument Establishing the Latin American Integration Association <http://www.sice.oas.org/trade/Montev_tr/indexe.asp>. The Constitution of the Association does not rule out the possibility of creating processes of sub-regional integration among the closest countries (geographically and historically), and thus allows for the establishment of such projects as the CAN and the MERCOSUR.

[88] MERCOSUR/CMC/DEC. No. 29/05.

[89] Andean Council of Foreign Affairs Ministers, Dec. No. 613 of 7 July 2005 on the Association of the Republic of Argentina, the Federal Republic of Brazil, the Republic of Paraguay and the Oriental Republic of Uruguay, States Parties of MERCOSUR, with the Andean Community [*Asociación de la República de Argentina, de la República Federativa de Brasil, de la República del Paraguay y de la República Oriental del Uruguay, Estados Parte del MERCOSUR, a la Comunidad Andina*].

[90] Framework Agreement on Regional Energy Complementarity between the States Parties of the MERCOSUR and Associated States [*Acuerdo Marco sobre Complementación Energética Regional entre los Estados Partes del MERCOSUR y Estados Asociados*], 8-9 Dec. 2005, Montevideo, Uruguay.

[91] Ibid., Art. 1 [*El presente Acuerdo marco tiene por objeto contribuir a avanzar en la integración energética regional en materia de los sistemas de producción, transporte, distribución y comercialización de energéticos en los Estados Partes, con el fin de asegurar los suministros energéticos y establecer las condiciones para minimizar los costos de las transacciones de intercambio energético entre dichos Estados, asegurando una valorización justa y razonable de dichos recursos, fortaleciendo los procesos de desarrollo de manera sustentable, respetando los compromisos internacionales vigentes, así como los marcos regulatorios vigentes en cada Estado Parte*].

Lastly, it is also worth mentioning the relations that exist between some of the social organs of the CAN and those of the MERCOSUR, for example the participation of the Economic and Social Consultative Forum of the MERCOSUR in the meetings of the Andean Community's Business and Labour Consultative Councils.[92]

6. Common Weaknesses of the Integration Processes in the MERCOSUR and the Andean Community

A brief summary of the main weaknesses of the integration projects currently underway in South America demonstrates that both the Andean Community and the MERCOSUR suffer from the same shortcomings:

- that any 'progress' that is made in terms of the free movement of persons is of a declaratory, empty nature, and that it does relatively little to achieve concrete results in practice;
- that both the goals of the organizations and the time-frames for their achievement display a lack of realism, which has resulted in the need for periodic revisions of the integration process;
- that both projects suffer from a high level of institutional weakness, which makes it difficult for them to ensure that the obligations assumed by their Member States are being respected.

7. Conclusions

Even taking into consideration all of the difficulties, noted above, that limit the possibilities of strengthening the sub-regional structures of integration and their ability to concretize the obligations that they generate, in particular with regard to their social dimension, there nonetheless remain many factors that should serve to encourage efforts to continue the development of these common markets. Firstly, sub-regional integration represents a valid alternative – and perhaps the only available response – to the demands of trade negotiations at the global level, which are focused on generating agreement between blocs of regions rather than

[92] During the last meeting held in 2005, the two sub-regional organs cooperated in the analysis of a document entitled 'For a new social contract in Latin America' [*Por un nuevo contrato social en América Latina*]. This document was examined once again in the Meeting of the Andean Community's Business and Labour Consultative Councils, held in February 2006, according to the press release published on the CAN's website. See the press release dated 7 Feb. 2006 <http://www.comunidadandina.org/prensa/notas/np7-2-06.htm> (Spanish text)).

bilateral relations between individual countries. Secondly, recent developments in both the MERCOSUR and the Andean Community demonstrate a renewed political will to strengthen the social dimension of the integration process, in recognition of the fact that, although mere economic growth can be generated by simply expanding the market, this alone brings neither more social justice nor a better quality of life to the inhabitants of the Member States. Lastly, the increasing involvement of workers, employers and civil society in enforcing the social elements of the sub-regional integration project seems to be based upon a more democratic vision of its institutional structures and processes.

In this context, even though the objective of guaranteeing the free movement of persons as a right for all citizens of each Member State of the MERCOSUR and the CAN does not appear to be achievable in the short-term, both have made progress towards the deepening of integration in border regions, the facilitation of free movement for the labour force in the services sector, and the promotion of a system for recognizing the rights of migrant workers, particularly in the field of social security.

Selected Bibliography

Bogado-Poisson, L., *Análisis comparado de las legislaciones migratoria y laboral en los países de la Comunidad Andina* [Comparative analysis of migration and labour legislation in the Countries of the Andean Community] (Buenos Aires, IOM 2001).

CELADE, *Migración Internacional en América Latina y el Caribe: Algunos antecedentes empíricos* [International Migration in Latin America and the Caribbean: An Empirical Record] (Santiago de Chile, CELADE 1999).

León Oliveros, R., 'La experiencia en el Pacto Andino' [The Experience of the Andean Pact], in *Las Migraciones Laborales en el MERCOSUR* [Labour Migration in the MERCOSUR] (Buenos Aires, CARI 1993).

Ermida Uriarte, O., *MERCOSUR y Derecho Laboral* [The MERCOSUR and Labour Law] (Montevideo, Fundación de Cultura Universitaria 1996).

—, *la Dimensión Social del MERCOSUR* [The Social Dimension of the MERCOSUR] (Montevideo, Fundación de Cultura Universitaria 2004).

Ferreira, M. and J. Ramos Olivera, *Mercosur. Enfoque laboral* [The MERCOSUR: A Labour Approach] (Montevideo, Fundación de Cultura Universitaria 1991).

Plá Rodríguez, A., 'Problemática de los trabajadores en el Mercosur' [The Issue of Workers in the MERCOSUR], in *El Derecho Laboral del Mercosur* [The Labour Law of the MERCOSUR] (Montevideo, Fundación de Cultura Universitaria 1994) p. 19.

Santestevan, A.M. and H. Barretto, 'Los problemas laborales y de seguridad social respecto a la migración de los trabajadores fronterizos' [Labour and Social Security Problems concerning the Migration of Frontier Workers], *XI Jornadas Rioplatenses de Derecho del Trabajo y de la Seguridad Social* (Montevideo, Fundación de Cultura Universitaria 2000).

Texidó, E., et al., *Migraciones Laborales en Sudamérica: el MERCOSUR Ampliado* [Labour Migration in South America: The Enlarged MERCOSUR], Estudio sobre Migraciones Internacionales [Studies in International Migration] No. 63 (Geneva, IOM 2003).

Torales, P., 'La situación migratoria en América del Sur' [The Migration Situation in South America], Segunda Conferencia Sudamericana sobre Migraciones [Second South American Conference on Migration] (Santiago de Chile, IOM 2001).

Torales, P., et al., *Migraciones Laborales en Sudamérica: la Comunidad Andina* [Labour Migration in South America: The Andean Community], Estudio sobre Migraciones Internacionales [Studies in International Migration] No. 60 (Geneva, IOM 2003).

Villatore, M.A.C., 'Direito do Trabalho no MERCOSUR e nas Constituições dos Estados Partes' [Labour Law in the MERCOSUR and in the Constitutions of the State Parties], 8 *Revista de Derecho Internacional y del Mercosur* (2004) p. 49.

Chapter 22
FREE MOVEMENT OF PERSONS IN THE CARIBBEAN COMMUNITY

Sophie Nonnenmacher*

1. Introduction

The Caribbean Community was established as the Caribbean Community and Common Market (CARICOM) in 1973 with the signing of the Treaty of Chaguaramas, bringing together all the Commonwealth Caribbean countries (Antigua and Barbuda, the Bahamas, Belize, Dominica, Grenada, Guyana, Jamaica, Saint Kitts and Nevis, Saint Lucia, Saint Vincent and Grenadines, Trinidad and Tobago, and Montserrat),[1] which were joined later by Suriname (in 1995) and Haiti (in 1997). The primary focus of the Common Market was on liberalizing trade in goods through the elimination of tariffs and non-tariff barriers to merchandise trade within the region.

The CARICOM Member States, with a total population of 14 million (6 million without Haiti), share several common features. All of them, apart from Haiti and Suriname, were former British colonies, and are English speaking. They are small countries; most are islands (except Guyana, Suriname and Belize). They are all developing countries, with economies that rely mainly on the extra-regional export of a limited number of goods, and services play an important role in their GDPs. The region is also characterized by wide economic disparity; for instance the difference in annual per capita income is 35:1 (the Bahamas with $17,432 is at the top end, and Haiti with $557 at the bottom).[2]

---

* Migration Policy Specialist in the Migration Policy Research and Communications Department, IOM Geneva. This chapter draws on material contributed by the author to the article by R. Cholewinski, S. Nonnenmacher, J. Redpath and J. Packer, 'The International Normative Framework with Reference to Migration in the Greater Caribbean', in *Intra-Caribbean Migration and the Conflict Nexus* (Human Rights Internet, International Organization, Association of Caribbean States and the University of West Indies, forthcoming 2006).

[1] The Seven Eastern Caribbean countries that are part of the CARICOM (Antigua and Barbuda, Dominica, Grenada, St. Kitts and Nevis, St. Vincent and Grenadines, St. Lucia, and Montserrat) formed, in 1981, the Organization of Eastern Caribbean States (OECS), and are at a more advanced stage in the integration process than the other CARICOM States.

[2] Inter-American Development Bank, *CARICOM Report No. 2* (Inter-American Development Bank, Buenos Aires 2005) p. 8 <http://www.iadb.org/intal/aplicaciones/uploads/publicaciones/CARICOM_Report_2.pdf>.

R. Cholewinski, R. Perruchoud and E. MacDonald, eds., International Migration Law

No recent data on intra-regional migration flows is available. The latest data provided from the CARICOM Census date back to 1991, and put the number of intra-CARICOM migrants at 105,000, equivalent to 2 per cent of the total CARICOM population (excluding Haiti, which has not yet been fully integrated into the Community). Over one third of the intra-Caribbean migrant population resides in Trinidad and Tobago and 12 per cent in Barbados, with the main source countries being Grenada (18 per cent), St. Vincent and the Grenadines (17 per cent), and Guyana (13 per cent).[3] With regard to recent trends, partial evidence suggests that intra-regional migration mainly occurs towards neighbouring and mostly prosperous economies, especially to those countries that have developed tourism industries (e.g., Antigua and Barbuda). While in the Bahamas most non-national workers are unskilled, in Jamaica professionals account for 46 per cent of the flows.[4] However, countries like the United States,[5] Canada and the United Kingdom exercise an even stronger attraction. It is likely that an important share of extra-regional flows is composed of low-skilled workers (e.g., agriculture labourers), but professionals attracted by higher earnings have also benefited from an increased demand in certain professions; countries like Jamaica and Trinidad and Tobago, for instance, are experiencing an important outward migration of their qualified labour, particularly teachers, nurses and other health professionals.[6] To give an idea of the importance of migration for the region, remittances accounted for 6 per cent of regional GDP during the period 1998-2003.[7]

2. Freedom of Movement under the CSME

In 1989, the CARICOM Heads of Government announced, in the Grand Anse Declaration,[8] their intention to deepen and strengthen the integration process by transforming the Community into a Caribbean Single Market and Economy (CSME) (Figure 1).[9] To complement the free movement of goods, the CSME

[3] World Bank, *A Time to Choose: Caribbean Development in the 21st Century*, Report No. 31725-LAC, p. 138 <http://wbln0018.worldbank.org/LAC/lacinfoclient.nsf/8d6661f6799ea8a48525673900537f95/fe9533fb44ff524185256ff0004d98b3/$FILE/Time%20to%20choose_report.pdf>.

[4] Ibid., at p. 139.

[5] According to the 2000 US Census, the stock of migrants from the Caribbean countries was 3 million, mainly from Cuba, the Dominican Republic, Jamaica and Haiti.

[6] About 460 nurses per annum are migrating from the Caribbean to Canada, the United States and the United Kingdom. See *A Managed Temporary Movement Programme for Teachers and Nurses, Preliminary Assessment of Policy for the Managed Temporary Movement of Caribbean Teachers and Nurses to Canada, the United Kingdom and the United States*, Study prepared for the Commonwealth Secretariat, Feb. 2005 <http://www.caribank-cfd.org/docs/cfddocs/healthed%20migration%20report.pdf>.

[7] See World Bank, op. cit. n. 3, at p. 212.

[8] Available on the CARICOM website at <http://www.caricom.org/jsp/communications/meeting_minutes/grandanse.jsp?menu=communications>, which also contains the legal instruments relevant to the establishment of the CARICOM Community, Single Market and Economy <http://www.caricom.org>.

[9] The deadline for the establishment of the single market covering the movement of goods, capital,

establishes a framework for the liberalization of services, the free movement of capital and skilled labour, and the freedom to establish business enterprises anywhere in the Community. It is only with the CSME that the issue of *freedom of movement* was introduced in the Caribbean integration agenda, which was considered an important missing element of the earlier integration initiatives of CARIFTA[10] and CARICOM. The Treaty of Chaguaramas[11] was revised by way of nine protocols,[12] which were subsequently incorporated into the Treaty.[13] The Revised Treaty is being applied provisionally,[14] pending ratification by all Member States, in order not to hamper the implementation of the CSME. However, only 13 states will participate in the CSME as the Bahamas (which is a member of the Community), and Haiti (which is not a full Member State[15]) have not indicated that they are interested in joining.

skills and services, and the right of establishment was 1 January 2006, while the creation of a single economy containing measures related to the harmonization of fiscal and investment policies, monetary integration, capital market integration and development should be completed by 31 December 2008. The CSME does not include political integration.

[10] A free trade agreement which came into force in 1968 and which gathered together newly independent Caribbean countries (Antigua and Barbuda, Barbados, Guyana, Trinidad and Tobago, Dominica, Grenada, St. Kitts-Nevis-Anguilla, St. Lucia, St. Vincent and the Grenadines, Montserrat, Jamaica, and Belize) to unite their economies and to give them a joint presence on the international scene.

[11] Treaty Establishing the Caribbean Community, 4 July 1973 <http://www.caricomlaw.org/docs/treaty-caricom.htm>.

[12] The nine protocols are as follows: Protocol I Amending the Treaty Establishing the Caribbean Community (19 July 1997); Protocol II on Establishment, Services and Capital (1 July 1997); Protocol III on Industrial Policy (30 June 2006); Protocol IV on Trade Policy (1997); Protocol V on Agricultural Policy (30 June 1998); Protocol VI on Transport Policy (4 July 1998); Protocol VII on Disadvantaged Countries, Regions and Sectors (4 July 1999); Protocol VIII on Competition Policy, Consumer Protection, Dumping and Subsidies (14 March 2000); and Protocol IX on Disputes Settlement (14 March 2000). They are all available at <http://www.sice.oas.org/trade/ccme/ccmetoc.asp>. Protocol II on Establishment, Services and Capital, which provides for the free movement of non-wage earners, either as service providers and/or to establish a business, entered into force in 1998, and was included in Chapter 3 of the revised Treaty. In addition, this chapter includes provisions related to the mobility of skilled Caribbean nationals for employment. The initiative of 'Free Movement of Skilled Community Nationals' originated in the 1989 Grand Anse Declaration, but the original concept has been modified over the years in order to facilitate the implementation of this mandate, and is now being introduced in phases.

[13] Revised Treaty of Chaguaramas establishing the Caribbean Community including the CARICOM Single Market and Economy (hereafter 'Revised Treaty'), July 2001 <http://www.caricomlaw.org/docs/revisedtreaty.pdf>.

[14] In order to enter into force the Treaty would have to be modified, as Article 234 prescribes that the Treaty will enter into force only when *all* CARICOM Members ratify the agreement; as not all of them have decided to be part of the CSME, it is unlikely that this condition will be fulfilled as it stands.

[15] Haiti has in fact been suspended from CARICOM deliberations since the political turmoil leading to the removal of President Jean Bertrand Aristide from office in February 2004. Furthermore, Haiti's final accession depends on the ratification by its Parliament of the already agreed terms and conditions of its accession.

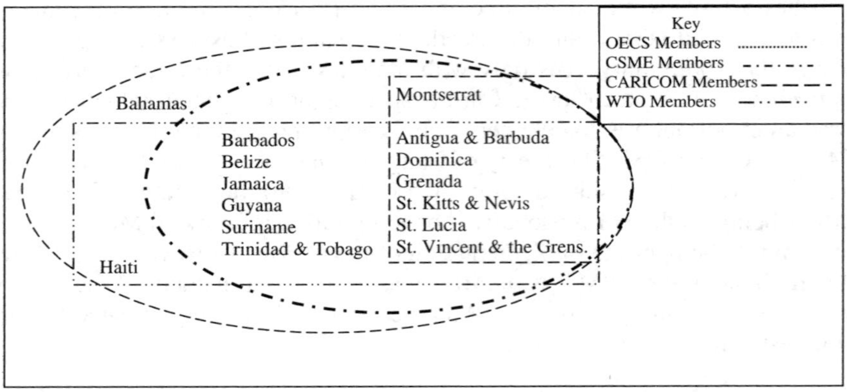

Figure 1: Member States of CARICOM and its inter-relationship with other regional and international trade regimes

CARICOM: Caribbean Community and Common Market
CSME: Caribbean Single Market and Economy
OECS: Organization of Eastern Caribbean States
WTO: World Trade Organization

While some commentators argue that liberalization of movement will not generate strong intra-regional flows (in line with current mobility patterns), it is nonetheless considered that the free movement of persons is a critical factor in the integration process of the CSME, especially as an important share of Caribbean economies rely on services (in particular, tourism and the off-shore sector).[16] It will allow, through better skill matching, for a more efficient distribution of human resources and wage adjustment. However, despite the adoption of the Revised Treaty, several obstacles to free movement remain. Hence, while the Treaty calls upon Member States to commit themselves to the goal of free movement of Community nationals,[17] it foresees a phased approach allowing first certain categories of skilled persons to move to another Member State to perform economic activities in addition to service providers, thus *de facto* excluding most of CARICOM citizens from the benefits of free movement.[18] The realization of the single economy, planned for 2008, will include the goal of complete dismantling of restrictions on free movement within the region.

[16] P.W. Wickham, C.L.A. Wharton, D.A. Marshall and H.A. Darlington-Weekes, 'Freedom of Movement: the Cornerstone of the Caribbean Single Market and Economy', paper prepared for the Caribbean Policy Development Center, Jan. 2004.

[17] Revised Treaty, loc. cit. n. 13, Art. 45.

[18] It is estimated that a maximum of 10 per cent of the CARICOM population would be categorized as 'skilled nationals', thus able to benefit from the freedom of movement provisions of the Revised Treaty. Ibid., at p. 9.

The provisions related to free movement of persons are found in various articles[19] of Chapter Three of the Revised Treaty, on Establishment, Services, Capital and Movement of Community Nationals. Free movement can be exercised under three different elements of the single market: the movement of skills, the movement of services, and the right of establishment. In addition, a certain number of supportive measures for labour mobility were introduced covering social security, 'hassle free travel',[20] and the free movement of spouses and immediate family members of the categories of migrants covered by Protocol II. The deadline for lifting all the restrictions under Chapter III of the Treaty (and thus those on the free movement of persons) was 1 January 2006, representing one of the prerequisite legal steps that Members had to take in order to be able to participate in the single market. Six states – Jamaica, Barbados, Belize, Guyana, Suriname, and Trinidad and Tobago – became the first full members of the CSME on this date. Another six states of the 13 planned CSME Members joined in July 2006. The British territory of Montserrat, which is also a member of the Caribbean Community, is seeking permission from the United Kingdom to become a part of the single market.[21]

2.1 Free movement of skilled community nationals

Free movement of skills entails the right to seek employment in any of the Member States and the elimination of the need for work permits. As mentioned above, it was decided that the liberalization of the movement of skills would be carried out in different phases. The categories covered so far are university graduates, media persons, artists, musicians, and sportspersons, all of whom can exercise their right to free movement only in pursuit of economic activities and not for residential purposes.[22] Discussions have since been under way for the expansion of the categories of skilled persons to include those possessing qualifications in technical and vocational fields as well as those acquiring associate degrees. It was agreed in the July 2006 Conference of the Heads of Government that nurses and teachers will also be covered, except in Antigua and Barbuda. However a deci-

[19] Prohibition of New Restrictions on the Right of Establishment (Art. 32), Removal of Restrictions on the Right of Establishment (Art. 33), Management of Removal of Restrictions on the Right of Establishment (Art. 34), Removal of Restrictions on Provision of Services (Art. 37), Movement of Community Nationals (Art. 45) and Movement of Skilled Community Nationals (Art. 46). The relevant provisions are discussed in greater detail below.

[20] This is how measures related to the freedom of CARICOM nationals to travel 'into and within the jurisdiction of any Member State without harassment or the imposition of impediments' (Art. 46(2)) are commonly referred to.

[21] Montserrat is a UK Overseas Territory.

[22] While the free movement initiative harks back to the Grand Anse Declaration of 1989, the Heads of Government only agreed, in their 1995 Conference, on the free movement of university graduates throughout the region, with was to take effect from January 1996 (the deadline was conditional on the adoption by each Member State of the proper legislation and administrative framework for processing the applications, and was not met). In 1996, the Heads of State decided to expand the initiative to include the other four categories mentioned above.

sion on artisans, domestic staff and hospitality workers was postponed pending the elaboration of procedures for certification and accreditation for these categories.

In order to demonstrate that they belong to an eligible category, CARICOM nationals should obtain a 'Certificate of Recognition of CARICOM Skills Qualification', which will facilitate their entry into another Member State.[23] To this end, the establishment of accreditation councils at the national and regional levels, which would establish a quality assurance framework for the registration and accreditation of tertiary level institutions, was planned. At the regional level, Member States have just begun this process, with the conclusion in 2005 of the Agreement on Accreditation for Education in Medical and other Health Professions.[24] This Agreement establishes an Authority responsible for accrediting doctors and other health care personnel across the region. The Agreement is in force among six states,[25] including Jamaica, where the headquarters of the Authority will be located. Parties are obliged to pass legislation incorporating the Agreement into domestic law. An Inter-Governmental Agreement has still to be finalized for the creation of a Regional Accreditation Body to oversee all accreditation and equivalency, although this role could be taken up by the CARICOM Regional Organization for Standards and Quality[26] (CROSQ).[27]

In addition to the mobility of skilled persons, Chapter III of the Revised Treaty provides for the movement of non-wage earners, such as service providers and/or to establish businesses, including managerial, supervisory and technical staff, and their spouses and immediate family members (previously Protocol II categories).

2.2 Movement of service providers

The Revised Treaty follows the General Agreement on Trade in Services (GATS)[28] model, and provides in its Article 36 for the removal of restrictions on

[23] The holder of the certificate will be granted a definite entry of six months by the receiving country, which will during this time assess the holder's qualifications, and, if satisfied, will grant indefinite entry.

[24] This sector was chosen because of its importance in the region, and the existence of national councils in many Member States.

[25] Antigua and Barbuda, Belize, Jamaica, Suriname, Trinidad and Tobago, and the Bahamas.

[26] Agreement establishing the CARICOM Regional Organization for Standards and Quality (CROSQ), 4 Feb. 2002 <http://www.caricom.org/jsp/secretariat/legal_instruments/agreement_crosq.jsp?menu=secretariat>. Article 4 of the Agreement stipulates that '[t]he primary objectives of CROSQ shall be the establishment and harmonisation of standards for the enhanced efficiency and improved quality in the production of goods and services in the Community, thereby facilitating consumer and environmental protection and improved trade within the Community and with third states'.

[27] At the national level, Jamaica, Belize and Trinidad and Tobago have a fully functioning accreditation body. The process of establishing Councils to regulate the licensing and professional activities of the various professions is at different levels of completion in the other Member States.

[28] Final Act Embodying the Results of the Uruguay Round of Multilateral Trade Negotiations

the provision of services according to the four modes of supply specified under Article I.2 of the GATS. The term 'services' is further defined according to remuneration, which should be other than wages.[29] This definition is very broad, and permits movement of service providers at all skills levels as long as they are not employees.[30] In this sense it is no different from the GATS, which does not include a skill threshold.[31]

One main difference between the GATS and the Revised Treaty is in their approach towards liberalization. CARICOM nationals should enjoy the same treatment as nationals when engaging in 'approved activities' in another Member State.[32] The CARICOM Member States have adopted a negative list approach, whereby all sectors and measures are to be liberalized unless otherwise specified.[33] In contrast, the GATS pursues a positive list approach, less conducive to liberalization, according to which countries limit the removal of restrictions to sectors and measures included in their national schedules.

While the Revised Treaty specifies that it applies to temporary movement, as does the GATS, it does not define the period of time covered (e.g., one day, several months or years). It is implied that service providers should supply the services and leave, having no right to take up residence (or enter the labour market) in the country in which they offer and provide the services (unless there is commercial presence – see Section 2.3 below). Free movement of service providers will be effective only with the removal of restrictions on certification, accreditation and licensing, which implies the establishment of common standards on procedures and/or for determining equivalency.[34] As observed above, while a regional body has been created for establishing standards and harmonizing the quality of goods and services (the CROSQ), which should ensure that a high qual-

(1994), Annex 1B General Agreement on Trade in Services (GATS) <http://www.wto.org/English/docs_e/legal_e/26-gats.pdf>.

[29] Revised Treaty, loc. cit. n. 13, Art. 36(4).

[30] Under the CARICOM mobility framework, two persons in the same profession may be subject to different rules. It will depend on whether they are wage earners or self-employed. For example, construction workers are not entitled to free movement under the 'skills' element as they are not included in the eligible categories, but they are able to move as (non-wage earning) service providers.

[31] Nonetheless, in practice most WTO Member States have decided in their GATS commitments to provide access to their labour market only to highly skilled persons.

[32] Revised Treaty, loc. cit. n. 13, Art. 36(2).

[33] The Revised Treaty, ibid., includes, in its Article 47, a safeguard clause, where restrictions on the rights provided under Chapter 3 can be applied to resolve difficulties in a sector of the economy or alleviate hardships in one region created by their application. In addition, Article 49 allows the Less Developed Countries (LDCs) within CARICOM to seek exemption from the Chapter III obligations in view of their special needs and circumstances. CARICOM considers the following countries as LDCs: Antigua and Barbuda, Belize, Dominica, Grenada, Haiti, Montserrat, St. Kitts and Nevis, St. Lucia, St. Vincent and Grenadines. As a corrective mechanism, the CSME has made provision for the establishment of a Development Fund to provide relief to Member States, regions or sectors disadvantaged by economic dislocations arising from the CSME, but the modalities of its functioning remain to be defined.

[34] Revised Treaty, ibid., Art. 35.

ity of output is associated with free movement in this context,[35] a regional body to oversee accreditation and equivalence has not yet been put in place.

2.3 Right of establishment

CARICOM nationals can move on a more permanent basis[36] to another Member State as self-employed or independent contractors by exercising their right of establishment (also referred to as 'commercial presence' under the services regime). It confers the right to engage in any non-wage earning activities[37] of a commercial, industrial, agricultural, professional or artisanal nature, as well as to create and manage economic enterprises for the production of or trade in goods or the provision of services.[38] The right of establishment requires, in addition, the removal of restrictions on the movement of managerial, technical and supervisory staff of economic enterprises, and on the establishment of agencies, branches and subsidiaries of companies.[39]

All CARICOM countries, except the Bahamas[40] and Montserrat, are Members of the WTO. Protocol II was submitted to the WTO Council for Trade in Services for a legal opinion on whether it was consistent with Article V of the GATS. This opinion is still pending. Article V allows parties to a regional agreement to treat the other parties to that agreement more favourably, subject to the conditions that it has substantial sectoral coverage and that each party must afford the services and service providers of other parties treatment no less favourable than it does its own. A positive legal opinion will thus ensure that the level of treatment afforded to CARICOM nationals under the CSME need not be extended to other WTO Members.

3. Additional Measures to Facilitate the Movement of Persons

Some additional measures have been envisaged to ensure the smooth implementation of policies on the free movement of persons. They cover the following areas: family reunion, 'hassle-free travel', social security and taxation.

---

[35] National bodies exist in all countries, apart from Montserrat and Suriname. See Wickham, et al., loc. cit. n. 16, at p. 27.

[36] That is, with the right of indefinite stay.

[37] These are defined as activities carried out by self-employed persons.

[38] Revised Treaty, loc. cit. n. 13, Art. 32.

[39] Ibid., Art. 34.

[40] On 10 May 2001, a request for accession under Article XII of the Agreement Establishing the World Trade Organization (1994) <http://www.wto.org/English/docs_e/legal_e/04-wto.pdf> was sent to the Director-General of the WTO by the Government of the Bahamas. However, the Bahamas has not yet submitted a Memorandum on the Foreign Trade Regime, which is part of the accession procedure.

The Revised Treaty provides rights to *family members* of those falling under the Protocol II categories[41] (related to the provision of services) to join the principal beneficiary, and to leave and re-enter the state in which the right of free movement has been exercised without further formalities. However, the issue of who constitutes a dependent in the context of the Revised Treaty is defined in accordance with the income tax legislation and the social security schemes of the respective Member States.[42] In the absence of a generalized and agreed definition of spouses and immediate dependent family members at the regional level, differences can occur within each Member State as to the categories of persons covered by this mobility right and to the transferability of social security benefits.

Other measures to encourage the movement of skills were introduced, although they also benefit other CARICOM nationals, namely 'hassle free travel', the transfer of social security benefits, and avoidance of double taxation. With regard to the first of these, the Revised Treaty envisaged the facilitation of intra-regional mobility, recognizing for CARICOM nationals the right to travel into and within the jurisdiction of any Member State 'without harassment or the imposition of impediments'.[43] In the Grand Anse Declaration, it was agreed that all CARICOM nationals should be free to travel within the Community without the need for passports, with a view to enhancing a sense of Community belonging and encouraging intra-Caribbean tourism. However, the scheme soon ran into implementation difficulties, as Member States could not agree on the forms of acceptable identity documents and on which nationals should be included. The idea of the introduction of a Caribbean passport has thus far faced similar problems, with only Suriname, St. Vincent and the Grenadines, St. Kitts and Nevis, Dominica, and Antigua and Barbuda issuing it to date; the other countries are expected to introduce the passport by 2007. Two accompanying elements have been introduced more successfully: the establishment of CARICOM nationals' lines at all ports of entry and the development and use of common embarkation/disembarkation forms.

The CARICOM Agreement on Social Security came into effect on 1 April 1997.[44] It protects all entitlements to long-term benefits by providing for the totalization of all periods in which contributions were paid to social security systems in Member States, and is operational in all Members but for Suriname (which does not have a similar social security system and is working on a system of transfer of benefits). Nonetheless, social security systems are not harmonized, and related benefits are unequal among Member States. Furthermore, only five

---

41 Art. 37(3)(c).

42 See 'The Role of Labour in Promoting the Caribbean Single Market and Economy', lecture by Rt. Hon. Owen Arthur, Prime Minister of Barbados, to the 15th Triennial Delegates' Congress, Caribbean Congress of Labour, Paramaribo, Suriname, 19 Oct. 2004, p. 41 <http://www.barbados.gov.bb/Docs/LecturetoCCLCongress.pdf>.

43 Revised Treaty, loc. cit. n. 13, Art. 46(2)(b).

44 CARICOM Agreement on Social Security, 1 March 1996 <http://www.caricom.org/jsp/secretariat/legal_instruments/agreement_socialsecurity.jsp?menu=secretariat>.

countries are currently processing social security claims under the Agreement (Barbados, Dominica, Guyana, St. Kitts and Nevis, and Trinidad and Tobago).[45] The Intra-Regional Double Taxation Agreement,[46] which entered into force in 1994, is currently applied by all Member States apart from the Bahamas, Grenada, Haiti, St. Kitts and Nevis, Suriname and Montserrat, and precludes self-employed CARICOM nationals from paying taxes twice on the same earnings.

These positive outcomes do not eliminate the broader issue of the need for Member States, as the labour market is liberalized, to put in place a satisfactory regime in respect of contingent rights. Contingent rights are those rights that Member nationals (and their dependents) should be entitled to when they exercise their freedom of movement (e.g., access to health, education and social services). The Revised Treaty only mentions the issue of contingent rights in the context of 'establishment, provision of services, and movement of capital in the Community', which are to be addressed in a separate Protocol to be elaborated by Member States.[47] Moreover it does not provide any information on what the substantive content of such rights might be. The Protocol referred to has still to be negotiated.

4. Implementation of the CSME Free Movement Provisions

Most of the migratory flows occurring today in the CARICOM region fall within the scope of national immigration frameworks established on a unilateral/discretionary basis. Persons seeking to find work must obtain a work permit and a resident permit from the receiving Member State. Although legislation on the free movement of skills has been adopted in most Member States for more than five years, relatively few skilled persons have actually moved to other Community States.[48] The bulk of those who have was made up of graduates moving to Barbados, Trinidad and Tobago, and Jamaica. For instance, Barbados granted freedom of movement to 998 persons between 1996 and April 2005 (of which one third were Guyanese nationals and another third were citizens of Trinidad and Tobago).[49] In contrast, there seem to have been more movements among unskilled per-

[45] Inter-American Development Bank, op. cit. n. 2, at p. 29.

[46] Agreement Among the Governments of Member States of the Caribbean Community for the Avoidance of Double Taxation and the Prevention of Fiscal Evasion with respect to Taxes on Income, Profits or Gains and Capital Gains and for the Encouragement of Regional Trade and Investment, July 1994 <http://www.caricomlaw.org/docs/agreement-doubletaxation.htm>.

[47] Revised Treaty, loc. cit. n. 13, Art. 239.

[48] H.R. Brewster, 'The Caribbean Single Market and Economy: Is it Realistic Without Commitment to Political Unity?', Washington, DC, 14 March 2003 <www.caricom.org/jsp/speeches/csme-politicalunity-brewster.htm>.

[49] S. McAndrew, 'Migration in the CARICOM Single Market and Economy', in *Regional and International Migration in the Caribbean and its Impact on Sustainable Development.* Compendium on Recent Research on Migration in the Caribbean, report presented at the Caribbean Expert Group Meeting on Migration, Human Rights and Development in the Caribbean, 14-15 Sept. 2005, Port of Spain, Trinidad and Tobago, p. 68, at p. 72 <http://www.eclac.org/publicaciones/xml/3/23203/L.61.pdf>.

sons, most of these occurring illegally, although such categories are not covered by the current regional liberalization agenda.

The implementation of the freedom of movement provisions has encountered several delays, with deadlines being passed and rescheduled. Problems relate to a lack of financial and human resources and institutional capacities, but also to a divergence of interests among countries on this issue, resulting in a lack of political will to move forward. On the one hand, the strongest economies fear attracting skilled workers from other states and thereby negatively affecting unemployment rates amongst their own nationals; and this argument is also used as a justification for maintaining general restrictions on the movement of unskilled labour. It is important to recall that this was the reason why the Bahamas, which has lower unemployment rates and higher per capita GDP than the Caribbean average, decided not to participate in the CSME process. On the other hand, less developed countries, with their small professional labour forces and absence of universities, gain only limited benefits from a regional open market for the highly skilled, and argue that one way to level the playing field is to immediately introduce free movement of unskilled labour. Apparently, this was one of the reasons why the Members of the OECS were not ready to join the Single Market on 1 January 2006.[50] The CSME also suffers from a general image problem in civil society (and from limited popular support as a result), with the perceived inequity of the distribution of the costs and benefits of economic integration, as well as a lack of knowledge on the exact content of free movement rights.

There is a broad consensus on the need to provide better information for citizens and policy makers within the region on the effects of free movement. This is currently impeded by, *inter alia*, the lack of statistical data on migration. To remedy this, it was decided that the CARICOM Secretariat should develop a database on the movement of skills,[51] and Trinidad and Tobago also submitted a proposal to the CARICOM Working Group on Services Negotiations for a register of service providers.[52] However, to understand the impact of regional integration arrangements, it is necessary to develop the capacity to capture a broader picture (beyond movements of persons covered by the regional agreement), including the recording of movements taking place under national immigration frameworks, some estimates of the number of irregular migrants, as well as a mapping of extra-regional mobility.

The case of service providers can be taken as one example of the relevance of shedding light on the relations between intra-regional and extra-regional flows. The lack of data on service providers impedes the assessment of the potential of

---

[50] M. La Rose, 'Trinidad Proposes Registration of Service Providers under CSME', 8 Jan. 2006, *Strabroek News* <http://www.stabroeknews.com>.

[51] S. McAndrew, op. cit. n. 49, at p.73.

[52] The aim is to facilitate their movement by making it easier for immigration officials to recognize service providers and facilitate their entry.

services exports by Caribbean countries under the GATS Mode 4.[53] Such monitoring is critical in certain sectors such as health and education, where negotiating market access should be based on a clear understanding of the effect of better access on the labour markets of developed countries, and the potential for 'brain drain', and whether a more open Caribbean market access for these services could counteract that loss.[54] In addition to statistics, other initiatives such as labour market analyses, evaluations of the actual implementation and operation of the regime on free movement (with an assessment of the positive and negative impact on each Member State), and proposals for corrective measures are much needed and should be developed by the Secretariat.[55]

Finally, it should be noted that the current level of progress in the elaboration of a regional freedom of movement regime is also a result of constraints emerging from the CARICOM institutional framework, which is one of a Community of sovereign states operating on the basis of the unanimity rule. With the exception of the Caribbean Court of Justice,[56] none of the institutions created to support the integration process has been given supranational decision-making powers. In addition, the majority of them lack sufficient funding. As a result, regional policy is moving at the pace of the lowest common denominator in the attempt to forge consensus; even when ambitious goals emerge from governmental consultations, the implementation of the decisions taken requires a separate legislative or administrative decision by every Member State, which often creates significant delays, especially in view of the lack of strong enforcement mechanisms. In order to achieve the goals of the CSME, many believe that it will be necessary to transfer some decision-making powers to a regional entity[57] that could speak with a common voice on the most important areas of the process, develop new policies, and monitor progress in their implementation.[58]

---

[53] Loc. cit. n. 28. For a detailed analysis of GATS Mode 4 in the context of migration, see Klein Solomon's chapter in this volume.

[54] UN Economic Commission for Latin America and the Caribbean (ECLAC), 'The Development of Services in the Caribbean', 17 Jan. 2003, p. 25 <www.cepal.org/id.asp?id=12285>.

[55] Address by the Hon. Clement J. Rohee, Minister of Foreign Trade and International Cooperation, Guyana, on the CARICOM Single Market and Economy (CSME), at a luncheon of the Georgetown Chamber of Commerce and Industry, 23 Aug. 2005, Georgetown, Guyana <www.CARICOM.org/jsp/speeches/gcci_csme_rohee.jsp>.

[56] The Caribbean Court of Justice, in its 'original jurisdiction' (i.e., when it is not functioning as a court of appeal), is responsible for the interpretation and application of the Revised Treaty, and will have to ensure that the benefits of free movement are realized.

[57] As was done in the European Union context with the transfer of competences to the European institutions, such as the Council of Ministers and European Commission.

[58] The need to reform the regional governance system is acknowledged by CARICOM Members themselves. In February 2003, the CARICOM Heads of Conference appointed a Prime Ministerial Expert Group on Governance, which, with the assistance of a technical group, provided recommendations on (a) enhancing the functioning of the Assembly of Caribbean Community Parliamentarians; (b) the establishment of a CARICOM Commission or other Executive Mechanism; and (c) automatic financing of regional institutions. However, no actions have been taken to date.

5. Conclusion

Progress on free movement has been slow. All Member States were required to remove existing restrictions on the rights of establishment, provision of services, movement of capital and movement of skills for the full implementation of the Single Market on 1 January 2006, or shortly thereafter; around 17 years after the Grand Anse Declaration referring to the free movement of persons was adopted. Even though the relevant legal actions should have now been put into place,[59] mobility will still be impeded by cumbersome administrative processes, significant variations in transposition of treaty requirements into domestic legislation (e.g., with regard to family reunion), and the absence of supportive regional instruments (e.g., an accreditation body). As a result, the translation of free movement from rhetoric into reality will not be completed by the end of 2006, and will require from Member States more actions at the national and regional level. In particular, CARICOM will need to continue to build its regional institutional frameworks to facilitate and/or encourage these movements. The establishment of a comprehensive accreditation system and an effective regional framework for the collection of statistics on migration flows, including service providers, will be particularly important.

Furthermore, the free movement of persons as envisioned in the CSME to date is specifically linked to economic activities, and concerns limited categories of persons. The question of its expansion to other categories of the labour force, especially unskilled labour, as well as to mobility unrelated to economic activities (e.g., for residential purposes), still has to be addressed. In view of the pace of the progress on free movement to date, the deadline of 2008 for providing access to this right to all CARICOM nationals seems rather optimistic. Even the realization of the more limited goal of full labour mobility, given the reluctance among Member States to liberalize the movement of unskilled labour region-wide, seems improbable by that time. Therefore, free movement of persons in the Caribbean, as in other regions (e.g., the EU), will prove to be a continuous and evolving process, requiring much fine-tuning over a long period of time.

The Caribbean Community experience with free movement illustrates the complexity of the relationships between trade liberalization and migration movements in the context of regional integration processes, and the integration of regional groupings into the world economy. Due to the small size of the region, CARICOM's integration strategy has focused on fostering intra-regional trade as a tool to improve the region's international competitiveness. The CSME was launched especially with a view to responding to the new challenges posed by a more globalized economy. It should allow, through free movement of goods, services, capital and skilled persons, for the emergence of a more efficient and dynamic regional market in a better position to take part in global market inte-

[59] However, for the time being, information is lacking on the level of implementation in a number of Member States.

gration. With regard to service providers, the creation of a regional market is expected to improve quality and competitiveness, and increasingly allow them to tap into the extra-regional market, while the CSME is expanding CARICOM's capacity to negotiate service agreements with extra-regional partners, or at the multilateral level under GATS Mode 4.

However, if CARICOM has been successful in the past in collectively negotiating trade and aid agreements, the increasingly powerful bargaining position and raised profile of individual members, coupled with regional integration and global liberalization processes leading to an erosion of trade preferences[60] in the context of declining external aid, might encourage countries to pursue their own economic interests in bilateral deals or wider regional settings[61] (e.g., the participation of Guyana and Suriname in the Initiative for the Integration of Regional Infrastructure in the Americas).[62] In the absence of the realization of the CSME, Caribbean states might find it hard to preserve their identity and economic space, in the context of a trend towards general trade liberalization in the Western Hemisphere[63] and at the global level.

Selected Bibliography

Brewster, H.R., 'The Caribbean Single Market and Economy: Is it Realistic Without Commitment to Political Unity?', Washington, DC, 14 March 2003 <www.caricom.org/jsp/speeches/csme-politicalunity-brewster.htm>.

Cholewinski, R., S. Nonnenmacher, J. Redpath and J. Packer, 'The International Normative Framework with Reference to Migration in the Greater Caribbean', in *Intra-Caribbean Migration and the Conflict Nexus* (Human Rights Internet, International Organization, Association of Caribbean States and the University of West Indies, forthcoming 2006).

Gonzales, A., 'Searching for the Optimal Response, CARICOM and NAFTA', in 65 *CARICOM Perspective* (1995).

Inter-American Development Bank, *CARICOM Report No. 2* (Inter-American Development Bank, Buenos Aires 2005) <http://www.iadb.org/intal/aplicaciones/uploads/publicaciones/CARICOM_Report_2.pdf>.

McAndrew, S., 'Migration in the CARICOM Single Market and Economy', in *Regional and International Migration in the Caribbean and its Impact on Sustainable Development*, Compendium on Recent Research on Migration in the Caribbean, report presented at the Caribbean

[60] These are, for example, preferential market access given to goods from certain countries due to past colonial links

[61] A. Gonzales, 'Searching for the Optimal Response, CARICOM and NAFTA', in 65 *CARICOM Perspective* (1995). See also the Section on Trade and Labour Migration in this volume.

[62] However, CARICOM Member States cannot offer more favourable treatment to non-CARICOM countries. Indeed, Article 8 of the Revised Treaty (loc. cit. n. 13) reads: 'Subject to the provisions of this Treaty, each Member State shall, with respect to any rights covered by this Treaty, accord to another Member State treatment no less favourable than that accorded to: (a) a third Member State; or (b) third States'.

[63] Inter-American Development Bank, op cit. n. 2, at p. 6; even if today the achievement of a Free Trade Area of the Americas encompassing 34 countries of the hemisphere is a very distant prospect.

Expert Group Meeting on Migration, Human Rights and Development in the Caribbean, 14-15 Sept. 2005, Port of Spain, Trinidad and Tobago, p. 68 <http://www.eclac.org/publicaciones/xml/3/23203/L.61.pdf>.

UN Economic Commission for Latin America and the Caribbean (ECLAC), 'The Development of Services in the Caribbean', 17 Jan. 2003 <www.cepal.org/id.asp?id=12285>.

Wickham, P.W., C.L.A. Wharton, D.A. Marshall and H.A. Darlington-Weekes, 'Freedom of Movement: the Cornerstone of the Caribbean Single Market and Economy', paper prepared for the Caribbean Policy Development Center (Jan. 2004).

World Bank, *A Time to Choose: Caribbean Development in the 21st Century*, Report No. 31725-LAC <http://wbln0018.worldbank.org/LAC/lacinfoclient.nsf/8d6661f6799ea8a48525673900537f95/fe9533fb44ff524185256ff0004d98b3/$FILE/Time%20to%20choose_report.pdf>.

Continuing and Emerging Issues of Significance

Chapter 23
COOPERATION MECHANISMS

Anne-Grethe Nielsen*

1. INTRODUCTION: THE NEED FOR INTERNATIONAL COOPERATION

The migration life-cycle is a process involving complex relationships between the migrant and various public and private stakeholders in the countries of destination, transit and origin. Effective management of this process and the relationships involved requires cooperation among all interested stakeholders in migration, including states, international organizations, NGOs, the private sector, civil society (including local migrant associations), and the migrants themselves. It is only through such an effort that the international community will be able to fully and effectively address the challenges and opportunities of migration. Cooperation in this field can take various forms, ranging from dialogue and sharing of information, experience and practice to cooperation in policy development and operational implementation. Cooperation at the international level will contribute to more effective national policy development, avoiding overlap and duplication and facilitating a more efficient use of resources at national, regional and international levels.[1]

However, the management of migration is a sovereign right and responsibility of states, and, consequently, migration policies have traditionally been developed at the national level. Yet, policy makers are becoming gradually more aware that migration cannot be managed at this level alone, and that international cooperation is needed. International migration is a transnational phenomenon, and as such affects more than one country. Over the years, states have therefore realized that any unilateral action taken by them has repercussions on

---

* Director of International Affairs at the Swiss Federal Office for Migration (previously the Federal Office for Refugees). With particular thanks to Alexandre Devillard, Cynthia Bryant and Karoline Popp for their research assistance in finalizing the references for this chapter.

[1] Concerning collective migration management in general, see 'Illustration of Multilateral, Regional and Bilateral Cooperative Arrangements in the Management of Migration', in T.A. Aleinikoff and V. Chetail (eds.), *Migration and International Legal Norms* (The Hague, T.M.C. Asser Press 2003) p. 305.

the regional or international levels, with direct consequences for other countries, such as, for example, an unexpected diversion of a stream of migrants to the borders of neighbouring states. Furthermore, there is a growing awareness that restrictive national measures in host states cannot be used in isolation, but have to be accompanied by long-term measures dealing with the roots of the problems in the countries of origin. These countries are also deeply affected by the management of migratory flows, facing important issues and challenges such as 'brain drain' or the re-integration of returning migrants; there is thus a growing interest in countries of origin in discussing with destination countries both the negative and the positive consequences of migration. And, last but not least, migratory movements often involve a passage through transit countries, thereby affecting issues such as border management and international security.

States are also becoming aware that, without better cooperation and partnership between concerned countries, irregular migration will continue to increase and to foster lasting negative attitudes towards non-citizens. The consequences of such developments may affect relations between states, as well as the delicate balance struck in the international trade and financial regimes and in terms of global security.

Profound changes are thus taking place in the understanding of, on the one hand, the phenomenon of migration itself, and, on the other, the role and nature of international collaboration in this field. This explains why a series of initiatives have been launched over recent years at the multilateral level with a view to better management of migration, characterized by a 'bottom-up' approach. They are largely initiated by states which see that their interests lie in building bridges for cooperation. These developments have begun to fundamentally alter the prospects for the realization of the positive potential of migration.

Consultation mechanisms play a significant role in facilitating effective migration management by states. Effective migration management needs to be consistent with principles of good governance, including transparency, predictability, participation, and responsiveness and accountability, among others. For many states, this is a new administrative field, often because they have not historically been affected by migration to a significant extent. For others, the capacity to manage migration is developed in one area but not in another. The regional and global inter-state consultation mechanisms described below can be instrumental in helping to develop states' capacity to deal with migration in a manner that is both effective and consistent with principles of good governance.

2. Cooperation at the Multilateral Level[2]

2.1 Inter-state consultations

2.1.1 *The Berne Initiative*

The Berne Initiative was launched by the Swiss Government in June 2001,[3] as a state-owned consultation mechanism with the goal of obtaining better management of migration at the national, regional and global levels through enhanced cooperation between states.[4] It assisted governments in identifying both their different policy priorities and, together with relevant stakeholders, a common orientation to migration management.

The most important outcome of the Berne Initiative has been the development of the International Agenda for Migration Management (IAMM).[5] The IAMM, a non-binding reference system and policy framework on migration management at the international level, was developed through a series of consultations involving interested states, as the principal actors in the field of migration management, with the advice and support of relevant regional and international organizations, NGOs and independent migration experts.

In 2004, four regional consultations were organized: in Addis Ababa, Ethiopia for Africa; in Budapest, Hungary for Europe and Central Asia; in Guilin, China for Asia and the Pacific; and in Santiago, Chile for the Americas region.[6] At these consultations, government officials and migration experts from all regions of the world explored the issues surrounding migration and contributed to the further development of the IAMM. In all four consultations, it was acknowledged that most countries share areas of common interest.

The IAMM gathers states' common perspectives and understandings on migration in a comprehensive and balanced framework in the form of a non-binding agenda, mapping out all major aspects of migration at the international level. It

---

[2] See generally IOM, *World Migration 2005, Costs and Benefits of International Migration* (Geneva, IOM 2005) pp. 368-371.

[3] The Berne Initiative, *Summary and Conclusions by the Chair*, International Symposium on Migration, Berne 14-15 June 2001.

[4] Further information and documentation related to the Berne Initiative are available at the Swiss Federal Office for Migration <http://www.bfm.admin.ch/index.php?id=226&L=3&S=1%2Findex.pjb> and the IOM website <http://www.iom.int/jahia/page1491.html>.

[5] *International Agenda for Migration Management; Common Understandings and Effective Practices for a Planned, Balanced, and Comprehensive Approach to the Management of Migration* (IAMM), Berne 16-17 Dec. 2004 (Geneva, IOM/Swiss Federal Office for Migration 2005).

[6] Berne Initiative Regional Consultations for Africa, 25-26 March 2004, Addis Ababa, Ethiopia; Berne Initiative Regional Consultations for Europe and Central Asia, 24-25 June 2004, Budapest, Hungary; Berne Initiative Consultations for Asia and the Pacific, 29-30 July 2004, Guilin, China; Berne Initiative Regional Consultations for the Americas, 9-10 Sept. 2004, Santiago de Chile. The reports of the Regional Consultations are available at <http://www.iom.int/jahia/page1494.html>.

includes such issues as migration and development,[7] human rights of migrants,[8] labour migration,[9] integration,[10] irregular migration, trafficking in human beings and migrant smuggling,[11] trade and health issues,[12] and return.[13]

The IAMM consists of two essential components:

- a set of Common Understandings outlining fundamental shared assumptions and principles underlying migration management, and summarizing the values and perceptions that governments bring to migration;[14] and
- an accompanying set of Effective Practices for a planned and coherent approach to migration management.[15]

It can be employed in the following ways:

- as a common reference document mapping out the constituent elements of a comprehensive migration policy strategy;
- as a planning instrument for the development of administrative structures and allocation of administrative responsibilities;
- as an instrument to facilitate inter-agency cooperation at the national level;
- as an evaluation tool for states in reviewing and developing their own national migration policies; and
- as a training instrument and capacity-building tool for governmental migration practitioners.[16]

The first IAMM-based capacity-building workshop took place in South Africa for the South African Development Community States in July 2005, organized by IOM and the Migration Dialogue for Southern Africa (MIDSA)[17] Secretariat. A second capacity-building workshop took place for West Africa in November

[7] IAMM, op. cit. n. 5, at pp. 58-61.
[8] Ibid., at pp. 45-49.
[9] Ibid., at pp. 40-42.
[10] Ibid., at pp. 51-52.
[11] Ibid., at pp. 42-45.
[12] Ibid., at pp. 61-64.
[13] Ibid., at pp. 53-57.
[14] Ibid., at ch. II, pp. 23-25.
[15] Ibid., at ch. III, pp. 27-70.
[16] On the different uses of the IAMM, see ibid., at pp. 13-14.
[17] See *infra* Section 3.4.2.

2005, held by the Migration Dialogue for West Africa (MIDWA).[18] Additional workshops were being considered for 2006.

The IAMM was made available to the Global Commission on International Migration (GCIM), and was provided to the UN General Assembly for its 2006 High-Level Dialogue on International Migration and Development,[19] to inform and support its work and serve as a complement to its activities and approaches.

2.1.2 *IOM's International Dialogue on Migration*

The IOM Council's International Dialogue on Migration (IDM) is an informal and non-binding consultation mechanism. The IDM's two primary activities are annual sessions, which take place at the IOM Council sessions, and inter-sessional workshops. The purpose of the IDM is to contribute to a better understanding of migration and to strengthen cooperative mechanisms between governments in order to comprehensively and effectively address migration issues. The IDM, which works through the IOM's Council, was launched at the eighty-second Council session in November 2001, on the occasion of the IOM's 50th anniversary.[20] The IDM represents the realization of one of the principal purposes of the IOM as set forth in its Constitution:

> 'to provide a forum to States as well as international and other organizations for the exchange of views and experiences, and the promotion of co-operation and co-ordination of efforts on international migration issues, including studies on such issues in order to develop practical solutions'.[21]

The discussions that take place at annual IDM sessions bring together migration policy makers from states around the world and are generally structured around a specific theme.

In addition to the IDM component of the annual Council sessions, two or three inter-sessional workshops are convened each year, to broaden and deepen reflection on migration-related issues. In recognition of the fact that other policy domains, such as development, trade, labour and health, are increasingly relevant to migration management, these inter-sessional workshops are also often structured around a theme that explores the links between international migration and other fields. In 2006, the inter-sessional workshops focused on migration and human resources for health and integration and migration.

---

[18] See *infra* Section 3.4.1.

[19] For further information on the High-Level Dialogue on International Migration and Development, see <http://www.un.int/iom/>.

[20] International Dialogue on Migration, 82nd Session of the Council, 27-29 Nov. 2001 (Geneva, IOM 2002) <http://www.iom.int/jahia/Jahia/cache/bypass/pid/8?entryId=7051>.

[21] Constitution of the IOM, Art. 1(1)(e).

Since its inception, the IDM has been driven by a clear statement of purpose – and it has been explicitly stated that this is not to develop norms or binding resolutions. Rather, it seeks to contribute to a better understanding of migration and to strengthen mechanisms for cooperation between governments in addressing relevant issues.[22]

2.1.3 *The Global Commission on International Migration*

On the encouragement of the UN Secretary-General Kofi Annan, a 'Core Group' of states (Brazil, Morocco, the Philippines, Sweden and Switzerland) established, in December 2003, the Global Commission on International Migration (GCIM). The mandate of the GCIM was to provide the framework for the formulation of a coherent, comprehensive and global response to the issue of international migration. Created as an independent body and consisting of 19 migration experts from all parts of the world with a variety of high-level international experience, it was given an 18-month mandate comprising the following tasks:

- to promote a comprehensive dialogue on international migration among governments, international organizations, civil society, the private sector and other relevant stakeholders;
- to analyze gaps in current policy approaches to migration and the linkages between international migration and other global policy issues;
- to present recommendations to the international community on ways to strengthen national, regional and global governance of international migration, and to maximize the benefits of migration while minimizing its potentially adverse consequences.[23]

To achieve these objectives, in 2004 and 2005 the Commission and its Geneva-based Secretariat met on a regular basis and undertook extensive consultations with a wide variety of stakeholders. These included five major regional hearings spread throughout the world, attended not only by government officials at the local, national, regional and international levels, but also by representatives of international organizations and NGOs, trade unions, migrant associations, and other civil society institutions, as well as employers, corporate managers, recruitment agents, academic experts and journalists. All stakeholders involved in migration, therefore, were included in the consultations; and this distinguishes the GCIM from other global consultative processes.

[22] Further information and documentation are available at <http://www.iom.int/jahia/page385.html>.

[23] See generally <http://www.gcim.org/en/>.

In addition to these activities, the GCIM convened a series of thematic workshops with stakeholder groups, including parliamentarians, the private sector, human rights organizations, the media, migration policy specialists and researchers. Throughout the process, the core Group of States – expanded to include more than 30 governments from all regions – acted as an informal consultative body to the Commission.

The GCIM presented its report[24] to the UN Secretary-General on 5 October 2005 in New York. This was followed by a series of other events in Geneva and elsewhere, aimed at encouraging reflection and discussion on the report, which formed an important part of the basis for discussion at the High-level Dialogue at the UN General Assembly in 2006.

2.1.4 *The International Labour Conference*

In 2004, the International Labour Organization (ILO) included in the 92nd Session of the International Labour Conference (ILC) a general discussion on the challenges of labour migration in an era of globalization. It sought a more integrated approach to policies and structures for the orderly flow of migration for employment, and improved migrant worker protection through the setting of appropriate standards. The ILC concluded with a resolution for a comprehensive plan of action for migrant workers, to include a non-binding multilateral framework for a rights-based approach to labour migration.[25] The framework was discussed and approved by a Tripartite Meeting of Experts at the beginning of November 2005[26] and was taken note of by the ILO Governing Body, which authorized its publication and dissemination, at its meeting in March 2006.

2.2 **Inter-agency cooperation**

2.2.1 *The Geneva (Global) Migration Group*

The Geneva Migration Group (GMG) was originally constituted by the heads of the IOM, the ILO, the UNHCR, the UN Office of the High Commissioner for Human Rights (OHCHR), the UN Office on Drugs and Crime (UNODC) and the UN Conference on Trade and Development (UNCTAD), which share com-

[24] GCIM, *Migration in a Interconnected World: New Directions for Action* (Geneva, GCIM 2005) <http://www.gcim.org/attachements/gcim-complete-report-2005.pdf>.

[25] Resolution Concerning a Fair Deal for Migrant Workers in a Global Economy, ILC, 92nd Session, 2004 <http://www.ilo.org/public/english/protection/migrant/download/ilcmig_res-eng.pdf>.

[26] *ILO Multilateral Framework on Labour Migration: Non-binding principles and guidelines for a rights-based approach to labour migration*, Tripartite Meeting of Experts on the ILO Multilateral Framework on Labour Migration, Geneva, 31 Oct.–2 Nov. 2005, Doc. TMMFLM/2005/1(Rev.) <http://www.ilo.org/public/english/protection/migrant/download/tmmflm-en.pdf>. See also the chapter by Ryszard Cholewinski in this volume.

plementary objectives and fields of work, both at operational and policy levels. It is designed to facilitate inter-agency cooperation and coordination and the exchange of migration-related information, to promote synergies between the agencies, to help avoid duplication of efforts, and to improve common understandings on migration. The members of the GMG aim to encourage good governance by working together for the promotion of all relevant international and regional instruments and norms relating to migration, and for the provision of more coherent and stronger leadership to improve the overall effectiveness of the international community's policy and operational response to current and future migration issues. They meet informally on a regular basis to discuss their migration-related work and endeavour to identify critical issues, opportunities, challenges, weaknesses, gaps and best practices. Each agency is able to highlight different aspects of, and contribute different perspectives on, the problems in question. Although only recently formed, the GMG has already led to spin-off collaborations between some of the agencies involved.

The GCIM report suggested the establishment of an inter-agency facility to strengthen cooperation between all international organizations and institutions dealing with migration issues.[27] The UN Secretary-General has confirmed the need for such cooperation; however, instead of establishing a new organ, he has recently given an enlarged GMG a mandate to perform this function. The new GMG now also includes the UN Development Programme (UNDP), the UN Department of Economic and Social Affairs (UNDESA), the UN Population Fund (UNFPA), and the World Bank. It has been renamed the Global Migration Group and its first meeting took place in Spring 2006.

2.2.2 *UN Coordination Meetings*

The UN Coordination Meetings on International Migration (hereafter, UN Coordination Meetings) are also designed to facilitate inter-agency cooperation and coordination and bring together technical-level participants from international, intergovernmental and other relevant organizations working on international migration issues.[28] The meetings help build a more solid basis for the collection, analysis and exchange of information on international migration; furthermore, they have provided a forum for the agencies to express their willingness to assist states in researching, developing and testing strategies aimed at maximizing the benefits of international migration.

---

[27] GCIM, op. cit. n. 24, pp. 76-78, 82.

[28] UN First Coordination Meeting on International Migration, 11-12 July 2002; UN Second Coordination Meeting on International Migration, 15-16 Oct. 2003; UN Third Coordination Meeting on International Migration, 27-28 Oct. 2004; UN Fourth Coordination Meeting on International Migration, 26-27 Oct. 2005. Further information and documentation are available at <http://www.un.org/esa/population/unpop.htm>.

3. Cooperation at the Regional Level[29]

Regional Consultative Processes (RCPs)[30] are informal groups made up of representatives of states in a given region, or like-minded states in one or more regions with common migration interests. Relevant international organizations and sometimes also NGOs participate in these consultations. These groups come together for informal and non-binding dialogue and information exchange on migration-related issues of common interest and concern, and have proliferated over the course of the past ten years in direct response to the need, identified by states, for greater inter-state dialogue and cooperation on migration. RCPs which have emerged outside of traditional institutional structures represent some of the most important 'bottom-up' migration management measures that have emerged since the Cairo Conference.[31] They reflect a major current trend in international migration management, a shift from *ad hoc* unilateral and bilateral approaches to regional multilateral strategies.

Through their role in identifying the shared interests of their members, allowing states to better understand each others' perspectives and needs, RCPs have served to build confidence in inter-state dialogue, information sharing, cooperation and exploration of collaborative approaches on migration issues. As a result, they have helped to create a climate conducive to the formation of other non-binding and informal platforms on migration management, including the Berne Initiative and the IOM's International Dialogue on Migration discussed in Sections 2.1.1 and 2.1.2 above.

3.1 **Europe**

3.1.1 *The EU*

The EU has now moved well beyond mere intergovernmental cooperation on migration. Originally, its focus was primarily on ensuring the right of EU citizens and their family members to move and reside freely within the territory of all Member States.[32] In 1999, with the entry into force of the Amsterdam Treaty, the

[29] See 'Illustration of Multilateral, Regional and Bilateral Cooperative Arrangements in the Management of Migration', loc. cit. n. 1.

[30] For a more detailed overview of RCPs, see A. Klekowski von Koppenfels, *The Role of Regional Consultative Processes in Managing International Migration*, IOM Migration Research Series No. 3 (Geneva, IOM 2001). See also *Interstate Cooperation and Migration*, Berne Initiative Studies (Geneva, IOM/Swiss Federal Office for Migration 2005); IOM, *World Migration 2005, Costs and Benefits of International Migration*, loc.cit. n. 2, at pp. 368-371; IOM, *World Migration 2003, Managing Migration, Challenges and Responses for People on the Move* (Geneva, IOM 2003) pp. 123-138.

[31] UN International Conference on Population and Development, Cairo, 5-13 Sept. 1994, Programme of Action, ch. X (International migration), UNFPA 2004 <http://www.unfpa.org/icpd/icpd_poa.htm>.

[32] EU law in this field has recently been consolidated in the EU Citizens' Directive, which EU Member States were to have transposed into their laws by 30 April 2006. See European Parliament and

conditions for entry and stay of third-country nationals also became subject to EU law-making.[33] Furthermore, joint border management and visa issues have been prominent in discussions between Member States and have resulted in the adoption of a number of recent legal measures.[34] There is, however, so far no common EU policy on legal migration, although numerous legally binding and operational measures have been adopted to deal with irregular movements.[35] The foundations for EU migration policy relating to third-country nationals were originally laid at the Tampere European Council in 1999,[36] and have been further developed in the Hague Programme on strengthening freedom, security and justice in the European Union, adopted in December 2004, which sets out the policy programme for the next five years.[37]

In the field of asylum, immigration and border control, the Hague Programme contains the following key policy goals:[38]

- a common European asylum system with a common procedure and a uniform status for those who are granted asylum or subsidiary protection by 2009;
- measures for foreigners to legally work in the EU in accordance with labour market requirements;[39]
- a European framework to guarantee the successful integration of migrants into host societies;

Council Directive 2004/38/EC of 29 April 2004 on the right of citizens of the Union and their family members to move and reside freely within the territory of the Member States, OJ 2004 L 158/77; OJ 2004 L 229/35 (Corrigendum).

[33] Treaty Establishing the European Community (OJ 2002 C 325), Part Three, Title IV on Visas, Asylum, Immigration and Other Policies Related to Free Movement of Persons.

[34] E.g., the EU borders Code and the EU Borders Agency, which are discussed by Steve Peers in this volume.

[35] E.g., Council Directive 2001/40/EC of 28 May 2001 on the mutual recognition of decisions on the expulsion of third country nationals, OJ 2001 L 149/34 and *Proposal for a Comprehensive Plan to Combat Illegal Immigration and Trafficking of Human Brings in the European Union*, OJ 2002 C 142/23.

[36] See *Presidency Conclusions*, Tampere European Council, 15-16 Oct. 1999 <http://europa.eu.int/european_council/conclusions/index_en.htm>. For further information on the programme initiated by the Tampere European Council, see <http://europa.eu.int/comm/justice_home/doc_centre/scoreboard_en.htm> and the chapter by Philippe De Bruycker in this volume.

[37] *The Hague Programme: Strengthening Freedom, Security and Justice in the European Union*, Council of the European Union, 13 Dec. 2004 <http://europa.eu.int/comm/justice_home/funding/doc/the_hague_programme.pdf>.

[38] See *Hague Programme – JHA Programme 2005-10* <http://www.euractiv.com>.

[39] See European Commission, *Policy Plan on Legal Migration* (COM (2005) 669, 21 Dec. 2005), which responds to the European Council's call to the Commission to develop measures on legal migration. For further information on the plan, see the chapter by Ryszard Cholewinski in this volume.

- partnerships with third countries to improve their asylum systems, better tackle illegal immigration and implement resettlement programmes;

- a policy to expel and return illegal immigrants to their countries of origin;[40]

- a fund for the management of external borders;

- the introduction of the second-generation Schengen Information System (SIS II) – a database of persons who have been issued with arrest warrants and of stolen objects, to be operational in 2007;

- further rules on visas (common application centres, introduction of biometrics in the development of the European Visa Information System,[41] etc.).

3.1.2 *The CIS Conference Process*

The CIS Conference Process was launched in 1996 following endorsement by the UN General Assembly, which, in its Resolution 50/151 of 1995,[42] called on the UNHCR to convene a regional conference to address the problems of refugees, displaced persons, other forms of involuntary displacement and returnees in the Commonwealth of Independent States and relevant neighbouring countries (the CIS conference). A Programme of Action was adopted in May 1996.[43] The CIS Conference Process was brought to a close in October 2005.

The process pursued three main aims:

- to provide a reliable forum for the CIS countries to discuss population displacement and refugee problems in a humanitarian and non-political way;

- to analyze all population movements in the region, and clarify the categories of concern;

---

[40] See European Commission, *Proposal for a Directive of the European Parliament and the Council on common standards and procedures in Member States for returning illegally staying third-country nationals* (COM (2005) 391, 1 Sept. 2005).

[41] See European Commission, *Proposal for a Regulation of the European Parliament and of the Council concerning the Visa Information System (VIS) and the exchange of data between Member States on short-stay visas* (COM (2004) 834, 28 Dec. 2004).

[42] See UNGA Resolution on Comprehensive consideration and review of the problems of refugees, returnees, displaced persons and related migratory movements, UN Doc. A/RES/50/151 (21 Dec. 1995) <http://www.un.org/documents/ga/res/50/a50r151.htm>.

[43] UNHCR publication for CIS Conference (Displacement in the CIS) – 'The CIS Conference on Refugees and Migrants', *Refugees Magazine,* May 1996 <http://www.unhcr.org/cgi-bin/texis/vtx/publ/opendoc.htm?tbl=PUBL&id=3b5588884>.

– To devise a comprehensive strategy at national, regional and international levels to cope with existing and possible future forms of involuntary movement.[44]

3.1.3 *The Budapest Group*

The Budapest Group was launched in 1991 at a ministerial meeting in Berlin with the immediate aim of preventing illegal migration from Eastern and Central Europe towards Western Europe.[45] It has evolved into a pan-European process not limited to Member States of the EU, and has gradually expanded its focus to the management of irregular migration, including the smuggling of migrants.

Through its work, it has contributed to the approximation of strategies in terms of the harmonization of laws, policies and practices in the field of irregular migration management, helping to bring about the successful alignment of the accession countries with EU standards, which was a necessary process before the enlargement of the EU could proceed. Increasingly, the Budapest Group today tackles migration control problems in the countries neighbouring the enlarged EU, notably Russia and other CIS countries. The International Centre for Migration Policy Development (ICMPD) in Vienna serves as its Secretariat.[46]

3.2 **The Americas**

3.2.1 *The Puebla Process*[47]

The first Regional Conference on Migration, involving Belize, Canada, Costa Rica, El Salvador, the United States of America, Guatemala, Honduras, Mexico, Nicaragua, Panama and the Dominican Republic, took place in Puebla, Mexico in 1996;[48] the second such conference, in Panama in 1997, established the Regional Consultative Group referred to as the Puebla Process, and adopted a Plan of Action aimed at better migration management in the region.[49] The Plan has been structured along three broad themes: migration policies and management; human rights of migrants, irrespective of their migration status; and migration and development. Furthermore, it focuses on the promotion of orderly and secure

[44] Ibid.

[45] See the Final Communiqué of the Ministerial Conference on Measures for Checking Illegal Immigration from and through Central and Eastern Europe, Berlin, Germany, 30-31 Oct. 1991 <http://www.icmpd.org/uploadimg/1991%20Berlin%20recommendations.pdf>.

[46] For further information, see the ICMPD website at <http://www.icmpd.org>.

[47] For an analysis of migration management in Central American countries, see IOM, *The State of Migration Management in Central America, an Applied Research* (Geneva, IOM 2002).

[48] Regional Conference on Migration, 13-14 March 1996, Puebla, Mexico. See the Joint Communiqué issued at the end of the Conference <http://www.un.org/documents/ga/docs/51/plenary/a51-90.htm>.

[49] Plan of Action, updated by the Regional Consultation Group on Migration, Panama City, Panama, 2-3 Dec. 2004 <http://www.rcmvs.org/plande.htm>.

migration, through dialogue and cooperation among countries and with the active participation of civil society.

3.2.2 *The Lima Process*

The South America Migration Dialogue, also known as the Lima Process, started in Lima, Peru, in July 1999, and brings together each year representatives from South American states to exchange views on the migration situation in their territories and to open up channels for dialogue and cooperation. In an effort to consolidate and apply the progress achieved at the regional level, the participants adopted the Lima Declaration.[50] The overall objective of these conferences is the drafting of regional plans of action on crucial migration issues, such as migrants' rights, irregular migration, trafficking in human beings, remittances, harmonization of migration systems and legislations, and the right of migrants to return to their countries of origin.

3.3 **Asia-Pacific**

3.3.1 *The Manila Process*

The Manila Process was launched by IOM in 1996, in order to address problems linked to migrant trafficking and irregular migration, and root causes of regular and irregular migration in the region.[51] The Process also focuses on return and reintegration, capacity-building, entry/border control, and remittances.

3.3.2 *The Bali Process*

The Bali Process on Human Trafficking was launched by Australia and Indonesia in 2002 as an intergovernmental process.[52] A number of countries outside the region participate in the conferences held under its auspices. Thus far, these have dealt not only with issues relating to human smuggling and trafficking, but also with topics as varied as the root causes of irregular movement, immigration administration issues, and the Afghan refugee crisis.

Areas addressed in the follow-up to the Bali Process include developing more effective information and intelligence sharing; improving cooperation among regional law enforcement agencies to deter and combat people smuggling and trafficking networks; enhancing cooperation on border and visa systems to detect and

[50] South American Meeting on Migration, Integration and Development, Lima Declaration, Lima, Peru, 14 July 1999 <http://www.iom.int/jahia/page852.html>.

[51] See 'Chairperson's Summary: IOM Regional Seminar on Irregular Migration and Migrant Trafficking in East and South-East Asia' (1996) <http://www.iom.int/jahia/page863.html>.

[52] Regional Ministerial Conference on People Smuggling, Trafficking in Persons and Related Transnational Crime, Bali, Indonesia, 26-28 Feb. 2002.

prevent illegal movements; increasing public awareness; enhancing the effectiveness of return as a strategy to deter people smuggling and trafficking, through the conclusion of appropriate arrangements; and enacting national legislation to criminalize people smuggling and trafficking in persons.[53]

3.3.3 *Asia-Pacific Consultations on Refugees, Displaced Persons and Migrants*

The Asia-Pacific Consultations on Refugees, Displaced Persons and Migrants (APC) were established in 1996. Themes of common concern include the nature, causes and consequences of population movements; data collection and information-sharing; prevention and preparedness; reintegration and its sustainability; comprehensive and durable solutions to refugee situations; trafficking in women and children; illegal immigrants/workers; people smuggling and irregular migration; emergency response and contingency planning; and the role of the country of origin and impact of economic crises.[54]

3.3.4 *The Colombo Process*

The Ministerial Consultations on Overseas Employment for Countries of Origin in Asia, also called the Colombo Process, was established in 2003. Participants from the main labour sending countries in Asia attended: Bangladesh, China, India, Indonesia, Nepal, Pakistan, the Philippines, Sri Lanka, Thailand and Vietnam. The second meeting was held in Manila in September 2004. The aim of the Ministerial Consultations is to provide a forum for Asian labour-sending countries to share experiences, discuss issues and identify steps for follow-up in the form of recommendations. The main policy emphases are on the protection of vulnerable migrants and provision of support services to them; optimizing benefits of organized labour migration; capacity building; data collection; and inter-state cooperation.[55] The third meeting took place in Bali in September 2005 and, for the first time, involved the participation of countries of destination, namely Bahrain, Italy, Kuwait, Malaysia, Qatar, Republic of Korea, Saudi Arabia and the United Arab Emirates.

---

[53] For further information see the Bali Process website at <http://www.baliprocess.net>.

[54] See APC Website at <http://www.apcprocess.net>.

[55] See R. Iredale, et al., 'Draft Regional Paper on the Asia Pacific', 2nd Berne Initiative Meeting, Towards the development of an International Agenda for Migration Management: Identification of common understandings and effective practices for a planned, balanced, and comprehensive approach to inter-state management of migration, 16-17 Dec. 2004, APMRN Secretariat, Australian National University, Canberra, ACT, Australia <http://apmrn.anu.edu.au/publications/BI%20AsiaPac.doc>. See also the chapter by Ryszard Cholewinski in this volume.

3.4 **Africa**

3.4.1 *The Migration Dialogue for West Africa*

The Migration Dialogue for West Africa (MIDWA) was established in October 2002 as a follow-up to the Dakar Declaration of October 2000,[56] which itself emerged from the Ministerial Meeting on the Participation of Migrants in the Development of their Country of Origin organized by the Economic Community of West African States (ECOWAS) and the West African Economic and Monetary Union (UEMOA) in collaboration with the IOM.[57] Its general goal is to encourage regional harmonization in migration management in order to enhance economic development. MIDWA focuses essentially on border management; data collection; labour migration; irregular migration; development; remittances; migrants' rights; trafficking and smuggling; and return and reintegration.

3.4.2 *The Migration Dialogue for Southern Africa*

The Migration Dialogue for Southern Africa (MIDSA) was established in 2000.[58] It aims to facilitate regional dialogue and cooperation on migration policy issues amongst the governments of the South African Development Community (SADC) by fostering greater understanding of migration and strengthening regional institutional and personnel capacities.[59]

The main issues for the MIDSA process include:

- information sharing and research: the importance of developing national and regional efforts to collect, analyze and share accurate information and data on the characteristics and volume of migration in each country as well as regionally;

- technical cooperation (capacity-building for migration management) and assistance: the establishment of effective migration systems, through such activities as the sharing of expertise, workshops, advisory services, practical and technical training of officials, institutional capacity-building, sup-

[56] West African Regional Ministerial Meeting on the Participation of Migrants in the Development of their Country of Origin, Dakar Declaration, Dakar, Senegal, 13 Oct. 2000 <http://www.iom.int/jahia/page862.html>.

[57] Inter-regional Conference on the Participation of Migrants in the Development of their Country of Origin – Preparatory Meeting, Dakar, Senegal, 12-13 Sept. 2000, *Unofficial Report* <http://www.iom.int/jahia/page862.html>. See also West African Regional Ministerial Meeting on the Participation of Migrants in the Development of their Country of Origin, Conference Report, *Supplement to the Report of the Preparatory Meeting*, Dakar, Senegal, 9-13 Oct. 2000 <http://www.iom.int/jahia/page862.html>.

[58] First MIDSA Forum for Southern Africa, *Report and Recommendations*, Mbabane, Swaziland, 6-9 Nov. 2000 <http://www.queensu.ca/samp/midsa/#activities>.

[59] Further information on MIDSA activities is available at the Southern African Migration Project website <http://www.queensu.ca/samp/midsa/#activities>.

ply of technical equipment and information management systems. A series of workshops have taken place focusing on technical aspects of migration management but also addressing a number of thematic issues;[60]

- information activities: the need to counteract xenophobic sentiments among the public, as well as to discourage potential migrants from irregular cross-border movements;
- combating irregular migration and trafficking of migrants: the need for a regional strategy to combat irregular migration and initiate new or further national and regional measures to alleviate conditions that compel migration in countries of origin.[61]

Both MIDWA and MIDSA were established with the support of the IOM and the International Migration Policy Programme (IMP).[62]

3.5 Inter-regional cooperation

3.5.1 *The 5 + 5 Dialogue*

The Forum for Dialogue in the Western Mediterranean, also known as the '5+5 Dialogue', was launched in Rome in December 1990.[63] The participating states are Algeria, France, Italy, Libya, Malta, Mauritania, Morocco, Portugal, Spain and Tunisia. The objective of this mechanism is to reinforce and to enrich the political, economic and cultural dialogue between the two shores of the Mediterranean. In 2002, the Tunis Declaration was adopted, which calls for information exchange and analysis of migration trends, with the objective of better cooperation and migration management.[64]

3.5.2 *Intergovernmental Consultations on Asylum, Refugee and Migration Policies*

The Inter-Governmental Consultations on Asylum, Refugee and Migration Policies in Europe, North America and Australia (IGC) came into life in 1985 as a discussion forum to deal with asylum-related issues.[65] The IGC has now ex-

[60] Recent workshops have taken place on issues such as capacity building (Centurion, July 2005); migration and health (Cape Town, Nov. 2004); trafficking (Malawi, Sept. 2004); migration and development (Zanzibar, March 2004); legal and policy harmonization (Maseru, Dec. 2003); and forced migration (Lusaka, Oct. 2003). The reports on these and earlier workshops are available at <http://www.iom.org.za/MIDSAPublications.html>.

[61] For further information, see <http://www.iom.int/jahia/page861.html>.

[62] For further information, see IMP Website at <http://www.impprog.ch/>.

[63] For further information, see <http://www.iom.int/jahia/page860.html>.

[64] 5+5 Dialogue, Ministerial Conference on Migration in the Western Mediterranean, Tunis Declaration, Tunis, Tunisia, 16-17 Oct. 2002 <http://www.iom.int/jahia/page860.html>.

[65] The participating states are Australia, Austria, Belgium, Canada, Denmark, Finland, Germany,

panded its area of interest to migration-related issues, but it remains an informal, non-decision-making forum focused on information exchange and discussion of policy directions among the participating governments. The IGC has its Secretariat in Geneva.

4. THEMATIC COOPERATION

The most obvious example of thematic cooperation is that on refugees, which draws its inspiration from the 1951 Geneva Convention Relating to the Status of Refugees and its 1967 Protocol.[66] Concrete examples in this area worthy of mention include, for example, the Comprehensive Plan of Action for Indo-Chinese Refugees (CPA), which was adopted following an International Conference on Indo-Chinese Refugees.[67] The CPA is a striking example of the use of a conference to forge an international consensus on solutions to a pressing international humanitarian problem.

Another example is the International Conference on Central American Refugees (CIREFCA), which addressed problems related to the regional crisis caused by the movement of approximately two million people, including refugees, displaced persons and returnees, in the aftermath of the conflicts in El Salvador, Guatemala and Nicaragua throughout the 1980s.[68] Moreover, the Convention Plus Initiative, launched by the UNHCR in 2002, represents a further attempt to find durable solutions to long-standing refugee situations through discussions with states and other UNHCR partners, leading to the conclusion of 'multilateral special agreements'.[69]

The theme of border management has also been the subject of regional cooperation in Europe, the Americas, and Africa. In Europe, the Schengen Agreements of 1985 and 1990[70] abolish passport control when crossing the internal

Ireland, Italy, the Netherlands, Norway, Spain, Sweden, Switzerland, the United Kingdom and the United States of America.

[66] Convention relating to the Status of Refugees, 28 July 1951, 189 *UNTS* 137; Protocol relating to the Status of Refugees, 31 Jan. 1967, 606 *UNTS* 267.

[67] See the Resolution adopted at the International Conference on Indo-Chinese Refugees, 15 Dec. 1989, UN Doc. A/RES/44/138 <http://www.un.org/documents/ga/res/44/a44r138.htm>. See also W. Courtland Robinson, 'The Comprehensive Plan of Action for Indochinese Refugees, 1989-1997: Sharing the Burden and Passing the Buck', 17 *Journal of Refugees Studies* (2004) p. 319.

[68] See 'International Conference on Central American Refugees (CIREFCA), Guatemala City, 29-31 May 1989 – Declaration and Concerted Plan of Action', 1 *International Journal of Refugee Law* (1989) p. 582. See also H. Gros Espiell, S. Picado and L. Valladares Lanza, 'Principles and Criteria for the Protection of and Assistance to Central American Refugees, Returnees and Displaced Persons in Latin America', 2 *International Journal of Refugee Law* (1990) p. 83.

[69] Further information on Convention Plus is available at <http://www.unhcr.org/cgi-bin/texis/vtx/protect?id=406d21802>.

[70] The Schengen Agreements, together with implementing measures, form the so-called 'Schengen *acquis*', which has been published in the *Official Journal of the European Communities*. See OJ 2000 L 239.

frontiers of States Parties. The Agreements also aim at reinforcing the security of citizens by improving police, judicial and administrative cooperation between the Member States, and establishing a common information system, known as the Schengen Information System (SIS). Most of the provisions of the Schengen Agreement of 1990 and the implementing measures adopted by the Schengen Executive Committee were integrated in the EC and EU treaties when the Treaty of Amsterdam came into force in 1999.

In the Americas, The Organization of American States (OAS) has expressed its commitment to a common security agenda, which includes the issue of border management.[71] In October 2003, the 34 OAS leaders and foreign ministers met for a Special Conference on Hemispheric Security in Mexico City, which aimed at strengthening the capacity to address security threats posed by terrorism, drugs, arms and human trafficking, and to ratify and implement the Inter-American Convention against Terrorism,[72] which includes a significant section on 'Cooperation on border controls'. The result of the conference was a joint declaration.[73] The OAS also organized various follow-up activities, such as a symposium on border management in the region.[74]

Lastly, the African Union is developing a strategic framework for policy in Africa that could contribute to addressing the challenges posed by migration and to ensuring the integration of migration and related issues into the national and regional agenda for security, stability, development and cooperation.[75] The draft strategic framework lists recommended actions on the following thematic issues, amongst others: labour migration, border migration, irregular migration, forced displacement, human rights of migrants, internal migration, migration data, migration and development, and inter-state cooperation and partnership.[76]

5. Bilateral Cooperation

The most common example of cooperation at the bilateral level in the field of migration is the return of non-nationals without authorization to stay. The return

---

[71] For further information, see OAS Website at <http://www.oas.org>.

[72] AG/RES. 1840 (XXXII-O/02).

[73] Declaration of Mexico on Security in the Americas, adopted at the Special Conference on Security in the Americas, Mexico City, Mexico, 28 Oct. 2003 <http://www.oas.org/main/main.asp?sLang=E&sLink=http://www.oas.org/csh/English>.

[74] OAS Symposium on Border Management: a Dialogue on Cross-Border Cooperation and Border Integrity, 30 Aug. – 2 Sept. 2004, Vancouver, Canada. The final report is available at <http://www.cicad.oas.org/Reduccion_Oferta/ENG/General_Info/FINAL%20REPORT_%20CD_%20English.pdf>.

[75] For further information, see the African Union Website at <http://www.africa-union.org/>.

[76] African Union, Expert Group Meeting on the Policy Framework on Migration in Africa, *Draft Strategic Framework for a Policy on Migration in Africa*, Addis Ababa, Ethiopia, 29-30 March 2004 <http://www.africa-union.org/Social%20Affairs/labour/LSC-6AU%20Migration%20policy%20revised%20BY%20Consultant.PDF>.

of irregular migrants and rejected asylum seekers is usually conducted through bilateral arrangements, often formalized through readmission agreements between the states concerned, in some cases with the supportive role of humanitarian organizations. Confirming the right of states under public international law to return non-citizens without authorization to stay and the obligation of states to readmit their own nationals, return arrangements contain provisions concerning the humane and effective treatment of persons, such as rejected asylum seekers, in accordance with relevant international standards and in a spirit of international cooperation.

Bilateral cooperation can also be achieved in the area of capacity-building in terms of migration management. Developing countries, and those that have only recently had to face the challenges of international migration, often lack adequate structures and legislation to deal with larger migratory movements. Capacity-building can, on some occasions, consist of a mere exchange of know-how, through, for example, the training of migration practitioners; at other times, however, it might entail more formal arrangements involving financial contributions towards the establishment of the necessary infrastructure.

6. Cooperation at the National Level

The proliferation of mechanisms, primarily on the regional level through RCPs, but also on the global level, reflects the awareness of governments that migration issues need to be addressed comprehensively and holistically. They realize that migration is not merely an international but also a multidisciplinary issue, and thus that, in order to be able to undertake concerted action in international fora, consultations have to take place between the various government departments involved, such as the ministries of foreign affairs, interior, justice, labour, health, and trade. Sadly, however, relatively few governments have taken steps to increase such interdisciplinary exchanges internally.

7. Cooperation with Other Stakeholders

Migration management is the responsibility of states, but governments increasingly invite NGOs to take part in both the regional and the global processes, including at the implementation stage. NGOs are included in the MIDSA and Puebla Processes, and they have also been involved in the Berne Initiative, the GCIM, and in other concrete capacity building projects. Furthermore, NGOs often also form their own migration fora, such as the Regional Network of Civil Organizations for Migration (RNCOM).[77]

---

77 See <http://www.enlacesamerica.org/rights/regional.html> and <http://www.enlacesamerica.org/rights/rncom_report_may02.pdf>.

7.1 The Hague Process

The Hague Process on Refugees and Migration (hereafter, the Hague Process) is a global initiative designed to advance the refugee and migration agenda through an innovative, multidisciplinary, complementary, and practical approach. It brings together a diverse range of stakeholders from the Northern and Southern hemispheres to develop concrete proposals for sustainable refugee and migration policies.[78] An important point of departure is the Declaration of The Hague on the Future of Refugee and Migration Policy.[79] The Declaration was issued in 2002 and endorsed by leading international figures, including UN Secretary-General Kofi Annan. The Hague Process was established in 2000 to build consensus on the key opportunities and challenges associated with migration, including refugees, asylum seekers and other displaced persons. The ambition is that the Process will provide a forum for the discussion and dissemination of advice on contentious issues related to refugees and migration. To this end, the 'Club of The Hague' has been established to provide guidance and advice. The Process was designed to include non-governmental actors as well as their governmental counterparts.

8. Conclusions

The value of all the processes described above is evident – migration stakeholders appreciate the opportunity to exchange experiences or to establish contacts for cooperative activities. Different interests and different goals require different approaches.

Bilateral mechanisms, for example, are characterized by cooperation between particular sending and destination countries. Their value is obvious – cooperation is initiated in order to solve concrete problems between the two states involved, for instance the return of irregular migrants, in an efficient manner and within a short time-frame. It can, however, develop into what is sometimes called a 'migration dialogue', or a 'migration partnership', in which an appreciation of the whole spectrum of issues related to migration come to form the basis for cooperation.

RCPs, on the other hand, often start as discussion fora, as governments realize that there is a need to consult with other countries in the region, either because they are faced with similar problems or due to migration movements actually taking place. Some of the RCPs (MIDSA, for example) develop over time to focus on more technical issues, under which concrete initiatives and action plans are worked out. Others (such as the IGC), however, remain restricted to providing a venue for dialogue and information sharing, allowing states to gain a better

[78] For further information, see <http://www.thehagueprocess.org>.

[79] Declaration of The Hague on the Future of Refugee and Migration Policy, 21 Nov. 2002 <http://www.thehagueprocess.org/activities/Declaration/DECLARATION%20ENGLISH.pdf>.

understanding of their respective priorities and positions, while at the same time focusing on the informal character of the intergovernmental consultations. The informal and non-binding nature of RCPs allows for a frank exchange of practices and experiences, as well as an immediate response to practical issues. Another advantage over global processes lies in the manageable size of the consultations, and in the fact that the states involved usually share common interests and perspectives.

At the global level, the first initiative towards cooperation in the migration field was taken at the 1994 United Nations International Conference on Population and Development, otherwise known as the Cairo Conference.[80] Chapter X of the Cairo Programme of Action was devoted to international migration. Some had hoped that the Conference would be followed by a global conference on migration; this, however, has not materialized. The reason behind the reticence of states to hold such a conference is no doubt to be found in their desire to maintain their sovereign right and responsibility to determine who enters into their territory. However, there is a growing perception that, as a consequence of globalization, any attempt to deal with migration in a comprehensive fashion requires a more multilateral approach. The emergence of global measures, such as the Berne Initiative, the IOM International Dialogue and the GCIM, has to be seen against this background.

The value of global or inter-regional processes certainly lies in the fact that they offer a forum for exchange between stakeholders with varying interests and experiences. Such processes allow states with little experience in migration management to learn from best practices adopted by other states, and enable them to find support for capacity-building projects. In contrast to bilateral or regional processes, they do not focus on concrete details but rather present a very comprehensive view on migration-related issues.

Twelve years after the Cairo Conference, the UN General Assembly will devote its High Level Dialogue (HLD) in 2006 to international migration and development. The preparation of the HLD gave states the opportunity to further reflect on the possible usefulness of a global framework and forum for migration. One major challenge, however, was to ensure that the debate did not become polarized as simply a clash between North and South.

It may be argued that a global framework for migration is needed, but there is no doubt that the informal intergovernmental consultations will continue to be the preferred mechanism for cooperation. These will make an important contribution to the better understanding of the relevant issues, and they will continue to influence the policy decisions of states in the very delicate areas that migration necessarily impacts upon. Through such processes states retain their sovereign authority and responsibility to determine which non-nationals may enter and stay in their territories, but, at the same time, they also acknowledge the common challenges that they face. Given all of the above, it seems unlikely that states will be ready to

[80] Loc. cit. n. 31.

enter into any 'hard' legal commitments at the international level at any point in the foreseeable future.

As can be seen, profound changes have taken place at the regional and global levels with regard to the necessity of international cooperation in the field of migration. Where much progress is still needed, however, is at the national level. Realization of the need for consultation between national ministries involved in dealing with various aspects of migration is only beginning to emerge. Even less is currently done to consult in an active way with the private sector, and to assess the effects of the interaction between migration flows and economic issues, such as trade and development.

Selected Bibliography

'Illustration of Multilateral, Regional and Bilateral Cooperative Arrangements in the Management of Migration', in T.A. Aleinikoff and V. Chetail (eds.), *Migration and International Legal Norms* (The Hague, T.M.C. Asser Press 2003) p. 305.

International Agenda for Migration Management; Common Understandings and Effective Practices for a Planned, Balanced, and Comprehensive Approach to the Management of Migration, Berne 16-17 Dec. 2004 (Geneva, IOM/Swiss Federal Office for Migration 2005).

GCIM, *Migration in an Interconnected World: New Directions for Action* (Geneva, GCIM 2005).

Gros Espiell, H., S. Picado and L. Valladares Lanza, 'Principles and Criteria for the Protection of and Assistance to Central American Refugees, Returnees and Displaced Persons in Latin America', 2 *International Journal of Refugee Law* (1990) p. 83.

Interstate Cooperation and Migration, Berne Initiative Studies (Geneva, IOM/Swiss Federal Office for Migration 2005).

IOM, *The State of Migration Management in Central America, an Applied Research* (Geneva, IOM 2002).

—, *World Migration 2003: Managing Migration, Challenges and Responses for People on the Move* (Geneva, IOM 2003).

—, *World Migration 2005: Costs and Benefits of International Migration* (Geneva, IOM 2005).

Klein Solomon, M., 'International Migration Management through Inter-State Consultation Mechanisms', UN Doc. UN/POP/MIG/2005/13 (5 July 2005) <http://www.un.org/esa/population/publications/ittmigdev2005/P13_MKSolomon.pdf>.

Klekowski von Koppenfels, A., *The Role of Regional Consultative Processes in Managing International Migration*, IOM Migration Research Series No. 3 (Geneva, IOM 2001).

Chapter 24
BIOMETRICS AND INTERNATIONAL MIGRATION

Jillyanne Redpath*

1. Introduction

The terrorist attacks of September 11 2001 radically affected the manner in which governments approach border security issues and international migration management. Since the events of that day, and subsequent terrorist attacks in Europe, Asia, and the Middle East, national security and migration have been brought sharply into focus, heightening the concern that weak migration management systems may endanger the security and safety of the destination country and its population. The call for tighter control of frontiers and safer travel documents, as well as significant increases in inter-departmental and cross-border cooperation, has been virtually unanimous among concerned states. Building capacities and increasing cooperation in these areas has become a priority in both domestic and foreign policy.

A key component of reinforcing the security aspect of international migration, particularly among developed countries, is the planned use of biometric systems in various areas of migration management. Biometric applications are being conceptualized and progressively implemented to promote and ensure national security at the borders, and to increase the integrity of international travel documents and their issuance systems. Not only are such systems being introduced at the national level, but there is an increasing call for, and expectation of, the collection and sharing of biometric data at the international level. In conjunction with this development there has been greater acceptance by the general public of the use of biometrics and the 'intrusion' of the state into the private sphere in the interests of national security.

As a result of these developments, states are increasing their accumulation of biometric data in relation to non-nationals seeking entry to their territory, and also in relation to their own nationals within the context of applications for travel documents. This has given rise to considerable concern amongst privacy and civil

* Senior Legal Officer in the Department of International Migration Law and Legal Affairs, IOM Geneva. Particular thanks to Charles Harns and Carla Edelenbos for their comments on this paper, and Katarína Tömölová for her research assistance. This paper is written in my personal capacity, and any errors remain my own.

R. Cholewinski, R. Perruchoud and E. MacDonald, eds., International Migration Law

rights advocates, who believe that the right to privacy and other interests of the individual are being overshadowed by, and in many cases subjugated to, the security interests of the state.

This chapter focuses on the impact of the rapid expansion in the use of biometric systems in migration management on the rights of individuals; it seeks to highlight legal issues for consideration in implementing such systems, taking as its starting point that the security interests of the state and the rights of the individual are not, and should not be, mutually exclusive. The first part of this chapter briefly describes the types of biometric applications available, how such systems function and how they can be used in migration management. The second part examines the potential offered by biometrics for greater security in migration management, and focuses on developments in the use of such data as a result of September 11. The third part discusses the impact of the use of biometrics in the management of migration on the individual's right to privacy and ability to move freely and lawfully. The chapter highlights the increasing need for domestic and indeed international frameworks to govern the use of biometric applications in the migration/security context, and proposes a number of issues that such frameworks could address.

2. Understanding Biometrics

Biometrics can be defined as the 'automated means of identifying an individual through the measurement of distinguishing physiological or behavioural traits'.[1] Biometric scanning is the process whereby biometric measurements are collected and enrolled in a computer system, with the purpose of using them to either verify a person's identity or to search for that identity. Most biometric systems are based on mathematical formulae used to detect statistically significant correlations between a live capture biometric[2] and biometric templates previously entered into the travel document or computer system.[3]

The main biometric techniques being used for verification and identification processes in all sectors of society include fingerprinting, iris scanning, facial imaging, hand geometry, voice recognition and signature verification.[4] Of most relevance to this chapter,

---

[1] *Biometrics Deployment of Machine Readable Travel Documents*, Technical Report, Version 2.0, ICAO TAG MRTD/NTWG (International Civil Aviation Organization (ICAO) 2004) p. 8.

[2] 'Live capture' can be defined as the process of capturing a biometric sample by an interaction between a machine readable travel document (such as a passport or visa) holder and a biometric system. Ibid., at p. 11.

[3] R. Feldman, 'Considerations on the Emerging Implementation of Biometric Technology', 25 *Hastings Communications and Entertainment Law Journal* (2003) p. 653 at p. 656.

[4] Examples of biometric identifiers under investigation include gait recognition, vein patterns, sweat pores, body odour measurements and brainwaves. See OECD, Working Party on Information Security and Privacy, *Biometric-Based Technologies* (2004), Doc. DSTI/ICCP/REG(2003)2/FINAL, for a comprehensive outline of biometric technologies.

- finger printing involves the placing of the finger/s on an electronic scanner which reads the unique ridges on the finger;
- iris scanning involves the photographic scanning of the unique coloured patterns of the iris;
- facial imaging involves capturing images of the face, preferably from a certain angle and with controlled light and background;
- hand geometry involves the placing of the hand on a scanner which measures the length, width and thickness of the hand and digits.

Thereafter, the biometric reading can be used to

a) verify that an individual is who he/she claims to be: this involves a one-to-one match between a subject's biometric data obtained at the point of verification and a biometric template created when the subject enrolled in the system. For example, when biometrics are used in the passport or visa application process, but not stored in the travel document itself, the live-capture biometric can be checked against the biometric stored in the visa or passport application record when the person arrives to pick up the new travel document. Similarly, once a biometric is included in a travel document, whether in a visa, passport or identification card, the person holding that document can be checked through live capture against the biometric data in the document. In both examples, the searching process is one-to-one: the biometric is used to verify that the person is the same one as in the document application record, or presented in the passport or travel document;

b) identify individuals when one-to-one verification is either not possible or insufficient: this involves a one-to-many search between a subject's biometric data, which can be either live-captured or taken from another source, and a collection of templates of the same biometric (facial, finger, etc.) of all the individuals enrolled in the system. For example, when an individual presents at a border, or when he/she applies for a passport or visa, his/her biometrics can be taken and searched against existing records in the database.

Of the two alternatives, one-to-one matches have the highest rate of accuracy. Rates of accuracy with one-to-many searches are, however, improving, and the use of multi-tiered biometric searching (searching more than one biometric identifier in a certain sequence) is one way of increasing the precision of these broader searches.

The most reliable biometric features are fingerprinting and iris scanning, both in one-to-one and one-to-many matches, and these are the most frequently used in migration management. Research into facial scanning is on-going, and it is anticipated that it will achieve high levels of accuracy in the future for identification and verification purposes.[5] The International Civil Aviation Organization (ICAO), the international organization leading the setting of standards for the use of biometrics in passports, has concluded that the face is the biometric most suited to the practicalities of travel document issuance, with fingerprint and/or iris available for choice by states for inclusion as complementary biometric technologies.[6] The considerations of ICAO Member States in choosing the biometric technologies for use in travel documents[7] provide an interesting insight into government concerns *vis-à-vis* biometrics in the migration/security context: these include the ease with which they build upon existing processes; the ease and mode of capture; and the degree of public familiarity with, and, tacitly, their acceptance of, the use of the biometric chosen.

3. Biometrics, Migration and Security

When compared to traditional forms of identification, such as photographs or data-only identity cards, the use of biometrics increases the certainty that the person presenting the identification is indeed who he/she claims to be, and ensures a stronger link between the holder of the document and the document itself. In the migration context, this has the obvious benefit of reducing document fraud and assisting in identifying *mala fide* travellers.

Further, the use of biometric systems in the management of migration can facilitate the efficient control of the border, particularly once the biometric is deployed in the travel document itself. When this is the case, those managing entry points can be quickly assured that the person holding the document is the one to whom it was issued. Routine and automated checks against a 'watch list' could still be required, as could a review of the usual security features present on most passports and visas to ensure that the entire document is not fraudulent. In the new biometric passports, this assurance could also be gained by electronically checking the validity of the issuance information encoded with the biometric on the travel document's chip against a database of authorized 'private keys', a kind

[5] Ibid., at p. 36.

[6] ICAO report, op. cit. n. 1, at p. 5.

[7] Considerations cited include that facial photographs do not disclose information that the subject does not routinely disclose to the general public; they are non-intrusive – the subject does not have to touch or interact with a physical device for a substantial timeframe to be enrolled; they are already collected and verified routinely as part of the application form process to produce a passport; they do not require the introduction of new and costly enrollment procedures; and they can be captured from an endorsed photograph, not requiring the subject to be physically present. In addition, for watch lists, face (photograph) is generally the only biometric available for comparison, and human verification of the biometric against the photograph/person is relatively simple and a familiar process for border control authorities. Ibid., at p. 17.

of electronic signature that guarantees the validity of the issuance systems.[8] Only in doubtful cases would border officers need then to instigate a secondary inspection process.[9]

Biometrics are most commonly used in the management of migration to secure the travel document and its issuance system through one or more of the following complementary applications:

a) providing a biometric log-on function for government officials who are issuing passports, thereby ensuring better security in the issuance process and a clear audit trail;

b) including biometric indicators in the travel document application process, thereby eliminating or greatly reducing the possibility of a single person being issued more than one passport under different names, and enabling better one-to-many checks against a pre-issuance watch list;

c) including the biometric indicator in the passport or other travel document in a standardized format.

In addition, the European Union is planning to use biometrics in a centralized database to record and screen persons seeking Schengen visas.[10] Under consideration are programmes to establish multi-country biometric databases of travellers, inclusive of watch list functions, to better manage the screening process and, in effect, to help manage the 'virtual border'.[11] Furthermore, biometrics are also being used in some destination countries to help manage services for migrant populations.[12]

The events of September 11 have had a dramatic impact on the use of biometric systems in the migration/security context. Prior to this date, such systems were emerging as a tool in migration management, and, as with any other emerging technology, were being implemented on an *ad hoc* basis as prototypes for testing.

---

[8] Biometric travel documents coupled with appropriately-equipped entry points could also lead to automated entry procedures at some borders, where travellers present their travel document to a scanner which can then open a gate or door for entry, or decline entry and refer the person for secondary inspection.

[9] European Commission, *Proposal for a Council Regulation on standards for security features and biometrics in EU Citizens' passports* (COM (2004) 116, 18 Feb. 2004) p. 4.

[10] European Commission, *Proposal for a Regulation of the European Parliament and of the Council concerning the Visa Information System (VIS) and the exchange of data between Member States on short-stay visas* (COM (2004) 835, 28 Dec. 2004); Council Decision 2004/512/EC of 8 June 2004 establishing the Visa Information System (VIS), OJ 2004 L 213/5; Council Conclusions on the Development of the Visa Information System (VIS) (Doc. 6535/04, 20 Feb. 2004).

[11] The 'virtual border' is the point of departure for entry into the target country (e.g., the air boarding point abroad for a direct flight to the country of destination's border).

[12] Such as the Netherlands or the United Kingdom, where biometric systems are used, for example, to monitor access to social benefits.

One use was to facilitate travel, enabling frequent travelers to enroll their biometric data and then use fast-track lanes upon departure and arrival. These systems were based on the voluntary enrollment of the subject and were used for personal convenience and speed of processing. In terms of security, biometric systems were primarily used for gaining access to restricted areas in airports, although there were examples of other uses, such as the EURODAC system.[13] It must be added, though, that the initiative to include biometrics in passports also predates September 11. The events of that day, however, undoubtedly led to redoubled efforts and specific timelines for implementation.

Since September 11, the biometric industry has been forced to develop at a rapid rate, driven by government demand for technology that enhances border security, combining a high degree of accuracy with the speed of processing necessary at border points. Whilst the call for greater security *vis-à-vis* non-nationals seeking to enter a country has resounded throughout many countries, this phenomenon has been most felt in, and in many ways driven by, the United States in its efforts to strengthen homeland security. Subsequent terrorist attacks in various regions around the globe have fortified other countries' resolve in this regard. Although several states are incorporating biometric applications into their migration management practices, the focus of this section is on post-September 11 developments in the United States and the European Union (EU), given the implications of these for governments and travellers worldwide.

A key US initiative affecting international progress in the use of biometrics is the Department of Homeland Security's (DHS) US Visitor and Immigrant Status Indicator Technology (US-VISIT) Program.[14] This programme collects biographic, travel and biometric information (photographs and fingerprints) of non-US nationals at the point of entry to assist border guards in verifying the individual's identity on arrival and departure.[15] The stated objective of the programme is to enhance the security of the United States while facilitating legitimate travel and trade. As a complement to the US-VISIT Program, in October

[13] The EURODAC system was introduced in the EU (with the exception of Denmark) in 2000, intended to create an EU database on asylum seekers and other non-EU nationals apprehended while illegally crossing borders in the EU territory or found illegally present within its territory. Its principal purpose is to facilitate the effective application of the former Dublin Convention (now Council Regulation 243/2003/EC, OJ 2003 L 50/1) for determining the EU Member State responsible for examining the asylum application. It uses a common asylum fingerprint database to check asylum applicants to ensure that no duplicate applications have been entered in different locations, or under different names. See Council Regulation 2725/2000/EC of 11 Dec. 2000 concerning the establishment of 'Eurodac' for the comparison of fingerprints for the effective application of the Dublin Convention, OJ 2002 L 316/1.

[14] The US-VISIT Program is based on The Illegal Immigration and Reform and Immigrant Responsibility Act of 1996; The Immigration and Naturalization Service Data Management Improvement Act of 2000; The USA PATRIOT Act of 2001; and The Enhanced Border Security and Visa Entry Reform Act of 2001.

[15] US-VISIT Program Privacy Policy, Nov. 2003, US Department of Homeland Security <http://www.dhs.gov/interweb/assetlibrary/USVISITPrivacyPolicy.pdf>.

2004, the State Department implemented a Biometric Visa Programme at all its non-immigrant visa-issuing overseas consulates, requiring that all applicants for US visas have fingerprints and digital photographs collected and cleared through the DHS Automated Biometric Identification System before receiving a visa.[16] A final component of the US migration/security approach is that, as a condition of continued participation in its visa waiver program, biometrics must be incorporated into tamper-resistant travel documents of participant countries.[17] The impact of these requirements has been felt around the globe and, as a result, several countries are introducing biometrics into their passports to ensure compliance with US requirements.

Parallel to these developments have been EU moves to establish a 'coherent approach… on biometric identifiers or biometric data for documents for third country nationals, EU passports and information systems'.[18] In September 2003, the European Commission advanced a proposal for a Regulation harmonizing the biometric identifiers for visas and residence permits of third country nationals,[19] and, in February 2004, a proposal for a Regulation harmonizing security standards for EU citizens' passports.[20] The Proposal concerning third-country national visas calls for the incorporation of a facial scan and fingerprint into visas and residence permits in a harmonized way, ensuring interoperability among Member States.[21]

The stated aim of the Proposal for the introduction of biometric indicators in EU passports is to render the passport more secure by setting minimum standards for harmonized security features, and, at the same time, to establish a reliable link between the genuine holder and the document through the use of biometrics. In addition, it would allow EU Member States to meet the requirements of the US

---

[16] *Border Security: State Department Rollout of Biometric Visas on Schedule, but Guidance is Lagging*, Report to the Chairman, Committee on Government Reform, House of Representatives, GAO-04-1001, 2004 US Government Accountability Office (GAO) <http://www.gao.gov/new.items/d041001.pdf>.

[17] In August 2004, the United States granted an extension from 26 October 2004 to 26 October 2005 for visa waiver countries to start issuing biometric passports. The EU has requested a second extension of the deadline to 28 August 2006: Europa IDABC, eGovernment News, 1 April 2005.

[18] Presidency Conclusions, European Council of Thessaloniki, 19-20 June 2003, *Bulletin EU* 6-2003.

[19] European Commission, *Proposal for a Council Regulation amending Regulation (EC) 1683/95 laying down a uniform format for visas; Proposal for a Council Regulation amending Regulation (EC) 1030/2002 laying down a uniform format for residence permits for third-country nationals* (COM (2003) 558, 24 Sept. 2003). See also Council Conclusions of 24 Feb. 2005 concerning, *inter alia*, the need for a 'period of consideration' to enable ongoing technical studies on the storage of biometric identifiers in visas to be completed: Council of the European Union, 2642nd Council Meeting, Brussels, 24 Feb. 2005, 6228/05 (Presse 28).

[20] European Commission, *Proposal for a Council Regulation on standards for security features and biometrics in EU Citizens' passports*, loc. cit. n. 9.

[21] The Proposal, loc cit. n. 19, reflects the European Council's intention to introduce a common identification system for visa data; see *supra*, n. 10.

Visa Waiver programme.[22] The Proposal required the inclusion of a facial image, with fingerprints in interoperable format as an option. In December 2004, the EU Council adopted a Regulation on standards for security features and biometrics in passports and travel documents issued by Member States,[23] requiring the mandatory, instead of optional, inclusion of fingerprints in passports. Member States are required to apply the Regulation within 18 months for facial images, and 36 months for fingerprints, of the date of adoption of the technical specifications to implement the Regulation.[24]

4. Human Rights Implications of the Use of Biometrics in Migration Management

Much discourse at the national and international levels has focused on biometrics as a tool to enhance state security. However, the impact of such systems on the rights of individuals, both nationals and non-nationals, cannot be overstated, and requires a full and genuine discussion of its implications, of the kind that has already taken place in the context of the use of biometrics in the general community. This is particularly relevant in the context of non-nationals seeking to enter a country; individuals who do not have the opportunity to participate in the decision-making process on the development and implementation of biometric systems in the context of migration management. This section focuses on the impact of the use of biometrics in migration management on the individual's right to privacy, and the implications for the individual's ability to move freely and lawfully in the event of an incorrect biometric reading, or a failure to obtain a reading at all.

4.1 Implications for the right to privacy

Biometrics are increasingly being used in all areas of life to promote convenience, accuracy and security in personal identification, which benefits both the individual and society. The pros and cons of the use of biometrics in the everyday life of the individual are well documented; so too is the potential impact that their use may have on the right to privacy.[25] The privacy concerns relating to the gen-

---

[22] European Commission, *Proposal for a Council Regulation on standards for security features and biometrics in EU Citizens' passports*, loc. cit. n. 9, at p. 8.

[23] Council Regulation 2252/2004/EC of 13 Dec. 2004, OJ 2004 L 385/1.

[24] Technical specifications *vis-à-vis* facial images were adopted by Commission Decision C (2005) 409 on 28 Feb. 2005.

[25] See for example, A. Alterman, 'A Piece of Yourself: Ethical Issues in Biometric Identification', 5 *Ethics and Information Technology* (2003) p. 139; D. Banisar, S. Davies, et al., 'Privacy and Human Rights: An International Survey of Privacy Laws and Practice', Global Internet Liberty Campaign <http://www.gilc.org/privacy/survey/>; R. Clarke, 'Biometrics and Privacy' (2001) <http://www.anu.edu.au/people/Roger.Clarke/DV/Biometrics.html>.

eral use of biometrics are equally applicable to their use in the migration/security context. In short, these include the risk of

a) functional creep: that biometric data collected for one purpose will be used for another without the consent of the individual. An example of this in the migration management context could be that data collected for immigration purposes are subsequently used for the prevention and detection of crime, or the regulation of access to state benefits. Indeed, in the absence of strict guidelines and their enforcement, information collected could potentially be used for any number of activities;

b) clandestine tracking: related to functional creep is the concern that the creation of large databases of information on individuals may enable a government to secretly monitor their activities. In the migration context, the aggressive collection and use of data on non-nationals could lead to the unwarranted monitoring of a non-national's movement once in a country;

c) divulging further information: biometric readings may divulge information about an individual in addition to the purposes for which it was collected. For example, an iris scan may provide information on a person's state of health;

d) access to information: that information may be used in a manner not permitted by law, whether by the authorized holder of the information or a third party. In the context of third-party access, computer systems used for the storage of biometric data are vulnerable to hacking and unauthorized use, just as any other computer system.[26]

These potential threats to the individual's right to privacy are usually limited to the domestic jurisdiction in which the system is being introduced. However, given the international scope of the use of biometric systems in the migration/security context, their potential impact on an individual's right to privacy is compounded.

Until now, the absence of standards of interoperability at the international level across broad applications in the migration sector has led to the incompatibility of different biometric solutions, meaning that there is potential for a lack of interoperability of systems between countries.[27] However, government policies

[26] For an interesting analysis of the potential threats posed by biometrics to the individual's right to privacy, see M. Crompton, 'Biometrics and Privacy: The End of the World as We Know It Or The White Knight of Privacy', 1st Biometrics Institute Conference, Australia, 20 March 2003 <http://www.privacy.gov.au/news/speeches/sp80notes.pdf>; see also Feldman, loc. cit. n. 3.

[27] For example, the EU, through the second-generation Schengen Information System (SIS II) (not yet operational, but expected to be so in 2007) and other national ID/passport issuance projects,

and the biometrics industry are increasingly moving towards worldwide applications for the use of such information in migration management and, before long, standards or marketing requirements will evolve increasing interoperability across various applications in the migration sector: including passports, visas, live capture at the border systems, and national identity cards. Devices, algorithms and protocols will follow suit. The result will likely be worldwide biometric systems that are increasingly interoperable.[28] Thus, migration/security management, *inter alia*, increasingly involves the prospect of biometric information being gathered and exchanged throughout the world, where principles of data and privacy protection are applied unevenly.

In addition, as noted by the ICAO, many actors and control procedures are often involved in the use of biometric systems. Not only are potentially several government authorities in a country entrusted with access to the data, but increasingly also private companies, such as airlines, have a responsibility in the field of control of travel documents and security.[29]

Given, therefore, the transnational nature of the migration/security phenomenon, the growth in the use of such systems, the disparity of privacy protection between domestic systems and the likely expansion of the number of actors having access to individuals' biometric information, consideration should be given to the establishment of national and, indeed, international standards which ensure that the privacy interests of the individual are adequately protected.

The definition of privacy depends on the context to which the concept is being applied. In its general use, it essentially equates to the right to protection from intrusion into one's private sphere, whether this be one's personal information, personal communications, physical integrity, or the physical space in which one lives.[30] The implications of biometrics on the privacy of one's personal information form the focus of this section. The right to privacy is found in various international instruments. It is contained in Article 12 of the Universal Declaration on Human Rights (UDHR), which states that

---

aims to ensure interoperability with EURODAC and the Visa Information System (VIS), and has thus taken the first step in this direction. The European Council has also discussed the issue of interoperability in the context of the Hague Programme (see European Council, *Presidency Conclusions of the Brussels European Council, 4-5 Nov. 2004*, Council Doc. 14292/1/04 REV 1, Annex 1, pp. 25-26 <http://ue.eu.int/ueDocs/cms_Data/docs/pressData/en/ec/82534.pdf>, and the European Commission issued a Communication on this matter in November 2005. See European Commission, *Communication to the Council and the European Parliament on improved effectiveness, enhanced interoperability and synergies among European databases in the area of Justice and Home Affairs* (COM (2005) 597, 24 Nov. 2005).

[28] Global interoperability can be defined as 'the capability of inspection systems in different states throughout the world to exchange data, to process data received from systems in other states, and to utilize that date in inspection operations in their respective states'. ICAO report, loc. cit. n. 1, at p. 10.

[29] Ibid., at p. 52.

[30] Crompton, loc. cit. n. 26, at p. 9.

> '[n]o one should be subject to arbitrary interference with his privacy, family, home or correspondence, nor to attacks on his honor or reputation. Everyone has the right to the protection of the law against such interferences or attacks'.[31]

This is reiterated in Article 17 of the International Covenant on Civil and Political Rights (ICCPR)[32] and various regional instruments,[33] and specifically recognized as applicable to migrants by the International Convention on the Protection of the Rights of All Migrant Workers and Members of Their Families (ICRMW).[34]

The right to privacy is a right of *all* individuals; it is not restricted to nationals of a country, nor is there a distinction between non-nationals in a regular or irregular situation in the entitlement to this right.[35] Whilst it may be derogated from in the interests of national security, such measures must be necessary and proportionate to the exigencies of the situation, and must not involve discrimination in their application. Further, as noted by the Human Rights Committee,[36] the right to privacy should be guaranteed against all arbitrary and unlawful interference, whether emanating from state authorities or from natural or legal persons.

A number of guidelines have been promulgated at the international level on privacy and the use of electronic data, which are also relevant to the use of biometrics in international migration management. These include the UN Guidelines for the Regulation of Computerized Personal Data Files,[37] the UN Human Rights Committee General Comment 16,[38] the OECD Guidelines Governing the Protection of Privacy and Transborder Data Flows of Personal Data,[39] and the OECD

---

[31] UNGA Res. 217A (III), UN Doc. A/810 at p. 71 (1948).

[32] UNGA Res. 2200A (XXI), 21 UN GAOR Supp. (No. 16) at p. 52, UN Doc. A/6316 (1966), 999 *UNTS* 171, entered into force 23 March 1976: 'No one shall be subjected to arbitrary or unlawful interference with his privacy, family, home or correspondence, nor to unlawful attacks on his honour and reputation'.

[33] Examples of the protection of the right to privacy at the regional level include Art. 8 of the European Convention for the Protection of Human Rights and Fundamental Freedoms, 4 Nov. 1950, *ETS* No. 5, entered into force 3 Sept. 1953, and Art. 11 of the American Convention on Human Rights, OAS Treaty Series No. 36, 1144 *UNTS* 123, entered into force 18 July 1978.

[34] ICRMW, UNGA Res. 45/158, Annex, 45 UN GAOR Supp. (No. 49A) at p. 262, UN Doc. A/45/49 (18 Dec. 1990), entered into force 1 July 2003, Art. 14: 'No migrant worker or member of his or her family shall be subjected to arbitrary or unlawful interference with his or her family, home, correspondence or other communications or to unlawful attacks on his or her honour and reputation. Each migrant worker and member of his or her family shall have the right to the protection of the law against such interference or attacks'.

[35] Whilst distinctions between nationals and non-nationals are permitted, such distinctions should not be discriminatory, i.e., they should pursue a legitimate state objective and be proportionately applied to that objective.

[36] General Comment No. 16: The right to respect of privacy, family, home and correspondence, and protection of honour and reputation (Art. 17) (8 April 1988).

[37] UNGA Res. 45/95 of 14 Dec. 1990, available at <http://www.unhchr.ch/html/menu3/b/71.htm>.

[38] General Comment No. 16, loc. cit. n. 36, at paras. 1 and 3.

[39] Annex to the Recommendation of the Council of 23 Sept. 1980 concerning Guidelines Governing the Protection of Privacy and Transborder Flows of Personal Data <http://www.oecd.org/document/18/0,2340,en_2649_34255_1815186_1_1_1_1,00.html>.

Security Principles.[40] A review of these standards reveals a list of common principles that should be applied in the collection and use of electronic data. These can be summarized as follows:

- Data should be obtained in accordance with the law and, where appropriate, with the knowledge or consent of the individual.
- The purposes of data collection should be known when collected; data collection should be relevant to the purposes for which it is used, and only be used in accordance with those purposes.
- Personal data should be kept accurate and up to date. It should be retained only for as long as needed for the purposes collected.
- Data likely to give rise to unlawful or arbitrary distinctions should not be compiled, unless domestic law provides appropriate safeguards.
- Personal data should be adequately safeguarded against human and non-human security risks.
- Policies and practices regarding the collection and use of personal data should be as transparent as possible.
- An individual should have the right, without undue delay or expense, to know whether or not a body holds data relating to him/her, to be able to access the information, to have incorrect information corrected, and to obtain a remedy if this is not complied with.
- The use of personal data should be monitored by an independent body.

The international principles outlined provide guidance for establishing a framework for achieving a balance between privacy and security interests in the collection, use and exchange of biometrics. However, certain of these principles give rise to a number of questions in the migration/security context. For example,

[40] *OECD Guidelines for the Security of Information Systems and Networks: Towards a Culture of Security* (OECD, Paris 2002) <http://www.oecd.org/dataoecd/16/22/15582260.pdf>. In addition, the following laws exist at the European level which reflects similar principles: Council of Europe Convention for the Protection of Individuals with regard to Automatic Processing of Personal Data, 1981, *ETS* No. 108; Directive 95/46/EC of the European Parliament and of the Council of 24 Oct. 1995 on the protection of individuals with regard to the processing of personal data and on the free movement of such data, OJ 1995 L 281/31 (as amended by Regulation 1882/2003/EC, OJ 2003 L 284/1); and Regulation 45/2001/EC of the European Parliament and of the Council of 18 Dec. 2000 on the protection of individuals with regard to the processing of personal data by the Community institutions and bodies and on the free movement of such data, OJ 2001 L 8/1.

- After how many years should biometric information of nationals and non-nationals collected in the migration/security context 'cease to be required'? Should there be a limit on the length of storage of such data? Should this vary depending on the type of travel document involved?

- At what age should the collection of biometric data of non-nationals commence? Is collecting the biometric data, for example, of a 2 year old child necessary/justifiable? Similarly, should there be an upper age limit on the collection or storage of such information?

- What mechanisms should be employed to keep information accurate and up to date? In the context, for example, of facial imaging, a digital image is stored in a contactless chip. Facial imaging has been proven to be less accurate as the photograph ages.

- What degree of information should be stored, in addition to the biometric, on a document with biometric identifiers? A biometric identifier does not, *per se*, give information on one's race, for example; supporting data may, however, be used for discriminatory purposes. Similarly, health-related information evident in iris readings may potentially be used for such purposes in the migration context.

- With whom, and in what circumstances, should biometric data collected in the migration/security context be shared, both at the national and international levels? Who is responsible and accountable if there is any improper use of the information? What recourse should be available?

- What degree of transparency should be expected in policies and practices *vis-à-vis* biometric data when a primary purpose of its collection is 'national security'?

It is important that these and related issues are addressed while the process of collection of biometric information in the migration/security context is in its infancy, to ensure a framework is in place that achieves a balance between the poles of the restless dichotomy of respecting the power of the state to take measures to protect its security, and ensuring adequate protection of the individual's right to privacy. Similarly, it is necessary that such a framework is established from the outset of system development to ensure that '... policy imperatives are driving the development of technology and not technology driving policy'.[41] The following elements are pivotal in achieving such balance, both at the national and international levels:

[41] *Biometrics: Implications and Applications for Citizenship and Immigration*, report on a Forum hosted by Citizenship and Immigration Canada, Ottawa, 7-8 Oct. 2003 <http://www.cic.gc.ca/english/pub/biometrics/index.html> p. 5.

- Appropriate mechanisms need to be put in place to ensure the accountability of those operating biometric systems.
- In particular, independent monitors, as with any area of application of biometrics, should be established at the national level to ensure accountability in the implementation and enforcement of privacy and data protection principles.
- Adequate security of biometric data needs to be built in at the outset of the creation of a system to ensure that the information cannot be accessed or used by people or for purposes other than those intended.[42]
- The collection and use of biometrics in migration management needs to be regulated by national, and where relevant regional, law. Legislation should apply to all entities having access to the data, both public and private.
- Only those individuals/entities whose participation is 'necessary' in order to achieve the purposes for which the biometric information was collected should have access to the data.
- The amount of biometric and related information collected, and its use, must be proportionate to the end sought to be achieved through its collection.
- Privacy legislation in domestic systems should afford equal protection to the biometric data collected from non-nationals to that provided to nationals. Any distinctions between the two must be justifiable.[43]
- Given the truly international nature of the migration phenomenon, and the burgeoning of biometric collection and exchange between countries, an international supervisory body could be established or mandated to monitor the use of biometrics in the migration/security context, and to facilitate the development of principles governing such data and its use that are acceptable to all countries involved. This body could also be responsible for establishing standards for the use by private entities, such as airlines and other carriers, of biometric data, and would ensure comprehensive regulation of both the use and the security of such information.

4.2 Implications for the ability to move freely and lawfully

As outlined above, the advantages of using biometric systems in migration management include greater accuracy in ascertaining the identity of an individual than

[42] OECD, op. cit. n. 4, at p. 37.

[43] See *supra*, n. 35.

traditional forms of identification, and greater security in linking the document holder to his/her document. It must be noted, however, that biometric systems are not infallible in performing either of these functions. The importance of this point in the migration/security context cannot be overstated, particularly given that the industry is being forced to rapidly develop to meet the security demands of governments, and the fact that the legal frameworks governing usage are evolving contemporaneously with, and often in response to, the emergence of new technology.

Biometric systems work on statistical matching and provide a 'degree of correlation' between the subject and biometric templates in a system, from which a human being must make a final decision regarding the identity of the individual in question.[44] Inherent to any biometric system is the occurrence of 'false positives' and 'false negatives'. False positives mean that a system will incorrectly correlate the individual presenting him/herself with the biometrics of someone else in the system. A false negative means that the system will incorrectly reject an individual as not being the person he/she is claiming to be. A system which has a low level of false positives means that it addresses security concerns; this, however, usually correlates to a high level of false negatives (that is, the wrongful rejection of individuals). As noted by Feldman, '... whether a system is reliable enough to implement may turn on policy choices concerning which goals are paramount and which goals are expendable'.[45] An obvious objective for the use of biometric systems in migration management in the current security environment is to ensure a low level of false positives; the risk to avoid is treating the interests of a small percentage of migrants as expendable.

In addition to false positives and negatives, each system involves rates of 'failure to acquire' and 'failure to enroll'. As described by the OECD,[46] the failure to acquire rate measures the degree to which a biometric system is unable to obtain or find an image of sufficient quality due, for example, to inadequate lighting. The failure to enroll rate measures the degree to which the system is unable to extract sufficient features and generate repeatable templates; for example, if the individual has no readable fingerprints.

Studies show that up to five per cent of individuals are unable to enroll biometric data due to the fact that they have no readable fingerprints or no fingerprints at all.[47] Similarly, in the context of false negatives, studies show that an error rate of 0.5 to 1 per cent is normal.[48] Thus, according to these results, if one

---

[44] OECD, op. cit. n. 4, at p. 10

[45] Feldman, loc. cit. n. 3, at p. 663.

[46] OECD, op. cit. n. 4, at p. 20

[47] Opinion of the European Data Protection Supervisor on the Proposal for a Regulation of the European Parliament and of the Council concerning the Visa Information System (VIS) and the exchange of data between Member States on short stay visas (COM (2004) 835, 23 March 2005).

[48] Ibid. See also A.K. Jain, et al., *Biometrics: A Grand Challenge*, Proceedings of the 17th International Conference on Pattern Recognition, Cambridge, UK, 23-26 Aug. 2004.

million people are seeking to travel, up to 50,000 may not be able to enroll biometric data, and between 5,000 and 10,000 will face wrongful rejection.

The limitations of biometric systems have prompted commentators to call for systems that provide for secondary inspections, and, where possible, the opportunity to appeal against a reading the individual alleges to be inaccurate.[49] This is of particular concern in the migration/security context where (a) in the passport or travel document application process, a 'false negative' is generated or there is a failure to enroll in the system; or (b) the individual presents at a border, real or 'virtual', and on the basis of an incorrect biometric reading, or a 'failure to acquire', he/she is refused entry. Both scenarios have the potential to arbitrarily infringe upon the individual's ability to move freely and lawfully.[50] In such instances, the impact for the migrant is far greater than for the state. For the individual this may seriously affect movement rights, and family, financial or security interests. For the state, it means one less migrant.

The following scenarios deserve particular attention:

a) In the context of the application process for passports incorporating biometric data, consideration should be given to allowing 'exceptional' procedures to ensure that those who cannot be enrolled in the system can nevertheless travel. This may be through the capacity to accept travel documents with only one biometric feature (where more than one is required), an alternative biometric feature, or a travel document without biometrics. Such a procedure would avoid discrimination against an individual based on physical features.

b) In the context of admission at the border, in order to ensure that the individual's interests are adequately protected, states should take measures to ensure border personnel are equipped to handle exceptions such as a failure to acquire, a damaged or badly functioning storage medium, a document that has been tampered with, or the production of a false negative by the verification software.[51] It should be noted that systems for managing the border without biometrics face similar challenges in terms of making judgments on questionable cases. This, in itself, is nothing new for border officials. The advent of biometrics will not change the need for judgment and secondary inspection and, in fact, the current capacities and methods

[49] See, for example, Feldman, loc. cit. n. 3, at p. 671.

[50] It should be noted here that the right to freedom of movement includes the right of a non-national lawfully within a territory to move freely in that territory, the right to leave one's own country, the right to return to one's own country, and the right to seek asylum: see Arts. 12(1), (2), (4) ICCPR (loc. cit. n. 32) and Art. 14 UDHR (loc. cit. n. 31). The right to *enter* a country is reserved to nationals of that country (noting, however that one's 'own country' has been interpreted to include the country of permanent residence). Thus, whilst there is generally no right of entry for a non-national, refusal to permit entry in such circumstances should not be based on an error of fact, or discrimination based on physical features (such as the absence of a readable fingerprint).

[51] ICAO report, op. cit. n. 1, at p. 27.

employed in this regard will continue to be useful and highly relevant. However, given the increasing government reliance on biometrics in this context and the perception of infallibility surrounding such systems, the ongoing need for secondary inspection and its entrenchment in the migration management process cannot be overstated.

c) The vulnerable position of non-nationals should be highlighted in relation to both the application for travel documents and admission at the real/virtual border. It is a fundamental principle of state sovereignty that states have the power to determine whether and which non-nationals enter their territory, and on what conditions. Indeed, it is well accepted that states have wide discretion on admission matters. However, such discretion should not be exercised on the basis of an error of fact *vis-à-vis* a biometric reading. States can and generally do simply refuse a visa or entry at the border if they believe a non-national poses a security or other risk.[52]

Given the potential for refusing a visa or entry based on a false negative biometric reading,[53] consideration should be given to establishing a process of administrative review for non-resident non-nationals alleging such an error.[54] In the travel document application process, this may include a paper appeal or interview process to establish the true identity of the individual. The practicalities of review/appeal on seeking entry or access to a border are complicated by the situation at control points, which are characterized by the prioritization of state security and speed of processing. Therefore, whilst it is unlikely that states would grant the right to appeal at that point, the possibility of an appeal 'post removal' would ensure an appropriate balance between the interests of the individual and the security needs of the state. In the context of resident non-nationals seeking re-entry to a state, given the possible family, economic and other ties that the individual may have there, the possibility of judicial review, with suspensive effect on removal, should be available in the event of a false negative.

In view of the above, mechanisms to ensure accuracy and accountability in document issuance and management of borders are vital. Greater attention should be paid by governments to the limitations of biometrics in the development and implementation of systems and protocols that make use of such information. Indeed,

---

[52] With the exception of international protection obligations precluding states from returning a person who arrives at the border to a country where there is a real risk that the person concerned will be subject to torture or to inhuman or degrading treatment (*refoulement*). This principle applies irrespective of whether he/she poses a security risk.

[53] Such a situation may arise when biometrics are checked against a watch list and the individual concerned is incorrectly correlated with a third person.

[54] Feldman, loc. cit. n. 3, at pp. 671-680.

further study is needed to examine the impact of these limitations, and to develop best practices addressing these challenges in a way that is responsive to the vulnerabilities of non-nationals without compromising national security.[55]

5. Conclusion

There is little doubt that the use of biometrics in migration management is increasing and will expand significantly in the near future. In addition to concerns over domestic security, most countries do not want to be perceived as being a 'weak link' when it comes to border security issues. Consequently, governments around the world are examining their immigration policies and procedures that are expected to affect the global security/migration management nexus.

Biometrics are now squarely on the international migration management agenda, and indeed provide many benefits for ensuring the security of national borders, the safety of international aviation, the security of travel documents, and the protection of the destination country and its population. However, clear, consistent parameters should be established at the national and international levels to ensure adequate protection for the privacy of the individual. Key to such protection is that the use of biometric information should be proportional to the objectives sought to be achieved through its collection, as is ensuring that appropriate safeguards exist in national systems to this end. Similarly, consideration should be given to the inclusion of secondary inspection and appeal procedures in migration management protocols, in order to avoid the arbitrary frustration of the individual's ability to move freely and lawfully. Such measures would promote the necessary balance between protecting the human rights of the individual and meeting the security objectives of the state.

Selected Bibliography

Alterman, A., 'A Piece of Yourself: Ethical Issues in Biometric Identification', 5 *Ethics and Information Technology* (2003) p. 139.

Banisar, D., S. Davies, et al., 'Privacy and Human Rights: An International Survey of Privacy Laws and Practice', Global Internet Liberty Campaign <http://www.gilc.org/privacy/survey/>.

Crompton, M., 'Biometrics and Privacy: The End of the World as We Know it or the White Knight of Privacy?', Paper presented at the 1st Biometrics Institute Conference, 20 March 2003, Australia <http://www.privacy.gov.au/news/speeches/sp80notes.pdf>.

Feldman, R., 'Considerations on the Emerging Implementation of Biometric Technology', 25 *Hastings Communications and Entertainment Law Journal* (2003) p. 653.

ICAO, *Biometrics Deployment of Machine Readable Travel Documents*, Technical Report, Version 2.0, ICAO TAG MRTD/NTWG, International Civil Aviation Organization (2004) <http://www.icao.int/mrtd/biometrics/intro.cfm>.

[55] One example being independent monitoring at the national, and where appropriate regional, level of false rejection and state responses thereto.

Koslowski, R., 'Possible Steps Towards an International Regime for Mobility and Security', 8 *Global Migration Perspectives*, Global Commission on International Migration <http://www.gcim.org/gmp/Global%20Migration%20Perspectives%20No%208.pdf>.

OECD, *Biometric-Based Technologies*, Working Party on Information Security and Privacy, Doc. DSTI/ICCP/REG(2003)2Final (Paris, OECD 2004).

—, *Background Material on Biometrics and Enhanced Network Systems for the Security of International Travel,* Working Party on Information Security and Privacy, Doc. DSTI/ICCP/REG(2003)3Final (Paris, OECD 2004).

Thomas, R.A.L., 'Biometrics, International Migrants and Human Rights', *Global Migration Perspectives No. 17* (2005) <http://www.gcim.org/gmp/Global%20Migration%20Perspectives%20No%2017.pdf>.

Chapter 25
ENHANCING COOPERATION ON BORDER CONTROLS IN THE EUROPEAN UNION

Steve Peers*

1. Introduction

The EU's convoluted and hotly disputed rules on the abolition of internal border checks and the imposition of standardized external border controls have recently been consolidated and amended, with the adoption by the Council and European Parliament (EP) of a Regulation establishing an EU Borders Code.[1] This measure is also of interest as it is the first binding measure in the area of EU immigration and asylum law to be agreed which was subject to the joint power of the Council and the EP (the co-decision procedure), entailing also qualified majority voting in the Council. As such, it is a test case to see whether the change in decision-making rules will lead to more liberal (or more conservative) EU measures in this field.

A detailed analysis of the agreed text shows that the EP had some success in getting a number of its more modest amendments accepted. However, the more radical changes have either been rejected by the Council or were not tabled at all by the EP. So while the new Code will introduce some important advances in terms of the position of EU citizens and their family members, the treatment of travellers by border guards and travellers' procedural rights in general, there will be more limited improvements concerning asylum seekers, the conditions of entry, and the reinstatement of controls at internal borders. A further significant development is the EU's new External Borders Agency (discussed briefly in Section 3 below), which is intended to increase the effectiveness of operational coordination between Member States.

The net result is that there will still be risks, in particular of breaches of international human rights and refugee law concerning asylum seekers who arrive at the external borders of EU Member States, as well as the human rights of demonstrators and protesters. There will also still be some practical difficulties as regards meeting the conditions to enter EU Member States.

---

* Professor of Law at the Human Rights Centre at the University of Essex.

[1] Regulation 562/2006/EC of the European Parliament and of the Council of 15 March 2006 establishing a Community Code governing the movement of persons across borders (Schengen Borders Code), OJ 2006 L 105/1.

R. Cholewinski, R. Perruchoud and E. MacDonald, eds., International Migration Law

2. THE EU BORDERS CODE: A DETAILED ANALYSIS

2.1 Overview

The EU's rules on border controls are complex and controversial. Controversy arises first from the ability of Member States to re-impose internal border controls (i.e., those between EU Member States) or police checks even though such controls are supposed to have been abolished between those EU Member States applying the Schengen rules (all of the 'old' Member States except the United Kingdom and Ireland, plus Norway and Iceland; the new Member States and Switzerland are due to apply the rules in several years' time).[2] In particular, these internal border checks can be used to stop the movement of protesters and demonstrators. Secondly, the EU's external border checks (on the land, air and sea borders between the Schengen and non-Schengen countries) are also controversial, not only because they are used to stop movement of protestors and demonstrators from outside the EU, but also because they are a chief means of restricting entry into the EU as part of a broader restrictive immigration policy, particularly in terms of limiting the movement of those who wish to claim asylum in a Member State.

The rules are complex because they have many overlapping sources. The primary source is the Schengen Convention,[3] Article 2 of which sets out the basic obligation to abolish internal border controls and the possible derogations from that obligation. Articles 3 to 8 then contain the basic rules on the conditions for crossing the external borders. A major additional source of external border rules is the Common Manual for Border Guards,[4] drawn up originally by the Schengen Member States in the Schengen Executive Committee (which consisted of the Interior Ministers of Member States) and amended several times since 1999 (when the Schengen *acquis* was integrated into EU law) by the Council, in particular to require use of a standard form where persons are refused entry at the border.[5] There are also border control rules in several other Schengen Executive

[2] See respectively the 2003 Accession Treaty (OJ 2003 L 236/33) and the EC-Swiss Treaty on the Application of the Schengen Rules (COM (2004) 593, 14 Sept. 2004; not yet in force).

[3] Convention implementing the Schengen Agreement of 14 June 1985 between the Governments of the States of the Benelux Economic Union, the Federal Republic of Germany and the French Republic on the gradual abolition of checks at their common borders (OJ 2000 L 239/19) (hereafter Schengen Convention).

[4] The first (and only) publication of a consolidated version of the Manual can be found in OJ 2002 C 313/97. The Manual was largely declassified in 2000 and 2002 (OJ 2000 L 303/29 and OJ 2002 L 123/49).

[5] Amendments solely to the Common Manual are set out in OJ 2002 L 123/47; OJ 2002 L 187/50; OJ 2004 L 157/36 and OJ 2004 L 261/36. Amendments to the Common Consular Instructions with a consequential effect upon the Manual are set out in: Arts. 1(2), 1(4) and 1(5) of Decision 2001/329/EC (OJ 2001 L 116/32); Art. 3 of Decision 2001/420/EC (OJ 2001 L 150/47); Art. 2 of Decision 2002/44/EC (OJ 2002 L 20/5); the Decision 2003/454/EC on fees for considering visa applications (OJ 2003 L 152/82); Decisions 2003/585/EC and 2003/586/EC on transit visa requirements (OJ 2003 L 198/13

Committee decisions,[6] as well as in Council acts adopted after the entry into force of the Treaty of Amsterdam.[7] This proliferation of acts is confusing, and, furthermore, the legal status and effect of Schengen measures is not yet clear, particularly in the case of the Common Manual, which was largely drawn up for practical use by border guards.[8]

In order to simplify and update the rules, the Commission proposed in May 2004 a Regulation establishing an EU Borders Code, with the intention of consolidating the texts of the various existing measures and amendments.[9] The Regulation also settles the question of the legal effect of the Common Manual, since any rules in the Common Manual which now appear in the Regulation are clearly 'normal' EU law (regulations are binding and 'directly applicable' in EU Member States' national law, according to Article 249 of the EC Treaty).

When the Commission made its proposal, measures concerning external borders still had to be agreed by a unanimous vote of the Council following consultation of the EP. However, since January 2005, following agreement on the Hague Programme, borders measures are to be adopted by a qualified majority vote in the Council and co-decision with the EP, giving the Parliament equal powers to the Council concerning the enactment of legislation.[10] Since the previous deci-

---

and 15); and Art. 2 of Decision 2004/17/EC on travel medical insurance requirements (OJ 2004 L 5/79). Legislation amending the Common Manual comprises: Art. 7(2) of Reg. 539/2001/EC (OJ 2001 L 81/3); Art. 2 of Reg. 334/2002/EC (OJ 2002 L 53/7); Art. 5(2) and (3) of Reg. 453/2003/EC (OJ 2003 L 64/1); and Art. 11(2) of Reg. 693/2003/EC (OJ 2003 L 99/8). Further amendments have been made unilaterally by the Member States, and by the 2003 Accession Treaty, loc. cit. n. 2.

[6] The Executive Committee measures comprise those solely concerning internal border abolition (Decisions on obstacles to traffic flows (SCH/Com-ex (94) 1, rev. 2), bringing the Convention into force (SCH/Com-ex (94) 29 rev. 2) and procedures for reintroducing border checks (SCH/Com-ex (95) 20 rev. 2): OJ 2000 L 239/157, 130 and 133), measures solely concerning external border checks (Decisions on introducing the Schengen system (SCH/Com-ex (94) 17, rev. 4) and the activities of a task force (SCH/Com-ex (98) 1, rev. 2): OJ 2000 L 239/168 and 191), and measures partly concerning external checks (Decisions on entry and exit stamps (SCH/Com-ex (94) 16 rev.), an action plan to combat illegal immigration (SCH/Com-ex (98) 37 def. 2) and a manual of documents to which visas may be affixed (SCH/Com-ex (99) 14): OJ 2000 L 239/166, 203 and 298).

[7] The first Council measure is Reg. 790/2001/EC (OJ 2001 L 116/5), which confers on the Council the power to amend the Common Manual (see also the parallel Reg. 789/2001/EC regarding the Common Consular Instructions, OJ 2001 L 116/2, which applies in part to the Border Manual). A challenge to the legality of these Regulations was rejected by the Court of Justice (Case C-257/01 *Commission* v. *Council* [2005] ECR I-345). The other five measures adopted comprise Decision 2004/581/EC concerning signs used by Member States' authorities at external borders (OJ 2004 L 261/119); Directive 2004/82/EC on the transmission of passenger data to border authorities (OJ 2004 L 261/24); Reg. 2007/2004/EC establishing a European Agency for the Management of Operational Cooperation at the External Borders of the Member States of the European Union (OJ 2004 L 349/1) – see Section 3 below; Reg. 2133/2004/EC on the stamping of travel documents at external borders (OJ 2004 L 369/5); and Reg. 2252/2004/EC on standard rules for security measures to be included in EU citizens' passports (OJ 2004 L 385/1). Regs. 2007/2004/EC and 2252/2004/EC have been challenged for failure to permit the UK to opt in: Cases C-77/05 and C-137/05 *UK* v. *Council*, pending.

[8] See Council doc. 12290/1/01, 10 Oct. 2001.

[9] COM (2004) 391, 26 May 2004.

[10] See the Hague Programme (OJ 2005 C 53/1) and Decision 2004/927/EC, providing for certain

sion-making system had clearly led to the adoption of immigration and asylum measures which were usually close to the 'lowest common denominator' of the most conservative Member States, the key question following the change to the new decision-making rules is whether the abolition of the veto and the granting of co-decision powers to the EP (which tends to have a majority favouring relatively liberal views on immigration and asylum) would lead to more liberal legislation in this area.

The Borders Code Regulation provides the first opportunity to see whether EU policy will change direction, as it was the first binding measure subjected to the new rules. Other EU legislative action on border control and visas subject to a qualified majority vote and co-decision (including rules on border traffic, the Visa Information System and the Schengen Information System) is pending,[11] and further proposals are expected in the near future.[12]

It appears that the EP committee in charge of the Borders Code issue, in particular its rapporteur in this area (Michael Cashman, a British Labour MEP), negotiated with the Council Presidency in the first half of 2005 (Luxembourg) a deal on this proposal, which incorporated many, but not all, of the amendments tabled by the rapporteur and others in the course of discussing a draft committee report.[13] While the compromise deal incorporated many positive features of the EP's proposals, a number of important suggested amendments were overlooked. The deal was accepted by the Council and the EP in June 2005, and formally adopted early in 2006.[14]

2.2 Asylum seekers

The Regulation contains a general provision in Article 3(b), specifying that the legislation does not affect 'the rights of refugees and persons requesting international protection, in particular as regards non-refoulement'. Article 4(3) provides

areas covered by Title IV of Part Three of the Treaty establishing the European Community to be governed by the procedure laid down in Article 251 of that Treaty (OJ 2004 L 396/45).

[11] The pending visas and borders measures subject to co-decision as of 1 January 2006 were the Regulation on the VIS (COM (2004) 835, 28 Dec. 2004); the Regulation on local border traffic (COM (2005) 56, 23 Feb. 2005); a Regulation establishing a borders fund (COM (2005) 123, 6 April 2005); the Regulation on SIS II (COM (2005) 236, 31 May 2005); and two Decisions relating to transit through new Member States and from Switzerland (COM (2005) 381, 22 Aug. 2005). Since the Borders Code was agreed in principle in June 2005, the EP and Council have agreed on and adopted Reg. 2046/2005/EC on visas and border control procedures for persons coming to the 2006 Winter Olympic Games in Turin (OJ 2005 L 334/1), which is therefore the first binding measure on visas and border controls to be *adopted* by means of the co-decision process.

[12] See the Hague Programme, loc. cit. n. 10, and the Action Plan on its implementation (OJ 2005 C 198/1).

[13] The proposed amendments can be found at on the EP's website at <http://www.europarl.eu.int/meetdocs/2004_2009/documents/pr/558/558830/558830en.pdf> and <http://www.europarl.eu.int/meetdocs/2004_2009/documents/am/563/563299/563299en.pdf>.

[14] Borders Code Regulation, loc. cit. n. 1; the Regulation applies from 13 Oct. 2006 (Art. 40).

expressly that the application of penalties to persons who cross the external borders without authorization is 'without prejudice to [Member States'] international protection obligations', and Article 13(1) states that 'special provisions on the right to asylum or to international protection' could trump an obligation to refuse entry at the external borders to an asylum seeker who does not meet the normal conditions for entry. These provisions were all found in the Commission's initial proposal, except that the reference to the 'right to international protection' was added.[15] None of the provisions adds any further detail on what they mean in practical terms.

As compared with the previous rules, the current Schengen Convention states that it is 'subject to' the Geneva Convention of 1951 relating to the Status of Refugees and the 1967 Protocol to that Convention (Refugee Convention),[16] although this provision was not integrated into EU law in 1999.[17] This can be contrasted to Article 3(b) of the Regulation, which will be useful because it reinstates a general provision on the rights of refugees and asylum seekers in Community law to replace Article 135 of the Schengen Convention, with more general wording, and also referring to requests for international protection. The Convention rules on conditions for crossing external borders specify that they 'shall not preclude the application of special provisions concerning the right of asylum';[18] this has been carried over into Article 13(1) of the Regulation, and augmented by the latter's addition of the reference to international protection. Article 3 of the Convention, which requires penalties to be imposed for unauthorized crossing of external borders, contains no such provision; as such, it conflicts with the Refugee Convention, Article 31 of which exempts refugees from penalties for unauthorized border crossing under certain conditions. Article 4(3) of the Regulation is therefore an improvement on this point.

Like the Regulation, the Schengen Convention adds no further detail on what the references to asylum mean in practical terms. There is little additional detail in the Common Manual. Point 1.3 of Part I of the Manual, which sets out exemptions from the penalties for unauthorized border crossing, does not provide for any exemption for refugees. There are special rules for refugees in points 6.3 and 6.10 of Part II, but these only address the issues of which travel documents are valid when a recognized refugee (i.e., not an asylum seeker claiming to be a refugee) crosses the border regularly and of which national law applies when asylum is requested at the border. The Manual does not further elaborate upon Articles 5(2) or 135 of the Convention to indicate what special rules apply to asylum seekers, and indeed the wording of point 6.10 of Part II of the Manual could be understood to mean that the treatment of asylum seekers at the border is left to the national law of each Schengen State to determine. These specific references

---

[15] Compare to Art. 11(1) of the initial proposal.

[16] Schengen Convention, loc. cit. n. 3, Art. 135.

[17] See the Decision 1999/435/EC on the definition of the Schengen *acquis* (OJ 1999 L 176/1).

[18] Schengen Convention, loc. cit. n. 3, Art. 5(2).

to asylum seekers and refugees contained in the Manual have not been taken over into the Regulation.

The practical impact of this is that the Regulation will not improve materially on the Schengen rules, which do not clearly and expressly prevent Member States from simply refusing to admit asylum seekers at their external borders. Such behaviour arguably infringes the Refugee Convention[19] and the European Convention of Human Rights (ECHR),[20] but it is less clear whether or not it infringes the Schengen rules or the Borders Code. The latter are subject to the jurisdiction of the Court of Justice, and accordingly might be more easily enforceable than the ECHR and Refugee Convention, given the direct effect and supremacy of EU law (assuming that the Schengen *acquis* within the scope of EU law is subject to these principles of EU law). While the references to the Refugee Convention and the right to asylum in the Schengen rules and the Borders Code, taken with the human rights protection accorded by the general principles of EU law (following the integration of the Schengen *acquis* into EU law), could be interpreted to mean that the Schengen rules and the Borders Code *do* preclude refusals of asylum seekers at the border, it would obviously be preferable to specify this (and other issues relating to asylum seekers) more precisely.

Amendment 23 proposed by the EP would have achieved this goal, as it would have specified that asylum seekers had the right to remain on the territory of a Member State until a final decision had been taken on their asylum application. Unfortunately, this proposed amendment was not taken on board by the Council, even in an amended form. The issue may not have been addressed in detail in the Borders Code because there is more detail on the topic in the EC's Directive on asylum procedures, which had been agreed in principle back in 2004 and has subsequently been formally adopted.[21] This Directive contains two sets of special rules on asylum applications made at the border,[22] one set providing for derogation from a number of key procedural safeguards, and another allowing Member States to skip some or all of the process of examination of an asylum application altogether for persons coming from countries which have ratified the ECHR and the Refugee Convention (without geographical reservations), subject to certain other conditions. There are grave doubts over the validity of these controversial provisions.[23]

---

[19] Convention relating to the Status of Refugees, 28 July 1951, 189 *UNTS* 137.

[20] Convention for the Protection of Human Rights and Fundamental Freedoms, 4 Nov. 1950, *ETS* No. 5.

[21] Directive 2005/85/EC (OJ 2005 L 326/13). Member States must implement this Directive by 1 December 2007.

[22] Ibid., Arts. 35 and 36.

[23] For detailed comments on their interpretation and validity, see ch. 14 in S. Peers and N. Rogers (eds.), *EU Immigration and Asylum Law: Text and Commentary* (Leiden, Martinus Nijhoff 2006).

2.3 EU citizens and their family members

The Commission's proposal for the new Regulation provided simply that it would not affect the entitlements of persons with EU free movement rights,[24] including EU citizens' family members.[25] It also suggested a distinction between a minimum check applicable to everyone and a thorough check for third-country nationals in Article 6 of the proposed Regulation, although it was not clear what the position of family members of EU citizens would be under these provisions.

This issue was the subject of divergent views between the EP and the Council during negotiations. The Council agreed to add a provision to Article 6 of the Regulation (which became Article 7 of the final text) which makes it clear that the minimum check applies in principle to both EU citizens and their family members with free movement rights, adopting in part the EP proposal. However, the Council insisted on adding a provision stating that border guards can consult national or European databases,

> 'occasionally, when carrying out minimum checks on persons enjoying the Community right of free movement … in order to ensure that a person does not represent a real, present and sufficiently serious danger to the internal security, public order, international relations of the Member States or a threat to the public health',

while specifying that this will not affect the right of entry of such persons.[26] A further Article 7(6), introduced to respond to another amendment proposed by the EP, states that Directive 2004/38/EC on the free movement rights of EU citizens (discussed further below) applies to checks on EU citizens and their family members; however, there appears to be a conflict here, as the Directive does not allow for checks in relation to threats to Member States' *international relations* or in relation to *internal security* (as distinct from public security). Nothing in EU free movement law allows for such exceptions; the international relations exception moreover appears to conflict with the right of freedom of expression and freedom of association if applied to demonstrators. The point of this provision is also unclear: if it does not authorize limits on free movement, what is the purpose of it?

The current rules on free movement of EU citizens and their family members are set out in Articles 12, 18, 39, 43 and 49 of the EC Treaty and diverse secondary legislation, which give EU citizens and their family members the right to move and reside freely in other Member States. The secondary legislation has been brought together in Directive 2004/38/EC, which Member States had to apply by the end of April 2006.[27] The EC Treaty articles and legislation allow EU citizens and their family members to enter and reside in other Member States if they meet the criteria to live there (essentially if they have a job, are in self-

[24] Art. 3(a) of the Commission proposal, loc. cit. n. 9.
[25] See definition in ibid., Art. 2(7).
[26] Art. 7(2), as amended.
[27] OJ 2004 L 229/35.

employment or have another source of income, rather than applying for benefits from the host state).

Directives 68/360/EEC and 73/148/EEC currently set out the immigration law rules applicable to EU citizens in another Member State and to their family members.[28] These rules also apply to EU citizens who move for other reasons unrelated to employment (along with their family members).[29] As regards exit (Article 2 of each Directive), this legislation provides that Member States must allow EU citizens and their family the right to leave their territory to enter another Member State, 'on production of a valid identity card or passport', and cannot demand exit visas or any equivalent document from their citizens. Member States must issue such documents to their nationals 'in accordance with their laws'. As for entry (Article 3 of each Directive), Member States must allow entry merely 'on production of a valid identity card or passport', and cannot demand entry visas or an equivalent document, except for family members who are non-EU nationals. In that case, 'Member States shall afford to such persons every facility for obtaining any necessary visas'. These visas must be free of charge (Article 9(2), Directive 68/360/EEC).

Interpreting these rules, the Court of Justice has ruled that a policy of imposing an entry clearance stamp in an EU citizen's passport upon entry is an equivalent measure to requiring a visa, and is therefore banned.[30] It is not permissible for border guards to ask EU citizens questions about the intended purpose of their visit, or their financial means.[31] On the other hand, the Court has ruled that sporadic checks on EU citizens, on occasion at the border, to see if they are carrying the correct permits, does not violate EU law if similar checks are carried out on that state's own nationals, unless those checks are 'carried out in a systematic, arbitrary or unnecessarily restrictive manner'.[32] As for third-country national family members of EU citizens, the Court has ruled that they can be turned back at the border if they lack an identity card or passport, or (if necessary) a visa, but they cannot be turned back if they are able to prove their identity and conjugal ties and if there is no evidence that they are a risk to public policy, public security, or public health. Moreover, in order to give the free movement Directives 'their full effect, a visa [where it is required] must be issued without delay and, as far as possible, on the place of entry into national territory'.[33] Third-country national family members are covered by the legislation setting out substantive limits to Member States' power to expel or deny entry to citizens of other EU Member States on grounds of public policy, public security, and public health, as well as procedural protection for those affected.[34]

[28] OJ Spec. Ed. 1968, L 257/13, p. 485 and OJ 1973 L 172/14.

[29] Directives 90/364/EEC (OJ 1990 L 180/26), 90/365/EEC (OJ 1990 L 180/28) and 93/96/EEC (OJ 1993 L 317/59).

[30] Case 157/79, *Pieck* [1980] ECR 2171.

[31] Case C-68/89, *Commission* v. *Netherlands* [1991] ECR I-2637.

[32] Case 321/87, *Commission* v. *Belgium* [1989] ECR I-997, para. 15.

[33] Case C-459/99, *MRAX* [2002] ECR I-6591, paras. 53-62.

[34] Directive 64/221/EEC, OJ Spec. Ed., 1963-64, 117.

As for the new Directive 2004/38/EC, the rules on visas and border controls are broadly the same as the old ones,[35] although a number of small differences do exist: the right of entry and exit is 'without prejudice to the provisions on travel documents applicable to national border controls'; there is an explicit reference to the EU visa list legislation 'or, where appropriate, ... national law' as regards family members' visa requirements; third-country national family members are exempt from the visa requirement where they hold a residence card issued to them as family members of an EU citizen who resides in a different Member State; visas must be issued to such persons 'as soon as possible and on the basis of an accelerated procedure'; passports of third-country national family members cannot be stamped if they present the aforementioned residence card; and EU citizens and family members without the required documents must be given the chance to obtain them or corroborate their identity before being turned back.

How do the new rules in the Borders Code compare to the old Schengen rules? Article 134 of the Schengen Convention provided that it only applies in so far as it is compatible with EU law. This provision was not taken over into EU law in 1999, but the Protocol to the EC and EU Treaties on the Schengen *acquis* sets out the same rule. The current Article 6 of the Schengen Convention, while badly drafted, appears to require that all persons, including EU citizens, should be checked to establish their identities on the basis of their travel documents, while third-country nationals should be subject to 'thorough checks'. This distinction appears more clearly from points 1.3.1 to 1.3.4 of Part I of the Common Manual, which moreover provides that EU citizens should be subject to 'random thorough checks' on entry and exit as well as checks where there are reasons to believe that the persons concerned might compromise public policy, national security or health. Furthermore, third-country national family members of EU citizens are not exempted from 'thorough checks'. The Borders Code has clarified this point, as well as the relationship between the borders rules and free movement rules.

Points 6.1 to 6.1.4 of Part II of the Common Manual also address the issue of EU citizens and their family members, stating that EU citizens can only be denied entry to another Member State if they pose a threat to public policy, national security or public health; if entry is refused, then the EU citizen must receive a written notification of the reason for refusal. Family members can only be refused on the same grounds, with addition of the absence of documents (although as with all third-country nationals, a residence permit is equivalent to a visa); their procedural rights are set out in point 1.4.1 of Part II, which provides that a ban on entry to one Member State is a ban on entry to all of them, and leaves the extent of appeal rights (if any) open to each Member State to determine. These provisions are clearly wholly in conflict with EC free movement law, and this was exacerbated by the secrecy of Part II of the Common Manual until its declassification and publication. These illegal provisions were deleted entirely by the Borders Code Regulation; this can only be heartily welcomed.

---

[35] Directive 2004/38/EC, loc. cit. n. 27, Arts. 4 and 5.

It is also worth noting that the Borders Code Regulation apparently drops the prior exception (retained in the Commission proposal and supported by the EP) which permitted Member States to exempt their own citizens from having to cross borders at authorized times and places, relieving them from penalties if they did not cross when and where they should.

2.4 Conditions of entry

A key issue concerning the EU's border rules is, of course, the conditions for obtaining entry into the Member States' territories across the Union's external borders. Article 5 of the Borders Code Regulation essentially retains the provisions of Article 5 of the Schengen Convention, which specify that entry can only be authorized if the person concerned has the correct travel documents, including a visa if required, and a justification for the proposed stay (including possibly a subsistence requirement); is not on the Schengen Information System (SIS) blacklist; and is not a threat to the public policy, national security or international relations of any (Schengen) Member State.[36] The Borders Code Regulation adds 'public health' to the grounds for refusal (clarified in accordance with EP amendments),[37] and offers a wider scope for travellers to prove that they have sufficient subsistence and justification for entry. In particular, Article 5(3) provides that means of subsistence shall be assessed in terms of the duration of the stay, in accordance with a reference amount to be established by Member States, taking into account the cash, credit cards and travellers' cheques a traveller holds, plus possibly (depending on national law) sponsorship letters and letters of guarantee. This does not clarify the situation any more than previously (see point 4.1.2 of Part I of the Common Manual) for persons in doubt as to what it will take to satisfy border guards that they have sufficient funds to satisfy the requirements for entry. A standardized rule on sponsorship and letters of guarantee would have been useful.

Moreover, the Council also added an explicit reference to checks in national databases as well as the SIS (although such databases are probably already checked in practice under the current rules); it is unclear if Member States are expected or permitted to check *each other's* databases to this end. The Commission had proposed a travel insurance requirement, but this was dropped.[38] The Council also rejected an EP amendment which would have ensured that a letter of guarantee from a host was conclusive proof that entry was justified.

The current exceptions from the conditions for entry have also been retained (humanitarian grounds, national interest or international obligations, without

[36] For a detailed analysis, see R. Cholewinski, 'No Right of Entry: The Legal Regime on Crossing the EU External Border', in K. Groenendijk, E. Guild and P. Minderhoud (eds.), *In Search of Europe's Borders* (The Hague, Kluwer 2003) p. 105 at pp. 115-127. On the national case-law on the issue, see H. Staples, 'Adjudicating the Schengen External Border', ibid., p. 215 at pp. 233-234.

[37] Borders Code Regulation, loc. cit. n. 1, Art. 5(1)(e).

[38] This requirement does apply to applications for Schengen visas: see OJ 2004 L 5/79.

prejudice to special asylum rules;[39] and entry in order to transit to a Member State where a person holds a residence permit or re-entry visa),[40] and another one has been added (exemption from the visa requirement where a person holds a residence permit issued by a Member State), although in fact it could previously be found in the Common Manual.

The net result of all this is that the conditions for entry have not changed significantly. It would have been preferable to focus more on abolition or further clarification of the criteria for entry, in particular abolishing or severely restricting the 'international relations' exception which could be used against demonstrators or protesters. However, there will be an obligation, not discretionary power, to admit any persons who meet the criteria for entry.[41]

2.5 Treatment by border guards

Article 6 of the Regulation provides that measures adopted by border guards must be subject to the principle of proportionality, must fully respect human dignity and cannot discriminate on grounds of sex, racial or ethnic origin, religion or belief, disability, age or sexual orientation. The Commission's proposal had only referred to proportionality; the improvements followed amendments tabled by the EP. This is the first non-discrimination clause inserted into the main text of an EU immigration or asylum measure (the Council has methodically removed such clauses from a number of prior legislative proposals). It should be pointed out, however, that the non-discrimination clause does not apply to the entire Regulation, including the conditions for entry, but only to the performance of border checks. Also, the Council accepted amendments based on EP proposals to specify that thorough checks should, where possible, be carried out in a non-public area, and that information should be given to a person subject to such a check, in particular their right to request the name or service number of the guard carrying it out.[42] But this still fell short of suggested EP amendments that would have ensured the right to be provided with the name and service number and to fuller information on the purpose of the checks. Nor did the Council accept an EP amendment to provide for a standard complaint form which aggrieved travellers could file in the event of a dispute.

2.6 Procedural rights

The Council accepted certain EP amendments designed to considerably enhance the procedural rights of persons at the border.[43] These amendments state that a

[39] Borders Code Regulation, loc. cit. n. 1, Art. 5(4)(c).
[40] Ibid., Art. 5(4)(a).
[41] Ibid., Arts. 5(1) and 13.
[42] Ibid., Arts. 7(5) and 7(6).
[43] Ibid., Art. 13(2) and (3).

person is entitled to know the precise reason for a refusal; that there is a 'right to appeal', although the details are left up to national law (previously, the Common Manual only stated that it is up to national law to determine any appeal rights); that the traveller must be given information on contacts regarding the appeal; and that, in addition to possible compensation, there must be a remedy of correction of the refusal of entry if the appeal is successful. These provisions still fall short of the EP's proposals, which also called for a refusal decision to be approved by a superior officer, for a clear right to compensation following a well-founded appeal, for a written and oral indication of appeal procedures, and for the appointment of representatives for travellers. The Council Presidency did, however, accept the basic features of an EP amendment requiring Member States to compile information on persons refused entry.

2.7 Internal border checks

The Regulation alters the rules concerning internal border checks by clarifying the cases in which police checks can take place behind borders, by amending the procedure applicable when a Member State seeks to derogate from the obligation to abolish internal checks (in particular to give the Commission a greater role), and by revising the provisions on reporting to the public and the EP.[44] The Commission's proposals to establish public health as a ground for re-imposition of border checks and setting out circumstances in which all Member States could reintroduce checks simultaneously in the event of a major terrorist threat were dropped after objections from both the Council and EP.[45]

2.8 Stamping of travel documents[46]

The Borders Code Regulation incorporates the provisions of the Regulation on the stamping of documents of third-country nationals adopted in 2004.[47] According to Article 1 of the latter Regulation, its purpose is to reiterate the obligation on Member States' authorities to stamp travel documents systematically when third-country nationals cross the external borders, and to specify the conditions under which the absence of such a stamp may lead to a presumption that the rules on short-term stays have been broken. Next, the Schengen Convention borders provisions were amended to provide that Member States may only relinquish this obligation in 'exceptional and unforeseen circumstances'.[48] The presumption that

[44] Ibid., Arts. 20-31.

[45] Arts. 20(1) and 24 of the Commission proposal, op. cit. n. 9.

[46] The following analysis is adapted from S. Peers, 'Key Legislative Developments on Migration in the European Union', 7 *European Journal of Migration Law* (2005) p. 87 at pp. 93-97.

[47] Reg. 2133/2004/EC, loc. cit. n. 7; Arts. 10 and 11 of the Borders Code Regulation, loc. cit. n. 1. The stamping of documents Regulation was based on the Commission's proposal (COM (2003) 664, 6 Nov. 2003) and followed the EP's opinion (vote of 21 April 2004 on the Angelilli report: Doc. A5-0229/2004).

[48] Art. 2(1) of Reg. 2133/2004/EC, loc. cit. n. 7, amending Art. 6(2)(e) of the Schengen Conven-

the rules on short-term stays have been broken may be rebutted by the person concerned, if he or she provides 'credible evidence', such as transport tickets or proof of presence outside the Member States, to demonstrate that the rules were not broken. This list is clearly non-exhaustive.[49] In that case, a Member State shall place an 'indication' in the travel document noting where the person crossed the external borders, and 'may' give the person concerned a standard form acknowledging the acceptance of evidence that the rules were not broken, which was attached to the Common Manual by the Regulation.[50] If the presumption is not overturned, the person concerned may be expelled from the Member State in which he or she was found.[51]

The Common Manual was also amended to provide that an event leading to intense traffic flows which can justify waiving systematic border checks must be 'unforeseen'.[52] It is unclear whether any other circumstances could justify waiving the checks. In any event, even where checks are relaxed, there is still an obligation to stamp all travel documents of third-country nationals on entry and exit;[53] presumably in such cases the national officials will simply have to stamp the documents hurriedly without examining them. Further amendments to the Common Manual specified that documents must be stamped on exit as well as entry, and the current rule exempting EU citizens from entry stamps in their passports was amended to exempt not only all EU citizens, but also nationals of European Economic Area States, Swiss citizens and their third-country national family members, provided that the latter can show a residence card issued pursuant to recent legislation on EU citizens' free movement rights.[54]

The Council deleted the proposed obligation for Member States to inform third-country nationals about the provisions of the Regulation.[55]

---

tion, loc. cit. n. 3. The Council deleted the obligation proposed by the Commission that in such cases Member States must inform the Council and Commission as soon as possible.

[49] New Art. 6b(2) of the Schengen Convention, loc. cit. n. 3, first sub-paragraph. The Commission had proposed that a declaration pursuant to Arts. 22 or 45 of the Convention should also be considered as evidence, but the Council deleted this provision.

[50] New Art. 6b(2) of the Schengen Convention, loc. cit. n. 3, second sub-paragraph. This provision, including the standard form, was added by the Council. A Member State applying Schengen in full must give an indication of where the person concerned crossed *any* external border, while a Member State not fully applying Schengen may give an indication only of where that person crossed *its* external border. Member States must inform the Commission and Council about their methods for providing such indications.

[51] New Art. 6b(3) of the Schengen Convention, loc. cit. n. 3.

[52] Art. 3(1), Reg. 2133/2004/EC, loc. cit. n. 7. The explanatory memorandum to the original proposal gave as examples of unforeseen events a 'major accident block[ing] the normal traffic routes' or 'sudden international transport strikes'.

[53] Ibid., Art. 3(2). The Commission had proposed instead that the national authorities would only have to stamp documents upon request of the person concerned in such cases.

[54] Ibid., Art. 3(3). The Commission had proposed exemption of third-country national family members without this condition. The free movement legislation referred to is Directive 2004/38/EC, loc. cit. n. 27.

[55] Art. 4 of the Commission's proposal, loc. cit. n. 47.

The underlying question about the stamping obligation is whether it is realistic to impose an absolute obligation to stamp all travel documents (except for the limited exceptions set out in the Common Manual), even on exit. In the explanatory memorandum to its proposal for the Regulation on stamping of documents, the Commission had proposed leaving a decision to stamp documents on exit to a future 'impact assessment'.[56] There is no indication that the Council carried out such an assessment, or considered the real possibility that an absolute stamping obligation on entry and exit would be an unrealistic burden in cases where border control points are overloaded. For example, the explanatory memorandum to the initial proposal refers to the practical difficulty of checking all documents on trains; is it realistic to stamp all documents of train travellers on entry and exit?

Moreover, the explanatory memorandum to the initial proposal justified the inclusion of a more limited stamping obligation on the grounds that the EC would be adopting streamlined border traffic rules and a Decision on border signs; but the former rules have not yet been adopted and the latter Decision will not fully apply in practice until 2009, and in any event does not oblige Member States to create separate lanes at sea and land crossings.[57] The Commission also justified its more limited initial proposal on the grounds that stamping of documents at the external borders of the first fifteen Member States would rarely be necessary after 1 May 2004, since the documents of nationals of the new Member States would no longer need to be stamped. This is obviously true, but the issue has simply moved further east, to the external land borders of the new Member States.

In any event, even if it is technically possible to satisfy the absolute stamping obligation if further resources are made available to the border authorities, surely there could be a better use for those limited resources from a border control perspective?

Nor is there any convincing reason why the Council dropped the Commission's proposal to warn third-country nationals that they will need to have their travel documents stamped, and to notify the Council and Commission of cases where border checks are relaxed. In the latter case, such notification might be thought irrelevant because of the absolute stamping obligation imposed by the final Regulation, but in the event that this obligation proves to be unrealistic (or simply ignored) in practice, this information would have been very useful, as the Commission pointed out in its explanatory memorandum, in order for third-country nationals to verify their position if necessary.

If the Council were confident that an absolute stamping obligation would actually be carried out by national authorities, there should be little or no need for the

---

[56] COM (2003) 664, loc. cit. n. 47. The EP's rapporteur similarly took the view that 'the regulation is a first step towards a more comprehensive reform of the present system, which would also require systematic stamping for those leaving the Schengen area' (Angelilli report, op. cit. n. 47). It might even be argued that the addition of an obligation to stamp all documents on exit was a sufficiently significant change to require the re-consultation of the EP.

[57] See Decision 2004/581/EC concerning signs used by Member States' authorities at external borders, loc. cit. n. 7.

provisions in the Regulation allowing persons to rebut the presumption that they crossed the border without authorization. The very fact that this presumption can be challenged is reason enough to maintain the obligation to inform the Council and Commission of cases where the obligation to check all persons at borders was not applied.

In conclusion, it is unfortunate that the efforts of the Commission in drafting a proportionate and balanced proposal on this issue were undone by the Council's final Regulation. It would have been more useful to begin with a more modest clarification of the rules on stamping of documents, and to take account of its impact before adopting more extensive measures. It is also unfortunate that the provisions concerning information to third-country nationals and notification to the Council and Commission were deleted. Time will tell whether the Council has chosen to follow the route of 'gesture politics' by adopting legislation so unrealistic as to be symbolic, instead of a more measured and achievable approach.

3. The EU Border Agency[58]

Regulation 2007/2004/EC, establishing a European Agency for the Management of Operational Cooperation at the External Borders of the Member States of the EU (hereafter Agency),[59] transferred the main tasks of the Council committee previously overseeing the application of the EU's operational border action plan to the new Agency.[60] The Regulation makes it clear that 'the responsibility for the control and the surveillance of external borders lies with the Member States'.[61] The Agency's main tasks are the coordination of operational cooperation between Member States, assistance with training (including common training standards), risk analysis, the follow-up to research on external borders, extra technical and operational assistance for Member States that need it, management of an inventory of Member States' equipment, and provision of support for joint return operations.[62] However, its powers are not exclusive; Member States can continue with bilateral cooperation between each other or cooperation with third states outside the framework of the Agency.[63] It is specified that executive acts by the Agency's staff on the territory of a Member State, or by the staff of one Member State on the territory of another, are subject to the national law of the host Member State; this obviously suggests that the Agency will be carrying out executive actions.[64]

---

[58] The following analysis is adapted from Peers, loc. cit. n. 46.

[59] Loc. cit. n. 7.

[60] The action plan is in Council doc. 10019/02. See also European Commission, *Communication to the European Parliament and the Council in view of the European Council of Thessaloniki on the development of a common policy on illegal immigration, smuggling and trafficking of human beings, external borders and the return of illegal residents* (COM (2003) 323, 3 June 2003).

[61] Regulation 2007/2004/EC, loc. cit. n. 7, Art. 1(2).

[62] Ibid., Art. 2(1) and see further details in Arts. 3-9.

[63] Ibid., Art. 2(2).

[64] Ibid., Art. 10.

The Regulation also provides for information exchange between the Agency, the Commission and the Member States, although it is not explicitly clear whether this would entail the collection or exchange of personal information.[65] However, a clause in the Preamble refers to the EU rules on personal data protection applicable to EU institutions, bodies or agencies, so it appears that the Agency could indeed be involved in processing personal data.[66] The Agency may also exchange non-personal data with the European Police Office (EUROPOL), third countries and international organizations.[67]

The Agency does not have a direct impact on individuals travelling to the European Union, and since it began operations in May 2005, it is too early to tell whether it is having (or will be able to have) a significant impact on operational cooperation between Member States.

4. Conclusion

The external borders rules of the Community are not, by themselves, as significant a barrier to entry as the rules concerning the obligation to obtain a visa and the conditions for obtaining it. These rules are even more convoluted than the current borders rules, and set out a very low level of procedural rights for visa applicants, who are frequently aggrieved by what they perceive to be arbitrary and irrational refusals of applications. The visa rules have also been criticized for unjustified discrimination.[68] Fortunately, the rules on conditions for obtaining visas are due to be reformed following a proposal in 2006, which will follow the model of the Borders Code Regulation.[69] It can only be hoped that the EU institutions can agree in particular on fair procedural rights, and that a separate exercise is undertaken to review the EU's visa list in light of objective and legitimate criteria for determining which states' nationals in fact present a genuine security or irregular immigration risk, justifying the imposition of a visa requirement.

For the present, though, the new Borders Code makes a modest contribution to clarifying and enhancing the following issues: the position of asylum seekers, EU citizens and their family members; conditions for entry; treatment by border guards; the procedural rights of individuals; and the rules concerning the EU's internal borders. But it seems, on the basis of this first measure subject to the codecision procedure, that, due to the requirement of having wide support in the EP for amendments to legislation at crucial stages of the procedure, the effect of the Parliament's enhanced powers in this area will be the adoption of incremental improvements to EU policies, rather than a radical rethink of them.

---

[65] Ibid., Art. 11.

[66] Ibid., Preamble, Recital 19.

[67] Ibid., Arts. 13 and 14.

[68] See R. Cholewinski, *Borders and Discrimination in the European Union* (London/Brussels, Immigration Law Practitioners' Association/Migration Policy Group 2002).

[69] See the Action Plan on implementing the Hague programme, loc. cit. n. 12.

Selected Bibliography

Cholewinski, R., *Borders and Discrimination in the European Union* (London, ILPA/Migration Policy Group 2002).

Gortazar, C., 'Abolishing Border Controls: Individual Rights and Common Control of EU External Borders', in E. Guild and C. Harlow (eds.), *Implementing Amsterdam* (Oxford, Hart Publishing 2001) p. 121.

Groenendijk, K., 'Reinstatement of Controls at the Internal Borders of Europe: Why and Against Whom?', 10 *European Law Journal* (2004) p. 150.

Guild, E., 'Adjudicating Schengen: National Judicial Control in France', 1 *European Journal of Migration and Law* (1999) p. 419.

Guild, E., P. Minderhoud and K. Groenendijk (eds.), *In Search of Europe's Borders* (The Hague, Kluwer 2003).

Hailbronner, K., 'Visa Regulations and Third-Country Nationals in EC Law', 31 *Common Market Law Review* (1994) p. 969.

Peers, S., *EU Justice and Home Affairs Law,* 2nd edn. (Oxford, Oxford University Press 2006), ch. 3.

Peers, S. and N. Rogers (eds.), *EU Immigration and Asylum Law: Text and Commentary* (Leiden, Martinus Nijhoff 2006).

Schermers, H., et al. (eds.), *Free Movement of Persons in Europe: Legal Problems and Experiences* (The Hague, Martinus Nijhoff 1993).

Steenbergen, J., 'Schengen and the Movement of Persons', in H. Meijers, et al., *Schengen: Internationalisation of Central Chapters of the law on aliens, refugees, privacy, security and the police*, 2nd edn. (Leiden, Stichting NJCM-Boekerij 1992).

Conclusion

Chapter 26
INTERNATIONAL LEGAL NORMS ON MIGRATION: SUBSTANCE WITHOUT ARCHITECTURE

T. Alexander Aleinikoff*

1. Introduction

The chapters in this volume display three broad perspectives on law and international migration. The first examines migration through the lens of the regulation of labour flows – low-skilled and high-skilled, lawful and unlawful, pursuant to unilateral national laws and bilateral and multilateral agreements.[1] The second adopts what is often termed a 'human rights approach', examining the causes of migration, the treatment of migrants in transit states, and discrimination and due process issues in the country of settlement.[2] The third perspective focuses on state control and security; issues such as border control, smuggling and trafficking, illegal entry, and terrorism.[3] The contributions also describe a variety of bilateral, regional and international agreements and processes that conceptualize, develop and promulgate norms and foster cooperation among states across the labour, human rights and security fields.[4]

These three perspectives are not exhaustive.[5] Legal norms from the fields of health and development, for example, have an impact on the international movement of persons.[6] Furthermore, the chapters in this book often combine the three approaches. For example, low-skilled immigration may be seen from all three

* Dean and Executive Vice President for Law Center Affairs at Georgetown University in Washington DC.

[1] See the chapters by Cholewinski, Flores-Macías, Klein Solomon, Martens, Nonnenmacher, Santestevan, and Orozco.

[2] See the chapters by Bagshaw, Byrne, Cholewinski, Grant, Legomsky, Perruchoud, Piotrowicz, Piper and Satterthwaite, Vohra, and Weissbrodt.

[3] See the chapters by Legomsky, Peers, Redpath, Schoenholtz, and Vohra.

[4] See the chapters by De Bruycker, Flores-Macías, Hailbronner, Klein Solomon, Martens, Nielsen, Nonnenmacher, Peers, and Santestevan.

[5] Moreover, not all of the chapters in the volume fit into one of these three categories; see, for example, the contributions by Gelazis, de Hart and Groenendijk, and Wühler.

[6] See S. Charnovitz, 'Trade Law Norms on International Migration', in T.A. Aleinikoff and V. Chetail (eds.), *Migration and International Legal Norms* (The Hague, T.M.C. Asser Press 2003) p. 241; P. van Krieken, 'Health and Migration: The Human Rights and Legal Context', in Aleinikoff and Chetail, ibid., p. 289.

R. Cholewinski, R. Perruchoud and E. MacDonald, eds., International Migration Law

perspectives: it clearly represents a flow of labour to the receiving state; the treatment of low-skilled workers gives rise to significant human rights issues; and to the extent that such flows occur without state permission, they bring into focus theoretical concerns of sovereignty and practical issues relating to enforcement. Likewise, the primary anti-trafficking norms – largely identified with the human rights approach – are located in a protocol to a security-based Convention.[7] I thus recognize the limitations of my tripartite classification of the contributions to this volume. Nonetheless, I think that these broad groupings provide a useful way to summarize and compare the conclusions of the various chapters here.

2. Major Conclusions

2.1 Labour migration

There is no comprehensive international regulation of labour flows. Policies and processes focus on three separate sets of issues. The first concerns the movement of unskilled and low-skilled migrants. At the national level, these workers generally enter through temporary worker programmes or are barred from admission altogether. The second is that of highly-skilled workers. There is growing competition among states for these migrants, and national programmes tend to facilitate their admission by providing either temporary or permanent status. The movement of skilled – and particularly professional – workers may also be included in multilateral trade agreements (such as the GATS and NAFTA). The third set of issues concerns regional agreements that look towards the free movement of workers among Member States. The EU has the most advanced set of norms in this regard.[8] In Africa, the Economic Community of West African States (ECOWAS) has taken significant steps toward free movement; the efforts of the South African Development Community have been less robust.[9] In the Western Hemisphere, the MERCOSUR[10] and Caribbean Community (CARICOM) states have discussed free movement as an objective but progress remains limited.[11]

In recent years, there has been increased focus on the human rights of migrant workers. The International Convention on the Protection of the Rights of All Migrant Workers and Members of Their Families,[12] which came into force on 1

[7] Protocol to Prevent, Suppress and Punish Trafficking in Persons, Especially Women and Children, supplementing the UN Convention against Transnational Organized Crime; UNGA Res. 55/25 of 15 Nov. 2000, UN Doc. A/55/25 (8 Jan. 2001); 111 parties (Jan. 2007) [hereafter, the Palermo Protocol].

[8] See the chapter by Hailbronner in this volume.

[9] See the chapter by Martens in this volume.

[10] *Mercado Común del Sur* [the Common Market of the South].

[11] See the contributions to this volume by Santestevan and Nonnenmacher.

[12] UNGA Res. 45/158 of 18 Dec. 1990, Annex, 45 UN GAOR Supp. (No. 49A) at p. 262, UN Doc. A/45/49 (1990).

July 2003, is recognized by the Office of the UN High Commissioner for Human Rights as one of the seven core international human rights treaties. Moreover, the ILO Governing Body is currently considering a draft multilateral framework on labor migration that identifies '[n]on-binding principles and guidelines for a rights-based approach to labour migration'.[13]

There appears to be little prospect of any significant, specific international mechanism for the regulation of labour flows. Such efforts – should they occur at all – are most likely to arise in the course of broadened trade negotiations.[14]

2.2 Human rights

It is common to speak of a rights-based approach to international migration, and a number of chapters in this volume note important ways in which human rights discourse now counterbalances traditional notions of state sovereignty, which view states as possessing unbridled authority to regulate immigration.[15] The recommendations of the Global Commission on International Migration (GCIM) state the enlightened consensus:

> 'States must protect the rights of migrants by strengthening the normative human rights framework affecting international migrants and by ensuring that its provisions are applied in a non-discriminatory manner.
>
> All states must ensure that the principle of state responsibility to protect those on their territory is put into practice, so as to reduce the pressures that induce people to migrate, protect migrants who are in transit and safeguard the human rights of those in destination countries.'[16]

Each of the seven core human rights conventions extends protections to non-citizens as well as citizens, and a number of international organizations – among them the UNHCHR, the UNHCR, the ILO and the IOM – now embrace a 'rights-based' approach. Despite general agreement at the international level on the applicability of human rights to migrants, however, non-citizens around the world are subject to discriminatory treatment, violations of due process, arbitrary detention and other forms of abuse. The chapters in this volume make clear that these human rights problems result not from a lack of human rights norms, principles and processes (although, as Weissbrodt notes, treaty bodies might do more to adopt specific standards or guidance on how generally recognized rights apply to non-citizens),[17] but from insufficient implementation and enforcement.

---

[13] See the chapter by Cholewinski in this volume.

[14] Klein Solomon notes, in her contribution to this volume, at p. 127, that 'the pressure to conclude a trade agreement is usefully serving as a catalyst for the greater exploration of ways of creating a more efficient, fair and safe approach to the management of global labour mobility'.

[15] See *supra* n. 2.

[16] Global Commission on International Migration (GCIM), *Migration in an Interconnected World: New Directions for Action* (GCIM 2005) (hereafter, GCIM Report) p. 81, para. 24.

[17] See the chapter by Weissbrodt in this volume at p. 233.

2.3 Security and control

Security and control issues are at the forefront of policy discussions for states for several reasons. First, legal routes for migration do not nearly exhaust either the demand for or supply of migrants. Thus, there are significant flows of unauthorized migrants in all regions of the world. Unauthorized migration is frequently seen as creating social, economic and cultural challenges in receiving states. Second, security concerns remain high in many states due to the perceived threat of international terrorist organizations. Finally, the trafficking of large numbers of migrants raises special problems of enforcement. States have cooperated on these issues at a number of levels – from the Palermo Protocol on Trafficking to the UN Convention against Transnational Organized Crime[18] to regional processes (such as EU directives, the Budapest Group, and the Bali Process on Human Trafficking)[19] to bi-national arrangements (such as US-Mexican efforts to prevent border smuggling).

The interest in increased control comes at the same time that many states are also recognizing the desirability of maintaining or increasing lawful levels of immigration, particularly in terms of high-skilled migrants. There is an obvious and deep tension here between facilitation and control – one that few states have successfully resolved.

One solution for states is to develop immigration agreements that allow free (or freer) movement for citizens from preferred states while adopting tougher enforcement measures against non-preferred states. These agreements are usually established among states within a region (examples include the EU and ECOWAS), but they may also be based on cultural or historical factors (consider Portugal's arrangements with other Lusophone states and Germany's policies regarding the *Aussiedler*).[20]

Technological advances offer the promise of a different kind of solution – we might call it 'smart enforcement'. Sensors and drone planes along the US southwest border can help border patrol agents identify routes of unauthorized migrants for targeted enforcement efforts. Further, as Redpath explains in her contribution to this volume, the increasing use of biometric information can provide benefits 'for ensuring the security of national borders, the safety of international aviation, the security of travel documents, and the protection of the destination country and its population'.[21] At the same time, however, she notes that biometrics raise serious questions regarding protection of the right to privacy. This point can be made in terms of security and control issues more generally. First, it is an open question whether increased enforcement – be it more border patrol agents and boats patrolling the waters between West Africa and the Canary Islands or hi-tech cards and

---

[18] Palermo Protocol, loc. cit. n. 7.

[19] See the contributions to this volume by Nielsen, Peers, and Piotrowicz.

[20] Ethnic Germans living on the territory of the former Soviet Union; on this, see the chapter by de Hart and Groenendijk, at p. 92.

[21] See Redpath's chapter, at p. 444.

devices – can ultimately achieve the full control states desire. Second, even if greater control is possible, its benefits must be weighed against the burden on migrants' and citizens' rights. In this regard, Schoenholtz's contribution here argues for more targeted enforcement strategies that run a lower risk of violating rights and alienating community members whose support would otherwise be of value in anti-terrorism activities.[22]

Taken together, the chapters provide both a comprehensive and sobering picture. They identify a wide range of conventions, norms, soft law and non-binding declarations that deal with various aspects of the sprawling set of issues that come under the general category of international migration; at the same time, they identify areas and issues in which further norm-development is advisable. Grant's chapter on 'stranded migrants' calls attention to an entire category of persons who 'find themselves outside any system of effective protection, and caught in a legal limbo'.[23] Similarly, the complexities of dual nationality remain generally unregulated at the international level.[24] The report of the GCIM notes other under- or unregulated topics of concern, such as principles of family unity and the actions of private agencies that recruit temporary workers across borders.[25]

The chapters in this volume demonstrate that there is no single, coherent body of norms that might be termed a regime of international migration law. In addition, they make clear that expertise in the field demands facility with the many sources of international norms as well as knowledge of a diverse set of fields of law (e.g., human rights, criminal, trade, diplomatic) that extend beyond those that relate specifically to migrants.

3. The Architecture of International Migration Law

In what follows, I want to raise briefly two possible foci for greater coherence in international migration law. The first, which I will consider in this section, concerns the question of legal architecture: is it time to think about more formal structures for the global governance of migration? The second, in the next section below, centres on attempts to bring together the various human rights norms that apply to migrants through the drafting of an International Bill of Rights for Migrants.

3.1 Modes of norm production, regime creation, and management

The papers in this volume identify a wide range of strategies for generating hard and soft norms, multilateral processes, and migration management tools. I will briefly outline a number of them here, moving from harder to softer.

---

22 See Schoenholtz's contribution to this volume.

23 See Grant's chapter on 'Stranded Migrants' in this volume, p. 46.

24 See, e.g., the chapter by de Hart and Groenendijk in this volume.

25 GCIM Report, op. cit. n. 16, at p. 56, para. 14.

3.1.1 *International conventions relating to migration and migrants*

International agreements constitute the 'hardest' norms, and, as noted above, the migration field includes several leading examples. The 1951 Convention on the Status of Refugees is an important example;[26] 146 states have ratified either the Convention or its 1967 Protocol.[27] Although the Convention provides no international adjudication structure, its norms defining refugee status and prohibited forms of discrimination against refugees have been widely adopted as a matter of national law (even if implementation of such norms at the national level has not been fully adequate). The Palermo Protocol on trafficking,[28] which seeks to promote cooperation among states to prevent and combat trafficking and assist its victims, has been ratified by 111 states. And the International Convention on the Protection of the Rights of All Migrant Workers and Members of Their Families (ICRMW) entered into force in 2003,[29] and has been ratified by 34 states.

3.1.2 *Other international agreements*

Several multilateral conventions have important implications for migrants. Most important are the major human rights treaties whose guarantees are not citizen-specific.[30] There are numerous other agreements: for example, as detailed in Perruchoud's chapter, the Vienna Convention on Consular Relations mandates that foreign nationals arrested or imprisoned be informed of their right to notify consular officials and that consular officials have the right to visit and communicate with detained nationals.[31] And although the GATS primarily concerns the cross-border provision of services, Mode 4 of the agreement concerns the movement of persons in the provision of services.[32]

3.1.3 *Regional norms*

Binding norms may be easier to establish among countries of a particular region that share similar histories, prospects and problems. The EU, of course, is the prime example here. The free movement regime for EU citizens among its Mem-

---

[26] Convention Relating to the Status of Refugees, 28 July 1951, 189 *UNTS* 137. Byrne deals with this treaty in her chapter.

[27] Protocol Relating to the Status of Refugees, 31 Jan. 1967, 606 *UNTS* 267.

[28] Palermo Protocol, loc. cit. n. 7. This is considered in more detail by Piotrowicz in this volume.

[29] Loc. cit. n. 12. This is discussed in more detail in Cholewinski's contribution to this volume.

[30] See, e.g., the International Covenant on Civil and Political Rights, 16 Dec. 1966, 999 *UNTS* 171, Art. 6: 'Every human being has the inherent right to life'; and the International Covenant on Economic, Social and Cultural Rights, 16 Dec. 1996, 993 *UNTS* 3, Art. 6, recognizing 'the right of everyone to the opportunity to gain his living by work which he freely chooses or accepts'.

[31] The Vienna Convention on Consular Relations, 24 April 1963, 596 *UNTS* 261, Art. 36(1).

[32] Final Act Embodying the Results of the Uruguay Round of Multilateral Trade Negotiations (1994), Annex 1B General Agreement on Trade in Services (GATS), discussed in detail by Klein Solomon in her chapter.

ber States is by now well-established.[33] Ongoing efforts in Africa, the Caribbean and South America continue but have generated less significant results.[34]

3.1.4 *Customary international law*

Customary legal norms at the international level may also be of direct relevance to migrants. The right of citizens to leave and return to their countries of origin, for example, is referred to in the (non-binding) Universal Declaration of Human Rights but is generally recognized as a binding norm as a matter of customary international law.[35] Likewise, the law relating to diplomatic immunity is, in part, secured by customary international norms.

3.1.5 *Principles (the Guiding Principles on Internal Displacement and the ILO multilateral framework on labour migration)*

The Guiding Principles on Internal Displacement[36] are described in detail in Bagshaw's chapter in this volume. Crafted by a Representative of the Secretary-General on Internally Displaced Persons, the Guidelines are a '"soft" restatement of existing international norms'.[37] They were presented to the Commission on Human Rights in 1998; and, as Bagshaw points out, resolutions of both the Commission and the General Assembly have noted with appreciation that an increasing number of states, as well as UN agencies and regional and non-governmental organizations, are using the Principles and have encouraged their further dissemination and application.[38]

Cholewinski's chapter explores the recent efforts of the ILO to focus attention on a comprehensive set of principles on the rights of migrant workers. Rather than drafting a new convention, the International Labour Conference called for the development of 'a non-binding multilateral framework for a rights-based approach to labour migration, which takes account of labour market needs'.[39] The Framework was adopted at a Tripartite Meeting of Experts in November 2005, and the Organization has invited governments, NGOs, employer and employee

---

[33] See Hailbronner's chapter in this volume.

[34] See Martens', Nonnenmacher's and Santestevan's chapters in this volume. In particular, Santestevan notes, at p. 385, that while free movement among the MERCOSUR countries and among the Andean Community states is not currently achievable, 'both have made progress towards the deepening of integration in border regions, the facilitation of free movement for the labour force in the services sector, and the promotion of a system for recognizing the rights of migrant workers'.

[35] GA Res. 217 A (III) of 10 Dec. 1948, UN Doc. A/810 (1948), Art. 13(2): 'Everyone has the right to leave any country, including his own, and to return to his country'.

[36] *Report of the Representative of the Secretary-General, Mr. Francis M. Deng, submitted pursuant to Commission on Human Rights resolution 1997/39. Addendum. Guiding Principles on Internal Displacement.* UN Doc. E/CN.4/1998/53/Add.2 (11 Feb. 1998).

[37] See the chapter by Bagshaw, at p. 191.

[38] Ibid., at p. 199.

[39] See the chapter by Cholewinski, at p. 268.

organizations 'to promote its contents and to observe the principles and guidelines embodied therein'.[40]

3.1.6 *National incorporation of international norms*

International norms, whether they have the status of hard or soft law at the international level, may be adopted by states into their domestic law. An example of the former is the Refugee Convention, which has been implemented in many states through the enactment of national legislation. The Guiding Principles on Internal Displacement provide an example of the latter: although the Principles are soft law at the international level, several states have given them formally binding status within their domestic legal systems.[41] Domestic courts may also recognize customary and conventional international legal norms relating to migrants in appropriate cases.[42]

3.1.7 *Cooperation/state-based processes*

The Nielsen chapter details a wide range of cooperative multi-state 'processes' both within and between regions. For example, the Berne Initiative has led to the development of an International Agenda for Migration Management,[43] a comprehensive non-binding framework that gathers states' common perspectives and understandings on such topics as migration and development, human rights, labour migration, integration of immigrants, irregular migration, trade, health, trafficking and return. Other processes are more focused, such as the Budapest Group, which concentrates on management of unauthorized migration, and the International Conference on Central American Refugees (CIREFCA).

3.2 **Towards global governance of migration?**

It would overstate the level of legal development to describe the foregoing strategies and norms as a regime. Not surprisingly, then, a number of scholars and practitioners have suggested the need for the establishment of a formal international legal regime relating to migration. Arthur Helton argued for the creation of

---

[40] ILO, Tripartite Meeting of Experts on the ILO Multilateral Framework on Labour Migration, Geneva, 31 Oct.-2 Nov. 2005, *ILO Multilateral Framework on Labour Migration*, Doc. TMMFLM/2005/1(Rev.), Preamble, Recital 10.

[41] See Bagshaw's contribution, at p. 200.

[42] See, e.g., the decision of the Inter-American Court of Human Rights on the Legal Status and Rights of Undocumented Migrants, Advisory Opinion OC-18/03 of 17 Sept. 2003, requested by the United Mexican States, *Inter-American Court of Human Rights* (Series A) No. 18 (2003); see also the decision by the UK House of Lords in *A (FC) and others (FC)* v. *Secretary of State for the Home Department* [2004] UKHL 56, on the detention of foreigners suspected of terrorism without criminal charge.

[43] *International Agenda for Migration Management*, Berne, 16-17 Dec. 2004 (IOM, Swiss Federal Office for Migration 2005).

a 'World Migration Organization' that would 'make and arbitrate global migration policy'.[44] Bimal Ghosh has suggested that it is time for a new international regime to facilitate the orderly movement of persons. This would include a shared set of objectives, an international normative framework, and the establishment of 'a coordinated institutional arrangement, including a monitoring mechanism'.[45] Philip Martin, Susan Martin and Patrick Weil have explored migration management on several continents and call for a 'strategy of cooperation' among sending and receiving states 'through a series of tradeoffs that facilitate the improved management of legal migration flows and better deal with illegal flows'.[46] These scholarly efforts, however, have not gathered steam on the international level or among states. Numerous international and regional 'processes' suggest 'best-practices' and information sharing, prepare agendas for action, and the like.[47] But they neither seek, nor have they produced, binding legal norms or building blocks of a general regime architecture.

To report these developments is not to slight them. I fully expect that the rather soft law in many migration-related areas will slowly harden. And law has, of course, hardened in some significant areas. Refugee law is the most noteworthy example; others include norms relating to consular protection (both in terms of treaty- and custom-based laws) and the free movement of EU citizens within the territory of the Union.

These examples are, however, far outnumbered by areas in which no significant supranational norms exist (such as citizenship), where existing norms are poorly implemented (such as human rights conventions), or where they have yet to be widely ratified. Emblematic of the latter is the ICRMW. The Convention provides a comprehensive set of rights for migrant workers – irrespective of their legal status in the host state – yet it has entered into force due to ratifications by primarily sending states and remains unratified by the major destination countries.

It was in the realm of possibility that the Report of the GCIM would call for the establishment of a new international organization or recommend first steps

[44] A. Helton, 'People movement: the need for a World Migration Organisation' (1 May 2003) p. 4 <http://www.opendemocracy.net/content/articles/PDF/1192.pdf>.

[45] B. Ghosh, 'New International Regime for Orderly Movements of People: What will it Look Like?', in B. Ghosh (ed.), *Managing Migration: Time for a New International Regime?* (Oxford, Oxford University Press 2000) p. 220, at p. 227.

[46] See P.L. Martin, S.F. Martin, and P. Weil, *Managing Migration: The Promise of Cooperation* (Lanham, Lexington Books 2006) p. 231; although they do note that '[m]oving from the current arrangements to a more robust international regime may be premature' (ibid., at p. 244). It is also worth considering in this regard Jagdish Bhagwati's early call for a 'brain drain tax', in terms of which developing countries would be entitled to receive revenue from the taxes paid by their skilled emigrants in the destination states. See, e.g., J.N. Bhagwati and M. Partington (eds.), *Taxing the Brain Drain: A Proposal* (Amsterdam, North-Holland 1976); J.N. Bhagwati (ed.), *The Brain Drain and Taxation: Theory and Analysis* (Amsterdam, North-Holland 1976).

[47] Nielsen provides an excellent overview of these processes in her contribution to the present volume.

towards an international legal regime on migration. Ultimately, however, it did neither. The Commission acknowledged both 'the paramount importance of interstate consultation and cooperation as a basis for the formulation and implementation of migration policies'[48] and 'that if the benefits of international migration are to be maximized and its adverse consequences minimized, then migration policies should be based on shared objectives and have a common vision'. [49] But it also recognized 'that there cannot be a single model for action by states and other stakeholders' and that 'there is currently no consensus concerning the introduction of a formal global governance system for international migration, involving the establishment of new international legal instruments or agencies'.[50] It was thus led to conclude that international, regional and domestic migration policies should be guided by a set of principles that might 'be employed by states and the international community as a guide to the formulation of comprehensive, coherent and effective migration policies'; these principles could be used to 'monitor and evaluate' the impact of immigration policies and to 'provide a framework for action that states and other stakeholders can use in their efforts to capitalize on the opportunities presented by international migration'.[51] In short, the Commission called for more coherent policies at the domestic level and greater consultation and cooperation at the regional and global level. Less dramatic conclusions are hard to imagine.

The chapters in this volume, taken as a whole, suggest that there can be no monolithic approach to migration management. Some areas might well benefit from norms adopted by way of an international convention; guiding principles might work best for areas in which a consensus is further away – perhaps in dealing with the problem of stranded migrants, for example.

While it seems plain that the establishment of an international organization to regulate migration – charged, for example, with the tasks of issuing universal rules regarding citizenship or dual nationality, controlling levels of migration, or establishing social benefit entitlement rules for migrants – is not on the cards, there may well be room for collective action across a fairly wide range of issues if agreement is reached from the bottom-up. That is, one can imagine a Conference, Platform or other multilateral process that would bring states together for discus-

[48] GCIM Report, op. cit. n. 16, at p. 3, para. 11.

[49] Ibid., at p. 3, para. 13. The report also noted the lack of coordination among international organizations with migration-related mandates: '[T]here is a need for enhanced cooperation and coordination between the different multilateral international organizations working in the field of migration. In meetings convened by the Commission, these organizations have acknowledged that they often work in a disconnected manner. While this situation derives in part from the competitive spirit that characterizes inter-agency relations, it is also a result of a lack of coherence at national level within those states that govern and fund these organizations. While steps have been taken to improve cooperation and coordination between the agencies concerned, more must be done to formulate and achieve shared objectives'. Ibid., at p. 3, para. 12.

[50] Ibid., at p. 3, para. 13.

[51] Ibid., at p. 3, para. 15.

sion and negotiation on the relevant issues. The idea here would not be that states should agree on a universal set of rules for international migration, but rather that they would put on the table their specific interests and then see if mutually advantageous bargains are possible.[52] For example, a sending state might bargain for enforcement of labour standards for its citizens working in another state; and that host state might agree to such enforcement if the sending state assists in combating visa fraud or undocumented migration.

4. Towards an International Bill of Rights for Migrants

The human rights approach to international migration is well-recognized in hard and soft law and in the scholarly and policy literature. Seven conventions establish wide-ranging rights that extend to non-citizens as well as citizens. The problem, as the Weissbrodt chapter makes clear, is with implementation – at all levels. The committees that monitor compliance with several of the conventions have no independent enforcement power; and those conventions left to national implementation are often not adequately enforced by domestic authorities. The GCIM thus noted that there is an

> 'urgent need to fill the gap that currently exists between the principles found in the legal and normative framework affecting international migrants and the way in which legislation, policies and practices are interpreted and implemented at the national level'.[53]

However, in a world of nation states where citizenship defines membership, immigrants will to some degree inevitably be treated differently. The task is to ensure that any differential treatment is fair, humane and justifiable.

Perhaps one way to move the human rights agenda forward would be to draft and promulgate an International Bill of Rights for Migrants. This would set out, in a clear and direct manner, a core set of guarantees for immigrants. It ought to include traditional negative rights – against cruel and inhumane treatment, detention without due process, and undue limits on speech and on the practice of religion – as well as some positive rights, such as guarantees of 'safety net' social benefits (e.g., emergency medical care, education and unemployment insurance). These might be formulated either as direct guarantees or as protections against

---

[52] Cf., Martin, Martin and Weil, op. cit. n. 46. The International Agenda for Migration Management (IAMM), discussed in the chapters by Cholewinski and Nielsen in this volume, is a potential source and/or basis for inter-state cooperative approaches as well as for the formulation of mutually acceptable principles. See *International Agenda for Migration Management*, Berne, 16-17 Dec. 2004 (IOM, Swiss Federal Office for Migration, 2005).

[53] GCIM report, op. cit. n. 16, at p. 58, para. 24.

discrimination.[54] Attention might be drawn to the special vulnerability of women, children and trafficked migrants.

Such a Bill of Rights could be proposed as hard law, seeking state ratification; it could be proposed as hortatory – like the Universal Declaration of Human Rights – in the hope that it might 'harden' over time; or it could be proposed as appropriate for direct incorporation into domestic law (as was the case, for example, with the suggested definition of the term 'refugee' in the Cartegena Declaration on Refugees).[55] The instrument could be the product of a state-based process (e.g., the Refugee Convention), a UN process (for example the ICRMW), or of efforts of civil society (such as the Landmines Convention).[56]

The proposal for an International Bill of Rights for Migrants might seem ill-advised for several reasons. First, it might be argued that the web of existing legal norms would adequately protect migrants if they were properly enforced; therefore, rather than proposing another instrument, it might be more advisable to devote energy to compliance. Second, it may be suggested that the ICRMW accomplishes much of the task I am proposing here. As Cholewinski points out in his contribution to the present volume, the Convention did not create many new rights; rather, it collected rights recognized in other instruments and under customary international law and applied them to the context of migrant workers and their families. Since most persons migrate either to work or to join family members who work, the Convention may fairly be said to cover a great majority of immigrants. A final objection may be that the prospect that such a Bill of Rights would actually be ratified by states is quite small in the current international and national climates.

These are not frivolous objections; however, I think there are persuasive answers to them. An International Bill of Rights for Migrants would not be a complex legal document designed only for lawyers and international tribunals. It would be a clear and concise statement of rights. Fitting perhaps on a single page (or computer screen), it could be easily circulated, read, and discussed – distributed to migrants, NGOs and state authorities, included in books, placed on posters, printed on T-shirts. It would demystify existing legal language and complex processes (how many migrants understand, for example, the current process for raising claims before the Human Rights Committee)? It would serve, then, as a rallying point. Even though a non-binding instrument, it could contribute to

[54] Compare the Refugee Convention, loc. cit. n. 26, in particular Arts. 16(1) (on the right of access to courts) and 15 (on the right of association on the most favourable terms granted to foreign nationals).

[55] See the Cartagena Declaration on Refugees, 22 Nov. 1984, Annual Report of the Inter-American Commission on Human Rights, OAS Doc. OEA/Ser.L/V/II.66/doc.10. For the text of the Declaration, see the UNHCR website at <http://www.unhcr.org/cgi-bin/texis/vtx/research/opendoc.htm?tbl=RSDLEGAL&id=3ae6b36ec>.

[56] Convention on the Prohibition of the Use, Stockpiling, Production and Transfer of Anti-Personnel Mines and on their Destruction, 18 Sept. 1997, reprinted in 36 *International Legal Materials* (1997) p. 1507.

the creation of a culture of rights which might engender and encourage better implementation of existing norms. The Universal Declaration of Human Rights provides an obvious analogy. Furthermore, even if not officially adopted at the international level – where the consensus necessary to formulate hard law may be difficult to attain – states could be encouraged to adopt an International Bill of Rights for Migrants into their domestic legal systems.

5. Conclusion

Legal norms and principles relating to international migration are both broad in scope and many in number, but they form no coherent regime. Moreover, it is not obvious that they either can or should. The sites and topics of governance may simply be too diffuse to permit a single edifice to be established, particularly at the international level. Nonetheless, there would seem to be enough overlapping concerns of states that some form of bottom-up negotiating process might produce a set of norms that could become widely shared, even if not fully comprehensive. Furthermore, the opportunity also exists, I would suggest, for civil society actors to draft, publicize and press for an International Bill of Rights for Migrants drawn from norms and principles in existing human rights instruments. Both would be of considerable help in providing some much needed architecture to the substance of international migration law.

INDEX

A

B

D

F

G

H

J

L

M